DATE DUE			

LOGICAL POSITIVISM

LOGICAL POSITIVISM

Edited by

A. J. AYER

GREENWOOD PRESS, PUBLISHERS
WESTPORT, CONNECTICUT

Library of Congress Cataloging in Publication Data

Ayer, Alfred Jules, Sir, 1910-   ed.
    Logical positivism.

    Reprint of the ed. published by Free Press, New York,
in series: The Library of philosophical movements.
    Bibliography: p.
    Includes index.
    1. Logical positivism--Addresses, essays, lectures.
[B824.6.A9 1978]   146'.4   78-6321
ISBN 0-313-20462-4

Reprinted with the permission of The Free Press, a Division of
Macmillan Publishing Co., Inc.

Reprinted in 1978 by Greenwood Press, Inc.,
51 Riverside Avenue, Westport, CT. 06880

Printed in the United States of America

10 9 8 7 6 5 4 3 2

Preface

Logical Positivism is the second in a series of books which will make available to the general public some of the most interesting work of philosophers of very diverse viewpoints. Each volume will deal with one or, in some cases, with two, philosophical "schools" or "movements." It is fortunate that philosophers are rarely united by the kind of common purpose which inspires political or religious "movements." Nevertheless, it is frequently helpful to consider the work of different writers according to the similarities in their aim and content; and this is the policy which has been adopted in designing the *Library of Philosophical Movements*.

This volume presents, for the first time in English, many of the most influential papers by leading members of the Vienna Circle. These and other articles contain authoritative expositions of the doctrines most commonly associated with logical positivism. However, for reasons explained by Professor Ayer in his introduction, several pieces which cannot be regarded as expositions or defenses of logical positivism have also been included. The scope of the bibliography, too, is broader than the title of the book would suggest. No volume dealing with other forms of analytic philosophy is contemplated in this series and it was therefore thought desirable to list the most important books and articles dealing with all types of analytic philosophy and not only with logical positivism.

I wish to express my gratitude to all the translators who generously contributed their labor, to Marvin Zimmerman, James Bayley, Irving Saltzmann, and a number of my students for helping to compile the bibliography, and to Leon Satinoff, Maxwell Grober, and José Huerta-Jourda for preparing the index. Special thanks are due to Professors Carnap and Hempel for supplying notes which indicate their present position on the issues dealt with in their papers. Professor Carnap was also kind enough to assist in the translation of his own articles.

PAUL EDWARDS

Contents

Knowledge and Truth

Ethics and Sociology

Analytical Philosophy

LOGICAL POSITIVISM

Editor's Introduction

I. History of the Logical Positivist Movement

THE TERM "Logical Positivism" was coined some thirty years ago to characterize the standpoint of a group of philosophers, scientists and mathematicians who gave themselves the name of the Vienna Circle. Since that time its reference has been extended to cover other forms of analytical philosophy; so that disciples of Bertrand Russell, G. E. Moore or Ludwig Wittgenstein at Cambridge, or members of the contemporary Oxford movement of linguistic analysis may also find themselves described as logical positivists. This wider usage is especially favored by those who are hostile to the whole modern development of philosophy as an analytical rather than a speculative enquiry. They wish to tar all their adversaries with a single brush. This is irritating to the analysts themselves who are rather more sensitive to their differences; they would prefer that the appellation of "logical positivist" be reserved for those who share the special outlook of the Vienna Circle. In compiling this anthology, I have not been quite so strict. I have drawn mainly on the writings of the members of the Vienna Circle, or of those who stand closest to them, but I have also included several pieces which fall outside this range. They are all, in some sense, analytical but the scope of what I regard as analytical philosophy is wide. It allows for serious disagreement, not only over technical niceties, but on major points of doctrine, including the method and purpose of analysis itself.

The Vienna Circle came into being in the early 1920's when Moritz Schlick, around whom it centered, arrived from Kiel to become professor of philosophy at the University of Vienna. On the philosophical side its leading members, besides Schlick himself, were Rudolf Carnap, Otto Neurath, Herbert Feigl, Friedrich Waismann, Edgar Zilsel and Victor Kraft; on the scientific and mathematical side, Philipp Frank, Karl Menger, Kurt Gödel and Hans Hahn. At the beginning, it was more of a club than an organized movement. Finding that they had a common interest in, and a

[3]

similar approach to, a certain set of problems, its members met regularly to discuss them. These meetings continued throughout the life of the Circle but they came to be supplemented by other activities which transformed the club into something more nearly resembling a political party. This process began in 1929 with the publication of a manifesto entitled "Wissenschaftliche Weltauffassung, Der Wiener Kreis"—The Vienna Circle; Its Scientific Outlook— which gave a brief account of the philosophical position of the group and a review of the problems in the philosophy of mathematics and of the physical and social sciences that they were chiefly concerned to solve. This pamphlet, which was written by Carnap, Neurath and Hahn, is also of interest as showing how the Circle situated itself in the history of philosophy. After claiming that they were developing a Viennese tradition which had flowered at the end of the nineteenth century in the work of such men as the physicists Ernst Mach and Ludwig Boltzmann, and, in spite of his theological interests, the philosopher Franz Brentano, the authors set out a list of those whom they regarded as their main precursors. As empiricists and positivists they named Hume, the philosophers of the enlightenment, Comte, Mill, Avenarius and Mach; as philosophers of science, Helmholtz, Riemann, Mach, Poincaré, Enriques, Duhem, Boltzmann and Einstein; as pure and applied logicians, Leibniz, Peano, Frege, Schröder, Russell, Whitehead and Wittgenstein; as axiomatists, Pasch, Peano, Vailati, Pieri and Hilbert; and as moralists and sociologists of a positivistic temper, Epicurus, Hume, Bentham, Mill, Comte, Spencer, Feuerbach, Marx, Müller-Lyer, Popper-Lynkeus and the elder Carl Menger. This list is surprisingly comprehensive, but it must be remembered that in most cases it is only a question of a special aspect of the author's works. Thus Leibniz is included for his logic, not for his metaphysics; Karl Marx is included neither for his logic nor his metaphysics but for his scientific approach to history. If we exclude contemporaries from the list, those who stand closest to the Vienna Circle in their general outlook are Hume and Mach. It is indeed remarkable how much of the doctrine that is now thought to be especially characteristic of logical positivism was already stated, or at least foreshadowed, by Hume.

Among contemporaries, Einstein, Russell, and Wittgenstein are singled out by the authors of the pamphlet for their kinship to the Vienna Circle and the extent of their influence upon it. Wittgenstein, indeed, stood to the Vienna Circle in a special relation. Having been a pupil of Russell's at Cambridge before the first world war he returned to Vienna and was there when his *Logisch-Philosophische*

Abhandlung was published in 1921. This famous book, which is better known as *Tractatus Logico-Philosophicus,* the title given to its English translation, had an enormous effect upon the positivist movement, both in Vienna and elsewhere. It would not be quite correct to say that the Vienna Circle drew its inspiration from it. Schlick himself, in his book on the theory of knowledge, *Allgemeine Erkenntnislehre,* of which the first edition appeared in 1918, had independently arrived at a similar conception of philosophy; and there is a hint of mysticism in the *Tractatus* which some members of the Circle, especially Neurath, found disquieting; but as a whole they accepted it, and it stood out as the most powerful and exciting, though not indeed the most lucid, exposition of their point of view. Wittgenstein did not officially adhere to the Circle but he maintained close personal relations at least with Schlick and Waismann whom he continued to influence even after his departure for Cambridge in 1929. In Cambridge, where he taught until 1947, four years before his death, he exercised an almost despotic sway over his pupils, and though he published nothing during these years except one short article his influence was strongly, if in most cases indirectly, felt by almost all the younger generation of British philosophers. He himself modified the rigors of his early positivism to an extent that can be measured by comparing the *Tractatus* with his posthumously published *Philosophical Investigations;* and it is to his influence, combined with that of Moore, that one may largely attribute the preoccupation of contemporary British philosophers with the everyday uses of language, and their tendency to deal with philosophical questions in an unsystematic, illustrative way, in contrast to the more rigorous would-be scientific method which was favored by the Vienna Circle. This is one reason why they are not happy to be described as Logical Positivists. But I shall have more to say about these alternative conceptions of analysis later on.

It was in 1929 also that the Vienna Circle organized its first international congress. It was held at Prague and was followed at intervals throughout the thirties by further congresses at Königsberg, Copenhagen, Prague, Paris and Cambridge. These meetings furthered the ambition of the Circle to develop Logical Positivism as an international movement. It had formed an early alliance with the so-called Berlin school of which Hans Reichenbach, Richard von Mises, Kurt Grelling and at a later date Carl Hempel were the leading members. The congresses helped it to make contact also with Scandinavian philosophers such as Eino Kaila, Arne Naess, Åke Petzäll, Joergen Joergensen, and the Uppsala school of empiricists, with the Dutch group around the philosopher Mannoury who pursued what they called the study of Significs, with the Münster group of logicians under Heinrich Scholtz, with American sympathizers such as Nagel, Charles Morris and Quine, and with British analysts of various shades of opinion, such as Susan Stebbing, Gilbert Ryle, R. B. Braithwaite, John Wisdom and myself. The brilliant Cambridge philosopher F. P. Ramsey was marked as an adherent, but he died in 1930 at the early age of 26. An alliance was also formed with the very important Polish groups of philosophers and logicians, of whom Lucasiewicz, Lesnievsky, Chwistek, Kotarbinski, Ajduciewicz and Tarski were perhaps the most prominent. The influence of Tarski's work, particularly on Carnap, was noticeably strong.

The missionary spirit of the Circle found a further outlet in its publications. In 1930 it took over a journal called *Annalen der Philosophie,* renamed it *Erkenntnis* and made it, under the editorship of Carnap and Reichenbach, the principal organ of the positivist movement. In the following years there also appeared a series of monographs with the collective title of *Einheitswissenschaft*—Unified Science—and a series of books, under the general editorship of Schlick and Philipp Frank, with the collective title of *Schriften zur Wissenschaftliche Weltauffassung.* Schlick himself contributed to it a book on ethics, of which the first chapter is included in this volume, and Frank a book on the law of causality and its limitations. Among the other volumes to appear in it were an important book by Carnap on the logical syntax of language, to which I shall have occasion to refer again, a book on sociology by Neurath with somewhat Marxist leanings, and Karl Popper's famous *Logik der Forschung* which was devoted to the philosophy of science. Popper was not in fact a member of the Circle and would at no time have wished to be classed as a positivist, but the affinities between him and the positivists whom he criticized appear more striking than the divergencies. In any case the members of the Circle did not in all points agree among themselves.

Though the logical positivist movement gathered strength throughout the thirties, the Vienna Circle itself was in the process of dissolution. By 1933, when I attended its meetings, Carnap and Frank had accepted chairs at the University of Prague and the discussions were chiefly carried on by Schlick, Neurath, Waismann and Hahn. But Hahn died in 1934 and two years later Schlick was murdered, at the age of 54, by a demented student who shot him as he was entering the University. The hostile tone of the obituaries which were devoted to Schlick in the governmental press, implying almost that logical

positivists deserved to be murdered by their pupils, foreshadowed
the troubles which were soon to fall upon the Circle. Except for
Neurath, who had participated in the revolutionary Spartacist Government in Munich at the end of the first world war, its members had
not been conspicuously active in politics, but their critical and
scientific temper made them suspect to the right-wing clerical govern-
ments of Dolfuss and Schuschnigg and still more so to the Nazis. The
majority of them were forced into exile. The advent of Nazism was
fatal also to the Berlin school, and the Polish groups were disrupted
by the war. Neurath, who had taken refuge in Holland, made a valiant
attempt to keep the movement going. The title of *Erkenntnis* was
changed to *The Journal of Unified Science* and its place of publication to the Hague. Arrangements were made for the publication by
the University of Chicago, where Carnap was established, of a series
of brochures ambitiously entitled the *International Encyclopedia of
Unified Science*. Further congresses were planned. But with the out-
break of war and Neurath's death in England some years later, the
movement lost its cohesion. Most of the volumes which were designed
to constitute the *Encyclopedia* have in fact appeared, but the *Journal
of Unified Science* very soon ceased publication and has not been
revived. Besides Carnap, Feigl, Gödel, Frank, Hempel and Tarski are
still at universities in the United States, and Waismann and Popper
at universities in England. Scholtz has remained at Münster and
Kotarbinski and Ajduciewicz in Poland; and Victor Kraft resumed
his chair of philosophy at the University of Vienna. But, however
much influence these philosophers may exert individually, they do
not constitute a school. In this sense, the logical positivist movement
has been broken up.

Nevertheless its tradition has been continued, especially in England, Scandinavia and the United States. In Scandinavia, Kaila has
been joined at Helsinki by Von Wright, a pupil of Wittgenstein's who
succeeded him for a time as professor of philosophy at Cambridge,
the Uppsala school still flourishes, under the direction of Hedenius,
Segerstedt and Marc-Wogau, with support from the logician
Wedberg in Stockholm, and Arne Naess in Oslo pursues his sociological researches into the current uses of language. Petzäll continued
to teach at Lund until his death in 1957 and Joergensen is still teaching in Copenhagen, though his positivism has been modified by an
injection of Marxism. In the United States a number of philosophers
like Quine, Nagel and Nelson Goodman conduct logical analysis in
a systematic scientific spirit that is probably closer to the original ideal
of the Vienna Circle than anything that is now to be met with else-

where. In this connection Nelson Goodman's book *The Structure of Appearance* (1951) and Quine's collection of essays *From a Logical Point of View* (1953) are especially notable. Their active interest in symbolic logic brings Quine and Goodman also into relation with Tarski, Gödel, Church and other members of the important contemporary group of American logicians. The same outlook is maintained by Carnap and his pupils, notably Bar Hillel, who is now teaching at the University of Jerusalem, and by Feigl and Hempel. Other philosophers in the United States such as Norman Malcolm, Max Black, Morris Lazerowitz and C. L. Stevenson owe more to the influence of G. E. Moore or the later Wittgenstein, and consequently display an approach to philosophical questions which is closer to that of the contemporary British schools.

In spite of the example of Bertrand Russell, there is not now among British philosophers the same interest in formal logic, or belief in the utility of symbolic techniques for clarifying philosophical issues, as is to be found in the United States. Neither is there the same desire to connect philosophy with science. My own *Language, Truth and Logic,* of which the first edition appeared in 1936, did something to popularize what may be called the classical position of the Vienna Circle; but since the war the prevailing tendency in England has been to replace this uncompromising positivism with its blanket rejection of metaphysics, its respect for scientific method, its assumption that in so far as philosophical problems are genuine at all they can be definitely solved by logical analysis, by an approach to philosophy which is empirical in the political sense, the sense in which Burke was a champion of empiricism. Generalizations are distrusted, particular examples are multiplied and carefully dissected. An attempt is made to illuminate every facet of a problem rather than to hammer or carve out a solution, common sense reigns as a constitutional, if not an absolute, monarch, philosophical theories are put to the touchstone of the way in which words are actually used. The metaphysician is treated no longer as a criminal but as a patient: there may be good reasons why he says the strange things that he does. This therapeutic technique, as it has been called, is well displayed in the work of John Wisdom, now a professor at Cambridge, whose collected volumes of articles, *Other Minds* and *Philosophy and Psycho-Analysis,* appeared in 1952 and 1953. A more robust form of therapy is practised by Gilbert Ryle, professor of metaphysics at Oxford, whose *Concept of Mind* (1949), with its attack on the Cartesian myth of "the ghost in the machine," has had a very great influence. Ryle shares with Wisdom a taste, and a gift, for analogy and metaphor, and a fondness for piling up examples, but he is less afraid of a generalization, less tolerant of departures from ordinary usage, more direct in his method than any present-day Wittgensteinian, and more ready to assume that a philosophical problem has a correct solution. What is now sometimes called the Oxford school, which takes its tone from J. L. Austin more than from Ryle, carries its interest in the ordinary use of language to a point where it may be thought that philosophical analysis has given way to the study of philology. But this tendency is not all-prevailing. The work of such philosophers as Stuart Hampshire, P. F. Strawson and David Pears shows that even within the framework of the Oxford manner there is still room for a fairly wide latitude of approach. The charge of scholasticism which is brought against "Oxford philosophy" is not entirely baseless; but it is not a truly warranted indictment.

At the present time, the philosophical world is curiously divided. If positivism be taken in its widest sense, the sense in which it embraces all shades of analytical, linguistic, or radically empirical philosophy, it is dominant in England and in Scandinavia, and commands considerable allegiance in Holland and Belgium, in Australia and in the United States. Elsewhere, it makes hardly any showing at all. Theoretically, it is not in all respects at odds with Marxism: the two at least have certain enemies in common: but it cannot flourish under Communist regimes, since Lenin's *Materialism and Empirio-Criticism,* an attack on Mach and his followers which appeared in 1905, declares it to be a form of bourgeois idealism. In other countries again, one finds philosophers subscribing to neo-Thomism or to neo-Kantianism or to neo-Hegelianism or to Existentialism or whatever form of German metaphysics may be in fashion. The ascendancy of Germany over France in this respect is especially remarkable. Conversely, in English-speaking countries there has been throughout the present century an almost complete disregard of the current extravagancies of German speculative thought. Such national divisions are indeed regrettable. They do not occur to anything like the same extent in other branches of learning. It is especially characteristic of philosophers that they tend to disagree not merely about the solution of certain problems but about the very nature of their subject and the methods by which it is to be pursued. Like others before them, the Vienna Circle believed that this could and should be remedied. They thought that they had succeeded, where Kant had failed, in finding a way "to set philosophy upon the sure path of a science." This end has not been attained: it may, indeed, be unattainable. All the same, there can be progress in philosophy and in one way and another the positivist movement is achieving it.

II. THE ATTACK ON METAPHYSICS

"When we run over libraries, persuaded of these principles, what havoc must we make? If we take in our hand any volume; of divinity or school metaphysics, for instance; let us ask, *Does it contain any abstract reasoning concerning quantity or number?* No. *Does it contain any experimental reasoning concerning matter of fact and existence?* No. Commit it then to the flames: for it can contain nothing but sophistry and illusion." This quotation is taken from David Hume's *Enquiry Concerning Human Understanding.* It is an excellent statement of the positivist's position. In the case of the logical positivists, the epithet "logical" was added because they wished to annex the discoveries of modern logic; they believed, in particular, that the logical symbolism which had been developed by Frege, Peano and Russell would be serviceable to them. But their general outlook was very much the same as Hume's. Like him, they divided significant propositions into two classes; formal propositions, like those of logic or pure mathematics, which they held to be tautological, in a sense that I shall presently explain, and factual propositions, of which it was required that they should be empirically verifiable. These classes were supposed to be exhaustive: so that if a sentence succeeded neither in expressing something that was formally true or false nor in expressing something that could be empirically tested, the view taken was that it did not express any proposition at all. It might have emotive meaning but it was literally nonsensical. A great deal of philosophical talk was held to fall into this category: talk about the absolute, or transcendent entities, or substance, or the destiny of man. Such utterances were said to be metaphysical; and the conclusion drawn was that if philosophy was to constitute a genuine branch of knowledge it must emancipate itself from metaphysics. The Viennese positivists did not go so far as to say that all metaphysical works deserved to be committed to the flames: they allowed, somewhat perfunctorily, that such writing might have poetic merit or even that it might express an exciting or interesting attitude to life. Their point was that even so it did not state anything that was either true or false and consequently that it could contribute nothing to the increase of knowledge. Metaphysical utterances were condemned not for being emotive, which could hardly be considered as objectionable in itself, but for pretending to be cognitive, for masquerading as something that they were not. Attacks on metaphysics occur fairly frequently in the history of philosophy. I have quoted Hume and I might also have quoted Kant who maintained that the human understanding lost itself in contradictions when it ventured beyond the bounds of possible experience. The originality of the logical positivists lay in their making the impossibility of metaphysics depend not upon the nature of what could be known but upon the nature of what could be said. Their charge against the metaphysician was that he breaks the rules which any utterance must satisfy if it is to be literally significant.

At the outset, their formulation of these rules was linked with a conception of language which Wittgenstein, who inherited it from Russell, made fully explicit in his *Tractatus*. The underlying assumption is that there are statements which are elementary in the sense that, if they are true, they correspond to absolutely simple facts. It may be that the language which we actually use does not contain the means of expressing these statements: the statements which it can serve to express may none of them be entirely elementary; but these more complex statements must still rest upon a foundation of elementary statements, even if the foundation be hidden. They are significant only in so far as they say what would be said by affirming certain elementary statements and denying certain others, that is, only in so far as they give a true or false picture of the ultimate "atomic" facts. They can, therefore, be represented as being constructed out of elementary statements by the logical operations of conjunction and negation, in such a way that their truth or falsehood is entirely dependent on the truth or falsehood of the elementary statements in question. Thus, assuming p and q to be elementary statements, the "molecular" statement "p or q" is taken to be equivalent to "not (not-p and not-q)"; and this means that it is false if both p and q are false, but true in the three remaining cases, namely that in which p and q are both true, that in which p is true and q false, and that in which p is false and q true. In general, given n elementary statements, where n is any finite number, there are 2^n possible distributions of truth and falsehood among them: and the meaning of the more complex statements which can be constructed out of them is constituted by the selection of truth distributions with which they agree or disagree.

As a rule, it will be found that a statement agrees with some truth distributions and disagrees with others: among the possible states of affairs with which it is concerned, some would make it true, and others would make it false. There are, however, two extreme cases; that in which a statement agrees with every truth distribution and that in which it agrees with none. In the former case it is true in any circumstances whatsoever, and in the latter case false. According to Wittgenstein, these two extremes are those of *tautology* and *contradiction*. On this view, all the truths of logic are tautologies; and if Russell and Whitehead succeeded in their attempt to show that mathematics is reducible to logic, so are the truths of mathematics. Wittgenstein himself did not allow that mathematical statements were tautologies; he said that they were identities: but apart from technical considerations, this comes to much the same thing. The point is that neither say anything about the world. The only way in which they can add to our knowledge is by enabling us to derive one statement from another: that is, by bringing out the implications of what, in a sense, we know already.

Tautologies say nothing because of their excessive modesty: since they agree with every possible state of affairs, they make no claim upon the facts. Thus, I obtain some information, whether true or false, about the habits of lions if I am told that they are carnivorous, and equally if I am told that they are not; but to tell me that they are either carnivorous or not is to tell me nothing about them at all. Similarly, contradictions say nothing because of their excessive cantankerousness; to disagree with every possible state of affairs is again to be disqualified from giving any information. I learn nothing, not even anything false, about the habits of lions if I am told that they are and are not carnivorous. On this interpretation, tautologies and contradictions are degenerate cases of factual statements. Metaphysical assertions, on the other hand, are meaningless because they bear no relation to fact. They are not constructed out of elementary statements in any way at all.

Since Wittgenstein did not say what he took his elementary statements to be, he did not make it quite clear at what point one is deemed to enter into metaphysics. It would seem, however, that any attempt to characterize reality as a whole, any such assertion as that the Universe is spiritual, or that everything happens for the best in the best of all possible worlds, must for him be metaphysical; for such assertions do not discriminate between possible states of affairs within the world—no matter what happens, it is to be characterized as spiritual, or regarded as happening for the best—from which it follows that they are not factual. Neither do they seem to be constructed out of factual statements in the way that tautologies are. And even if they were they would still say nothing.

Whatever may have been Wittgenstein's own view, his followers took it for granted that the elementary statements which yielded this criterion of meaning were reports of observations. As we shall see later on, they soon came to disagree about the character of these reports. There was a dispute over the question whether they were infallible, and whether they referred to the private sensations of the speaker, or to public physical events. But it was agreed that, in one form or another, they provided the touchstone by reference to which all other statements were empirically verified. And since, according to Wittgenstein's theory, they alone furnished these statements with their factual content, they were also responsible for their meaning. This view was then summed up in the famous slogan that the meaning of a proposition is its method of verification.

The assumption behind this slogan was that everything that could be said at all could be expressed in terms of elementary statements. All statements of a higher order, including the most abstract scientific hypotheses, were in the end nothing more than shorthand descriptions of observable events. But this assumption was very difficult to sustain. It was particularly vulnerable when the elementary statements were taken to be records of the subject's immediate experiences: for while it has sometimes been maintained that statements about physical objects can be faithfully translated into statements about sense-data, no such translation has ever been achieved: there are, indeed, good grounds for supposing that it is not feasible. Moreover this choice of a basis raised the question of solipsism; the problem of making the transition from the subject's private experiences to the experiences of others and to the public world. Carnap, indeed, in his *Der logische Aufbau der Welt* (1928) made a valiant attempt to reconstruct our whole apparatus of empirical concepts on a solipsistic foundation, taking as his starting-point the single undefined notion of remembered similarity: but he later acknowledged that this enterprise did not succeed. The position was easier for those who treated elementary statements as descriptions of physical events, though their right to do this remained in question: they at least were not troubled by the problem of solipsism or by the difficulty of reducing physical objects to sense-data. But other difficulties remained. The most serious of all, perhaps, was presented by the case of universal statements of law. For while the truth of such a statement may be confirmed by the accumulation of favorable instances, it is not formally entailed by them; the possibility that a further instance will refute it must always remain open: and this means that statements of this sort are not conclusively verifiable. On the other hand, they can be conclusively falsified in the sense that a negative instance formally contradicts them. For this reason Karl Popper suggested in his

Logik der Forschung that what should be required of a factual statement was just that it be capable in theory of being falsified. And he argued that apart from the logical superiority of this criterion it was more in accord with scientific practice; for scientists set up hypotheses which they test by looking for counter-examples: when a counter-example is discovered the hypothesis is rejected or modified; otherwise it is retained. But Popper's criterion has demerits of its own. For instance, as he himself recognizes, it allows one to deny an indefinite existential statement but not to affirm it. One can say that there are no abominable snowmen, for this could be falsified by finding them, but one cannot say that there are abominable snowmen, for this could not be falsified; the fact that one had failed to find any would not prove conclusively that none existed. What could be disproved would be that any of them existed at a particular place and time, and it is only if this further specification is given that the statement becomes legitimate: otherwise it is to be counted as metaphysical. But this is to bring the frontiers of metaphysics rather close.

Because of this and other difficulties the view which came to prevail among the logical positivists was that the demands that a statement be conclusively verifiable, or that it be conclusively falsifiable, were both too stringent as criteria of meaning. They chose instead to be satisfied with a weaker criterion by which it was required only that a statement be capable of being in some degree confirmed or disconfirmed by observation; if it were not itself an elementary statement, it had to be such that elementary statements could support it, but they did not need to entail it or to entail its negation. Unfortunately, this notion of "support" or "confirmation" has never yet been adequately formalized. Various attempts have been made to give "the verification principle," in this weaker form, a thoroughly precise expression, but the results have not been altogether satisfactory. However, the employment of the principle did not wait upon its proper formulation; its general purport was held to be sufficiently clear. I have already given examples of the kind of philosophical talk that it served to eliminate: but its destructiveness was not confined to what one might call the grosser forms of metaphysics. As employed by the Viennese positivists, it made short work of most of the perennial problems of philosophy. Thus, the questions at issue between monists and pluralists, or between realists and idealists, were accounted no less spurious than questions about the limitations of Being, or a transcendent world of values. For what empirical test could possibly go to decide whether the world is one or many, or whether the things that we perceive do or do not exist outside someone's mind? It is characteristic of such rival philosophical theses as realism and idealism that each is consistent with all the appearances, whatever their content may happen to be. But, for the positivist, it is just this that condemns them.

An obvious objection to the verification principle, which the positivists' opponents were quick to seize on, is that it is not itself verifiable. I suppose that it might be taken as an empirical hypothesis about the way in which people actually use the word "meaning," but in that case it would appear to be false; for it is not contrary to ordinary usage to say that metaphysical utterances are meaningful. Neither did its sponsors put the principle forward as the result of any such empirical investigation. But then what status did they think it had? Might it not itself be metaphysical? Surprisingly, Wittgenstein acceded to this charge. "My propositions," he said at the end of the *Tractatus,* "are elucidatory in this way: he who understands me finally recognizes them as senseless, when he has climbed out through them, on them, over them. (He must so to speak throw away the ladder, after he has climbed up on it.) He must surmount these propositions; then he sees the world rightly." But this is a vain attempt to have it both ways. No doubt some pieces of nonsense are more suggestive than others, but this does not give them any logical force. If the verification principle really is nonsensical, it states nothing; and if one holds that it states nothing, then one cannot also maintain that what it states is true.

The Vienna Circle tended to ignore this difficulty: but it seems to me fairly clear that what they were in fact doing was to adopt the verification principle as a convention. They were propounding a definition of meaning which accorded with common usage in the sense that it set out the conditions that are in fact satisfied by statements which are regarded as empirically informative. Their treatment of *a priori* statements was also intended to provide an account of the way in which such statements actually function. To this extent their work was descriptive; it became prescriptive with the suggestion that only statements of these two kinds should be regarded as either true or false, and that only statements which were capable of being either true or false should be regarded as literally meaningful.

But why should this prescription be accepted? The most that has been proved is that metaphysical statements do not fall into the same category as the laws of logic, or as scientific hypotheses, or as historical narratives, or judgments of perception, or any other common sense descriptions of the "natural" world. Surely it does not follow that they are neither true nor false, still less that they are nonsensical?

No, it does not follow. Or rather, it does not follow unless one makes it follow. The question is whether one thinks the difference between metaphysical and common sense or scientific statements to be sufficiently sharp for it to be useful to underline it in this way. The defect of this procedure is that it tends to make one blind to the interest that metaphysical questions can have. Its merit is that it removes the temptation to look upon the metaphysician as a sort of scientific overlord. Neither is this a trivial matter. It has far too often been assumed that the metaphysician was doing the same work as the scientist, only doing it more profoundly; that he was uncovering a deeper layer of facts. It is therefore important to emphasize that he is not in this sense describing any facts at all.

But then what is he doing? What is the point of saying, like McTaggart, that time is unreal or, like Berkeley, that physical objects are ideas in the mind of God or, like Heidegger, that the "nothing nihilates itself"? It should not be assumed that there is a general answer to this question, that metaphysicians are always doing the same sort of thing. One must begin in any case by looking at the context in which such pronouncements occur. Heidegger's remark is a piece of verbiage, but it contributes in its fashion to his development of the theme that it is a matter for wonder that the world exists. "Why is there anything at all," he asks, "and not rather nothing?" This is indeed the kind of question that people expect philosophers to put: it has an air of profundity about it. The trouble is that it does not admit of any answer. On the face of it, McTaggart's contention that time is unreal seems hardly more sensible. If taken literally, as implying that nothing ever happens, it is grotesquely false. And if it is not to be taken literally, what does it mean? The answer is to be found by looking at McTaggart's arguments. He shows himself there to be perplexed by the idea of the passage of time; he tries to prove that the notion of an event's being successively future, present, and past involves a vicious infinite regress. The proof is invalid, but we can learn something from it. In defending our use of temporal expressions against McTaggart's arguments we may reach a clearer understanding of all that it implies. Berkeley, again, was concerned to discover what could be meant by saying that physical objects exist: he convinced himself by plausible arguments that when we speak of physical objects we can be referring only to collections of "sensible qualities," the existence of which consists in their being perceived; and he then brought in God as the permanent sensorium which was needed to keep things in being. His arguments can be withstood; but they do raise important philosophical problems about the meaning and justification of the statements that we make about the "external world."

The Viennese positivists were chiefly interested in the formal and the natural sciences. They did not identify philosophy with science, but they believed that it ought to contribute in its own way to the advance of scientific knowledge. They therefore condemned metaphysics because it failed to meet this condition. The logical analysts of to-day are more indulgent. They too are opposed to metaphysics in so far as it is merely rhapsodical: even in the sphere of ethics they wish to dissociate philosophy from preaching. But they allow that the metaphysician may sometimes be seeing the world in a fresh and interesting way; he may have good reason for being dissatisfied with our ordinary concepts, or for proposing to revise them. In many cases no doubt he is the victim of a logical error; but such errors may be instructive. If philosophical problems arise, as Wittgenstein thought, because we are led astray by certain features of our language, the metaphysician, by his very extravagancies, may also contribute to their dissolution.

III. Language and Fact

With their elimination of metaphysics, the Viennese positivists hoped that they had also put the theory of knowledge behind them, but in this they were deceived. The first source of trouble was the notion of elementary statements. Both their character and status became a matter of dispute.

At the outset, as I have said, the prevailing view was that these statements referred to the subject's introspectible or sensory experiences. This view was adopted because it seemed to follow from the equation of the meaning of a statement with the method of its verification. For in the last resort it is only through someone's having some experience that any statement is actually verified. In most cases, the verification would consist in the perception of some physical object; but it was held, following Russell and ultimately Berkeley, that perceiving physical objects was to be analyzed in terms of having sensations, or as Russell put it, of sensing sense-data. Though physical objects might be publicly accessible, sense-data were taken to be private. There could be no question of our literally sharing one another's sense-data, any more than we can literally share one another's thoughts or images or feelings. The result was that the truth of an elementary statement could be directly checked only by the person to whose experience it referred. And not only was his judgment sovereign; in the most favorable case, it was held to be infallible. One can indeed be mistaken about the experiences that one is going to have in the future, or even about those that one has had in the past; it is not maintained that our memories cannot deceive us: but if one sets out merely to record an experience that one is actually having, then, on this view, there is no possibility of error. Since one can lie, one's statement may be false; but one cannot be in doubt or mistaken about its truth. If it is false one knows it to be so. A way in which this point is sometimes put is by saying that statements of this kind are "incorrigible."

This conception of elementary statements was exposed to attack on various grounds. There were some to whom it seemed that no empirical statement could be incorrigible, in the sense required. They were therefore inclined to maintain either that one could be mistaken about the character of one's present experience, so that the statements which purported to record it were fallible like the rest, or that these "direct records of experience" were not genuine statements, since they purchased their security at the expense of sacrificing all descriptive content. But the most serious difficulty lay in the privacy of the objects to which the elementary statements were supposed to refer. If each one of us is bound to interpret any statement as being ultimately a description of his own private experiences, it is hard to see how we can ever communicate at all. Even to speak of "each one of us" is to beg a question; for it would seem that on this view the supposition that other people exist can have no meaning for me unless I construe it as a hypothesis about my own observations of them, that is, about the course of my own actual or possible experiences. It was maintained by Carnap and others that the solipsism which seemed to be involved in this position was only methodological; but this was little more than an avowal of the purity of their intentions. It did nothing to mitigate the objections to their theory.

At first, it was thought that the difficulty about communication could be met by drawing a distinction between the content of experiences and their structure. Content, it was maintained, was incommunicable. Since other people cannot sense my sense-data, or share my thoughts or feelings, they cannot verify the statements that I make about them; neither can I verify the corresponding statements that they make about their experiences. And if I cannot verify them, I cannot understand them either. To this extent we inhabit entirely different worlds. What can be verified, however, is that these worlds have a similar structure. I have no means of telling that the feeling which another person records when he says that he is in pain is at all like the feeling that I call pain: I have no means of telling that the colors which he identifies by the use of certain words look at all the same to him as the colors for which I use these words look to me. But at least I can observe that we apply the words on the same occasions, that his classification of objects according to their color coincides with mine; I can observe that when he says he is in pain he displays what I regard as the appropriate signs. And this is all that is required for communication. It does not matter to me what my neighbour's experiences actually are: for all that I can ever know they are utterly different from mine. What matters is that the structure of our respective worlds is sufficiently alike for me to be able to rely on the information that he gives me. And it is in this sense only that we have a common language; we have, as it were, the same canvas which each of us paints in his own private fashion. It follows that if there are propositions, like the propositions of science, which have an inter-subjective meaning, they must be interpreted as descriptions of structure.

As I have already remarked, the fundamental objection to this view is that it inconsistently puts the "private worlds" of other people on a level with one's own; it results in a curious, and indeed contradictory, theory of multiple solipsism. But, apart from this, the distinction which it tries to make between content and structure does not seem to be tenable. For what would be an example of a statement which referred only to structure? There is an echo here of Locke's "primary qualities." But statements which refer to the "geometrical" properties of objects, to "figure, extension, number and motion" have to be interpreted in terms of content, just as much as statements which refer to colors and sounds. If I have no means of knowing that my neighbor means the same as I do by his use of color-words, I have equally no means of knowing that he means the same by his use of words which refer to spatial relations or to numerical quantities. I cannot tell even that what I take to be the same word really is the same for him. All that I am left with is the apparent harmony of our behavior. Moreover it seems that the attempt to draw a distinction *within* the boundaries of descriptive language between what can and cannot be communicated must be self-defeating. It leads to the absurdity to which Ramsey draws attention in his short paper on "Philosophy," which is included in this volume: "the position of the child in the following dialogue: 'Say breakfast.' 'Can't.' 'What can't you say?' 'Can't say breakfast.' "

Because of such difficulties, Neurath, and subsequently Carnap, rejected this whole conception of elementary statements. They argued that if elementary statements were to serve as the basis for the inter-subjective statements of science, they must themselves be inter-subjective. They must refer, not to private incommunicable experi-ences, but to public physical events. More generally, statements which ostensibly refer to experiences, or to "mental" states or processes of any kind, whether one's own or anybody else's, must all be equiva-lent to "physical statements": for it is only in this way that they can be publicly intelligible. This is the thesis of physicalism. I shall not dwell upon it here, as I have inserted an article by Carnap, "Psychology in Physical Language," which sets it out at length.

The view that they were included in "the physical language" took away from elementary, or, as Neurath and Carnap called them, "protocol," statements their privileged position. They were no longer thought to be incorrigible. Their truth, like that of any other physical statements, was always open to question. But, more than this, they lost even their judicial status. If a protocol-statement conflicted with a statement of a higher order, such as a scientific hypothesis, one or other of them would have to be abandoned, but it need not necessarily be the scientific hypothesis: in certain circumstances it might be more convenient to reject the protocol-statement instead.

As can be seen from his paper on the foundation of knowledge ("Über das Fundament der Erkenntnis") Schlick found this con-clusion unacceptable. He argued that to treat the reports of observa-tion, which was what protocol-statements were supposed to be, in this cavalier fashion, was to put scientific hypotheses, and indeed all would-be empirical statements, outside the control of fact. Neurath and Carnap, however, were not impressed by this argument. They had decided by this time that it was metaphysical to talk of comparing statements with facts. For what could this "comparison" be if not a logical relation? And the only thing to which a statement could stand in any logical relation was another statement. Consequently, they were led to adopt a coherence theory of truth.

Their version of the coherence theory was in some ways less objectionable than that which the Hegelian idealists had made familiar. Even so, for the reasons which I set out in my paper on Verification and Experience, it seems to me quite untenable. Carnap himself abandoned it after he had been convinced by Tarski of the respectability of semantics; for semantics provides us with the means of referring to the relationship between sentences and what they are used to signify. It provides, as Tarski showed, an adequate reformulation of the correspondence theory of truth. On the other hand Carnap has not, so far as I know, abandoned the thesis of physicalism. But, if he does still hold it, I think that he is mistaken. It now seems clear to me that statements about the experiences of others can not be *logically* equivalent to statements about their overt behavior; while to maintain that the statements which one makes about one's own experiences are equivalent to statements about the publicly observable condition of one's body is, as Ramsey put it, to feign anaesthesia. Nevertheless, the difficulties which this thesis was designed to meet remain. Neither is it easy to see how else they can be avoided. I suggest, however, that much of the trouble may arise from the acceptance of two false assumptions, the first being that for a language to be public it must refer to public objects, and the second that in making an empirical statement one is always referring to one's own experiences. I still think that empirical statements must refer to experiences, in the sense that they must be verifiable; but the reference need not be to the experiences of any one person, as opposed to any other. But I acknowledge that this attempt to "neutralize" the verification principle meets with considerable difficulties of its own.

IV. ETHICS

One of the attractions, especially for Neurath, of the thesis of physicalism was that it supported the doctrine of the Unity of Science. In one aspect, this was less of a doctrine than a program; it was desired that scientists of different disciplines should collaborate more closely with each other and with philosophers than they usually do: but it was also maintained that they were, or should be, speaking a common language, that the vocabulary of the sciences should be unified. Thus, the Vienna Circle rejected the view, which many still hold, that there is a radical distinction between the natural and the social sciences. The scale and diversity of the phenomena with which the social sciences dealt made them less successful in establishing scientific laws, but this was a difficulty of practice, not of principle: they too were concerned in the end with physical events.

Even those who did not accept the thesis of physicalism agreed that there was no essential difference in aim or method between the various branches of science. In the social sciences, no less than in the natural, an attempt was made to formulate hypotheses which could be tested by observation. Thus Schlick, who included ethics among the social sciences, denied that its results depended upon the use of any special faculty of moral intuition. The questions which

arise in ethics are, in his opinion, questions of fact; why people hold
the principles that they do, what it is that they desire, and how their
desires can be fulfilled. In short, his general position is very similar
to that of the Utilitarians. It has much the same merits and much the
same defects.

The Vienna Circle as a whole was not very greatly interested in
ethics; but it did not dispute Schlick's view that if ethical statements
were to be brought into the scientific fold, they must be handled in the
way that he proposed. The only question was whether they belonged
within the fold, whether they were statements of fact at all. Carnap,
for example, maintained that they were not; he said that they were
disguised imperatives. He did not develop this suggestion, but it has
since been given substance by R. M. Hare in his book on *The
Language of Morals* (1952). This imperative theory of ethics may
be regarded as a version of the so-called Emotive Theory which,
mainly through the work of English and American philosophers, has
come to be most closely associated with logical positivism. The
salient point is that ethical statements are not descriptive of natural
facts, still less of an alleged non-natural world of values: they are
not *descriptive* of anything at all. The problem is then to determine
how they do function. In C. L. Stevenson's book *Ethics and Language* (1944), where the emotive theory was first worked out in
detail, it was argued that ethical statements served the dual purpose
of expressing their author's approval, or disapproval, of whatever
was in question and recommending others to share his attitude. He
laid particular emphasis upon the *persuasive* use of ethical terms. His
views have not passed without criticism even from those who share
his general standpoint; but the alternative accounts of ethics which
these critics have put forward belong, as it were, to the same family.

In discussions of logical positivism, this theory of ethics is apt
to receive a disproportionate measure of attention, considering that it
stands on the periphery of the system. One reason for this is that it
has been thought, quite wrongly, that it was an onslaught upon
morals. It has even been asserted, without a shadow of empirical
evidence, that its advocates were corrupters of youth. In fact, the
theory only explores the consequences of a sound and respectable
point of logic which was already made by Hume; that normative
statements are not derivable from descriptive statements, or, as Hume
puts it, that "ought" does not follow from "is." To say that moral
judgments are not fact-stating is not to say that they are unimportant,
or even that there cannot be arguments in their favor. But these
arguments do not work in the way that logical or scientific arguments
do. It is not as if the intuitionists had discovered grounds for moral

judgments which the emotivists tried to take away. On the contrary, as Mr. Strawson shows in his paper on "Ethical Intuitionism," the intuitionists themselves do not supply any foundation for moral judgments. It is therefore only on personal grounds that they can be entitled to put themselves forward as the guardians of virtue.

V. PHILOSOPHICAL ANALYSIS

Some of the dissatisfaction that is aroused by the emotive theory of ethics, and indeed by logical positivism in general, may be due to the fact that people are still inclined to look to philosophy for guidance as to the way they ought to live. When this function is denied to it, and when it is denied even the possibility of penetrating the veil of appearance and exploring the hidden depths of reality, they feel that it is being trivialized. If this time-honored program is nonsensical, what remains? As Ramsey says, "philosophy must be of some use, and we must take it seriously." But what function do the positivists leave it to perform?

From the point of view of Wittgenstein's *Tractatus,* its function would appear to be purely negative, though not for that reason unimportant. "The right method of philosophy," said Wittgenstein, "would be this. To say nothing except what can be said, i.e. the propositions of natural science, i.e. something that has nothing to do with philosophy: and then always, when someone wished to say something metaphysical, to demonstrate to him that he had given no meaning to certain signs in his propositions. This method would be unsatisfying to the other—he would not have the feeling that we were teaching him philosophy—but it would be the only strictly correct method." This rather depressing view of the philosopher's duty was not strictly maintained by Wittgenstein himself. The *Philosophical Investigations* contains a great deal more than a series of proofs that people have failed to attach any meaning to certain signs in their propositions. Nevertheless it still gives the impression that to philosophize is to get into a muddle, or to rescue oneself or others from one. Philosophy is "a battle against the bewitchment of our intelligence by means of language." "What is your aim in philosophy? To show the fly the way out of the fly bottle." All the same, it is meritorious of the fly to be there. It is the critical intelligences that get themselves bewitched.

The *Tractatus* left no room for philosophical propositions. The whole field of significant discourse was covered by formal statements on the one hand and empirical statements on the other. There remained nothing for philosophy to be about. It was for this reason that Wittgenstein, and also Schlick, maintained that philosophy was not a doctrine but an activity. The result of philosophizing, said Schlick, would not be to accumulate a stock of philosophical propositions, but to make other propositions clear.

But to make propositions clear it must be possible to talk about them. As Russell points out in his introduction to the *Tractatus,* Wittgenstein appeared not to allow for this, or to allow for it only to a limited extent. He implied that an attempt to describe the structure of language, as opposed to exhibiting it in use, must result in nonsense. But though this conclusion may have been formally accepted by Schlick, it was in practice disregarded by the Vienna Circle. Thus, Carnap, in his *Der Logische Aufbau der Welt,* explicitly set himself to describe the structure of language by devising what he called a "Konstitution-System," in which the various types of linguistic expressions, or concepts, were assigned their proper places in a deductive hierarchy. If he had been questioned about the status of his own propositions, I suppose that he would have said that they were analytic; consisting, as they did, of definitions and their logical consequences, they would belong to the realm of formal truths. However this may be, he certainly believed that these propositions were significant; and he carried the Vienna Circle with him in holding that they were the sort of propositions that a philosopher should be expected to put forward.

The attempt to bring philosophy within the domain of logic was carried further by Carnap in his book on the *Logical Syntax of Language.* "Philosophy," he says in the foreword to this book, "is to be replaced by the logic of science—that is to say by the logical analysis of the concepts and sentences of the sciences, for the logic of science is nothing other than the logical syntax of the language of science." Though he speaks here of *the* language of science, he does not hold that there need be only one. Alternative language-systems may be devised, and the choice between them is a matter of convenience: this is an important departure from the position of Wittgenstein's *Tractatus.* According to Carnap, a language is characterized by its formation-rules, which specify what sequences of signs are to count as proper sentences of the language, and by its transformation-rules, which lay down the conditions under which sentences are validly derivable from one another. It might be thought that if the language was to have any empirical application it must also contain meaning-rules; rules which would correlate its expressions with observable states of affairs: but Carnap, in this formalist stage of his philosophy, thought that he could dispense with them. He believed, quite mistakenly, that statements of verbal equivalences could do the work not only of semantic statements but even of ostensive definitions.

It is in this book that Carnap makes his famous distinction between the material and the formal modes of speech. He distinguishes three kinds of sentences: "object-sentences," such as "5 is a prime number" or "Babylon was a big town," "pseudo-object sentences," such as "Five is not a thing, but a number" "Babylon was treated of in yesterday's lecture," and "syntactical sentences" such as " 'Five' is not a thing-word, but a number word" "The word 'Babylon' occurred in yesterday's lecture." The pseudo-object sentences are said to be "quasi-syntactical," because they are syntactical sentences masquerading as object-sentences. They are "quasi-syntactical sentences of the material mode of speech." Translation from the material into the formal mode replaces them by their syntactical equivalents. To put it less technically, when one speaks in the formal mode one is overtly speaking about words; when one speaks in the material mode one is speaking about words while seeming to speak about things. This distinction does not of course apply to object-sentences. Carnap was not maintaining, as some critics have supposed, that all discourse is about words. What he did appear to overlook, however, was the existence of a further category, that of pseudo-syntactical sentences; sentences which were about things but seemed to be about words. As a result, he was apt to fall into the error of treating these sentences as if they were syntactical.

It is with the opposite error that he reproached most other philosophers. He maintained that philosophical statements were syntactical, but that they had been treated as if they were object-statements, because of the fashion for expressing them in the material mode of speech. Thus, to take a selection of his examples, he argued that "The world is the totality of facts, not of things," the first proposition of Wittgenstein's *Tractatus,* was equivalent to "Science is a system of sentences, not of names": "This circumstance is logically necessary; . . . logically impossible; . . . logically possible" became "This sentence is analytic; . . . contradictory; . . . not contradictory": Kronecker's epigram "God created the natural numbers; everything else in mathematics is the work of man" was a way of saying "The natural-number symbols are primitive symbols; other numerical expressions are introduced by definition." "The only primitive data are relations between experiences" was equivalent to "Only two-or more-termed predicates whose arguments belong to the genus of experience-expressions occur as descriptive primitive symbols": "Time is infinite in both directions" to "Every positive or negative real-number expression can be used as a time-co-ordinate." Even the

question of determinism was said to "concern a syntactical difference
in the system of natural laws." In this way rival philosophical theses,
if they made any sense at all, were represented as alternative pro-
posals about the way one's language should be formed. They were
not true or false, but only more or less convenient.

I think that Carnap's distinction between the material and formal
modes was fruitful, in that it called attention to the fact that many
philosophical statements are disguised statements about language.
Where he went wrong for the most part was in supposing that they
were syntactical. For what they are concerned with is not the form
or order of words, but their use. This does not come out in Carnap's
examples because he illicitly smuggles semantics into syntax. Thus,
"experience-expressions" is not a syntactical term. What makes an
expression an "experience-expression" is not its having any particular
form but its being used to refer to an experience. But then the
question what is to count as an experience becomes important.
Neither is it to be settled by an arbitrary decision.

In his more recent works, Carnap has recognized the legitimacy
of semantics, and indeed devoted considerable attention both to the
development of semantic theory and to building up semantic systems. An interesting effect of this has been a marked relaxation of
his philosophical austerity. Having acquired the right to speak of
the reference of words to things, he has allowed almost any type
of word to denote its special sort of object, thus recreating the
baroque universe which Russell had labored to depopulate. His defense
of this apparent extravagance is to be found in his paper on "Empiricism, Semantics and Ontology," where he distinguishes between
"internal" questions which arise within a given conceptual framework and "external" questions which concern the status and legitimacy of the framework itself. He himself has always been chiefly
interested in the external questions: he has thought it his business
as a philosopher to devise linguistic systems and elaborate concepts
that will be useful to the scientist. And no one should deny that this
is a serious and legitimate activity. Where he is wrong, I think, is
in assuming that the external questions present no serious problem:
that nothing more is at issue than a choice of linguistic forms.

It is this disregard of questions about the status of his linguistic
frameworks that separates Carnap from the American philosophers,
like Quine and Goodman, who resemble him in their systematic
approach to philosophy and in their preference for formal techniques.
These philosophers are interested in what they call ontology, that
is, in the question how far one's choice of language commits one to
saying that certain things exist. "To be," says Quine, "is to be

the value of a variable": and this means that the extent of what Russell called the "furniture" of the world depends upon the range of predicates that are needed to describe it. Both Quine, and Goodman wish this furniture to be as hard and spare as possible. They "renounce abstract entities" not just because they wish to exercise their logical ingenuity in seeing how well they can do without them, but because they cannot bring themselves to believe that they exist. In the same spirit, Goodman forgoes making any use of the notion of possible, as opposed to actual, things, or of the distinction between causal and accidental connections, or of that between analytic and synthetic statements. "You may," he says, "decry some of these scruples and protest that there are more things in heaven and earth than are dreamt of in my philosophy. I am concerned, rather, that there should not be more things dreamt of in my philosophy than there are in heaven or earth." It is not clear, however, either in his case or in Quine's, on what this demand for stringent economy is based. Quine, indeed, allows in the end that the question of what there is must be settled on pragmatic grounds. And so he rejoins Carnap; but his pragmatism is much less serene.

An interest in categories, which is another way of approaching the problem of what there is, is characteristic also of the British philosophers who have been influenced by the later work of Wittgenstein. But, for the most part, they are concerned not so much with trying to eliminate certain types of entity, or to "reduce" one to another, as with bringing out the resemblances and differences in the functioning of the statements which ostensibly refer to them. A technique which Wittgenstein himself uses for this purpose is that of devising what he calls language games. The idea is that by studying distorted or simplified models of our actual language we can obtain a clearer insight into the way it really works. This is one way of protecting us against the error, into which we so easily fall, of assuming that something must be the case, instead of looking and seeing what actually is the case. "Where our language suggests a body and there is none, there, we should like to say, is a *spirit*." But this is to forsake description for bogus explanation. Very often the mental processes which we are led to postulate just do not occur. For instance, "it is no more essential to the understanding of a proposition that we should imagine anything in connection with it than that we should make a sketch from it." Such remarks foreshadow Ryle's attack upon the myth of "the ghost in the machine." And much as Wittgenstein disliked Carnap's methods, there is an echo of physicalism in his dictum that "an 'inner process' stands in need of outward criteria."

I suppose that Wittgenstein is mainly responsible for the prevalent interest in the question how words are ordinarily used, though account has also to be taken of the influence of G. E. Moore. It does not seem to me, however, that Moore has ever been so greatly concerned with ordinary usage as such. He has been concerned with upholding the "commonsense view" of the world and with analyzing the propositions which exemplify it; but he has not insisted that we limit ourselves to ordinary usage in carrying out this analysis. When he does appeal to ordinary usage it is mainly as a weapon for dealing with other philosophers. He shows that if their words are taken literally, they are using them to make statements which are manifestly false. It remains possible that they are saying something quite different from what they would appear to be saying, but then the discovery of their meaning presents a problem. If they are not using words in any ordinary sense, the sense in which they are using them has to be made clear.

To my mind, the main achievement of the "ordinary-language school" has been their examination and dissection of the "unscientific" uses of language. A good example of this is J. L. Austin's description of what he calls performative statements: statements like "I know . . ." or "I promise . . ." of which the purpose is not to assert a fact but to commit the speaker in certain ways or to offer some sort of guarantee. To what imaginative lengths this greater flexibility in the approach to language can lead is indicated by Dr. Waismann's paper which concludes this volume. It shows that the current conception of philosophical analysis has spread far beyond Ramsey's idea of philosophy as simply issuing in definitions. But Ramsey was right in saying that it is "all part of the vital work of clarifying and organizing our thought."

VI.

In compiling this anthology I have tried to illustrate the historical development of logical positivism, the range of its interests and the main points of controversy. Lack of space has obliged me to pass over many pieces that I should have liked to include. In particular, I am sorry to have had no room for Quine's paper on "Truth by Convention," in which the positivists' account of *a priori* statements is effectively criticized, or for Carnap's influential articles on "Testability and Meaning." It is especially to be regretted that the volume contains nothing of Wittgenstein. But neither the *Tractatus Logico-Philosophicus* nor the *Philosophical Investigations,* for all their episodic character, is a work to which one can do justice by selecting passages. They have to be read as a whole.

Logical Atomism

1

Logical Atomism

BY BERTRAND RUSSELL

THE PHILOSOPHY which I advocate is generally regarded as a species of realism, and accused of inconsistency because of the elements in it which seem contrary to that doctrine. For my part, I do not regard the issue between realists and their opponents as a fundamental one; I could alter my view on this issue without changing my mind as to any of the doctrines upon which I wish to lay stress. I hold that logic is what is fundamental in philosophy, and that schools should be characterized rather by their logic than by their metaphysic. My own logic is atomic, and it is this aspect upon which I should wish to lay stress. Therefore I prefer to describe my philosophy as "logical atomism," rather than as "realism," whether with or without some prefixed adjective.

A few words as to historical development may be useful by way of preface. I came to philosophy through mathematics, or rather through the wish to find some reason to believe in the truth of mathematics. From early youth, I had an ardent desire to believe that there can be such a thing as knowledge, combined with a great difficulty in accepting much that passes as knowledge. It seemed clear that the best chance of finding indubitable truth would be in pure mathematics, yet some of Euclid's axioms were obviously doubtful, and the infinitesimal calculus, as I was taught it, was a mass of sophisms, which I could not bring myself to regard as anything else. I saw no reason to doubt the truth of arithmetic, but I did not then know that arithmetic can be made to embrace all traditional pure mathematics. At the age of eighteen I read Mill's *Logic,* but was profoundly dissatisfied with his reasons for accepting arithmetic and geometry. I had not read Hume, but it seemed to me that pure empiricism (which I was disposed to accept) must lead to scep-

This essay was Russell's contribution to *Contemporary British Philosophy,* first series (ed. J. H. Muirhead), a book published in 1924. It is here reprinted by the kind permission of the author and George Allen and Unwin Ltd., London.

ticism rather than to Mill's support of received scientific doctrines.
At Cambridge I read Kant and Hegel, as well as Mr. Bradley's
Logic, which influenced me profoundly. For some years I was a
disciple of Mr. Bradley, but about 1898 I changed my views, largely
as a result of arguments with G. E. Moore. I could no longer believe
that knowing makes any difference to what is known. Also I found
myself driven to pluralism. Analysis of mathematical propositions
persuaded me that they could not be explained as even partial
truths unless one admitted pluralism and the reality of relations.
An accident led me at this time to study Leibniz, and I came to the
conclusion (subsequently confirmed by Couturat's masterly researches) that many of his most characteristic opinions were due
to the purely logical doctrine that every proposition has a subject
and a predicate. This doctrine is one which Leibniz shares with
Spinoza, Hegel, and Mr. Bradley; it seemed to me that, if it is
rejected, the whole foundation for the metaphysics of all these
philosophers is shattered. I therefore returned to the problem which
had originally led me to philosophy, namely, the foundations of
mathematics, applying to it a new logic derived largely from Peano
and Frege, which proved (at least, so I believe) far more fruitful
than that of traditional philosophy.

In the first place, I found that many of the stock philosophical
arguments about mathematics (derived in the main from Kant)
had been rendered invalid by the progress of mathematics in the
meanwhile. Non-Euclidean geometry had undermined the argument
of the transcendental aesthetic. Weierstrass had shown that the
differential and integral calculus do not require the conception of
the infinitesimal, and that, therefore, all that had been said by
philosophers on such subjects as the continuity of space and time
and motion must be regarded as sheer error. Cantor freed the
conception of infinite number from contradiction, and thus disposed
of Kant's antinomies as well as many of Hegel's. Finally Frege
showed in detail how arithmetic can be deduced from pure logic,
without the need of any fresh ideas or axioms, thus disproving Kant's
assertion that "$7 + 5 = 12$" is synthetic—at least in the obvious
interpretation of that dictum. As all these results were obtained, not
by any heroic method, but by patient detailed reasoning, I began
to think it probable that philosophy had erred in adopting heroic
remedies for intellectual difficulties, and that solutions were to be
found merely by greater care and accuracy. This view I have come
to hold more and more strongly as time went on, and it has led me
to doubt whether philosophy, as a study distinct from science and

possessed of a method of its own, is anything more than an unfortunate legacy from theology.

Frege's work was not final, in the first place because it applied only to arithmetic, not to other branches of mathematics; in the second place because his premises did not exclude certain contradictions to which all past systems of formal logic turned out to be liable. Dr. Whitehead and I in collaboration tried to remedy these two defects, in *Principia Mathematica,* which, however, still falls short of finality in some fundamental points (notably the axiom of reducibility). But in spite of its shortcomings I think that no one who reads this book will dispute its main contention, namely, that from certain ideas and axioms of formal logic, by the help of the logic of relations, all pure mathematics can be deduced, without any new undefined idea or unproved propositions. The technical methods of mathematical logic, as developed in this book, seem to me very powerful, and capable of providing a new instrument for the discussion of many problems that have hitherto remained subject to philosophic vagueness. Dr. Whitehead's *Concept of Nature* and *Principles of Natural Knowledge* may serve as an illustration of what I mean.

When pure mathematics is organized as a deductive system— i.e. as the set of all those propositions that can be deduced from an assigned set of premises—it becomes obvious that, if we are to believe in the truth of pure mathematics, it cannot be solely because we believe in the truth of the set of premises. Some of the premises are much less obvious than some of their consequences, and are believed chiefly because of their consequences. This will be found to be always the case when a science is arranged as a deductive system. It is not the logically simplest propositions of the system that are the most obvious, or that provide the chief part of our reasons for believing in the system. With the empirical sciences this is evident. Electro-dynamics, for example, can be concentrated into Maxwell's equations, but these equations are believed because of the observed truth of certain of their logical consequences. Exactly the same thing happens in the pure realm of logic; the logically first principles of logic—at least some of them—are to be believed, not on their own account, but on account of their consequences. The epistemological question: "Why should I believe this set of propositions?" is quite different from the logical question: "What is the smallest and logically simplest group of propositions from which this set of propositions can be deduced?" Our reasons for believing logic and pure mathematics are, in part, only inductive and probable, in spite of the fact that, in their *logical* order, the propositions of logic and pure mathematics follow from the premises of logic by pure deduction. I think this point important, since errors are liable to arise from assimilating the logical to the epistemological order, and also, conversely, from assimilating the epistemological to the logical order. The only way in which work on mathematical logic throws light on the truth or falsehood of mathematics is by disproving the supposed antinomies. This shows that mathematics *may* be true. But to show that mathematics *is* true would require other methods and other considerations.

One very important heuristic maxim which Dr. Whitehead and I found, by experience, to be applicable in mathematical logic, and have since applied in various other fields, is a form of Ockham's razor. When some set of supposed entities has neat logical properties, it turns out, in a great many instances, that the supposed entities can be replaced by purely logical structures composed of entities which have not such neat properties. In that case, in interpreting a body of propositions hitherto believed to be about the supposed entities, we can substitute the logical structures without altering any of the detail of the body of propositions in question. This is an economy, because entities with neat logical properties are always inferred, and if the propositions in which they occur can be interpreted without making this inference, the ground for the inference fails, and our body of propositions is secured against the need of a doubtful step. The principle may be stated in the form: "Wherever possible, substitute constructions out of known entities for inferences to unknown entities."

The uses of this principle are very various, but are not intelligible in detail to those who do not know mathematical logic. The first instance I came across was what I have called "the principle of abstraction," or "the principle which dispenses with abstraction."[1] This principle is applicable in the case of any symmetrical and transitive relation, such as equality. We are apt to infer that such relations arise from possession of some common quality. This may or may not be true; probably it is true in some cases and not in others. But all the formal purposes of a common quality can be served by membership of the group of terms having the said relation to a given term. Take magnitude, for example. Let us suppose that we have a group of rods, all equally long. It is easy to suppose that there is a certain quality, called their length, which they all share. But all propositions in which this supposed quality occurs will

1. *Our Knowledge of the External World*, p. 42.

retain their truth-value unchanged if, instead of "length of the rod *x*" we take "membership of the group of all those rods which are as long as *x*." In various special cases—e.g. the definition of real numbers—a simpler construction is possible.

A very important example of the principle is Frege's definition of the cardinal number of a given set of terms as the class of all sets that are "similar" to the given set—where two sets are "similar" when there is a one-one relation whose domain is the one set and whose converse domain is the other. Thus a cardinal number is the class of all those classes which are similar to a given class. This definition leaves unchanged the truth-values of all propositions in which cardinal numbers occur, and avoids the inference to a set of entities called "cardinal numbers," which were never needed except for the purpose of making arithmetic intelligible, and are now no longer needed for that purpose.

Perhaps even more important is the fact that classes themselves can be dispensed with by similar methods. Mathematics is full of propositions which seem to require that a class or an aggregate should be in some sense a single entity—e.g. the proposition "the number of combinations of *n* things any number at a time is 2^n." Since 2^n is always greater than *n,* this proposition leads to difficulties if classes are admitted because the number of classes of entities in the universe is greater than the number of entities in the universe, which would be odd if classes were some among entities. Fortunately all the propositions in which classes appear to be mentioned can be interpreted without supposing that there are classes. This is perhaps the most important of all the applications of our principle. (See *Principia Mathematica,* *20.)

Another important example concerns what I call "definite descriptions," i.e. such phrases as "the even prime," "the present King of England," "the present King of France." There has always been a difficulty in interpreting such propositions as "the present King of France does not exist." The difficulty arose through supposing that "the present King of France" is the subject of this proposition, which made it necessary to suppose that he subsists although he does not exist. But it is difficult to attribute even subsistence to "the round square" or "the even prime greater than 2." In fact, "the round square does not subsist" is just as true as "the present King of France does not exist." Thus the distinction between existence and subsistence does not help us. The fact is that, when the words "the so-and-so" occur in a proposition, there is no corresponding single constituent of the proposition, and when the proposition is fully analyzed the words "the so-and-so" have disappeared. An important consequence of the theory of descriptions is that it is meaningless to say "A exists" unless "A" is (or stands for) a phrase of the form "the so-and-so." If the so-and-so exists, and x is the so-and-so, to say "x exists" is nonsense. Existence, in the sense in which it is ascribed to single entities, is thus removed altogether from the list of fundamentals. The ontological argument and most of its refutations are found to depend upon bad grammar. (See *Principia Mathematica*, *14.)

There are many other examples of the substitution of constructions for inferences in pure mathematics, for example, series, ordinal numbers, and real numbers. But I will pass on to the examples in physics.

Points and instants are obvious examples: Dr. Whitehead has shown how to construct them out of sets of events all of which have a finite extent and a finite duration. In relativity theory, it is not points or instants that we primarily need, but event-particles, which correspond to what, in older language, might be described as a point at an instant, or an instantaneous point. (In former days, a point of space endured throughout all time, and an instant of time pervaded all space. Now the unit that mathematical physics wants has neither spatial nor temporal extension.) Event-particles are constructed by just the same logical process by which points and instants were constructed. In such constructions, however, we are on a different plane from that of constructions in pure mathematics. The possibility of constructing an event-particle depends upon the existence of sets of events with certain properties; whether the required events exist can only be known empirically, if at all. There is therefore no *a priori* reason to expect continuity (in the mathematical sense), or to feel confident that event-particles can be constructed. If the quantum theory should seem to demand a discrete space-time, our logic is just as ready to meet its requirements as to meet those of traditional physics, which demands continuity. The question is purely empirical, and our logic is (as it ought to be) equally adapted to either alternative.

Similar considerations apply to a particle of matter, or to a piece of matter of finite size. Matter, traditionally, has two of those "neat" properties which are the mark of a logical construction; first, that two pieces of matter cannot be at the same place at the same time; secondly, that one piece of matter cannot be in two places at the same time. Experience in the substitution of constructions for inferences makes one suspicious of anything so tidy and exact. One cannot help feeling that impenetrability is not an empirical fact, derived from observation of billiard-balls, but is something logically necessary. This feeling is wholly justified, but it could not be so if matter were not a logical construction. An immense number of occurrences coexist in any little region of space-time; when we are speaking of what is not logical construction, we find no such property as impenetrability, but, on the contrary, endless overlapping of the events in a part of space-time, however small. The reason that matter is impenetrable is because our definitions make it so. Speaking roughly, and merely so as to give a notion of how this happens, we may say that a piece of matter is all that happens in a certain track in space-time, and that we construct the tracks called bits of matter in such a way that they do not intersect. Matter is impenetrable because it is easier to state the laws of physics if we make our constructions so as to secure impenetrability. Impenetrability is a logically necessary result of definition, though the fact that such a definition is convenient is empirical. Bits of matter are not among the bricks out of which the world is built. The bricks are events, and bits of matter are portions of the structure to which we find it convenient to give separate attention.

In the philosophy of mental occurrences there are also opportunities for the application of our principle of constructions *versus* inferences. The subject, and the relation of a cognition to what is known, both have that schematic quality that arouses our suspicions. It is clear that the subject, if it is to be preserved at all, must be preserved as a construction, not as an inferred entity; the only question is whether the subject is sufficiently useful to be worth constructing. The relation of a cognition to what is known, again, cannot be a straightforward single ultimate, as I at one time believed it to be. Although I do not agree with pragmatism, I think William James was right in drawing attention to the complexity of "knowing." It is impossible in a general summary, such as the present, to set out the reasons for this view. But whoever has acquiesced in our principle will agree that here is prima facie a case for applying it. Most of my *Analysis of Mind* consists of applications of this principle. But as psychology is scientifically much less perfected than physics, the opportunities for applying the principle are not so good. The principle depends, for its use, upon the existence of some fairly reliable body of propositions, which are to be interpreted by the logician in such a way as to preserve their truth while minimizing the element of inference to unobserved entities. The principle therefore presupposes a moderately advanced science, in the absence of which the logician does not know what he ought to construct. Until recently, it would have seemed necessary to construct geometrical points; now it is event-particles that are wanted. In view of such a change in an advanced subject like physics, it is clear that constructions in psychology must be purely provisional.

I have been speaking hitherto of what it is *not* necessary to assume as part of the ultimate constituents of the world. But logical constructions, like all other constructions, require materials, and it is time to turn to the positive question, as to what these materials are to be. This question, however, requires as a preliminary a discussion of logic and language and their relation to what they try to represent.

The influence of language on philosophy has, I believe, been profound and almost unrecognized. If we are not to be misled by this influence, it is necessary to become conscious of it, and to ask ourselves deliberately how far it is legitimate. The subject-predicate logic, with the substance-attribute metaphysic, are a case in point. It is doubtful whether either would have been invented by people speaking a non-Aryan language; certainly they do not seem to have arisen in China, except in connection with Buddhism, which brought Indian philosophy with it. Again, it is natural, to take a different kind of instance, to suppose that a proper name which can be used significantly stands for a single entity; we suppose that there is a certain more or less persistent being called "Socrates," because the same name is applied to a series of occurrences which we are led to regard as appearances of this one being. As language grows more abstract, a new set of entities come into philosophy, namely, those represented by abstract words—the universals. I do not wish to maintain that there are no universals, but certainly there are many abstract words which do not stand for single universals—e.g. triangularity and rationality. In these respects language misleads us both by its vocabulary and by its syntax. We must be on our guard in both respects if our logic is not to lead to a false metaphysic.

Syntax and vocabulary have had different kinds of effects on philosophy. Vocabulary has most influence on common sense. It might be urged, conversely, that common sense produces our vocabulary. This is only partially true. A word is applied at first to things which are more or less similar, without any reflection as to whether they have any point of identity. But when once usage has fixed the objects to which the word is to be applied, common sense is influenced by the existence of the word, and tends to suppose that one word must stand for one object, which will be a universal in the case of an adjective or an abstract word. Thus the influence of vocabulary is towards a kind of platonic pluralism of things and ideas.

The influence of syntax, in the case of the Indo-European languages, is quite different. Almost any proposition can be put into a form in which it has a subject and a predicate, united by a copula. It is natural to infer that every fact has a corresponding form, and consists in the possession of a quality by a substance. This leads, of course, to monism, since the fact that there were several substances (if it were a fact) would not have the requisite form. Philosophers, as a rule, believe themselves free from this sort of influence of linguistic forms, but most of them seem to me to be mistaken in this belief. In thinking about abstract matters, the fact that the words for abstractions are no more abstract than ordinary words always makes it easier to think about the words than about what they stand for, and it is almost impossible to resist consistently the temptation to think about the words.

Those who do not succumb to the subject-predicate logic are apt to get only one step further, and admit relations of two terms, such as before-and-after, greater-and-less, right-and-left. Language lends itself to this extension of the subject-predicate logic, since we say *"A* precedes *B," "A* exceeds *B,"* and so on. It is easy to prove that the fact expressed by a proposition of this sort cannot consist of the possession of a quality by a substance, or of the possession of two or more qualities by two or more substances. (See *Principles of Mathematics,* § 214.) The extension of the subject-predicate logic is therefore right so far as it goes, but obviously a further extension can be proved necessary by exactly similar arguments. How far it is necessary to go up the series of three-term, four-term, five-term . . . relations I do not know. But it is certainly necessary to go beyond two-term relations. In projective geometry, for example, the order of points on a line or of planes through a line requires a four-term relation.

A very unfortunate effect of the peculiarities of language is in connection with adjectives and relations. All words are of the same logical type; a word is a class of series, of noises or shapes according as it is heard or read. But the meanings of words are of various different types; an attribute (expressed by an adjective) is of a different type from the objects to which it can be (whether truly or falsely) attributed; a relation (expressed perhaps by a preposition, perhaps by a transitive verb, perhaps in some other way) is of a different type from the terms between which it holds or does not hold. The definition of a logical type is as follows: *A* and *B* are of the same logical type if, and only if, given any fact of which *A* is a constituent, there is a corresponding fact which has *B* as a constituent, which either results by substituting *B* for *A,* or is the negation of what so results. To take an illustration, Socrates and Aristotle are of the same type, because "Socrates was a philosopher" and "Aristotle was a philosopher" are both facts; Socrates and Caligula are of the same type, because "Socrates was a philosopher" and "Caligula was not a philosopher" are both facts. To love and to kill are of the same type, because "Plato loved Socrates" and "Plato did not kill Socrates" are both facts. It follows formally from the definition that, when two words have meanings of different types, the relations of the words to what they mean are of different types; that is to say, there is not one relation of meaning between words and what they stand for, but as many relations of meaning, each of a different logical type, as there are logical types among the objects for which there are words. This fact is a very potent source of error and confusion in philosophy. In particular, it has made it extraordinarily difficult to express in words any theory of relations which is logically capable of being true, because language cannot preserve the difference of type between a relation and its terms. Most of the arguments for and against the reality of relations have been vitiated through this source of confusion.

At this point, I propose to digress for a moment, and to say, as shortly as I can, what I believe about relations. My own views on the subject of relations in the past were less clear than I thought them, but were by no means the views which my critics supposed them to be. Owing to lack of clearness in my own thoughts, I was unable to convey my meaning. The subject of relations is difficult, and I am far from claiming to be now clear about it. But I think certain points are clear to me. At the time when I wrote *The Principles of Mathematics,* I had not yet seen the necessity of logical types. The doctrine of types profoundly affects logic, and I think shows what, exactly, is the valid element in the arguments of those who oppose "external" relations. But so far from strengthening their main position, the doctrine of types leads, on the contrary, to a more complete and radical atomism than any that I conceived to be possible twenty years ago. The question of relations is one of the most important that arise in philosophy, as most other issues turn on it: monism and pluralism; the question whether anything is wholly true except the whole of truth, or wholly real except the whole of reality; idealism and realism, in some of their forms; perhaps the very existence of philosophy as a subject distinct from science and possessing a method of its own. It will serve to make my meaning clear if I take a passage in Mr. Bradley's *Essays on Truth and Reality,* not for controversial purposes, but because it raises exactly the issues that ought to be raised. But first of all I will try to state my own view, without argument.[2]

Certain contradictions—of which the simplest and oldest is the one about Epimenides the Cretan, who said that all Cretans were liars, which may be reduced to the man who says "I am lying"— convinced me, after five years devoted mainly to this one question, that no solution is technically possible without the doctrine of types. In its technical form, this doctrine states merely that a word or symbol may form part of a significant proposition, and in this sense have meaning, without being always able to be substituted for another word or symbol in the same or some other proposition without producing nonsense. Stated in this way, the doctrine may seem like a truism. "Brutus killed Caesar" is significant, but "Killed killed Caesar" is nonsense, so that we cannot replace "Brutus" by "killed," although both words have meaning. This is plain common sense, but unfortunately almost all philosophy consists in an attempt to forget it. The following words, for example, by their very nature, sin against it: attribute, relation, complex, fact, truth, falsehood, not, liar, omniscience. To give a meaning to these words, we have to make a detour by way of words or symbols and the different ways in which they may mean; and even then, we usually arrive, not at one meaning, but at an infinite series of different meanings. Words, as we saw, are all of the same logical type; therefore when the meanings of two words are of different types, the relations of the two words to what they stand for are also of different types. Attribute-words and relation-words are of the same type, therefore we can say significantly "attribute-words and relation-words have different uses." But we cannot say significantly "attributes are not relations." By our definition of types, since relations are relations, the form of words "attributes are relations" must be not false, but meaningless, and the form of words "attributes are not relations," similarly, must be not true, but meaningless. Nevertheless, the statement "attribute-words are not relation-words" is significant and true.

---

2. I am much indebted to my friend Wittgenstein in this matter. See his *Tractatus Logico-Philosophicus,* Kegan Paul, 1922. I do not accept all his doctrines, but my debt to him will be obvious to those who read his book.

We can now tackle the question of internal and external relations, remembering that the usual formulations, on both sides, are inconsistent with the doctrine of types. I will begin with attempts to state the doctrine of external relations. It is useless to say "terms are independent of their relations," because "independent" is a word which means nothing. Two events may be said to be causally independent when no causal chain leads from one to the other; this happens, in the special theory of relativity, when the separation between the events is space-like. Obviously this sense of "independent" is irrelevant. If, when we say "terms are independent of their relations," we mean "two terms which have a given relation would be the same if they did not have it," that is obviously false; for, being what they are, they have the relation, and therefore whatever does not have the relation is different. If we mean—as opponents of external relations suppose us to mean —that the relation is a third term which comes between the other two terms and is somehow hooked on to them, that is obviously absurd, for in that case the relation has ceased to be a relation, and all that is truly relational is the hooking of the relation to the terms. The conception of the relation as a third term between the other two sins against the doctrine of types, and must be avoided with the utmost care.

What, then, can we mean by the doctrine of external relations? Primarily this, that a relational proposition is not, in general, logically equivalent formally to one or more subject-predicate propositions. Stated more precisely: Given a relational propositional function "xRy," it is not in general the case that we can find predicates α, β, γ, such that, for all values of x and y, xRy is equivalent to $x\alpha$, $y\beta$, $(x, y)\gamma$ (where (x, y) stands for the whole consisting of x and y), or to any one or two of these. This, and this only, is what I mean to affirm when I assert the doctrine of external relations; and this, clearly, is at least part of what Mr. Bradley denies when he asserts the doctrine of internal relations.

In place of "unities" or "complexes," I prefer to speak of "facts." It must be understood that the word "fact" cannot occur significantly in any position in a sentence where the word "simple" can occur significantly, nor can a fact occur where a simple can occur. We must not say "facts are not simples." We can say, "The symbol for a fact must not replace the symbol for a simple, or vice versa, if significance is to be preserved." But it should be observed that, in this sentence, the word "for" has different meanings on the two occasions of its use. If we are to have a language which is to safeguard us from errors as to types, the symbol for a fact must be a proposition, not a single word or letter. Facts can be asserted or denied, but cannot be named. (When I say "facts cannot be named," this is, strictly speaking, nonsense. What can be said without falling into nonsense is: "The symbol for a fact is not a name.") This illustrates how meaning is a different relation for different types. The way to mean a fact is to assert it; the way to mean a simple is to name it. Obviously naming is different from asserting, and similar differences exist where more advanced types are concerned, though language has no means of expressing the differences.

There are many other matters in Mr. Bradley's examination of my views which call for reply. But as my present purpose is explanatory rather than controversial, I will pass them by, having, I hope, already said enough on the question of relations and complexes to make it clear what is the theory that I advocate. I will only add, as regards the doctrine of types, that most philosophers assume it now and then, and few would deny it, but that all (so far as I know) avoid formulating it precisely or drawing from it those deductions that are inconvenient for their systems.

I come now to some of Mr. Bradley's criticisms (*loc. cit.,* p. 280 ff.). He says:

"Mr. Russell's main position has remained to myself incomprehensible. On the one side I am led to think that he defends a strict pluralism, for which nothing is admissible beyond simple terms and external relations. On the other side Mr. Russell seems to assert emphatically, and to use throughout, ideas which such a pluralism surely must repudiate. He throughout stands upon unities which are complex and which cannot be analysed into terms and relations. These two positions to my mind are irreconcilable, since the second, as I understand it, contradicts the first flatly."

With regard to external relations, my view is the one I have just stated, not the one commonly imputed by those who disagree. But with regard to unities, the question is more difficult. The topic is one with which language, by its very nature, is peculiarly unfitted to deal. I must beg the reader, therefore, to be indulgent if what I say is not exactly what I mean, and to try to see what I mean in spite of unavoidable linguistic obstacles to clear expression.

To begin with, I do not believe that there are complexes or unities in the same sense in which there are simples. I did believe this when I wrote *The Principles of Mathematics,* but, on account of the doctrine of types, I have since abandoned this view. To speak loosely, I regard simples and complexes as always of different types. That is to say, the statements "There are simples" and "There are complexes" use the words "there are" in different senses. But if I use the words "there are" in the sense which they have in the statement "there are simples," then the form of words "there are not complexes" is neither true nor false, but meaningless. This shows how difficult it is to say clearly, in ordinary language, what I want to say about complexes. In the language of mathematical logic it is much easier to say what I want to say, but much harder to induce people to understand what I mean when I say it.

When I speak of "simples" I ought to explain that I am speaking of something not experienced as such, but known only inferentially as the limit of analysis. It is quite possible that, by greater logical skill, the need for assuming them could be avoided. A logical language will not lead to error if its simple symbols (i.e. those not having any parts that are symbols, or any significant structure) all stand for objects of some one type, even if these objects are not simple. The only drawback to such a language is that it is incapable of dealing with anything simpler than the objects which it represents by simple symbols. But I confess it seems obvious to me (as it did to Leibniz) that what is complex must be composed of simples, though the number of constituents may be infinite. It is also obvious that the logical uses of the old notion of substance (i.e. those uses which do not imply temporal duration) can only be applied, if at all, to simples; objects of other types do not have that kind of being which one associates with substances. The essence of a substance, from the symbolic point of view, is that it can only be named—in old-fashioned language, it never occurs in a proposition except as the subject or as one of the terms of a relation. If what we take to be simple is really complex, we may get into trouble by naming it, when what we ought to do is to assert it. For example, if Plato loves Socrates, there is not an entity "Plato's love for Socrates," but only the fact that Plato loves Socrates. And in speaking of this as "a fact," we are already making it more substantial and more of a unity than we have any right to do.

Attributes and relations, though they may be not susceptible of analysis, differ from substances by the fact that they suggest a structure, and that there can be no significant symbol which symbolizes them in isolation. All propositions in which an attribute or a relation *seems* to be the subject are only significant if they can be brought into a form in which the attribute is attributed or the relation relates. If this were not the case, there would be significant propositions in which an attribute or a relation would occupy a position appropriate to a substance, which would be contrary to the doctrine of types, and would produce contradictions. Thus the proper symbol for "yellow" (assuming for the sake of illustration that this is an attribute) is not the single word "yellow," but the propositional function "*x* is yellow," where the structure of the symbol shows the position which the word "yellow" must have if it is to be significant. Similarly the relation "precedes" must not be represented by this one word, but by the symbol "*x* precedes *y*," showing the way in which the symbol can occur significantly. (It is here assumed that values are not assigned to *x* and *y* when we are speaking of the attribute or relation itself.)

The symbol for the simplest possible kind of fact will still be of the form "*x* is yellow" or "*x* precedes *y*," only that "*x*" and "*y*" will be no longer undetermined variables, but names.

In addition to the fact that we do not experience simples as such, there is another obstacle to the actual creation of a correct logical language such as I have been trying to describe. This obstacle is vagueness. All our words are more or less infected with vagueness, by which I mean that it is not always clear whether they apply to a given object or not. It is of the nature of words to be more or less general, and not to apply only to a single particular, but that would not make them vague if the particulars to which they applied were a definite set. But this is never the case in practice. The defect, however, is one which it is easy to imagine removed, however difficult it may be to remove it in fact.

The purpose of the foregoing discussion of an ideal logical language (which would of course be wholly useless for daily life) is twofold: first, to prevent inferences from the nature of language to the nature of the world, which are fallacious because they depend upon the logical defects of language; secondly, to suggest, by inquiring what logic requires of a language which is to avoid contradiction, what sort of a structure we may reasonably suppose the world to have. If I am right, there is nothing in logic that can help us to decide between monism and pluralism, or between the view that there are ultimate relational facts and the view that there are none. My own decision in favor of pluralism and relations is taken on empirical grounds, after convincing myself that the *a priori* arguments to the contrary are invalid. But I do not think these arguments can be adequately refuted without a thorough treatment of logical types, of which the above is a mere sketch.

This brings me, however, to a question of method which I

believe to be very important. What are we to take as data in philosophy? What shall we regard as having the greatest likelihood of being true, and what as proper to be rejected if it conflicts with other evidence? It seems to me that science has a much greater likelihood of being true in the main than any philosophy hitherto advanced (I do not, of course, except my own). In science there are many matters about which people are agreed; in philosophy there are none. Therefore, although each proposition in a science may be false, and it is practically certain that there are some that are false, yet we shall be wise to build our philosophy upon science, because the risk of error in philosophy is pretty sure to be greater than in science. If we could hope for certainty in philosophy the matter would be otherwise, but so far as I can see such a hope would be chimerical.

Of course those philosophers whose theories, *prima facie,* run counter to science always profess to be able to interpret science so that it shall remain true on its own level, with that minor degree of truth which ought to content the humble scientist. Those who maintain a position of this sort are bound—so it seems to me—to show in detail how the interpretation is to be effected. In many cases, I believe that this would be quite impossible. I do not believe, for instance, that those who disbelieve in the reality of relations (in some such sense as that explained above) can possibly interpret those numerous parts of science which employ asymmetrical relations. Even if I could see no way of answering the objections to relations raised (for example) by Mr. Bradley, I should still think it more likely than not that some answer was possible, because I should think an error in a very subtle and abstract argument more probable than so fundamental a falsehood in science. Admitting that everything we believe ourselves to know is doubtful, it seems, nevertheless, that what we believe ourselves to know in philosophy is more doubtful than the detail of science, though perhaps not more doubtful than its most sweeping generalizations.

The question of interpretation is of importance for almost every philosophy, and I am not at all inclined to deny that many scientific results require interpretation before they can be fitted into a coherent philosophy. The maxim of "constructions *versus* inferences" is itself a maxim of interpretation. But I think that any valid kind of interpretation ought to leave the detail unchanged, though it may give a new meaning to fundamental ideas. In practice, this means that *structure* must be preserved. And a test of this is that all the propositions of a science should remain, though new meanings may be found for their terms. A case in point, on a non-philosophical level, is the relation of the physical theory of light to our perceptions of color. This provides different physical occurrences corresponding to different seen colors, and thus makes the structure of the physical spectrum the same as that of what we see when we look at a rainbow. Unless structure is preserved, we cannot validly speak of an interpretation. And structure is just what is destroyed by a monistic logic.

I do not mean, of course, to suggest that, in any region of science, the structure revealed at present by observation is exactly that which actually exists. On the contrary, it is in the highest degree probable that the actual structure is more fine-grained than the observed structure. This applies just as much to psychological as to physical material. It rests upon the fact that, where we perceive a difference (e.g. between two shades of color), there is a difference, but where we do not perceive a difference it does not follow that there is not a difference. We have therefore a right, in all interpretation, to demand the preservation of observed differences, and the provision of room for hitherto unobserved differences, although we cannot say in advance what they will be, except when they can be inferentially connected with observed differences.

In science, structure is the main study. A large part of the importance of relativity comes from the fact that it has substituted a single four-dimensional manifold (space-time) for the two manifolds, three-dimensional space and one-dimensional time. This is a change of structure, and therefore has far-reaching consequences, but any change which does not involve a change of structure does not make much difference. The mathematical definition and study of structure (under the name of "relation-numbers") form Part IV of *Principia Mathematica.*

The business of philosophy, as I conceive it, is essentially that of logical analysis, followed by logical synthesis. Philosophy is more concerned than any special science with relations of different sciences and possible conflicts between them; in particular, it cannot acquiesce in a conflict between physics and psychology, or between psychology and logic. Philosophy should be comprehensive, and should be bold in suggesting hypotheses as to the universe which science is not yet in a position to confirm or confute. But these should always be presented *as* hypotheses, not (as is too often done) as immutable certainties like the dogmas of religion. Although, moreover, comprehensive construction is part of the business of philosophy, I do not believe it is the most important part. The most important part, to my mind, consists in criticizing and clarifying notions which are apt to be regarded as fundamental and accepted uncritically. As instances I might mention: mind, matter, consciousness, knowledge, experience, causality, will, time. I believe all these notions to be inexact and approximate, essentially infected with vagueness, incapable of forming part of any exact science. Out of the original manifold of events, logical structures can be built which will have properties sufficiently like those of the above common notions to account for their prevalence, but sufficiently unlike to allow a great deal of error to creep in through their acceptance as fundamental.

I suggest the following as an outline of a possible structure of the world; it is no more than an outline, and is not offered as more than possible.

The world consists of a number, perhaps finite, perhaps infinite, of entities which have various relations to each other, and perhaps also various qualities. Each of these entities may be called an "event"; from the point of view of old-fashioned physics, an event occupies a short finite time and a small finite amount of space, but as we are not going to have an old-fashioned space and an old-fashioned time, this statement cannot be taken at its face value. Every event has to a certain number of others a relation which may be called "compresence"; from the point of view of physics, a collection of compresent events all occupy one small region in space-time. One example of a set of compresent events is what would be called the contents of one man's mind at one time—i.e. all his sensations, images, memories, thoughts, etc., which can coexist temporally. His visual field has, in one sense, spatial extension, but this must not be confused with the extension of physical space-time; every part of his visual field is compresent with every other part, and with the rest of "the contents of his mind" at that time, and a collection of compresent events occupies a minimal region in space-time. There are such collections not only where there are brains, but everywhere. At any point in "empty space," a number of stars could be photographed if a camera were introduced; we believe that light travels over the regions intermediate between its source and our eyes, and therefore something is happening in these regions. If light from a number of different sources reaches a certain minimal region in space-time, then at least one event corresponding to each of these sources exists in this minimal region, and all these events are compresent.

We will define a set of compresent events as a "minimal region." We find that minimal regions form a four-dimensional manifold,

and that, by a little logical manipulation, we can construct from
them the manifold of space-time that physics requires. We find also
that, from a number of different minimal regions, we can often
pick out a set of events, one from each, which are closely similar
when they come from neighboring regions, and vary from one region
to another according to discoverable laws. These are the laws of the
propagation of light, sound, etc. We find also that certain regions
in space-time have quite peculiar properties; these are the regions
which are said to be occupied by "matter." Such regions can be
collected, by means of the laws of physics; into tracks or tubes, very
much more extended in one dimension of space-time than in the
other three. Such a tube constitutes the "history" of a piece of
matter; from the point of view of the piece of matter itself, the
dimension in which it is most extended can be called "time," but
it is only the private time of that piece of matter, because it does
not correspond exactly with the dimension in which another piece of
matter is most extended. Not only is space-time very peculiar within
a piece of matter, but it is also rather peculiar in its neighborhood,
growing less so as the spatio-temporal distance grows greater; the
law of this peculiarity is the law of gravitation.

All kinds of matter to some extent, but some kinds of matter
(viz. nervous tissue) more particularly, are liable to form "habits,"
i.e. to alter their structure in a given environment in such a way that,
when they are subsequently in a similar environment, they react
in a new way, but if similar environments recur often, the reaction
in the end becomes nearly uniform, while remaining different from
the reaction on the first occasion. (When I speak of the reaction
of a piece of matter to its environment, I am thinking both of the
constitution of the set of compresent events of which it consists,
and of the nature of the track in space-time which constitutes what
we should ordinarily call its motion; these are called a "reaction
to the environment" in so far as there are laws correlating them
with characteristics of the environment.) Out of habit, the peculiarities of what we call "mind" can be constructed; a mind is a track
of sets of compresent events in a region of space-time where there
is matter which is peculiarly liable to form habits. The greater the
liability, the more complex and organized the mind becomes. Thus
a mind and a brain are not really distinct, but when we speak of a
mind we are thinking chiefly of the set of compresent events in the
region concerned, and of their several relations to other events forming parts of other periods in the history of the spatio-temporal tube
which we are considering, whereas when we speak of a brain we

are taking the set of compresent events as a whole, and considering its external relations to other sets of compresent events, also taken as wholes; in a word, we are considering the shape of the tube, not the events of which each cross-section of it is composed.

The above summary hypothesis would, of course, need to be amplified and refined in many ways in order to fit in completely with scientific facts. It is not put forward as a finished theory, but merely as a suggestion of the kind of thing that may be true. It is of course easy to imagine other hypotheses which may be true, for example, the hypothesis that there is nothing outside the series of sets of events constituting my history. I do not believe that there is any method of arriving at one sole possible hypothesis, and therefore certainty in metaphysics seems to me unattainable. In this respect I must admit that many other philosophies have the advantage, since in spite of their differences *inter se,* each arrives at certainty of its own exclusive truth.

Philosophy, Metaphysics and Meaning

2

The Turning Point in Philosophy

BY MORITZ SCHLICK

(TRANSLATED BY DAVID RYNIN)

FROM TIME to time prizes have been established for essays on the question what progress philosophy has made in a given period. The period tends to be limited on the one side by the name of some great thinker, on the other by "the present." It was thus assumed that there is some degree of clarity regarding the philosophic progress of mankind up to the time of that thinker, but that it is dubious what further contributions have been made in recent times.

Such questions clearly express a certain mistrust concerning the philosophy of the period which had recently elapsed. One has the impression of being presented only with an embarrassed formulation of the question: Has philosophy in that period made any progress whatever? For if one were sure that contributions had been made one would also know in what they consisted.

If the more remote past is regarded with less scepticism and one is rather inclined to see in its philosophy a continuous development, the explanation may be that one's attitude towards everything whose place is established in history is tinged with greater respect. A further point is that the older philosophers have at least demonstrated their historical influence. Hence in considering them one can take as one's base their historical rather than their substantive importance, especially since one often does not venture to distinguish between the two.

But it is just the ablest thinkers who most rarely have believed that the results of earlier philosophizing, including that of the classical models, remain unshakable. This is shown by the fact that basically every new system starts again from the beginning, that every thinker

"Die Wende Der Philosophie," as this piece is called in German, opened the first number of Volume I of *Erkenntnis* (1930/31). It is here published with the kind permission of Mrs. Schlick and Professor Carnap, the co-editor of *Erkenntnis*.

seeks his own foundation and does not wish to stand on the shoulders of his predecessors. Descartes (not without reason) felt himself to be making a wholly new beginning; Spinoza believed that in introducing the (to be sure quite adventitious) mathematical form he had found the ultimate philosophical method; and Kant was convinced that on the basis of the way taken by him philosophy would at last adopt the sure path of a science. Further examples are superfluous, for practically all great thinkers have sought for a radical reform of philosophy and considered it essential.

This peculiar fate of philosophy has been so often described and bemoaned that it is indeed pointless to discuss it at all. Silent scepticism and resignation seem to be the only appropriate attitudes. Two thousand years of experience seem to teach that efforts to put an end to the chaos of systems and to change the fate of philosophy can no longer be taken seriously. To point out that man has finally succeeded in solving the most stubborn problems, for example that of Daedelus, gives an informed person no comfort; for what he fears is just that philosophy will never arrive at a genuine "problem."

I refer to this anarchy of philosophical opinions which has so often been described, in order to leave no doubt that I am fully conscious of the scope and weighty significance of the conviction that I should now like to express. For I am convinced that we now find ourselves at an altogether decisive turning point in philosophy, and that we are objectively justified in considering that an end has come to the fruitless conflict of systems. We are already at the present time, in my opinion, in possession of methods which make every such conflict in principle unnecessary. What is now required is their resolute application.

These methods have been quietly developed, unnoticed by the majority of those who teach or write philosophy; and thus a situation has been created which is not comparable to any earlier one. That the situation is unique and that the turning embarked upon is really decisive can be understood only by becoming acquainted with the new paths and by looking back, from the standpoint to which they lead, upon all those efforts that have ever passed as "philosophical."

The paths have their origin in logic. Leibniz dimly saw their beginning. Bertrand Russell and Gottlob Frege have opened up important stretches in the last decades, but Ludwig Wittgenstein (in his *Tractatus Logico-Philosophicus*, 1922) is the first to have pushed forward to the decisive turning point.

It is well known that in recent decades mathematicians have developed new logical methods, at first primarily for the solution of their own problems which could not be overcome by the traditional methods of logic. But the logic thus developed has also long since shown its superiority in other ways over the old forms, and doubtless will very soon supplant them. Was I referring to this logic as the powerful means which is in principle capable of raising us above all philosophical conflicts? Does it give us general rules with those help all the traditional problems of philosophy can at least in principle be resolved?

If this were so I should hardly have had the right to say that a wholly new situation had been created. For then there would have been only a gradual, as it were, technical progress, as for example, when the invention of the internal combustion engine finally made possible the solution of the problem of flight. However highly the value of the new methods is to be esteemed, it is plain that nothing so fundamental can be brought about by the mere development of a method. The great turning point is therefore not to be attributed to logic itself but to something quite different which was indeed stimulated and made possible by it, but which proceeds on a much deeper level: the insight into the nature of logic itself.

That the logical is in some sense the purely *formal* has been expressed early and often; however, one was not really clear concerning the nature of pure forms. The clue to their nature is to be found in the fact that every cognition is an expression or representation. That is, it expresses a fact which is cognized in it. This can happen in any number of ways, in any language, by means of any arbitrary system of signs. All these possible modes of representation—if they otherwise actually express the same knowledge—must have something in common; and what is common to them is their logical form.

So all knowledge is such only by virtue of its form. It is through its form that it represents the fact known. But the form cannot itself in turn be represented. It alone is concerned in cognition. Everything else in the expression is inessential and accidental material, not different, say, from the ink by means of which we write down a statement.

This simple insight has consequences of the very greatest importance. Above all, it enables us to dispose of the traditional problems of "the theory of knowledge." Investigations concerning the human "capacity for knowledge," in so far as they do not become part of psychology, are replaced by considerations regarding the nature of expression, of representation, i.e. concerning every possible "language" in the most general sense of the term. Questions regarding the "validity and limits of knowledge" disappear. Everything is knowable which can be expressed, and this is the total subject matter concerning which meaningful questions can be raised. There are consequently no questions which are in principle unanswerable, no problems which are in principle insoluble. What have been considered such up to now are not genuine questions, but meaningless sequences of words. To be sure, they look like questions from the outside, since they seem to satisfy the customary rules of grammar, but in truth they consist of empty sounds, because they transgress the profound inner rules of logical syntax discovered by the new analysis.

Wherever there is a meaningful problem one can in theory always give the path that leads to its solution. For it becomes evident that giving this path coincides with the indication of its meaning. The practical following out of this path may of course be hindered by factual circumstances—by deficient human capacities, for example. The act of verification in which the path to the solution finally ends is always of the same sort: it is the occurrence of a definite fact that is confirmed by observation, by means of immediate experience. In this manner the truth (or falsity) of every statement, of daily life or science, is determined. There is thus no other testing and corroboration of truths except through observation and empirical science. Every science, (in so far as we take this word to refer to the content and not to the human arrangements for arriving at it) is a system of cognitions, that is, of true experiential statements. And the totality of sciences, including the statements of daily life, is the system of cognitions. There is, in addition to it, no domain of "philosophical" truths. Philosophy is not a system of statements; it is not a science.

But what is it then? Well, certainly not a science, but nevertheless something so significant and important that it may henceforth, as before, be honored as the Queen of the Sciences. For it is nowhere written that the Queen of the Sciences must itself be a science. The great contemporary turning point is characterized by the fact that we see in philosophy not a system of cognitions, but a system of *acts*; philosophy is that activity through which the meaning of statements is revealed or determined. By means of philosophy statements are explained, by means of science they are verified. The latter is concerned with the truth of statements, the former with what they actually mean. The content, soul and spirit of science is lodged naturally in what in the last analysis its statements actually mean; the philosophical activity of giving meaning is therefore the Alpha and Omega of all scientific knowledge. This was indeed correctly surmised when it was said that philosophy supplied both the foundation and the apex of the edifice of science. It was a mistake, however, to suppose that the foundation was made up of "philosophical" statements (the statements of theory of knowledge), and crowned by a dome of philosophical statements (called metaphysics).

It is easy to see that the task of philosophy does not consist in asserting statements—that bestowing meaning upon statements cannot be done in turn by statements. For if, say, I give the meaning of my words through explanatory statements and definitions, that is by help of other words, one must ask further for the meaning of these words, and so on. This process cannot proceed endlessly. It always comes to an end in actual pointings, in exhibiting what is meant, thus in real acts; only these acts are no longer capable of, or in need of, further explanation. The final giving of meaning always takes place therefore, through *deeds*. It is these deeds or acts which constitute philosophical activity.

It was one of the most serious errors of former times to have believed that the actual meaning and ultimate content was in turn to be formulated in statements, and so was representable in cognitions. This was the error of "metaphysics." The efforts of metaphysicians were always directed upon the absurd end of expressing the content of pure quality (the "essence" of things) by means of cognitions, hence of uttering the unutterable.[1] Qualities cannot be "said." They can only be shown in experience. But with this showing, cognition has nothing to do.

Thus metaphysics collapses not because the solving of its tasks is an enterprise to which the human reason is unequal (as for example Kant thought) but because there is no such task. With the disclosure of the mistaken formulation of the problem the history of metaphysical conflict is likewise explained.

If our conception is in general correct we must be able to establish it historically. It would have to be capable of giving some account of the change in meaning of the word "philosophy."

Now this is actually the case. If in ancient times, and actually until recently, philosophy was simply identical with every purely theoretical scientific investigation, this points to the fact that science found itself in a state in which it saw its main task still in the clarification of its fundamental concepts. The emancipation of the special sciences from their common mother, philosophy, indicates that the meaning of certain fundamental concepts became clear enough to make successful further work with them possible. If, today, ethics

1. See my article "Erleben, Erkennen, Metaphysik," *Kantstudien*, Vol. 31 (1930).

and aesthetics, and frequently also psychology, are considered branches of philosophy, this is a sign that these studies do not yet possess sufficiently clear basic concepts, that their efforts are still chiefly directed upon the *meaning* of their statements. Finally, if within a well-established science the necessity suddenly arises at some point of reflecting anew on the true meaning of the fundamental concepts, and thereby a more profound clarification of their meaning is achieved, this will be felt at once as an eminent philosophical achievement. All are agreed that, for instance, Einstein's work, proceeding from an analysis of the meaning of statements about time and space, was actually a philosophical achievement. Here we should add that the decisive epoch-making forward steps of science are always of this character; they signify a clarification of the meaning of the fundamental statements and only those succeed in them who are endowed for philosophical activity. The great investigator is also always a philosopher.

Frequently also the name of philosophy is bestowed on mental activities which have as their concern not pure knowledge but the conduct of life. This is readily understandable. For the wise man rises above the uncomprehending mass just by virtue of the fact that he can point out more clearly than they the meaning of statements and questions concerning life relationships, facts and desires.

The great turning point of philosophy signifies also a decisive turning away from certain erroneous paths which have been embarked upon since the second half of the 19th century and which must lead to quite a wrong assessment and evaluation of philosophy. I mean the attempts to claim for it an inductive character and accordingly to believe that it consists solely of statements of hypothetical validity. The idea of claiming only probability for its statements was remote from earlier thinkers. They would have rejected it as incompatible with the dignity of philosophy. In this was expressed a healthy instinct for the fact that philosophy must supply the ultimate support of knowledge. The reverse side of the medal is the dogma that philosophy supplies unconditionally true *a priori* axioms, which we must regard as an extremely unfortunate expression of this instinct, particularly since philosophy does not consist of statements at all. But we too believe in the dignity of philosophy and deem incompatible with it the character of being uncertain and only probable; and we are happy that the decisive turning point makes it impossible to attribute any such character to it. For the concept of probability or uncertainty is simply not applicable to the acts of giving meaning which constitute philosophy. It is a matter of positing the meaning of statements as something simply final. Either we *have* this meaning, and then we know what is meant by the statement, or we do not possess it, in which case mere empty words confront us, and as yet no statement at all. There is nothing in between and there can be no talk of the probability that the meaning is the right one. Thus after the great turning point philosophy shows its decisive character even more clearly than before.

It is only, indeed, because of this character that the conflict of systems can be ended. I repeat: in consequence of the insights which I have sketched we may today consider it as in principle already ended. I hope that this may become increasingly clear in the pages of this journal* in the new period of its existence.

Certainly there will still be many a rear-guard action. Certainly many will for centuries continue to wander further along the traditional paths. Philosophical writers will long continue to discuss the old pseudo-questions. But in the end they will no longer be listened to; they will come to resemble actors who continue to play for some time before noticing that the audience has slowly departed. Then it will no longer be necessary to speak of "philosophical problems" for one will speak philosophically concerning all problems, that is: clearly and meaningfully.

----

* Sc. *Erkenntnis*, Ed.

3

The Elimination of Metaphysics

Through Logical Analysis

of Language

BY RUDOLF CARNAP

(TRANSLATED BY ARTHUR PAP)

1. INTRODUCTION

THERE HAVE BEEN many *opponents of metaphysics* from the Greek skeptics to the empiricists of the 19th century. Criticisms of very diverse kinds have been set forth. Many have declared that the doctrine of metaphysics is *false*, since it contradicts our empirical knowledge. Others have believed it to be *uncertain*, on the ground that its problems transcend the limits of human knowledge. Many antimetaphysicians have declared that occupation with metaphysical questions is *sterile*. Whether or not these questions can be answered, it is at any rate unnecessary to worry about them; let us devote ourselves entirely to the practical tasks which confront active men every day of their lives!

The development of *modern logic* has made it possible to give a new and sharper answer to the question of the validity and justification of metaphysics. The researches of applied logic or the theory of knowledge, which aim at clarifying the cognitive content of scientific statements and thereby the meanings of the terms that occur in the statements, by means of logical analysis, lead to a positive and to a negative result. The positive result is worked out in the domain of empirical science; the various concepts of the various branches of science are clarified; their formal-logical and epistemological connections are made explicit. In the domain of *metaphysics,*

This article, originally entitled "Überwindung der Metaphysik durch Logische Analyse der Sprache," appeared in *Erkenntnis*, Vol. II (1932). It is published here with the kind permission of Professor Carnap.

including all philosophy of value and normative theory, logical analysis yields the negative result *that the alleged statements in this domain are entirely meaningless.* Therewith a radical elimination of metaphysics is attained, which was not yet possible from the earlier antimetaphysical standpoints. It is true that related ideas may be found already in several earlier trains of thought, e.g. those of a nominalistic kind; but it is only now when the development of logic during recent decades provides us with a sufficiently sharp tool that the decisive step can be taken.

In saying that the so-called statements of metaphysics are *meaningless,* we intend this word in its strictest sense. In a loose sense of the word a statement or a question is at times called meaningless if it is entirely sterile to assert or ask it. We might say this for instance about the question "what is the average weight of those inhabitants of Vienna whose telephone number ends with '3'?" or about a statement which is quite obviously false like "in 1910 Vienna had 6 inhabitants" or about a statement which is not just empirically, but logically false, a contradictory statement such as "persons A and B are each a year older than the other." Such sentences are really meaningful, though they are pointless or false; for it is only meaningful sentences that are even divisible into (theoretically) fruitful and sterile, true and false. In the strict sense, however, a sequence of words is *meaningless* if it does not, within a specified language, constitute a statement. It may happen that such a sequence of words looks like a statement at first glance; in that case we call it a *pseudo-statement.* Our thesis, now, is that logical analysis reveals the alleged statements of metaphysics to be pseudo-statements.

A language consists of a vocabulary and a syntax, i.e. a set of words which have meanings and rules of sentence formation. These rules indicate how sentences may be formed out of the various sorts of words. Accordingly, there are two kinds of pseudo-statements: either they contain a word which is erroneously believed to have meaning, or the constituent words are meaningful, yet are put together in a counter-syntactical way, so that they do not yield a meaningful statement. We shall show in terms of examples that pseudo-statements of both kinds occur in metaphysics. Later we shall have to inquire into the reasons that support our contention that metaphysics in its entirety consists of such pseudo-statements.

2. The Significance of a Word

A word which (within a definite language) has a meaning, is usually also said to designate a concept; if it only seems to have a meaning while it really does not, we speak of a "pseudo-concept." How is the origin of a pseudo-concept to be explained? Has not every word been introduced into the language for no other purpose than to express something or other, so that it had a definite meaning from the very beginning of its use? How, then, can a traditional language contain meaningless words? To be sure, originally every word (excepting rare cases which we shall illustrate later) had a meaning. In the course of historical development a word frequently changes its meaning. And it also happens at times that a word loses its old sense without acquiring a new one. It is thus that a pseudo-concept arises.

What, now, is *the meaning of a word?* What stipulations concerning a word must be made in order for it to be significant? (It does not matter for our investigation whether these stipulations are explicitly laid down, as in the case of some words and symbols of modern science, or whether they have been tacitly agreed upon, as is the case for most words of traditional language.) First, the *syntax* of the word must be fixed, i.e. the mode of its occurrence in the simplest sentence form in which it is capable of occurring; we call this sentence form its *elementary sentence*. The elementary sentence form for the word "stone" e.g. is "x is a stone"; in sentences of this form some designation from the category of things occupies the place of "x," e.g. "this diamond," "this apple." Secondly, for an elementary sentence S containing the word an answer must be given to the following question, which can be formulated in various ways:

(1.) What sentences is S *deducible* from, and what sentences are deducible from S?

(2.) Under what conditions is S supposed to be true, and under what conditions false?

(3.) How is S to be *verified?*

(4.) What is the *meaning* of S?

(1) is the correct formulation; formulation (2) accords with the phraseology of logic, (3) with the phraseology of the theory of knowledge, (4) with that of philosophy (phenomenology). Wittgenstein has asserted that (2) expresses what philosophers mean by (4): the meaning of a sentence consists in its truth-condition. ((1) is the "metalogical" formulation; it is planned to give elsewhere a detailed exposition of metalogic as the theory of syntax and meaning, i.e. relations of deducibility.)

In the case of many words, specifically in the case of the overwhelming majority of scientific words, it is possible to specify their meaning by reduction to other words ("constitution," definition).

E.g. " 'arthropodes' are animals with segmented bodies and jointed legs." Thereby the above-mentioned question for the elementary sentence form of the word "arthropode," that is for the sentence form "the thing x is an arthropode," is answered: it has been stipulated that a sentence of this form is deducible from premises of the form "x is an animal," "x has a segmented body," "x has jointed legs," and that conversely each of these sentences is deducible from the former sentence. By means of these stipulations about deducibility (in other words: about the truth-condition, about the method of verification, about the meaning) of the elementary sentence about "arthropode" the meaning of the word "arthropode" is fixed. In this way every word of the language is reduced to other words and finally to the words which occur in the so-called "observation sentences" or "protocol sentences." It is through this reduction that the word acquires its meaning.

For our purposes we may ignore entirely the question concerning the content and form of the primary sentences (protocol sentences) which has not yet been definitely settled. In the theory of knowledge it is customary to say that the primary sentences refer to "the given"; but there is no unanimity on the question what it is that is given. At times the position is taken that sentences about the given speak of the simplest qualities of sense and feeling (e.g. "warm," "blue," "joy" and so forth); others incline to the view that basic sentences refer to total experiences and similarities between them; a still different view has it that even the basic sentences speak of things. Regardless of this diversity of opinion it is certain that a sequence of words has a meaning only if its relations of deducibility to the protocol sentences are fixed, whatever the characteristics of the protocol sentences may be; and similarly, that a word is significant only if the sentences in which it may occur are reducible to protocol sentences.

Since the meaning of a word is determined by its criterion of application (in other words: by the relations of deducibility entered into by its elementary sentence-form, by its truth-conditions, by the method of its verification), the stipulation of the criterion takes away one's freedom to decide what one wishes to "mean" by the word. If the word is to receive an exact meaning, nothing less than the criterion of application must be given; but one cannot, on the other hand, give more than the criterion of application, for the latter is a sufficient determination of meaning. The meaning is implicitly contained in the criterion; all that remains to be done is to make the meaning explicit.

Let us suppose, by way of illustration, that someone invented the new word "teavy" and maintained that there are things which are teavy and things which are not teavy. In order to learn the meaning of this word, we ask him about its criterion of application: how is one to ascertain in a concrete case whether a given thing is teavy or not? Let us suppose to begin with that we get no answer from him: there are no empirical signs of teavyness, he says. In that case we would deny the legitimacy of using this word. If the person who uses the word says that all the same there are things which are teavy and there are things which are not teavy, only it remains for the weak, finite intellect of man an eternal secret which things are teavy and which are not, we shall regard this as empty verbiage. But perhaps he will assure us that he means, after all, something by the word "teavy." But from this we only learn the psychological fact that he associates some kind of images and feelings with the word. The word does not acquire a meaning through such associations. If no criterion of application for the word is stipulated, then nothing is asserted by the sentences in which it occurs, they are but pseudo-statements.

Secondly, take the case when we are given a criterion of application for a new word, say "toovy"; in particular, let the sentence "this thing is toovy" be true if and only if the thing is quadrangular (It is irrelevant in this context whether the criterion is explicitly stated or whether we derive it by observing the affirmative and the negative uses of the word). Then we will say: the word "toovy" is synonymous with the word "quadrangular." And we will not allow its users to tell us that nevertheless they "intended" something else by it than "quadrangular"; that though every quadrangular thing is also toovy and conversely, this is only because quadrangularity is the visible manifestation of toovyness, but that the latter itself is a hidden, not itself observable property. We would reply that after the criterion of application has been fixed, the synonymy of "toovy" and "quadrangular" is likewise fixed, and that we are no further at liberty to "intend" this or that by the word.

Let us briefly summarize the result of our analysis. Let "a" be any word and "S(a)" the elementary sentence in which it occurs. Then the sufficient and necessary condition for "a" being meaningful may be given by each of the following formulations, which ultimately say the same thing:

1. The *empirical criteria* for a are known.

2. It has been stipulated from what protocol sentences "S(a)" is *deducible*.

3. The *truth-conditions* for "S(a)" are fixed.
4. The method of *verification* of "S(a)" is known.[1]

3. METAPHYSICAL WORDS WITHOUT MEANING

Many words of metaphysics, now, can be shown not to fulfill the above requirement, and therefore to be devoid of meaning.

Let us take as an example the metaphysical term "principle" (in the sense of principle of being, not principle of knowledge or axiom). Various metaphysicians offer an answer to the question which is the (highest) "principle of the world" (or of "things," of "existence," of "being"), e.g. water, number, form, motion, life, the spirit, the idea, the unconscious, activity, the good, and so forth. In order to discover the meaning of the word "principle" in this metaphysical question we must ask the metaphysician under what conditions a statement of the form "x is the principle of y" would be true and under what conditions it would be false. In other words: we ask for the criteria of application or for the definition of the word "principle." The metaphysician replies approximately as follows: "x is the principle of y" is to mean "y arises out of x," "the being of y rests on the being of x," "y exists by virtue of x" and so forth. But these words are ambiguous and vague. Frequently they have a clear meaning; e.g., we say of a thing or process y that it "arises out of" x when we observe that things or processes of kind x are frequently or invariably followed by things or processes of kind y (causal connection in the sense of a lawful succession). But the metaphysician tells us that he does not mean this empirically observable relationship. For in that case his metaphysical theses would be merely empirical propositions of the same kind as those of physics. The expression "arising from" is not to mean here a relation of temporal and causal sequence, which is what the word ordinarily means. Yet, no criterion is specified for any other meaning. Consequently, the alleged "metaphysical" meaning, which the word is supposed to have here in contrast to the mentioned empirical meaning, does not exist. If we reflect on the original meaning of the word "principium" (and of the corresponding Greek word ἀρχή), we notice the same development. The word is explicitly deprived of its original meaning "beginning"; it is not supposed to mean the temporally prior any more, but the prior in some other, specifically metaphysical, respect. The criteria for this "metaphysical respect," however, are lacking. In both cases,

---

1. For the logical and epistemological conception which underlies our exposition, but can only briefly be intimated here, cf. Wittgenstein, *Tractatus Logico-Philosophicus*, 1922, and Carnap, *Der logische Aufbau der Welt*, 1928.

then, the word has been deprived of its earlier meaning without being given a new meaning; there remains the word as an empty shell. From an earlier period of significant use, it is still associatively connected with various mental images; these in turn get associated with new mental images and feelings in the new context of usage. But the word does not thereby become meaningful; and it remains meaningless as long as no method of verification can be described.

Another example is the word "God." Here we must, apart from the variations of its usage within each domain, distinguish the linguistic usage in three different contexts or historical epochs, which however overlap temporally. In its *mythological* use the word has a clear meaning. It, or parallel words in other languages, is sometimes used to denote physical beings which are enthroned on Mount Olympus, in Heaven or in Hades, and which are endowed with power, wisdom, goodness and happiness to a greater or lesser extent. Sometimes the word also refers to spiritual beings which, indeed, do not have manlike bodies, yet manifest themselves nevertheless somehow in the things or processes of the visible world and are therefore empirically verifiable. In its *metaphysical* use, on the other hand, the word "God" refers to something beyond experience. The word is deliberately divested of its reference to a physical being or to a spiritual being that is immanent in the physical. And as it is not given a new meaning, it becomes meaningless. To be sure, it often looks as though the word "God" had a meaning even in metaphysics. But the definitions which are set up prove on closer inspection to be pseudo-definitions. They lead either to logically illegitimate combinations of words (of which we shall treat later) or to other metaphysical words (e.g. "primordial basis," "the absolute," "the unconditioned," "the autonomous," "the self-dependent" and so forth), but in no case to the truth-conditions of its elementary sentences. In the case of this word not even the first requirement of logic is met, that is the requirement to specify its syntax, i.e. the form of its occurrence in elementary sentences. An elementary sentence would here have to be of the form "x is a God"; yet, the metaphysician either rejects this form entirely without substituting another, or if he accepts it he neglects to indicate the syntactical category of the variable x. (Categories are, for example, material things, properties of things, relations between things, numbers etc.).

The *theological* usage of the word "God" falls between its mythological and its metaphysical usage. There is no distinctive meaning here, but an oscillation from one of the mentioned two uses to the other. Several theologians have a clearly empirical (in our terminology, "mythological") concept of God. In this case there are no pseudo-statements; but the disadvantage for the theologian lies in the circumstance that according to this interpretation the statements of theology are empirical and hence are subject to the judgment of empirical science. The linguistic usage of other theologians is clearly metaphysical. Others again do not speak in any definite way, whether this is because they follow now this, now that linguistic usage, or because they express themselves in terms whose usage is not clearly classifiable since it tends towards both sides.

Just like the examined examples "principle" and "God," most of the other *specifically metaphysical terms are devoid of meaning,* e.g. "the Idea," "the Absolute," "the Unconditioned," "the Infinite," "the being of being," "non-being," "thing in itself," "absolute spirit," "objective spirit," "essence," "being-in-itself," "being-in-and-for-itself," "emanation," "manifestation," "articulation," "the Ego," "the non-Ego," etc. These expressions are in the same boat with "teavy," our previously fabricated example. The metaphysician tells us that empirical truth-conditions cannot be specified; if he adds that nevertheless he "means" something, we know that this is merely an allusion to associated images and feelings which, however, do not bestow a meaning on the word. The alleged statements of metaphysics which contain such words have no sense, assert nothing, are mere pseudo-statements. Into the explanation of their historical origin we shall inquire later.

4. THE SIGNIFICANCE OF A SENTENCE

So far we have considered only those pseudo-statements which contain a meaningless word. But there is a second kind of pseudo-statement. They consist of meaningful words, but the words are put together in such a way that nevertheless no meaning results. The syntax of a language specifies which combinations of words are admissible and which inadmissible. The grammatical syntax of natural languages, however, does not fulfill the task of elimination of senseless combinations of words in all cases. Let us take as examples the following sequences of words:

1. "Caesar is and"
2. "Caesar is a prime number"

The word sequence (1) is formed countersyntactically; the rules of syntax require that the third position be occupied, not by a conjunction, but by a predicate, hence by a noun (with article) or by an adjective. The word sequence "Caesar is a general," e.g., is formed in accordance with the rules of syntax. It is a meaningful word sequence, a genuine sentence. But, now, word sequence (2) is likewise syntactically correct, for it has the same grammatical form as the sentence just mentioned. Nevertheless (2) is meaningless. "Prime number" is a predicate of numbers; it can be neither affirmed nor denied of a person. Since (2) looks like a statement yet is not a statement, does not assert anything, expresses neither a true nor a false proposition, we call this word sequence a "pseudo-statement." The fact that the rules of grammatical syntax are not violated easily seduces one at first glance into the erroneous opinion that one still has to do with a statement, albeit a false one. But "a is a prime number" is false if and only if a is divisible by a natural number different from a and from 1; evidently it is illicit to put here "Caesar" for "a." This example has been so chosen that the nonsense is easily detectable. Many so-called statements of metaphysics are not so easily recognized to be pseudo-statements. The fact that natural languages allow the formation of meaningless sequences of words without violating the rules of grammar, indicates that grammatical syntax is, from a logical point of view, inadequate. If grammatical syntax corresponded exactly to logical syntax, pseudo-statements could not arise. If grammatical syntax differentiated not only the word-categories of nouns, adjectives, verbs, conjunctions etc., but within each of these categories made the further distinctions that are logically indispensable, then no pseudo-statements could be formed. If, e.g., nouns were grammatically subdivided into several kinds of words, according as they designated properties of physical objects, of numbers etc., then the words "general" and "prime number" would belong to grammatically different word-categories, and (2) would be just as linguistically incorrect as (1). In a correctly constructed language, therefore, all nonsensical sequences of words would be of the kind of example (1). Considerations of grammar would already eliminate them as it were automatically; i.e. in order to avoid nonsense, it would be unnecessary to pay attention to the meanings of the individual words over and above their syntactical type (their "syntactical category," e.g. thing, property of things, relation between things, number, property of numbers, relation between numbers, and so forth). It follows that if our thesis that the statements of metaphysics are pseudo-statements is justifiable, then metaphysics could not even be expressed in a logically constructed language. This is the great philosophical importance of the task, which at present occupies the logicians, of building a logical syntax.

5. METAPHYSICAL PSEUDO-STATEMENTS

Let us now take a look at some examples of metaphysical pseudo-statements of a kind where the violation of logical syntax is especially obvious, though they accord with historical-grammatical syntax. We select a few sentences from that metaphysical school which at present exerts the strongest influence in Germany.[2]

"What is to be investigated is being only and—*nothing* else; being alone and further—*nothing;* solely being, and beyond being—*nothing. What about this Nothing? . . . Does the Nothing exist only because the Not, i.e. the Negation, exists?* Or is it the other way around? *Does Negation and the Not exist only because the Nothing exists? . . .* We assert: *the Nothing is prior to the Not and the Negation. . . .* Where do we seek the Nothing? How do we find the Nothing. . . . We know the Nothing. . . . *Anxiety reveals the Nothing.* . . . That for which and because of which we were anxious, was 'really'—nothing. Indeed: the Nothing itself—as such—was present. . . . *What about this Nothing?—The Nothing itself nothings.*"

In order to show that the possibility of forming pseudo-statements is based on a logical defect of language, we set up the schema below. The sentences under I are grammatically as well as logically impeccable, hence meaningful. The sentences under II (excepting B3) are in grammatical respects perfectly analogous to those under I. Sentence form IIA (as question and answer) does not, indeed, satisfy the requirements to be imposed on a logically correct language. But it is nevertheless meaningful, because it is translatable into correct language. This is shown by sentence IIIA, which has the same meaning as IIA. Sentence form IIA then proves to be undesirable because we can be led from it, by means of grammatically faultless operations, to the meaningless sentence forms IIB, which are taken from the above quotation. These forms cannot even be constructed in the correct language of Column III. Nonetheless, their nonsensicality is not obvious at first glance, because one is easily deceived by the analogy with the meaningful sentences IB. The fault of our language identified here lies, therefore, in the circumstance that, in contrast to a logically correct language, it admits of the same grammatical form for meaningful and meaningless word sequences. To each sentence in words we have added a corresponding formula in the

---

2. The following quotations (original italics) are taken from M. Heidegger, *Was Ist Metaphysik?* 1929. We could just as well have selected passages from any other of the numerous metaphysicians of the present or of the past; yet the selected passages seem to us to illustrate our thesis especially well.

notation of symbolic logic; these formulae facilitate recognition of
the undesirable analogy between IA and IIA and therewith of the
origin of the meaningless constructions IIB.

I.	II.	III.
Meaningful Sentences of Ordinary Language	*Transition from Sense to Nonsense in Ordinary Language*	*Logically Correct Language*
A. What is outside? Ou(?) Rain is outside Ou(r)	A. What is outside? Ou(?) Nothing is outside Ou(no)	A. There is nothing (does not exist any-thing) which is outside. $\sim(\exists x).Ou(x)$
B. What about this rain? (i.e. what does the rain do? or: what else can be said about this rain? ?(r)	B. "What about this Nothing?" ?(no)	B. None of these forms can even be constructed.
1. We know the rain K(r)	1. "We seek the Nothing" "We find the Nothing" "We know the Nothing" K(no)	
2. The rain rains R(r)	2. "The Nothing nothings" No(no)	
	3. "The Nothing exists only because . . ." Ex(no)	

On closer inspection of the pseudo-statements under IIB, we also
find some differences. The construction of sentence (1) is simply
based on the mistake of employing the word "nothing" as a noun,
because it is customary in ordinary language to use it in this form in
order to construct a negative existential statement (see IIA). In
a correct language, on the other hand, it is not a particular *name,*
but a certain *logical form* of the sentence that serves this purpose

(see IIIA). Sentence IIB2 adds something new, viz. the fabrication of the meaningless word "to nothing." This sentence, therefore, is senseless for a twofold reason. We pointed out before that the meaningless words of metaphysics usually owe their origin to the fact that a meaningful word is deprived of its meaning through its metaphorical use in metaphysics. But here we confront one of those rare cases where a new word is introduced which never had a meaning to begin with. Likewise sentence IIB3 must be rejected for two reasons. In respect of the error of using the word "nothing" as a noun, it is like the previous sentences. But in addition it involves a contradiction. For even if it were admissible to introduce "nothing" as a name or description of an entity, still the existence of this entity would be denied in its very definition, whereas sentence (3) goes on to affirm its existence. This sentence, therefore, would be contradictory, hence absurd, even if it were not already meaningless.

In view of the gross logical errors which we find in sentences IIB, we might be led to conjecture that perhaps the word "nothing" has in Heidegger's treatise a meaning entirely different from the customary one. And this presumption is further strengthened as we go on to read there that anxiety reveals the Nothing, that the Nothing itself is present as such in anxiety. For here the word "nothing" seems to refer to a certain emotional constitution, possibly of a religious sort, or something or other that underlies such emotions. If such were the case, then the mentioned logical errors in sentences IIB would not be committed. But the first sentence of the quotation at the beginning of this section proves that this interpretation is not possible. The combination of "only" and "nothing else" shows unmistakably that the word "nothing" here has the usual meaning of a logical particle that serves for the formulation of a negative existential statement. This introduction of the word "nothing" is then immediately followed by the leading question of the treatise: "What about this Nothing?".

But our doubts as to a possible misinterpretation get completely dissolved as we note that the author of the treatise is clearly aware of the conflict between his questions and statements, and logic. *"Question and answer* in regard to the Nothing are equally *absurd* in themselves. . . . The fundamental rule of thinking commonly appealed to, the law of prohibited contradiction, general *'logic,'* destroys this question." All the worse for logic! We must abolish its sovereignty: "If thus the power of the *understanding* in the field of questions concerning Nothing and Being is broken, then the fate of the sovereignty of 'logic' within philosophy is thereby decided as

well. The very idea of 'logic' dissolves in the whirl of a more basic
questioning." But will sober science condone the whirl of counter-
logical questioning? To this question too there is a ready answer:
"The alleged sobriety and superiority of science becomes ridiculous
if it does not take the Nothing seriously." Thus we find here a good
confirmation of our thesis; a metaphysician himself here states that
his questions and answers are irreconcilable with logic and the scientific way of thinking.

The difference between our thesis and that of the *earlier antimetaphysicians* should now be clear. We do not regard metaphysics
as "mere speculation" or "fairy tales." The statements of a fairy
tale do not conflict with logic, but only with experience; they are
perfectly meaningful, although false. Metaphysics is not *"superstition"*; it is possible to believe true and false propositions, but not
to believe meaningless sequences of words. Metaphysical statements
are not even acceptable as *"working hypotheses";* for an hypothesis
must be capable of entering into relations of deducibility with (true
or false) empirical statements, which is just what pseudo-statements
cannot do.

With reference to the so-called *limitation of human knowledge*
an attempt is sometimes made to save metaphysics by raising the
following objection: metaphysical statements are not, indeed, verifiable by man nor by any other finite being; nevertheless they might
be construed as conjectures about the answers which a being with
higher or even perfect powers of knowledge would make to our
questions, and as such conjectures they would, after all, be meaningful. To counter this objection, let us consider the following. If
the meaning of a word cannot be specified, or if the sequence of
words does not accord with the rules of syntax, then one has not
even asked a question. (Just think of the pesudo-questions: "Is this
table teavy?", "is the number 7 holy?", "which numbers are darker,
the even or the odd ones?"). Where there is no question, not even
an omniscient being can give an answer. Now the objector may say:
just as one who can see may communicate new knowledge to the
blind, so a higher being might perhaps communicate to us metaphysical knowledge, e.g. whether the visible world is the manifestation of a spirit. Here we must reflect on the meaning of "new knowledge." It is, indeed, conceivable that we might encounter animals
who tell us about a new sense. If these beings were to prove to us
Fermat's theorem or were to invent a new physical instrument or
were to establish a hitherto unknown law of nature, then our knowledge would be increased with their help. For this sort of thing we

can test, just the way even a blind man can understand and test the whole of physics (and therewith any statement made by those who can see). But if those hypothetical beings tell us something which we cannot verify, then we cannot understand it either; in that case no information has been communicated to us, but mere verbal sounds devoid of meaning though possibly associated with images. It follows that our knowledge can only be quantitatively enlarged by other beings, no matter whether they know more or less or everything, but no knowledge of an essentially different kind can be added. What we do not know for certain, we may come to know with greater certainty through the assistance of other beings; but what is unintelligible, meaningless for us, cannot become meaningful through someone else's assistance, however vast his knowledge might be. Therefore no god and no devil can give us metaphysical knowledge.

6. MEANINGLESSNESS OF ALL METAPHYSICS

The examples of metaphysical statements which we have analyzed were all taken from just one treatise. But our results apply with equal validity, in part even in verbally identical ways, to other metaphysical systems. That treatise is completely in the right in citing approvingly a statement by Hegel ("pure Being and pure Nothing, therefore, are one and the same"). The metaphysics of Hegel has exactly the same logical character as this modern system of metaphysics. And the same holds for the rest of the metaphysical systems, though the kind of phraseology and therewith the kind of logical errors that occur in them deviate more or less from the kind that occurs in the examples we discussed.

It should not be necessary here to adduce further examples of specific metaphysical sentences in diverse systems and submit them to analysis. We confine ourselves to an indication of the most frequent kinds of errors.

Perhaps the majority of the logical mistakes that are committed when pseudo-statements are made, are based on the logical faults infecting the use of the word "to be" in our language (and of the corresponding words in other languages, at least in most European languages). The first fault is the ambiguity of the word "to be." It is sometimes used as copula prefixed to a predicate ("I am hungry"), sometimes to designate existence ("I am"). This mistake is aggravated by the fact that metaphysicians often are not clear about this ambiguity. The second fault lies in the form of the verb in its second meaning, the meaning of *existence*. The verbal form feigns a predicate where there is none. To be sure, it has been known for a long time that existence is not a property (cf. Kant's refutation of the ontological proof of the existence of God). But it was not until the advent of modern logic that full consistency on this point was reached: the syntactical form in which modern logic introduces the sign for existence is such that it cannot, like a predicate, be applied to signs for objects, but only to predicates (cf. e.g. sentence IIIA in the above table). Most metaphysicians since antiquity have allowed themselves to be seduced into pseudo-statements by the verbal, and therewith the predicative form of the word "to be," e.g. "I am," "God is."

We meet an illustration of this error in Descartes' "cogito, ergo sum." Let us disregard here the material objections that have been raised against the premise—viz. whether the sentence "I think" adequately expresses the intended state of affairs or contains perhaps an hypostasis—and consider the two sentences only from the formal-logical point of view. We notice at once two essential logical mistakes. The first lies in the conclusion "I am." The verb "to be" is undoubtedly meant in the sense of existence here; for a copula cannot be used without predicate; indeed, Descartes' "I am" has always been interpreted in this sense. But in that case this sentence violates the above-mentioned logical rule that existence can be predicated only in conjunction with a predicate, not in conjunction with a name (subject, proper name). An existential statement does not have the form "a exists" (as in "I am," i.e. "I exist"), but "there exists something of such and such a kind." The second error lies in the transition from "I think" to "I exist." If from the statement "P(a)" ("a has the property P") an existential statement is to be deduced, then the latter can assert existence only with respect to the predicate P, not with respect to the subject a of the premise. What follows from "I am a European" is not "I exist," but "a European exists." What follows from "I think" is not "I am" but "there exists something that thinks."

The circumstance that our languages express existence by a verb ('to be" or "to exist") is not in itself a logical fault; it is only inappropriate, dangerous. The verbal form easily misleads us into the misconception that existence is a predicate. One then arrives at such logically incorrect and hence senseless modes of expression as were just examined. Likewise such forms as "Being" or "Not-Being," which from time immemorial have played a great role in metaphysics, have the same origin. In a logically correct language such forms cannot even be constructed. It appears that in the Latin and the German languages the forms "ens" or "das Seiende" were, perhaps under the seductive influence of the Greek example, introduced specifically for use by metaphysicians; in this way the language deteriorated logically whereas the addition was believed to represent an improvement.

Another very frequent violation of logical syntax is the so-called *"type confusion"* of concepts. While the previously mentioned mistake consists in the predicative use of a symbol with non-predicative meaning, in this case a predicate is, indeed, used as predicate yet as predicate of a different type. We have here a violation of the rules of the so-called theory of types. An artificial example is the sentence we discussed earlier: "Caesar is a prime number." Names of persons and names of numbers belong to different logical types, and so do accordingly predicates of persons (e.g. "general") and predicates of numbers ("prime number"). The error of type confusion is, unlike the previously discussed usage of the verb "to be," not the prerogative of metaphysics but already occurs very often in conversational language also. But here it rarely leads to nonsense. The typical ambiguity of words is here of such a kind that it can be easily removed.

Example: 1. "This table is larger than that." 2. "The height of this table is larger than the height of that table." Here the word "larger" is used in (1) for a relation between objects, in (2) for a relation between numbers, hence for two distinct syntactical categories. The mistake is here unimportant; it could, e.g., be eliminated by writing "larger1" and "larger2"; "larger1" is then defined in terms of "larger2" by declaring statement form (1) to be synonymous with (2) (and others of a similar kind).

Since the confusion of types causes no harm in conversational language, it is usually ignored entirely. This is, indeed, expedient for the ordinary use of language, but has had unfortunate consequences in metaphysics. Here the conditioning by everyday language has led to confusions of types which, unlike those in everyday language, are no longer translatable into logically correct form. Pseudo-statements of this kind are encountered in especially large quantity, e.g., in the writings of Hegel and Heidegger. The latter has adopted many peculiarities of the Hegelian idiom along with their logical faults (e.g. predicates which should be applied to objects of a certain sort are instead applied to predicates of these objects or to "being" or to "existence" or to a relation between these objects).

Having found that many metaphysical statements are meaningless, we confront the question whether there is not perhaps a core of meaningful statements in metaphysics which would remain after elimination of all the meaningless ones.

Indeed, the results we have obtained so far might give rise to the view that there are many dangers of falling into nonsense in metaphysics, and that one must accordingly endeavor to avoid these traps with great care if one wants to do metaphysics. But actually the situation is that meaningful metaphysical statements are impossible. This follows from the task which metaphysics sets itself: to discover and formulate a kind of knowledge which is not accessible to empirical science.

We have seen earlier that the meaning of a statement lies in the method of its verification. A statement asserts only so much as is verifiable with respect to it. Therefore a sentence can be used only to assert an empirical proposition, if indeed it is used to assert anything at all. If something were to lie, in principle, beyond possible experience, it could be neither said nor thought nor asked.

(Meaningful) statements are divided into the following kinds. First there are statements which are true solely by virtue of their form ("tautologies" according to Wittgenstein; they correspond approximately to Kant's "analytic judgments"). They say nothing about reality. The formulae of logic and mathematics are of this kind. They are not themselves factual statements, but serve for the transformation of such statements. Secondly there are the negations of such statements (*"contradictions"*). They are self-contradictory, hence false by virtue of their form. With respect to all other statements the decision about truth or falsehood lies in the protocol sentences. They are therefore (true or false) *empirical statements* and belong to the domain of empirical science. Any statement one desires to construct which does not fall within these categories becomes automatically meaningless. Since metaphysics does not want to assert analytic propositions, nor to fall within the domain of empirical science, it is compelled to employ words for which no criteria of application are specified and which are therefore devoid of sense, or else to combine meaningful words in such a way that neither an analytic (or contradictory) statement nor an empirical statement is produced. In either case pseudo-statements are the inevitable product.

Logical analysis, then, pronounces the verdict of meaninglessness on any alleged knowledge that pretends to reach above or behind experience. This verdict hits, in the first place, any speculative metaphysics, any alleged knowledge by *pure thinking* or by *pure intuition* that pretends to be able to do without experience. But the verdict equally applies to the kind of metaphysics which, starting from experience, wants to acquire knowledge about that which *transcends experience* by means of special *inferences* (e.g. the neo-vitalist thesis of the directive presence of an "entelechy" in organic processes, which supposedly cannot be understood in terms of physics; the question concerning the "essence of causality," transcending the ascertainment of certain regularities of succession; the talk about the "thing in itself"). Further, the same judgment must be passed on all *philosophy of norms,* or *philosophy of value,* on any ethics or esthetics as a normative discipline. For the objective validity of a value or norm is (even on the view of the philosophers of value) not empirically verifiable nor deducible from empirical statements; hence it cannot be asserted (in a meaningful statement) at all. In other words: Either empirical criteria are indicated for the use of "good" and "beautiful" and the rest of the predicates that are employed in the normative sciences, or they are not. In the first case, a statement containing such a predicate turns into a factual judgment, but not a value judgment; in the second case, it becomes a pseudo-statement. It is altogether impossible to make a statement that expresses a value judgment.

Finally, the verdict of meaninglessness also hits those metaphysical movements which are usually called, improperly, epistemological movements, that is *realism* (insofar as it claims to say more than the empirical fact that the sequence of events exhibits a certain regularity, which makes the application of the inductive method possible) and its opponents: subjective *idealism,* solipsism, phenomenalism, and *positivism* (in the earlier sense).

But what, then, is left over for *philosophy,* if all statements whatever that assert something are of an empirical nature and belong to factual science? What remains is not statements, nor a theory, nor a system, but only a *method*: the method of logical analysis. The foregoing discussion has illustrated the negative application of this method: in that context it serves to eliminate meaningless words, meaningless pseudo-statements. In its positive use it serves to clarify meaningful concepts and propositions, to lay logical foundations for factual science and for mathematics. The negative application of the method is necessary and important in the present historical situation. But even in its present practice, the positive application is more fertile. We cannot here discuss it in greater detail. It is the indicated task of logical analysis, inquiry into logical foundations, that is meant by *"scientific philosophy"* in contrast to metaphysics.

The question regarding the logical character of the statements which we obtain as the result of a logical analysis, e.g. the statements occurring in this and other logical papers, can here be answered only tentatively: such statements are partly analytic, partly empirical. For these statements about statements and parts of statements belong in part to pure *metalogic* (e.g. "a sequence consisting of the existence-symbol and a noun, is not a sentence"), in part to descriptive metalogic (e.g. "the word sequence at such and such a place in such and such a book is meaningless"). Metalogic will be discussed elsewhere. It will also be shown there that the metalogic which speaks about the sentences of a given language can be formulated in that very language itself.

7. METAPHYSICS AS EXPRESSION OF AN ATTITUDE TOWARD LIFE

Our claim that the statements of metaphysics are entirely meaningless, that they do not assert anything, will leave even those who agree intellectually with our results with a painful feeling of strangeness: how could it be explained that so many men in all ages and nations, among them eminent minds, spent so much energy, nay veritable fervor, on metaphysics if the latter consisted of nothing but mere words, nonsensically juxtaposed? And how could one account for the fact that metaphysical books have exerted such a strong influence on readers up to the present day, if they contained not even errors, but nothing at all? These doubts are justified since metaphysics does indeed have a content; only it is not theoretical content. The (pseudo)statements of metaphysics do not serve for the *description of states of affairs,* neither existing ones (in that case they would be true statements) nor non-existing ones (in that case they would be at least false statements). They serve for the *expression of the general attitude of a person towards life* ("Lebenseinstellung, Lebensgefühl").

Perhaps we may assume that metaphysics originated from *mythology.* The child is angry at the "wicked table" which hurt him. Primitive man endeavors to conciliate the threatening demon of earthquakes, or he worships the deity of the fertile rains in gratitude. Here we confront personifications of natural phenomena, which are the quasi-poetic expression of man's emotional relationship to his environment. The heritage of mythology is bequeathed on the one hand to poetry, which produces and intensifies the effects of mythology on life in a deliberate way; on the other hand, it is handed down to theology, which develops mythology into a system. Which, now, is the historical role of metaphysics? Perhaps we may regard it as a substitute for theology on the level of systematic, conceptual thinking. The (supposedly) transcendent sources of knowledge of theology are here replaced by natural, yet supposedly trans-empirical sources of knowledge. On closer inspection the same content as that of mythology is here still recognizable behind the repeatedly varied dressing: we find that metaphysics also arises from the need to give expression to a man's attitude in life, his emotional and volitional reaction to the environment, to society, to the tasks to which he devotes himself, to the misfortunes that befall him. This attitude manifests itself, unconsciously as a rule, in everything a man does or says. It also impresses itself on his facial features, perhaps even on the character of his gait. Many people, now, feel a desire to create over and above these manifestations a special expression of their attitude, through which it might become visible in a more succinct and penetrating way. If they have artistic talent they are able to express themselves by producing a work of art. Many writers have already clarified the way in which the basic attitude is manifested through the style and manner of a work of art (e.g. Dilthey and his students). [In this connection the term "world view" ("Weltanschauung") is often used; we prefer to avoid it because of its ambiguity, which blurs the difference between attitude and theory, a difference which is of decisive importance for our analysis.] What is here essential for our considerations is only the fact that art is an adequate, metaphysics an inadequate means for the expression of the basic attitude. Of course, there need be no intrinsic objection to one's using any means of expression one likes. But in the case of metaphysics we find this situation: through the form of its works it pretends to be something that it is not. The form in question is that of a system of statements which are apparently related as premises and conclusions, that is, the form of a theory. In this way the fiction of theoretical content is generated, whereas, as we have seen, there is no such content. It is not only the reader, but the metaphysician himself who suffers from the illusion that the metaphysical statements say something, describe states of affairs. The metaphysician believes that he travels in territory in which truth and falsehood are at stake. In reality, however, he has not asserted anything, but only expressed something, like an artist. That the metaphysician is thus deluding himself cannot be inferred from the fact that he selects language as the medium of expression and declarative sentences as the form of expression; for lyrical poets do the same without succumbing to self-delusion. But the metaphysician supports his statements by arguments, he claims assent to their content, he polemicizes against metaphysicians of divergent persuasion by attempting to refute their assertions in his treatise. Lyrical poets, on the other hand, do not try to refute in their poem the statements in a poem by some other lyrical poet; for they know they are in the domain of art and not in the domain of theory.

Perhaps music is the purest means of expression of the basic attitude because it is entirely free from any reference to objects. The harmonious feeling or attitude, which the metaphysician tries to express in a monistic system, is more clearly expressed in the music of Mozart. And when a metaphysician gives verbal expression to his dualistic-heroic attitude towards life in a dualistic system, is it not perhaps because he lacks the ability of a Beethoven to express this attitude in an adequate medium? Metaphysicians are musicians without musical ability. Instead they have a strong inclination to work within the medium of the theoretical, to connect concepts and thoughts. Now, instead of activating, on the one hand, this inclination in the domain of science, and satisfying, on the other hand, the need for expression in art, the metaphysician confuses the two and produces a structure which achieves nothing for knowledge and something inadequate for the expression of attitude.

Our conjecture that metaphysics is a substitute, albeit an inadequate one, for art, seems to be further confirmed by the fact that the metaphysician who perhaps had artistic talent to the highest degree, viz. Nietzsche, almost entirely avoided the error of that confusion. A large part of his work has predominantly empirical content. We find there, for instance, historical analyses of specific artistic phenomena, or an historical-psychological analysis of morals. In the work, however, in which he expresses most strongly that which others express through metaphysics or ethics, in *Thus Spake Zarathustra,* he does not choose the misleading theoretical form, but openly the form of art, of poetry.

REMARKS BY THE AUTHOR (1957)

To section 1, "metaphysics." This term is used in this paper, as usually in Europe, for the field of alleged knowledge of the essence of things which transcends the realm of empirically founded, inductive science. Metaphysics in this sense includes systems like those of Fichte, Schelling, Hegel, Bergson, Heidegger. But it does not include endeavors towards a synthesis and generalization of the results of the various sciences.

To section 1, "meaning." Today we distinguish various kinds of meaning, in particular cognitive (designative, referential) meaning on the one hand, and non-cognitive (expressive) meaning components, e.g. emotive and motivative, on the other. In the present paper, the word "meaning" is always understood in the sense of "cognitive meaning." The thesis that the sentences of metaphysics are meaningless, is thus to be understood in the sense that they have no cognitive meaning, no assertive content. The obvious psychological fact that they have expressive meaning is thereby not denied; this is explicitly stated in Section 7.

To section 6, "metalogic." This term refers to the theory of expressions of a language and, in particular, of their logical relations. Today we would distinguish between logical syntax as the theory of purely formal relations and semantics as the theory of meaning and truth-conditions.

To section 6, realism and idealism. That both the affirmative and the negative theses concerning the reality of the external world are pseudo-statements, I have tried to show in the monograph *Scheinprobleme in der Philosophie: Das Fremdpsychische und der Realismusstreit,* Berlin, 1928. The similar nature of the ontological theses about the reality or unreality of abstract entities, e.g., properties, relations, propositions, is discussed in "Empiricism, Semantics, and Ontology," *Revue Intern. de Philos.* 4, 1950, 20-40, reprinted in: *Meaning and Necessity,* second edition, Chicago, 1956.

4

Positivism and Realism

BY MORITZ SCHLICK

(TRANSLATED BY DAVID RYNIN)

1. PRELIMINARY QUESTIONS

EVERY PHILOSOPHICAL POINT OF VIEW is defined by the principles which it considers fundamental and to which it constantly recurs in argument. But in the course of the historical development of such a view these principles tend to change—whether they be reformulated, extended, or restricted, or even gradually altered in meaning. At some time then the question arises whether we should still speak of the development of the one point of view at all, and retain its old name; or whether a new viewpoint has arisen.

If, along with the developed view there also exists an "orthodox" viewpoint which retains the first principles in their original form and meaning, sooner or later some terminological distinction between the old and the new will arise automatically. But where this is not clearly the case, where rather the different exponents of a "viewpoint" employ extremely different, even contradictory, formulations and meanings of the principles, confusion arises; the adherents and opponents of the view talk at cross purposes; each selects those statements which can be used in defense of his own opinions, and all ends in fatal misunderstanding and obscurity. These confusions disappear only when the different principles are distinguished, and each is tested separately for its meaning and truth. In such an examination of principles one quite ignores, for the time, the question of the historical contexts of their origins, and of their names.

I should like to apply these considerations to the modes of think-

This article first appeared in *Erkenntnis*, Volume III (1932/33) and is here republished with the kind permission of Mrs. Schlick and Professor Carnap. It was written in response to criticisms of positivism in a lecture by Max Planck entitled "Positivismus und Reale Aussenwelt," published in 1931 by the Akademische Verlagsgesellschaft, Leipzig.

ing grouped together under the name "positivism." They have, from the time August Comte invented the term until the present, undergone a development which furnishes a good example of what has just been said. But I do not do this with the historical aim, say, of determining a strict concept of positivism as it has appeared in history, but rather in order to contribute something to a positive settlement of the dispute carried on nowadays concerning certain principles which pass as fundamental to positivism. Such a settlement concerns me the more because I myself advocate some of these principles. I am concerned here only to make their meaning as clear as possible; whether or not one will, after this clarification, attribute them to "positivism" is a question of very little importance.

If one wishes to characterize every view which denies the possibility of metaphysics as positivistic this is quite unobjectionable, as a mere definition; and I should in this sense call myself a strict positivist. But this holds, of course, only under the presupposition of a special definition of "metaphysics." What the definition of metaphysics is which must be adopted here need not interest us at the moment; but it hardly agrees with the formulations usual in philosophic literature, and further determinations of positivism which refer to such formulations lead at once into confusions and difficulties.

If we say, as frequently has been said, that metaphysics is the theory of "true being," of "reality in itself," of "transcendent being" this obviously implies a (contradictory) spurious, lesser, apparent being; as has indeed been assumed by all metaphysicians since the time of Plato and the Eleatics. This apparent being is the realm of "appearances," and while the true transcendent reality is to be reached only with difficulty, by the efforts of the metaphysician, the special sciences have to do exclusively with appearances which are perfectly accessible to them. The difference between the ways in which these two "modes of being" are to be known, is then explained by the fact that the appearances are immediately present, "given," to us, while metaphysical reality must be inferred from them in some roundabout manner. And thus we seem to arrive at a fundamental concept of the positivists, for they always speak of the "given," and usually formulate their fundamental principle in the proposition that the philosopher as well as the scientist must always remain within the given, that to go beyond it, as the metaphysician attempts, is impossible or senseless.

Thus it amounts to identifying the "given" of the positivist with the "appearances" of metaphysics, and to believing that positivism is at bottom a metaphysics, from which one has left, or stricken, out the transcendent; and such an opinion may indeed often enough have inspired the arguments of the positivists, as well as those of their opponents. But this belief finds us well on our way to dangerous errors.

The term "the given" itself is a cause of grave misunderstandings. "To give" usually connotes a three term relation: it presupposes first, someone who gives, secondly, one to whom is given, and thirdly, something given. The metaphysician finds this quite in order, for what gives is the transcendent reality, what receives is the knowing mind, which makes what is given to it into its "content." But evidently the positivist will from the very outset have nothing to do with such notions; the given is for him but a word for what is most simple and no longer questionable. No matter what word we choose, every one will be capable of misinterpretations; if we speak of "experiences" we seem to presuppose the distinction between what experiences and what is experienced; with the use of the phrase "content of consciousness" we seem burdened with a similar distinction, and in addition with the complicated concept of "consciousness," which in any case did not exist until invented by philosophy.

But even apart from such difficulties it is perhaps still not clear what is actually meant by the given. Do only such "qualities" as "blue," "warm," "pain," come under this heading, or e.g. also relations between them, or their order? Is the similarity of two qualities "given" in the same sense as the qualities themselves? And if the given is somehow worked up or interpreted or judged is this working-up or judging not also in some sense something given?

But it is not obscurities of this sort that give rise to the current matter of dispute: the bone of contention appears among the various parties only with the question of "reality."

If the rejection of metaphysics by positivism signifies the denial of transcendent reality then it seems the most natural conclusion in the world that the positivist attributes reality only to non-transcendent being. The fundamental principle of the positivist then seems to run: "Only the given is real." If one enjoys word-play one can lend to this proposition the semblance of tautological self-evidence by making use of a peculiarity of the German language in thus formulating it: "Es gibt nur das Gegebene." (There is only the given.)

What shall we make of this proposition? Many positivists may have expressed and advocated it (especially, perhaps, those who represented physical objects as "mere logical constructions," or "mere auxiliary concepts"), while this view has been attributed to others by their opponents. We must insist, however, that whoever states this proposition seeks to establish an assertion which is metaphysical in exactly the same sense and degree as its apparent contradictory: "There is a transcendent reality."

The problem about which the matter revolves here is evidently the so-called problem of the reality of the external world, and there seem to be two parties: that of "realism" which believes in the reality of the external world, and that of "positivism" which does not. In truth, I am convinced that it is quite senseless to set two views in opposition in this manner, for neither party really knows what it wants to say (which is the case with every metaphysical proposition.) But before I explain this I should like to show how the more obvious interpretations of the proposition "only the given is real" actually lead at once to well-known metaphysical views.

This problem can take the form of the question about the existence of the "external" world only if somehow we can distinguish between inner and outer; and this distinction is made by considering the given as a "content" of consciousness, as belonging to one or several subjects *to whom* it is given. Thus the immediate datum would have attributed to it some sort of mental character, the character of a representation or an idea; and the proposition would then state that this character pertained to all reality: no being outside of consciousness. But this is nothing but the fundamental principle of metaphysical *idealism*. If the philosopher thinks himself able to speak only of what is given to himself we have before us a solipsistic metaphysics, but if he thinks he may assume that the given is distributed among many subjects we have a metaphysics of the Berkeleyan variety.

On this interpretation positivism would be simply identical with the older idealistic metaphysics. But since its founders certainly desired something quite different from a renewal of that idealism, this interpretation is to be rejected as contrary to the anti-metaphysical attitude of positivism. Idealism and positivism are incompatible. The positivist Ernst Laas has written a work of several volumes to demonstrate the irreconcilable opposition which exists on all points between them; and if his student Hans Vaihinger gave to his "Philosophy of As If" the subtitle an "idealistic positivism" it is but one of the contradictions from which this work suffers. Ernst Mach especially emphasized that his own positivism developed in an opposite direction to that of Berkeleyan metaphysics; and he and Avenarius laid great stress upon not taking the given as a content of consciousness. They tried to exclude this concept from their philosophy altogether.

In view of the uncertainty in the camp of the positivists themselves it is no wonder that the "realist" fails to observe the distinctions we have discussed, and directs his arguments against the thesis: "There is nothing but the contents of consciousness," or "There is only an internal world." But this proposition belongs to idealistic metaphysics, and has no place in an anti-metaphysical positivism, which is not affected by these realistic arguments.

Of course the realist can think that it is simply inevitable to conceive the given as contents of consciousness, as subjective, as mental—or whatever expression is used; and he will then consider as a failure the attempt of Mach and Avenarius to take the given as neutral and to resolve the distinction between inner and outer, and will believe that a view free of any metaphysical basis is impossible. But this line of thought is rarely met with. And however it may fare, in any case, the whole business is much ado about nothing, for the "problem of the reality of the external world" is a meaningless pseudo-problem. This must now be made evident.

2. ON THE MEANING OF PROPOSITIONS

It is the peculiar business of philosophy to ascertain and make clear the *meaning* of statements and questions. The chaotic state in which philosophy has found itself during the greater part of its history is due to the unfortunate fact that, in the *first* place, it took certain formulations to be real questions before carefully ascertaining whether they really made any sense, and, in the *second* place, it believed that the answers to the questions could be found by the aid of special philosophical methods, different from those of the special sciences. But we cannot by philosophical analysis decide whether anything is real, but only what it *means* to say that it is real; and whether this is then the case or not can be decided only by the usual methods of daily life and of science, that is, through *experience*. Hence we have here the task of making clear to ourselves whether any meaning can be attached to the problem of the reality of the "external world."

When, in general, are we sure that the meaning of a question is clear to us? Evidently when and only when we are able to state exactly the conditions under which it is to be answered in the affirmative, or, as the case may be, the conditions under which it is to be answered in the negative. By stating these conditions, and by this alone, is the meaning of a question defined.

It is the first step of any philosophizing, and the foundation of all reflection, to see that it is simply impossible to give the meaning of any statement except by describing the fact which must exist if the statement is to be true. If it does not exist then the statement is false. The meaning of a proposition consists, obviously, in this alone, that it expresses a definite state of affairs. And this state of affairs must be pointed out in order to give the meaning of the proposition. One can, of course, say that the proposition itself already gives this state of affairs. This is true, but the proposition indicates the state of affairs only to the person who understands it. But when do I understand a proposition? When I understand the meanings of the words which occur in it? These can be explained by definitions. But in the definitions new words appear whose meanings cannot again be described in propositions, they must be indicated directly: the meaning of a word must in the end be *shown,* it must be *given.* This is done by an act of indication, of pointing; and what is pointed at must be given, otherwise I cannot be referred to it.

Accordingly, in order to find the meaning of a proposition, we must transform it by successive definitions until finally only such words occur in it as can no longer be defined, but whose meanings can only be directly pointed out. The criterion of the truth or falsity of the proposition then lies in the fact that under definite conditions (given in the definition) certain data are present, or not present. If this is determined then everything asserted by the proposition is determined, and I know its meaning. If I am *unable,* in principle, to verify a proposition, that is, if I am absolutely ignorant of how to proceed, of what I must do in order to ascertain its truth or falsity, then obviously I do not know what the proposition actually states, and I should then be unable to interpret the proposition by passing from the words, with the aid of the definitions, to possible experiences. For in so far as I am able to do this I am also able in the same way to state at least in principle the method of verification (even though, often, because of practical difficulties I am unable to carry it out). The statement of the conditions under which a proposition is true is *the same* as the statement of its meaning, and not something different.

And these *"conditions,"* we have already seen, must finally be discoverable in the given. Different conditions mean differences in the given. The *meaning* of every proposition is finally to be determined by the given, and by nothing else.

I do not know if this insight ought to be called positivistic; but of course I should like to believe that it underlay all those efforts which appear by this name in the history of philosophy, whether or not it was ever clearly formulated. We may indeed assume that it constitutes the real nucleus and motive force of many quite perverted formulations which we find among positivists.

If we but once attain the insight that the meaning of every proposition can be determined only by means of the given we can no longer conceive the *possibility* of another opinion, for we see that we have discovered simply the conditions under which opinions in general can be formulated. Hence it would be quite mistaken to see, somehow, in what we have said a "theory of meaning" (in Anglo-Saxon countries this insight, that the meaning of a proposition is determined wholly and alone by its verification in the given, is often called the "experimental theory of meaning"). What precedes every formulation of a theory cannot itself be a theory.

The content of our insight is indeed quite simple (and this is the reason why it is so sensible). It says: a proposition has a statable meaning only if it makes a verifiable difference whether it is true or false. A proposition which is such that the world remains the same whether it be true or false simply says nothing about the world; it is empty and communicates nothing; I can give it no meaning. We have a *verifiable* difference, however, only when it is a difference in the given, for verifiable certainly means nothing but "capable of being exhibited in the given."

It is obvious that verifiability is used here in the sense of "verifiable in principle," for the meaning of a proposition is, of course, independent of whether the conditions under which we find ourselves at a specified time allow or prevent the actual verification. There is not the least doubt that the proposition "there is a mountain of a height of 3000 meters on the other side of the moon" makes good sense, even though we lack the technical means of verifying it. And it would remain just as meaningful if one knew with certainty, on scientific grounds, that no man would ever reach the other side of the moon. The verification remains *conceivable;* we are always able to state what data we should have to experience in order to decide the truth or falsity of the proposition; the verification is *logically* possible, whatever be the case regarding its practical feasibility, and this alone concerns us.

But if someone should say: within every electron there is a nucleus, which, though always present, never has in any way any external effects, so that its existence never manifests itself in nature—this would be a meaningless assertion. For we should have to ask the maker of the hypothesis: what do you really *mean* by the presence of that "nucleus"?; and he could answer only: I mean that something exists there in the electron. We should inquire further: what does that mean? What would be the case if it didn't exist? And he would have to answer: everything would remain exactly the same as before.

For according to his assertion, the "somewhat" in the electron has no effects, and there would simply be no observable change: the realm of the given would not be affected in any way. We should judge that he had not succeeded in communicating the meaning of his hypothesis, and that therefore it made no sense. In this case the impossibility of verification is not factual, but *logical,* for by reason of the utter ineffectiveness of that nucleus a decision regarding it based on differences in the given is *in principle* excluded.

One cannot here suppose that the distinction between the impossibility of verifying something in principle and the mere factual, empirical impossibility is not clear, and is therefore sometimes difficult to draw; for the impossibility *in principle* is logical impossibility which does not differ in degree from empirical impossibility, but in very essence. What is empirically impossible still remains conceivable, but what is logically impossible is contradictory, and cannot therefore be thought at all. As a matter of fact we find that in scientific thinking this distinction is always clearly and instinctively felt. The physicists were the first to reject the statement given in our example regarding the forever hidden nucleus of the electron, with the criticism that it was no hypothesis at all, but mere empty word play. And in all times the most successful scientific investigators have adopted this standpoint with respect to the meaning of their statements, since they have acted in accordance with it, even if for the most part unconsciously.

For science, then, our standpoint does not represent something foreign and out of the ordinary, but it has in a certain sense always been more or less taken for granted. It could not be otherwise, because only from this standpoint is a proposition verifiable at all; and since all the activities of science consist in examining the truth of propositions, it continuously acknowledges the correctness of our insight by its practice.

If express confirmation were still necessary, it would be found most conspicuously at critical points in the development of science where investigation is forced to bring the self-evident presuppositions to light. This is the case where difficulties of principle lead one to suppose that something may be wrong with these presuppositions. The most famous example of this sort, which will remain forever memorable, is Einstein's analysis of the concept of time, which consists in nothing but the analysis of the *meaning* of our statements about the simultaneity of spatially separate events. Einstein said to the physicists (and to the philosophers): you must first state what you *mean* by simultaneity, and you can do this only by showing how the proposition "two events are simultaneous" is verified. But with this you have *completely* determined its meaning. What is true of the concept of simultaneity holds of every other concept: every proposition has meaning only in so far as it can be verified, and it *says* only what is verified, and simply nothing more. If one should say that it did contain something more he must be able to say what more this is, and to do this he would have to tell us how the world would differ if he were mistaken. But this cannot be done, since by assumption all the observable differences are already included in the verification.

In the example of simultaneity the analysis of the meaning, as is appropriate for the physicist, is carried only to the point where the decision regarding the truth or falsity of a proposition about time is based on the occurrence or non-occurrence of a definite physical event (e.g. the coincidence of a pointer with a point on a scale). But it is clear that one can ask further: what does it *mean* to say that the pointer indicates a definite point on the scale? And the answer can only be made by reference to the occurrence of certain data, or as one generally says, certain "sense-impressions." This will be generally admitted, especially by physicists. "For positivism will always be right in this, that there is no other source of knowledge than sense-impressions" says Planck[1] and this evidently means that the truth or falsity of a physical statement depends entirely upon the occurrence of certain sense-impressions (which constitute a special class of data).

But there will always be many who are inclined to say: granted that the truth of a physical statement can be tested only by the occurrence of certain sense-impressions, this is not the same as asserting that the *meaning* of the statement is also thereby exhaustively given. This latter must be denied: a proposition can contain more than can be verified; that the pointer stands at a definite point on the scale means *more* than the existence of certain sensations (namely "the existence of a definite fact in the external world").

In answer to this denial of the identity of meaning and verification we must point out the following: 1) This denial is found among physicists only when they leave the actual sphere of physical statements and begin to philosophize. (In physics, obviously, there occur only statements about the properties or behavior of things or events, an express statement concerning their "reality" is not a scientific statement but a philosophical one). In his own sphere the physicist admits entirely the correctness of our standpoint. We mentioned this earlier, and illustrated it in the example of simultaneity. There are

1. *Positivismus und Reale Aussenwelt,* p. 14.

indeed many philosophers who say: of course we can determine only relative simultaneity, but it does not follow from this that there is no such thing as absolute simultaneity, and we continue to believe in it! The falsity of this statement cannot in any sense be demonstrated, but the overwhelming majority of physicists is rightly of the opinion that it is meaningless. However it must be sharply emphasized that in both cases we have to do with the same situation. There is in principle no difference whether I ask: does the proposition "two events are simultaneous" mean more than can be verified? Or whether I ask: does the proposition "the pointer points toward the fifth line on the scale" mean more than can be verified? The physicist who handles these two cases differently is guilty of an inconsistency. He will of course justify himself, believing that in the second case where the question concerns the "reality of the external world" much more is at stake, philosophically. This argument is too vague for us to attach much weight to it, but we shall see presently whether anything lies behind it.

2) It is perfectly true that every statement about a physical object or an event *means* more than is verified, say, by the occurrence of a single experience. It is rather presupposed that the experience occurred under very definite conditions, whose realization of course can only be verified by something given, and it is presupposed further that ever more verifications are possible (confirmations etc.), which in their turn, naturally, reduce to certain given events. In this manner one can and must give an account of illusions of sense, and of error, and it is easy to see how those cases are to be included in which we should say the observer was merely dreaming, that the pointer indicated a definite line, or that he did not carefully observe, etc. The assertions of Blondlot about N-Rays which he believed himself to have discovered were certainly *more* than statements that under certain conditions he had experienced certain visual sensations; and because of this, of course, they could be refuted.[2] Strictly speaking, the meaning of a proposition about physical objects would be exhausted only by an indefinitely large number of possible verifications, and we gather from this that such a proposition can in the last analysis never be shown to be absolutely true. It is indeed generally recognized that even the most certain propositions of science are always to be taken as hypotheses, which remain open to further refinement and improvement. This has certain consequences for the logical nature of such propositions, but these do not interest us here.

Once again: the meaning of a physical statement is never de-

---

2. Cf. Planck, *op. cit.,* p. 11.

termined by a single isolated verification, but it must be thought of in the form: If conditions x are given, the data y occur, where we can substitute an indefinitely large number of conditions for x, the proposition remaining true for each case. (This holds even when the statement refers to a single happening—a historical event, for such an event has innumerable consequences whose occurrences are verifiable). Thus the meaning of every physical statement is lodged finally in an endless concatenation of data; the isolated datum therefore is here uninteresting. Hence if any positivist ever said that the only objects of science are the given experiences themselves he was certainly quite mistaken; what alone the scientists seek are the rules which govern the connections among experiences, and by means of which they can be predicted. No one will deny that the sole verification of natural laws lies in the fact that they yield such true predictions. The common objection that the immediately given, which at most can be but the object of psychology, is thus falsely made into the object of physics is in this way refuted.

3) Most important however: if anyone is of the opinion that the meaning of a proposition is nevertheless not exhausted by what can be verified in the given, but extends far beyond it, he must at least admit that this additional meaning cannot in any way be described, stated, or expressed in language. For let him try to communicate this additional meaning! To the extent to which he succeeds in *communicating* something about this additional meaning he will find that the communication consists in the fact that he has indicated certain conditions which can serve for verification in the given, and thus he finds our position confirmed. Or else he believes himself to have given a meaning, but closer examination shows that his words express only that *something* more is there, concerning whose nature simply nothing is said. And then in fact he has communicated nothing, and his assertion is meaningless. For one cannot assert the existence of something without saying *what* one asserts to exist. This is obvious in the case of our example of the "nucleus of the electron" which in principle lies beyond experience; yet for clarity's sake we shall consider another example which brings out an important point of principle.

I observe two pieces of green paper and determine that they have the same color. The proposition which asserts the sameness of color is verified, among other ways, by the fact that at the same time I have two experiences of the same color. The proposition: "there are two spots of the same color before me now" cannot be reduced to any others; it is verified by the fact that it describes the given. It has a clear meaning: by virtue of the meanings of the words involved in the proposition, it signifies just the existence of color sameness; and by virtue of linguistic usage the proposition expresses just that experience. Now I show one of these two pieces of paper to a second observer, and ask the question: does he see the green as I do? Is his color experience *like* my color experience? This case differs *in principle* from that just considered. While there the statement was verifiable by the experience of color sameness, here, brief reflection shows, such a verification is simply impossible. Of course the second observer, if he is not color blind, calls the paper *green,* and if I describe this green to him more closely by saying: it is yellower than this carpet, but bluer than the billiard cloth, darker than this plant, etc., he will find the same to hold in his experience, i.e. he will agree with my statements. But even if all his judgments about color agree entirely with mine I cannot infer from this that he experiences this same quality. It could be the case that on looking at the green paper he would have a color experience which I would call "red," that on the other hand, when I see red he would see green, calling it "red" of course, and so on. Indeed it might even be that my color sensations correspond to his tone experiences, or to any other data. It would nevertheless forever be impossible to discover these differences, between his and my experience. We should always understand one another perfectly, and could never be of different opinions regarding our environment if (and this is the only assumption that need be made) the inner *order* of his experiences agreed with that of mine. There is no question here of their "quality," all that is required is that they can be arranged into systems in the same manner.

All this is indeed admitted, and philosophers have often pointed it out. But, for the most part, while they have allowed that such subjective differences are theoretically possible, and that this possibility raises a very interesting question of principle, they have held it to be "highly probable" that the other observer and I do in fact have the *same* experience. But, we must point out, the statement that different individuals have the same experience has its sole verifiable meaning in the fact that all their assertions (and of course all the rest of their behavior) exhibit certain agreements. Hence it follows that the statement *means* nothing but this. It is only to express the same thing in a different manner if we say that we here are concerned with the similarity of two system-orders. The proposition that two experiences of different subjects not only occupy the same place in the order of a system but are, in addition, qualitatively similar has no meaning for us. Note well, it is not false, but meaningless: we have no idea what it means.

Experience shows, however, that most people find it very difficult to agree to this. We must make it clear that here we have to do with a logical impossibility of verification. It makes good sense to speak of the similarity of data in the *same* consciousness, for it can be verified through an immediate experience. But if we want to speak of the similarity of data in *different* consciousnesses we are dealing with a new concept, which has to be newly defined. For the statements in which it occurs are no longer verifiable in the old manner. The new definition is simply the similarity of all relevant reactions of the two individuals; we can find no other. Most people, of course, believe that no definition is required here; one knows the meaning of "similar" without it, and the meaning in both cases is the same. But, to recognize this as a mistake we need only remember the concept of simultaneity, in which the situation is exactly the same. To the concept of "simultaneity at a place" there corresponds the concept of "similarity of the experiences of the same individual," and to "simultaneity at different places" there corresponds the notion of "similarity of the experiences of different persons." The second notion is, with respect to the first, a new concept in each case, and must be specially defined. We can no more indicate a directly experiencable quality which would verify the similarity of two greens in different consciousnesses than we can for simultaneity at different points: *both* must be determined by a system of relations.

Many philosophers have sought to overcome the difficulty which seemed to confront them here by all sorts of speculations and ideal experiments, speaking, say, of a universal consciousness comprehending all individuals (God) or thinking perhaps that by means of some artificial connection of the nervous systems of two individuals the sensations of one would be made accessible to the other, and thus be rendered comparable. But of course all this is in vain. For even in this fantastic way in the end only the contents of one and the same consciousness would be directly compared. The question, however, concerns the possibility of the comparison of qualities in so far as they belong to different, and *not* the same, consciousnesses.

Hence it must be granted that a statement concerning the similarity of the experiences of two persons has no other *communicable* meaning than a certain agreement of their reactions. Of course everyone is free to believe that such a proposition also possesses another more direct meaning; but so much is sure: no such meaning is verifiable, and one cannot in any way state or show what this meaning is. Hence it follows that such a meaning simply cannot in any way become the object of discussion. We can say absolutely nothing about it, and it can in no way enter into any language by means of which we communicate with one another. And what has, I hope, become clear here holds generally. We can understand in a proposition only what it communicates, and a meaning is communicable only if it is verifiable. Since propositions are nothing but vehicles for communication we can include in their meanings only what they can communicate. For this reason I should maintain that "meaning" can mean only "verifiable meaning."

But even if someone should insist that there is a non-verifiable meaning this would not help in the least. For *such* a meaning can in no way enter into anything he says or asks, or into what we ask him or answer him. In other words: if there were any such thing, all our utterances, arguments, and modes of behavior would remain quite unaffected by it, whether we were dealing with daily life, ethical or aesthetic attitudes, with science or philosophy. Everything would remain as if there were no unverifiable meaning. For if there were a difference this very difference would make it verifiable.

This is a serious situation, and we must insist that it be taken seriously. Above all one must guard against confusing this logical impossibility with an empirical incapacity, as if some technical difficulty and human imperfection were responsible for the fact that only what is verifiable can be expressed, and as if there were still some rear entrance through which an unverifiable meaning might slip in and make itself evident in our discourse and behavior. No! The incommunicability is absolute; he who believes (or rather imagines that he believes) in a non-verifiable meaning must nevertheless admit that with respect to it only *one* course is open to him: utter silence. Neither he nor we gain anything, no matter how often he asserts: "yet there is a non-verifiable meaning!" For this statement itself is devoid of meaning, it tells us nothing.

3. What is the Meaning of "Reality," of "External World"?

We are now prepared to apply what has been said to the so-called problem of the reality of the external world.

We ask: What is the meaning of the realist's assertion, "there is an external world?" or what is the meaning of the statement (attributed to the positivist by the realist) "there is no external world"?

In order to answer the question it is of course necessary to make clear the meanings of the words, "there is," and "external world." We begin with the first. "There is an x" means the same as "x is real" or "x is actual." Hence what do we mean when we attribute reality to an object? It is an old, very important logical or philosophical insight, that the proposition "x is real" is of quite a different sort from a proposition which ascribes some *property* to x (e.g. "x is hard.") In other words: reality or existence is not a predicate. The statement "the dollar in my pocket is round" has a completely different logical form from that of the statement "the dollar in my pocket is real." In modern logic this distinction is expressed by means of two very different symbolisms, but it was already clearly drawn by Kant, who, as we know, in his critique of the so-called ontological proof of God's existence, correctly found the source of error of this proof in the fact that existence is treated as a predicate.

In daily life we constantly speak of reality or existence, and for this reason it cannot be very difficult to discover its meaning. In a law-suit it is often necessary to determine whether a certain document actually exists, or whether it is merely wrongly asserted to exist; and it is not altogether unimportant to me whether the dollar in my pocket is only imagined or is real. Now everyone knows how such an assertion of the reality of something is verified, and there cannot be the slightest doubt that the reality of the dollar is verified and verified only by the fact that, as a result of certain suitable manipulations, I obtain certain sensations of touch and sight upon whose presence I am accustomed to say "this is a dollar." The same holds of the document, except that in this case we would content ourselves with certain statements of others who claim to have seen the document, i.e. to have had perceptions of a very definite sort. And the "statements of others" consist again of certain acoustic, or, if they were written statements, of certain visual perceptions. No special analysis is required of the fact that the occurrence of certain sense-perceptions among the data always constitutes the sole criterion of statements concerning the reality of a "physical" object or event in everyday life, as well as in the most subtle propositions of science. That there are okapis in Africa can be determined only by the fact that such animals are observed there. However it is not necessary that the object or event "itself" be perceived. We can, for example, imagine the existence of a transneptunian planet to be inferred with as much certainty from the observation of perturbations as from the direct perception of a spot of light in the telescope. The reality of atoms furnishes us with another example. And the same is true of the other side of the moon.

It is of great importance to realize that the occurrence of a definite single experience in the verification of a proposition about nature is often not accepted as verifying the proposition, but that throughout we are concerned with uniformities, with connections obeying natural laws: in this manner genuine verifications are distinguished from illusions and hallucinations. When we say of any object or event—which must be designated by a description—that it is *real* this means that there exists a very definite connection between perceptions or other experiences, that under certain conditions certain data appear. Such a statement is verified in this manner alone, and therefore it has only this communicable meaning.

This was in principle already formulated by Kant, whom no one would charge with "positivism." Reality for him is a category, and if we apply it in any way, and say of an object that it is real this means, according to Kant, that it belongs to a collection of perceptions connected according to some natural law.

We see that for us (as for Kant; and the same applies to every philosopher who understands his business) it is simply a matter of saying what it means in everyday life or in science to ascribe real existence to a thing. Our task is in no sense that of correcting the statements of everyday life or of science. I must confess that I should repudiate and consider absurd any philosophical system that involved the assertion that clouds and stars, mountains and sea were unreal, that the chair by the wall ceased to exist whenever I turned my back. Nor do I credit any serious thinker with any such statement. It would for example surely be quite a perverse interpretation of Berkeley's philosophy to see in it such a system. He too didn't deny the reality of the world of bodies, but merely tried to explain what we mean when we ascribe reality to it. He who says that unperceived ideas exist in God's mind does not thereby deny their existence but seeks to understand it. John Stuart Mill himself did not wish to deny the reality of physical bodies, but to clarify it, when he declared them to be "permanent possibilities of sensation," though in my opinion his manner of expression was very ill chosen.

Therefore if one understands by "positivism" a view which denies the reality of bodies I must declare positivism to be simply absurd. But I do not believe that such an interpretation of positivistic views would be historically just, at least so far as their ablest representatives are concerned. Be this as it may, we are not concerned with it, but with the view itself. And in this connection we have seen that our principle, that the meaning of a proposition is identical with its verification, leads to the insight that the assertion of the reality of a thing is a statement regarding a regular connection of experiences. It does not lead to the conclusion that the assertion is false. (Therefore reality is not denied to physical things in favor of sensations.)

But opponents of the view just expounded are not at all satisfied with this. They would probably offer the following answer: "You do, indeed, admit the reality of the physical world, but, as it seems to us, only verbally. You simply *call* that real which we would describe as a mere conceptual construction. When *we* use the word reality we mean by it something quite different from what you mean. Your definition of reality refers back to experiences; but we mean something altogether independent of experience. We mean something which possesses that same independence evidently attributed by you to the data alone, in the sense that you reduce everything to them as to something not further reducible."

Even though it would suffice as a rebuttal to invite our opponents to reconsider how existential propositions are verified, and how verification and meaning are connected, I think it necessary to consider the psychological attitude from which this argument arises, and to request attention for the following remarks, which may result in a modification of that attitude.

We ask first whether on our view a reality is attributed to a "content of consciousness" which is denied to a physical object. Thus we inquire whether the assertion of the reality of a feeling or a sensation has a different meaning from that of the reality of a physical body? This can mean for us only: do we have different modes of verification in each case? The answer is: No! In order to make this clear it is necessary to undertake some slight analysis of the logical form of existential propositions. The general logical insight that an existential proposition about a datum is possible only if it is referred to by a description, and not if it is given by direct indication holds of course for "data of consciousness." (In the language of symbolic logic this is expressed by the fact that an existential proposition must contain an "operator.") In B. Russell's symbolism, for example, an existential proposition has the form $(\exists x)\ fx$, or in words: "there is an x having the property f." The combination of words "there is an a," where "a" is the proper name of an object directly present, and therefore means the same as "this," is meaningless, and cannot be written in Russell's symbolism. We must attain the insight that Descartes' statement "I am"—or, to use a less misleading formulation, "my contents of consciousness exist"—is simply meaningless; it expresses nothing and contains no knowledge. This is because "contents of consciousness" occurs in this context simply as a *name* for the given: no characteristic is expressed whose presence could be tested. A proposition only has meaning, is verifiable only, if I can state the conditions under which it would be true and under which it would be false. But how shall I describe the conditions under which the proposition "my contents of consciousness exist" would be false? Every attempt would lead to absurdity, for example to such statements as "it is the case that nothing is the case," or something of the sort. Therefore it is self-evident that I cannot describe the conditions which make the proposition true (try to do so!). There is indeed also no doubt that Descartes failed to gain any knowledge through his statement, and was no wiser at the end than he was at the beginning of his inquiry.

No, a question concerning the reality of an experience makes sense only if its reality can significantly be *doubted*. I can for example ask: Is it really true that I felt happy upon hearing that news? This can be verified or falsified in exactly the same way as, say, the question: is it true that Sirius has a satellite (that this satellite is real)? That on a given occasion I experienced pleasure can for example be verified by examining the statements of others concerning my behavior at the time, by finding a letter written by me at the time, or even simply by a veridical memory of the emotion experienced. Hence there is here absolutely no difference in principle: to be real always means to stand in a definite relationship to the given. And this also holds, say, for an experience at this very moment. For example, I can significantly ask (say in the course of a physiological experiment): do I, or do I not, experience a pain at this moment? Observe that here "pain" does not function as a proper name for a this-here, but represents a concept which stands for a describable class of experiences. Here, too, the question is answered by determining that an experience having certain describable properties occurs in conjunction with certain conditions (experimental conditions, concentration of attention etc.). Such describable properties would be, for instance, similarity to an experience occurring under certain other conditions; the tendency to produce certain reactions, etc.

No matter how we twist and turn: it is impossible to interpret an existential proposition except as a statement regarding a connection of perceptions. It is reality of *the same* sort that one must attribute to data of consciousness and, say, to physical events. Hardly anything in the history of philosophy has produced greater confusion than the attempt to distinguish one of the two as true "being." Wherever the word "real" is significantly used it means one and the same thing.

The opponent of this view will perhaps not feel that what has been said upsets his own view in any way, but will be of the impression that the preceding arguments presuppose a point of departure he is from the outset unwilling to adopt. He must indeed grant that a decision regarding the reality or unreality of a fact in experience is always made in the way described, but he claims that in this way one arrives only at what Kant called *empirical* reality. This method defines the realm of the observations of everyday life and of science, but beyond this limit lies something more, the *transcendent* reality, which cannot be deduced by strict logic, and therefore is not a postulate of the understanding, but is perhaps a postulate of *reason*. This is the only real *external world,* and it alone is relevant to the philosophical problem of the existence of the external world. Thus our discussion leaves the question of the meaning of the word "reality," and turns to that of the phrase "external world."

The phrase "external world" is evidently used in two different ways: first in the language of everyday life, and secondly as a technical term in philosophy.

Wherever it occurs in daily life it has, as do most of the expressions used in practical affairs, a sensible meaning which can be stated. In opposition to the "inner world," which includes memories, thoughts, dreams, desires, feelings, the external world is simply the world of mountains and trees, of animals and men. Every child knows what is meant when we assert the existence of definite objects of this world; and we must insist that it really means absolutely nothing *more* than what the child knows. We all know how to verify the statement, say, that "there is a castle in the park outside the city." We act in certain ways and then if certain clearly describable facts are experienced we say: "Yes, there really is a castle there," otherwise we say the statement was wrong, or a lie. And if someone asks us: "Was the castle also there at night, when no one saw it?" We answer: "Undoubtedly! For it would have been impossible to build it since this morning; furthermore the condition of the building shows that not only was it there yesterday, but for hundreds of years, hence before we were born." Thus we possess quite definite empirical criteria with which to determine whether houses and trees existed when we did not see them, and whether they already existed before our birth, and whether they will exist after our death. This means that the statement that those things "exist independently of us" has a clear verifiable meaning, and is obviously to be affirmed. We can very well distinguish empirically things of this sort from those that are only "subjective" and "dependent upon us." If, for instance, because of some visual defect I see a dark spot when I look at the adjacent wall I say that the spot is there only when I look at it, but I say that the wall is there even when I do not look at it. The verification of this distinction is indeed quite easy, and both these statements say just what is contained in the verifications, and nothing else.

Hence if the phrase external world is taken with the signification it has in everyday life then the question regarding its existence is simply the question: are there in addition to memories, desires and ideas also stars, clouds, plants, animals, and my own body? We have just seen that it would be simply absurd to answer this question in the negative. There are, quite evidently, houses, clouds, and animals existing independently of us, and I said above that any thinker who denied the existence of the external world in this sense would have no claim on our respect. Instead of telling us what we mean when we speak of mountains and plants he would convince us that there aren't any such things at all!

But science! Does it, in opposition to common sense, mean something other than things like houses and trees when it speaks of the external world? It seems to me that nothing of the sort is the case. For atoms and electric fields, or whatever the physicist may speak of, are just what constitute houses and trees according to their theory; and therefore the one must be real in the same sense as the other. The objectivity of mountains and clouds is exactly the same as that of protons and energies—these latter stand in no greater opposition to "subjectivity," say to feelings and hallucinations, than do the former. In fact we are at last convinced that the existence of even the most subtle "invisible things," assumed by the scientist, is, in principle, verified exactly as is the reality of a tree or a star.

In order to settle the dispute concerning realism it is of very great importance to draw the physicist's attention to the fact that his external world is simply *nature,* which also surrounds us in daily life, and not the "transcendent world" of the metaphysician. The distinction between the two is again especially clear in Kant's philosophy. Nature, and everything of which the physicist can and must speak belongs, according to Kant, to empirical reality, and what that means is (as we have already said) explained by him in just the way that it must be by us. Atoms in Kant's system have no transcendent reality, they are not "things in themselves." Hence the physicist cannot appeal to the Kantian philosophy; its arguments lead only to the empirical external world which we all acknowledge, not to a transcendent world; his electrons are not metaphysical entities.

Nevertheless many scientists speak of the necessity of assuming the existence of an external world as a metaphysical hypothesis. To be sure, they do not do this within their own science (even though all the necessary hypotheses of a science ought to be found *within* it), but only where they leave this realm and begin to philosophize. In fact the transcendent external world is something dealt with only in philosophy, never in a science, nor in daily life. It is simply a technical term into whose meaning we must now inquire.

How is the transcendent or metaphysical external world distinguished from the empirical world? In philosophical systems it is thought of as somehow standing behind the empirical world, where the word "behind" indicates that it cannot be *known* in the same sense as can the empirical world, that it lies beyond a boundary which separates the accessible from the inaccessible.

This distinction has its original source in the view, formerly held by most philosophers, that in order to know an object it is necessary to perceive it directly; knowledge is a sort of intuition, and is perfect only when the object is directly present to the knower as a sensation or feeling. Hence according to this view what cannot be immediately experienced or perceived remains unknowable, incomprehensible, transcendent; it belongs to the realm of things in themselves. Here there is simply a confusion, which I have revealed elsewhere many times, between knowledge and mere acquaintance or experience. But modern scientists will certainly be guilty of no such confusion. I do not believe that any physicist is of the opinion that knowledge of the electron consists in the fact that it enters bodily into the consciousness of the investigator through an act of intuition. He will, rather, hold the view that for complete knowledge it is only necessary to state the laws governing the behavior of the electron so exhaustively that all formulae into which its properties enter in any way are completely confirmed by experience. In other words: the electron, and equally all physical realities are *not* unknowable things in themselves, they do not belong to transcendent reality, if this is characterized by the fact that it contains the unknowable.

Therefore we again come to the conclusion that all physical hypotheses can refer only to *empirical* reality, if by this we mean the knowable. In fact it would be a self-contradiction to assume hypothetically something unknowable. For there must always be definite *reasons* for setting up an hypothesis, the hypothesis has a certain function to fulfill. Therefore what is assumed in the hypothesis must have the property of fulfilling this function, and must be so constituted that it is justified by those reasons. But in just this way certain statements are made regarding the assumed entity and these express our *knowledge* of it. And of course they contain *complete* knowledge of it. For *only* that can be assumed hypothetically for which there are grounds in experience.

Or does the "realistic" scientist want to designate the theory of objects which are not directly experienced as a metaphysical hypothesis for some other reason than that of their unknowableness, which is not under consideration at all? To this he will perhaps answer affirmatively. In fact we learn from numerous statements in the literature that the physicist does not add any statement of its unknowable character to his affirmation of a transcendent world; quite the contrary, he is rightly of the opinion that the nature of the extra-mental things is correctly represented by his equations. Thus the external world of the physical realist is not that of traditional metaphysics. He uses the technical term of the philosopher, but what he means by it has appeared to us to be nothing but the external world of everyday life, whose existence no one, not even the "positivist," doubts.

What, then, is that other reason which leads the "realist" to conceive his external world as a metaphysical hypothesis? Why does he want to distinguish it from the empirical external world which we have described? The answer to this question leads us back again to an earlier point in our discussion. The physical "realist" is quite satisfied with our description of the external world except in one point: he does not believe that we have granted it enough *reality*. It is not because it is unknowable, or for any such reason that he thinks his "external world" differs from the empirical, but only because a different, higher reality pertains to it. This often shows itself in his language; the word "real" is frequently reserved for that external world in contrast with the merely "ideal," "subjective" contents of consciousness, and in opposition to mere "logical" constructions, "positivism" being reproached with the attempt to reduce reality to such logical constructs.

But the physical realist, too, feels obscurely that, as we know, reality is not a "predicate," hence he cannot well pass from our empirical to his transcendent external world by ascribing to it, in addition to the characteristics which we also attribute to physical objects, the characteristic of "reality." Nevertheless he expresses himself in this way; and this illegitimate leap, which carries him beyond the realm of significance, would indeed be "metaphysical," and will be felt by him to be such.

Now we see the situation clearly, and can base our final judgment on the foregoing considerations.

Our principle that the truth and falsity of all statements, including those concerning the reality of a physical object, can be tested only in the "given," and that *therefore* the meaning of all propositions can be formulated and understood only with the help of the given—this principle is mistakenly conceived as if it asserted or presupposed that only the given is real. Therefore the "realist" feels impelled to contradict this principle and to establish the contrary: that the meaning of an existential proposition is in no sense exhausted by mere propositions of the form "under these definite conditions that definite experience will occur" (those propositions constituting an infinite set according to our view), but that their meaning lies *beyond* all this in something else, which is to be designated, say, as "independent existence," as "transcendent being," or similarly, and to which our principle fails to do justice.

And here we inquire: Well, how *do* you do justice to it? What do these phrases "independent existence" and "transcendent being" *mean?* In other words: what verifiable difference does it make in the world whether transcendent being pertains to an object or not?

Two answers are given to this question. The first is that it makes a very great difference. For a scientist who believes in a "real" external world will feel and work very differently from one who believes himself to be "describing sensations." The former will observe the starry heavens, whose view makes him conscious of his own puny nature, and the incomprehensible sublimity and grandeur of the world with very different feelings of fervor and awe from the latter, for whom the most distant galactic systems are merely "complexes of his own sense-impressions." The former will devote himself to his task with an inspiration and will feel a satisfaction in the knowledge of the external world which is denied to the latter, because he believes himself to be dealing only with his own constructions.

In answer to this we offer the following comment. Let us assume that somewhere in the behavior of two scientists there does exist a difference such as has been described here. Such a difference would of course be an observable difference. Suppose now somebody insists on expressing this difference by saying that one of the scientists believes in a real external world and the other does not. In that event the *meaning* of this statement would consist solely in what we observe in the behavior of the two men. That is, the words "absolute reality" or "transcendent being," or whatever expressions we might choose to employ, mean here simply certain states of feeling, which occur in the men when they observe the world, or make statements about it, or philosophize. It is, indeed, the case that the use of the words "independent existence," "transcendent reality," etc., is simply and only the expression of a feeling, of a psychological attitude of the speaker (this, moreover, may, in the final analysis, be true of all metaphysical propositions). If someone assures us that there is a real external world in the trans-empirical sense of the word, he of course believes himself to have communicated some truth about the world. But in actual fact, his words express something very different; they merely express certain feelings which give rise to various linguistic and other reactions on his part.

If this self-evident point requires any further emphasis I should like to call attention to the fact—and with the greatest stress on the *seriousness* of what is said—that the non-metaphysician is not distinguished from the metaphysician by, say, the absence in him of those feelings which the other expresses in terms of the statements of a realistic philosophy, but only by the fact that he recognizes that these statements simply do not have the meaning they seem to have, and are therefore to be avoided. The non-metaphysician will express these same feelings in a *different* way. In other words: the contrast drawn in the first answer of the "realist" between the two types of thinkers was misleading and unjust. If one is unfortunate enough not to feel the sublimity of the starry heavens something other than a logical analysis of the concepts of reality and external world is to be blamed. To assume that the opponents of metaphysics are unable justly to comprehend, say, the greatness of Copernicus, because in a certain sense the Ptolemaic view represents the empirical facts as well as the Copernican, seems to me to be as strange as to believe that the "positivist" cannot be a good parent because according to his theory his children are merely complexes of his own sense-impressions, and it is therefore senseless to take measures for their welfare after his death. No: the world of the non-metaphysician is the same world as that of all other men; it lacks nothing which is needed to bestow meaning on all the propositions of science and the whole conduct of life. He merely avoids adding meaningless statements to his description of the world.

We come now to the *second* answer which can be given to the question concerning the meaning of the assertion of a transcendent reality. It consists in granting that it makes no difference at all for experience whether or not one assumes something further to exist behind the empirical world, that metaphysical realism therefore cannot be tested and is actually unverifiable. Hence one cannot indicate any further what is meant by this assertion; but nevertheless it does mean something, and this meaning can be understood even without verification.

This is nothing but the view, criticized in the previous section, that the meaning of a proposition has nothing to do with its verification, and we need only apply our earlier general criticism to this special case. Therefore we must say: you designate here by existence or reality something which simply cannot in any way be given or explained. Yet despite this you believe that those words make sense. We shall not quarrel with you over this point. But this much is certain: according to the admission just made this sense can in no way become evident, it cannot be expressed in any written or spoken communication, nor by any gesture or conduct. For if this were possible we should have before us a verifiable empirical fact, and the world would be *different* if the proposition "there is an external world" were true, from what it would be if it were false. This difference would then constitute the meaning of the phrase "real external world," hence it would be an empirical meaning; that is, this real external world would again be only the empirical world, which, like all human beings, we also acknowledge. Even to speak of any other world is logically impossible. There can be no discussion concerning it, for a non-verifiable existence cannot enter meaningfully into any possible proposition. Whoever still believes—or believes himself to believe—in it must do so only silently. Arguments can relate only to what can be said.

The results of our discussion may be summarized as follows:

1) The justified unassailable nucleus of the "positivistic" tendency seems to me to be the principle that the meaning of every proposition is completely contained within its verification in the given.

But this principle has seldom been clearly apparent within that general tendency, and has so frequently been mixed with so many untenable propositions that a logical purification is necessary. If one wishes to call the result of the purification positivism, which would perhaps be historically justifiable, at least a differentiating adjective must be added. Sometimes the term "logical" or else "logistic positivism" is used.[3] Otherwise the designation "consistent empiricism" seems to me to be appropriate.

---

3. See the article by Blumberg and Feigl in the *Journal of Philosophy*, Vol. XXVIII (1931), the article by E. Kaila in the *Annales Universitatis Aboensis*, Vol. XIII, Ser. B. (Turku, 1930), and the one by A. Petzäll in the *Schriften der Universität Göteborg*.

2) This principle does not mean and does not imply that only the given is real. Such an assertion does not make sense.

3) Hence also, consistent empiricism does *not* deny the existence of an external world; it merely points out the empirical meaning of this existential proposition.

4) It is not a "Theory of As If." It does not assert that everything behaves as if there were physical independent bodies; but for it, too, everything is real which the non-philosophizing scientist calls real. The subject-matter of physics is *not* sensations, but laws. The formulation, used by some positivists, that bodies are only "complexes of sensations" is therefore to be rejected. What is correct is only that propositions concerning bodies are transformable into equivalent propositions concerning the occurrence of sensations in accordance with laws.

5) Hence logical positivism and realism are not in opposition; whoever acknowledges our fundamental principle must be an empirical realist.[4]

6) An opposition exists only between the consistent empiricist and the metaphysician, and indeed no more against the realist than against the idealist metaphysician (the former has been referred to in our discussion as "realist" in quotation marks).

7) The denial of the existence of a transcendent external world would be just as much a metaphysical statement as its affirmation. Hence the consistent empiricist does not deny the transcendent world, but shows that both its denial and affirmation are meaningless.

This last distinction is of the greatest importance. I am convinced that the chief opposition to our view derives from the fact that the distinction between the falsity and the meaninglessness of a proposition is not observed. The proposition "Discourse concerning a metaphysical external world is meaningless" does *not* say: "There is no external world," but something altogether different. The empiricist does not say to the metaphysician "what you say is false," but, "what you say asserts nothing at all!" He does not contradict him, but says "I don't understand you."

---

4. On this point and on the entire subject of the present essay the reader is also referred to Hans Cornelius' "Zur Kritik der Wissenschaftlichen Grundbegriffe," *Erkenntnis,* Vol. II. The formulations there are, however, open to objections. See also the splendid remarks in Chapter X of Phillip Frank's fine work, *Das Kausalgesetz und seine Grenzen,* and Rudolf Carnap's *Scheinprobleme der Philosophie.*

5

The Empiricist Criterion

of Meaning

BY CARL G. HEMPEL

1. INTRODUCTION

THE FUNDAMENTAL TENET of modern empiricism is the view that all non-analytic knowledge is based on experience. Let us call this thesis the principle of empiricism.[1] Contemporary logical empiricism has added[2] to it the maxim that a sentence makes a cognitively meaningful assertion, and thus can be said to be either true or false, only if it is either (1) analytic or self-contradictory or (2) capable, at least in principle, of experiential test. According to this so-called *empiricist criterion of cognitive meaning, or of cognitive significance,* many of the formulations of traditional metaphysics and large parts of epistemology are devoid of cognitive significance—however rich some of them may be in non-cognitive import by virtue of their emotive appeal or the moral inspiration they offer. Similarly certain doctrines which have been, at one time or another, formulated within empirical science or its border disciplines are so contrived as to be incapable of test by any conceivable evidence; they are therefore qualified as pseudo-hypotheses, which assert nothing, and which

This article first appeared in Vol. 4 of *Revue Internationale de Philosophie* (1950). It is republished here with the kind permission of Professor Hempel and the editor of that journal.

1. This term is used by Benjamin (2) in an examination of the foundations of empiricism. For a recent discussion of the basic ideas of empiricism see Russell (27), Part Six.
2. In his stimulating article, "Positivism," W. T. Stace argues, in effect, that the testability criterion of meaning is not logically entailed by the principle of empiricism. (See (29), especially section 11.) This is correct: according to the latter, a sentence expresses knowledge only if it is either analytic or corroborated by empirical evidence; the former goes further and identifies the domain of cognitively significant discourse with that of potential knowledge; i. e., it grants cognitive import only to sentences for which—unless they are either analytic or contradictory—a test by empirical evidence is conceivable.

therefore have no explanatory or predictive force whatever. This verdict applies, for example, to the neo-vitalist speculations about entelechies or vital forces, and to the "telefinalist hypothesis" propounded by Lecomte du Noüy.[3]

The preceding formulations of the principle of empiricism and of the empiricist meaning criterion provide no more, however, than a general and rather vague characterization of a basic point of view, and they need therefore to be elucidated and amplified. And while in the earlier phases of its development, logical empiricism was to a large extent preoccupied with a critique of philosophic and scientific formulations by means of those fundamental principles, there has been in recent years an increasing concern with the positive tasks of analyzing in detail the logic and methodology of empirical science and of clarifying and restating the basic ideas of empiricism in the light of the insights thus obtained. In the present article, I propose to discuss some of the problems this search has raised and some of the results it seems to have established.

2. CHANGES IN THE TESTABILITY CRITERION OF EMPIRICAL MEANING

As our formulation shows, the empiricist meaning criterion lays down the requirement of experiential testability for those among the cognitively meaningful sentences which are neither analytic nor contradictory; let us call them sentences with empirical meaning, or empirical significance. The concept of testability, which is to render precise the vague notion of being based—or rather baseable —on experience, has undergone several modifications which reflect an increasingly refined analysis of the structure of empirical knowledge. In the present section, let us examine the major stages of this development.

For convenience of exposition, we first introduce three auxiliary concepts, namely those of observable characteristic, of observation predicate, and of observation sentence. A property or a relation of physical objects will be called an *observable characteristic* if, under suitable circumstances, its presence or absence in a given instance can be ascertained through direct observation. Thus, the terms "green," "soft," "liquid," "longer than," designate observable characteristics, while "bivalent," "radioactive," "better electric conductor," and "introvert" do not. Terms which designate observable characteristics will be called *observation predicates*. Finally, by an

---

3. Cf. (19), Ch. XVI.

observation sentence we shall understand any sentence which—correctly or incorrectly—asserts of one or more specifically named objects that they have, or that they lack, some specified observable characteristic. The following sentences, for example, meet this condition: "The Eiffel Tower is taller than the buildings in its vicinity," "The pointer of this instrument does not cover the point marked '3' on the scale," and even, "The largest dinosaur on exhibit in New York's Museum of Natural History had a blue tongue"; for this last sentence assigns to a specified object a characteristic—having a blue tongue—which is of such a kind that under suitable circumstances (e.g., in the case of my Chow dog) its presence or absence can be ascertained by direct observation. Our concept of observation sentence is intended to provide a precise interpretation of the vague idea of a sentence asserting something that is "in principle" ascertainable by direct observation, even though it may happen to be actually incapable of being observed by myself, perhaps also by my contemporaries, and possibly even by any human being who ever lived or will live. Any evidence that might be adduced in the test of an empirical hypothesis may now be thought of as being expressed in observation sentences of this kind.[4]

We now turn to the changes in the conception of testability, and thus of empirical meaning. In the early days of the Vienna Circle, a sentence was said to have empirical meaning if it was capable, at least in principle, of complete verification by observational evidence; i.e., if observational evidence could be described which, if actually obtained, would conclusively establish the truth of the sentence.[5] With the help of the concept of observation sen-

---

4. Observation sentences of this kind belong to what Carnap has called the thing-language (cf., e. g., (7), pp. 52-53). That they are adequate to formulate the data which serve as the basis for empirical tests is clear in particular for the intersubjective testing procedures used in science as well as in large areas of empirical inquiry on the common-sense level. In epistemological discussions, it is frequently assumed that the ultimate evidence for beliefs about empirical matters consists in perceptions and sensations whose description calls for a phenomenalistic type of language. The specific problems connected with the phenomenalistic approach cannot be discussed here; but it should be mentioned that at any rate all the critical considerations presented in this article in regard to the testability criterion are applicable, *mutatis mutandis,* to the case of a phenomenalistic basis as well.

5. Originally, the permissible evidence was meant to be restricted to what is observable by the speaker and perhaps his fellow-beings during their lifetimes. Thus construed, the criterion rules out, as cognitively meaningless, all statements about the distant future or the remote past, as has been pointed out, among others, by Ayer in (1), Chapter I; by Pap in (21), Chapter 13, esp. pp. 333 ff.; and by Russell in (27), pp. 445-47. This difficulty is avoided, however, if we permit the evidence to consist of any finite set of "logically possible observation data," each of them formulated in an observation sentence. Thus, e. g., the sentence S_1, "The tongue of the largest dinosaur in New York's Museum of Natural History was blue

tence, we can restate this requirement as follows: A sentence S has empirical meaning if and only if it is possible to indicate a finite set of observation sentences, O_1, O_2, . . . , O_n, such that if these are true, then S is necessarily true, too. As stated, however, this condition is satisfied also if S is an analytic sentence or if the given observation sentences are logically incompatible with each other. By the following formulation, we rule these cases out and at the same time express the intended criterion more precisely:

(2.1) *Requirement of complete verifiability in principle:* A sentence has empirical meaning if and only if it is not analytic and follows logically from some finite and logically consistent class of observation sentences.[6]

---

or black" is completely verifiable in our sense; for it is a logical consequence of the Sentence S_2, "The tongue of the largest dinosaur in New York's Museum of Natural History was blue"; and this is an observation sentence, as has been shown above.

And if the concept of *verifiability in principle* and the more general concept of *confirmability in principle*, which will be considered later, are construed as referring to *logically possible evidence* as expressed by observation sentences, then it follows similarly that the class of statements which are verifiable, or at least confirmable, in principle includes such assertions as that the planet Neptune and the Antarctic Continent existed before they were discovered, and that atomic warfare, if not checked, may lead to the extermination of this planet. The objections which Russell (cf. (27), pp. 445 and 447) raises against the verifiability criterion by reference to those examples do not apply therefore if the criterion is understood in the manner here suggested. Incidentally, statements of the kind mentioned by Russell, which are not actually verifiable by any human being, were explicitly recognized as cognitively significant already by Schlick (in (28), Part V), who argued that the impossibility of verifying them was "merely empirical." The characterization of verifiability with the help of the concept of observation sentence as suggested here might serve as a more explicit and rigorous statement of that conception.

6. As has frequently been emphasized in empiricist literature, the term "verifiability" is to indicate, of course, the conceivability, or better, the logical possibility of evidence of an observational kind which, if actually encountered, would constitute conclusive evidence for the given sentence; it is not intended to mean the technical possibility of performing the tests needed to obtain such evidence, and even less does it mean the possibility of actually finding directly observable phenomena which constitute conclusive evidence for that sentence—which would be tantamount to the actual existence of such evidence and would thus imply the truth of the given sentence. Analogous remarks apply to the terms "falsifiability" and "confirmability." This point has been disregarded in some recent critical discussions of the verifiability criterion. Thus, e.g., Russell (cf. (27), p. 448) construes verifiability as the actual existence of a set of conclusively verifying occurrences. This conception, which has never been advocated by any logical empiricist, must naturally turn out to be inadequate since according to it the empirical meaningfulness of a sentence could not be established without gathering empirical evidence, and moreover enough of it to permit a conclusive proof of the sentences in question! It is not surprising, therefore, that his extraordinary interpretation of verifiability leads Russell to the conclusion: "In fact, that a proposition is verifiable is itself not verifiable" (*l. c.*) Actually, under the empiricist interpretation of complete verifiability, any statement asserting the verifiability of some sentence S whose text is quoted, is either analytic or contradictory; for the decision whether there exists a class of observation sentences which entail S, i. e., whether such observation sentences can be formulated, no matter whether they are true or false—that decision

This criterion, however, has several serious defects. The first of those here to be mentioned has been pointed out by various writers:

(*a*) The verifiability requirement rules out all sentences of universal form and thus all statements purporting to express general laws; for these cannot be conclusively verified by any finite set of observational data. And since sentences of this type constitute an integral part of scientific theories, the verifiability requirement must be regarded as overly restrictive in this respect. Similarly, the criterion disqualifies all sentences such as "For any substance there exists some solvent," which contain both universal and existential quantifiers (i.e., occurrences of the terms "all" and "some" or their equivalents); for no sentences of this kind can be logically deduced from any finite set of observation sentences.

Two further defects of the verifiability requirement do not seem to have been widely noticed:

(*b*) Suppose that S is a sentence which satisfies the proposed criterion, whereas N is a sentence such as "The absolute is perfect," to which the criterion attributes no empirical meaning. Then the alternation SvN (i.e., the expression obtained by connecting the two sentences by the word "or"), likewise satisfies the criterion; for if S is a consequence of some finite class of observation sentences, then trivially SvN is a consequence of the same class. But clearly, the empiricist criterion of meaning is not intended to countenance sentences of this sort. In this respect, therefore, the requirement of complete verifiability is too inclusive.

(*c*) Let "P" be an observation predicate. Then the purely existential sentence "(E*x*)P(*x*)" ("There exists at least one thing that has the property P") is completely verifiable, for it follows from any observation sentence asserting of some particular object that it has the property P. But its denial, being equivalent to the universal

___

is a matter of pure logic and requires no factual information whatever.

A similar misunderstanding is in evidence in the following passage in which W. H. Werkmeister claims to characterize a view held by logical positivists: "A proposition is said to be 'true' when it is 'verifiable in principle'; i. e., when we know the conditions which, when realized, will make 'verification' possible (cf. Ayer)." (cf. (31), p. 145). The quoted thesis, which, again, was never held by any logical positivist, including Ayer, is in fact logically absurd. For we can readily describe conditions which, if realized, would verify the sentence "The outside of the Chrysler Building is painted a bright yellow"; but similarly, we can describe verifying conditions for its denial; hence, according to the quoted principle, both the sentence and its denial would have to be considered true. Incidentally, the passage under discussion does not accord with Werkmeister's perfectly correct observation, *l. c.*, p. 40, that verifiability is intended to characterize the meaning of a sentence—which shows that verifiability is meant to be a criterion of cognitive significance rather than of truth.

sentence "$(x) \backsim P(x)$" ("Nothing has the property P") is clearly
not completely verifiable, as follows from comment (*a*) above.
Hence, under the criterion (2.1), the denials of certain empirically
—and thus cognitively—significant sentences are empirically meaningless; and as they are neither analytic nor contradictory, they are
cognitively meaningless. But however we may delimit the domain
of significant discourse, we shall have to insist that if a sentence falls
within that domain, then so must its denial. To put the matter more
explicitly: The sentences to be qualified as cognitively meaningful
are precisely those which can be significantly said to be either true
or false. But then, adherence to (2.1) would engender a serious
dilemma, as is shown by the consequence just mentioned. We would
either have to give up the fundamental logical principle that if a
sentence is true or false, then its denial is false or true, respectively
(and thus cognitively significant); or else, we must deny, in a manner
reminiscent of the intuitionistic conception of logic and mathematics,
that "$(x) \backsim P(x)$" is logically equivalent to the negation of
"$(Ex) P (x)$." Clearly, the criterion (2.1), which has disqualified
itself on several other counts, does not warrant such drastic measures
for its preservation; hence, it has to be abandoned.[7]

Strictly analogous considerations apply to an alternative criterion,
which makes complete falsifiability in principle the defining characteristic of empirical significance. Let us formulate this criterion
as follows: A sentence has empirical meaning if and only if it is
capable, in principle, of complete refutation by a finite number of
observational data; or, more precisely:

(2.2) *Requirement of complete falsifiability in principle:* A sentence has empirical meaning if and only if its denial is not analytic
and follows logically from some finite logically consistent class of
observation sentences.[8]

---

7. The arguments here adduced against the verifiability criterion also prove the
inadequacy of a view closely related to it, namely that two sentences have the same
cognitive significance if any set of observation sentences which would verify one
of them would also verify the other, and conversely. Thus, e. g., under this criterion,
any two general laws would have to be assigned the same cognitive significance, for
no general law is verified by any set of observation sentences. The view just referred
to must be clearly distinguished from a position which Russell examines in his
critical discussion of the positivistic meaning criterion. It is "the theory that two
propositions whose verified consequences are identical have the same significance"
((27), p. 448). This view is untenable indeed, for what consequences of a statement
have actually been verified at a given time is obviously a matter of historical accident which cannot possibly serve to establish identity of cognitive significance. But
I am not aware that any logical positivist ever subscribed to that "theory."

8. The idea of using theoretical falsifiability by observational evidence as the
"criterion of demarcation" separating empirical science from mathematics and logic
on the one hand and from metaphysics on the other is due to K. Popper (cf. (22),

This criterion qualifies a sentence as empirically meaningful if its denial satisfies the requirement of complete verifiability; as is to be expected, it is therefore inadequate on similar grounds as the latter:

(*a*) It rules out purely existential hypotheses, such as "There exists at least one unicorn," and all sentences whose formulation calls for mixed—i.e., universal and existential—quantification; for none of these can possibly be conclusively falsified by a finite number of observation sentences.

(*b*) If a sentence S is completely falsifiable whereas N is a sentence which is not, then their conjunction, S.N. (i.e., the expression obtained by connecting the two sentences by the word "and") is completely falsifiable; for if the denial of S is entailed by some class of observation sentences, then the denial of S.N. is, *a fortiori,* entailed by the same class. Thus, the criterion allows empirical significance to many sentences which an adequate empiricist criterion should rule out, such as, say "All swans are white and the absolute is perfect."

(*c*) If "P" is an observation predicate, then the assertion that all things have the property P is qualified as significant, but its denial, being equivalent to a purely existential hypothesis, is disqualified (cf. (*a*)). Hence, criterion (2.2) gives rise to the same dilemma as (2.1).

In sum, then, interpretations of the testability criterion in terms of complete verifiability or of complete falsifiability are inadequate because they are overly restrictive in one direction and overly inclusive in another, and because both of them require incisive changes in the fundamental principles of logic.

Several attempts have been made to avoid these difficulties by construing the testability criterion as demanding merely a partial and possibly indirect confirmability of empirical hypotheses by observational evidence.

(2.3) A formulation suggested by Ayer[9] is characteristic of these attempts to set up a clear and sufficiently comprehensive criterion of confirmability. It states, in effect, that a sentence S has empirical import if from S in conjunction with suitable subsidiary

---

section 1-7 and 19-24; also see (23), vol. II, pp. 282-285). Whether Popper would subscribe to the proposed restatement of the falsifiability criterion, I do not know.

9. (1), Ch. I.—The case against the requirements of verifiability and of falsifiability, and favor of a requirement of partial confirmability and disconfirmability is very clearly presented also by Pap in (21), Chapter 13.

hypotheses it is possible to derive observation sentences which are not derivable from the subsidiary hypotheses alone.

This condition is suggested by a closer consideration of the logical structure of scientific testing; but it is much too liberal as it stands. Indeed, as Ayer himself has pointed out in the second edition of his book, *Language, Truth, and Logic*,[10] his criterion allows empirical import to any sentence whatever. Thus, e.g., if S is the sentence "The absolute is perfect," it suffices to choose as a subsidiary hypothesis the sentence "If the absolute is perfect then this apple is red" in order to make possible the deduction of the observation sentence "This apple is red," which clearly does not follow from the subsidiary hypothesis alone.[11]

(2.4) To meet this objection, Ayer has recently proposed a modified version of his testability criterion. The modification restricts, in effect, the subsidiary hypotheses mentioned in (2.3) to sentences which are either analytic or can independently be shown to be testable in the sense of the modified criterion.[12]

But it can readily be shown that this new criterion, like the requirement of complete falsifiability, allows empirical significance to any conjunction S.N, where S satisfies Ayer's criterion while N is a sentence such as "The absolute is perfect," which is to be disqualified by that criterion. Indeed: whatever consequences can be

---

10. (1), 2d ed., pp. 11-12.

11. According to Stace (cf. (29), p. 218), the criterion of partial and indirect testability, which he calls the positivist principle, presupposes (and thus logically entails) another principle, which he terms the *Principle of Observable Kinds*: "A sentence, in order to be significant, must assert or deny facts which are of a kind or class such that it is logically possible directly to observe some facts which are instances of that class or kind. And if a sentence purports to assert or deny facts which are of a class or kind such that it would be logically impossible directly to observe any instance of that class or kind, then the sentence is non-significant." I think the argument Stace offers to prove that this principle is entailed by the requirement of testability is inconclusive (mainly because of the incorrect tacit assumption that "on the transformation view of deduction," the premises of a valid deductive argument must be necessary conditions for the conclusion (*l. c.*, p. 225). Without pressing this point any further, I should like to add here a remark on the principle of observable kinds itself. Professor Stace does not say how we are to determine what "facts" a given sentence asserts or denies, or indeed whether it asserts or denies any "facts" at all. Hence, the exact import of the principle remains unclear. No matter, however, how one might choose the criteria for the factual reference of sentences, this much seems certain: If a sentence expresses any fact at all, say *f*, then it satisfies the requirement laid down in the first sentence of the principle; for we can always form a class containing *f* together with the fact expressed by some observation sentence of our choice, which makes *f* a member of a class of facts at least one of which is capable, in principle, of direct observation. The first part of the principle of observable kinds is therefore all-inclusive, somewhat like Ayer's original formulation of the empiricist meaning criterion.

12. This restriction is expressed in recursive form and involves no vicious circle. For the full statement of Ayer's criterion, see (1), second edition, p. 13.

deduced from S with the help of permissible subsidiary hypotheses can also be deduced from S.N. by means of the same subsidiary hypotheses, and as Ayer's new criterion is formulated essentially in terms of the deducibility of a certain type of consequence from the given sentence, it countenances S.N together with S. Another difficulty has been pointed out by Professor A. Church, who has shown[13] that if there are any three observation sentences none of which alone entails any of the others, then it follows for any sentence S whatsoever that either it or its denial has empirical import according to Ayer's revised criterion.

3. TRANSLATABILITY INTO AN EMPIRICIST LANGUAGE AS A NEW CRITERION OF COGNITIVE MEANING

I think it is useless to continue the search for an adequate criterion of testability in terms of deductive relationships to observation sentences. The past development of this search—of which we have considered the major stages—seems to warrant the expectation that as long as we try to set up a criterion of testability for individual sentences in a natural language, in terms of logical relationship to observation sentences, the result will be either too restrictive or too inclusive, or both. In particular it appears likely that such criteria would allow empirical import, in the manner of (2.1)(b) or of (2.2)(b), either to any alternation or to any conjunction of two sentences of which at least one is qualified as empirically meaningful; and this peculiarity has undesirable consequences because the liberal grammatical rules of English as of any other natural language countenance as sentences certain expressions ("The absolute is perfect" was our illustration) which even by the most liberal empiricist standards make no assertion whatever; and these would then have to be permitted as components of empirically significant statements.

The predicament would not arise, of course, in an artificial language whose vocabulary and grammar were so chosen as to preclude altogether the possibility of forming sentences of any kind which the empiricist meaning criterion is intended to rule out. Let us call any such language an *empiricist language*. This reflection suggests an entirely different approach to our problem: Give a general characterization of the kind of language that would qualify as empiricist, and then lay down the following

(3.1) *Translatability criterion of cognitive meaning:* A sentence

---
13. Church (11).

has cognitive meaning if and only if it is translatable into an empiricist language.

This conception of cognitive import, while perhaps not explicitly stated, seems to underlie much of the more recent work done by empiricist writers; as far as I can see it has its origin in Carnap's essay, *Testability and Meaning* (especially part IV).

As any language, so also any empiricist language can be characterized by indicating its vocabulary and the rules determining its logic; the latter include the syntactical rules according to which sentences may be formed by means of the given vocabulary. In effect, therefore, the translatability criterion proposes to characterize the cognitively meaningful sentences by the vocabulary out of which they may be constructed, and by the syntactical principles governing their construction. What sentences are singled out as cognitively significant will depend, accordingly, on the choice of the vocabulary and of the construction rules. Let us consider a specific possibility:

(3.2) We might qualify a language L as empiricist if it satisfies the following conditions:

(a) *The vocabulary of L* contains:

(1) The customary locutions of logic which are used in the formulation of sentences; including in particular the expressions "not," "and," "or," "if . . . then . . . ," "all," "some," "the class of all things such that . . . ," ". . . is an element of class . . .";

(2) Certain *observation predicates*. These will be said to constitute the basic empirical vocabulary of L;

(3) Any expression definable by means of those referred to under (1) and (2).

(b) *The rules of sentence formation for L* are those laid down in some contemporary logical system such as *Principia Mathematica*.

Since all defined terms can be eliminated in favor of primitives, these rules stipulate in effect that a language L is empiricist if all its sentences are expressible, with the help of the usual logical locutions, in terms of observable characteristics of physical objects. Let us call any language of this sort a thing-language in the narrower sense. Alternatively, the basic empirical vocabulary of an empiricist language might be construed as consisting of phenomenalistic terms, each of them referring to some aspect of the phenomena of perception or sensation. The construction of adequate phenomenalistic languages, however, presents considerable difficulties,[14] and in recent empiricism, attention has been focussed primarily on the potential-

---

14. Important contributions to the problem have been made by Carnap (5) and by Goodman (15).

ities of languages whose basic empirical vocabulary consists of observation predicates; for the latter lend themselves more directly to the description of that type of intersubjective evidence which is invoked in the test of scientific hypotheses.

If we construe empiricist languages in the sense of (3.2), then the translatability criterion (3.1) avoids all of the shortcomings pointed out in our discussion of earlier forms of the testability criterion:

(a) Our characterization of empiricist languages makes explicit provision for universal and existential quantification, i.e., for the use of the terms "all" and "some"; hence, no type of quantified statement is generally excluded from the realm of cognitively significant discourse;

(b) Sentences such as "The absolute is perfect" cannot be formulated in an empiricist language (cf. (d) below); hence there is no danger that a conjunction or alternation containing a sentence of that kind as a component might be qualified as cognitively significant;

(c) In a language L with syntactical rules conforming to *Principia Mathematica,* the denial of a sentence is always again a sentence of L. Hence, the translatability criterion does not lead to the consequence, which is entailed by both (2.1) and (2.2), that the denials of certain significant sentences are non-significant;

(d) Despite its comprehensiveness, the new criterion does not attribute cognitive meaning to *all* sentences; thus, e.g., the sentences "The absolute is perfect" and "Nothingness nothings" cannot be translated into an empiricist language because their key terms are not definable by means of purely logical expressions and observation terms.

4. THE PROBLEM OF DISPOSITION TERMS AND OF THEORETICAL CONSTRUCTS

Yet, the new criterion is still too restrictive—as are, incidentally, also its predecessors—in an important respect which now calls for consideration. If empiricist languages are defined in accordance with (3.2), then, as was noted above, the translatability criterion (3.1) allows cognitive import to a sentence only if its constitutive empirical terms are explicitly definable by means of observation predicates. But as we shall argue presently, many terms even of the physical sciences are not so definable; hence the criterion would oblige us to reject, as devoid of cognitive import, all scientific hypotheses containing such terms—an altogether intolerable consequence.

The concept of temperature is a case in point. At first glance, it seems as though the phrase "Object x has a temperature of c degrees centigrade," or briefly "$T(x) = c$" could be defined by the following sentence, (D): $T(x) = c$ if and only if the following condition is satisfied: If a thermometer is in contact with x, then it registers c degrees on its scale.

Disregarding niceties, it may be granted that the definiens given here is formulated entirely in reference to observables. However, it has one highly questionable aspect. In *Principia Mathematica* and similar systems, the phrase "if p then q" is construed as being synonymous with "not p or q"; and under this so-called material interpretation of the conditional, a statement of the form "if p then q" is obviously true if (though not only if) the sentence standing in the place of "p" is false. If, therefore, the meaning of "if . . . then . . ." in the definiens of (D) is understood in the material sense, then that definiens is true if (though not only if) x is an object not in contact with a thermometer—no matter what numerical value we may give to c. And since the definiendum would be true under the same circumstances, the definition (D) would qualify as true the assignment of any temperature value whatsoever to any object not in contact with a thermometer! Analogous considerations apply to such terms as "electrically charged," "magnetic," "intelligent," "electric resistance," etc., in short to all disposition terms, i.e., terms which express the disposition of one or more objects to react in a determinate way under specified circumstances. A definition of such terms by means of observation predicates cannot be effected in the manner of (D), however natural and obvious a mode of definition this may at first seem to be.[15]

There are two main directions in which a resolution of the difficulty might be sought. On the one hand, it could be argued that the definition of disposition terms in the manner of (D) is perfectly adequate provided that the phrase "if . . . then . . ." in the definiens is construed in the sense it is obviously intended to have, namely as implying, in the case of (D), that even if x is not actually in contact with a thermometer, still if it *were* in such contact, then the thermometer *would* register c degrees. In sentences such as this, the phrase "if . . . then . . ." is said to be used counterfactually;

---

15. This difficulty in the definition of disposition terms was first pointed out and analyzed by Carnap (in (6); see esp. section 7).

and it is in this "strong" sense, which implies a counterfactual conditional, that the definiens of (D) would have to be construed. This suggestion would provide an answer to the problem of defining disposition terms if it were not for the fact that no entirely satisfactory account of the exact meaning of counterfactual conditionals seems to be available at present. Thus, the first way out of the difficulty has the status of a program rather than that of a solution. The lack of an adequate theory of counterfactual conditionals is all the more deplorable as such a theory is needed also for the analysis of the concept of general law in empirical science and of certain related ideas. A clarification of this cluster of problems constitutes at present one of the urgent desiderata in the logic and methodology of science.[16]

An alternative way of dealing with the definitional problems raised by disposition terms was suggested, and developed in detail, by Carnap. It consists in permitting the introduction of new terms, within an empiricist language, by means of so-called reduction sentences, which have the character of partial or conditional definitions.[17] Thus, e.g., the concept of temperature in our last illustration might be introduced by means of the following reduction sentence, (R): If a thermometer is in contact with an object x, then $T(x) = c$ if and only if the thermometer registers c degrees.

This rule, in which the conditional may be construed in the material sense, specifies the meaning of "temperature," i.e., of statements of the form "$T(x) = c$," only partially, namely in regard to those objects which are in contact with a thermometer; for all other objects, it simply leaves the meaning of "$T(x) = c$" undetermined. The specification of the meaning of "temperature" may then be gradually extended to cases not covered in (R) by laying down further reduction sentences, which reflect the measurement of temperature by devices other than thermometers.

Reduction sentences thus provide a means for the precise formulation of what is commonly referred to as operational definitions.[18]

16. The concept of strict implication as introduced by C. I. Lewis would be of no avail for the interpretation of the strong "if . . . then . . ." as here understood, for it refers to a purely logical relationship of entailment, whereas the concept under consideration will, in general, represent a nomological relationship, i. e., one based on empirical laws. For recent discussions of the problems of counterfactuals and laws, see Langford (18); Lewis (20), pp. 210-230; Chisholm (10); Goodman (14); Reichenbach (26), Chapter VIII; Hempel and Oppenheim (16), Part III; Popper (24).

17. Cf. Carnap (6); a brief elementary exposition of the central idea may be found in Carnap (7), Part III. The partial definition (R) formulated above for the expression "$T(x) = c$" illustrates only the simplest type of reduction sentence, the so-called bilateral reduction sentence.

18. On the concept of operational definition, which was developed by Bridgman, see, for example, Bridgman (3, 4) and Feigl (12).

At the same time, they show that the latter are not definitions in the strict sense of the word, but rather partial specifications of meaning.

The preceding considerations suggest that in our characterization (3.2) of empiricist languages we broaden the provision *a* (3) by permitting in the vocabulary of L all those terms whose meaning can be specified in terms of the basic empirical vocabulary by means of definitions or reduction sentences. Languages satisfying this more inclusive criterion will be referred to as thing-languages in the wider sense.

If the concept of empiricist language is broadened in this manner, then the translatability criterion (3.1) covers—as it should— also all those statements whose constituent empirical terms include "empirical constructs," i.e., terms which do not designate observables, but which can be introduced by reduction sentences on the basis of observation predicates.

Even in this generalized version, however, our criterion of cognitive meaning may not do justice to advanced scientific theories, which are formulated in terms of "theoretical constructs," such as the terms "absolute temperature," "gravitational potential," "electric field," "Ψ function," etc. There are reasons to think that neither definitions nor reduction sentences are adequate to introduce these terms on the basis of observation predicates. Thus, e.g., if a system of reduction sentences for the concept of electric field were available, then—to oversimplify the point a little—it would be possible to describe, in terms of observable characteristics, some necessary and some sufficient conditions for the presence, in a given region, of an electric field of any mathematical description, however complex. Actually, however, such criteria can at best be given only for some sufficiently simple kinds of fields.

Now theories of the advanced type here referred to may be considered as hypothetico-deductive systems in which all statements are logical consequences of a set of fundamental assumptions. Fundamental as well as derived statements in such a system are formulated either in terms of certain theoretical constructs which are not defined within the system and thus play the role of primitives, or in terms of expressions defined by means of the latter. Thus, in their logical structure such systems equal the axiomatized uninterpreted systems studied in mathematics and logic. They acquire applicability to empirical subject matter, and thus the status of theories of empirical science, by virtue of an empirical interpretation. The latter is effected by a translation of some of the sentences of the theory—often derived rather than fundamental ones—into an empiricist language, which may contain both observation predicates and empirical constructs. And since the sentences which are thus given empirical meaning are logical consequences of the fundamental hypotheses of the theory, that translation effects, indirectly, a partial interpretation of the latter and of the constructs in terms of which they are formulated.[19]

In order to make translatability into an empiricist language an adequate criterion of cognitive import, we broaden therefore the concept of empiricist language so as to include thing-languages in the narrower and in the wider sense as well as all interpreted theoretical systems of the kind just referred to.[20] With this understanding, (3.1) may finally serve as a general criterion of cognitive meaning.

5. On "The Meaning" of an Empirical Statement

In effect, the criterion thus arrived at qualifies a sentence as cognitively meaningful if its non-logical constituents refer, directly or in certain specified indirect ways, to observables. But it does not make any pronouncement on what "the meaning" of a cognitively significant sentence is, and in particular it neither says nor implies that that meaning can be exhaustively characterized by what the totality of possible tests would reveal in terms of observable phenomena. Indeed, *the content of a statement with empirical import cannot, in general, be exhaustively expressed by means of any class of observation sentences.*

For consider first, among the statements permitted by our criterion, any purely existential hypothesis or any statement involving

---

19. The distinction between a formal deductive system and the empirical theory resulting from it by an interpretation has been elaborated in detail by Reichenbach in his penetrating studies of the relations between pure and physical geometry; cf., e. g., Reichenbach (25). The method by means of which a formal system is given empirical content is characterized by Reichenbach as "coordinating definition" of the primitives in the theory by means of specific empirical concepts. As is suggested by our discussion of reduction and the interpretation of theoretical constructs, however, the process in question may have to be construed as a partial interpretation of the non-logical terms of the system rather than as a complete definition of the latter in terms of the concepts of a thing-language.

20. These systems have not been characterized here as fully and as precisely as would be desirable. Indeed, the exact character of the empirical interpretation of theoretical constructs and of the theories in which they function is in need of further investigation. Some problems which arise in this connection—such as whether, or in what sense, theoretical constructs may be said to denote—are obviously also of considerable epistemological interest. Some suggestions as to the interpretation of theoretical constructs may be found in Carnap (8), section 24, and in Kaplan (17); for an excellent discussion of the epistemological aspects of the problem, see Feigl (13).

mixed quantification. As was pointed out earlier, under (2.2)(*a*), statements of these kinds entail no observation sentences whatever; hence their content cannot be expressed by means of a class of observation sentences.

And secondly, even most statements of purely universal form (such as "All flamingoes are pink") entail observation sentences (such as "That thing is pink") only when combined with suitable other observation sentences (such as "That thing is a flamingo").

This last remark can be generalized. The use of empirical hypotheses for the prediction of observable phenomena requires, in practically all cases, the use of subsidiary empirical hypotheses.[21] Thus, e.g., the hypothesis that the agent of tuberculosis is rod-shaped does not by itself entail the consequence that upon looking at a tubercular sputum specimen through a microscope, rod-like shapes will be observed: a large number of subsidiary hypotheses, including the theory of the microscope, have to be used as additional premises in deducing that prediction.

Hence, what is sweepingly referred to as "the (cognitive) meaning" of a given scientific hypothesis cannot be adequately characterized in terms of potential observational evidence alone, nor can it be specified for the hypothesis taken in isolation. In order to understand "the meaning" of a hypothesis within an empiricist language, we have to know not merely what observation sentences it entails alone or in conjunction with subsidiary hypotheses, but also what other, non-observational, empirical sentences are entailed by it, what sentences in the given language would confirm or disconfirm it, and for what other hypotheses the given one would be confirmatory or disconfirmatory. In other words, the cognitive meaning of a statement in an empiricist language is reflected in the totality of its logical relationships to all other statements in that language and not to the observation sentences alone. In this sense, the statements of empirical science have a surplus meaning over and above what can be expressed in terms of relevant observation sentences.[22]

6. The Logical Status of the Empiricist Criterion of Meaning

What kind of a sentence, it has often been asked, is the empiricist meaning criterion itself? Plainly it is not an empirical hypothesis;

---

21. This point is clearly taken into consideration in Ayer's criteria of cognitive significance, which were discussed in section 2.

22. For a fuller discussion of the issues here involved cf. Feigl (13) and the comments on Feigl's position which will be published together with that article.

but it is not analytic or self-contradictory either; hence, when judged
by its own standard, is it not devoid of cognitive meaning? In that
case, what claim of soundness or validity could possibly be made
for it?

One might think of construing the criterion as a definition which
indicates what empiricists propose to understand by a cognitively
significant sentence; thus understood, it would not have the character of an assertion and would be neither true nor false. But this
conception would attribute to the criterion a measure of arbitrariness
which cannot be reconciled with the heated controversies it has en-
gendered and even less with the fact, repeatedly illustrated in the
present article, that the changes in its specific content have always
been determined by the objective of making the criterion a more
adequate index of cognitive import. And this very objective illumi-
nates the character of the empiricist criterion of meaning: It is intended to provide a clarification and *explication* of the idea of a
sentence which makes an intelligible assertion.[23] This idea is admittedly vague, and it is the task of philosophic explication to replace it by a more precise concept. In view of this difference of
precision we cannot demand, of course, that the "new" concept,
the explicatum, be strictly synonymous with the old one, the explicandum.[24] How, then, are we to judge the adequacy of a proposed
explication, as expressed in some specific criterion of cognitive
meaning?

First of all, there exists a large class of sentences which are
rather generally recognized as making intelligible assertions, and
another large class of which this is more or less generally denied.
We shall have to demand of an adequate explication that it take into
account these spheres of common usage; hence an explication which,
let us say, denies cognitive import to descriptions of past events or
to generalizations expressed in terms of observables has to be rejected as inadequate. As we have seen, this first requirement of
adequacy has played an important rôle in the development of the
empiricist meaning criterion.

---

23. In the preface to the second edition of his book, Ayer takes a very similar
position: he holds that the testability criterion is a definition which, however, is not
entirely arbitrary, because a sentence which did not satisfy the criterion "would not
be capable of being understood in the sense in which either scientific hypotheses
or commonsense statements are habitually understood" ((1), p. 16).

24. Cf. Carnap's characterization of explication in his article (9), which examines in outline the explication of the concept of probability. The Frege-Russell
definition of integers as classes of equivalent classes, and the semantical definition
of truth—cf. Tarski (30)—are outstanding examples of explication. For a lucid
discussion of various aspects of logical analysis see Pap (21), Chapter 17.

But an adequate explication of the concept of cognitively significant statement must satisfy yet another, even more important, requirement: together with the explication of certain other concepts, such as those of confirmation and of probability, it has to provide the framework for a general theoretical account of the structure and the foundations of scientific knowledge. Explication, as here understood, is not a mere description of the accepted usages of the terms under consideration: it has to go beyond the limitations, ambiguities, and inconsistencies of common usage and has to show how we had better construe the meanings of those terms if we wish to arrive at a consistent and comprehensive theory of knowledge. This type of consideration, which has been largely influenced by a study of the structure of scientific theories, has prompted the more recent extensions of the empiricist meaning criterion. These extensions are designed to include in the realm of cognitive significance various types of sentences which might occur in advanced scientific theories, or which have to be admitted simply for the sake of systematic simplicity and uniformity,[25] but on whose cognitive significance or non-significance a study of what the term "intelligible assertion" means in everyday discourse could hardly shed any light at all.

As a consequence, the empiricist criterion of meaning, like the result of any other explication, represents a linguistic proposal which itself is neither true nor false, but for which adequacy is claimed in two respects: first in the sense that the explication provides a reasonably close *analysis* of the commonly accepted meaning of the explicandum—and this claim implies an empirical assertion; and secondly in the sense that the explication achieves a *"rational reconstruction"* of the explicandum, i.e., that it provides, together perhaps with other explications, a general conceptual framework which permits a consistent and precise restatement and theoretical systematization of the contexts in which the explicandum is used—and this claim implies at least an assertion of a logical character.

Though a proposal in form, the empiricist criterion of meaning is therefore far from being an arbitrary definition; it is subject to revision if a violation of the requirements of adequacy, or even a way of satisfying those requirements more fully, should be discov-

---

25. Thus, e. g., our criterion qualifies as significant certain statements containing, say, thousands of existential or universal quantifiers—even though such sentences may never occur in everyday nor perhaps even in scientific discourse. For indeed, from a systematic point of view it would be arbitrary and unjustifiable to limit the class of significant statements to those containing no more than some fixed number of quantifiers. For further discussion of this point, cf. Carnap (6), sections 17, 24, 25.

ered. Indeed, it is to be hoped that before long some of the open
problems encountered in the analysis of cognitive significance will
be clarified and that then our last version of the empiricist meaning
criterion will be replaced by another, more adequate one.

BIBLIOGRAPHIC REFERENCES

(1) Ayer, A. J., *Language, Truth and Logic,* Gollancz, London, 1936;
2nd ed., 1946.
(2) Benjamin, A. C., "Is Empiricism Self-refuting?" (*Journal of Philos.,*
Vol. 38, 1941).
(3) Bridgman, P. W., *The Logic of Modern Physics,* The Macmillan
Co., New York, 1927.
(4) Bridgman, P. W., "Operational Analysis" (*Philos. of Science,*
Vol. 5, 1938).
(5) Carnap, R., *Der logische Aufbau der Welt,* Berlin, 1928.
(6) Carnap, R., "Testability and Meaning" (*Philos. of Science,* Vol.
3, 1936, and Vol. 4, 1937).
(7) Carnap, R., *Logical Foundations of the Unity of Science,* In:
Internat. Encyclopedia of Unified Science, I, 1; Univ. of Chicago
Press, 1938.
(8) Carnap, R., *Foundations of Logic and Mathematics. Internat. Encyclopedia of Unified Science,* I, 3; Univ. of Chicago Press, 1939.
(9) Carnap, R., "The Two Concepts of Probability" (*Philos. and
Phenom. Research,* Vol. 5, 1945).
(10) Chisholm, R. M., "The Contrary-to-Fact Conditional" (*Mind,*
Vol. 55, 1946).
(11) Church, A., Review of (1), 2nd. ed. (*The Journal of Symb. Logic,*
Vol. 14, 1949, pp. 52-53).
(12) Feigl, H., "Operationism and Scientific Method" (*Psychol. Review,*
Vol. 52, 1945). (Also reprinted in Feigl and Sellars, *Readings
in Philosophical Analysis,* New York, 1949.)
(13) Feigl, H., "Existential Hypotheses; Realistic vs. Phenomenalistic
Interpretations," (*Philos. of Science,* Vol. 17, 1950).
(14) Goodman, N., "The Problem of Counterfactual Conditionals"
(*Journal of Philos.,* Vol. 44, 1947).
(15) Goodman, N., *The Structure of Appearance.* Harvard University
Press, 1951.
(16) Hempel, C. G., and Oppenheim, P., "Studies in the Logic of Explanation" (*Philos. of Science,* Vol. 15, 1948).
(17) Kaplan, A., "Definition and Specification of Meaning" (*Journal
of Philos.,* Vol. 43, 1946).
(18) Langford, C. H., Review in *The Journal of Symb. Logic,* Vol. 6
(1941), pp. 67-68.

(19) Lecomte du Noüy, *Human Destiny*, New York, London, Toronto, 1947.
(20) Lewis, C. I., *An Analysis of Knowledge and Valuation*, Open Court Publ., La Salle, Ill., 1946.
(21) Pap, A., *Elements of Analytic Philosophy*, The Macmillan Co., New York, 1949.
(22) Popper, K., *Logik der Forschung*, Springer, Vienna, 1935.
(23) Popper, K., *The Open Society and Its Enemies*, 2 vols., Routledge, London, 1945.
(24) Popper, K., "A Note on Natural Laws and So-called 'Contrary-to-Fact Conditionals' " (*Mind*, Vol. 58, 1949).
(25) Reichenbach, H., *Philosophie der Raum-Zeit-Lehre*, Berlin, 1928.
(26) Reichenbach, H., *Elements of Symbolic Logic*, The Macmillan Co., New York, 1947.
(27) Russell, B., *Human Knowledge*, Simon and Schuster, New York, 1948.
(28) Schlick, M., "Meaning and Verification" (*Philos. Review*, Vol. 45, 1936). (Also reprinted in Feigl and Sellars, *Readings in Philosophical Analysis*, New York, 1949).
(29) Stace, W. T. "Positivism" (*Mind*, Vol. 53, 1944).
(30) Tarski, A., "The Semantic Conception of Truth and the Foundations of Semantics" (*Philos. and Phenom. Research*, Vol. 4, 1944). (Also reprinted in Feigl and Sellars, *Readings in Philosophical Analysis*, New York, 1949.)
(31) Werkmeister, W. H., *The Basis and Structure of Knowledge*, Harper, New York and London, 1948.
(32) Whitehead, A. N., and Russell, B., *Principia Mathematica*, 3 vols., 2nd ed., Cambridge, 1925-1927.

REMARKS BY THE AUTHOR (1958)

If I were to write a revised version of this article, I would qualify the objections (2.1)(b) and (2.2)(b) against complete verifiability or falsifiability as criteria of empirical meaningfulness, or empirical significance. The first of these objections argues that if a sentence S is empirically significant under the verifiability criterion, then so is $S \vee N$, even when N is cognitively meaningless in the sense of being (i) neither analytic nor self-contradictory and (ii) devoid of empirical meaning in the sense of the verifiability criterion; for whatever class of observation sentences completely verifies S also completely verifies $S \vee N$, since $S \vee N$ is a logical consequence of S.—But the rule underlying this latter assertion, i.e., the rule that an alternation is logically implied by either of its components, applies only if N, no less than S, is a *statement*, i.e. a sentence which is either true or false; and if the verifiability criterion is taken to characterize all sentences, other than the analytic and the self-contradictory ones, which can significantly be said to be either true or false, then clearly N cannot be significantly said to be either true or false and thus is no statement at all; hence the inference from S to SvN fails.—The case against objection (2.2)(b) is analogous.[1] However, the latter objection still applies against the view of those who propound falsifiability as a criterion which will separate off the statements of empirical science from those of logic and mathematics and from those of metaphysics, without denying truth or falsity to the latter. For then $S.N$ qualifies as a significant scientific statement if S does, even though N be a purely metaphysical utterance. The remaining arguments mentioned in section 2 of my article seems to me fully sufficient, however, to disqualify both complete verifiability and complete falsifiability as criteria of cognitive significance.

I have more serious doubts concerning the idea of a translatability criterion of the kind proposed in sections 3 and 4 of the article. For the notion of translatability needed in this context is by no means fully clear, and an attempt to explicate it faces considerable difficulties.[2] It seems desirable, therefore, to do without that idea. In a sequel[3] to the article here under consideration, I did just that and considered instead the possibility of characterizing cognitively significant sentences as being built up, according to specified syntactical rules, from a given logical vocabulary and from cognitively (better: empirically) significant terms; each of the latter would have to be either an observational predicate or an expression connected with a set of observational terms by sentences of specified types, such as definitions or reduction sentences, which could then be said to introduce the non-observational term in question.[4] There remains the problem of specifying the types of sentences which are to be permissible for this purpose. This issue, which is briefly examined in section 4 of the present article, has been dealt with in much greater detail in two more recent essays of mine.[5]

---

1. A criticism to this effect was put forth some years ago by students in a graduate seminar of mine; recently, the same point was made explicitly and forcefully by D. Rynin in his presidential address, "Vindication of L*G*C*L P*S*T*V*SM*," *Proceedings and Addresses of The American Philosophical Association*, Vol. 30 (1957), p. 45-67; cf. especially pp. 57-58.

2. This has recently been pointed out very lucidly by I. Scheffler in "Prospects of a Modest Empiricism," *The Review of Metaphysics*, Vol. 10, pp. 383-400, 602-625 (1957); cf. especially sections 7-11.

3. C. G. Hempel, "The Concept of Cognitive Significance: A Reconsideration," *Proc. Amer. Acad. of Arts and Sciences*, Vol. 80, No. 1, pp. 61-77 (1951).

4. This procedure seems closely related in spirit to one recently suggested by Scheffler (*loc. cit.*, section 9), namely replacement of the translatability condition by the following criterion: S is cognitively significant if and only if it *is* a sentence of some empiricist language.

5. "A Logical Appraisal of Operationism," *The Scientific Monthly*, Vol. 79, pp. 215-220 (1954), reprinted in Philipp Frank, ed., *The Validation of Scientific Theories*, the Beacon Press, Boston, 1957.—"The Theoretician's Dilemma," in H. Feigl, M. Scriven, and G. Maxwell, eds., *Minnesota Studies in the Philosophy of Science*, Vol. II. University of Minnesota Press, 1958. For a critical discussion of the issues raised in these articles, see especially R. Carnap, "The Methodological Character of Theoretical Concepts," in H. Feigl and M. Scriven, eds., *Minnesota*

But no matter how one might reasonably delimit the class of sentences qualified to introduce empirically significant terms, this new approach seems to me to lead to the realization that cognitive significance cannot well be construed as a characteristic of individual sentences, but only of more or less comprehensive systems of sentences (corresponding roughly to scientific theories). A closer study of this point suggests strongly that, much like the analytic-synthetic distinction, the idea of cognitive significance, with its suggestion of a sharp distinction between significant and non-significant sentences or systems of such, has lost its promise and fertility as an explicandum, and that it had better be replaced by certain concepts which admit of differences in degree, such as the formal simplicity of a system; its explanatory and predictive power; and its degree of confirmation relative to available evidence.[6] The analysis and theoretical reconstruction of these concepts seems to offer the most promising way of advancing further the clarification of the issues implicit in the idea of cognitive significance.

Studies in the Philosophy of Science, Vol. I. University of Minnesota Press, 1956; and sections 12-19 of Scheffler's article cited in note 28.

6. This point is developed in detail in my article cited in note 3.

Logic and Mathematics

6

The Old and the New Logic

BY RUDOLF CARNAP

(TRANSLATED BY ISAAC LEVI)

1. LOGIC AS A METHOD OF PHILOSOPHIZING

THE NEW SERIES of this journal, which begins with this volume, will be devoted to the development of a *new, scientific method of philosophizing*. Perhaps this method can be briefly characterized as consisting in the *logical analysis of the statements and concepts of empirical science*. This description indicates the two most important features that distinguish this method from the methods of traditional philosophy. First, this type of philosophizing goes strictly hand in hand with empirical science. Thus, philosophy is no longer viewed as a domain of knowledge in its own right, on a par with, or superior to, the empirical sciences. Secondly, this description indicates the part that philosophy plays in empirical science: it consists in the clarification of the statements of empirical science; more specifically, in the decomposition of statements into their parts (concepts), the step by step reduction of concepts to more fundamental concepts and of statements to more fundamental statements. This way of setting the problem brings out the value of logic for philosophical enquiries. Logic is no longer merely one philosophical discipline among others, but we are able to say outright: Logic is the method of philosophizing. Logic is understood here in the broadest sense. It comprehends pure, formal logic and applied logic or the theory of knowledge.

The desire to replace metaphysical concept-poetry by a rigorous, scientific method of philosophizing would have remained a pious hope if the system of traditional logic had been the only logical in-

This article, originally entitled "Die alte und die neue Logik," appeared in the first issue of *Erkenntnis*. Vol. I of *Erkenntnis* (1930-31) was at the same time Vol. IX of *Annalen der Philosophie* (see Editor's Introduction, p. 6 above). It is published here with the kind permission of Professor Carnap.

strument available. Traditional logic was totally incapable of satisfying the requirement of richness of content, formal rigor and technical
utility which its new role demanded of it. Formal logic rested on the
aristotelian-scholastic system which in the course of its further development had been only slightly improved and extended. In the
field of applied logic (methodology), there were indeed a great many
individual studies and several comprehensive works, some of them
containing interesting material. But with regard to their precision
in forming concepts and profundity of analysis, they remained at a
rather primitive stage. This is no reproach against these works, at
least not against those belonging to the previous century. For the
state of applied logic was determined by the inadequacy of its formal
foundations.

The creation of a new and efficient instrument in the place of
the old and useless one took a long time. It is perhaps to be doubted
whether the logicians could have brought this about under their own
power. Fortunately an instrument has been found, a new logic which
has been developed almost entirely by mathematicians in the last
fifty years. Difficulties in mathematics gave rise to this development.
General applications of a philosophically significant nature were not
at first envisaged. The majority of philosophers have even now taken
little cognizance of the new logic and have extracted even less advantage from it for their own work. Indeed, the caution and uneasy timidity with which they approach or, more generally, circum-
vent the new logic is striking. To be sure, the formal garb demanded
by mathematics frightens many away. However, an instinctive feeling of opposition lies at the root of the philosophers' fear. And for
once they have caught the scent correctly: in the new logic—this is
not yet realized by many of its advocates—lies the point at which
the old philosophy is to be removed from its hinges. Before the
inexorable judgment of the new logic, all philosophy in the old
sense, whether it is connected with Plato, Thomas Aquinas, Kant,
Schelling or Hegel, or whether it constructs a new "metaphysic of
Being" or a "philosophy of spirit," proves itself to be not merely
materially false, as earlier critics maintained, but logically untenable
and therefore meaningless.

2. THE NEW LOGIC

The new logic came into existence in the final decades of the
last century. Following on Leibniz's ideas and making use of the
earlier contributions (De Morgan 1847; Boole 1854), Frege, Peano

and Schröder made the first attempts at a new and comprehensive reconstruction of logic. On the basis of this previous work, Whitehead and Russell created the great basic work of the new logic, *Principia Mathematica* (1910-1913). All further contributions to the new logic depend upon this work. They attempt either to supplement or revise it. (A few names may be mentioned here; the Göttingen School: Hilbert, Ackermann, Bernays, Behmann, *et al.;* the Warsaw School: Lukasiewicz, Lesniewski, Chwistek, Tarski, *et al.;* Wittgenstein and his associate Ramsey.)

The most important stimulus for the development of the new logic lay in the need for a critical re-examination of the foundations of mathematics. Mathematics, especially since the time of Leibniz and Newton, had made enormous advances and acquired an abundance of new knowledge. But the securing of the foundations had not kept in step with the rapid growth of the edifice. Therefore, about a century ago, a more vigorous effort began to be made to clarify the fundamental concepts. This effort was successful in many instances. Mathematicians succeeded in defining in a rigorous form such important concepts as, for example, limit, derivative and complex number. For a long time, these concepts had been fruitfully applied in practice without having adequate definitions. We have only the sure instincts of great mathematicians and not the clarity of concepts to thank for the fact that the inadequacy of the concept formation caused no mischief in mathematics.

Efforts at a clarification of fundamental concepts went forward step by step. People were not satisfied with reducing the various concepts of mathematical analysis to the fundamental concept of number; they required that the concept of number should itself be logically clarified. This inquiry into the *logical foundations of arithmetic* with a *logical analysis of number* as its goal, called peremptorily for a logical system which had the comprehensiveness and precision to do the work demanded of it. Thus, these inquiries gave an especially strong impetus to the development of the new logic. Peano, Frege, Whitehead, Russell and Hilbert were led to do their work on logic primarily for this reason.

The necessity for a new reconstruction of logic became even more pressing when certain contradictions ("antinomies") were noticed in the realm of mathematics which soon proved themselves to be of a general, logical nature. These contradictions could be overcome only by a fundamental reconstruction of logic.

In the following pages, some of the important characteristics of the new logic will be stated. Above all, mention will be made of those traits which distinguish the new logic from the old and by means of which the new logic has gained a special significance for the whole of science. First we shall take a look at the symbolic garb in which the new logic customarily appears. Then a few remarks will be made about the enrichment in content which consists primarily in taking account of relations instead of restricting oneself to predicates. In addition, it will be briefly shown how the contradictions to which we have just referred are overcome by the so-called theory of types. After dealing with these points, which are significant chiefly for logic itself, we shall examine the several points of general scientific importance: the possibility of deriving mathematics from logic; the explanation of the essentially tautological character of logical sentences, a point which is very important for philosophy; the analysis of concepts by means of which science is rendered a unified whole; and finally the elimination of metaphysics by logical analysis.

3. THE SYMBOLIC METHOD

When a reader looks at a treatise in modern logic, the first outward feature that strikes him is the use of symbolic forms which appear similar to those of mathematics. This symbolism was originally constructed in imitation of mathematics. However, forms more suitable for the special purposes of logic were subsequently developed.

In mathematics, the advantage of the symbolic method of representation over verbal language is obvious. Consider the sentence: "if one number is multiplied by another, the result is the same as that obtained by multiplying the second by the first." It is evidently much clearer and more convenient to say, "For any numbers x and y, it is the case that $x.y = y.x$" or more briefly, using the logical sign for universality, "$(x,y).x.y = y.x$."

By employing symbolism in logic, inferences acquire a rigor which is otherwise unobtainable. Inferences are made by means of arithmetical operations on formulae analogous to calculations (hence the designation "calculus," "propositional calculus," "functional calculus"). To be sure, material considerations guide the course of deduction, but they do not enter into the deduction itself. This method guarantees that no unnoticed assumptions will slip into the deduction, a thing which it is very difficult to avoid in a word-language. Such deductive rigor is especially important in the axiomatization of any domain, e.g. geometry. The history of geometry furnishes numerous examples of impure deductions, such as the various attempts to derive the axiom of parallels from the other axioms of Euclidean geometry. A sentence equivalent to the axiom of parallels was always tacitly assumed and employed in these derivations. Rigor and neatness is required in the constitution of concepts just as much as in the derivation of sentences. With the methods of the new logic, analysis has shown that many philosophical concepts do not satisfy the higher standards of rigor; some have to be interpreted differently and others have to be eliminated as meaningless. (See Section 9 below.)

As will become clearer presently, the theory of knowledge, which is after all nothing but applied logic, can no more dispense with symbolic logic than physics can dispense with mathematics.

4. THE LOGIC OF RELATIONS

The new logic is distinguished from the old not only by the form in which it is presented but chiefly also by the increase of its range. The most important new domains are the theory of relational sentences and the theory of sentential functions. Only the theory of relations will be (briefly) considered here.

The only form of statements (sentences) in the old logic was the predicative form: "Socrates is a man," "All (or some) Greeks are men." A predicate-concept or property is attributed to a subject-concept. Leibniz had already put forward the demand that logic should consider sentences of relational form. In a relational sentence such as, for example, "a is greater than b," a relation is attributed to two or more objects, (or, as it might be put, to several subject-concepts). Liebniz's idea of a theory of relations has been worked out by the new logic. The old logic conceived relational sentences as sentences of predicative form. However, many inferences involving relational sentences thereby become impossible. To be sure, one can interpret the sentence "a is greater than b" in such a way that the predicate "greater than b" is attributed to the subject a. But the predicate then becomes a unity; one cannot extract b by any rule of inference. Consequently, the sentence "b is smaller than a" cannot be inferred from this sentence. In the new logic, this inference takes place in the following way: The relation "smaller than" is defined as the "converse" of the relation "greater than." The inference in question then rests on the universal proposition: If a relation holds between x and y, its converse holds between y and x. A further example of a statement that cannot be proved in the old logic: "Wherever there is a victor someone is vanquished." In the new logic, this follows from the logical proposition: If a relation has a referent, it also has a relatum.

Relational statements are especially indispensable for the mathematical sciences. Let us consider as an example the geometrical concept of the three-place relation "between" (on an open straight line). The geometrical axioms "If a lies between b and c, b does not lie between c and a" can be expressed only in the new logic. According to the predicative view, in the first case we would have the predicates "lying between b and c" and "lying between c and a." If these are left unanalyzed, there is no way of showing how the first is transformed into the second. If one takes the objects b and c out of the predicate, the statement "a lies between b and c" no longer serves to characterize only one object, but three. It is therefore a three-place relational statement.

The relations "greater than" and "between" are of such a kind that the order of their terms cannot be altered at will. The determination of any order in any domain rests essentially on relations of this kind. If among a class of persons it is known which of any pair is the taller, this class of persons is thereby serially ordered. It might be held that this could also be done by means of predicative ascriptions—namely, by attributing a definite measure as a property to each person. But in that case it would again have to be assumed that with respect to any two of these quantities, it was known which was the greater. Thus without an ordering relation no series can be constructed. This shows the indispensability of the theory of relations for all those sciences which deal with series and orderings: arithmetic (number series), geometry (point series), physics (all scales of measurement: those of space and time and the various state magnitudes).

Restriction to predicate-sentences has had disastrous effects on subjects outside logic. Perhaps Russell is right when he made this logical failing responsible for certain metaphysical errors. If every sentence attributes a predicate to a subject, there can, after all, be only one subject, the Absolute, and every state of affairs must consist in the possession of a certain attribute by the Absolute. In the same way perhaps all metaphysical theories about mysterious "substances" could be traced to this mistake.

However this may be, it is certain that this restriction has for a long time been a serious drag upon physics—e.g., the idea that physical matter is substance in the philosophical sense. Above all, we may well assume that this logical error is responsible for the concept of absolute space. Because the fundamental form of a proposition had to be predicative, it could only consist in the specification of the position of a body. Since Leibniz had recognized the possibility of relational sentences, he was able to arrive at a correct conception of space: the elementary fact is not the position of a body but its positional relations to other bodies. He upheld the view on epistemological grounds: there is no way of determining the absolute position of a body, but only its positional relations. His campaign in favor of the relativistic view of space, as against the absolutistic views of the followers of Newton, had as little success as his program for logic.

Only after two hundred years were his ideas on both subjects taken up and carried through: in logic with the theory of relations (De Morgan 1858; Peirce 1870), in physics with the theory of relativity (anticipatory ideas in Mach 1883; Einstein 1905).

5. THE LOGICAL ANTINOMIES

Around the turn of the century, certain strange contradictions ("paradoxes") appeared in the new mathematical discipline of set theory. Closer investigation soon showed that these contradictions were not specifically mathematical but were of a general logical character, the so-called "logical antinomies." The new logic had not yet developed to the point where it was able to overcome these contradictions. This was a defect which it shared with the old logic, and it provided a further motive for rebuilding the system of logic from its foundations. Russell succeeded in eliminating the contradictions by means of the "theory of types." The gulf between the new and the old logic thereby became still wider. The old logic is not only significantly poorer in content than the new, but, because the contradictions are not removed from it, it no longer counts at all. (Most logical textbooks are still unaware of this.)

Let us consider the simplest example of an antinomy (following Russell). A concept is to be called "predicable" if it is applicable to itself. For example: The concept "abstract" is abstract. A concept is to be called "impredicable" if it does not apply to itself. For example: The concept "virtuous" is not virtuous. According to the law of excluded middle, the concept "impredicable" is either predicable or impredicable. Assume that it is predicable; then, according to the definition of "predicable," it can be ascribed to itself and is, therefore, impredicable. Assume that the concept "impredicable" is impredicable; then the concept is ascribed to itself; consequently, according to the definition of "predicable," it is predicable. Therefore, both assumptions are self-contradictory. There are many similar antinomies.

The *theory of types* consists in the fact that all concepts, both properties and relations, are classified according to "types." For simplicity's sake, let us restrict ourselves to properties. A distinction is made between "individuals," i.e. objects which are not properties (zero level); properties of individuals (first level); properties of properties of individuals (second level) and so on. Let us take for example bodies to be individuals; then "square" and "red" are properties of the first level; "spatial property" and "color" are properties of the second level. The theory of types says: a property of the first level can be attributed or denied only to individuals but cannot apply to properties of the first or higher levels at all; a property of the second level can be attributed or denied only to properties of the first level but cannot apply to individuals or to properties of the second or higher levels, and so on. For example: If a and b are bodies, the sentences "a is square" and "b is red" are either true or false but in either case meaningful. Further, the sentences "Square-ness is a spatial property" and "Red is a color" are true. On the other hand, the series of words "a is a spatial property," "Square-ness is red" and "Color is a spatial property" are neither true nor false but meaningless. They are mere pseudo-sentences. Such pseudo-sentences are avoided if a property of the nth level is applied only to concepts of the level n-1. A particularly important special case follows from this: The assumption that a certain property belongs or does not belong to itself can be neither true nor false, but is meaningless.

As one can easily see, if the rules of the theory of types are obeyed, the above-mentioned antinomy of "impredicable" does not arise. For the stated definitions of "predicable" and impredicable" cannot be formulated. They are therefore meaningless. The remaining antinomies which have not been referred to here can be eliminated in a similar manner.

6. MATHEMATICS AS A BRANCH OF LOGIC

As has been mentioned, the logical analysis of arithmetic is one of the goals of the new logic. Frege had already come to the conclusion that mathematics is to be considered a branch of logic. This view was confirmed by Whitehead and Russell who carried through the con-struction of the system of mathematics on the basis of logic. It was shown that every mathematical concept can be derived from the fundamental concepts of logic and that every mathematical sentence (insofar as it is valid in every conceivable domain of any size) can be derived from the fundamental statements of logic.

The most important concepts of the new logic (they are in part reducible to one another) are the following: 1. Negation: "not"; 2. the logical connectives for two sentences: "and," "or," "if—then"; 3. "every" (or "all"), "there is"; 4. "identical." The possibility of deriving arithmetical concepts may be illustrated by a simple example: the number *two* as a cardinal, i.e., as the number of a concept. Definition: "The cardinal number of a concept f is two" is to mean "There is an x and there is a y such that x is not identical with y, x falls under f, y falls under f, and for every z it is the case that if z falls under f, z is identical with x or with y." We see that only the logical concepts which have just been listed are employed in this definition of "two"; this can be shown rigorously only in a symbolic representation. All the natural numbers can be defined in a similar manner. Furthermore, the positive and negative numbers, fractions, real numbers, complex numbers, and finally even the concepts of analysis—limit, convergence, derivative, integral, continuity, etc.—can also be defined in this way.

Since every mathematical concept is derived from the fundamental concepts of logic, every mathematical sentence can be translated into a sentence about purely logical concepts; and this translation is then deducible (under certain conditions, as has been indicated) from the fundamental logical sentences. Let us take as an example the arithmetical sentence "$1+1=2$." Its translation into a sentence of pure logic reads: "If a property f has the cardinal number 1 and a property g has the cardinal number 1, and f and g are mutually exclusive, and if the concept h is the union of f and g, then h has the cardinal number 2." This translation represents a sentence from the logic of properties (theory of sentential functions) which is derivable from the fundamental sentences of logic. In a similar way, all the remaining sentences of arithmetic and analysis (to the extent that they are universally valid in the widest sense) are provable as sentences of logic.

7. The Tautological Character of Logic

On the basis of the new logic, the essential character of logical sentences can be clearly recognized. This has become of the greatest importance for the theory of mathematical knowledge as well as for the clarification of controversial philosophical questions.

The usual distinction in logic between fundamental and derived sentences is arbitrary. It is immaterial whether a logical sentence is derived from other sentences. Its validity can be recognized from its form. This may be illustrated by a simple example.

With the aid of the logical connectives, one can construct other sentences from two sentences "A" and "B", e.g., "not-A," "A or B," "A and B." The truth of these compound sentences obviously does not depend upon the meanings of the sentences "A" and "B" but only upon their truth-values, i.e., upon whether they are true or false. Now there are four combinations of truth-values for "A" and "B," namely, 1. "A" is true and "B" is true: TT, 2. TF, 3. FT, 4. FF. The meaning of a logical connective is determined by the fact that the sentences constructed with the help of this connective are true in certain of the four possible cases and false in the others. For example, the meaning of "or" (in the non-exclusive sense) is determined by the stipulation that the sentence "A or B" is true in the first three cases and false in the fourth. Compound sentences can be combined further to make new compound sentences. Let us take as an example: "(not-A and not-B) or (A or B)." We can now establish the truth-values in the four cases first for the constituent sentences and then for the sentence as a whole. We thereby in this example arrive at a remarkable result. "Not-A" is true only in the third and fourth cases. "Not-B is true only in the second and fourth cases. Consequently, "not-A and not-B" is true only in the fourth case.

	A B	not-A	not-B	not-A and not-B	A or B	(not-A and not-B) or (A or B)
1	T T	F	F	F	T	T
2	T F	F	T	F	T	T
3	F T	T	F	F	T	T
4	F F	T	T	T	F	T

"A or B" is true in the first three cases. Therefore, the entire sentence "(not-A and not-B) or (A or B)" is true in every case. Such a formula, which depends neither on the meanings nor the truth-values of the sentences occurring in it but is necessarily true, whether its constituent sentences are true or false, is called a *tautology*. A tautology is true in virtue of its mere form. It can be shown that all the sentences of logic and, hence, according to the view advocated here, all the sentences of mathematics are tautologies.

If a compound sentence is communicated to us, e.g., "It is raining here and now or it is snowing," we learn something about reality. This is so because the sentence excludes certain of the relevant states-of-affairs and leaves the remaining ones open. In our example, there are four possibilities: 1. It is raining and snowing, 2. It is raining and not snowing, 3. It is not raining but it is snowing, 4. It is not raining and not snowing. The sentence excludes the fourth possibility and leaves the first three open. If, on the other hand, we are told a tautology, no possibility is excluded but they all remain open. Consequently, we learn nothing about reality from the tautology, e.g., "It is raining (here and now) or it is not raining." Tautologies, therefore, are empty. They say nothing; they have, so-to-speak, zero-content. However, they need not be trivial on this account. The above-mentioned tautology is trivial. On the other hand, there are other sentences whose tautological character cannot be recognized at first glance.

Since all the sentences of logic are tautological and devoid of content, we cannot draw inferences from them about what was necessary or impossible in reality. Thus the attempt to base metaphysics on pure logic which is chiefly characteristic of such a system as Hegel's, is shown to be unwarranted.

Mathematics, as a branch of logic, is also tautological. In the Kantian terminology: The sentences of mathematics are analytic. They are not synthetic *a priori*. Apriorism is thereby deprived of its strongest argument. Empiricism, the view that there is no synthetic *a priori* knowledge, has always found the greatest difficulty in interpreting mathematics, a difficulty which Mill did not succeed in overcoming. This difficulty is removed by the fact that mathematical sentences are neither empirical nor synthetic *a priori* but analytic.

8. UNIFIED SCIENCE

We distinguish *applied logic,* the logical analysis of the concepts and sentences of the different branches of science, from pure logic with its formal problems. Though up to now most of the work in the new logic has dealt with formal subjects, it has also attained successful results in this domain.

The analysis of the concepts of science has shown that all these concepts, no matter whether they belong, according to the usual classification, to the natural sciences, or to psychology or the social sciences, go back to a common basis. They can be reduced to root concepts which apply to the "given," to the content of immediate experience. To begin with, all concepts relating to one's own experience, i.e. those which apply to the psychological events of the knowing subject, can be traced back to the given. All physical concepts can be reduced to concepts relating to one's own experience, for every physical event is in principle confirmable by means of perceptions. All concepts relating to other minds, that is, those that apply to the psychological processes of subjects other than oneself, are constituted out of physical concepts. Finally the concepts of the social sciences go back to concepts of the kinds just mentioned. Thus, a genealogical tree of concepts results in which every concept must in principle find its place according to the way it is derived from other concepts and ultimately from the given. The constitution theory, i.e. the theory of the construction of a system of all scientific concepts on a common basis, shows further that in a corresponding manner every statement of science can be retranslated into a statement about the given ("methodological positivism").

A second constitution system, which likewise includes all concepts, has physical concepts for its basis, i.e., concepts which apply to events in space and time. The concepts of psychology and the social sciences are reduced to physical concepts according to the principle of behaviorism ("methodological materialism").

We speak of "methodological" positivism or materialism because we are concerned here only with methods of deriving concepts, while completely eliminating both the metaphysical thesis of positivism about the reality of the given and the metaphysical thesis of materialism about the reality of the physical world. Consequently, the positivist and materialist constitution systems do not contradict one another. Both are correct and indispensable. The positivist system corresponds to the epistemological viewpoint because it proves the validity of knowledge by reduction to the given. The materialist system corresponds to the viewpoint of the empirical sciences, for in this system all concepts are reduced to the physical, to the only domain which exhibits the complete rule of law and makes intersubjective knowledge possible.

Thus, with the aid of the new logic, logical analysis leads to a *unified science*. There are not different sciences with fundamentally different methods or different sources of knowledge, but only *one* science. All knowledge finds its place in this science and, indeed, is knowledge of basically the same kind; the appearance of fundamental differences between the sciences are the deceptive result of our using different sub-languages to express them.

9. THE ELIMINATION OF METAPHYSICS

The tautological character of logic shows that all inference is tautological. The conclusion always says the same as the premises (or less), but in a different linguistic form. One fact can never be inferred from another. (According to the usual view this does occur in inductive inference, but this subject cannot be discussed here.) From this follows the impossibility of any metaphysics which tries to draw inferences from experience to something transcendent which lies beyond experience and is not itself experiencable; e.g. the "thing in itself" lying behind the things of experience, the "Absolute" behind the totality of the relative, the "essence" and "meaning" of events behind the events themselves. Since rigorous inference can never lead from experience to the transcendent, metaphysical inferences must leave out essential steps. The appearance of transcendence stems from this. Concepts are introduced which are irreducible either to the given or to the physical. They are therefore mere illusory concepts which are to be rejected from the epistemological viewpoint as well as from the scientific viewpoint. No matter how much they are sanctified by tradition and charged with feeling, they are meaningless words.

With the aid of the rigorous methods of the new logic, we can treat science to a thoroughgoing process of decontamination. Every sentence of science must be proved to be meaningful by logical analysis. If it is discovered that the sentence in question is either a tautology or a contradiction (negation of a tautology), the statement belongs to the domain of logic including mathematics. Alternatively the sentence has factual content, i.e., it is neither tautological nor contradictory; it is then an empirical sentence. It is reducible to the given and can, therefore, be discovered, in principle, to be either true or false. The (true or false) sentences of the empirical sciences are of this character. There are no questions which are in principle unanswerable. There is no such thing as speculative philosophy, a system of sentences with a special subject matter on a par with those of the sciences. To pursue philosophy can only be to clarify the concepts and sentences of science by logical analysis. The instrument for this is the new logic.

REMARKS BY THE AUTHOR (1957)

The position explained in sections 8 and 9 of the foregoing paper was modified in the years following its publication in the following respect. The reduction of scientific concepts to the concepts of either of the two bases indicated (viz., to the given, i.e., sense-data, or to observable properties of physical things) cannot generally be carried out in the form of explicit definitions. Therefore scientific sentences are in general not translatable into sentences of either of the two bases; the relation between them is more complicated. Consequently a scientific sentence is not simply decidable as true or as false; it can only be more or less confirmed on the basis of given observations. Thus the earlier principle of verifiability, first pronounced by Wittgenstein, was replaced by the weaker requirement of confirmability. The thesis of the unity of science remained, however, intact in virtue of the common basis of confirmation for all branches of empirical science. The modification here indicated was explained in the article "Testability and Meaning" (1936-37). For the later development of the conception of the nature of scientific concepts, see the article "The Methodological Character of Theoretical Concepts" (1956), in H. Feigl and M. Scriven eds., *Minnesota Studies in the Philosophy of Science,* Vol. I.

7

Logic, Mathematics and

Knowledge of Nature

BY HANS HAHN

(TRANSLATED BY ARTHUR PAP)

I

EVEN A CURSORY glance at the statements of physics shows that they are obviously of a very diverse character. There are statements like "if a stretched string is plucked, a tone is heard" or "if a ray of sunlight is passed through a glass prism, then a colored band, interspersed with dark lines, is visible on a screen placed behind the prism," which can be tested at any time by observation. We also find statements like "the sun contains hydrogen," "the satellite of Sirius has a density of about 60,000," "a hydrogen atom consists of a positively charged nucleus around which a negatively charged electron revolves," which cannot by any means be tested by immediate observation but which are made only on the basis of theoretical considerations and likewise are testable only with the help of theoretical considerations. And thus we are confronted by the urgent question: what is the relationship between *observation* and *theory* in physics—and not just in physics, but in science generally. For there is but one science, and wherever there is scientific investigation it proceeds ultimately according to the same methods; only we see everything with the greatest clarity in the case of physics, because it is the most advanced, neatest, most scientific of all the sciences. And in physics, indeed, the interaction of observation and theory is

This contribution comprises the first four sections of the pamphlet "Logik, Mathematik und Naturerkennen," published in Vienna in 1933 as the second volume of the series entitled "Einheitswissenschaft." It is reproduced here with the kind permission of Mrs. Lilly Hahn, Gerold & Co., Vienna, and Professor Rudolf Carnap, the co-editor of *Einheitswissenschaft*. The last two sections of Hahn's pamphlet which are omitted do not deal with the nature of logical or mathematical propositions.

especially pronounced, even officially recognized by the institution of special professorships for experimental physics and for theoretical physics.

Now, presumably the usual conception is roughly speaking the following: we have two sources of knowledge, by means of which we comprehend "the world," "the reality" in which we are "placed": *experience,* or *observation* on the one hand, and *thinking* on the other. For example, one is engaged in experimental physics or in theoretical physics according to one's using the one or the other of these sources of knowledge in physics.

Now, in philosophy we find a time-honored controversy about these two sources of knowledge: which parts of our knowledge derive from observation, are "a posteriori," and which derive from thinking, are "a priori"? Is one of these sources of knowledge superior to the others, and if so, which?

From the very beginning philosophy has raised doubts about the reliability of *observation* (indeed, these doubts are perhaps the source of all philosophy). It is quite understandable that such doubts arose: they spring from the belief that sense-perception is frequently deceptive. At sunrise or at sunset the snow on distant mountains appears red, but "in reality" it is surely white! A stick which is immersed in water appears crooked, but "in reality" it is surely straight! If a man recedes from me, he appears smaller and smaller to me, but surely he does not change size "in reality"!

Now, although all the phenomena to which we have been referring have long since been accounted for by physical theories, so that nobody any longer regards them as deceptions caused by sense-perception, the consequences which flow from this primitive, long discarded conception still exert a powerful influence. One says: if observation is sometimes deceptive, perhaps it is always so! Perhaps everything disclosed by the senses is mere illusion! Everybody knows the phenomenon of dreams, and everybody knows how difficult it is at times to decide whether a given experience was "real life" or "a mere dream." Perhaps, then, whatever we observe is merely a dream object! Everybody knows that hallucinations occur, and that they can be so vivid that the subject cannot be dissuaded from taking his hallucination for reality. Perhaps then, whatever we observe is only a hallucination! If we look through appropriately polished lenses, everything appears distorted; who knows whether perhaps we do not always, unknowingly, look at the world as it were through distorting glasses, and therefore see everything distorted, different from what it really is! This is one of the basic themes of the philosophy of Kant.

But let us return to antiquity. As we said, the ancients believed that they were frequently deceived by observation. But nothing of this kind ever happened in the case of thought: there were plenty of *delusions of sense,* but no *delusions of thought!* And thus, as confidence in observation got shaken, the belief may have arisen that *thinking* is a method of knowledge which is absolutely superior to observation, indeed the only reliable method of knowledge: observation discloses mere appearance, thought alone grasps true being.

This, "rationalistic," doctrine that thinking is a source of knowledge which surpasses observation, that it is indeed the only reliable source of knowledge, has remained dominant from the climax of Greek philosophy until modern times. I cannot even intimate what peculiar fruits matured on the tree of such knowledge. At any rate, they proved to have extraordinarily little nourishing value; and thus the "empiricist" reaction, originating in England, slowly gained the upper hand, supported by the tremendous success of modern natural science—the philosophy which teaches that observation is superior to thought, indeed is the only source of knowledge: *nihil est in intellectu, quod non prius fuerit in sensu;* in English: "nothing is in the intellect which was not previously in the senses."

But at once this empiricism faces an apparently insuperable difficulty: how is it to account for the real validity of logical and mathematical statements? Observation discloses to me only the transient, it does not reach beyond the observed; there is no bond that would lead from one observed fact to another, that would compel future observations to have the same result as those already made. The laws of logic and mathematics, however, claim *absolutely universal* validity: that the door of my room is now closed, I know by observation; next time I observe it it may be open. That heated bodies expand, I know by observation; yet the very next observation may show that some heated body does not expand; but that two and two make four, holds not only for the case in which I verify it by counting I know with certainty that it holds always and everywhere. Whatever I know by observation could be otherwise: the door of my room might have been open now, I can easily imagine it; and I can easily imagine that a body does not expand on being heated; but two and two could not occasionally make five, I cannot imagine in any way what it would be like for twice two to equal five.

The conclusion seems inevitable: since the propositions of logic and mathematics have absolutely universal validity, are apodeictically certain, since it must be as they say and cannot be otherwise, these propositions cannot be derived from experience. In view of the tremendous importance of logic and mathematics in the system of our knowledge, empiricism, therefore, seems to be irrevocably refuted. To be sure, in spite of all this the older empiricists have attempted to found logic and mathematics upon experience. According to them we now believe that something must be this way and cannot be otherwise simply because the relevant experience is so old and the relevant observations have been repeated innumerable times. On this view, therefore, it is entirely conceivable that, just as an observation might show that a heated body does not expand, two and two might sometimes make five. This is alleged to have escaped our notice so far because it happens with such extraordinary rarity, like finding a piece of four-leaved clover which for superstitious people is a sign of good luck, an occurrence which is not so very rare—how much more promise of fortune would there be in the discovery of a case where two and two make five! One can safely say that on closer sight these attempts to derive logic and mathematics from experience are fundamentally unsatisfactory, and it is doubtful whether anybody seriously holds this view today.

Rationalism and empiricism having thus, as it were, suffered shipwreck—rationalism, because its fruits lacked nourishing value, empiricism, because it could not do justice to logic and mathematics —*dualistic* conceptions gained the upper hand, with the view that thinking and observation are equally legitimate sources of knowledge which are both indispensable to our comprehension of the world and play a distinctive role in the system of our knowledge. *Thought* grasps the most general laws of all being, as formulated perhaps in logic and mathematics; *observation* provides the detailed filling of this framework. As regards the limits set to the two sources of knowledge, opinions diverge.

Thus it is, for instance, disputed whether geometry is *a priori* or *a posteriori,* whether it is based on pure thinking or on experience. And the same dispute is encountered in connection with the most fundamental physical laws, e.g. the law of inertia, the laws of the conservation of mass and energy, the law of attraction of masses: all of them have already been acclaimed as *a priori,* as necessities of thought, by various philosophers—but always after they had been established and well confirmed as empirical laws in physics. This was bound to lead to a skeptical attitude, and as a matter of fact there is probably a prevalent tendency among physicists to regard the framework which can be grasped by pure thinking as being as wide and general as possible, and to acknowledge experience as the source of our knowledge of everything that is somehow concrete.

The usual conception, then, may be described roughly as follows: from experience we learn certain facts, which we formulate as "laws of nature"; but since we grasp by means of thought the most general lawful connections (of a logical and mathematical character) that pervade reality, we can control nature on the basis of facts disclosed by observation to a much larger extent than it has actually been observed. For we know in addition that anything which can be deduced from observed facts by application of logic and mathematics must be found to exist. According to this view, the experimental physicist provides knowledge of laws of nature by direct observation. The theoretical physicist thereafter enlarges this knowledge tremendously by thinking, in such a way that we are in a position also to assert propositions about processes that occur far from us in space and time and about processes which, on account of their magnitude or minuteness, are not directly observable but which are connected with what is directly observed by the most general laws of being, grasped by thought, the laws of logic and mathematics. This view seems to be strongly supported by numerous discoveries that have been made with the help of theory, like—to mention just some of the best known—the calculation of the position of the planet Neptune by Leverrier, the calculation of electric waves by Maxwell, the calculation of the bending of light rays in the gravitational field of the sun by Einstein and the calculation of the redshift in the solar spectrum, also by Einstein.

Nevertheless we are of the opinion that this view is entirely untenable. For on closer analysis it appears that the function of thought is immeasurably more modest than the one ascribed to it by this theory. The idea that thinking is an instrument for learning more about the world than has been observed, for acquiring knowledge of something that has absolute validity always and everywhere in the world, an instrument for grasping general laws of all being, seems to us wholly mystical. Just how should it come to pass that we could predict the necessary outcome of an observation before having made it? Whence should our thinking derive an executive power, by which it could compel an observation to have this rather than that result? Why should that which compels our thoughts also compel the course of nature? One would have to believe in some miraculous pre-established harmony between the course of our thinking and the course of nature, an idea which is highly mystical and ultimately theological.

There is no way out of this situation except a return to a purely

empiricist standpoint, to the view that observation is the only source
of knowledge of facts: there is no *a priori* knowledge about matters
of fact, *there is no "material" a priori*. However, we shall have to
avoid the error committed by earlier empiricists, that of interpreting
the propositions of logic and mathematics as mere facts of experience. We must look out for a different interpretation of logic and
mathematics.

II

Let us begin with logic. The old conception of logic is approximately as follows: logic is the account of the most universal properties of things, the account of those properties which are common
to all things; just as ornithology is the science of birds, zoology the
science of all animals, biology the science of all living beings, so
logic is the science of *all* things, the science of being as such. If
this were the case, it would remain wholly unintelligible whence
logic derives its certainty. For we surely do not know all things.
We have not observed everything and hence we cannot know how
everything behaves.

Our thesis, on the contrary, asserts: logic does not by any means
treat of the totality of things, it does not treat of objects at all but
only of our way of speaking about objects; logic is first generated
by language. The certainty and universal validity, or better, the
irrefutability of a proposition of logic derives just from the fact that
it says nothing about objects of any kind.

Let us clarify the point by an example. I talk about a well-known
plant: I describe it, as is done in botanical reference books, in terms
of the number, color and form of its blossom leaves, its calyx leaves,
its stamina, the shape of its leaves, its stem, its root, etc., and I
make the stipulation: let us call any plant of this kind "snow rose,"
but let us also call it "helleborus niger." Thereupon I can pronounce with absolute certainty the universally valid proposition:
"every snow rose is a helleborus niger." It is certainly valid, always
and everywhere; it is not refutable by any sort of observation; but
it says nothing at all about facts. I learn nothing from it about the
plant in question, when it is in bloom, where it may be found,
whether it is common or rare. It tells me nothing about the plant;
it cannot be disconfirmed by any observation. This is the basis of
its certainty and universal validity. The statement merely expresses
a convention concerning the way we wish to talk about the plant
in question.

Similar considerations apply to the principles of logic. Let us make the point with reference to the two most famous laws of logic: the law of contradiction and the law of the excluded middle. Take, for example, colored objects. We learn, by training as I am tempted to say, to apply the designation "red" to some of these objects, and we stipulate that the designation "not red" be applied to all other objects. On the basis of this stipulation we now can assert with absolute certainty the proposition that there is no object to which both the designation "red" and the designation "not red" is applied. It is customary to formulate this briefly by saying that nothing is both red and not red. This is the law of contradiction. And since we have stipulated that the designation "red" is to be applied to some objects and the designation "not red" to *all* other objects, we can likewise pronounce with absolute certainty the proposition: everything is either designated as "red" or as "not red," which it is customary to formulate briefly by saying that everything is either red or not red. This is the law of the excluded middle. These two propositions, the law of contradiction and the law of the excluded middle, say nothing at all about objects of any kind. They do not tell me of any of them whether they are red or not red, which color they have, or anything else. They merely stipulate a method for applying the designations "red" and "not red" to objects, i.e. they prescribe a *method of speaking about things.* And their universal validity and certainty, their irrefutability, just derives from the fact that they say nothing at all about objects.

The same is to be said of all the other principles of logic. We shall presently return to this point. But first let us insert another consideration. We have previously maintained that there can be no material *a priori,* i.e. no *a priori* knowledge about matters of fact. For we cannot know the outcome of an observation before the latter takes place. We have made clear to ourselves that no material *a priori* is contained in the laws of contradiction and of excluded middle, since they say nothing about facts. There are those, however, who would perhaps admit that the nature of the laws of logic is as described, yet would insist that there is a material *a priori* elsewhere, e.g. in the statement "nothing is both red and blue" (of course what is meant is: at the same time and place) which is alleged to express real *a priori* knowledge about the nature of things. Even before having made any observation, they say, one can predict with absolute certainty that it will not disclose a thing which is both blue and red; and it is maintained that such *a priori* knowledge is obtained by "eidetic insight" or an intuitive grasp of the essence of colors. If one desires to adhere to our thesis that there is no kind of material *a priori,* one must somehow face statements like "nothing is both blue and red." I want to attempt this in a few suggestive words, though they cannot by any means do full justice to this problem which is not easy. It surely is correct that we can say with complete certainty before having made any observations: the latter will not show that a thing is both blue and red—just as we can say with complete certainty that no observation will yield the result that a thing is both red and not red, or that a snow rose is not a helleborus niger. The first statement, however, is not a case of a material *a priori* any more than the second and third. Like the statements "every snow rose is a helleborus niger": and "nothing is both red and not red," the statement "nothing is both blue and red" says nothing at all about the nature of things; it likewise refers only to our proposed manner of speaking about objects, of applying designations to them. Earlier we said: there are some objects that we call "red," every other object we call "not red," and from this we derive the laws of contradiction and excluded middle. Now we say: some objects we call "red," some *other* objects we call "blue," and *other* objects again we call "green," etc. But if it is in this way that we ascribe color designations to objects, then we can say with certainty in advance: in this procedure no object is designated both as "red" and as "blue," or more briefly: no object is both red and blue. The reason why we can say this with certainty is that we have regulated the ascription of color designations to objects in just this way.

We see, then, that there are two totally different kinds of statements: those which really say something about objects, and those which do not say anything about objects but only stipulate rules for speaking about objects. If I ask "what is the color of Miss Erna's new dress?" and get the answer "Miss Erna's new dress is not both red and blue (all over)," then no information about this dress has been given to me at all. I have been made no wiser by it. But if I get the answer "Miss Erna's new dress is red," then I have received some genuine information about the dress.

Let us clarify this distinction in terms of one more example. A statement which really says something about the objects which it mentions, is the following: "If you heat this piece of iron up to 800°, it will turn red, if you heat it up to 1300°, it will turn white." What makes the difference between this statement and the statements cited above, which say nothing about facts? The application of temperature designations to objects is *independent* of the application of color designations, whereas the color designations "red" and "not red," or "red" and "blue" are applied to objects in *mutual dependence*. The statements "Miss Erna's new dress is either red or not red" and "Miss Erna's new dress is not both red and blue" merely express this dependence, hence make no assertion about that dress, and are for that reason absolutely certain and irrefutable. The above statement about the piece of iron, on the other hand, relates independently given designations, and therefore really says something about that piece of iron and is for just that reason not certain nor irrefutable by observation.

The following example may make the difference between these two kinds of statements particularly clear. If someone were to tell me: "I raised the temperature of this piece of iron to 800° but it did not turn red," then I would test his assertion; the result of the test may be that he was lying, or that he was the victim of an illusion, but perhaps it would turn out that—contrary to my previous beliefs—there are cases where a piece of iron heated to 800° does not become red-hot, and in that case I would just change my opinion about the reaction of iron to heating. But if someone tells me "I raised the temperature of this piece of iron to 800°, and this made it turn both red and not red" or "it became both red and white," then I will certainly make no test whatever. Nor will I say "he has told me a lie," or "he has become the victim of an illusion" and it is quite certain that I would not change my beliefs about the reaction of iron to heating. The point is—it is best to express it in language which any card player is familiar with—that the man has revoked: he has violated the rules in accordance with which we want to speak, and I shall refuse to speak with him any longer. It is as though one attempted in a game of chess to move the bishop orthogonally. In this case too, I would not make any tests, I would not change my beliefs about the behavior of things, but I would refuse to play chess with him any longer.

To sum up: we must distinguish two kinds of statements: those which say something about facts and those which merely express the way in which the rules which govern the application of words to facts depend upon each other. Let us call statements of the latter kind *tautologies*: they say nothing about objects and are for this very reason certain, universally valid, irrefutable by observation; whereas the statements of the former kind are not certain and are refutable by observation. The logical laws of contradiction and of the excluded middle are tautologies, likewise, e.g., the statement "nothing is both red and blue."

And now we maintain that in the same way all the other laws of logic are tautologies. Let us, therefore, return to logic once more in order to clarify the matter by an example. As we said, the designation "red" is applied to certain objects and the convention is adopted of applying the designation "not red" to any other object. It is this convention about the use of negation which is expressed by the laws of contradiction and of the excluded middle. Now we add the convention—still taking our examples from the domain of colors—that any object which is called "red" is also to be called "red or blue," "blue or red," "red or yellow," "yellow or red," etc., that every object which is called "blue," is also called "blue or red," "red or blue," "blue or yellow," "yellow or blue," etc., and so on. On the basis of this convention, we can again assert with complete certainty the proposition: "every red object is either red or blue." This is again a tautology. We do not speak about the objects, but only about our manner of talking about them.

If once more we remind ourselves of the way in which the designations "red," "not red," "blue," "red or blue," etc. are applied to objects, we can moreover assert with complete certainty and irrefutability: everything to which both designations "red or blue" and "not red" are applied, is also designated as "blue"—which is usually put more briefly: if a thing is red or blue and not red, then it is blue. Which is again a tautology. No information about the nature of things is contained in it, it only expresses the sense in which the logical words "not" and "or" are used.

Thus we have arrived at something fundamental: our conventions regarding the use of the words "not" and "or" is such that in asserting the two propositions "object A is either red or blue" and "object A is not red," I have implicitly already asserted "object A is blue." This is the essence of so-called *logical deduction*. It is not, then, in any way based on real connections between states of affairs, which we apprehend in thought. On the contrary, it has nothing at all to do with the nature of things, but derives from our manner of speaking about things. A person who refused to recognize logical deduction would not thereby manifest a different belief from mine about the behavior of things, but he would refuse to speak about things according to the same rules as I do. I could not convince him, but I would have to refuse to speak with him any longer, just as I should refuse to play chess with a partner who insisted on moving the bishop orthogonally.

What logical deduction accomplishes, then, is this: it makes us aware of all that we have implicitly asserted—on the basis of conventions regarding the use of language—in asserting a system of propositions, just as, in the above example, "object A is blue" is implicitly asserted by the assertion of the two propositions "object A is red or blue" and "object A is not red."

In saying this we have already suggested the answer to the question, which naturally must have forced itself on the mind of every reader who has followed our argument: if it is really the case that the propositions of logic are tautologies, that they say nothing about objects, what purpose does logic serve?

The logical propositions which were used as illustrations derived from conventions about the use of the words "not" and "or" (and it can be shown that the same holds for all the propositions of so-called propositional logic). Let us, then, first ask for what purpose the words "not" and "or" are introduced into language. Presumably the reason is that we are not omniscient. If I am asked about the color of the dress worn by Miss Erna yesterday, I may not be able to remember its color. I cannot say whether it was red or blue or green; but perhaps I will be able to say at least "it was not yellow." Were I omniscient, I should know its color. There would be no need to say "it was not yellow": I could say "it was red." Or again: my daughter has written to me that she received a cocker-spaniel as a present. As I have not seen it yet, I do not know its color; I cannot say "it is black" nor "it is brown"; but I *am* able to say "it is black or brown." Were I omniscient, I could do without this "or" and could say immediately "it is brown."

Thus logical propositions, though being purely tautologous, and logical deductions, though being nothing but tautological transformations, have significance for us because we are not omniscient. Our language is so constituted that in asserting such and such propositions we implicitly assert such and such other propositions—but we do not see immediately all that we have implicitly asserted in this manner. It is only logical deduction that makes us conscious of it. I assert, e.g., the propositions "the flower which Mr. Smith wears in his buttonhole, is either a rose or a carnation," "if Mr. Smith wears a carnation in his buttonhole, then it is white," "the flower which Mr. Smith wears in his buttonhole is not white." Perhaps I am not consciously aware that I have implicitly asserted also "the flower which Mr. Smith wears in his buttonhole is a rose"; but logical deduction brings it to my consciousness. To be sure, this does not mean that I know whether the flower which Mr. Smith wears in his buttonhole really is a rose; if I notice that it is not a rose, then I must not maintain my previous assertions—otherwise I sin against the rules of speaking, I revoke.

III

If I have succeeded in clarifying somewhat the role of logic, I may now be quite brief about the role of *mathematics*. The propositions of mathematics are of exactly the same kind as the propositions of logic: they are tautologous, they say nothing at all about the objects we want to talk about, but concern only the manner in which we want to speak of them. The reason why we can assert apodeictically with universal validity the proposition: $2 + 3 = 5$, why we can say even before any observations have been made, and can say it with complete certainty, that it will not turn out that $2 + 3 = 7$, is that by "$2 + 3$" we mean the same as by "5"—just as we mean the same by "helleborus niger" as by "snow rose." For this reason no botanical investigation, however subtle, could disclose that an instance of the species "snow rose" is not a *helleborus niger*. We become aware of meaning the same by "$2 + 3$" and by "5," by going back to the meanings of "2," "3," "5," "$+$," and making tautological transformations until we just see that "$2 + 3$" means the same as "5." It is such successive tautological transformation that is meant by "calculating"; the operations of addition and multiplication which are learnt in school are directives for such tautological transformation; every mathematical proof is a succession of such tautological transformations. Their utility, again, is due to the fact that, for example, we do not by any means see immediately that we mean by "24×31" the same as by "744"; but if we calculate the product "24×31," then we transform it step by step, in such a way that in each individual transformation we recognize that on the basis of the conventions regarding the use of the signs involved (in this case numerals and the signs "$+$" and "$\times$") what we mean after the transformation is still the same as what we meant before it, until finally we become consciously aware of meaning the same by "744" as by "24×31."

To be sure, the proof of the tautological character of mathematics is not yet complete in all details. This is a difficult and arduous task; yet we have no doubt that the belief in the tautological character of mathematics is essentially correct.

There has been prolonged opposition to the interpretation of mathematical statements as tautologies; Kant contested the tautological character of mathematics emphatically, and the great mathematician Henri Poincaré, to whom we are greatly indebted also for philosophical criticism, went so far as to argue that since mathematics cannot possibly be a huge tautology, it must somewhere contain an *a priori* principle. Indeed, at first glance it is difficult to believe that the whole of mathematics, with its theorems that it cost such labor to establish, with its results that so often surprise us, should admit of being resolved into tautologies. But there is just one little point which this argument overlooks: it overlooks the fact that we are not omniscient. An omniscient being, indeed, would at once know everything that is implicitly contained in the assertion of a few propositions. It would know immediately that on the basis of the conventions concerning the use of the numerals and the multiplication sign, "24 $\times$ 31" is synonymous with "744." An omniscient being has no need for logic and mathematics. We ourselves, however, first have to make ourselves conscious of this by successive tautological transformations, and hence it may prove quite surprising to us that in asserting a few propositions we have implicitly also asserted a proposition which seemingly is entirely different from them, or that we do mean the same by two complexes of symbols which are externally altogether different.

IV

And now let us be clear what a world-wide difference there is between our conception and the traditional—perhaps one may say: platonizing—conception, according to which the world is made in accordance with the laws of logic and mathematics ("God is perennially doing mathematics"), and our thinking, a feeble reflection of God's omniscience, is an instrument given to us for comprehending the eternal laws of the world. No! Our thinking cannot give insight into any sort of reality. It cannot bring us information of any fact in the world. It only refers to the manner in which we speak about the world. All it can do is to transform tautologically what has been said. There is no possibility of piercing through the sensible world disclosed by observation to a "world of true being": any metaphysics is impossible! Impossible, not because the task is too difficult for our human thinking, but because it is meaningless, because every attempt to do metaphysics is an attempt to speak in a way that contravenes the agreement as to how we wish to speak, comparable to the attempt to capture the queen (in a game of chess) by means of an orthogonal move of the bishop.

Let us return now to the problem which was our point of departure: what is the relationship between observation and theory in physics? We said that the usual view was roughly this: experience teaches us the validity of certain laws of nature, and since our thinking gives us insight into the most general laws of all being, we know that likewise anything which is deducible from these laws of nature by means of logical and mathematical reasoning must be found to exist. We see now that this view is untenable; for thinking does not grasp any sort of laws of being. Never and nowhere, then, can thought supply us with knowledge about facts that goes beyond the observed. But what, then, should we say about the discoveries made by means of theory on which, as we pointed out, the usual view so strongly relies for its support? Let us ask ourselves, e.g., what was involved in the computation of the position of the planet Neptune by Leverrier! Newton noticed that the familiar motions, celestial as well as terrestrial, can be well described in a unified way by the assumption that between any two mass points a force of attraction is exerted which is proportional to their masses and inversely proportional to the square of their distance. And it is because this assumption enables us to give a satisfactory description of the familiar motions, that he *made* it, i.e. he asserted tentatively, as an hypothesis, the law of gravitation: between any two mass points there is a force of attraction which is proportional to their masses and inversely proportional to the square of their distance. He could not pronounce this law as a *certainty,* but only as an hypothesis. For nobody can know that such is really the behavior of every pair of mass points— nobody can observe all mass points. But having asserted the law of gravitation, one has implicitly asserted many other propositions, that is, all propositions which are deducible from the law of gravitation (together with data immediately derivable from observation) by calculation and logical inference. It is the task of theoretical physicists and astronomers to make us conscious of everything we implicitly assert along with the law of gravitation. And Leverrier's calculations made people aware that the assertion of the law of gravitation implies that at a definite time and definite place in the heavens a hitherto unknown planet must be visible. People looked and actually saw that new planet—the hypothesis of the law of gravitation was confirmed. But it was not Leverrier's calculation that proved that this planet existed, but the looking, the observation. This observation could just as well have had a different result. It could just as well have happened that nothing was visible at the computed place in the heavens—in which case the law of gravitation would not have been confirmed and one would have begun to doubt whether it is really a suitable hypothesis for the description of the observable motions. Indeed, this is what actually happened later: in asserting the law of gravitation, one implicitly asserts that at a certain time the planet Mercury must be visible at a certain place in the heavens. Whether it would actually be visible at that time at that place, only observation could disclose; but observations showed that it was not visible at exactly the required position in the heavens. And what happened? They said: since in asserting the law of gravitation we implicitly assert propositions which are not true, we cannot maintain the hypothesis of the law of gravitation. Newton's theory of gravitation was replaced by Einstein's.

It is not the case, then, that we know through experience that certain laws of nature are valid, and—since by our thinking we grasp the most general laws of all being—therefore also know that whatever is deducible from these laws by reasoning must exist. On the contrary, the situation is this: there is not a single law of nature which we know to be valid; the laws of nature are *hypotheses* which we assert tentatively. But in asserting such laws of nature we implicitly assert also many other propositions, and it is the task of thinking to make us conscious of the implicitly asserted propositions. So long, now, as these implicitly asserted propositions, to the extent that they are about the directly observable, are confirmed by observation, these laws of nature are confirmed and we adhere to them; but if these implicitly asserted propositions are not confirmed by observation, then the laws of nature have not been confirmed and are replaced by others.

Knowledge and Truth

8

Psychology in Physical Language

BY RUDOLF CARNAP

(TRANSLATED BY GEORGE SCHICK)

1. INTRODUCTION. PHYSICAL LANGUAGE AND PROTOCOL LANGUAGE

IN WHAT FOLLOWS, we intend to explain and to establish the thesis that *every sentence of psychology may be formulated in physical language.* To express this in the material mode of speech: *all sentences of psychology describe physical occurrences, namely, the physical behavior of humans and other animals.* This is a sub-thesis of the general thesis of *physicalism* to the effect that *physical language is a universal language,* that is, a language into which every sentence may be translated. The general thesis has been discussed in an earlier article,[1] whose position shall here serve as our point of departure. Let us first briefly review some of the conclusions of the earlier study.

In meta-linguistic discussion we distinguish the customary *material mode of speech* (e.g. "The sentences of this language speak of this and that object.") from the more correct *formal mode of speech* (e.g. "The sentences of this language contain this and that word and are constructed in this and that manner.") In using the material mode of speech we run the risk of introducing confusions and pseudo-problems. If, because of its being more easily understood, we occasionally do use it in what follows, we do so only as a paraphrase of the formal mode of speech.

Of first importance for epistemological analyses are the *protocol*

This article was originally published in Volume III of *Erkenntnis* (1932/33). It is reproduced here with the kind permission of Professor Carnap.

1. Carnap, "Die Physikalische Sprache als Universalsprache der Wissenschaft," *Erkenntnis* II, 1931, pp. 432-465. [The English translation of this article by Max Black was published as a monograph under the title "The Unity of Science" (London: Kegan Paul, 1934).]

language, in which the primitive protocol sentences (in the material mode of speech: the sentences about the immediately given) of a particular person are formulated, and the *system language,* in which the sentences of the system of science are formulated. A person S *tests* (verifies) a system-sentence by deducing from it sentences of his own protocol language, and comparing these sentences with those of his actual protocol. The possibility of such a deduction of protocol sentences constitutes the *content* of a sentence. If a sentence permits no such deductions, it has no content, and is meaningless. If the same sentences may be deduced from two sentences, the latter two sentences have the same content. They say the same thing, and may be translated into one another.

To every sentence of the system language there corresponds some sentence of the physical language such that the two sentences are inter-translatable. It is the purpose of this article to show that this is the case for the sentences of psychology. Moreover, every sentence of the protocol language of some specific person is inter-translatable with some sentence of physical language, namely, with a sentence about the physical state of the person in question. The various protocol languages thus become sub-languages of the physical language. The *physical language is universal and inter-subjective.* This is the thesis of physicalism.

If the physical language, on the grounds of its universality, were adopted as the system language of science, all science would become physics. Metaphysics would be discarded as meaningless. The various domains of science would become parts of unified science. In the material mode of speech: there would, basically, be only one kind of object—physical occurrences, in whose realm law would be all-encompassing.

Physicalism ought not to be understood as requiring psychology to concern itself only with physically describable situations. The thesis, rather, is that psychology may deal with whatever it pleases, it may formulate its sentences as it pleases—these sentences will, in every case, be translatable into physical language.

We say of a sentence P that it is *translatable* (more precisely, that it is reciprocally translatable) into a sentence Q if there are rules, independent of space and time, in accordance with which Q may be deduced from P and P from Q; to use the material mode of speech, P and Q describe the same state of affairs; epistemologically speaking, every protocol sentence which confirms P also confirms Q and *vice versa.* The definition of an expression "a" by means of expressions "b," "c" . . . , represents a translation-rule with the help of which any sentence in which "a" occurs may be translated into a sentence in which "a" does not occur, but "b," "c," . . . do, and *vice versa*. The translatability of all the sentences of language L_1 into a (completely or partially) different language L_2 is assured if, for every expression of L_1, a definition is presented which directly or indirectly (i.e., with the help of other definitions) derives that expression from expressions of L_2. Our thesis thus states that a definition may be constructed for every psychological concept (i.e. expression) which directly or indirectly derives that concept from physical concepts. We are not demanding that psychology formulate each of its sentences in physical terminology. For its own purposes psychology may, as heretofore, utilize its own terminology. All that we are demanding is the production of the definitions through which psychological language is linked with physical language. We maintain that these definitions can be produced, since, implicitly, they already underlie psychological practice.

If our thesis is correct, the generalized sentences of psychology, the *laws* of psychology, are also translatable into the physical language. They are thus physical laws. Whether or not these physical laws are deducible from those holding in inorganic physics, remains, however, an open question. This question of the deducibility of the laws is completely independent of the question of the definability of concepts. We have already considered this matter in our discussion of biology.[2] As soon as one realizes that the sentences of psychology belong to the physical language, and also overcomes the emotional obstacles to the acceptance of this provable thesis, one will, indeed, incline to the conjecture, which cannot as yet be proved, that the laws of psychology are special cases of physical laws holding in inorganic physics as well. But we are not concerned with this conjecture here.

Let us permit ourselves a brief remark—apart from our principal point—concerning the emotional resistance to the thesis of physicalism. Such resistance is always exerted against any thesis when an Idol is being dethroned by it, when we are asked to discard an idea with which dignity and grandeur are associated. As a result of Copernicus' work, man lost the distinction of a central position in the universe; as a result of Darwin's, he was deprived of the dignity of a special supra-animal existence; as a result of Marx's, the factors by means of which history can be causally explained were degraded from the realm of ideas to that of material events; as a result of

2. "Die Physikalische Sprache," *op. cit.*, p. 449 ff., (*The Unity of Science*, p. 68 ff.).

Nietzsche's, the origins of morals were stripped of their halo; as a result of Freud's, the factors by means of which the ideas and actions of men can be causally explained were located in the darkest depths, in man's nether regions. The extent to which the sober, objective examination of these theories was obstructed by emotional opposition is well known. Now it is proposed that psychology, which has hitherto been robed in majesty as the theory of spiritual events, be degraded to the status of a part of physics. Doubtless, many will consider this an offensive presumption. Perhaps we may therefore express the request that the reader make a special effort in this case to retain the objectivity and openness of mind always requisite to the testing of a scientific thesis.

2. THE FORMS OF PSYCHOLOGICAL SENTENCES

The distinction between singular and general sentences is as important in psychology as in other sciences. A *singular psychological sentence,* e.g. "Mr. A was angry at noon yesterday" (an analogue of the physical sentence, "Yesterday at noon the temperature of the air in Vienna was 28 degrees centigrade"), is concerned with a particular person at a particular time. *General psychological sentences* have various forms, of which the following two are perhaps the most important. A sentence may describe a specific quality of a specific kind of event, e.g. "An experience of surprise always (or: always for Mr. A, or: always for people of such and such a society) has such and such a structure." A physical analogy would be: "Chalk (or: chalk of such and such a sort) always is white." The second important form is that of universal-conditional statements concerning sequences of events, that is, of causal laws. For instance, "When, under such and such circumstances, images of such and such a sort occur to a person (or: to Mr. A, or: to anyone of such and such a society), an emotion of such and such a sort always (or: frequently, or: sometimes) is aroused." A physical analogy would be: "When a solid body is heated, it usually expands."

Research is primarily directed to the discovery of general sentences. These cannot, however, be established except by means of the so-called method of induction from the available singular sentences, i.e. by means of the construction of hypotheses.

Phenomenology claims to be able to establish universal synthetic sentences which have not been obtained through induction. These sentences about psychological qualities are, allegedly, known either *a priori* or on the basis of some single illustrative case. In our view, knowledge cannot be gained by such means. We need not, however, enter upon a discussion of this issue here, since even on the view of phenomenology itself, these sentences do not belong to the domain of psychology.

In physics it sometimes seems to be the case that a general law is established on the basis of some single event. For instance, if a physicist can determine a certain physical constant, say, the heat-conductivity of a sample of some pure metal, in a single experiment, he will be convinced that, on other occasions, not only the sample examined but any similar sample of the same substance will, very probably, be characterizable by the same constant. But here too induction is applied. As a result of many previous observations the physicist is in possession of a universal sentence of a higher order which enables him in this case to follow an abbreviated method. This higher-order sentence reads roughly: "All (or: the following) physical constants of metals vary only slightly in time and from sample to sample."

The situation is analogous for certain conclusions drawn in psychology. If a psychologist has, as a result of some single experiment, determined that the simultaneous sounding of two specific notes is experienced as a dissonance by some specific person A, he infers (under favorable circumstances) the truth of the general sentence which states that the same experiment with A will, at other times, have the same result. Indeed, he will even venture—and rightly—to extend this result, with some probability, to pairs of tones with the same acoustic interval if the pitch is not too different from that of the first experiment. Here too the inference from a singular sentence to a general one is only apparent. Actually, a sentence inductively obtained from many observations is brought into service here, a sentence which, roughly, reads: "The reaction of any specific person as to the consonance or dissonance of a chord varies only very slightly with time, and only slightly on a not too large transposition of the chord." It thus remains the case that every general sentence is inductively established on the basis of a number of singular ones.

Finally, we must consider sentences about psycho-physical inter-relations, such as for instance, the connection between physical stimulus and perception. These are likewise arrived at through induction, in this case through induction in part from physical and in part from psychological singular sentences. The most important sentences of gestalt psychology belong also to this kind.

General sentences have the character of hypotheses in relation

to concrete sentences, that is, the testing of a general sentence consists in testing the concrete sentences which are deducible from it.
A general sentence has content insofar and only insofar as the concrete sentences deducible from it have content. Logical analysis must
therefore primarily be directed towards the examination of the
latter sort of sentences.

If A utters a singular psychological sentence such as "Yesterday
morning B was happy," the epistemological situation differs according as A and B are or are not the same person. Consequently, we
distinguish between sentences about *other minds* and sentences about
one's own mind. As we shall presently see, this distinction cannot
be made among the sentences of inter-subjective science. For the
epistemological analysis of subjective, singular sentences it is, however, indispensable.

3. Sentences about Other Minds

The epistemological character of a singular sentence about other
minds will now be clarified by means of an analogy with a sentence
about a physical property, defined as a disposition to behave (or
respond) in a specific manner under specific circumstances (or
stimuli). To take an example: a substance is called "plastic" if,
under the influence of deforming stresses of a specific sort and a
specific magnitude, it undergoes a permanent change of shape, but
remains intact.

We shall try to carry out this analogy by juxtaposing two examples. We shall be concerned with the epistemological situation of
the example taken from psychology; the parallel example about the
physical property is intended only to facilitate our understanding
of the psychological sentence, and not to serve as a specimen of an
argument from analogy. (For the sake of convenience, where the
text would have been the same in both columns, it is written only
once.)

A Sentence about a property of a physical substance.
Example: I assert the sentence P_1: "This wooden support is very firm."

A Sentence about a condition of some other mind.
Example: I assert the sentence P_1: "Mr. A is now excited."

There are two different ways in which sentence P_1 may be derived.
We shall designate them as the "rational" and the "intuitive" methods. The *rational* method consists of inferring P_1 from some protocol

sentence p_1 (or from several like it), more specifically, from a perception-sentence

about the shape and color of the wooden support.	about the behavior of A, e.g. about his facial expressions, his gestures, etc., or about physical effects of A's behavior, e.g. about characteristics of his handwriting.

In order to justify the conclusion, a major premise O is still required, namely the general sentence which asserts that

when I perceive a wooden support to be of this color and form, it (usually) turns out to be firm. (A sentence about the perceptual signs of firmness.)	when I perceive a person to have this facial expression and handwriting he (usually) turns out to be excited. (A sentence about the expressional or graphological signs of excitement.)

The content of P_1 does not coincide with that of p_1, but goes beyond it. This is evident from the fact that to infer P_1 from p_1 O is required. The cited relationship between P_1 and p_1 may also be seen in the fact that under certain circumstances, the inference from p_1 to P_1 may go astray. It may happen that, though p_1 occurs in a protocol, I am obliged, on the grounds of further protocols, to retract the established system sentence P_1. I would then say something like, "I made a mistake. The test has shown

that the support was not firm, even though it had such and such a form and color."	that A was not excited, even though his face had such and such an expression."

In practical matters the *intuitive* method is applied more frequently than this rational one, which presupposes theoretical knowledge and requires reflection. In accordance with the intuitive method, P_1 is obtained without the mediation of any other sentence from the identically sounding protocol sentence p_2.

"The support is firm."	"A is excited."

Consequently, one speaks in this case of *immediate perceptions*

of properties of substances, e.g., of the firmness of supports.	of other minds, e.g., of the excitement of A.

But in this case too the protocol sentence p_2 and the system sentence P_1 have different contents. The difference is generally not noted because, on the ordinary formulation, both sentences sound alike.

Here too we can best clarify the difference by considering the possibility of error. It may happen that, though p_2 occurs in my protocol, I am obliged, on the basis of further protocols, to retract the established system sentence P_1. I would then say "I made a mistake. Further tests have shown

that the support was not firm, although I had the intuitive impression that it was."	that A was not excited, although I had the intuitive impression that he was."

[The difference between p_2 and P_1 is the same as that between the identically sounding sentences p and P_1: "A red marble is lying on this table," of an earlier example.[3] The argument of that article shows that the inference of P_1 from p_2, if it is to be rigorous, also requires a major premise of general form, and that it is not in the least simple. Insofar as ordinary usage, for convenience's sake, assigns to both sentences the same sequence of words, the inference is, in practice, simplified to the point of triviality.]

Our problem now is: *what does sentence P_1 mean?* Such a question can only be answered by the presentation of a sentence (or of several sentences) which has (or which conjointly have) the same content as P_1. The viewpoint which will here be defended is that P_1 has the same content as a sentence P_2 which asserts the existence of a physical structure characterized by the disposition to react in a specific manner to specific physical stimuli. In our example, P_2 asserts the existence of that physical structure (microstructure)

of the wooden support that is characterized by the fact that, under a slight load, the support undergoes no noticeable distortion, and, under heavier loads, is bent in such and such a manner, but does not break.	of Mr. A's body (especially of his central nervous system) that is characterized by a high pulse and rate of breathing, which, on the application of certain stimuli, may even be made higher, by vehement and factually unsatisfactory answers to questions, by the occurrence of agitated movements on the application of certain stimuli, etc.

On my view, there is here again a thoroughgoing analogy between the examples from physics and from psychology. If, however, we were to question the experts concerning the examples from their

---

3. See *Erkenntnis*, Vol. II, p. 460 (*The Unity of Science*, p. 92).

respective fields, the majority of them nowadays would give us thoroughly non-analogous answers. The identity of the content of P_2

and of the content of the physical sentence P_1 would be agreed to as a matter of course by all physicists.	and of the content of the psychological sentence P_1 would be denied by almost all psychologists (the exceptions being the radical behaviorists).

The contrary view which is most frequently advocated by psychologists is that, "A sentence of the form of P_1 asserts the existence of a state of affairs not identical with the corresponding physical structure, but rather, only accompanied by it, or expressed by it. In our example:

P_1 states that the support not only has the physical structure described by P_2, but that, besides, there exists in it a certain force, namely its *firmness*.	P_1 states that Mr. A not only has a body whose physical structure (at the time in question) is described by P_2, but that—since he is a *psychophysical being*—he has, besides, a consciousness, a certain power or entity, in which that excitement is to be found.
This firmness is not identical with the physical structure, but stands in some parallel relation to it in such a manner that the firmness exists when and only when a physical structure of the characterized sort exists.	This excitement cannot, consequently, be identical with the cited structure of the body, but stands in some parallel relation (or in some relation of interaction) to it in such a manner that the excitement exists when and only when (or at least, frequently when) a physical, bodily structure of the characterized sort exists.
Because of this parallelism one may consider the described reaction to certain stimuli—which is causally dependent upon that structure—to be an *expression* of firmness.	Because of this parallelism one may consider the described reaction to certain stimuli to be an *expression* of excitement.
Firmness is thus an occult property, an obscure power which stands behind physical structure, appears in it, but itself remains unknowable."	Excitement, or the consciousness of which it is an attribute, is thus an occult property, an obscure power which stands behind physical structure, appears in it, but itself remains unknowable."

This view falls into the error of a hypostatization as a result of which a remarkable duplication occurs: besides or behind a state of affairs whose existence is empirically determinable, another, *parallel* entity is assumed, whose existence is not determinable. (Note that we are here concerned with a sentence about other minds.) But—one may now object—is there not really at least one possibility of testing this claim, namely, by means of the protocol sentence p_2 about the intuitive impression of

the firmness of the support?   the excitement of A?

The objector will point out that this sentence, after all, occurs in the protocol along with the perception sentence p_1. May not then a system sentence whose content goes beyond that of P_2 be founded on p_2? This may be answered as follows. A sentence says no more than what is testable about it. If, now, the testing of P_1 consisted in the deduction of the protocol sentence p_2, these two sentences would have the same content. But we have already seen that this is impossible.

There is no other possibility of testing P_1 except by means of protocol sentences like p_1 or like p_2. If, now, the content of P_1 goes beyond that of P_2, the component not shared by the two sentences is not testable, and is therefore meaningless. If one rejects the interpretation of P_1 in terms of P_2, P_1 becomes a metaphysical pseudo-sentence.

The various sciences today have reached very different stages in the process of their decontamination from metaphysics. Chiefly because of the efforts of Mach, Poincaré, and Einstein, physics is, by and large, practically free of metaphysics. In psychology, on the other hand, the work of arriving at a science which is to be free of metaphysics has hardly begun. The difference between the two sciences is most clearly seen in the different attitudes taken by experts in the two fields towards the position which we rejected as metaphysical and meaningless. In the case of the example from physics, most physicists would reject the position as anthropomorphic, or mythological, or metaphysical. They thereby reveal their anti-metaphysical orientation, which corresponds to our own. On the other hand, in the case of the example from psychology (though, perhaps, not when it is so crudely formulated), most psychologists would today consider the view we have been criticizing to be self-evident on intuitive grounds. In this one can see the metaphysical orientation of psychologists, to which ours is opposed.

4. REJOINDER TO FOUR TYPICAL CRITICISMS

Generalizing the conclusion of the argument which, with reference to a special case, we have been pursuing above, we arrive at the thesis that *a singular sentence about other minds always has the same content as some specific physical sentence.* Phrasing the same thesis in the material mode of speech—a sentence about other minds states that the body of the person in question is in a physical state of a certain sort. Let us now discuss several objections against this thesis of physicalism.

A. *Objection on the ground of the undeveloped state of physiology:* "Our current knowledge of physiology—especially our knowledge of the physiology of the central nervous system—is not yet sufficiently advanced to enable us to know to what class of physical conditions something like excitement corresponds. Consequently, when today we use the sentence 'A is excited,' we cannot mean by it the corresponding physical state of affairs."

Rebuttal. Sentence P_1, "A is excited" cannot, indeed, today be translated into a physical sentence P_3 of the form "such and such a physico-chemical process is now taking place in A's body" (expressed by a specification of physical state-coordinates and by chemical formulae). Our current knowledge of physiology is not adequate for this purpose. Even today, however, P_1 may be translated into another sentence about the physical condition of A's body, namely into the sentence P_2, to which we have already referred. This takes the form "A's body is now in a state which is characterized by the fact that when I perceive A's body the protocol sentence p_1 (stating my perception of A's behavior) and (or) the protocol sentence p_2 (stating my intuitive impression of A's excitement) or other, analogous, protocol sentences of such and such a sort are produced." Just as, in our example from physics, sentence P_1, "The wooden support is firm," refers to the physical structure of the wooden support—and this even though the person using the sentence may sometimes not be capable of characterizing this physical structure by specifying the distribution of the values of the physical state-coordinates, so also does the psychological sentence P_1, "A is excited," refer to the physical structure of A's body—though this structure can only be characterized by potential perceptions, impressions, dispositions to react in a specific manner, etc., and not by any specification of state-coordinates. Our ignorance of physiology can therefore affect only the mode of our characterization of the physical state of affairs in question. It in no way touches upon the principal point: that sentence P_1 refers to a physical state of affairs.

B. *Objection on the ground of analogy:* "When I myself am angry, I not only act out the behavior-pattern of an angry man, I experience a special *feeling* of anger. If, consequently, I observe someone else acting out the same behavior-pattern I may, on grounds of analogy, conclude (if not with certainty, at least with probability) that he too, besides acting as he does, now has a *feeling* of anger (which is not meant as a physical state of affairs)."

Rebuttal. Though arguments from analogy are not certain, as probability arguments they are undoubtedly admissible. By way of an example let us consider an everyday argument from analogy. I see a box of a certain shape, size, and color. I discover that it contains matches. I find another box of a similar appearance, and now, by analogy, draw the probability inference that it too contains matches. Our critic believes that the argument from analogy he presents is of the same logical form as the argument just presented. If this were the case, his conclusion would certainly be sound. But this is not the case. In our critic's argument, the conclusion is *meaningless*—a mere pseudo-sentence. For, being a sentence about other minds, not to be physically interpreted, it is in principle not testable. This was the result of our previous considerations; objection D will offer us an opportunity for discussing it again. In the non-testability of our critic's conclusion rests also the difference between his arguments and the example just cited. That the second box also contains matches may in principle be tested and confirmed by observation sentences of one's protocol. The two analogous sentences, "The first box contains matches" and "The second box contains matches" are both logically and epistemologically of the same sort. This is why the analogy holds here. The case is different with "I am angry" and "That person is angry." We consider the former of these two sentences to be meaningful and the latter (if its physical interpretation is rejected) to be meaningless. Our critic, who considers the latter as well as the former sentence to be meaningful, will believe that the person who asserts the sentence finds it testable, only in a manner altogether different from that in which the former is testable. Thus both of us agree that the latter sentence is epistemologically different from the former. The use of the same grammatical structure in these two sentences is logically illegitimate. It misleads us into believing that the two sentences are of the same logical form, and that one may be used as an analogue of the other.

If the conclusion is acknowledged to be meaningless, it remains to be explained how this pseudo-sentence was introduced into the argument. The logical analysis of concept formation and of sentences in science and (especially) in philosophy very frequently discloses pseudo-sentences. However, a pseudo-sentence rarely turns up as the conclusion of an argument from analogy with meaningful premises. This may readily be accounted for. An argument from analogy has (in a simple case) the following form. Premises: If A has the property E, it always also has the property F; A′ resembles A in many respects; A′ has the property E. We conclude (with probability): A′ also has the property F. Now, according to semantics, if "A" and "B" are object-names, "E" and "F" property-names, and "E(A)" means that A has the property E, then a) if "E(A)" and "E(B)" are meaningful (i.e. either true or false), "A" and "B" belong to the same semantic type; b) if two names, "A" and "B," belong to the same semantic type, and "F(A)" is meaningful, then "F(B)" is also meaningful. In the case under discussion here "E(A)" and "E(A′)" are meaningful, and consequently—in accordance with b)—"F(A′)," the conclusion of the argument from analogy, is also meaningful. Thus if the premises of an argument from analogy are meaningful and yet the conclusion is meaningless, the formulation of the premises must be in some way logically objectionable. And this is indeed the case with the argument from analogy presented by our critic. The predicative expression "I am angry" does not adequately represent the state of affairs which is meant. It asserts that a certain property belongs to a certain entity. All that exists, however, is an experienced feeling of anger. This should have been formulated as, roughly, "now anger." On this correct formulation the possibility of an argument from analogy disappears. For now the premises read: when I (i.e. my body) display angry behavior, anger occurs; the body of another person resembles mine in many respects; the body of the other person is now displaying angry behavior. The original conclusion can now no longer be drawn, since the sentence "Anger occurs" contains no "I" which may be replaced by "the other person." If one wanted to draw the appropriate conclusion, in which no substitution is made but the form of the premises simply retained, one would arrive at the meaningful but plainly false conclusion, "Anger occurs"—which states what would be expressed in ordinary language by "I am now angry."

C. *Objection on the ground of mental telepathy.* "The telepathic transmission of the contents of consciousness (ideas, emotions, thoughts) occurs without any determinable physical mediation. Here we have an instance of the knowledge of other minds which involves no perception of other people's bodies. Let us consider an example. I wake up suddenly one night, have a distinct sensation of fear, and know that my friend is now experiencing fear; later, I discover that at that very moment my friend was in danger of death. In this case, my knowledge of my friend's fear cannot refer to any state of his body, for I know nothing of that; my knowledge concerns itself immediately with my friend's sensation of fear."

Rebuttal. Psychologists are not yet unanimously decided on the degree to which they ought properly to credit the occurrence of cases of telepathy. This is an empirical problem which it is not our business to solve here. Let us concede the point to our critic, and assume that the occurrence of cases of telepathic transmission has been confirmed. We shall show that, even so, our earlier contentions are not affected in the least. The question before us is: what does sentence P_1, "My friend now experiences fear" mean, if I take P_1 to be a statement of telepathically derived cognition? We maintain that the meaning of P_1 is precisely the same as it would be if we used it on the grounds of some normally (rationally or intuitively) derived cognition. The occurrence of telepathy in no way alters the meaning of P_1.

Let us consider a precisely analogous situation involving the cognition of some physical event. I suddenly have the impression that a picture has fallen from the wall at my house, and this when neither I nor anyone else can in any normal way perceive that this has happened. Later, I discover that the picture has, indeed, fallen from the wall. I now express this cognition which I have obtained by clairvoyance in sentence Q, "The picture has now fallen from the wall." What is the meaning of this sentence? The meaning of Q here is clearly the same as it would be if I used it on the ground of some normally derived cognition, that is, on the ground of some cognition by direct perception of the event in question. For in both cases Q asserts that a physical event of a certain sort, a specific displacement of a specific body, has taken place.

The case is the same with telepathic cognition. We have already considered the case in which the state of some other mind is intuitively grasped, though by means of a perception of the other person's body. If a telepathic cognition of the state of some other mind occurs, it too is based on an intuitive impression, this time without a simultaneous perception. That which is cognized, however, is the same in both cases. Earlier, we remarked that P_1 does not have the same content as the protocol sentence p_2 about the (normally) intuitive impression, and that p_2 cannot support a sentence about something beside or behind the physical condition of the other person's body. Our remarks hold equally for telepathically intuitive impressions.

D. *Objection on the ground of statements by others.* "We are, to begin with, agreed that A is in a certain physical state which is manifested by behavior of a certain sort and produces in me, apart from sense-perceptions, an intuitive impression of A's anger. Beyond this, however, I can find out that A really does experience anger by questioning him. He himself will testify that he experienced anger. Knowing him to be a truthful person and a good observer, why should I not consider his statement to be true—or at least probably true?"

Rebuttal. Before I can decide whether I should accept A's statement as true, or false, or probably true—before, indeed, I can consider this question at all—I must first of all understand the statement. It must have meaning for me. And this is the case only if I can test it, if, that is, sentences of my protocol are deducible from it. If the expression is interpreted physically it is testable by means of protocol sentences such as my p_1 and p_2, that is, by sentences about specific perceptions and intuitive expressions. Since, however, our critic rejects the physical interpretation of the expression, it is in principle impossible for me to test it. Thus it is meaningless for me, and the question whether I should consider it to be true, or false, or probable, cannot even be posed.

Should unusual, brilliant patterns suddenly appear in the sky— even if they took the form of letters which seemed to compose a sentence—science could not comprehend them except by first conceiving them, describing them, and explaining them (i.e. subsuming them under general causal-sentences) as physical facts. The question whether such an arrangement of symbols constitutes a meaningful sentence must be decided without taking into consideration whether or not it appears in the sky. If this symbol-arrangement is not a meaningful sentence at other times, it cannot become one no matter how effulgent an appearance it makes in the sky. Whether a sentence is true or false is determined by empirical contingencies; but whether a sentence is or is not meaningful is determined solely by the syntax of language.

It is no different in the case of those acoustic phenomena that issue from the mouths of certain vertebrates. They are first of all facts, physical occurrences, and specifically, sound waves of a certain sort. We can, further, also interpret them as symbols. But whether or not such an arrangement of symbols is meaningful cannot depend on its occurrence as an acoustic phenomenon. If the sentence "A was angry yesterday at noon" has no meaning for me —as would be the case if (insofar as our critic rejects its physical meaning) I could not test it—it will not be rendered meaningful by the fact that a sound having the structure of this sentence came from A's own mouth.

But—it will be asked—do we not need the statements of our fellow-men for the elaboration of inter-subjective science? Would not physics, geography, and history become very meager studies if I had to restrict myself in them to occurrences which I myself had directly observed? There is no denying that they would. But there is a basic difference between a statement by A about the geography of China or about some historical event in the past on the one hand, and, on the other, a statement by A about the anger he felt yesterday. I can, in principle, test the statements of the first sort by means of perception sentences of my own protocol, sentences about my own perceptions of China, or of some map, or of historical documents. It is, however, in principle impossible for me to test the statement about anger if our critic asks me to reject the physical meaning of the sentence. If I have often had occasion to note that the geographical or historical reports that A makes can be confirmed by me, then, on the basis of an inductive probability inference, I consider myself justified in using his other statements—insofar as they are meaningful to me—in the elaboration of my scientific knowledge. It is in this way that inter-subjective science is developed. A sentence, however, which is not testable and hence not meaningful prior to its statement by A is not any the more meaningful after such a statement. If, in accordance with our position, I construe A's statement about yesterday's anger as a statement about the physical condition of A's body yesterday, this statement *may* be used for the development of inter-subjective science. For we use A's sentence as evidence (just to the extent to which we have found A to be trustworthy) in support of the attribution of a corresponding physical structure to the corresponding spatio-temporal region of our physical world. Neither do the consequences which we draw from this attribution generically differ from those that are obtained from any other physical statement. We build our expectations of future perceptions on it—in this case with respect to A's behavior, as in other cases with respect to the behavior of other physical systems.

The assertions of our fellow men contribute a great deal to extending the range of our knowledge. But they cannot bring us anything *basically* new. that is, anything which cannot also be learned in some other way. For the assertions of our fellow men are, at bottom, no different from other physical events. Physical events are different from one another as regards the extent to which they may be used as signs of other physical events. Those physical events which we call "assertions of our fellow man" rank particularly high on this scale. It is for this reason that science, quite rightly, treats these events with special consideration. However, between the contribution of these assertions to our scientific knowledge and the contributions of a barometer there is, basically, at most a difference of degree.

5. BEHAVIORISM AND "INTUITIVE" PSYCHOLOGY

The position we are advocating here coincides in its broad out-lines with the psychological movement known as "behaviorism"—when, that is, its epistemological principles rather than its special methods are considered. We have not linked our exposition with a statement of behaviorism since our only concern is with epistemo-logical foundations while behaviorism is above all else interested in a specific method of research and in specific concept formations.

The advocates of behaviorism were led to their position through their concern with animal psychology. In this domain, when the material given to observation does not include statements but only inarticulate behavior, it is most easy to arrive at the correct method of approach. This approach leads one to the correct interpretation of the statements of human experimental subjects, for it suggests that these statements are to be conceived as acts of verbalizing be-havior, basically no different from other behavior.

Behaviorism is confronted with views, more influential in Ger-many than in the United States, which uphold the thesis that psy-chology's concern is not with behavior in its physical aspect, but rather, with *meaningful behavior*. For the comprehension of mean-ingful behavior the special method known as "intuitive understand-ing" ("Verstehen") is said to be required. Physics allegedly knows nothing of this method. Neither meaningful behavior considered collectively nor the individual instances of such behavior which psychology investigates can possibly—so it is maintained—be char-acterized in terms of physical concepts.

In intuitive psychology this view is generally linked with the view that beside physical behavior there is yet another, psychical event, which constitutes the true subject-matter of psychology, and to which intuitive understanding leads. We do not want to consider this idea any further here, since we have already thoroughly examined it.

But even after one puts this idea aside, intuitive psychology poses the following objection to physicalism.

Objection based on the occurrence of "meaningful behavior." "When psychology considers the behavior of living creatures (we disregard here the question whether it deals only with such behavior), it is interested in it as meaningful behavior. This aspect of behavior cannot, however, be grasped in terms of physical concepts, but only by means of the method of intuitive understanding. And this is why psychological sentences cannot be translated into physical sentences."

Rebuttal. Let us recall a previous example of the *physicalization* of an intuitive impression, i.e. of a qualitative designation in the protocol language.[4] We there showed that it is possible by investigating optical state-coordinates, to determine the entirety of those physical conditions which correspond to "green of this specific sort" and to subsume them under laws. The same is the case here. It simply depends on the physical nature of an act—say, of an arm-movement —whether I can intuitively understand it—as, say, a beckoning-motion—or not. Consequently, physicalization is possible here too. The class of arm-movements to which the protocol-designation "beckoning motion" corresponds can be determined, and then described in terms of physical concepts. But perhaps doubts may be raised as to whether the classification of arm-movements as intelligible or unintelligible, and, further, the classification of intelligible arm-movements as beckoning motions or others really depends, as our thesis claims, solely on the physical constitution of the arms, the rest of the body, and the environment. Such doubts are readily removed if, for instance, one thinks of films. We understand the *meaning* of the action on the movie screen. And our understanding would doubtless be the same if, instead of the film presented, another which resembled it in every physical particular were shown. Thus one can see that both our understanding of meaning and the particular forms it takes are, in effect, completely determined by the physical processes impinging on our sense-organs (in the film-example, those impinging on our optic and auditory sense-organs).

The problem of physicalization in this area, that is, the problem of the characterization of *understandable* behavior as such and of the various kinds of such behavior by means of concepts of systematized physics, is not as yet solved. But does not then our basic thesis rest on air? It states that all psychological sentences can be translated into physical sentences. One may well ask to what extent

---

4. *Erkenntnis*, Vol. II, *op. cit.*, pp. 444 ff. (*The Unity of Science*, p. 58 ff.).

such a translation is possible, given the present state of our knowledge. Even today every sentence of psychology *can* be translated into a sentence which refers to the physical behavior of living creatures. In such a physical characterization terms do indeed occur which have not yet been physicalized, i.e. reduced to the concepts of physical science. Nevertheless, the concepts used *are* physical concepts, though of a primitive sort—just as "warm" and "green" (applied to bodies) were physical concepts before one could express them in terms of physical state-coordinates (temperature and electromagnetic field, respectively).

We should like, again, to make the matter clear by using a *physical example*. Let us suppose that we have found a substance whose electrical conductivity is noticeably raised when it is irradiated by various types of electro-magnetic radiation. We do not yet, however, know the internal structure of this substance and so cannot yet explain its behavior. We want to call such a substance a "detector" for radiation of the sort involved. Let us suppose, further, that we have not yet systematically determined to what sorts of radiation the detector reacts. We now discover that the sorts of radiation to which it responds share still another characteristic, say, that they accelerate specific chemical reactions. Now suppose that we are interested in the photo-chemical effects of various sorts of radiation, but that the determination of these effects, in the case of a specific sort of radiation, is difficult and time-consuming, while the determination of the detector's reaction to it is easy and quickly accomplished; then we shall find it useful to adopt the detector as a test-instrument. With its aid we can determine for any particular sort of radiation whether or not it is likely to have the desired photo-chemical effect. This practical application will not be impeded by our ignorance of the detector's micro-structure and our inability to explain its reaction in physical terms. In spite of our ignorance, we can certainly say that the detector isolates a certain physically specified class of rays. The objection that this is not a physical class since we cannot characterize it by a specification of optical state-coordinates but only by the behavior of the detector will not stand. For to begin with, we know that if we carried out a careful empirical investigation of the electro-magnetic spectrum, we could identify the class of rays to which the detector responds. On the basis of this identification we could then physicalize the characterization of the rays in terms of detector-reactions, by substituting for it a characterization in terms of systematic physical concepts. But even our present way of characterizing the radiation in terms of the detector-test is a physical characterization, though an indirect one. It is distinguished from the direct characterization which is our goal only through being more circumstantial. There is no difference of kind between the two characterizations, only one of degree, though the difference of degree is indeed sufficiently great to give us a motive for pursuing the empirical investigations which might bring the direct physical characterization within our grasp.

Whether *the detector is organic or inorganic* is irrelevant to the epistemological issue involved. The function of the detector is basically the same whether we are dealing with a physical detector of specific sorts of radiation or with a tree-frog as a detector of certain meteorological states of affairs or (if one may believe the newspapers) with a sniffing dog as a detector of certain human diseases. People take a practical interest in meteorological forecasts. Where barometers are not available they may, consequently, use a tree-frog for the same purpose. But let us be clear about the fact that this method does not determine the state of the tree-frog's soul, but a physically specified weather condition, even if one cannot describe this condition in terms of the concepts of systematized physics. People, likewise, have a practical interest in medical diagnoses. When the directly determinable symptoms do not suffice, they may, consequently, enlist a dog's delicate sense of smell for the purpose. It is clear to the doctor that, in doing so, he is not determining the state of the dog's soul, but a physically specified condition of his patient's body. The doctor may not be able, given the present state of physiological knowledge, to characterize the diseased condition in question in terms of the concepts of systematic physics. Nonetheless, he knows that his diagnosis—whether it is based on the symptoms he himself has directly observed or on the reactions of the diagnostic dog—determines nothing and can determine nothing but the physical condition of his patient. Even apart from this, the physiologist acknowledges the need for physicalization. This would here consist in describing the bodily condition in question, i.e. defining the disease involved in purely physiological terms (thus eliminating any mention of the dog's reaction). A further task would be to trace these back to chemical terms, and these, in turn, to physical ones.

The case with *intuitive psychology* is precisely analogous. The situation here happens to be complicated for epistemological analysis (though for psychological practice it is simplified) by the fact that in the examination of an experimental subject the intuitive psychologist is both the observer and detector. The doctor here is his own diagnostic dog; which, indeed, is also often the case in medical diagnoses—in their intuitive phases. The psychologist calls the behavior of the experimental subject "understandable" or, in a special case, for instance, "a nod of affirmation," when his detector responds to it, or—in our special case—when it results in his protocols registering "A nods affirmatively." Science is not a system of experiences, but of sentences; it does not include the psychologist's experience of understanding, but rather, his protocol sentence. The utterance of the psychologist's protocol sentence is a reaction whose epistemological function is analogous to the tree-frog's climbing and to the barking of the diagnostic dog. To be sure, the psychologist far surpasses these animals in the variety of his reactions. As a result, he is certainly very valuable to the pursuit of science. But this constitutes only a difference of degree, not a difference of kind.

In the light of these considerations, two demands are to be made of the psychologist. First, we shall expect him (as we expect the doctor) to be clear about the fact that, in spite of his complicated diagnostic reaction, he establishes nothing but the existence of some specific physical condition of the experimental subject, though a condition which can be characterized only indirectly—by his own diagnostic reaction. Secondly, he must acknowledge (as the physiologist does) that it is a task of scientific research to find a way of physicalizing the indirect characterization. Psychology must determine what are the physical conditions to which people's detector-reactions correspond. When this is carried out for every reaction of this sort, i.e. for every result of intuitive understanding, psychological concept formation can be physicalized. The indirect definitions based on detector-reactions will be replaced by direct definitions in terms of the concepts of systematized physics. Psychology, like the other sciences, must and will reach the level of development at which it can replace the tree-frog by the barometer. But even in the tree-frog stage psychology already uses physical language, though of a primitive sort.

6. PHYSICALIZATION IN GRAPHOLOGY

The purpose of this section is not to justify physicalism, but only to show how psychological concepts can in fact be physicalized. To this end we shall examine a branch of psychology in which physicalization has already been undertaken with some success. In doing so we may perhaps also meet the criticism which is occasionally voiced, that the achievement of physicalization, assuming it were possible, would in any case be fruitless and uninteresting. It is held that, given sufficient information concerning the social group and the circumstances of the people involved, one might perhaps be able to specify arm-movements which are interpreted as beckoning-motions in such a way that they would be characterizable in terms of kinematic (i.e. spatio-temporal) concepts. But it is alleged that this procedure would not provide us with any further insight into anything of interest, least of all into the connections of these with other events.

Remarkably enough, physicalization can show significant success in a branch of psychology which until comparatively recent times was pursued in a purely intuitive (or at most a pseudo-rational) manner and with wholly inadequate empirical data, so that it then had no claim to scientific status. This is graphology. Theoretical graphology—we shall concern ourselves here with no other sort—investigates the law-like relationships which hold between the formal properties of a person's handwriting and those of his psychological properties that are commonly called his "character."

We must first of all explain what is meant by *character* in physical psychology. Every psychological property is marked out as a disposition to behave in a certain way. By "actual property" we shall understand a property which is defined by characteristics that can be directly observed: by "disposition" (or "dispositional concept") we shall understand a property which is defined by means of an implication (a conditional relationship, an if-then sentence). Examples of familiar dispositional concepts of physics may serve to illustrate this distinction, and will, at the same time, illustrate the distinction between occurrent and continuant properties, a distinction which is important in psychology. An example of a physical *occurrent property* is a specific degree of temperature. We define "Body K has temperature T" to mean "When a sufficiently small quantity of mercury is brought into contact with K, then . . . " When defined in this way, the concept of temperature is a dispositional concept. Now that physics has disclosed the micro-structure of matter and determined the laws of molecular motion, a different definition of temperature is used: temperature is the mean kinetic energy of molecules. Here, then, temperature is no longer a dispositional concept, but an actual property. The *occurrent properties of psychology* are logically analogous to the familiar dispositional concepts of physics. Indeed, on our view, they are themselves nothing else than physical concepts. Example: "Person X is excited" means "If, now, stimuli of such and such a sort were applied, X would react in such and such a manner" (both stimuli and reactions being physical events). Here too the aim of science is to change the form of the definition; more accurate insight into the micro-structure of the human body should enable us to replace dispositional concepts by actual properties. That this is not a utopian aim is shown by the fact that even at the present time, a more accurate knowledge of physiological macro-events has yielded us a set of actual characteristics of occurrent states (e.g. for feelings of various sorts: frequency and intensity of pulse and respiration, glandular secretion, innervation of visceral muscles, etc.). Such a change of definitions is markedly more difficult when the states which have to be delimited are not emotional, for it then presupposes a knowledge of the micro-structure of the central nervous system which far surpasses the knowledge currently available.

Physical constants, e.g. heat-conductivity, coefficient of refraction, etc. might be taken as examples of physical *continuant properties*. These too were originally defined as dispositional concepts, e.g. "A substance has a coefficient of refraction n" means "If a ray of light enters the substance, then . . . " Here again the aim of transforming the definition has already been achieved for some concepts, and is being pursued in the case of the remainder. The reference to dispositions gives way to an actual designation of the composition (in terms of atoms and electrons) of the substance in question. The *psychological continuant properties* or "character properties" (the word "character" is here being used in a broad, neutral sense—to mean more than volitional or attitudinal properties) can, at present, be defined only in the form of dispositional concepts. Example: "X is more impressionable than Y" means "If both X and Y have the same experience under the same circumstances, more intense feelings are experienced by X than by Y." In these definitions, both in the characterization of the stimuli (the statement of the circumstances) and in that of the reaction, there are names which still designate psychological occurrent properties, for which the problem of physicalization has not yet been solved. To physicalize the designations of continuant properties will be possible only when the designations of occurrent properties have been dealt with. So long as these are not completely physicalized, the physicalization of continuant properties and, as a result, that of characterology as a whole, must remain in a scientifically incomplete state, and this no matter how rich our stock of intuitive knowledge may be.

There is no sharp division between occurrent and continuant designations. Nonetheless, the difference of degree is large enough to justify their being differently labelled and differently treated, and, consequently, large enough to justify the separation of characterology from psychology as a whole (considered as the theory of behavior). Graphology sets itself the task of finding in the features of a person's handwriting indications of his character and, to some extent, of his occurrent properties. The practising graphologist does not intend the rational method to replace intuition, but only to support or to correct it. It has, however, become clear that the pursuit of the task of physicalization will serve even this purpose. Along these lines graphology has already, of late, made some significant discoveries.

Since the problem of graphology is to discover the correspondences holding between the properties of a person's handwriting and those of his character, we may here divide the problem of physicalization into three parts. The physicalization of the properties of handwriting constitutes the *first part of the problem*. A certain script gives me, for instance, an intuitive impression of something full and juicy. In saying so, I do not primarily refer to characteristics of the writer, but to characteristics of his script. The problem now is to replace intuitively identified script-properties of this sort by properties of the script's shape, i.e. by properties which may be defined with the aid of geometrical concepts. That this problem can be solved is clear. We need only thoroughly investigate the system of forms which letters, words, and lines of script might possibly take in order to determine which of these forms make the intuitive impression in question on us. So, for instance, we might find that a script appears full or two-dimensional (as opposed to thin or linear) if rounded connections are more frequent than angles, the loops broader than normal, the strokes thicker, etc. This task of the physicalization of the properties of handwriting has in many cases been accomplished to a large extent.[5] We are not objecting to the retention of the intuitively derived descriptions (in terms, for instance, of "full," "delicate," "dynamic," etc.). Our requirement will be adequately met as soon as a definition in exclusively geometric terms is provided for each such description. This problem is precisely analogous to the problem, to which we have frequently referred, of identifying in quantitative terms those physical conditions which correspond to a qualitative designation—such as "green of such and such a sort"—in the protocol language.

The *second part of the problem* consists of the physicalization of the character properties referred to in graphological analyses. The traditional concepts of characterology—whose meaning is as a

5. *Cf.* Klages, L., *Handschrift und Character,* Leipzig, 1920. Several of our examples are taken from this book or suggested by it.

rule not clearly defined, but left to be expressed in our everyday vocabulary or by means of metaphorical language—have to be systematized and given physicalistic (behavioristic) definitions. We have already seen that such a definition refers to a disposition to behave in a certain way, and further, that the task of the construction of such definitions is difficult and presupposes the physicalization of psychological occurrent properties.

We can see that in both parts of the problem the task is one of replacing primitive, intuitive concept formations by systematic ones, of replacing the observer with a tree-frog by the observer with a barometer (in graphology, as in intuitive medical diagnoses, the observer and the tree-frog coincide).

In addition to these questions there is a third aspect of the problem to be considered: the basic empirical task of graphology. This consists of the search for the correlations which hold between the properties of handwriting and those of character. Here too, a systematization, though of a different sort, takes place. The correspondence of a specific property of handwriting to a specific property of character may, at first, be recognized intuitively—for instance, as a result of an empathetic reflection on the arm-movements which produced the script in question. The problem of systematization here is to determine the degree of correlation of the two properties by a statistical investigation of many instances of script of the type in question and the characters of the corresponding writers.

Our position now is that the further development and clarification of the concepts of psychology as a whole must take the direction we have illustrated in our examination of graphology, the direction, that is, of physicalization. But, as we have already emphasized several times, psychology is a physical science even prior to such a clarification of its concepts—a physical science whose assignment it is to describe systematically the (physical) behavior of living creatures, especially that of human beings, and to develop laws under which this behavior may be subsumed. These laws are of quite diverse sorts. A hand movement, for instance, may be examined from various aspects: first, semiotically, as a more or less conventional sign for some designated state of affairs; secondly, mimically, as an expression of the contemporaneous psychological state—the occurrent properties of the person in question; thirdly, physiognomically, as an expression of the continuant properties—the character of the person in question. In order to investigate, say, the hand movements of people (of certain groups) in their mimical and physiognomic aspects one might perhaps take motion pictures of them, and, from these, derive kinematic diagrams of the sort which engineers construct for machine parts. In this manner the shared kinematic (i.e., spatio-temporal) characteristics of the hand movements with whose perception certain intuitive protocol designations tend to be associated (e.g. "This hand movement looks rushed," ". . . grandiose," etc.) would have to be determined. It will now be clear why precisely graphology—the characterological investigation of writing movements, a very special sort of hand movements, identifiable in terms of their specific purpose—should be the only study of this sort which can as yet show any results. The reason is that writing movements themselves produce something resembling kinematic diagrams, namely, the letters on the paper. To be sure, only the track of the movements is drawn. The passage of time is not recorded —the graphologist can subsequently only infer this, imperfectly, from indirect signs. More accurate results would be demonstrable if the complete three-dimensional spatio-temporal diagram, not only its projection on the writing plane, were available. But even the conclusions to which graphology currently subscribes allay whatever misgivings there might have been that investigations directed at the physicalization of psychological concepts would prove to be uninteresting. It may not even be too rash a conjecture that interesting parallels may be found to hold between the conclusions of characterological investigations of both the involuntary and the voluntary motions of the various parts of the human body on the one hand, and on the other hand the conclusions of graphology which are already available to us. If specific properties of a person's character express themselves both in a specific form of handwriting and in a specific form of arm motion, a specific form of leg motion, specific facial features, etc., might not these various forms resemble one another? Perhaps, after having first given fruitful suggestions for the investigation of other sorts of bodily movements, graphology may, in turn, be stimulated by the results to examine script properties it had previously overlooked. These, of course, are mere conjectures; whether or not they are justifiable cannot affect the tenability of our thesis, which maintains the possibility of translating all psychological sentences into physical language. This translatability holds regardless of whether or not the concepts of psychology are physicalized. Physicalization is simply a higher-level, more rigorously systematized scientific form of concept formation. Its accomplishment is a practical problem which concerns the psychologist rather than the epistemologist.

7. SENTENCES ABOUT ONE'S OWN MIND;
"INTROSPECTIVE PSYCHOLOGY"

Our argument has shown that a sentence about other minds refers to physical processes in the body of the person in question. On any other interpretation the sentence becomes untestable in principle, and thus meaningless. The situation is the same with sentences about one's own mind, though here the emotional obstacles to a physical interpretation are considerably greater. The relationship of a sentence about one's own mind to one about someone else's may most readily be seen with respect to a sentence about some *past state* of one's own mind, e.g. P_1: "I was excited yesterday." The testing of this sentence involves either a *rational* inference from protocol sentences of the form of p_1—which refer to presently perceived script, photographs, films, etc. originating with me yesterday; or it involves an *intuitive* method, e.g. utilizing the protocol sentence p_2, "I recall having been excited yesterday." The content of P_1 exceeds both that of the protocol sentence p_1 and that of the protocol sentence p_2, as is most clearly indicated by the possibility of error and disavowal where P_1 is concerned. P_1 can only be progressively better confirmed by sets of protocol sentences of the form of p_1 and p_2. The very same protocol sentences, however, also confirm the physical sentence P_2: "My body was yesterday in that physical condition which one tends to call 'excitement.'" P_1 has, consequently, the same content as the physical sentence P_2.

In the case of a sentence about the *present state* of one's own mind, *e.g.* P_1: "I now am excited" one must clearly distinguish between the system sentence P_1 and the protocol sentence p_2, which, likewise, may read "I now am excited." The difference rests in the fact that the system sentence P_1 may, under certain circumstances, be disavowed, whereas a protocol sentence, being an epistemological point of departure, cannot be rejected. The protocol sentences p_1 which rationally support P_1 have here some such form as "I feel my hands trembling," "I see my hands trembling," "I hear my voice quavering," etc. Here too, the content of P_1 exceeds that of both p_1 and p_2, in that it subsumes all the possible sentences of this sort. P_1 has the same content as the physical sentence P_2, "My body is now in that condition which, both under my own observation and that of others, exhibits such and such characteristics of excitement," the characteristics in question being those which are mentioned both in my own protocol sentences of the sort of p_1

and p_2 and in other people's protocol sentences of corresponding sorts (discussed above in our example of sentences about other minds).

The table opposite shows the analogous application of the physicalist thesis to the three cases we have discussed by exhibiting the parallelism of sentences about other minds, sentences about some past condition of one's own mind, and sentences about the present condition of one's own mind, with the physical sentence about the wooden support.

Objection from introspective psychology: "When the psychologist is not investigating other experimental subjects, but pursues self-observation, or "introspection," instead, he grasps, in a direct manner, something non-physical—and this is the proper subject-matter of psychology."

Rebuttal. We must distinguish between a question of the justification of the use of some prevalent practical method of inquiry and a question of the justification of some prevalent interpretation of the results of that method. *Every* method of inquiry is justified; disputes can arise only over the question of the purpose and fruitfulness of a given method, which is a question our problem does not involve. We may apply any method we choose; we cannot, however, interpret the obtained sentences as we choose. The meaning of a sentence, no matter how obtained, can unequivocally be determined by a logical analysis of the way in which it is derived and tested. A psychologist who adopts the method of what is called "introspection" does not thereby expose himself to criticism. Such a psychologist admits sentences of the form "I have experienced such and such events of consciousness" into his experiment-protocol and then arrives at general conclusions of his own by means of inductive generalization, the construction of hypotheses, and, finally, a comparison of his hypotheses with the conclusions of other persons. But again we must conclude, both on logical and epistemological grounds, that the singular as well as the general sentences must be interpreted physically. Let us say that psychologist A writes sentence p_2: "(I am) now excited" into his protocol. An earlier investigation[6] has shown that the view which holds that protocol sentences cannot be physically interpreted, that, on the contrary, they refer to something non-physical (something "psychical," some "experience-content," some "datum of consciousness," etc.) leads directly to the consequence that every protocol sentence is meaningful only to its author. If A's protocol sentence p_2 were not subject to a

---

6. *Erkenntnis,* Vol. II, p. 454, (*The Unity of Science,* pp. 78-79).

THE PHYSICALISTIC INTERPRETATION OF PSYCHOLOGICAL SENTENCES

	1. Sentence about the Wooden Support (As an Analogy)	2. Sentence about the State of Someone Else's Mind	3. Sentence about the State of One's Own Mind at Some Time in the Past	4. Sentence about the Present State of One's Own Mind
System sentence P_1: a) *rationally* derived from protocol sentence p_1:	"The support is firm"	"A is excited"	"I was excited yesterday"	"I am now excited"
or b) *intuitively* derived from protocol sentence p_2:	"The support has such and such a color and shape"	"A has such and such an expression"	"These letters (written by me yesterday) have such and such a shape"	"My hands are now trembling"
	"The support looks firm"	"A is excited (A looks excited)"	"Now a recollection of excitement"	"Now a recollection of 'Now excited'"
P_1 has the same content as the *physical sentence* P_2:	"The support is physically firm"	"A's body is physically excited"	"My body was physically excited yesterday."	"My body is now physically excited"
The physical term: is hereby defined as a disposition to react under certain circumstances in a specified way:	"physically firm"	"physically excited"	"physically excited"	
	"Under such and such a load, such and such a distortion occurs; under such and such a load, breakage occurs"	"Under such and such circumstances, such and such gestures, expressions, actions, and words occur."		

physical interpretation, it could not be tested by B, and would, thus, be meaningless to B. On the previous occasion in question we showed, further, that the non-physical interpretation leads one into insoluble contradictions. Finally, we found that every protocol sentence has the same content as some physical sentence,[7] and that this physical translation does not presuppose an accurate knowledge of the physiology of the central nervous system, but is feasible even at present. Sentences about one's own mind—whether one takes these to be inter-subjective system sentences or so-called introspective protocol sentences—are thus in every case translatable into sentences of the physical language.

One may perhaps object that there is, after all, a difference between an experience and an utterance about it, and that not every experience has to be expressed in a protocol sentence. The difference referred to certainly exists, though we would formulate it differently. Sentences P_1: "A now sees red" and P_2: "A now says 'I see red'" do not have exactly the same content. Nor does P_1 justify the inference of P_2; only the conditional sentence "If this and that occurs, then P_2" may be inferred. For P_1 ascribes a physical state to A of such a kind that, under certain circumstances, it leads to the event of speaking the sentence referred to in P_2.

If we consider the method in accordance with which the conclusions of so-called introspection are generally integrated with the body of scientific knowledge, we shall note that these conclusions are, indeed, physically evaluated. It so happens that the physicalism adopted in practice is generally not acknowledged in theory. Psychologist A announces his experimental results; reader B reads in them, among others, the sentence "A was excited" (for the sake of clarity we write "A" instead of the word "I" which B in reading must replace by "A"). For B, this is a sentence about someone else's mind; nothing of its claim can be verified except that A's body *was* in such and such a physical condition at the time referred to. (We argued this point in our analysis of sentence P_1 about someone else's mind.) B himself could not, indeed, have observed this condition, but he can now indirectly infer its having existed. For, to begin with, he sees the sentence in question in a book on whose title-page A is identified as the author. Now, on the basis of a general sentence for which he has already obtained indirect evidence, B infers (with some degree of probability) that A wrote the sentences printed in this book; from this, in its turn, on the basis of

---

7. *Ibid.*, pp. 457 ff., (*The Unity of Science*, pp. 84 ff.).

a general sentence, with regard to A's reliability, for which he again has good inductive evidence, B infers that, had he observed A's body at the relevant time he would (probably) have been able to confirm the existence of the state of (physical) excitement. Since this confirmation can refer only to some physical state of A's body, the sentence in question can have only a physical meaning for B.

Generally speaking, a psychologist's spoken, written, or printed protocol sentences, when they are based on so-called introspection, are to be interpreted by the reader, and so figure in inter-subjective science, *not chiefly as scientific sentences, but as scientific facts.* The epistemological confusion of contemporary psychology stems, to a large extent, from this confusion of facts in the form of sentences with the sentences themselves considered as parts of science. (Our example of the patterns in the sky is relevant here.) The introspective statements of a psychologist are not, in principle, to be interpreted any differently from the statements of his experimental subjects, which he happens to be reporting. The only distinction the psychologist enjoys is that, when the circumstances justify it, one may accept his statements as those of an exceptionally reliable and well-trained experimental subject. Further, the statements of an experimental subject are not, in principle, to be interpreted differently from his other voluntary or involuntary movements—though his speech movements may, under favorable circumstances, be regarded as especially informative. Again, the movements of the speech organs and of the other parts of the body of an experimental subject are not, in principle, to be interpreted differently from the movements of any other animal—though the former may, under favorable circumstances, be more valuable in the construction of general sentences. The movements of an animal are not, again, in principle, to be interpreted any differently from those of a volt-meter—though under favorable circumstances, animal movements may serve scientific purposes in more ways than do the movements of a volt-meter. Finally, the movements of a volt-meter are not, in principle, to be interpreted differently from the movements of a raindrop—though the former offer more opportunities for drawing inferences to other occurrences than do the latter. In all these cases, the issue is basically the same: from a specific physical sentence, other sentences are inferred by a causal argument, i.e. with the help of general physical formulae—the so-called natural laws. The examples cited differ only in the degree of fruitfulness of their premises. Volt-meter readings will, perhaps, justify the inference of a greater number of scientifically important sentences than the behavior of some specific raindrop will; speech movements will, in a certain respect, justify more such inferences than other human bodily movements will. Now, in the case with which we are concerned here, the inference from the sign to the state of affairs signified has a quite remarkable form. In using someone's introspective statement about the state of his own mind (e.g. A's statement: "A is excited"), the statement, taken as an acoustic event, is the sign; under favorable conditions, which are frequently satisfied in scientific contexts, the state of affairs referred to is such that it can be described by a sentence ("A is excited") of the very same form as the acoustic event which functions as a sign of it. [The requisite conditions are that the person in question be considered reliable and qualified to make psychological reports, and further that the language of these reports be the same as that of the scientific system.] This identity of the form of the acoustic fact and the scientific sentence which is to be inferred from it explains why the two are so easily and so obstinately confused. The disastrous muddle into which this confusion leads us is cleared up as soon as we realize that here, as in the other cases cited, it is only a question of drawing an inference from a sign to that which it indicates.

It becomes all the more clear that so-called introspective statements cannot be given a non-physical interpretation when we consider how their use is learned. A tired child says "Now I am happy to be in bed." If we investigated how the child learned to talk about the states of his own mind we would discover that, under similar circumstances, his mother had said to him, "Now you are happy to be in bed." Thus we see that A learns to use the protocol sentence p_2 from B—who, however, interprets this series of words as constituting the system sentence P_2, a sentence, for B, about someone else's mind. Learning to talk consists of B's inducing a certain habit in A, a habit of "verbalizing" (as the behaviorists put it) in a specific manner in specific circumstances. And, indeed one tends so to direct this habit that the series of words produced by the speech movements of the child A coincides with the sentence of the intersubjective physical language which not only describes the appropriate state of A, but—and this is the essential point—describes A's state *as B perceives it,* that is, the physical state of A's body. The example of the child shows this especially clearly. The sentence, "You are happy," spoken by the mother, is a sentence about someone else's mind, and thus, according to our earlier analysis, can designate nothing but some physical state of affairs. The child is thus induced to develop the habit of responding to specific circumstances by uttering a sentence which expresses a physical state observed by some other person (or inferred by some other person from observed signs). If the child utters the same sounds again on some other occasion, no more can be inferred than that the child's body is again in that physical state.

8. Summary

So-called psychological sentences—whether they are concrete sentences about other minds, or about some past condition of one's own mind, or about the present condition of one's own mind, or, finally, general sentences—are always translatable into physical language. Specifically, every psychological sentence refers to physical occurrences in the body of the person (or persons) in question. On these grounds, psychology is a part of the domain of unified science based on physics. By "physics" we wish to mean, not the system of currently known physical laws, but rather the science characterized by a mode of concept formation which traces every concept back to state-coordinates, that is, to systematic assignments of numbers to space-time points. Understanding "physics" in this way, we can rephrase our thesis—a particular thesis of physicalism—as follows: *psychology is a branch of physics.*

REMARKS BY THE AUTHOR (1957)

While I would still maintain the essential content of the main thesis of this article, I would today modify some special points. Perhaps the most important of them is the following. In the article I regarded a psychological term, say "excited," as designating a state characterized by the disposition to react to certain stimuli with overt behavior of certain kinds. This may be admissible for the psychological concepts of everyday language. But at least for those of scientific psychology, as also of other fields of science, it seems to me more in line with the actual procedure of scientists, to introduce them not as disposition concepts, but rather as theoretical concepts (sometimes called "hypothetical constructs"). This means that they are introduced as primitives by the postulates of a theory, and are connected with the terms of the observation language, which designate observable properties, by so-called rules of correspondence. This method is explained and discussed in detail in my article "The Methodological Character of Theoretical Concepts," in H. Feigl and M. Scriven, (eds., *Minnesota Studies in the Philosophy of Science, Vol. I.*

The main thesis of physicalism remains the same as before. It says that psychological statements, both those of everyday life and of scientific psychology, say something about the physical state of the person in question. It is different from the corresponding statements in terms of micro-physiology or micro-physics (which at the present stage of scientific development are not yet known, comp. § 4A above) by using the conceptual framework of psychology instead of those of the two other fields. To find the specific features of the correspondence will be an empirical task (comp. § 6, the third part of the procedure of physicalization). Once known, the correspondence can be expressed by empirical laws or, according to our present view, by theoretical postulates. Our present conception of physicalism, the arguments for it, and the development which led to it, are represented in the following two articles by Herbert Feigl: (1) "Physicalism, Unity of Science and the Foundations of Psychology," in: P. A. Schilpp, editor, *The Philosophy of Rudolf Carnap* (Library of Living Philosophers); see also my reply to Feigl in the same volume; (2) "The 'Mental' and the 'Physical,'" in Vol. II of *Minnesota Studies in Philosophy of Science.*

9

Protocol Sentences

BY OTTO NEURATH

(TRANSLATED BY GEORGE SCHICK)

WITH THE PROGRESS of knowledge, the number of expressions which are formulated with a high degree of precision in the language of Unified Science is continually on the increase. Even so, no such scientific term is wholly precise; for they are all based upon terms which are essential for *protocol sentences;* and it is immediately obvious to everyone that these terms must be vague.

The fiction of an ideal language constructed out of pure atomic sentences is no less metaphysical than the fiction of Laplace's demon. The language of science, with its ever increasing development of symbolic systems, cannot be regarded as an approximation to such an ideal language. The sentence "Otto is observing an angry person" is less precise than the sentence "Otto is observing a thermometer reading 24 degrees," insofar as the expression "angry person" cannot be so exactly defined as "thermometer reading 24 degrees." But "Otto" itself is in many ways a vague term. The phrase "Otto is observing" could be replaced by the phrase "The man, whose carefully taken photograph is listed no. 16 in the file, is observing": but the term "photograph listed no. 16 in the file" still has to be replaced by a system of mathematical formulae, which is unambiguously correlated with another system of mathematical formulae,

This article first appeared in Volume III of *Erkenntnis* (1932/33). It is published here with the kind permission of Mrs. Marie Neurath and Professor Rudolf Carnap. At the beginning of his article Neurath had the following note: "References will be to Rudolf Carnap's article, 'Die Physikalische Sprache als Universalsprache der Wissenschaft,' *Erkenntnis,* 1932, Vol. II, pp. 432ff.* Since there is widespread agreement with Carnap, we shall adopt his terminology. So that I need not repeat what I have already written elsewhere, I refer the reader to my articles 'Physikalismus,' *Scientia,* 1931, pp. 297 ff. and 'Soziologie im Physikalismus,' *Erkenntnis,* Vol. II, 1932, pp. 393 ff."

[* There is an English translation of this article by Max Black under the title "The Unity of Science." It was published as a monograph by Kegan Paul, London.]

the terms of which take the place of "Otto," "angry Otto," "friendly Otto," etc.

What is originally given to us is our *ordinary natural language* with a stock of imprecise, unanalyzed terms. We start by purifying this language of metaphysical elements and so reach the *physicalistic ordinary language*. In accomplishing this we may find it very useful to draw up a list of proscribed words.

There is also the *physicalistic language of advanced science* which we can so construct that it is free from metaphysical elements from the start. We can use this language only for special sciences, indeed only for parts of them.

If one wished to express all of the unified science of our time in one language, one would have to combine terms of ordinary language with terms of the language of advanced science, since, in practice, the two overlap. There are some terms which are used only in ordinary language, others which occur only in the language of advanced science, and still others which appear in both languages. Consequently, in a scientific treatise concerned with the entire field of unified science only a "slang" comprising words of both languages will serve.

We believe that every word of the physicalistic ordinary language will prove to be replaceable by terms taken from the language of advanced science, just as one may also formulate the terms of the language of advanced science with the help of the terms of ordinary language. Only the latter is a very unfamiliar proceeding, and sometimes not easy. Einstein's theories are expressible (somehow) in the language of the Bantus—but not those of Heidegger, unless linguistic abuses to which the German language lends itself are introduced into Bantu. A physicist must, in principle, be able to satisfy the demand of the talented writer who insisted that: "One ought to be able to make the outlines of any rigorously scientific thesis comprehensible in his own terms to a hackney-coach-driver."

The language of advanced science and ordinary language coincide today primarily in the domain of arithmetic. But, in the system of radical physicalism, even the expression "2 times 2 is 4," a *tautology,* is linked to protocol sentences. Tautologies are defined in terms of sentences which state how tautologies function as codicils appended to certain commands under certain circumstances. For instance: "Otto says to Karl 'Go outside when the flag waves *and* when 2 times 2 is four.'" The addition of the tautology here does not alter the effect of the command.

Even considerations of rigorous scientific method restrict us to the use of a *"universal slang."* Since there is as yet no general agreement as to its composition, each scholar who concerns himself with these matters must utilize a universal slang to which he himself has contributed new terms.

There is no way of taking conclusively established pure protocol sentences as the starting point of the sciences. No *tabula rasa* exists. We are like sailors who must rebuild their ship on the open sea, never able to dismantle it in dry-dock and to reconstruct it there out of the best materials. Only the metaphysical elements can be allowed to vanish without trace. Vague linguistic conglomerations always remain in one way or another as components of the ship. If vagueness is diminished at one point, it may well be increased at another.

We shall, from the very first, teach children the universal-slang —purged of all metaphysics—as the language of the historically transmitted unified science. Each child will be so trained that it starts with a simplified universal-slang, and advances gradually to the use of the universal-slang of adults. In this connection, it is meaningless to segregate this children's language from that of the adults. One would, in that case, have to distinguish several universal-slangs. The child does not learn a *primitive* universal-slang from which the universal-slang of the adults derives. He learns a "poorer" universal-slang, which is gradually filled in. The expression "ball of iron" is used in the language of adults as well as in that of children. In the former it is defined by a sentence in which terms such as "radius" and "π" occur, while in the children's definition words such as "nine-pins," "present from Uncle Rudi," etc. are used. But "Uncle Rudi" also crops up in the language of rigorous science, if the physical ball is defined by means of protocol sentences in which "Uncle Rudi" appears as "the observer who perceives a ball."

Carnap, on the other hand, speaks of a *primitive* protocol language.[1] His comments on the primitive protocol language—on the protocol sentences which "require no verification"—are only marginal to his significant anti-metaphysical views, the mainspring of which is not affected by the objections here brought forward. Carnap speaks of a primary language, also referred to as an experiential or as a phenomenalistic language. He maintains that "at the present stage of inquiry, the question of the precise characterization of this language cannot be answered." These comments might induce

1. *Op. cit., Erkenntnis,* Vol. II, pp. 437 ff. and 453 ff. (*Unity of Science,* pp. 42 ff. and 76 ff.).

younger men to search for a protocol language of the sort described: and this might easily lead to metaphysical deviations. Although metaphysical speculation cannot altogether be restrained by argument, it is important, as a means of keeping waverers in line, to maintain physicalism in its most radical version.

Apart from tautologies, unified science consists of factual sentences. These may be sub-divided into

(a) protocol sentences
(b) non-protocol sentences.

Protocol sentences are factual sentences of the same form as the others, except that, in them, a personal noun always occurs several times in a specific association with other terms. A complete protocol sentence might, for instance, read: "Otto's protocol at 3:17 o'clock: [At 3:16 o'clock Otto said to himself: (at 3:15 o'clock there was a table in the room perceived by Otto)]." This factual sentence is so constructed that, within each set of brackets, further factual sentences may be found, viz.: "At 3:16 o'clock Otto said to himself: (At 3:15 o'clock there was a table in the room perceived by Otto)" and "At 3:15 o'clock there was a table in the room perceived by Otto." These sentences are, however, not protocol sentences.

Each term occurring in these sentences may, to some extent, be replaced at the very outset by a group of terms of the language of advanced science. One may introduce a system of physicalistic designations in place of "Otto," and this system of designations may, in turn, further be defined by referring to the "position" of the name "Otto" in a group of signs composed of the names "Karl," "Heinrich," etc. All the words used in the expression of the above protocol sentence are either words of the universal-slang or may without difficulty be replaced at any moment by words of the universal-slang.

For a protocol sentence to be complete it is essential that the name of some person occur in it."Now joy," or "Now red circle," or "A red die is lying on the table" are not complete protocol sentences.[2] They are not even candidates for a position within the innermost set of brackets. For this they would, on our analysis, at least have to read "Otto now joy," or "Otto now sees a red circle," or "Otto now sees a red die lying on the table"—which would roughly correspond to the children's language. That is, in a full protocol sen-

2. Cf. Carnap, op. cit., Erkenntnis, Vol. II, pp. 438 ff. (Unity of Science, pp. 43 ff.).

tence the expression within the innermost set of brackets is a sentence which again features a personal noun and a term from the domain of perception-terms. The relative extent to which terms of ordinary language and of the language of advanced science are used is of no significance, since the universal-slang may be used with considerable flexibility.

The expression "said to himself," after the first bracket, recommends itself when, as above, one wants to construct various groups of sentences, as, for instance, sentences incorporating reality-terms, or hallucination-terms, or dream-terms, and especially when one wants to identify unreality as such. For instance, one could say: "Otto actually said to himself, 'There was nothing in the room but a bird perceived by Otto' but, in order to amuse himself, he wrote, 'There was nothing in the room but a table perceived by Otto.' " This is especially pertinent to the discussion in the next section, in which we reject Carnap's thesis to the effect that protocol sentences are those "which require no verification."

The transformation of the sciences is effected by the discarding of sentences utilized in a previous historical period, and, frequently, their replacement by others. Sometimes the same form of words is retained, but their definitions are changed. *Every law and every physicalistic sentence of unified-science or of one of its sub-sciences is subject to such change. And the same holds for protocol sentences.*

In unified science we try to construct a non-contradictory system of protocol sentences and non-protocol sentences (including laws).[3] When a new sentence is presented to us we compare it with the system at our disposal, and determine whether or not it conflicts with that system. If the sentence does conflict with the system, we may discard it as useless (or false), as, for instance, would be done with "In Africa lions sing only in major scales." One may, on the other hand, *accept* the sentence and so change the system that it remains consistent even after the adjunction of the new sentence. The sentence would then be called "true."

The fate of being discarded may befall even a protocol sentence. No sentence enjoys the *noli me tangere* which Carnap ordains for protocol sentences. Let us consider a particularly drastic example. We assume that we are acquainted with a scholar called "Kalon," who can write with both hands simultaneously. He writes with his left hand, "Kalon's protocol at 3:17 o'clock: [At 16 minutes 30

---

3. Cf. Carnap, *op. cit., Erkenntnis*, Vol. II, pp. 439 ff. (*Unity of Science*, pp. 47 ff.).

seconds past 3 o'clock Kalon said to himself: (There was *nothing* in the room at 3:16 o'clock except a table perceived by Kalon)]." At the same time, with his right hand, he writes, "Kalon's protocol at 3:17 o'clock: [At 16 minutes 30 seconds past 3 o'clock Kalon said to himself: (There was *nothing* in the room at 3:16 o'clock except a bird perceived by Kalon)]." What is he—and what are we—to make of the conjunction of these two sentences? We may, of course, make statements such as "Marks may be found on this sheet of paper, sometimes shaped this way and sometimes that." With respect to these marks on paper, however, Carnap's word "verification" finds no application. "Verification" can only be used with reference to sentences, that is, with reference to sequences of marks which are used in a context of a reaction-test and which may systematically be replaced by other marks.[4] Synonymous sentences may be characterized as stimuli which under specific reaction-tests evoke the same responses. Chains of ink-marks on paper and chains of air-vibrations which may under specific conditions be co-ordinated with one another are called "sentences."

Two conflicting protocol sentences cannot both be used in the system of unified science. Though we may not be able to tell which of the two is to be excluded, or whether both are not to be excluded, it is clear that not both are verifiable, that is, that both do not fit into the system.

If a protocol sentence must in such cases be discarded, may not the same occasionally be called for when the contradiction between protocol sentences on the one hand and a system comprising protocol sentences and non-protocol sentences (laws, etc.) on the other is such that an extended argument is required to disclose it? On Carnap's view, one could be obliged to alter only non-protocol sentences and laws. *We also allow for the possibility of discarding protocol sentences. A defining condition of a sentence is that it be subject to verification, that is to say, that it may be discarded.*

Carnap's contention that protocol sentences do not require verification, however it may be understood, may without difficulty be related to the belief in *immediate experiences* which is current in traditional academic philosophy. According to this philosophy there are, indeed, certain *basic elements* out of which the world-picture is to be constructed. On this academic view, these *atomic experiences* are, of course, above any kind of critical scrutiny; they do not require verification.

Carnap is trying to introduce a kind of *atomic protocol,* with

---

4. Cf. my article in *Scientia,* p. 302.

his demand that "a clear-cut distinction be made in scientific procedure between the adoption of a protocol and the interpretation of the protocol sentences," as a result of which "no indirectly acquired sentences would be accepted into the protocol."[5] The above formulation of a complete protocol sentence shows that, insofar as personal nouns occur in a protocol, interpretation must *always* already have taken place. When preparing scientific protocols, it may be useful to phrase the expression within the innermost set of brackets as simply as possible, as, for instance, "At 3 o'clock Otto was seeing red," or—another protocol—"At 3 o'clock Otto was hearing C sharp," etc. But a protocol of such a sort is not primitive in Carnap's sense, since one cannot, after all, get around Otto's act of perception. There are no sentences in the universal-slang which one may characterize as "more primitive" than any others. All are of equal primitiveness. Personal nouns, words denoting perceptions, and other words of little primitiveness occur in all factual sentences, or, at least, in the hypotheses from which they derive. All of which means that *there are neither primitive protocol sentences nor sentences which are not subject to verification.*

The universal-slang, in the sense explained above, is the same for the child as for the adult. It is the same for a Robinson Crusoe as for a human society. If Crusoe wants to relate what he registered ("protokolliert") yesterday with what he registers today, that is, when he wants to have any sort of recourse to a language, he cannot but have recourse to the inter-subjective language. The Crusoe of yesterday and the Crusoe of today stand to one another in precisely the relation in which Crusoe stands to Friday. Consider a man who has both lost his memory and been blinded, who is now learning afresh to read and to write. The notes which he himself took in the past and which now, with the aid of a special apparatus, he reads again are for him as much the notes of some other man as notes actually written by someone else. And the same would still be the case after he had realized the tragic nature of his circumstances, and had pieced together the story of his life.

In other words, *every* language *as such* is inter-subjective. The protocols of one moment must be subject to incorporation in the protocols of the next, just as the protocols of A must be subject to incorporation in the protocols of B. *It is therefore meaningless to talk, as Carnap does, of a private language,* or of a set of disparate protocol languages which may ultimately be drawn together.

5. *Op. cit.,* p. 437 (*Unity of Science,* p. 42).

The protocol languages of the Crusoe of yesterday and of the Crusoe of today are as close and as far apart from one another as are the protocol languages of Crusoe and of Friday. If, under certain circumstances, the protocol languages of yesterday's Crusoe and of today's are called the *same* language, then one may also, under the same circumstances, call the protocol language of Crusoe and that of Friday the same language.

In Carnap's writings we also encounter an emphasis on the "I" familiar to us from idealistic philosophy. In the universal-slang it is as meaningless to talk of a *personal* protocol as to talk of a *here* or a *now*. In the physicalistic language personal nouns are simply replaced by co-ordinates and coefficients of physical states. One can distinguish an *Otto-protocol* from a *Karl-protocol,* but not a protocol of one's own from a protocol of others. The whole puzzle of *other minds* is thus resolved.

Methodological solipsism and *methodological positivism*[6] do not become any the more serviceable because of the addition of the word "methodological."[7]

For instance, had I said above, "Today, the 27th of July, I examine protocols both of my own and of others," it would have been more correct to have said "Otto Neurath's protocol at 10:00 a.m., July 27, 1932; [At 9:35 o'clock Otto Neurath said to himself: (Otto Neurath occupied himself between 9:40 and 9:57 with a protocol by Neurath and one by Kalon, to both of which the following two sentences belong: . . .)]." Even though Otto Neurath himself formulates the protocol concerning the utilization of these protocols, he does not link his own protocol with the system of unified science in any different way from that in which he links Kalon's. It may well happen that Neurath discards one of Neurath's protocols, and adopts in its stead one of Kalon's. The fact that men generally retain their own protocol sentences more obstinately than they do those of other people is a historical accident which is of no real significance for our purposes. Carnap's contention that "every individual can adopt only his own protocol as an epistemological basis" cannot be accepted, for the argument presented in its favor is *not* sound: "S_1 can, indeed, also utilize the protocol of S_2—and the incorporation of both protocol languages in physicalistic language makes this utilization particularly easy. The utilization is, however, indirect: S_1 must first state in his own protocol that he sees a piece of writing

6. Cf. Carnap, *op. cit., Erkenntnis,* Vol. II, p. 461 (*Unity of Science,* p. 93).
7. Cf. my article in *Erkenntnis,* Vol. II, p. 401. [Translated in the present volume, see p. 282 below.]

of such and such a form."[8] *But Neurath must describe Neurath's protocol in a manner analogous to that in which he describes Kalon's!* He describes how Neurath's protocol looks to him as well as how Kalon's does.

In this way we can go on to deal with everyone's protocol sentences. Basically, it makes no difference at all whether Kalon works with Kalon's or with Neurath's protocols, or whether Neurath occupies himself with Neurath's or with Kalon's protocols. In order to make this quite clear, we could conceive of a sorting-machine into which protocol sentences are thrown. The laws and other factual sentences (including protocol sentences) serving to mesh the machine's gears sort the protocol sentences which are thrown into the machine and cause a bell to ring if a contradiction ensues. At this point one must either replace the protocol sentence whose introduction into the machine has led to the contradiction by some other protocol sentence, or rebuild the entire machine. *Who* rebuilds the machine, or *whose* protocol sentences are thrown into the machine is of no consequence whatsoever. Anyone may test his own protocol sentences as well as those of others.

SUMMING UP:

Unified science utilizes a universal-slang, in which terms of the physicalistic ordinary language necessarily also occur.

Children can be trained to use the universal-slang. Apart from it we do not employ any specially distinguishable "basic" protocol sentences, nor do different people make use of different protocol languages.

We find no use in unified science for the expressions "methodological solipsism" and "methodological positivism."

One cannot start with conclusively established, pure protocol sentences. Protocol sentences are factual sentences like the others, containing names of persons or names of groups of people linked in specific ways with other terms, which are themselves also taken from the universal-slang.

The Vienna Circle devotes itself more and more to the task of expressing unified science (which includes sociology as well as chemistry, biology as well as mechanics, psychology—more properly termed "behavioristics"—as well as optics) in a unified language, and with the displaying of the inter-connections of the various sciences which are so often neglected; so that one may without

---

8. Cf. Carnap, *op. cit., Erkenntnis*, Vol. II, p. 461 (*The Unity of Science*, p. 93).

difficulty relate the terms of any science to those of any other. The word "man" which is prefixed to "makes assertions" is to be defined in just the same way as the word "man" occurring in sentences which contain the words "economic system" and "production."

The Vienna Circle has received powerful encouragement from various sources. The achievements of Mach, Poincaré, and Duhem have been turned to as good account as the contributions of Frege, Schröder, and Russell. Wittgenstein's writings have been extraordinarily stimulating, both through what has been taken from them and through what has been rejected. His original plan—to use philosophy as a ladder which it is necessary to climb in order to see things clearly —may, however, be considered to have come to grief. The main issue in this, as in all other intellectual activities, will always be to bring the sentences of unified science—both protocol sentences and non-protocol sentences—into consonance with one another. For this, a *logical syntax* of the sort toward which Carnap is working is required—Carnap's *logical reconstruction of the world* being the first step in this direction.

The discussion I have initiated here—for Carnap will certainly find much in the corrections to correct again and to develop—serves, as do so many of our other efforts, to secure ever more firmly the common, broad foundations on which all the adherents of physicalism base their studies. Discussions of peripheral issues, such as this one, are, however, going to play a continuously diminishing role. The rapid progress of the work of the Vienna Circle shows that the planned co-operative project dedicated to the construction of unified science is in constant development. The less time we find it necessary to devote to the elimination of ancient confusions and the more we can occupy ourselves with the formulation of the inter-connections of the sciences, the quicker and more successful will this construction be. To this end it is of the first importance that we learn how to use the physicalistic language, on behalf of which Carnap, in his article, entered the lists.

10

The Foundation of Knowledge

BY MORITZ SCHLICK

(TRANSLATED BY DAVID RYNIN)

ALL IMPORTANT ATTEMPTS at establishing a theory of knowledge grow out of the problem concerning the certainty of human knowledge. And this problem in turn originates in the wish for absolute certainty.

The insight that the statements of daily life and science can at best be only probable, that even the most general results of science, which all experiences confirm, can have only the character of hypotheses, has again and again stimulated philosophers since Descartes, and indeed, though less obviously, since ancient times, to search for an unshakeable, indubitable, foundation, a firm basis on which the uncertain structure of our knowledge could rest. The uncertainty of the structure was generally attributed to the fact that it was impossible, perhaps in principle, to construct a firmer one by the power of human thought. But this did not inhibit the search for the bedrock, which exists prior to all construction and does not itself vacillate.

This search is a praiseworthy, healthy effort, and it is prevalent even among "relativists" and "sceptics, who would rather not acknowledge it." It appears in different forms and leads to odd differences of opinion. The problem of "protocol statements," their structure and function, is the latest form in which the philosophy or rather the decisive empiricism of our day clothes the problem of the ultimate ground of knowledge.

What was originally meant by "protocol statements," as the name indicates, are those statements which express the *facts* with absolute simplicity, without any moulding, alteration or addition, in whose elaboration every science consists, and which precede all know-

This article, originally entitled "Über das Fundament der Erkenntnis," first appeared in *Erkenntnis,* Vol. IV (1934). It is published here with the kind permission of Mrs. Schlick and Professor Carnap.

ing, every judgment regarding the world. It makes no sense to speak of uncertain facts. Only assertions, only our knowledge can be uncertain. If we succeed therefore in expressing the raw facts in "protocol statements," without any contamination, these appear to be the absolutely indubitable starting points of all knowledge. They are, to be sure, again abandoned the moment one goes over to statements which are actually of use in life or science (such a transition appears to be that from "singular" to "universal" statements), but they constitute nevertheless the firm basis to which all our cognitions owe whatever validity they may possess.

Moreover, it makes no difference whether or not these so-called protocol statements have ever actually been made, that is, actually uttered, written down or even only explicitly "thought"; it is required only that one know what statements form the basis for the notations which are actually made, and that these statements be at all times reconstructible. If for example an investigator makes a note, "Under such and such conditions the pointer stands at 10.5," he knows that this means "two black lines coincide," and that the words "under such and such conditions" (which we here imagine to be specified) are likewise to be resolved into definite protocol statements which, if he wished, he could in principle formulate exactly, although perhaps with difficulty.

It is clear, and is so far as I know disputed by no one, that knowledge in life and science in *some* sense *begins* with confirmation of facts, and that the "protocol statements" in which this occurs stand in the same sense at the *beginning* of science. What is this sense? Is "beginning" to be understood in the temporal or logical sense?

Here we already find much confusion and oscillation. If I said above that it is not important whether the decisive statements have been actually made or uttered, this means evidently that they need not stand at the beginning *temporally,* but can be arrived at later just as well if need be. The necessity for formulating them would arise when one wished to make clear to oneself the meaning of the statement that one had actually written down. Is the reference to protocol statements then to be understood in the *logical* sense? In that event they would be distinguished by definite logical properties, by their structure, their position in the system of science, and one would be confronted with the task of actually specifying these properties. In fact, this is the form in which, for example, Carnap used explicitly to put the question of protocol statements, while later[1] declaring it to be a question which is to be settled by an arbitrary decision.

1. See Carnap, "Über Protokollsätze," *Erkenntnis,* Vol. III, pp. 216 ff.

On the other hand, we find many expositions which seem to presuppose that by "protocol statements" only those assertions are to be understood that also temporally precede the other assertions of science. And is this not correct? One must bear in mind that it is a matter of the ultimate basis of knowledge of *reality,* and that it is not sufficient for this to treat statements as, so to speak, "ideal constructions" (as one used to say in Platonic fashion), but rather that one must concern oneself with real occurrences, with events that take place in time, in which the making of judgments consists, hence with psychic acts of "thought," or physical acts of "speaking" or "writing." Since psychic acts of judgment seem suitable for establishing inter-subjectively valid knowledge only when translated into verbal or written expressions (that is, into a physical system of symbols) "protocol statements" come to be regarded as certain spoken, written or printed sentences, i.e., certain symbol-complexes of sounds or printer's ink, which when translated from the common abbreviations into full-fledged speech, would mean something like: "Mr. N. N. at such and such a time observed so and so at such and such a place." (This view was adopted particularly by O. Neurath).[2] As a matter of fact, when we retrace the path by which we actually arrive at all our knowledge, we doubtless always come up against this same source: printed sentences in books, words out of the mouth of a teacher, our own observations (in the latter case we are ourselves N. N.).

On this view protocol statements would be real happenings in the world and would temporally precede the other real processes in which the "construction of science," or indeed the production of an individual's knowledge consists.

I do not know to what extent the distinction made here between the logical and temporal priority of protocol statements corresponds to differences in the views actually held by certain authors—but that is not important. For we are not concerned to determine who expressed the correct view, but what the correct view *is.* And for this our distinction between the two points of view will serve well enough.

As a matter of fact, these two views are compatible. For the statements that register simple data of observation and stand temporally at the beginning could at the same time be those that by virtue of their structure would have to constitute the logical starting-point of science.

---

2. Neurath, "Protokollsätze," *Erkenntnis,* Vol. III, pp. 104 ff. (This article is translated in the present volume, see pp. 199-208 above.)

II

The question which will first interest us is this: What progress is achieved by formulating the problem of the ultimate basis of knowledge in terms of protocol statements? The answer to this question will itself pave the way to a solution of the problem.

I think it a great improvement in method to try to aim at the basis of knowledge by looking not for the primary *facts* but for the primary *sentences*. But I also think that this advantage was not made the most of, perhaps because of a failure to realize that what was at issue, fundamentally, was just the old problem of the basis. I believe, in fact, that the position to which the consideration of protocol statements has led is not tenable. It results in a peculiar relativism, which appears to be a necessary consequence of the view that protocol statements are empirical facts upon which the edifice of science is subsequently built.

That is to say: when protocol statements are conceived in this manner, then directly one raises the question of the certainty with which one may assert their truth, one must grant that they are exposed to all possible doubts.

There appears in a book a sentence which says, for example, that N. N. used such and such an instrument to make such and such an observation. One may under certain circumstances have the greatest confidence in this sentence. Nevertheless, it and the observation it records, can never be considered *absolutely* certain. For the possibilities of error are innumerable. N. N. can inadvertently or intentionally have described something that does not accurately represent the observed fact; in writing it down or printing it, an error may have crept in. Indeed the assumption that the symbols of a book retain their form even for an instant and do not "of themselves" change into new sentences is an empirical hypothesis, which as such can never be strictly verified. For every verification would rest on assumptions of the same sort and on the presupposition that our memory does not deceive us at least during a brief interval, and so on.

This means, of course—and some of our authors have pointed this out almost with a note of triumph—that protocol statements, so conceived, have in principle exactly the same character as all the other statements of science: they are hypotheses, nothing but hypotheses. They are anything but incontrovertible, and one can use them in the construction of the system of science only so long as they are supported by, or at least not contradicted by, other hypotheses. We therefore always reserve the right to make protocol statements subject to correction, and such corrections, quite often indeed, do occur when we eliminate certain protocol statements and declare that they must have been the result of some error.

Even in the case of statements which we ourselves have put forward we do not in principle exclude the possibility of error. We grant that our mind at the moment the judgment was made may have been wholly confused, and that an experience which we now say we had two minutes ago may upon later examination be found to have been an hallucination, or even one that never took place at all.

Thus it is clear that on this view of protocol statements they do not provide one who is in search of a firm basis of knowledge with anything of the sort. On the contrary, the actual result is that one ends by abandoning the original distinction between protocol and other statements as meaningless. Thus we come to understand how people come to think[3] that any statements of science can be selected at will and called "protocol statements," and that it is simply a question of convenience which are chosen.

But can we admit this? Are there really only reasons of convenience? It is not rather a matter of where the particular statements come from, what is their origin, their history? In general, what is meant here by convenience? What is the end that one pursues in making and selecting statements?

The end can be no other than that of science itself, namely, that of affording a *true* description of the facts. For us it is self-evident that the problem of the basis of knowledge is nothing other than the question of the criterion of truth. Surely the reason for bringing in the term "protocol statement" in the first place was that it should serve to mark out certain statements by the truth of which the truth of all other statements comes to be measured, as by a measuring rod. But according to the viewpoint just described this measuring rod would have shown itself to be as relative as, say, all the measuring rods of physics. And it is this view with its consequences that has been commended as the banishing of the last remnant of "absolutism" from philosophy.[4]

But what then remains at all as a criterion of truth? Since the proposal is not that all scientific assertions must accord with certain definite protocol statements, but rather that all statements shall accord with one another, with the result that every single one is consid-

---

3. K. Popper as quoted by Carnap, *op. cit., Erkenntnis*, Vol. III, p. 223.
4. Carnap, *op. cit.*, p. 228.

ered as, in principle, corrigible, truth can consist only in a *mutual agreement of statements*.

III

This view, which has been expressly formulated and represented in this context, for example, by Neurath, is well known from the history of recent philosophy. In England it is usually called the "coherence theory of truth," and contrasted with the older "correspondence theory." It is to be observed that the expression "theory" is quite inappropriate. For observations on the nature of truth have a quite different character from scientific theories, which always consist of a system of hypotheses.

The contrast between the two views is generally expressed as follows: according to the traditional one, the truth of a statement consists in its agreement with the facts, while according to the other, the coherence theory, it consists in its agreement with the system of other statements.

I shall not in general pursue the question here whether the latter view can not also be interpreted in a way that draws attention to something quite correct (namely, to the fact that in a quite definite sense we cannot "go beyond language" as Wittgenstein puts it). I have here rather to show that, on the interpretation required in the present context, it is quite untenable.

If the truth of a statement is to consist in its coherence or agreement with the other statements, one must be clear as to what one understands by "agreement," and *which* statements are meant by "other."

The first point can be settled easily. Since it cannot be meant that the statement to be tested asserts the same thing as the others, it remains only that they must be *compatible* with it, that is, that no contradictions exist between them. Truth would consist simply in absence of contradiction. But on the question whether truth can be identified simply with the absence of contradiction, there ought to be no further discussion. It should long since have been generally acknowledged that only in the case of statements of a tautological nature are truth (if one will apply this term at all) and absence of contradiction to be equated, as for instance with the statements of pure geometry. But with such statements every connection with reality is purposely dissolved; they are only formulas within a determinate calculus; it makes no sense in the case of the statements of *pure* geometry to ask whether they agree with the facts of the world: they need only be compatible with the axioms arbitrarily laid down at the beginning (in addition, it is usually also required that they follow from them) in order to be called true or correct. We have before us precisely what was earlier called *formal* truth and distinguished from *material* truth.

The latter is the truth of synthetic statements, assertions of matters of fact, and if one wishes to describe them by help of the concept of absence of contradiction, of agreement with other statements, one can do so only if one says that they may not contradict *very special* statements, namely just those that express "facts of immediate observation." The criterion of truth cannot be compatibility with any statements whatever, but agreement is required with certain exceptional statements which are not chosen arbitrarily at all. In other words, the criterion of absence of contradiction does not by itself suffice for material truth. It is, rather, entirely a matter of compatibility with very special peculiar statements. And for this compatibility there is no reason not to use—indeed I consider there is every justification for using—the good old expression "agreement with reality."

The astounding error of the "coherence theory" can be explained only by the fact that its defenders and expositors were thinking only of such statements as actually occur in science, and took them as their only examples. Under these conditions the relation of non-contradiction was in fact sufficient, but only because these statements are of a very special character. They have, that is, in a certain sense (to be explained presently) their "origin" in observation statements, they derive, as one may confidently say in the traditional way of speaking, "from experience."

If one is to take coherence seriously as a general criterion of truth, then one must consider arbitrary fairy stories to be as true as a historical report, or as statements in a textbook of chemistry, provided the story is constructed in such a way that no contradiction ever arises. I can depict by help of fantasy a grotesque world full of bizarre adventures: the coherence philosopher must believe in the truth of my account provided only I take care of the mutual compatibility of my statements, and also take the precaution of avoiding any collision with the usual description of the world, by placing the scene of my story on a distant star, where no observation is possible. Indeed, strictly speaking, I don't even require this precaution; I can just as well demand that the others have to adapt themselves to my description; and not the other way round. They cannot then object that, say, this happening runs counter to the observations, for according

to the coherence theory there is no question of observations, but only
of the compatibility of statements.

Since no one dreams of holding the statements of a story book
true and those of a text of physics false, the coherence view fails
utterly. Something more, that is, must be added to coherence, namely,
a principle in terms of which the compatibility is to be established,
and this would alone then be the actual criterion.

If I am given a set of statements, among which are found some
that contradict each other, I can establish consistency in a number of
ways, by, for example, on one occasion selecting certain statements
and abandoning or altering them and on another occasion doing
the same with the other statements that contradict the first.

Thus the coherence theory is shown to be logically impossible;
it fails altogether to give an unambiguous criterion of truth, for by
means of it I can arrive at any number of consistent systems of statements which are incompatible with one another.

The only way to avoid this absurdity is not to allow any statements whatever to be abandoned or altered, but rather to specify
those that are to be maintained, to which the remainder have to be
accommodated.

IV

The coherence theory is thus disposed of, and we have in the
meantime arrived at the second point of our critical considerations,
namely, at the question whether *all* statements are corrigible, or
whether there are also those that cannot be shaken. These latter
would of course constitute the "basis" of all knowledge which we
have been seeking, without so far being able to take any step towards it.

By what mark, then, are we to distinguish these statements
which themselves remain unaltered, while all others must be brought
into agreement with them? We shall in what follows call them not
"protocol statements," but "basic statements" for it is quite dubious
whether they occur at all among the protocols of science.

The most obvious recourse would doubtless be to find the rule
for which we are searching in some kind of economy principle,
namely, to say: we are to choose those as basic statements whose
retention requires a *minimum* of alteration in the whole system of
statements in order to rid it of all contradictions.

It is worth noticing that such an economy principle would not
enable us to pick out certain statements as being basic once and
for all, for it might happen that with the progress of science the

basic statements that served as such up to a given moment would be again degraded, if it appeared more economical to abandon them in favor of newly found statements which from that time on— until further notice—would play the basic role. This would, of course, no longer be the pure coherence viewpoint, but one based on economy; "relativity," however, would characterize it also.

There seems to me no question but that the representatives of the view we have been criticizing did in fact take the economy principle as their guiding light, whether explicitly or implicitly; I have therefore already assumed above that on the relativity view there are purposive grounds which determine the selection of protocol statements, and I asked: Can we admit this?

I now answer this question in the negative. It is in fact not economic purposiveness but quite other characteristics which distinguish the genuine basic statements.

The procedure for choosing these statements would be called economic if it consisted say in conforming to the opinions (or "protocol statements") of the majority of investigators. Now it is of course the case that we do not doubt the existence of a fact, for example a fact of geography or history, or even of a natural law, when we find that in the relevant contexts its existence is very frequently reported. It does not occur to us in those cases to wish to investigate the matter ourselves. We acquiesce in what is universally acknowledged. But this is explained by the fact that we have precise knowledge of the manner in which such factual statements tend to be made, and that this manner wins our confidence; it is not that it agrees with the view of the majority. Quite the contrary, it could only arrive at universal acceptance because everyone feels the same confidence. Whether and to what extent we hold a statement to be corrigible or annulable depends solely on its *origin,* and (apart from very special cases) not at all upon whether maintaining it requires the correction of very many other statements and perhaps a reorganization of the whole system of knowledge.

Before one can apply the principle of economy one must know to *which* statements it is to be applied. And if the principle were the *only* decisive rule the answer could only be: to *all* that are asserted with any claim to validity or have ever been so asserted. Indeed, the phrase "with any claim to validity" should be omitted, for how should we distinguish such statements from those which were asserted quite arbitrarily, as jokes or with intent to deceive? This distinction cannot even be formulated without taking into consideration *the derivation* of the statements. So we find ourselves once more referred to the question of their origin. Without having classified statements according to their origin, any application of the economy principle of agreement would be quite absurd. But once one has examined the statements with respect to their origin it becomes immediately obvious that one has thereby already ordered them in terms of their validity, and that there is no place left for the application of the principle of economy (apart from certain very special cases in still unfinished areas of science). We can see also that the establishment of this order points the way to the basis of which we are in search.

V

Here of course the greatest care is necessary. For we are treading on the path which has been followed from ancient times by all those who have ever embarked upon the journey towards the ultimate grounds of truth. And always they have failed to reach the goal. In the ordering of statements according to their origin which I undertake for the purpose of judging their certainty, I start by assigning a special place to those that I make *myself*. And here a secondary position is occupied by those that lie in the past, for we believe that their certainty can be impaired by "errors of memory"—and indeed in general the more so the farther back in time they lie. On the other hand, the statements which stand at the top, free from all doubt, are those that express facts of one's own "perception," or whatever you like to call it. But in spite of the fact that statements of this sort seem so simple and clear, philosophers have found themselves in a hopeless labyrinth the moment they actually attempted to use them as the foundation of all knowledge. Some puzzling sections of this labyrinth are for example those formulations and deductions that have occupied the center of so many philosophical disputes under the heading "evidence of inner perception," "solipsism," "solipsism of the present moment," "self-conscious certainty," etc. The Cartesian *cogito ergo sum* is the best-known of the destinations to which this path has led—a terminating point to which indeed Augustine had already pushed through. And concerning *cogito ergo sum* our eyes have today been sufficiently opened: we know that it is a mere pseudo-statement, which does not become genuine by being expressed in the form *"cogitatio est"*—"the contents of consciousness exist."[5] Such a statement, which does not express anything itself, cannot in any sense serve as the basis of anything.

---

5. Cf. "Positivismus und Realismus," *Erkenntnis,* Vol. III, p. 20 (see the present volume, p. 82 above).

It is not itself a cognition, and none rests upon it. It cannot lend certainty to any cognition.

There exists therefore the greatest danger that in following the path recommended one will arrive at empty verbiage instead of the basis one seeks. The critical theory of protocol statements originated indeed in the wish to avoid this danger. But the way out proposed by it is unsatisfactory. Its *essential* deficiency lies in ignoring the different rank of statements, which expresses itself most clearly in the fact that for the system of science which one takes to be the "right" one, one's *own* statements in the end play the only decisive role.

It would be theoretically conceivable that my own observations in no way substantiate the assertions made about the world by other men. It might be that all the books that I read, all the teachers that I hear are in perfect agreement among themselves, that they never contradict one another, but that they are simply incompatible with a large part of my own observation statements. (Certain difficulties would in this case accompany the problem of learning the language and its use in communication, but they can be removed by means of certain assumptions concerning the place in which the contradictions are to appear.) According to the view we have been criticizing I would in such a case simply have to sacrifice my own "protocol statements," for they would be opposed by the overwhelming mass of other statements which would be in mutual agreement themselves, and it would be impossible to expect that these should be corrected in accordance with my own limited fragmentary experience.

But what would actually happen in such a case? Well, under no circumstances would I abandon my own observation statements. On the contrary, I find that I can accept only a system of knowledge into which they fit unmutilated. And I can always construct such a system. I need only view the others as dreaming fools, in whose madness lies a remarkable method, or—to express it more objectively—I would say that the others live in a different world from mine, which has just so much in common with mine as to make it possible to achieve understanding by means of the same language. In any case no matter what world picture I construct, I would test its truth always in terms of my own experience. I would never permit anyone to take this support from me: my own observation statements would always be the ultimate criterion. I should, so to speak, exclaim "What I see, I see!"

VI

In the light of these preliminary critical remarks, it is clear where we have to look for the solution of these confusing difficulties: we must use the Cartesian road in so far as it is good and passable, but then be careful to avoid falling into the *cogito ergo sum* and related nonsense. We effect this by making clear to ourselves the role which really belongs to the statements expressing "the immediately observed."

What actually lies behind one's saying that they are "absolutely certain"? And in what sense may one describe them as the ultimate ground of all knowledge?

Let us consider the second question first. If we imagine that I at once recorded every observation—and it is in principle indifferent whether this is done on paper or in memory—and then began from that point the construction of science, I should have before me genuine "protocol statements" which stood temporally at the beginning of knowledge. From them would gradually arise the rest of the statements of science, by means of the process called "induction," which consists in nothing else than that I am stimulated or induced by the protocol statements to establish tentative generalizations (hypotheses), from which those first statements, but also an endless number of others, follow logically. If now these others express *the same* as is expressed by later observation statements that are obtained under quite definite conditions which are exactly specifiable beforehand, then the hypotheses are considered to be confirmed so long as no observation statements appear that stand in contradiction to the statements derived from the hypotheses and thus to the hypotheses themselves. So long as this does not occur we believe ourselves to have hit correctly upon a law of nature. Induction is thus nothing but methodically conducted guessing, a psychological, biological process whose conduct has certainly nothing to do with "logic."

In this way the actual procedure of science is described schematically. It is evident what role is played in it by the statements concerning what is "immediately perceived." They are not identical with those written down or memorized, with what can correctly be called "protocol statements," but they are the *occasions* of their formation. The protocol statements observed in a book or memory are, as we acknowledged long ago, so far as their validity goes, doubtless to be compared to hypotheses. For, when we have such a statement before us, it is a mere assumption that it is true, that it agrees with the observation statements that give rise to it. (Indeed it may have been occasioned by no observation statements, but derived from some game or other.) What I call an observation statement cannot be identical with a genuine protocol statement, if only because in a certain sense it cannot be written down at all—a point which we shall presently discuss.

Thus in the schema of the building up of knowledge that I have described, the part played by observation statements is first that of standing temporally at the beginning of the whole process, stimulating it and setting it going. How much of their content enters into knowledge remains in principle at first undetermined. One can thus with some justice see in the observation statements the ultimate origin of all knowledge. But should they be described as the basis, as the ultimate certain ground? This can hardly be maintained, for this "origin" stands in a too questionable relation to the edifice of knowledge. But in addition we have conceived of the true process as schematically simplified. In reality what is actually expressed in protocols stands in a less close connection with the observed, and in general one ought not to assume that any pure observation statements ever slip in between the observation and the "protocol."

But now a second function appears to belong to these statements about the immediately perceived, these "confirmations"* as we may also call them, namely, the corroboration of hypotheses, their *verification*.

Science makes prophecies that are tested by "experience." Its essential function consists in making predictions. It says, for example: "If at such and such a time you look through a telescope adjusted in such and such a manner you will see a point of light (a star) in coincidence with a black mark (cross wires)." Let us assume that in following out these instructions the predicted experience actually occurs. This means that we make an anticipated

---

* The term used by the author is "Konstatierung" which he sometimes equates with "observation statement" i.e., "Beobachtungssatz," and generally tends to quote, in a manner indicating his awareness that it is a somewhat unusual usage and perhaps a not altogether adequate technical term. Wilfred Sellars in a recently published essay ("Empiricism and the Philosophy of Mind," *Minnesota Studies in the Philosophy of Science*, Volume I, University of Minnesota Press, 1956) uses the term "report" in referring to what seems to be the kind of statement Schlick is discussing. I do not adopt this term, despite some undoubted advantages it has over "confirmation," because of the close connection that "Konstatierung" has with confirmation or verification, a connection so close that Schlick uses the same term unquoted to refer to confirmation. Furthermore, as the text shows, confirmations are never false, as Schlick understands them; but this is certainly not a characteristic of reports, as the term "report" is used in everyday or even scientific language. (Translator's note.)

confirmation, we pronounce an expected judgment of observation, we obtain thereby a feeling of *fulfilment,* a quite characteristic satisfaction: we are *satisfied*. One is fully justified in saying that the confirmation or observation statements have fulfilled their true mission as soon as we obtain this peculiar satisfaction.

And it is obtained in the very moment in which the confirmation takes place, in which the observation statement is made. This is of the utmost importance. For thus the function of the statements about the immediately experienced itself lies in the immediate present. Indeed we saw that they have so to speak no duration, that the moment they are gone one has at one's disposal in their place inscriptions, or memory traces, that can play only the role of hypotheses and thereby lack ultimate certainty. One cannot build any logically tenable structure upon the confirmations, for they are gone the moment one begins to construct. If they stand at the beginning of the process of cognition they are logically of no use. Quite otherwise however if they stand at the end; they bring verification (or also falsification) to completion, and in the moment of their occurrence they have already fulfilled their duty. Logically nothing more depends on them, no conclusions are drawn from them. They constitute an absolute end.

Of course, psychologically and biologically a new process of cognition begins with the satisfaction they create: the hypotheses whose verification ends in them are considered to be upheld, and the formulation of more general hypotheses is sought, the guessing and search for universal laws goes on. The observation statements constitute the origin and stimuli for these events that follow in time, in the sense described earlier.

It seems to me that by means of these considerations a new and clear light is cast upon the problem of the ultimate basis of knowledge, and we see clearly how the construction of the system of knowledge takes place and what role the "confirmations" play in it.

Cognition is originally a means in the service of life. In order to find his way about in his environment and to adjust his actions to events, man must be able to foresee these events to a certain extent. For this he makes use of universal statements, cognitions, and he can make use of them only in so far as what has been predicted actually occurs. Now in science this character of cognition remains wholly unaltered; the only difference is that it no longer serves the purposes of life, is not sought because of its utility. With the confirmation of prediction the scientific goal is achieved: the joy in cognition is the joy of verification, the triumphant feeling of having guessed correctly. And it is this that the observation statements bring about. In them science as it were achieves its goal: it is for their sake that it exists. The question hidden behind the problem of the absolutely certain basis of knowledge is, as it were, that of the legitimacy of this satisfaction with which verification fills us. Have our predictions actually come true? In every single case of verification or falsification a "confirmation" answers unambiguously with a yes or a no, with joy of fulfilment or disappointment. The confirmations are final.

Finality is a very fitting word to characterize the function of observation statements. They are an absolute end. In them the task of cognition at this point is fulfilled. That a new task begins with the pleasure in which they culminate, and with the hypotheses that they leave behind does not concern them. Science does not rest upon them but leads to them, and they indicate that it has led correctly. They are really the absolute fixed points; it gives us joy to reach them, even if we cannot stand upon them.

VII

In what does this fixity consist? This brings us to the question we postponed earlier: in what sense can one speak of observation statements as being "absolutely certain"?

I should like to throw light on this by first saying something about a quite different kind of statement, namely about *analytic* statements. I will then compare these to the "confirmations." In the case of analytic statements it is well known that the question of their validity constitutes no problem. They hold *a priori;* one cannot and should not try to look to experience for proof of their correctness for they say nothing whatever about objects of experience. For this reason only "formal truth" pertains to them, i.e., they are not "true" because they correctly express some fact. What makes them true is just their being correctly constructed, i.e. their standing in agreement with our arbitrarily established definitions.

However, certain philosophical writers have thought themselves obliged to ask: Yes, but how do I know in an individual case whether a statement really stands in agreement with the definition, whether it is really analytic and therefore holds without question? Must I not carry in my head these definitions, the meaning of all the words that are used when I speak or hear or read the statement even if it endures only for a second? But can I be sure that my psychological capacities suffice for this? Is it not possible, for example, that at the end of the statement I should have forgotten or incorrectly remembered the beginning? Must I not thus agree that for psychological reasons I can never be sure of the validity of an analytic judgment also?

To this there is the following answer: the possibility of a failure of the psychic mechanism must of course always be granted, but the consequences that follow from it are not correctly described in the sceptical questions just raised.

It can be that owing to a weakness of memory, and a thousand other causes, we do not understand a statement, or understand it erroneously (i.e. differently from the way it was intended)—but what does this signify? Well, so long as I have not understood a sentence it is not a statement at all for me, but a mere series of words, of sounds or written signs. In this case there is no problem, for only of a statement, not of an uncomprehended series of words, can one ask whether it is analytic or synthetic. But if I have misinterpreted a series of words, but nevertheless interpreted it as a statement, then I know of just *this* statement whether it is analytic or synthetic and therefore valid *a priori* or not. One may not suppose that I could comprehend a statement as such and still be in doubt concerning its analytic character. For if it is analytic I have understood it only when I have understood it as analytic. To understand means nothing else, that is, than to be clear about the rules governing the use of the words in question; but it is precisely these rules of usage that make statements analytic. If I do not know whether a complex of words constitutes an analytic statement or not, this simply means that at that moment I lack the rules of usage: that therefore I have simply not understood the statement. Thus the case is that either I have understood nothing at all, and then nothing more is to be said, or I know whether the statement *which* I understand is synthetic or analytic (which of course does not presuppose that these words hover before me, that I am even acquainted with them). In the case of an analytic statement I know at one and the same time that it is valid, that formal truth belongs to it.

The above doubt concerning the validity of analytic statements was therefore out of order. I may indeed doubt whether I have correctly grasped the meaning of some complex of signs, in fact whether I shall ever understand the meaning of any sequence of words. But I cannot raise the question whether I can ascertain the correctness of an analytic statement. For to understand its meaning and to note its *a priori* validity are in an analytic statement *one and the same* process. In contrast, a synthetic assertion is characterized by the fact that I do not in the least know whether it is true or false if I have only ascertained its meaning. Its truth is determined only by comparison with experience. The process of grasping the meaning is here quite distinct from the process of verification.

There is but one exception to this. And we thus return to our "confirmations." These, that is, are always of the form "Here now so and so," for example "Here two black points coincide," or "Here yellow borders on blue," or also "Here now pain," etc. What is common to all these assertions is that *demonstrative* terms occur in them which have the sense of a present gesture, i.e. their rules of usage provide that in making the statements in which they occur some experience is had, the attention is directed upon something observed. What is referred to by such words as "here," "now," "this here," cannot be communicated by means of general definitions in words, but only by means of them together with pointings or gestures. "This here" has meaning only in connection with a gesture. In order therefore to understand the meaning of such an observation statement one must simultaneously execute the gesture, one must somehow point to reality.

In other words: I can understand the meaning of a "confirmation" only by, and when, comparing it with the facts, thus carrying out that process which is necessary for the verification of all synthetic statements. While in the case of all other synthetic statements determining the meaning is separate from, distinguishable from, determining the truth, in the case of observation statements they coincide, just as in the case of analytic statements. However different therefore "confirmations" are from analytic statements, they have in common that the occasion of understanding them is at the same time that of verifying them: I grasp their meaning at the same time as I grasp their truth. In the case of a confirmation it makes as little sense to ask whether I might be deceived regarding its truth as in the case of a tautology. Both are absolutely valid. However, while the analytic, tautological, statement is empty of content, the observation statement supplies us with the satisfaction of genuine knowledge of reality.

It has become clear, we may hope, that here everything depends on the characteristic of immediacy which is peculiar to observation statements and to which they owe their value and disvalue; the value of absolute validity, and the disvalue of uselessness as an abiding foundation.

A misunderstanding of this nature is responsible for most of the unhappy problems of protocol statements with which our enquiry began. If I make the confirmation "Here now blue," this is *not* the same as the protocol statement "M. S. perceived blue on the nth of April 1934 at such and such a time and such and such a place." The latter statement is a hypothesis and as such always characterized by uncertainty. The latter statement is equivalent to "M. S. made . . . (here time and place are to be given) the confirmation 'here now blue.' " And that this assertion is not identical with the confirmation occurring in it is clear. In protocol statements there is *always* mention of perceptions (or they are to be added in thought—the identity of the perceiving observer is important for a scientific protocol), while they are never mentioned in confirmations. A genuine confirmation cannot be written down, for as soon as I inscribe the demonstratives "here," "now," they lose their meaning. Neither can they be replaced by an indication of time and place, for as soon as one attempts to do this, the result, as we saw, is that one unavoidably substitutes for the observation statement a protocol statement which as such has a wholly different nature.

VIII

I believe that the problem of the basis of knowledge is now clarified.

If science is taken to be a system of statements in which one's interest as a logician is confined to their logical connections, the question of its basis, which would then be a 'logical" question, can be answered quite arbitrarily. For one is free to define the basis as one wishes. In an abstract system of statements there is no priority and no posteriority. For instance, the most general statements of science, thus those that are normally selected as axioms, could be regarded as its ultimate foundation; but this name could just as well be reserved for the most particular statements, which would then more or less actually correspond to the protocols written down. Or any other choice would be possible. But all the statements of science are collectively and individually *hypotheses* the moment one considers them from the point of view of their truth value, their validity.

If attention is directed upon the relation of science to reality the system of its statements is seen to be that which it really is, namely, a means of finding one's way among the facts; of arriving at the joy of confirmation, the feeling of finality. The problem of the "basis" changes then automatically into that of the unshakeable point of contact between knowledge and reality. We have come to know these absolutely fixed points of contact, the confirmations, in their individuality: they are the only synthetic statements that are not *hypotheses*. They do not in any way lie at the base of science; but like a flame, cognition, as it were, licks out to them, reaching each but for a moment and then at once consuming it. And newly fed and strengthened, it flames onward to the next.

These moments of fulfilment and combustion are what is essential. All the light of knowledge comes from them. And it is for the source of this light the philosopher is really inquiring when he seeks the ultimate basis of all knowledge.

Verification and Experience

BY A. J. AYER

WHAT IS IT that determines the truth or falsehood of empirical propositions? The customary answer is, in effect, that it is their agreement or disagreement with reality. I say "in effect" because I wish to allow for alternative formulations. There are some who would speak of correspondence or accordance rather than agreement; some who for the word "reality" would substitute "facts" or "experience." But I do not think that the choice of different words here reflects any important difference of meaning. This answer, though I believe it to be correct, requires some elucidation. To quote William James; "Pragmatists and Intellectualists both accept (it) as a matter of course. They begin to quarrel only after the question is raised as to what precisely may be meant by the term 'agreement' and what by the term 'reality' when reality is taken as something for our ideas to agree with."[1] I hope at least to throw some light upon this question in the course of this paper.

It will simplify our undertaking if we can draw a distinction between those empirical propositions whose truth or falsehood can be determined only by ascertaining the truth or falsehood of other propositions and those whose truth or falsehood can be determined directly by observation. To the former class belong all universal propositions. We cannot, for example, directly establish the truth or falsehood of the proposition that gold is dissoluble in *aqua regia,* unless of course we regard this as a defining attribute of gold and so make the proposition into a tautology. We test it by establishing the truth or falsehood of singular propositions relating, among other things, to particular pieces of gold. We may indeed deduce one uni-

This paper was originally published in the *Proceedings of the Aristotelian Society,* Volume 37 (1936-37). It is reprinted here with the permission of the secretary of the Aristotelian Society.

1. *Pragmatism*, p. 198.

versal proposition from another, or even infer it by analogy, but in all such cases we must finally arrive at a proposition for which the evidence consists solely in the truth or falsehood of certain singular propositions. It is here to be remarked that no matter how many such singular propositions we succeed in establishing we are never entitled to regard the universal proposition as conclusively verified. However often we may have observed the dissolution of pieces of gold in *aqua regia,* we must still allow it to be possible that the next piece with which we experiment will not so dissolve. On the other hand the falsity of any one of the relevant singular propositions does entail the falsity of the universal proposition. It is this logical assymetry in the relationship of universal and singular propositions that has led some philosophers[2] to adopt the possibility of falsification rather than that of verification as their criterion of empirical significance.

We said that the way to test the validity of a universal proposition about the dissolubility of gold was to ascertain the truth or falsehood of singular propositions referring to particular pieces of gold. But these propositions in their turn depend for their verification upon the verification of other propositions. For a piece of gold is a material thing; and to test the validity of propositions referring to material things we must ascertain the truth or falsehood of propositions referring to sense-data. Here we have another instance of logical assymetry. A proposition referring to a material thing may entail propositions referring to sense-data but cannot itself be entailed by any finite number of them.

Now at last we seem to have reached propositions which need not wait upon other propositions for the determination of their truth or falsehood, but are such that they can be directly confronted with the given facts. These propositions I propose to call basic propositions. If the distinction which we have drawn between them and other propositions is legitimate, we may confine ourselves, for our present purpose, to questions concerning the nature of basic propositions and the manner in which our determination of their validity depends upon our experience.

It is noteworthy that the legitimacy of the distinction which we have drawn is implicitly acknowledged even by philosophers who reject the notion of agreement with reality as a criterion of truth. Neurath and Hempel, for example, have recently been maintaining that it is nonsensical to speak of comparing propositions with facts

2. Notably Karl Popper. See his *Logik der Forschung.*

or reality or experience.[3] A proposition, they say, can be compared only with another proposition. At the same time they assign a status corresponding to that of our basic propositions to a class of propositions which they call protocol propositions. According to Neurath, for a sentence to express a protocol proposition it is necessary that it should contain the name or description of an observer and some words referring to an act of observation. He gives the following as an example. "Otto's protocol at 3.17/Otto's speech-thought at 3.16 was (there was in the room at 3.15 a table observed by Otto)/." This is not regarded by Neurath as the only legitimate way of formulating a protocol proposition. If others care to adopt a different convention, they are, as far as he is concerned, at liberty to do so. But he claims for the peculiar form that he has chosen that it has the advantage of giving protocol propositions greater stability than they might otherwise have.

It is easy enough to see why he says this. He is thinking of the case in which it turns out that Otto has been having a hallucination or that in which he is found to be lying. In the former case the proposition in the interior bracket must be held to be false; in the latter, the proposition in the main bracket. But the whole proposition is not a truth-function of the propositions within the brackets, any more than they are truth-functions of one another. We may therefore continue to accept it even when we have rejected them. In itself, this is a valid point. But it is surely inconsistent with Neurath's main position. For how, if we are debarred from appealing to the facts, can we ever discover that Otto has lied or had a hallucination? Neurath makes the truth and falsehood of any proposition whatsoever depend upon its compatibility or incompatibility with other propositions. He recognizes no other criterion. In this respect, his protocol propositions are not allowed any advantage. If we are presented with a protocol proposition and also with a non-protocol proposition which is incompatible with it we are not obliged to accept the protocol proposition and reject the other. We have an equal right to reject either. But if this is so we need not bother to devise a special form for protocol propositions in order to ensure their stability. All we have to do if we wish a proposition to be stable is to decide to accept it and to reject any proposition that is incompatible with it. The question whether such a decision is em-

---

3. Otto Neurath, "Protokollsätze." *Erkenntnis,* Volume III, p. 223, [see above, p. 199], and "Radikaler Physikalismus und 'Wirkliche Welt,' " *Erkenntnis,* Vol. IV; Carl Hempel, "On the Logical Positivists' Theory of Truth," *Analysis,* Vol. II, "Some Remarks on Empiricism," *Analysis,* Vol. III, and "Some Remarks on 'Facts' and Propositions," *Analysis,* Vol. II.

pirically justified or not is one to which, according to the implications of Neurath's doctrine, no meaning can be attached.

One wonders indeed why he and Hempel pay so much attention to protocol propositions, inasmuch as the only distinction which they are able to draw between them and other propositions is a distinction of form. They do not mean by a protocol proposition one which can be directly verified by observation, for they deny that this is possible. They use the term "protocol" purely as a syntactical designation for a certain assemblage of words. But why should one attach special significance to the *word* "observation"? It·may be that there is no error involved in constructing sentences of a peculiar type and dignifying them with the title of *Protokollsätze,* but it is arbitrary and misleading. There is no more justification for it than there would be for making a collection of all the propositions that could be correctly expressed in English by sentences beginning with the letter B, and choosing to call them Basic propositions. If Neurath and Hempel do not recognize this it is probably because, in writing about *Protokollsätze,* they unconsciously employ the forbidden criterion of agreement with experience. Though they say that the term "protocol" is nothing more than a syntactical designation, they do not use it merely as such. We shall see later on that Carnap equivocates with this term in a similar way.

It is not, however, a sufficient reason for rejecting a theory that some of its advocates have failed consistently to adhere to it. And it is necessary for us to investigate more closely the view that in order to determine the validity of a system of empirical propositions one cannot and need not go beyond the system itself. For if this view were satisfactory we should be absolved from troubling any further about the use of the phrase "agreement with experience."

The theory which we now have to examine is that which is commonly known as the coherence theory of truth. It should be noted that the theory is not, as we interpret it, concerned with the definition of truth and falsehood but only with the means by which they are determined. According to it a proposition is to be accepted if it is found to be compatible with other accepted propositions, rejected if it is not. If, however, we are anxious to accept a proposition which conflicts with our current system we may abandon one or more of the propositions which we had previously accepted. In such a case we should, it is sometimes said, be guided by a principle of economy. We should make the smallest transformation of the system which ensured self-consistency. I think it is usually assumed also that we have, or ought to have, a preference for large and highly integrated systems; systems containing a great number of propositions which support one another to a high degree.

One strong objection to this theory is well put by Professor Price in his lecture on *Truth and Corrigibility*. "Suppose," he says, "we have a group of mutually supporting judgments. The extraordinary thing is that however large the group may be, and however great the support which the members give to each other, the entire group hangs, so to speak, in the air. If we accept one member, no doubt it will be reasonable to accept the rest. But why must we accept any of them? Why should we not reject the whole lot? Might they not all be false, although they all support each other?"[4] He goes on to argue that we cannot consider such a system of judgments to have even any probability unless we can attribute to at least one of its constituents a probability which is derived from some other ground than its membership of the system. He suggests therefore that the only way to save the theory would be to maintain that some propositions were intrinsically probable. But this, though he does not say so, is to reduce it to absurdity. There is no case at all to be made out for the view that a proposition can be probable independently of all evidence. The most that could be said in favor of anyone who accepted Price's suggestion would be that he had chosen to give the word "probability" an unfamiliar sense.

A point which Price appears to have overlooked is that according to one well-known version of the coherence theory there can be only one completely coherent system of propositions. If this were so the theory would give us at least an unequivocal criterion for determining the truth of any proposition; namely, the possibility of incorporating it in this single system. It would not, however, afford us any ground for supposing that the enlargement of an apparently coherent system of propositions increased its probability. On the contrary, we ought rather to hold that it decreased it. For *ex hypothesi* any set of propositions which is internally coherent is the only one that is so. If, therefore, we have a set of propositions which appears to be self-consistent, either it is *the* unique coherent system or it contains a contradiction which we have failed to discover; and the larger the set the greater the probability that it contains a contradiction which we have failed to discover. But in saying this we are assuming the truth of a proposition about the limited powers of the human understanding, which may or may not find a place in the one coherent system. Perhaps, therefore, it would be

4. *Truth and Corrigibility* (Inaugural lecture, Oxford University Press, 1936), p 19.

better to say that the advocates of this form of the coherence theory dispense with the notion of probability altogether.

But now we must ask, Why should it be assumed that only one completely coherent system of propositions is conceivable? However many empirical propositions we succeed in combining into an apparently self-consistent system we seem always able to construct a rival system which is equally extensive, appears equally free from contradiction, and yet is incompatible with the first. Why should it be held that at least one of these systems must contain a contradiction, even though we are unable to detect it? I can see no reason at all for this assumption. We may not be able to demonstrate that a given system is free from contradiction; but this does not mean that it is probable that it contains one. This indeed is recognized by the more recent advocates of what we are calling a coherence theory. They admit the possibility of inventing fictitious sciences and histories which would be just as comprehensive, elegant and free from contradiction as those in which we actually believe. But how then do they propose to distinguish the true systems from the false?

The answer given[5] is that the selection of the true system does not depend upon any internal features of the system itself. It cannot be effected by purely logical means. But it can be carried out inside the realm of descriptive syntax. We are to say that the true system is that which is based upon true protocol propositions; and that true protocol propositions are those which are produced by accredited observers, including notably the scientists of our era. Logically, it might be the case that the protocol propositions which each of us expressed were so divergent that no common system of science or only a very meagre system could be based upon them. But fortunately this is not so. People do occasionally produce inconvenient protocol propositions. But being in a small minority they are over-ridden. They are said to be bad observers or liars or, in extreme cases, mad. It is a contingent, historical fact that the rest of us agree in accepting an "increasingly comprehensive, common, scientific system." And it is to this, so the theory runs, that we refer when out of the many coherent systems of science that are conceivable we speak of only one as being true.

This is an ingenious answer; but it will not do. One reason why we trust "the scientists of our era" is that we believe that they give an accurate account of their observations. But this means that we shall be involved in a circle if we say that the reason why we accept

5. *E.g.*, by Rudolf Carnap, "Erwiderung auf die Aufsätze von E. Zilsel und K. Duncker," *Erkenntnis*, Vol. III, pp. 179-180.

certain evidence is merely that it comes from the scientists of our era. And furthermore, How are we to determine that a particular system is accepted by contemporary scientists except by appealing to the facts of experience? But once it is conceded that such an appeal is possible there is no longer any need to bring in the contemporary scientists. However great our admiration for the achievements of the scientists of our era we can hardly maintain that it is only with reference to their behavior that the notion of agreement with reality has any meaning. Hempel[6] has indeed attempted to meet this objection by telling us that instead of saying that "the system of protocol-statements which we call true may only be characterized by the historical fact that it is actually adopted by the scientists of our culture circle" we ought to express ourselves "formally" and say: "The following statement is sufficiently confirmed by the protocol-statements adopted *in our science;* 'Amongst the numerous imaginable consistent sets of protocol-statements, there is in practice exactly one which is adopted by the vast majority of instructed scientific observers; at the same time, it is just this set which we generally call true.' " But this does not remove the difficulty. For now we must ask, How is it determined that the protocol-statements which support the statement quoted really are adopted in our science? If Hempel is really speaking formally, as he says he is, then the phrase "adopted in our science" must be regarded merely as an arbitrary syntactical designation of a certain set of sentences. But it is clear that he does not intend it to be nothing more than this. He intends it to convey the information that the propositions expressed by these sentences actually are adopted. But this is to re-introduce the reference to historical fact which he is trying to eliminate. We have here a fallacy which is akin to the fallacy of the ontological argument. It is not legitimate to use the phrase "adopted in our science" simply as a means of naming certain statements and then proceed to infer from this that these statements really are adopted in it. But Hempel cannot dispense with this fallacious inference. For each of many incompatible systems might contain the statement that it alone was accepted by contemporary scientists, together with the protocol propositions that were needed to support it.

We may conclude then that the attempt to lay down a criterion for determining the truth of empirical propositions which does not contain any reference to "facts" or "reality" or "experience," has not proved successful. It seems plausible only when it involves a tacit introduction of that very principle of agreement with reality

---

6. *Analysis,* Vol. III, pp. 39-40.

which it is designed to obviate. Accordingly, we may return to our original question concerning the nature of basic propositions and the manner in which their validity depends upon fact. And first of all I wish to consider how far this question admits of a purely conventional answer.

According to Professor Carnap it is wholly a matter of convention what propositions we take as basic. "Every concrete proposition," he tells us,[7] "belonging to the physicalistic system-language can in suitable circumstances serve as a protocol proposition. Let G be a law (that is a general proposition belonging to the system language). For the purpose of verification one must in the first instance derive from G concrete propositions referring to particular space-time points (through substitution of concrete values for the space-time co-ordinates x, y, z, t which occur in G as free variables). From these concrete propositions one may with the help of additional laws and logico-mathematical rules of inference derive further concrete propositions, until one comes to propositions which in the particular case in question one is willing to accept. It is here a matter of choice which propositions are employed at any given time as the terminating points of this reduction, that is as protocol propositions. In every case the process of reduction, which serves the purpose of verification, must be brought to an end somewhere. But one is never obliged to call a halt at any one point rather than another."

In reasoning thus, Carnap says that he is following the example of Karl Popper. Actually Popper adopts a rather narrower convention. He proposes, and takes the view that there can in this matter be no warrant for anything more than a proposal, that basic propositions should have the form of singular existentials. They must, according to his convention, refer to particular spatio-temporal points and the events which are said to be occurring at these points must be observable events. But in case anyone should think that the use of the word "observable" brings in an element of psychology he hastens to add that instead of an "observable" event he might equally well have spoken of an event of motion located in (macroscopic) physical bodies.[8] His views concerning the verification of these propositions are summed up as follows: "The basic propositions are accepted by an act of will, by convention. *Sie sind Festsetzungen.*"[9]

7. "Über Protokollsätze." *Erkenntnis,* Vol. III, p. 224.
8. *Logik der Forschung,* p. 59.
9. *Op. cit.,* p. 62.

The verification of all other empirical propositions is held to depend upon that of the basic propositions. So that if we take the remark I have quoted literally, we are presented with the view that our acceptance or rejection of any empirical proposition must be wholly arbitrary. And this is surely wrong. Actually, I do not think that Popper himself wishes to maintain this. His stipulation that basic propositions should refer to observable events suggests that he recognizes that our acceptance of them somehow depends upon our observations. But he does not tell us how.

There is indeed this much truth in what Popper says. The propositions which he calls basic refer to material things. As such, they can be tested by observation, but never conclusively established. For, as we have already remarked, although they may entail propositions referring to sense-data they cannot be entailed by them. It follows that there is in our acceptance of them an element of convention. I cannot carry out all the tests which would bear upon the truth of even so simple a proposition as that my pen is lying on my table. In practice, therefore, I accept such a proposition after making only a limited number of tests, perhaps only a single test, which leaves it still possible that it is false. But this is not to say that my acceptance of it is the result of an arbitrary decision. I have collected some evidence in favor of the proposition, even though it may not be conclusive evidence. I might have accepted it without having any evidence at all; and then my decision would, in fact, have been arbitrary. There is no harm in Popper's insisting that our acceptance of such propositions as he calls basic is not wholly dictated by logic; but he ought still to distinguish the cases in which our acceptance of a "basic" proposition is reasonable from those in which it is not. We may say that it is reasonable when the proposition is supported by our observations. But what is meant by saying that a proposition is supported by our observations? This is a question which in his discussion of the "Basis-problem" Popper does not answer.

We find, therefore, that this "discovery" of Popper's which has been fastened on to by Carnap amounts to no more than this; that the process of testing propositions referring to physical objects can be extended as far as we choose. What is conventional is our decision to carry it in any given case just so far and no farther. To express this, as Carnap does, by saying that it is a matter of convention what propositions we take as protocols is simply to give the term "protocol proposition" an unfamiliar meaning. We understand that he now proposes to use it to designate any singular proposition, be-

longing to "the physicalistic system-language," which we are prepared to accept without further tests. This is a perfectly legitimate
usage. What is not legitimate is to ignore the discrepancy between it
and his former usage according to which protocol propositions were
said to "describe directly given experience." And in abandoning the
original usage he has incidentally shelved the problem which it was
designed to meet.

Elsewhere,[10] Carnap has suggested that problems concerning the
nature of basic propositions, in our sense of the term, depend for
their solution only on conventions about forms of words. I think
that this, too, can be shown to be a mistake. Most people are by
now familiar with his division of propositions into factual propositions such as "the roses in my garden are red," pseudo-factual propositions such as "a rose is a thing," which are also said to be syntactical propositions, expressed in the material mode of speech, and
propositions such as " 'rose' is a thing-word," which are syntactical
and expressed in the formal mode of speech. Now when he raises
the question "What objects are the elements of given, direct experience?" he treats it as if it were a syntactical question, expressed in
the material mode of speech. That is, he considers it to be a loose
way of raising the question "What kinds of word occur in protocol-
statements?"[11] And he sets out various possible answers both in
what he calls the material and in what he calls the formal mode.
Thus, he says that it may be the case that "the elements that are
directly given are the simplest sensations and feelings" or "more
complex objects such as partial *gestalts* of single sensory fields" or
that "material things are elements of the given"; and he takes these
to be misleading ways of saying that "protocol-statements are of
the same kind as: 'joy now,' 'here, now, blue' " or that "protocol-
statements are of forms similar to 'red circle, now' " or that they
have "approximately the same kind of form as 'a red cube is on the
table.' "[12] In this way he assumes that questions about the nature of
immediate experience are linguistic in character. And this leads him
to dismiss all the "problems of the so-called given or primitive data"
as depending only upon our choice of a form of language.[13] But
this is to repeat the error of Neurath and Hempel, which we have
already exposed. If the term "protocol-statement" was being used
merely as a syntactical designation for certain combinations of

10. *Logical Syntax of Language,* pp. 305-6.
11. *The Unity of Science,* p. 45.
12. *The Unity of Science,* pp. 46-7.
13. *The Logical Syntax of Language,* pp. 305-6.

symbols then our choice of the sentences to which we applied it would indeed be a matter of convention. It would involve no more reference to truth than a decision to apply the designation "basic" to all English sentences beginning with B. But this is not the sense in which Carnap is supposed to be using the term. He is using it not to mark out the form of certain statements, but rather to express the fact that they refer to what is immediately given. Accordingly, our answer to his question "What kinds of word occur in protocol-statements?" cannot depend simply upon a conventional choice of linguistic forms. It must depend upon the way in which we answer the question "What objects are the elements of given, direct experience?" And this is not a matter of language, but a matter of fact. It is a plain question of fact whether the atomistic or the *gestalt* theory of sensation is correct.

Thus we see that the proposition that "the elements that are directly given are the simplest sensations and feelings" which Carnap takes to be a syntactical proposition expressed in the material mode of speech, is not syntactical at all. And the proposition which he gives as its formal equivalent, namely, that "protocol-statements are of the same kind as: 'joy now,' 'here, now, blue; there, red' " is not syntactical either. If we want to give it a label we may call it a pseudo-syntactical proposition. And by this we shall mean that it seems to be about words but is really about objects. It is important that the existence of such propositions should not be overlooked; for they are quite as dangerous in their way as the pseudo-factual propositions of which Carnap has made so much. In this instance the source of confusion is the use of the term "protocol." It cannot without contradiction be interpreted both as a purely formal designation and as involving a covert reference to a matter of fact. But this is precisely how Carnap does interpret it; and it is thus that he is led to make the mistake of supposing that questions about the nature of basic propositions can be decided merely by convention. It is indeed a matter of convention that we should use a word consisting of the letters "j o y" to denote joy. But the proposition that joy is immediately experienced, which is implied in saying that "joy" is a protocol word, is one whose truth or falsehood is not to be decided by convention but only by referring to the facts. The psychology of sensation is not an *a priori* branch of science.

We conclude therefore that the forms of basic propositions depend partly indeed upon linguistic conventions but partly also upon the nature of the given; and this is something that we cannot determine *a priori*. We may hold indeed that a person's sensations are

always private to himself; but this is only because we happen so to
use words that it does not make sense to say "I am acquainted with
your sense-data" or "You and I are experiencing the same sense-
datum."[14] This is a point about which we are apt to be confused.
One says mournfully "I cannot experience your toothache" as
though it revealed a lack of mental power. That is, we are inclined
to think of the contents of another person's mind, or the immediate
objects of his experience, as being concealed from us by some sort
of natural obstacle, and we say to ourselves: "If only we had a ray
which would penetrate this obstacle!" (Intuition!) or "Perhaps we
can construct a reflector which will show us what is going on behind."
But in fact there is no obstacle but our usage of words. To say that
whatever is directly "given" to me is mine and mine only is to express a tautology. A mistake which I, for one, have made in the past
is to confuse this with the proposition "Whatever is directly 'given'
is mine." This is not a tautology. It is an empirical proposition, and
it is false.

A further point which it is advisable to make clear is that we
are not setting any arbitrary boundaries to the field of possible experience. As an illustration of this let us consider the case of the
man who claims to have an immediate, non-sensory experience of
God. So long as he uses the word "God" simply as a name for the
content of his experience, I have no right to disbelieve him. Not
having such experiences myself I cannot understand him fully. I do
not myself know what it is like to be acquainted with God. But I
can at least understand that he is having some experience of a kind
that I do not have. And this I may readily believe. I should certainly not be justified in assuming that the sort of experiences that I
myself had were the only sort that could be had at all. At the same
time it must be remarked that "God," in this usage, cannot be the
name of a transcendent being. For to say that one was immediately
acquainted with a transcendent being would be self-contradictory.
And though it might be the name of a person who in fact endured
for ever one could not say that one was immediately acquainted with
Him as enduring for ever. For this, too, would be self-contradictory.
Neither would the fact that people were acquainted with God, in
this sense, afford a valid ground for inferring that the world had a
first cause, or that human beings survived death, or in short that
anything existed which had the attributes that are popularly ascribed

---

14. This point has been forcibly made by G. A. Paul, *vide* "Is there a Problem
About Sense-Data?" *Supp. Proc. Arist. Soc.*, 1936, also reprinted in A. Flew (ed.),
Essays in Logic and Language, First Series.

to God. And the same thing applies to the case of moral experience. We should certainly not be justified in denying *a priori* the possibility of moral experience. But this does not mean that we recognize that there is any ground for inferring the existence of an ideal, objective world of values. It is necessary to say this because the use of "God" or "value" as a designation of the content of a certain kind of experience often misleads people into thinking that they are entitled to draw such inferences; and we must make it clear that in admitting the possibility of such experiences we are not also upholding the conclusions which are illegitimately drawn from them.

We have tried to show that neither the form nor the validity of basic propositions is dependent merely on convention. Since it is their function to describe what can be immediately experienced, their form will depend upon the general nature of the "given," their validity upon their agreement with it in the relevant particular case. But what is this relation of agreement? What kind of correspondence do we suppose to exist between basic propositions and the experiences that verify them?

It is sometimes suggested that this relation of agreement is of the same kind as that which holds between a picture and that of which it is a picture. I do not think that this is true. It is possible indeed to construct picture-languages; no doubt they have their advantages; but it surely cannot be maintained that they alone are legitimate; or that a language such as English is really a picture-language although we do not know it. But if English is not a picture-language and propositions expressed in English are sometimes verified, as they surely are, then it cannot be the case that this relation of agreement with which we are concerned is one of picturing. Besides, there is this further difficulty. If any propositions are pictures, presumably false propositions are so as well as true ones. In other words, we cannot tell from the form of the proposition, that is, merely by looking at the picture, whether it depicts a real situation or not. But how then are we to distinguish the true picture from the false? Must we not say that the true picture agrees with reality whereas the false one does not? But in that case the introduction of the notion of picturing does not serve our purpose. It does not enable us to dispense with the notion of agreement.

The same objections hold against those who say that this relation of agreement is one of identity of structure. This is to treat propositions as if they were maps. But then it is to be supposed that a false proposition is also a map. The mere form of the proposition will not tell us whether the country which it purports to map is imaginary or real. Can we then avoid saying that we test the truth of such a map by seeing whether it agrees with reality? But then the notion of agreement is still left unclarified. And, in any case, why should it be assumed that if a proposition is to describe what is directly given it must have the same structure as the given? One might, perhaps, allow the possibility of creating a language in which all basic propositions were expressed by sentences functioning as maps, though I am by no means sure that it would be possible to draw a map of our internal sensations; but I can see no ground at all for assuming that only a language of this.kind is legitimate, or that any of the European languages with which I am acquainted is a language of this kind. Yet propositions, expressed in these languages, are frequently verified. There is, perhaps, a historical connection between the view that basic propositions must be identical in structure with the facts that verify them and the view that only structure can be known or expressed.[15] But this too is arbitrary, and indeed self-defeating. To maintain that content is inexpressible is to behave like Ramsey's child. " 'Say breakfast.' 'Can't.' 'What can't you say?' 'Can't say breakfast.' "[16]

What is being assumed in the theories which we have just been discussing is not so much that a proposition cannot be verified as that it, or, to speak more accurately, the sentence expressing it, cannot have a sense at all unless it is a picture or a map. The difficulty with regard to sentences that express false propositions is got round by saying that they depict or map possible facts. But surely this assumption is quite gratuitous. If I am speaking English I may use the words "I am angry" to say that I am angry. You may say, if you like, that in doing so I am obeying a meaning-rule[17] of the English language. For this to be possible it is not in the least necessary that my words should in any way resemble the state of anger which they describe. That "this is red" is used to say that this is red does not imply that it bears any relation of resemblance, whether of structure or content, to an actual or hypothetical red patch.

But if the words "I am angry" are used to say that I am angry, then it does not seem in any way mysterious that my being angry should verify the proposition that they express. But how do I know that I am angry? I feel it. How do I know that there is now a loud sound? I hear it. How do I know that this is a red patch? I see it.

15. Cf. E. Zilsel, "Bemerkungen zur Wissenschaftslogik," *Erkenntnis*, Vol. III, p. 143.

16. *Foundations of Mathematics*, p. 268. [*Vide* pp. 321-6 of this volume.]

17. Cf. K. Ajdukiewicz, "Sprache und Sinn," *Erkenntnis*, Vol. IV, pp. 114-116.

If this answer is not regarded as satisfactory, I do not know what other can be given.

It may be suggested that we ought in this connection to introduce the notion of causation. The relation, it may be said, between the proposition "I am in pain" and the fact that verifies it is that the fact causes me to assert the proposition, or at any rate to believe it. That such a relation often exists is not to be denied. But we cannot analyze verification in terms of it. For if I am a habitual liar my being in pain may cause me to deny that I am in pain; and if I am a sufficiently hidebound Christian Scientist it may not cause me to believe it. But in either case my being in pain will verify the proposition that I am in pain. Why? Because when I say "I am in pain" I mean that I am in pain, and if p then p. But how do I establish p? How do I know that I really am in pain? Again the answer can only be "I feel it."

Does this mean that basic propositions must be regarded as incorrigible? I find this question difficult to answer because I do not know what precise meaning those who have discussed it have been giving to the term "incorrigible." Probably, different philosophers have given it different meanings. Professor Price, for example, when he argues that basic propositions are incorrigible appears to mean no more than that our reasons for accepting them are found in our experience; that if one is justified in saying of a visual sense-datum "this is red," it is because one sees it so. For the only arguments which he gives in favor of the view that some first-order propositions are incorrigible are arguments against the coherence theory of truth.[18] I should of course agree that basic propositions were incorrigible, in this rather unnatural sense. Dr. von Juhos makes the same statement.[19] But what he appears to mean by it is that there can never be any ground for abandoning a basic proposition; that once it is accepted it cannot subsequently be doubted or denied. In a sense, we may agree that this is so. For we may say that what is subsequently doubted or denied is always a different proposition. What I accept now is the proposition "this is red"; what I may doubt or deny in thirty seconds' time is the proposition "I was seeing something red thirty seconds ago." But in this sense every proposition which contains a demonstrative is incorrigible, and not only basic propositions. And if von Juhos wishes to maintain that some special sacrosanctity attaches to propositions which purport to be records of our immediate experiences, I think that he is wrong. If I find the

18. *Vide Truth and Corrigibility.*
19. See his articles in *Analysis,* Vol. II, and *Erkenntnis,* Vol. IV.

sentence "I feel happy" written in my diary under the heading February 3rd I am not obliged to believe that I really did feel happy on February 3rd, merely because the sentence has the same form as that which I should utter if I felt happy now. I may indeed believe it on the ground that I am not in the habit of writing down false statements in my diary. But that is a different matter.

Professor Moore has suggested to me that what some of those who say that basic propositions are incorrigible may have in mind is that we cannot be mistaken about them in the way that we can be mistaken about other empirical propositions. If I say "I am in pain" or "this is red" I may be lying, or I may be using words wrongly; that is, I may be classifying as "pain" or as "red" something that would not normally be so classified. But I cannot be mistaken in any other way. I cannot be mistaken in the way that I can be mistaken if I take this red patch to be the cover of a book. If this is a fact, it is not a fact about human psychology. It is not just a merciful dispensation of Providence that we are secured from errors of a certain kind. It is, if anything, a fact about language.[20] If Moore is right, it does not make sense to say "I doubt whether this is red" or "I think that I am in pain but I may be mistaken," unless it is merely meant that I am doubting whether "pain" or "red" is the correct word to use. I believe now that Moore is right on this point. But whether it is a fact from which any important conclusions follow I do not profess to know.

20. Cf. John Wisdom, "Philosophical Perplexity," *Proc. Arist. Soc.*, 1936-7, p. 81.

Ethics and Sociology

12

What Is the Aim of Ethics?

by MORITZ SCHLICK

(TRANSLATED BY DAVID RYNIN)

1. ETHICS SEEKS NOTHING BUT KNOWLEDGE

IF THERE ARE ethical questions which have meaning, and are therefore capable of being answered, then ethics is a science. For the correct answers to its questions will constitute a system of true propositions, and a system of true propositions concerning an object is
the "science" of that object. Thus ethics is a system of *knowledge,*
and nothing else; its only goal is the truth. Every science is, as such,
purely theoretical; it seeks to understand; hence the questions of
ethics, too, are purely theoretical problems. As philosophers we try
to find their correct solutions, but their practical application, if such
is possible, does not fall within the sphere of ethics. If anyone studies
these questions in order to apply the results to life and action, his
dealing with ethics has, it is true, a practical end; but ethics itself
never has any other goal than the truth.

So long as the philosopher is concerned with his purely theoretical questions, he must forget that he has a human interest as well
as a cognitive interest in the object of his investigation. For him
there is no greater danger than to change from a philosopher into
a moralist, from an investigator into a preacher. Desire for the truth
is the only appropriate inspiration for the thinker when he philoso-
phizes; otherwise his thoughts run the danger of being led astray
by his feelings. His wishes, hopes, and fears threaten to encroach
upon that objectivity which is the necessary presupposition of all
honest inquiry. Of course, the prophet and the investigator can be
one and the same person; but one cannot at the same moment serve

This is Chapter I of Schlick's *Problems of Ethics,* copyright 1939 by Prentice-Hall
Inc., New York. It is reprinted here with the kind permission of the translator and
the publishers. Schlick's book was first published in Vienna in 1930.

both interests, for whoever mixes the two problems will solve neither.

A glance at the great ethical systems will show how necessary these remarks are. There is hardly one in which we do not occasionally find an appeal to the feeling or the morality of the reader where a scientific analysis would have been appropriate.

Nevertheless, I do not point out the purely theoretical character of ethics merely to warn my reader, and myself. I do it also because it will help us to define the problems with which ethics is concerned and which we shall try to solve.

2. THE SUBJECT-MATTER OF ETHICS

To what object, or realm of objects, do the questions of ethics relate? This object has many names, and we use them so often in daily life that one might think we should know exactly what we mean by them. The ethical questions concern "morality," or what is morally "valuable," what serves as a "standard" or "norm" of human conduct, what is "demanded" of us; or, finally, to name it by the oldest, simplest word, ethical questions concern the "good."

And what does ethics do with this object? We have already answered this question: ethics seeks to *understand* it, to gain knowledge of it, and would and can under no circumstances do anything else with it. Since ethics is, in essence, theory or knowledge, its task cannot be to produce morality, or to establish it, or call it to life. It does not have the task of producing the good—neither in the sense that its business is to invest the good with reality in human affairs, nor in the sense that it has to stipulate or decree what the word "good" ought to signify. It creates neither the concept nor the objects which fall under the concept, nor does it provide the opportunity of applying the concept to the objects. All this it finds, as every science finds the materials it works with, in experience. It is obvious that no science can have any other beginning. The misleading view (introduced by the "Neo-Kantians") according to which objects of a science are not simply "given" to it but are themselves always "given as problems" will not lead anyone to deny that whoever wishes to understand anything must first know *what* it is he wishes to understand.

Where and how, then, is "the good" of ethics given?

We must from the outset be clear on the point that here there is only *one* possibility, the same that lies before all other sciences. Wherever an instance of the object to be known occurs, there must be exhibited a certain mark (or group of marks) which characterizes the thing or event as one of a certain definite kind, thus distinguishing it from all others in a special way. If this were not so we would have no opportunity and no motive to call it by a special name. Every name which is used in discourse for communication must have a meaning capable of being indicated. This is indeed self-evident, and it would not be doubted of the object of any other science—only in ethics has it sometimes been forgotten.

Let us consider some examples outside the field of ethics. Biology, the science of life, finds its sphere limited by a group of characteristics (a special kind of motion, regeneration, growth, and so forth) which belong to all living things, and stand out so clearly for everyday observation that—apart from certain critical instances—the difference between the animate and inanimate is very sharply distinguished, without the use of any scientific analysis. It is only because of this that the concept of life could have first been formed, and obtained its special name. If the biologist succeeds, with progressive knowledge, in establishing new and sharper definitions of life, in order better to bring the events of life under general laws, this means only more precision in, and perhaps extension of, the concept, without however altering its original meaning.

Similarly the word "light" had a definite meaning before there was a science of light, that is, optics, and this meaning determined the subject-matter of optics. The distinguishing mark was in this case that immediate experience which we call "light-sensation," that is, a not-further-definable datum of consciousness, known only to the perceiver, the occurrence of which—again apart from critical instances—indicates the presence of those events which constitute the subject-matter of optics. The fact that optics in its modern developed form is the science of Roentgen rays and radio-telegraphic waves as well (because their laws are identical with the laws of light) enlarges the meaning of the word "optics" without changing its basis.

As certainly, then, as the expression "moral good" makes good sense, just as certainly must we be able to discover it in a way analogous to that by which one discovers the meaning of the word "life" or "light." But many philosophers see in this a serious difficulty of ethics, indeed *the* difficulty, and they are of the opinion that the sole task of ethics is the discovery of the definition of "good."

3. ON THE DEFINITION OF GOOD

This view can be interpreted in two ways. In the first place, it could mean that the task of the philosopher is exhausted in describing exactly the sense in which the word "good"—or *bon* or *gut* or *buono* or ἀγαθόν—in its moral signification is actually used. It would concern itself merely with making clear the already well-known meaning, by a strict formulation of it in other words (were it not already well known one would not know that, for example, "good" is the translation of *bonum*). Is this really the goal of ethics? The statement of the meaning of words by definitions is (as G. E. Moore in his *Principia Ethica* has pointed out in a similar connection) the business of the science of language. Ought we really to believe that ethics is a branch of linguistics? Perhaps a branch that has split off from it because the definition of "good" harbors special difficulties we meet in no other word? A very peculiar case, that a whole science should be necessary to find merely the definition of a concept! And in any case, who is interested in mere definitions? They are, after all, only means to an end; they stand at the *beginning* of the real cognitive task. If ethics ended with a definition it would be at most the introduction to a science, and the philosopher would interest himself only in what comes after it. No, the real problems of ethics are certainly of a very different sort. Even though the task of ethics could be formulated as that of stating what the good "really is," this could not be understood as consisting in the mere determination of the meaning of a concept (as also, in our example, optics does not strive for a mere definition of "light"). Rather it would have to be understood as the task of explanation, of complete cognition of the good—which presupposes that the meaning of the concept is already known and then relates it to something else, orders it in more general connections (just as optics does with light, which tells us what light "really is" by pointing out the place in the sphere of natural events to which the well-known phenomenon belongs, by describing to the last detail its laws, and by recognizing their identity with the laws of certain electrical events).

Secondly, the view according to which the goal of ethics consists of a correct determination of the concept "good" could be interpreted as not being concerned with the formulation of the content of the concept, but rather with giving it a content. This would, however, be exactly that view which we have from the start recognized to be quite senseless. It would mean that the philosopher made, or created, the concept of the good, while without him there existed merely the word "good." He would of course have to invent it quite arbitrarily. (But inasmuch as in formulating his definition he could not act completely arbitrarily, since he would be bound by some norm, some guiding principle, the concept of the good would already be determined by these norms. The philosopher would have merely to find a formulation of it, and we should have before us the previously considered case.) However, it would be quite absurd to demand of ethics nothing but the arbitrary establishment of the meaning of a word. That would be no achievement at all. Even the prophet, the creator of a new morality, never forms a new concept of morality, but presupposes one, and asserts only that other modes of behavior are subsumed under it than those which people have believed up to that time. In logical terms, the prophet holds that the acknowledged content of the concept has a different range from that supposed. This alone can be the meaning when he declares: "Not that is 'good' which you have held as such, but something else!"

Thus we see the view confirmed that in no way is the formulation of the concept of the moral good to be considered as the final task of ethics; it cannot be regarded as anything but a mere preparation.

To be sure, this preparation is not to be neglected; ethics ought not to spare itself the task of determining the meaning of its concept, even though, as we have said, the meaning of the word "good" may in one sense be assumed as known.

4. IS THE GOOD INDEFINABLE?

It is very dangerous to withdraw from this task under the pretext that the word "good" is one of those whose meaning is simple and unanalyzable, of which therefore a definition, a statement of the connotation, is impossible. What is demanded here need not be a definition in the strictest sense of the word. It is sufficient to indicate how we can get the content of the concept; to state what must be done in order to become acquainted with its content. It is, strictly speaking, also impossible to define what the word "green" means—but we can nevertheless fix its meaning unambiguously, for example, by saying it is the color of a summer meadow, or by pointing to the foliage of a tree. We mentioned above that a "light-sensation" which furnishes us with the fundamental concept of optics is not definable; however, we know exactly what is meant by it, because we can give the exact conditions under which we have a light-sensation. In the same way, in ethics we must be able to give the exact conditions under which the word "good" is applied, even though its fundamental concept be indefinable. In this manner it must be possible to give the meaning of any word, for otherwise it would have no meaning at all. It must even be capable of being given easily; profound philosophical analysis cannot be necessary for this, for the matter concerns merely a question of fact, namely, a description of those conditions under which the word "good" (or its equivalent in other languages, or its contrary, "evil") is actually used.

It is difficult for many philosophers to stick to the realm of facts even temporarily, without immediately inventing a theory to describe the facts. And thus the theory has been frequently propounded that the fundamental concept of ethics is given as is the fundamental concept of optics. Just as we possess a special sense, namely the sense of sight, for the perception of light, so it is supposed that a special "moral sense" indicates the presence of good or evil. Accordingly, good and evil would be objective characters, to be determined and investigated as are the physical events which optics investigates, and which it considers to be the causes of light-sensations.

This theory is of course wholly hypothetical. The moral sense is merely assumed; its organs cannot be pointed out as can the human eye. But the hypothesis is also false, it fails to account for the variations in moral judgment among men, since the further assumption that the moral sense is poorly developed in many persons, or completely absent, does not suffice to explain these variations.

No, it is not the distinguishing characteristic of the subject-matter of ethics that it is the object of a special kind of perception. Its characteristics must be capable of exhibition by simply pointing to certain known facts, without any artifice. This can happen in different ways. Two ways are here distinguished: first, one can seek for an external, formal characteristic of good and evil; and, second, one can search for a material characteristic, one of content.

5. The Formal Characteristic of the Good

The formal characteristic, on which Kant placed the whole weight of his moral philosophy, and which he made prominent by his greatest eloquence, is this: the good always appears as something that is demanded, or commanded; the evil, as something forbidden. Good conduct is such as is demanded or desired of us. Or, as it has generally been expressed since Kant: those actions are good which we *ought to do*. Now, to a demand, a claim, or a desire there belongs someone who demands, claims, or desires. This author of the moral law must also be given in order that the characterization by means of the formal property of the command be unambiguous.

Here opinions differ. In theological ethics this author is God, and according to one interpretation the good is good because God desires it; in this case the formal characteristic (to be a command of God) would express the very essence of the good. According to another, perhaps profounder, interpretation, God desires the good because it is good. In this case its essence must be given by certain material characters previously to and independently of those formal determinations. In traditional philosophical ethics the opinion prevails that the author is, for example, human society (utilitarianism) or the active self (eudaimonism) or even no one (the categorical imperative). From this last proceeds Kant's doctrine of the "absolute ought," that is, a demand without a demander. One of the worst errors of ethical thought lies in his belief that the concept of the moral good is completely exhausted by the statement of its purely formal property, that it has no content except to be what is demanded, "what should be."

6. MATERIAL CHARACTERISTICS

In opposition to this, it is clear that the discovery of the formal characters of the good constitutes only a preliminary step in the determination of the content of the good, in the statement of material characteristics. If we know that the good is what is demanded, we must still ask: What is it then that is actually demanded? In answer to this question we must turn to the author of the command and investigate his will and desire, for the content of his desire is that which he wishes to happen. When I recommend an action to someone as being "good," I express the fact that I *desire* it.

So long as the lawgiver is not known with certainty, we must stick to the laws as they are generally observed, to the formulations of moral rules as we find them among men. We must discover which ways of acting (or dispositions, or whatever be the term used) are called "good" by different people, at different times, by different wise men or religious writers. Only in this way do we come to know the content of this concept. From the content it may then be possible to infer the lawgiving authority, if it cannot be ascertained otherwise.

In grouping together the individual cases in which something is designated as morally good, we must search for the common elements, the characters in which these examples agree or show similarities. These similar elements are the characters of the concept "good"; they constitute its content, and within them must lie the reason why one and the same word, "good," is used for the several cases.

To be sure, one will at once come upon cases in which nothing

common can be found, in which there seems to be a complete incompatibility; one and the same thing—for example, polygamy—will
be considered moral in one community, and in another a crime. In
such a situation there are two possibilities. First, there could be several irreducibly different concepts of "good" (which agree in the
purely formal property of being somehow "demanded"); if this
were so there would not be a single morality, but many. Or, second,
it could be that the divergence in moral judgments was only apparent
and not final; that, namely, in the end one and the same goal was
approved, but that a difference of opinion prevailed as to which way
leads to it, which actions should therefore be demanded. (For instance, polygamy and monogamy are not in themselves judged
morally. The real object of valuation is perhaps the peace of family
life, or the least troublesome order of sexual relationships. One person
believes that this end can be attained only through monogamous marriage, and considers it, therefore, to be morally good; another believes the same of polygamy. One may be right, the other wrong;
they differ, not by their final valuations, but only by virtue of their
insight, capacity of judgment, or experience.)

Whether there is actually among men a multiplicity of moralities
incompatible with one another, or whether the differences in the
moral world are only specious, so that the philosopher would find
everywhere, under the many disguises and masks of morality, one
and the same face of the one Good, we cannot now decide. In any
case, there are wide regions in which the unanimity and security of
moral judgments is substantiated. The modes of behavior which we
group together under the names reliability, helpfulness, sociability
are everywhere judged to be "good," while, for example, thievery,
murder, quarrelsomeness pass for "evil" so unanimously that here
the question of the common property can be answered with practically universal validity. If such characters are found for a large
group of actions, then one can apply himself to the "exceptions" and
irregularities, that is, to those cases in which the same behavior evokes
divergent moral judgments in different times, among different peoples.
Here one finds either that there is no different ground for the judgment from that in all ordinary cases, but that it is merely more remote, hidden, or applied under altered circumstances; or one must
simply note the fact as indicating a new or ambiguous meaning of
the word "good." And finally, it happens, of course, that certain
individuals hold different opinions regarding good and evil from
those held by people of their time and community. In these cases it
is quite as important to make out the content and causes of their

opinions as in any other more regular cases, if the persons in question are important as prophets, moral writers, or morally creative men; or if their teachings disclose hidden currents or impress their moral judgments on humanity and the future.

7. MORAL NORMS AND MORAL PRINCIPLES

The common characteristics which a group of "good" acts or dispositions exhibits can be combined in a *rule* of the form: A mode of action must have such and such properties in order to be called "good" (or "evil"). Such a rule can also be called a "norm." Let it be understood at once, however, that such a "norm" is nothing but a mere expression of fact; it gives us only the conditions under which an act or disposition or character is actually called "good," that is, is given a moral value. The setting up of norms is nothing but the determination of the concept of the good, which ethics undertakes to understand.

This determination would proceed by seeking ever new groups of acts that are recognized to be good, and showing for each of them the rule or norm which all of their members satisfy. The different norms, so obtained, would then be compared, and one would order them into new classes such that the individual norms of each class had something in common, and thus would all be subsumed under a higher, that is, a more general, norm. With this higher norm the same procedure would be repeated, and so on, until, in a perfect case, one would at last reach a highest, most general rule that included all others as special cases, and would be applicable to every instance of human conduct. This highest norm would be the definition of "the good" and would express its universal essence; it would be what the philosopher calls a "moral principle."

Of course, one cannot know beforehand whether one will actually arrive at a single moral principle. It might well be that the highest series of rules to which the described way leads simply shows no common character, that one has, therefore, to stop with several norms as highest rules, because despite all attempts none higher can be found to which these could be reduced. There would then be several mutually independent meanings of the expression "moral good," several mutually independent moral principles which only in their totality would determine the concept of morality, or perhaps several different concepts of the moral, depending upon the time and the people. It is significant how little these possibilities have, in general, been considered by philosophers; almost all have at once sought a single moral principle. Quite the contrary is true of the practical moral systems, which ordinarily do not attempt to establish an all-inclusive principle; as in the case of the catechism, which stops at the ten commandments.

For those who believe that the sole task of ethics consists in the determination of the concept of the good, that is, in the establishment of one or several moral principles, the completion of the described procedure would exhaust the theme of ethics. It would be a pure "normative science"; for its end would lie in the discovery of a hierarchy of norms or rules which culminated in one or several points, the moral principles, and in which the lower levels would be explained or "justified" by the higher. To the question, "Why is this act moral?" the explanation can be given, "Because it falls under these definite rules"; and if one asks further, "Why are all the acts falling under this rule moral?" this would be explained by saying, "Because they all fall under that next higher rule." And only with the highest norm—with the moral principle or moral principles —is the knowledge of the validating grounds, a justification, no longer possible in this way. There ethics is at an end for him who sees it as a mere normative science.

8. Ethics as a "Normative Science"

We now see clearly what meaning the phrase "normative science" can have, and in what sense alone ethics can "justify" an act or its valuation. In modern philosophy since Kant, the idea repeatedly appears that ethics as a normative science is something completely different from the "factual sciences." It does not ask, "When is a person judged to be good?" or, "Why is he judged to be good?" These questions concern mere facts and their explanation. But it does ask, "With *what right* is that person judged to be good?" It does not trouble itself with what is actually valued, but asks: "What is valuable? What should be valued?" And here obviously the question is quite different.

But *this* manner of opposing normative and factual sciences is fundamentally false. For if ethics furnishes a justification it does so only in the sense just explained, namely, in a relative-hypothetical way, not absolutely. It "justifies" a certain judgment only to the extent that it shows that the judgment corresponds to a certain norm; that this norm itself is "right," or justified, it can neither show nor, by itself, determine. Ethics must simply recognize this as a fact of human nature. Even as a normative science, a science can do no more than *explain*; it can never set up or establish a norm (which alone would be equivalent to an absolute justification). It is never able to do more than to discover the rules of the judgment, to read them from the facts before it; the origin of norms always lies outside and before science and knowledge. This means that their origin can only be apprehended by the science, and does not lie within it. In other words: if, or in so far as, the philosopher answers the question "What is good?" by an exhibition of norms, this means only that he tells us what "good" *actually* means; he can never tell us what good *must* or *should* mean. The question regarding the validity of a valuation amounts to asking for a higher acknowledged norm under which the value falls, and this is a question of *fact*. The question of the justification of the highest norms or the ultimate values is senseless, because there is nothing higher to which these could be referred. Since modern ethics, as we remarked, often speaks of this absolute justification as *the* fundamental problem of ethics, it must be said, unfortunately, that the formulation of the question from which it proceeds is simply meaningless.

The perversity of such a formulation of the question will be exhibited by a famous example. John Stuart Mill has often been justly criticized because he thought himself able to deduce from the fact that a thing was desired that it was in itself *desirable*. The double meaning of the word desirable ("capable of being desired" and "worth desiring") misled him. But his critics were also wrong, for they rested their criticism upon the same false presupposition (expressly formulated by neither), namely, that the phrase "in itself desirable" had a definite meaning (by "in itself" I mean "for its own sake," not merely as a means to an end); but in fact they could give it no meaning. If I say of a thing that it is desirable, and mean that one must desire it as a means if one desires a certain end, then everything is perfectly clear. If, however, I assert that a thing is desirable simply in itself, I cannot say what I mean by this statement; it is not verifiable and is therefore meaningless. A thing can be desirable only with respect to something else, not in itself. Mill believed himself able to deduce what is in itself desirable from what actually is desired; his opponents held that these had nothing to do with one another. But ultimately neither side knew what it said, for both failed to give an absolute meaning to the word "desirable." The question whether something is desirable for its own sake is no question at all, but mere empty words. On the other hand, the question of what actually is desired for its own sake is of course quite sensible, and ethics is actually concerned only with answering this question.

Mill succeeded in arriving at this real question, in the passage criticized, and thus freed himself of the senseless form of the question, to be sure, less by his false argument than by his healthy instinct, while his opponents remained tied to it and continued to search for an absolute justification of desire.

9. ETHICS AS FACTUAL SCIENCE

Such norms as are recognized as the ultimate norms, or highest values, must be derived from human nature and life as facts. Therefore, no result of ethics can stand in contradiction to life; ethics cannot declare as evil or false those values which lie at the foundation of life; its norms cannot demand or command anything that is in a real opposition to those final norms recognized by life. Where such opposition occurs it is a sure sign that the philosopher has misunderstood his problem, and has failed to solve it; that he has unwittingly become a moralist, that he feels uncomfortable in the role of a knower and would prefer to be a creator of moral values. The demands and claims of a morally creative person are merely subjects for investigation for the philosopher, mere objects for cognitive consideration; and this holds also if he should by chance, at other times, be this creative man himself.

We just said that there could be no real opposition between the meaning of the word "good" that is actually accepted in life, and the meaning found by the philosopher. An *apparent* difference can of course occur, for language and thought are very imperfect in daily life. Often the speaker and valuer is himself not clear as to what he expresses, and often his valuations rest on a false interpretation of the facts, and would at once change with a correction of the mistake. The philosopher would have the task of discovering such errors and faulty expressions, and would have to recognize the true norms that lie at the root of moral judgments, and place them in opposition to the apparent ones which the agent, or valuer, believes himself to follow. And in so doing he would, perhaps, find it necessary to delve deep into the human soul. Always, however, it would be an actual, already fundamental norm that he would find there.

The ultimate valuations are facts existing in human consciousness, and even if ethics were a normative science it would not cease because of this to be a science of *facts*. Ethics has to do entirely with the *actual*; this seems to me to be the most important of the propositions which determine its task. Foreign to us is the pride of those philosophers who hold the questions of ethics to be the most noble and elevated of questions just because they do not refer to the common *is* but concern the pure *ought*.

Of course, after one is in the possession of such a system of norms, of a system of applications of the concepts good and evil, one can consider the connections of the members of the hierarchy, the order of the individual rules, quite independently of any relation to actuality; one can investigate merely the inner structure of the system. And this holds even if the norms are not the really valid ones, but are falsely considered such, or are freely imagined and arbitrarily established. The last case would indeed possess only the interest of a game and would make no claim to the name of "ethics." Ethics as a normative science would, however, furnish a hierarchical order of rules, in which all acts and attitudes and characters would possess a definite place with respect to their moral value. And of course this would be true not only of existing acts and attitudes, but also of all possible ones; for if the system is to be of any value it must beforehand supply a place for every possibility of human behavior. After becoming acquainted with the highest norms, one can consider the whole system without any reference to actual behavior, by merely considering the possible. Thus Kant emphasized that for his moral philosophy it was indifferent whether or not any moral will actually existed. Hence ethics conceived as a theory of norms would exhibit the characteristics of an "ideal science"; it would have to do with a system of ideal rules, which could, of course, be applied to actuality, and would only thereby possess any interest, but the rules would have meaning quite independently of this application, and could be investigated in their relations to one another. Thus someone might have invented the rules of chess, and might have considered their application to the individual matches even if the game had never been played, except in his mind, between imaginary opponents.

10. ETHICS SEEKS CAUSAL EXPLANATION

To recapitulate: We began with the position that the task of ethics is to "explain the moral good," and we asked, first, what sort of thing this "good" is which we want to explain. We found that this subject-matter of ethics is not given to us as simply as, say, the subject-matter of optics, light, that is, by a mere sensation; but that for its determination the discovery of a "moral principle" or a whole system of principles or rules is necessary. If we call a discipline that concerns itself with such a system a "normative science," we see that this theory of norms affords nothing more than the discovery of the meaning of the concept "good." In this it exhausts itself. There is no question in it of a real explanation of the good. It offers ethics only the object which is to be explained. Therefore we have from the outset rejected the view of those philosophers who consider ethics to be merely a normative science. No, only where the theory of norms ends does ethical explanation begin. The former fails completely to see the important, exciting questions of ethics, or, worse, turns them aside as foreign in essence to ethics; in truth it fails, except through mistakes, to get beyond the mere linguistic result of determining the meanings of the words "good" and "evil."

It does of course also give us a kind of pseudo-explanation, namely, that which we call justification. Explanation always consists of the reduction of what is to be explained to something else, to something more general; and actually the norms are thus referred back to one another, until the highest are reached. These, the moral principles (or *the* moral principle), according to definition, cannot be referred to other ethical *norms*, and cannot therefore be morally justified.

But this does not mean that all further reduction must be impossible. It might be that the *moral* good could be shown to be a special case of a more general kind of good. Actually the word "good" is used in an extra-moral sense (one speaks not only of good men, but also of good riders, good mathematicians, of a good catch, a good machine, and so forth); it is therefore probable that the ethical and the extra-ethical meanings of the word are somehow connected. If the moral good can in this manner be subsumed under a wider concept of the good, then the question, "Why is moral behavior good?" could be answered by, "Because it is good in a more general sense of the word." The highest moral norm would be justified by means of an extra-moral norm; the moral principle would be referred back to a higher principle of life.

Possibly the reduction could go on a few more steps, but the final norm, the highest principle, can in no way be justified, for the very reason that it is the last. It would be senseless to ask for a further justification, a further explanation. It is not the norms, principles, or values themselves that stand in need of and are capable of explanation, but rather the actual facts from which they are abstracted. These facts are the acts of giving rules, of valuation, of approbation in human consciousness; they are thus real events in the life of the soul. "Value," "the good," are mere abstractions, but valuation, approbation, are actual psychic occurrences, and separate acts of this sort are quite capable of explanation, that is, can be reduced to one another.

And here lies the proper task of ethics. Here are the remarkable facts which excite philosophic wonder, and whose explanation has always been the final goal of ethical inquiry. That man actually approves of certain actions, declares certain dispositions to be "good," appears not at all self-explanatory to the philosopher, but often very astonishing, and he therefore asks his "Why?" Now, in all of the natural sciences every explanation can be conceived as a *causal* explanation, a truth which we need not prove here; therefore the "why" has the sense of a question concerning the *cause* of that psychical process in which man makes a valuation, establishes a moral claim. (We must make clear that when we speak of the discovery of the "cause," we mean by the term "cause" only a popular abbreviation for the statement of the complete laws governing the event to be known.)

In other words, the *determination* of the contents of the concepts of good and evil is made by the use of moral principles and a system of norms, and affords a relative justification of the lower moral rules by the higher; scientific *knowledge* of the good, on the other hand, does not concern norms, but refers to the cause, concerns not the justification but the explanation of moral judgments. The theory of norms asks, *"What* does actually serve as the standard of conduct?" Explanatory ethics, however, asks *"Why* does it serve as the standard of conduct?"

11. Formulation of the Fundamental Question

It is clear that in essence the first question is a dry, formal matter that could win little interest from man did it not have such importance for practice, and if the path to its answer did not offer so many opportunities for profound insight into human nature. The second question, however, leads directly to these profundities. It concerns the real grounds, the actual causes and motives that drive one to distinguish between good and evil, and call forth the acts of moral judgment. Not only judgments, but also *conduct,* for this follows upon judgment. The explanation of moral judgment cannot be separated from the explanation of conduct. To be sure, one should not believe, without further reason, that everyone arranges his conduct according to his moral judgments. Obviously, that would be a false assumption. The connection, although indissoluble, is more complicated. What a man values, approves, and desires is finally inferred from his actions—better from these than from his assertions, though these, too, are kinds of action. What kind of demands one makes of himself and others can only be known from one's conduct. A man's valuations must somehow appear among the motives of his acts; they cannot, in any case, be discovered anywhere else. He who traces the causes of conduct far enough must come upon the causes of all approbation. The question of the causes of conduct is, therefore, more general than that of the grounds of moral judgments; its answer would give more comprehensive knowledge, and it would be methodologically profitable to start with it even if it were not necessary to begin with the study of conduct as the only thing observable.

Therefore, we may and should replace the question raised above, "What motives cause us to establish moral norms?" by the other question, "What are the motives of conduct in general?" (We formulate the question in this general way and do not at once restrict it to *moral* actions because, according to what has been said, it might be possible to deduce valuations and their motives just as well, if not better, from immoral or neutral acts.) We are the more warranted in relating our question at once to *conduct,* since man interests himself in valuations only because conduct depends upon them. If moral approbation were something that remained enclosed in the depths of the heart, if it could never appear in any way and could not exert the least influence on the life, happiness and unhappiness of man, no one would bother himself with it, and the philosopher would become acquainted with this unimportant phenomenon only by an act of introspection. That wonder concerning the moral judgments of man, which we have described as the earliest impulse leading to the formulation of ethical questions, is above all wonder at his own actual moral behavior.

Therefore, we inquire into the causes, that is, the regularity and order, of all human actions, with the aim of discovering the motives of moral actions. And we profit in so doing because we can postpone the question regarding the essence of morality, the moral principle, until we solve the problem of the natural law governing behavior in general. When, however, we come to know about action in general, it will certainly be much easier to learn what is peculiar to moral actions and to define the content of the concept "good" without difficulty. Perhaps it will turn out that we no longer feel the necessity of determining a sharp boundary for it (just as, after the physical explanation of light, the question of how and whether the concept of "light" is to be distinguished from that of heat radiation or ultra-violet radiation loses all interest).

12. THE METHOD OF ETHICS IS PSYCHOLOGICAL

Thus the central problem of ethics concerns the causal explanation of moral behavior; all others in relation to it sink to the level of preliminary or subordinate questions. The moral problem was most clearly formulated in this way by Schopenhauer, whose sound sense of reality led him to the correct path here (if not in the solution) and guarded him from the Kantian formulation of the problem and from the post-Kantian philosophy of value.

The problem which we must put at the center of ethics is a purely psychological one. For, without doubt, the discovery of the motives or laws of any kind of behavior, and therefore of moral behavior, is a purely psychological affair. Only the empirical science of the laws which describe the life of the soul can solve this problem. One might wish to derive from this a supposedly profound and destructive objection to our formulation of the problem. For, one might say, "In such case there would be no ethics at all; what is called ethics would be nothing but a part of psychology!" I answer, "Why shouldn't ethics be a part of psychology?" Perhaps in order that the philosopher have his science for himself and govern autonomously in this sphere? He would, indeed, thereby be freed of many burdensome protests of psychology. If he laid down a command, *"Thus shall man act,"* he would not have to pay attention to the psychologist who said to him, "But man *cannot* act so, because it contradicts psychological laws!" I fear greatly that here and there this motive, though hidden, is at work. However, if one says candidly that "there is no ethics," because it is not necessary to label a part of psychology by a special name, then the question is merely terminological.

It is a poor recommendation of the philosophical spirit of our age that we so often attempt to draw strict lines of division between the sciences, to separate ever new disciplines, and to prove their autonomy. The true philosopher goes in the opposite direction; he does not wish to make the single sciences self-sufficient and independent, but, on the contrary, to unify and bring them together; he wishes to show that what is common to them is what is most essential, and that what is different is accidental and to be viewed as belonging to practical methodology. *Sub specie aeternitatis* there is for him only *one* reality and *one* science.

Therefore, if we decide that the fundamental question of ethics, "Why does man act morally?" can be answered only by psychology, we see in this no degradation of, nor injury to, science, but a happy simplification of the world-picture. In ethics we do not seek independence, but only the truth.

13

The Emotive Meaning

of Ethical Terms

BY C. L. STEVENSON

I

ETHICAL QUESTIONS first arise in the form "Is so and so good?" or "Is this alternative better than that?" These questions are difficult partly because we don't quite know what we are seeking. We are asking, "Is there a needle in that haystack?" without even knowing just what a needle is. So the first thing to do is to examine the questions themselves. We must try to make them clearer, either by defining the terms in which they are expressed, or by any other method that is available.

The present paper is concerned wholly with this preliminary step of making ethical questions clear. In order to help answer the question "Is X good?" we must *substitute* for it a question which is free from ambiguity and confusion.

It is obvious that in substituting a clearer question we must not introduce some utterly different kind of question. It won't do (to take an extreme instance of a prevalent fallacy) to substitute for "Is X good?" the question "Is X pink with yellow trimmings?" and then point out how easy the question really is. This would beg the original question, not help answer it. On the other hand, we must not expect the substituted question to be strictly "identical" with the original one. The original question may embody hypostatization, anthropomorphism, vagueness, and all the other ills to which our ordinary discourse is subject. If our substituted question is to be clearer, it must remove these ills. The questions will be identical only in the sense that a child is identical with the man he later becomes. Hence we must not demand that the substitution strike us, on immediate introspection, as making no change in meaning.

This article first appeared in *Mind,* 1937. It is reprinted with the kind permission of Professor Stevenson and the editor of *Mind.*

Just how, then, must the substituted question be related to the original? Let us assume (inaccurately) that it must result from replacing "good" by some set of terms which define it. The question then resolves itself to this: How must the defined meaning of "good" be related to its original meaning?

I answer that it must be *relevant*. A defined meaning will be called "relevant" to the original meaning under these circumstances: Those who have understood the definition must be able to say all that they then want to say by using the term in the defined way. They must never have occasion to use the term in the old, unclear sense. (If a person did have to go on using the word in the old sense, then to this extent his meaning would not be clarified, and the philosophical task would not be completed.) It frequently happens that a word is used so confusedly and ambiguously that we must give it *several* defined meanings, rather than one. In this case only the whole set of defined meanings will be called "relevant," and any one of them will be called "partially relevant." This is not a rigorous treatment of *relevance,* by any means; but it will serve for the present purposes.

Let us now turn to our particular task—that of giving a relevant definition of "good." Let us first examine some of the ways in which others have attempted to do this.

The word "good" has often been defined in terms of *approval,* or similar psychological attitudes. We may take as typical examples: "good" means *desired by me* (Hobbes); and "good" means *approved by most people* (Hume, in effect).* It will be convenient to refer to definitions of this sort as "interest theories," following Mr. R. B. Perry, although neither "interest" nor "theory" is used in the most usual way.

Are definitions of this sort relevant?

It is idle to deny their *partial* relevance. The most superficial inquiry will reveal that "good" is exceedingly ambiguous. To maintain that "good" is *never* used in Hobbes's sense, and never in Hume's, is only to manifest an insensitivity to the complexities of language. We must recognize, perhaps, not only these senses, but a variety of similar ones, differing both with regard to the kind of interest in question, and with regard to the people who are said to have the interest.

---

* [The author has requested that the following note be added here: For a more adequate treatment of Hume's views see my *Ethics and Language* (Yale University Press, 1944), Chap. XII, Sect. 5. In the present paper the references to Hume are to be taken as references to the general *family* of definitions of which Hume's is typical; but Hume's own definition is somewhat different from any that is here specifically stated. Perhaps the same should be said of Hobbes.]

But this is a minor matter. The essential question is not whether interest theories are *partially* relevant, but whether they are *wholly* relevant. This is the only point for intelligent dispute. Briefly: Granted that some senses of "good" may relevantly be defined in terms of interest, is there some *other* sense which is *not* relevantly so defined? We must give this question careful attention. For it is quite possible that when philosophers (and many others) have found the question "Is X good?" so difficult, they have been grasping for this *other* sense of "good," and not any sense relevantly defined in terms of interest. If we insist on defining "good" in terms of interest, and answer the question when thus interpreted, we may be begging *their* question entirely. Of course this *other* sense of "good" may not exist, or it may be a complete confusion; but that is what we must discover.

Now many have maintained that interest theories are *far* from being completely relevant. They have argued that such theories neglect the very sense of "good" which is most vital. And certainly, their arguments are not without plausibility.

Only . . . what *is* this "vital" sense of "good"? The answers have been so vague, and so beset with difficulties, that one can scarcely determine.

There are certain requirements, however, with which this "vital" sense has been expected to comply—requirements which appeal strongly to our common sense. It will be helpful to summarize these, showing how they exclude the interest theories.

In the first place, we must be able sensibly to *disagree* about whether something is "good." This condition rules out Hobbes's definition. For consider the following argument: "This is good." "That isn't so; it's not good." As translated by Hobbes, this becomes: "I desire this." "That isn't so, for *I* don't." The speakers are not contradicting one another, and think they are, only because of an elementary confusion in the use of pronouns. The definition, "good" means *desired by my community,* is also excluded, for how could people from different communities disagree?[1]

In the second place, "goodness" must have, so to speak, a magnetism. A person who recognizes X to be "good" must *ipso facto* acquire a stronger tendency to act in its favor than he otherwise would have had. This rules out the Humian type of definition. For according to Hume, to recognize that something is "good" is simply to recognize that the majority approve of it. Clearly, a man may see that the majority approve of X without having, himself, a

1. See G. E. Moore's *Philosophical Studies,* pp. 332-334.

stronger tendency to favor it. This requirement excludes any attempt to define "good" in terms of the interest of people *other* than the speaker.[2]

In the third place, the "goodness" of anything must not be verifiable solely by use of the scientific method. "Ethics must not be psychology." This restriction rules out all of the traditional interest theories, without exception. It is so sweeping a restriction that we must examine its plausibility. What are the methodological implications of interest theories which are here rejected?

According to Hobbes's definition, a person can prove his ethical judgments, with finality, by showing that he is not making an introspective error about his desires. According to Hume's definition, one may prove ethical judgments (roughly speaking) by taking a vote. *This* use of the empirical method, at any rate, seems highly remote from what we usually accept as proof, and reflects on the complete relevance of the definitions which imply it.

But aren't there more complicated interest theories which are immune from such methodological implications? No, for the same factors appear; they are only put off for a while. Consider, for example, the definition: "X is good" means *most people would approve of X if they knew its nature and consequences.* How, according to this definition, could we prove that a certain X was good? We should first have to find out, empirically, just what X was like, and what its consequences would be. To this extent the empirical method, as required by the definition, seems beyond intelligent objection. But what remains? We should next have to discover whether most people would approve of the sort of thing we had discovered X to be. This couldn't be determined by popular vote—but only because it would be too difficult to explain to the voters, beforehand, what the nature and consequences of X really were. Apart from this, voting would be a pertinent method. We are again reduced to counting noses, as a *perfectly final* appeal.

Now we need not scorn voting entirely. A man who rejected interest theories as irrelevant might readily make the following statement: "If I believed that X would be approved by the majority, when they knew all about it, I should be strongly *led* to say that X was good." But he would continue: *"Need* I say that X was good, under the circumstances? Wouldn't my acceptance of the alleged 'final proof' result simply from my being democratic? What about the more aristocratic people? They would simply say that the approval of most people, even when they knew all about the object

2. See G. C. Field's *Moral Theory,* pp. 52, 56-57.

of their approval, simply had nothing to do with the goodness of anything, and they would probably add a few remarks about the low state of people's interests." It would indeed seem, from these considerations, that the definition we have been considering has presupposed democratic ideals from the start; it has dressed up democratic propaganda in the guise of a definition.

The omnipotence of the empirical method, as implied by interest theories and others, may be shown unacceptable in a somewhat different way. Mr. G. E. Moore's familiar objection about the open question is chiefly pertinent in this regard. No matter what set of scientifically knowable properties a thing may have (says Moore, in effect), you will find, on careful introspection, that it is an open question to ask whether anything having these properties is *good*. It is difficult to believe that this recurrent question is a totally confused one, or that it seems open only because of the ambiguity of "good." Rather, we must be using some sense of "good" which is not definable, relevantly, in terms of anything scientifically knowable. That is, the scientific method is not sufficient for ethics.[3]

These, then, are the requirements with which the "vital" sense of "good" is expected to comply: (1) goodness must be a topic for intelligent disagreement; (2) it must be "magnetic"; and (3) it must not be discoverable solely through the scientific method.

II

Let us now turn to my own analysis of ethical judgments. First let me present my position dogmatically, showing to what extent I vary from tradition.

I believe that the three requirements, given above, are perfectly sensible; that there is some *one* sense of "good" which satisfies all three requirements; and that no traditional interest theory satisfies them all. But this does not imply that "good" must be explained in terms of a Platonic Idea, or of a Categorical Imperative, or of an unique, unanalyzable property. On the contrary, the three requirements can be met by a *kind* of interest theory. *But we must give up a presupposition which all the traditional interest theories have made.*

Traditional interest theories hold that ethical statements are *descriptive* of the existing state of interests—that they simply *give information* about interests. (More accurately, ethical judgments are said to describe what the state of interests is, was, or will be,

---

3. See G. E. Moore's *Principia Ethica*, chap. i. I am simply trying to preserve the spirit of Moore's objection, and not the exact form of it.

or to indicate what the state of interests *would* be under specified circumstances.) It is this emphasis on description, on information, which leads to their incomplete relevance. Doubtless there is always *some* element of description in ethical judgments, but this is by no means all. Their major use is not to indicate facts, but to *create an influence*. Instead of merely describing people's interests, they *change* or *intensify* them. They *recommend* an interest in an object, rather than state that the interest already exists.

For instance: When you tell a man that he oughtn't to steal, your object isn't merely to let him know that people disapprove of stealing. You are attempting, rather, to get *him* to disapprove of it. Your ethical judgment has a quasi-imperative force which, operating through suggestion, and intensified by your tone of voice, readily permits you to begin to *influence,* to *modify,* his interests. If in the end you do not succeed in getting *him* to disapprove of stealing, you will feel that you've failed to convince him that stealing is wrong. You will continue to feel this, even though he fully acknowledges that you disapprove of it, and that almost everyone else does. When you point out to him the consequences of his actions—consequences which you suspect he already disapproves of—these *reasons* which support your ethical judgment are simply a means of facilitating your influence. If you think you can change his interests by making vivid to him how others will disapprove of him, you will do so; otherwise not. So the consideration about other people's interest is just an additional means you may employ, in order to move him, and is not a part of the ethical judgment itself. Your ethical judgment doesn't merely describe interests to him, it directs his very interests. The difference between the traditional interest theories and my view is like the difference between describing a desert and irrigating it.

Another example: A munition maker declares that war is a good thing. If he merely meant that he approved of it, he would not have to insist so strongly, nor grow so excited in his argument. People would be quite easily convinced that he approved of it. If he merely meant that most people approved of war, or that most people would approve of it if they knew the consequences, he would have to yield his point if it were proved that this wasn't so. But he wouldn't do this, nor does consistency require it. He is not *describing* the state of people's approval; he is trying to *change* it by his influence. If he found that few people approved of war, he might insist all the more strongly that it was good, for there would be more changing to be done.

This example illustrates how "good" may be used for what most of us would call bad purposes. Such cases are as pertinent as any others. I am not indicating the *good* way of using "good." I am not influencing people, but am describing the way this influence sometimes goes on. If the reader wishes to say that the munition maker's influence is bad—that is, if the reader wishes to awaken people's disapproval of the man, and to make him disapprove of his own actions—I should at another time be willing to join in this undertaking. But this is not the present concern. I am not using ethical terms, but am indicating how they *are* used. The munition maker, in his use of "good," illustrates the persuasive character of the word just as well as does the unselfish man who, eager to encourage in each of us a desire for the happiness of all, contends that the supreme good is peace.

Thus ethical terms are *instruments* used in the complicated interplay and readjustment of human interests. This can be seen plainly from more general observations. People from widely separated communities have different moral attitudes. Why? To a great extent because they have been subject to different social influences. Now clearly this influence doesn't operate through sticks and stones alone; words play a great part. People praise one another, to encourage certain inclinations, and blame one another, to discourage others. Those of forceful personalities issue commands which weaker people, for complicated instinctive reasons, find it difficult to disobey, quite apart from fears of consequences. Further influence is brought to bear by writers and orators. Thus social influence is exerted, to an enormous extent, by means that have nothing to do with physical force or material reward. The ethical terms facilitate such influence. Being suited for use in *suggestion,* they are a means by which men's attitudes may be led this way or that. The reason, then, that we find a greater similarity in the moral attitudes of one community than in those of different communities is largely this: ethical judgments propagate themselves. One man says "This is good"; this may influence the approval of another person, who then makes the same ethical judgment, which in turn influences another person, and so on. In the end, by a process of mutual influence, people take up more or less the same attitudes. Between people of widely separated communities, of course, the influence is less strong; hence different communities have different attitudes.

These remarks will serve to give a general idea of my point of view. We must now go into more detail. There are several questions which must be answered: How does an ethical sentence acquire its power of influencing people—why is it suited to suggestion? Again, what has this influence to do with the *meaning* of ethical terms? And finally, do these considerations really lead us to a sense of "good" which meets the requirements mentioned in the preceding section?

Let us deal first with the question about *meaning*. This is far from an easy question, so we must enter into a preliminary inquiry about meaning in general. Although a seeming digression, this will prove indispensable.

III

Broadly speaking, there are two different *purposes* which lead us to use language. On the one hand we use words (as in science) to record, clarify, and communicate *beliefs*. On the other hand we use words to give vent to our feelings (interjections), or to create moods (poetry), or to incite people to actions or attitudes (oratory).

The first use of words I shall call "descriptive"; the second, "dynamic." Note that the distinction depends solely upon the *purpose* of the *speaker*.

When a person says "Hydrogen is the lightest known gas," his purpose *may* be simply to lead the hearer to believe this, or to believe that the speaker believes it. In that case the words are used descriptively. When a person cuts himself and says "Damn," his purpose is not ordinarily to record, clarify, or communicate any belief. The word is used dynamically. The two ways of using words, however, are by no means mutually exclusive. This is obvious from the fact that our purposes are often complex. Thus when one says "I want you to close the door," part of his purpose, ordinarily, is to lead the hearer to believe that he has this want. To that extent the words are used descriptively. But the major part of one's purpose is to lead the hearer to *satisfy* the want. To that extent the words are used dynamically.

It very frequently happens that the same sentence may have a dynamic use on one occasion, and may not have a dynamic use on another; and that it may have different dynamic uses on different occasions. For instance: A man says to a visiting neighbor, "I am loaded down with work." His purpose may be to let the neighbor know how life is going with him. This would *not* be a dynamic use of words. He may make the remark, however, in order to drop a hint. This *would* be dynamic usage (as well as descriptive). Again, he may make the remark to arouse the neighbor's sympathy. This would be a *different* dynamic usage from that of hinting.

Or again, when we say to a man, "Of course you won't make those mistakes any more," we *may* simply be making a prediction. But we are more likely to be using "suggestion," in order to encourage him and hence *keep* him from making mistakes. The first use would be descriptive; the second, mainly dynamic.

From these examples it will be clear that we can't determine whether words are used dynamically or not, merely by reading the dictionary—even assuming that everyone is faithful to dictionary meanings. Indeed, to know whether a person is using a word dynamically, we must note his tone of voice, his gestures, the general circumstances under which he is speaking, and so on.

We must now proceed to an important question: What has the dynamic use of words to do with their *meaning?* One thing is clear —we must not define "meaning" in a way that would make meaning vary with dynamic usage. If we did, we should have no use for the term. All that we could say about such "meaning" would be that it is very complicated, and subject to constant change. So we must certainly distinguish between the dynamic use of words and their meaning.

It doesn't follow, however, that we must define "meaning" in some non-psychological fashion. We must simply restrict the psychological field. Instead of identifying meaning with *all* the psychological causes and effects that attend a word's utterance, we must identify it with those that it has a *tendency* (causal property, dispositional property) to be connected with. The tendency must be of a particular kind, moreover. It must exist for all who speak the language; it must be persistent; and must be realizable more or less independently of determinate circumstances attending the word's utterance. There will be further restrictions dealing with the interrelation of words in different contexts. Moreover, we must include, under the psychological responses which the words tend to produce, not only immediately introspectable experiences, but *dispositions* to react in a given way with appropriate stimuli. I hope to go into these matters in a subsequent paper. Suffice it now to say that I think "meaning" may be thus defined in a way to include "propositional" meaning as an important kind. Now a word may *tend* to have causal relations which in fact it sometimes doesn't; and it may sometimes have causal relations which it *doesn't tend* to have. And since the tendency of words which constitutes their meaning must be of a particular kind, and may include, as responses, dispositions to reactions, of which any of *several* immediate experiences may be a sign, then there is nothing surprising in the fact that words have a permanent meaning, in spite of the fact that the immediately intro-spectable experiences which attend their usage are so highly varied.

When "meaning" is defined in this way, meaning will not include dynamic use. For although words are sometimes accompanied by dynamic purposes, they do not *tend* to be accompanied by them in the way above mentioned. E.g., there is no tendency realizable inde-pendently of the determinate circumstances under which the words are uttered.

There will be a kind of meaning, however, in the sense above defined, which has an intimate relation to dynamic usage. I refer to "emotive" meaning (in a sense roughly like that employed by Ogden and Richards).[4] The emotive meaning of a word is a tendency of a word, arising through the history of its usage, to produce (result from) *affective* responses in people. It is the immediate aura of feeling which hovers about a word. Such tendencies to pro-duce affective responses cling to words very tenaciously. It would be difficult, for instance, to express merriment by using the inter-jection "alas." Because of the persistence of such affective tenden-cies (among other reasons) it becomes feasible to classify them as "meanings."

Just *what* is the relation between emotive meaning and the dynamic use of words? Let us take an example. Suppose that a man is talking with a group of people which includes Miss Jones, aged 59. He refers to her, without thinking, as an "old maid." Now even if his purposes are perfectly innocent—even if he is using the words purely descriptively—Miss Jones won't think so. She will think he is encouraging the others to have contempt for her, and will draw in her skirts, defensively. The man might have done better if instead of saying "old maid" he had said "elderly spinster." The latter words could have been put to the same descriptive use, and would not so readily have caused suspicions about the dynamic use.

"Old maid" and "elderly spinster" differ, to be sure, only in emotive meaning. From the example it will be clear that certain words, because of their emotive meaning, are suited to a certain kind of dynamic use—so well suited, in fact, that the hearer is likely to be misled when we use them in any other way. The more pro-nounced a word's emotive meaning is, the less likely people are to use it purely descriptively. Some words are suited to encourage people, some to discourage them, some to quiet them, and so on.

----

4. See *The Meaning of Meaning,* by C. K. Ogden and I. A. Richards. On p. 125, second edition, there is a passage on ethics which was the source of the ideas embodied in this paper.

Even in these cases, of course, the dynamic purposes are not to be identified with any sort of meaning; for the emotive meaning accompanies a word much more persistently than do the dynamic purposes. But there is an important contingent relation between emotive meaning and dynamic purpose: the former assists the latter. Hence if we define emotively laden terms in a way that neglects their emotive meaning, we are likely to be confusing. *We lead people to think that the terms defined are used dynamically less often than they are.*

IV

Let us now apply these remarks in defining "good." This word may be used morally or non-morally. I shall deal with the non-moral usage almost entirely, but only because it is simpler. The main points of the analysis will apply equally well to either usage.

As a preliminary definition, let us take an inaccurate approximation. It may be more misleading than helpful, but will do to begin with. Roughly, then, the sentence "X is good" means *We like X.* ("We" includes the hearer or hearers.)

At first glance this definition sounds absurd. If used, we should expect to find the following sort of conversation: A. "This is good." B. "But I *don't* like it. What led you to believe that I did?" The unnaturalness of B's reply, judged by ordinary word-usage, would seem to cast doubt on the relevance of my definition.

B's unnaturalness, however, lies simply in this: he is assuming that "We like it" (as would occur implicitly in the use of "good") is being used descriptively. This won't do. When "We like it" is to take the place of "This is good," the former sentence must be used not purely descriptively, but dynamically. More specifically, it must be used to promote a very subtle (and for the non-moral sense in question, a very easily resisted) kind of *suggestion.* To the extent that "we" refers to the hearer, it must have the dynamic use, essential to suggestion, of leading the hearer to *make* true what is said, rather than merely to believe it. And to the extent that "we" refers to the speaker, the sentence must have not only the descriptive use of indicating belief about the speaker's interest, but the quasi-interjectory, dynamic function of giving direct expression to the interest. (This immediate expression of feelings assists in the process of suggestion. It is difficult to disapprove in the face of another's enthusiasm.)

For an example of a case where "We like this" is used in the dynamic way that "This is good" is used, consider the case of a mother who says to her several children, "One thing is certain, *we all like to be neat.*" If she really believed this, she wouldn't bother to say so. But she is not using the words descriptively. She is *encouraging* the children to like neatness. By telling them that they like neatness, she will lead them to *make* her statement true, so to speak. If, instead of saying "We all like to be neat" in this way, she had said "It's a good thing to be neat," the effect would have been approximately the same.

But these remarks are still misleading. Even when "We like it" is used for suggestion, it isn't quite like "This is good." The latter is more subtle. With such a sentence as "This is a good book," for example, it would be practically impossible to use instead "We like this book." When the latter is used, it must be accompanied by so exaggerated an intonation, to prevent its becoming confused with a descriptive statement, that the force of suggestion becomes stronger, and ludicrously more overt, than when "good" is used.

The definition is inadequate, further, in that the definiens has been restricted to dynamic usage. Having said that dynamic usage was different from meaning, I should not have to mention it in giving the *meaning* of "good."

It is in connection with this last point that we must return to emotive meaning. The word "good" has a pleasing emotive meaning which fits it especially for the dynamic use of suggesting favorable interest. But the sentence "We like it" has no such emotive meaning. Hence my definition has neglected emotive meaning entirely. Now to neglect emotive meaning is likely to lead to endless confusions, as we shall presently see; so I have sought to make up for the inadequacy of the definition by letting the restriction about dynamic usage take the place of emotive meaning. What I should do, of course, is to find a definiens whose emotive meaning, like that of "good," simply does *lead* to dynamic usage.

Why didn't I do this? I answer that it isn't possible, if the definition is to afford us increased clarity. No two words, in the first place, have quite the same emotive meaning. The most we can hope for is a rough approximation. But if we seek for such an approximation for "good," we shall find nothing more than synonyms, such as "desirable" or "valuable"; and these are profitless because they do not clear up the connection between "good" and favorable interest. If we reject such synonyms, in favor of non-ethical terms, we shall be highly misleading. For instance: "This is good" has something like the meaning of "I *do* like this; do so as well." But this is certainly not accurate. For the imperative makes an appeal to the conscious efforts of the hearer. Of course he can't like something just by trying. He must be led to like it through suggestion. Hence an ethical sentence differs from an imperative in that it enables one to make changes in a much more subtle, less fully conscious way. Note that the ethical sentence centers the hearer's attention not on his interests, but on the object of interest, and thereby facilitates suggestion. Because of its subtlety, moreover, an ethical sentence readily permits counter-suggestion, and leads to the give and take situation which is so characteristic of arguments about values.

Strictly speaking, then, it is impossible to define "good" in terms of favorable interest if emotive meaning is not to be distorted. Yet it is possible to say that "This is good" is *about* the favorable interest of the speaker and the hearer or hearers, and that it has a pleasing emotive meaning which fits the words for use in suggestion. This is a rough description of meaning, not a definition. But it serves the same clarifying function that a definition ordinarily does; and that, after all, is enough.

A word must be added about the moral use of "good." This differs from the above in that it is about a different kind of interest. Instead of being about what the hearer and speaker *like,* it is about a stronger sort of approval. When a person *likes* something, he is pleased when it prospers, and disappointed when it doesn't. When a person *morally approves* of something, he experiences a rich feeling of security when it prospers, and is indignant, or "shocked" when it doesn't. These are rough and inaccurate examples of the many factors which one would have to mention in distinguishing the two kinds of interest. In the moral usage, as well as in the nonmoral, "good" has an emotive meaning which adapts it to suggestion.

And now, are these considerations of any importance? Why do I stress emotive meanings in this fashion? Does the omission of them really lead people into errors? I think, indeed, that the errors resulting from such omissions are enormous. In order to see this, however, we must return to the restrictions, mentioned in section I, with which the "vital" sense of "good" has been expected to comply.

V

The first restriction, it will be remembered, had to do with disagreement. Now there is clearly some sense in which people disagree on ethical points; but we must not rashly assume that all disagreement is modelled after the sort that occurs in the natural sciences. We must distinguish between "disagreement in belief" (typical of the sciences) and "disagreement in interest." Disagreement in belief occurs when A believes *p* and B disbelieves it. Disagreement in interest occurs when A has a favorable interest in X, when B has an unfavorable one in it, and when neither is content to let the other's interest remain unchanged.

Let me give an example of disagreement in interest. A. "Let's go to a cinema to-night." B. "I don't want to do that. Let's go to the symphony." A continues to insist on the cinema, B on the symphony. This is disagreement in a perfectly conventional sense. They can't agree on where they want to go, and each is trying to redirect the other's interest. (Note that imperatives are used in the example.)

It is disagreement in *interest* which takes places in ethics. When C says "This is good," and D says "No, it's bad," we have a case of suggestion and counter-suggestion. Each man is trying to redirect the other's interest. There obviously need be no domineering, since each may be willing to give ear to the other's influence; but each is trying to move the other nonetheless. It is in this sense that they disagree. Those who argue that certain interest theories make no provision for disagreement have been misled, I believe, simply because the traditional theories, in leaving out emotive meaning, give the impression that ethical judgments are used descriptively only; and of course when judgments are used purely descriptively, the only disagreement that can arise is disagreement *in belief*. Such disagreement may be disagreement in belief *about* interests; but this is not the same as disagreement *in* interest. My definition doesn't provide for disagreement in belief about interests, any more than does Hobbes's; but that is no matter, for there is no reason to believe, at least on common-sense grounds, that this kind of disagreement exists. There is only disagreement *in* interest. (We shall see in a moment that disagreement in interest does not remove ethics from sober argument—that this kind of disagreement may often be resolved through empirical means.)

The second restriction, about "magnetism," or the connection between goodness and actions, requires only a word. This rules out *only* those interest theories which do *not* include the interest of the speaker, in defining "good." My account does include the speaker's interest; hence is immune.

The third restriction, about the empirical method, may be met in a way that springs naturally from the above account of disagreement. Let us put the question in this way: When two people disagree over an ethical matter, can they completely resolve the disagreement through empirical considerations, assuming that each applies the empirical method exhaustively, consistently, and without error?

I answer that sometimes they can, and sometimes they cannot; and that at any rate, even when they can, the relation between empirical knowledge and ethical judgments is quite different from the one which traditional interest theories seem to imply.

This can best be seen from an analogy. Let's return to the example where A and B couldn't agree on a cinema or a symphony. The example differed from an ethical argument in that imperatives were used, rather than ethical judgments; but was analogous to the extent that each person was endeavoring to modify the other's interest. Now how would these people argue the case, assuming that they were too intelligent just to shout at one another?

Clearly, they would give "reasons" to support their imperatives. A might say, "But you know, Garbo is at the Bijou." His hope is that B, who admires Garbo, will acquire a desire to go to the cinema when he knows what play will be there. B may counter, "But Toscanini is guest conductor tonight, in an all-Beethoven program." And so on. Each supports his imperative (*"Let's* do so and so") by reasons which may be empirically established.

To generalize from this: disagreement in interest may be rooted in disagreement in belief. That is to say, people who disagree in interest would often cease to do so if they knew the precise nature and consequences of the object of their interest. To this extent disagreement in interest may be resolved by securing agreement in belief, which in turn may be secured empirically.

This generalization holds for ethics. If A and B, instead of using imperatives, had said, respectively, "It would be *better* to go to the cinema," and "It would be better to go to the symphony," the reasons which they would advance would be roughly the same. They would each give a more thorough account of the object of interest, with the purpose of completing the redirection of interest which was begun by the suggestive force of the ethical sentence. On the whole, of course, the suggestive force of the ethical statement merely exerts enough pressure to start such trains of reasons, since the reasons are much more essential in resolving disagreement in interest than the persuasive effect of the ethical judgment itself.

Thus the empirical method is relevant to ethics simply because our knowledge of the world is a determining factor to our interests. But note that empirical facts are not inductive grounds from which the ethical judgment problematically follows. (This is what traditional interest theories imply.) If someone said "Close the door," and added the reason "We'll catch cold," the latter would scarcely be called an inductive ground of the former. Now imperatives are related to the reasons which support them in the same way that ethical judgments are related to reasons.

Is the empirical method *sufficient* for attaining ethical agreement? Clearly not. For empirical knowledge resolves disagreement in interest only to the extent that such disagreement is rooted in disagreement in belief. Not all disagreement in interest is of this sort. For instance: A is of a sympathetic nature, and B isn't. They are arguing about whether a public dole would be good. Suppose that they discovered all the consequences of the dole. Isn't it possible, even so, that A will say that it's good, and B that it's bad? The disagreement in interest may arise not from limited factual knowledge, but simply from A's sympathy and B's coldness. Or again, suppose, in the above argument, that A was poor and unemployed, and that B was rich. Here again the disagreement might not be due to different factual knowledge. It would be due to the different social positions of the men, together with their predominant self-interest.

When ethical disagreement is not rooted in disagreement in belief, is there *any* method by which it may be settled? If one means by "method" a *rational* method, then there is no method. But in any case there is a "way." Let's consider the above example, again, where disagreement was due to A's sympathy and B's coldness. Must they end by saying, "Well, it's just a matter of our having different temperaments"? Not necessarily. A, for instance, may try to *change* the temperament of his opponent. He may pour out his enthusiasms in such a moving way—present the sufferings of the poor with such appeal—that he will lead his opponent to see life through different eyes. He may build up, by the contagion of his feelings, an influence which will modify B's temperament, and create in him a sympathy for the poor which didn't previously exist. This is often the only way to obtain ethical agreement, if there is any way at all. It is persuasive, not empirical or rational; but that is no reason for neglecting it. There is no reason to scorn it, either, for it is only by such means that our personalities are able to grow, through our contact with others.

The point I wish to stress, however, is simply that the empirical method is instrumental to ethical agreement only to the extent that disagreement in interest is rooted in disagreement in belief. There is little reason to believe that all disagreement is of this sort. Hence the empirical method is not sufficient for ethics. In any case, ethics is not psychology, since psychology doesn't endeavor to *direct* our interests; it discovers facts about the ways in which interests are or can be directed, but that's quite another matter.

To summarize this section: my analysis of ethical judgments meets the three requirements for the "vital" sense of "good" that were mentioned in section I. The traditional interest theories fail to meet these requirements simply because they neglect emotive meaning. This neglect leads them to neglect dynamic usage, and the sort of disagreement that results from such usage, together with the method of resolving the disagreement. I may add that my analysis answers Moore's objection about the open question. Whatever scientifically knowable properties a thing may have, it *is* always open to question whether a thing having these (enumerated) qualities is good. For to ask whether it is good is to ask for *influence*. And whatever I may know about an object, I can still ask, quite pertinently, to be influenced with regard to my interest in it.

VI

And now, have I really pointed out the "vital" sense of "good"?

I suppose that many will still say "No," claiming that I have simply failed to set down *enough* requirements which this sense must meet, and that my analysis, like all others given in terms of interest, is a way of begging the issue. They will say: "When we ask 'Is X good?' we don't want mere influence, mere advice. We decidedly don't want to be influenced through persuasion, nor are we fully content when the influence is supported by a wide scientific knowledge of X. The answer to our question will, of course, modify our interests. But this is only because an unique sort of *truth* will be revealed to us—a truth which must be apprehended *a priori*. We want our interests to be guided by this truth, and by nothing else. To substitute for such a truth mere emotive meaning and suggestion is to conceal from us the very object of our search."

I can only answer that I do not understand. What is this truth to be *about*? For I recollect no Platonic Idea, nor do I know what to *try* to recollect. I find no indefinable property, nor do I know what to look for. And the "self-evident" deliverances of reason, which so many philosophers have claimed, seem, on examination, to be deliverances of their respective reasons only (if of anyone's) and not of mine.

I strongly suspect, indeed, that any sense of "good" which is expected both to unite itself in synthetic *a priori* fashion with other concepts, and to influence interests as well, is really a great confusion. I extract from this meaning the power of influence alone, which I find the only intelligible part. If the rest is confusion, however, then it certainly deserves more than the shrug of one's shoulders. What I should like to do is to *account* for the confusion—to examine the psychological needs which have given rise to it, and to show how these needs may be satisfied in another way. This is *the* problem, if confusion is to be stopped at its source. But it is an enormous problem, and my reflections on it, which are at present worked out only roughly, must be reserved until some later time.

I may add that if "X is good" is essentially a vehicle for suggestion, it is scarcely a statement which philosophers, any more than many other men, are called upon to make. To the extent that ethics predicates the ethical terms of anything, rather than explains their meaning, it ceases to be a reflective study. Ethical statements are social instruments. They are used in a co-operative enterprise in which we are mutually adjusting ourselves to the interests of others. Philosophers have a part in this, as do all men, but not the major part.

14

Sociology and Physicalism

BY OTTO NEURATH

(TRANSLATED BY MORTON MAGNUS AND RALPH RAICO)

I. PHYSICALISM: A NON-METAPHYSICAL STANDPOINT

CONTINUING the work of Mach, Poincaré, Frege, Wittgenstein and others, the "Vienna Circle for the Dissemination of the Scientific World-Outlook (*Weltauffassung*) seeks to create a climate which will be free from metaphysics in order to promote scientific studies in all fields by means of logical analysis. It would be less misleading to speak of a "Vienna Circle for Physicalism," since "world" is a term which does not occur in the language of science, and since world-outlook (Weltauffassung) is often confused with world-view (Weltanschauung). All the representatives of the Circle are in agreement that "philosophy" does not exist as a discipline, alongside of science, with propositions of its own: the body of scientific propositions exhausts the sum of all meaningful statements.

When reduced to unified science, the various sciences are pursued in precisely the same manner as in their disassociation. Up to now their uniform logical character has not always been sufficiently emphasized. Unified science is the outgrowth of comprehensive *collective labor*—in the same way as the structure of chemistry, geology, biology or even mathematics and logic.

Unified science will be pursued in the same fashion as the individual sciences have been pursued hitherto. Thus, the "thinker without a school" will have no more significance than he had when the sciences were disunited. The individual can here achieve just as much or just as little with isolated notions as he could before. Every proposed innovation must be so formulated that it may be expected

This article, originally entitled "Soziologie im Physikalismus," first appeared in Volume II of *Erkenntnis* (1931/2). It is included in the present work with the kind permission of Mrs. Marie Neurath and Professor Rudolf Carnap.

to gain universal acceptance. Only through the cooperative effort of many thinkers do all its implications become clear. If it is false or meaningless, i.e., metaphysical, then, of course, it falls outside the range of unified science. Unified science, alongside of which there exists no "philosophy" or "metaphysics," is not the achievement of isolated individuals, but of a generation.

Some representatives of the "Vienna Circle" who, like all their colleagues in this group, explicitly declare that there are no peculiarly "philosophic truths," nevertheless still occasionally employ the word "philosophy." By this they mean to designate "philosophizing," the "operation whereby concepts are clarified." This concession to traditional linguistic usage, though understandable for a number of reasons, easily gives rise to misconceptions. In the present exposition the term is not employed. We are not here seeking to oppose a new "Weltanschauung" to an old one, or to improve on an old one by the clarification of concepts. The opposition, rather, is between all world-views and science which is "free of any world-view." In the opinion of the "Vienna Circle," the traditional edifice of metaphysics and other constructions of a similar nature, consist, insofar as they do not "accidentally" contain scientific statements, of meaningless sentences. But the objection to the expression, "philosophizing," is not merely a terminological one; the "clarification of the meaning of concepts" cannot be separated from the "scientific method," to which it belongs. The two are inextricably intertwined.

The contributions to unified science are closely interrelated, whether it be a question of thinking out the implications of new astronomical observation-statements, or of inquiring into the chemical laws which are applicable to certain digestive processes, or of re-examining the concepts of various branches of science in order to find out the degree to which they are already capable of being connected with one another, in the way that unified science demands. That is to say, every law in unified science must be capable of being connected, under given conditions, with every other law, in order to reach new formulations.

It is, of course, possible to delimit different kinds of laws from one another, as for instance, chemical, biological or sociological. *But one may not assert that the prediction of a concrete individual event depends solely on laws of one of these kinds.* Whether, for example, the burning down of a forest at a certain spot on the earth will proceed in a certain way depends just as much on the weather as on whether or not human beings will undertake certain measures. These measures, however, can only be predicted if the laws of human behavior are known. *That is to say, all types of laws must, under given conditions, be capable of being connected with one another.* All laws, whether chemical, climatological or sociological, must, therefore, be conceived of as constituents of a system, viz., of unified science.

For the construction of unified science a unified language (*"Einheitsprache"*)[1], with its unified syntax, is required. To the imperfections of syntax in the period preparatory to unified science one may trace the respective positions of particular schools and ages.

Wittgenstein and other proponents of the scientific world-outlook, who deserve great credit for their rejection of metaphysics, i.e., for the elimination of meaningless statements, are of the opinion that every individual, in order to arrive at scientific knowledge, has temporary need of meaningless word-sequences for "elucidation" (Wittgenstein, *Tractatus* 6. 54): "My propositions are elucidatory in this way: he who understands me finally recognizes them as senseless, when he has climbed out through them, on them, over them. (He must, so to speak, throw away the ladder after he has climbed up on it.)" This sentence seems to suggest that one must as it were undergo repeated purgations of meaningless, i.e., metaphysical, statements, that one must repeatedly make use of and then discard this ladder. Only with the help of elucidations, consisting of what are later recognized to be mere meaningless sequences of words, is one able to arrive at the unified language of science. These elucidations, which may, indeed, be pronounced metaphysical, do not, however, appear in isolation in Wittgenstein's writings: we find there further expressions which resemble less the rungs of a ladder than parts of an unobtrusively formulated subsidiary metaphysical doctrine. The conclusion of the *Tractatus,* "Whereof one cannot speak, thereof one must be silent," is, at least grammatically, misleading. It sounds as if there were a "something" of which one could not speak. We should rather say: if one really wishes to avoid the metaphysical attitude entirely, then one will "be silent," but not "about something."

We have no need of any metaphysical ladder of elucidation. We cannot follow Wittgenstein in this matter, although his great significance for logic is not, for that reason, to be less highly valued. We owe him, among other things, the distinction between "tautologies" and "statements about empirical events." Logic and mathematics show us what linguistic transformations are possible *without any*

---

1. Kurt Lewin has pointed out that the term has been employed, although in a somewhat different sense, by Franz Oppenheimer.

extension of meaning, independently of the way in which we choose to formulate the facts.

Logic and mathematics do not require any observation statements to complete their structures. Logical and mathematical errors can be eliminated without recourse to any outside field. This is not contradicted by the fact that empirical statements may be the occasion for such corrections. Let us suppose that a captain sails his ship on to a reef. All the rules of calculation have been correctly applied, and the reef is to be found on the maps. In this way an error in the logarithm tables, which was responsible for the misfortune, could be discovered, but it also could be discovered independently of such an experience.

In his "elucidations," which may also be characterized as "mythological introductory remarks," Wittgenstein seems to be attempting to investigate, as it were, a pre-linguistic state from the point of view of a pre-linguistic stage of development. These attempts must not only be rejected as meaningless; they are also not required as a preliminary step towards unified science. One part of language can, to be sure, be used to discuss other parts; but one cannot make pronouncements concerning language as a whole from a "not yet linguistic" standpoint, as Wittgenstein and certain representatives of the "Vienna Circle" seek to do. A part of these endeavors, although in a modified form, may be suitably incorporated into scientific work. The rest would have to be discarded.

Nor may language as a whole be set against "experience as a whole," "the world," or "the given." Thus, every statement of the kind, "The very possibility of science depends on the fact of order in the universe," is meaningless. Such statements cannot be salvaged by counting them as "elucidations," to which a somewhat less rigorous criterion applies. There is little difference between such an attempt and metaphysics in the conventional sense. The possibility of science is demonstrated by the existence of science. We extend its domain by augmenting the *body of scientific propositions,* by comparing new propositions with the legacy of past scientists, and thus creating a self-consistent system of unified science capable of being utilized for successful *prediction.* We cannot as deponents stand aside, as it were, from our depositions and serve simultaneously as plaintiff, defendant and judge.

That science keeps within the domain of propositions, that propositions are its starting point and terminus, is often conceded even by metaphysicians, of course with the rider that besides science there exists yet another domain, containing statements which are to some degree figurative. In contrast to the dovetailing of science and metaphysics which is so frequently proposed, this separation of science and metaphysics (without, however, eliminating the latter) is carried out by Reininger,[2] who also, when it comes to scientific questions, adopts a position towards behaviorism which is similar to that of the Vienna Circle.

Unified science formulates statements, corrects them, and makes predictions. But it cannot anticipate its own future state. There is no "true" system of statements as distinct from that which is accepted at the present time. It would be meaningless to speak of such a thing even as a limiting concept. We can only ascertain that we are operating today with the space-time system to which that of physics corresponds, and thus achieve successful predictions. This system of statements is that of unified science. This is the point of view which may be designated *physicalism*.[3] If this term should become established, then it would be advisable to speak of "physicalistic" when one has in mind any spatio-temporal description framed in the spirit of contemporary physics, e.g., a behavioristic description. The term "physical" would then be reserved for "physical statement in the narrower sense," e.g., for those of mechanics, electrodynamics, etc. Ignoring all meaningless statements, the unified science proper to a given historical period proceeds from proposition to proposition, blending them into a self-consistent system which is an instrument for successful prediction, and, consequently, for life.

II. THE UNIFIED LANGUAGE OF PHYSICALISM

Unified science comprises all scientific *laws*. These are capable, without exception, of being combined with one another. Laws are not statements, but merely directions for proceeding from observation statements to *predictions*. (Schlick)

Unified science expresses everything in its unified language, common to the blind and the seeing, the deaf and the hearing. It is "intersensual" and "intersubjective." It connects what the soliloquizer asserts today with what he asserted yesterday, the statements he makes when his ears are closed with those he makes when he opens them. The only thing essential in language is *ordering,* something present even in a Morse Code message. "Intersubjective" or "intersensual" language depends above all on *ordering* ("next to," "between," etc.), that is, on that which is expressed in the symbol

---

2. *Metaphysik der Wirklichkeit,* 1931.
3. Cf. Otto Neurath, *Empirische Soziologie,* p. 2.

sequences of logic and mathematics. It is in this language that all predictions are formulated.

The unified language of unified science, which is derivable by and large from modifications of the language of everyday life, is the language of physics. In this connection, it is a matter of indifference for the uniformity of the language of physicalism what particular language the physics of a given period may use. It is of no significance whether it explicitly employs a four-dimensional continuum in its more highly refined formulations, whether it recognizes a spatio-temporal order of such a type that the locus of every event is precisely determined, or whether couplings of placer and velocity-dispersions, *whose precision is limited in principle,* figure as basic elements. It is essential only that the concepts of unified science, both where they are thought out in the most subtle detail and where the description remains imprecise, be made to share the current fate of fundamental physical concepts. It is precisely in this that the point of view of physicalism is expressed. But all predictions, in whose confirmation or rejection we see the measure of science, are reducible to observation-statements, to statements involving percipient individuals and objects emitting stimuli.

The belief that with the abandonment, as in modern physics, of the ideal of complete precision, the more or less complex relations which this yields provide a less intelligible picture than we should obtain by the introduction of hypothetical electron paths is probably due to our persistence in certain habitual ways of thinking.[4]

The unified language of physicalism confronts us wherever we make a scientific prediction on the basis of laws. When someone says that if he sees a certain color he will hear a certain sound, or *vice versa,* or when he speaks of the "red patch" next to the "blue patch," which will appear under certain conditions, he is already operating within the framework of physicalism. As a percipient he is a physical structure: he must localize perception, e.g., in the central nervous system or in some other place. Only in this way can he make predictions and reach agreement with others and with himself at different times. Every temporal designation is already a physical formulation.

Science endeavors to transform the statements of everyday life. They are presented to us as "agglomerations," consisting of physicalistic and pre-physicalistic components. We replace them by the "unification" of physicalistic language. If one says, for instance, "the

---

4. Cf. Concerning this, Philipp Frank, "Der Charakter der heutigen physikalischen Theorien," *Scientia,* March 1931.

screeching saw cuts through the blue wooden cube," "cube" is obviously an "intersensual" and "intersubjective" concept, equally available for the blind and the deaf. If a man soliloquizes and makes predictions, which he can himself control, he is able to compare what he said of the cube when he saw it with what he communicates in the dark when he touches it.

With the word "blue," on the other hand, there is, at first, a doubt as to how it is to be incorporated into the unified language. It can be used in the sense of the rate of vibration of electromagnetic waves. But it can also be used in the sense of a "field statement," meaning: when a seeing man (defined in a certain way) enters, as a test body, the range of this cube, he behaves in a certain manner, describable physicalistically; e.g., he says, "I see 'blue.'" While there may be doubt as to what people mean when they use "blue" in colloquial speech, "screeching" would be chiefly intended as a "field statement," i.e., as an expression in which the auditor is always included. Closer consideration, however, reveals that "cube," "blue" and "screeching" are all words of the same type.

Let us attempt to follow up our analysis by giving a more exact rendering of the above sentence, in accordance with physicalism, and reformulating it in a way that will make it more suitable for prediction.

"Here is a blue cube." (This formulation, like those which follow, may be restated as a physical formula, in which the locus is determined by means of coordinates.)

"Here is a screeching saw." (The screeching enters into the formulation, at first, only as vibrations of the saw and the air, which could be expressed in physical formulae.)

"Here is a percipient man." (Possibly a "field statement" could be added indicating that under certain conditions the percipient enters into a relationship with the physical blue and the physical screeching.)

This perceiving may perhaps be divided into:

"Neural changes are occurring here."

"Cerebral changes are occurring here in the perception area and, perhaps, in the speech area also." (It is immaterial for our purposes whether these areas can be defined locationally or whether they have to be defined structurally. Neither is it necessary to discuss whether changes in the speech area—the "speech-thought" of the behaviorists—are connected with the larynx or laryngeal innervation.)

Perhaps, in order to exhaust the physicalistic meaning of this simple sentence, something more has still to be added, e.g., particulars concerning time, or positional coordinates; but the essential thing is that, in every case, the additions should be statements involving physical concepts.

It would be a mistake to suppose, because physical formulae of a very complex nature, which are still not fully at our disposal, are required for the computation of certain correlations, that, therefore, the physicalistic expressions of everyday life must also be complex. Physicalistic everyday language will arise from existing common speech, only parts of which will have to be discarded; others will be integrated, while supplements will make up for certain deficiencies. The occurrence of a perception will be, from the outset, more closely connected than hitherto with the observation statement and with the identification of the object. The analysis of certain groups of statements, e.g., observation statements, will proceed in a different manner from before.

Children are capable of learning physicalistic every-day language. They are able to advance to the rigorous symbolic language of science and learn how to make successful predictions of all kinds, without having to resort to "elucidations" supposedly functioning as a meaningless introduction. It is a question of a more lucid mode of speech, so formulated as to omit such expressions, for instance as "illusion of the senses," which create so much confusion. But even though the physicalistic language has the capacity some day to become the universal language of social intercourse, we must continue to devote ourselves, for the present, to cutting away the metaphysical appendages from the "agglomerations" of our language and to defining physicalistically everything that remains. When the metaphysical cord is no longer present, much of what is left may present itself as disconnected heaps. The further use of such remnants would not be profitable, and a reconstruction would be indispensable.

We can often continue to make use of available "agglomerations" by reinterpreting them. But caution is required here: men who are ready enough to adjust their views, but at the same time comfort-loving, frequently console themselves with the belief that a great deal can be "systematically" reinterpreted. It is more than questionable whether it would be convenient to continue to employ terms like "instinct," "motive," "memory," "world," etc., attaching to them a wholly unusual sense, which one may easily forget when one goes on using these terms for the sake of peace. Certainly there are many cases in which a reconstruction of language is superfluous, or even dangerous. So long as one expresses oneself "approximately," one must guard against the desire to be, at the same time, excessively subtle.

Since the views presented here are most nearly similar to the ideas of Carnap, let it be emphasized that they exclude the special "phenomenal" language from which Carnap seeks to derive the physical language. The elimination of the "phenomenal" language, which does not even seem to be usable for "prediction"—the essence of science—in the form it has assumed up to now, will probably necessitate many modifications in his system of concept construction.* In the same way, we must exclude "methodological solipsism" (Carnap, Driesch), which seems to be an attenuated residue of idealistic metaphysics, a position from which Carnap himself constantly attempts to get away. The thesis of "methodological solipsism," as even Carnap would probably concede, cannot be scientifically formulated. Nor can it be used to indicate a particular standpoint, which would be an alternative to some other standpoint, because there exists only *one* physicalism, and everything susceptible of scientific formulation is contained in it.

There can be no contrasting of the "ego" or the "thinking personality," or anything else with "experience," "what is experienced," or "thought." The statements of physicalism are based on statements connected with seeing, hearing, feeling and other "sense perceptions" (as physical events), but also with "organic perceptions," which, for the most part, are only roughly noted. We can, of course, close our eyes, but we cannot stop the process of digestion, the circulation of the blood, or the occurrence of muscular innervations. What people are at pains to separate off as "the ego" are, in the language of physicalism, events of this sort also, of which we are not informed through our ordinary "external" senses. All "personality co-efficients" which separate one individual from another are of a physicalistic kind!

Although the "ego" cannot be set off against either the "world or "thinking," one is able, without abandoning physicalism, to distinguish statements about the "physicalistically described person," besides those concerning the "physicalistically described cube," and can, under certain conditions, make "observation statements," thereby creating a substitute for the "phenomenal language." But careful investigation will show that the mass of *observation statements is contained in the mass of physical statements.*

* [This is a reference to the "Konstitutionssystem" elaborated by Carnap in his book *Der Logische Aufbau der Welt. Vide* the Introduction p. 24. Ed.]

The protocol statements of an astronomer or a chronicler (appearing as physical formulations) will, of course, be distinguished from statements having a precisely determined position in the context of a physical system, despite the fact that between the two there are fluid transitional stages. But there is no special "phenomenal" as opposed to physicalistic language. *Every one of our statements can, from the very outset, be a physicalistic one—and it is this that distinguishes what is said here from all the pronouncements of the "Vienna Circle,"* which otherwise constantly stresses the importance of predictions and their verification. Unified language is the language of predictions, which are the very heart of physicalism.

In a certain sense, the doctrine here proposed proceeds from a given condition of everyday language, which in the beginning is essentially physicalistic, and, in the usual course of events, is gradually developed in a metaphysical direction. This forms a point of contact with the "natural concept of the world" ("Natürlicher Weltbegriff") in Avenarius. The language of physicalism is, so to speak, in no way new; it is the language familiar to certain "naive" children and peoples.

It is always science as a system of statements which is at issue. *Statements are compared with statements,* not with "experiences," "the world," or anything else. All these meaningless *duplications* belong to a more or less refined metaphysics and are, for that reason, to be rejected. Each new statement is compared with the totality of existing statements previously coordinated. To say that a statement is correct, therefore, means that it can be incorporated in this totality. What cannot be incorporated is rejected as incorrect. The alternative to rejection of the new statement is, in general, one accepted only with great reluctance: the whole previous system of statements can be modified up to the point where it becomes possible to incorporate the new statement. Within unified science there is important work to be done in making transformations. The definition of "correct" and "incorrect" proposed here departs from that customary among the "Vienna Circle," which appeals to "meaning" and "verification." In our presentation we confine ourselves always to the sphere of linguistic thought. Systems of statements are subjected to transformation. Generalizing statements, however, as well as statements elaborated by means of determinate relations, can be compared with the totality of protocol statements.

Unified science thus comprehends a variety of types of statements. So, for example, whether one is dealing with "statements about reality," "hallucination statements," or "untruths" depends on the degree to which one can employ the statements in drawing inferences about physical events other than oral movements. One is confronted by an "untruth" when one can infer a certain excitation of the speech center of the brain, but not corresponding events in the perception centers; the latter events are, on the other hand, essential for a hallucination. If, besides excitation in the perception centers, one can also infer, in a manner to be specified, events outside the body, then one is dealing with "statements about reality." In this case, we can continue to employ the statement—for example, "a cat is sitting in this room"—as a physicalistic statement. A statement is always compared with another statement or with the system of statements, never with a "reality." Such a procedure would be metaphysical; it would be meaningless. "The" reality is not, however, replaced by "the" physicalistic system, but by groups of such systems, one of which is employed in practice.

From all this it becomes clear that within a consistent physicalism there can be no "theory of knowledge," at least not in the traditional form. It could consist only of defensive operations against metaphysics, that is to say, of the unmasking of meaningless phrases. Many of the problems of the theory of knowledge will, perhaps, be transformed into empirical questions in such a way that they can be accommodated in unified science.

This problem can no more be discussed here than the question of how all "statements" can be incorporated in physicalism as physicalistic constructions. "Two statements are equivalent" could, perhaps, be expressed in this way. Let a man be acted on by a system of commands connected with all sorts of statements, e.g., "If A behaves in such and such a way, do this and that." Now one can fix certain conditions, and observe that the *addition of a certain statement* produces the same change in his reactions as the addition of another. Then one will say that the first statement is *equivalent* to the second. When tautologies are added, the stimulus offered by the system of commands remains *unchanged*.

All this could be developed experimentally with the aid of a "thinking machine" such as Jevons proposed. By means of this machine, syntax could be formulated and logical errors automatically avoided. The machine would not even be able to write the sentence, "two times red is hard."

The views suggested here are best combined with a *behavioristic* orientation. One will not then speak of "thought," but of "speech-thought," i.e., of *statements as physical events*. Whether a perception statement about the past (e.g., "I recently heard a melody") can be traced back to a past speech-thought, or whether previous stimuli are only now evoking a reaction in speech-thought, is, in this regard, of no essential importance. All too often the discussion is conducted as if the refutation of some minor assertions of the behaviorists had somehow shaken the fundamental principle that only *physicalistic statements* have a meaning, i.e., can become part of unified science.

We begin with statements, and we conclude with statements. There are no "elucidations" which are not physicalistic statements. If someone wished to conceive of "elucidations" as exclamations, then, like whistles and caresses, they would be subject to no logical analysis. The physicalistic language, *unified language,* is the Alpha and Omega of all science. There is no "phenomenal language" beside the "physical language," no "methodological solipsism" beside some other possible position, no "philosophy," no "theory of knowledge," no new "Weltanschauung" beside the others: there is only *Unified Science,* with its laws and predictions.

III. SOCIOLOGY NO "MORAL SCIENCE"

Unified science makes predictions about the behavior of machines just as it does about that of animals, about the behavior of stones as about that of plants. Some of its complex statements we could analyze even today, while the analysis of others temporarily eludes us. There are "laws" of the behavior of animals and of machines. The "laws" of machines can be reduced to physical laws. But even in this sphere, a law in terms of mass and metrical measurement often suffices, without recourse to atoms or other elements. In the same way, the laws of the animal body are often so formulated that there is no need to fall back on micro-structural laws. Admittedly, where much has been hoped for from the investigation of macro-structural laws, they have often turned out to be inadequate: certain irregularities remain incalculable.

There is a constant search for *correlations* between magnitudes appearing in the physicalistic description of events. It makes no fundamental difference whether *statistical* or *nonstatistical* descriptions are involved. No matter whether one is investigating the statistical behavior of atoms, plants or animals, the methods employed in establishing correlations are always the same. As we saw above, all the laws of unified science must be capable of being connected with one another if they are to be equal to the task of serving, as often as possible, to *predict* individual events or certain groups of events.

This does away, at the outset, with any fundamental division of unified science, for instance, into the "natural sciences" and the "moral sciences," the latter being often referred to also in other ways, e.g., "Kulturwissenschaften" ("sciences of culture"). The theses by which it is intended to establish this division vary, but are always of a metaphysical character, that is, meaningless. It is senseless to speak of different "essences" reposing "behind" events. What cannot be expressed in terms of relations among elements cannot be expressed at all. It is consequently meaningless *to go beyond correlations and speak of the "essence of things."* Once it is understood what the unified language of science really means, there will be no more talk of "different kinds of causality." One can only compare the organization of one field and its laws with the organization of another, and ascertain, perhaps, that the laws in one field are more complex than those in another, or that certain modes of organization lacking in one are found in another; that, for example, certain mathematical formulae are required in one case but not in the other.

If the "natural sciences" cannot be delimited from the "moral sciences," it is even less possible to make the distinction between the "philosophy of nature" and the "philosophy of the moral sciences." Even leaving aside the fact that the former term is unsuitable because, as mentioned above, it still contains the word "philosophy," by "philosophy of nature" one can only understand a sort of introduction to the whole work of unified science. For how should "nature" be distinguished from "non-nature"?

One cannot even adduce the practical exigencies of everyday life or of the conduct of scientific investigations as justification for this dichotomy. Is the theory of human behavior seriously to be opposed to that of the behavior of all other objects? Is it seriously intended that the theory of human societies should be fitted into one discipline and the theory of animal societies into another? Are the natural sciences to deal with "cattle-breeding," "slavery" and "warfare" among ants, and the moral sciences with these same institutions among men? If this is not meant, then the distinction is no sharper than that between different "scientific fields" in the older sense.

Or is there something to be said, perhaps, for the linguistic usage according to which one simply speaks of "moral sciences" whenever "social sciences" are meant? But, to be consistent, one would have to count the theory of animal societies together with the theory of human societies as social sciences, and therefore as "moral sciences," an implication from which most people would recoil. And quite understandably so, for then where would be the great cleavage concealed behind all this, the cleavage depending on the maintenance of the centuries-old theological habit of thought which divides up all existence into at least two departments, e.g., a "noble"' and an "ignoble"? The dualism of "natural sciences" and "moral sciences," and the dualism of "philosophy of nature" and "philosophy of culture" are, in the last analysis, *residues of theology.*

The ancient languages are, on the whole, more physicalistic than the modern. They are full of magical elements, to be sure, but above all they treat "body" and "soul"· as simply two forms of matter: the soul is a diminutive, shadowy body which issues from the mouth of the individual at death. It is theology which first replaces the contrast of "matter-soul" and "matter-body" with that of "non-matter-soul" and "matter-body," as well as "non-matter-God" and "matter-world," adding a whole hierarchy of subordinate and superior entities, natural and supernatural. The opposition of "natural" and "supernatural" can be formulated only by means of meaningless phrases. These phrases, because they are meaningless, do not contradict the statements of unified science; neither are they in accord with them. But they are certainly the cause of great confusion. It is when it is asserted that these expressions are just as meaningful as those of science that the trouble starts.[5]

What part the mental habit of theological dualism plays in the creation of such dichotomies can perhaps be gathered from the fact that as soon as one such division is discarded another easily establishes itself. The opposition of the "Is" and the "Ought," which is encountered especially among philosophers of law, may be mentioned here. In part, of course, this may be traced to the theological opposition of "Ideal" to "Reality." But the capacity of language for forming nouns facilitates all these meaningless schemes. One can, without violating syntactical rules, as serenely say "the Ought" as "the sword." And then people go on to make statements about this "Ought" just as they would about a "sword," or at least as they would about the "Is."

The "moral sciences," the "psychical world," the world of the "categorical imperative," the realm of *Einfühlung* (empathy), the realm of *Verstehen* ("the 'understanding' characteristic of the historian")—these are more or less interpenetrating, often mutually substitutable, expressions. Some authors prefer one group of meaningless phrases, some another, some combine and accumulate them.

---

5. Cf. Hans Hahn, *Überflüssige Wesenheiten* (Publications of the Verein Ernst Mach, Vol. II).

While such phrases provide only the marginal decorations of science in the case of many writers, with others they influence the entire body of their pronouncements. Even if the practical effect of the doctrines on which the school of "moral sciences" is based are not over-rated, even if the confusion in empirical investigation wrought by it is not exaggerated, still, in the systematic establishment of physicalism and sociology, clarity requires that a clean sweep be made here. It is the duty of the practitioners of unified science to take a determined position against such distinctions; this is not a matter for their arbitrary choice.

If there is uncertainty over these questions even among anti-metaphysically minded thinkers, it is partly connected with the fact that there does not exist sufficient clarity about the subject matter and method of "psychology." The detachment of the "moral "sciences" from other disciplines is concurrent with the separation of "psychical" objects from others in other fields. This detachment has only been systematically eliminated by *behaviorism,* which, in this essay, we always understand in the widest sense. Only physicalistic statements about human behavior are incorporated into its system. When the sociologist makes predictions about human groups in the same way as the behaviorist does about individual men or animals, sociology may appropriately be called *social behaviorism.*

Our conclusion is as follows: sociology is not a "moral science" or "the study of man's spiritual life" (Sombart's "Geisteswissenschaft") standing in fundamental opposition to some other sciences, called "natural sciences"; no, *as social behaviorism, sociology is a part of unified science.*

IV. SOCIOLOGY AS SOCIAL BEHAVIORISM

It is possible to speak in the same terms of men's painting, housebuilding, religion, agriculture, poetry. And yet, it is maintained again and again that "understanding" human beings is fundamentally different from "merely" observing them and determining regularities expressible as laws. The area of "understanding," of "empathy" with other personalities is closely connected with that traditionally claimed by the "moral sciences." We find here a resurrection of the division on grounds of principle—already eliminated on a previous level—between "internal" and "external" perceptions (experience, mind, etc.), which possess the same empirical character.

Philosophical literature, especially the literature of the philosophy of history, frequently insists that without "empathy" and "understanding" it would be impossible to pursue historical studies or comprehensively to arrange and describe human actions at all.

How can we attempt to dispose in general of these obstacles from the point of view of physicalism? It must be assumed from the outset that the persistent asseverations of many sociologists and philosophers of history concerning the unavoidability of recourse to "understanding" are also aimed at preserving the results of some very worthy scientific researches. Here, as so often elsewhere, it may be a case of a not easily disentangled combination of the dualistic habits of mind, originating in theology, and the actual procedure of science. It will be apparent to anyone familiar with the *monism of unified science* that even statements which are fully capable of formulation in physicalistic terms have been presented in an unphysicalistic form.

Sentences such as "I see a blue table in this room," and "I feel angry" do not lie far apart. The "I" is appropriately replaced by some personal name, since all such statements may be applied to anyone, and an "I-statement," therefore, must be capable of being asserted by someone else. Now we have: "There is a blue table in this room," and "There is anger in this man." The discussions concerning "primary" and "secondary" qualities are at an end when it is realized that, in the last analysis, all statements about qualities are of one type, only tautologies being excluded from the class of such statements. Then all statements about qualities become physicalistic statements. Besides these, there are tautologies, rules for the combination and connection of statements. The propositions of geometry can be interpreted as physicalistic statements or as tautologies, thereby removing many difficulties.

What, among other things, is characteristic of the sentence, "There is anger in this man"? Its peculiarity is that it is open only to inadequate analysis. It is as if someone were able to tell us, "Here is a severe storm" without being in a position to state in what manner it was composed of lightning, thunder, rain, etc., nor yet whether he arrived at his discoveries by means of his eyes, ears or nose.

When one speaks of anger, *organic perceptions* are made use of. Changes in the intestinal tract, internal secretions, blood pressure and muscle contraction are essentially equivalent to changes in the eye, ear or nose. In the systematic construction of behaviorism, a man's statement, "I am angry" is incorporated into physicalism *not only as the reaction* of the speaker, but also as the formulation of his "organic perceptions." Just as, from the enunciation of "color perceptions," one can infer physicalistic statements about retinal changes and other events, so from assertions about anger, i.e., about "organic perceptions," one can derive physicalistic statements about "intestinal changes," "changes in blood pressure," etc., phenomena which become known to others often only by means of such statements. This may be appended as a supplement to Carnap's discussions on this subject, where the full value of statements about "organic perceptions" (in the older sense) has not been taken into consideration.

If someone says that he requires this experience of "organic perceptions" in order to have empathy with another person, his statement is unobjectionable. That is to say, the employment of physicalistic statements concerning one's own body in making physicalistic statements about another's is completely in line with our scientific work, which throughout makes this sort of "extrapolation." Our commitment to induction leads us constantly to such extensions. The same principle is involved in making statements about the other side of the moon on the basis of our experience concerning the side which faces us. That is to say, one may speak of "empathy" in the physicalistic language if one means no more by it than that one draws inferences about physical events in other persons on the basis of formulations concerning organic changes in one's own body. What is involved here, as in so many other cases, is a physicalistic induction, the usual attempt at establishing certain correlations. The linguistic clarity achieved so far in regard to many of these events leaves, to be sure, much to be desired. One would come very close to the actual state of affairs if one were to say that the moral sciences are, above all, the sciences in which correlations are asserted between events which are very inadequately described and for which only complex names are available.

When we analyze the concepts of "understanding" and "empathy" more closely, everything in them that is usable in a physicalistic way proves to be a statement about order, exactly as in all sciences. The alleged distinction between "natural sciences" and "moral sciences," to the effect that the former concern themselves "only" with arrangement, the latter with understanding as well, is non-existent.

If, wherever non-metaphysical formulations are encountered, they are subjected to systematic formulation, physicalistic statements will be achieved throughout. There will no longer be a special sphere of the "psychical." It is a matter of indifference for the position here maintained whether certain individual theses of Watson's, Pavlov's or others are upheld or rejected. What is essential is that only *physicalistically formulated correlations be employed in the description of living things, whatever may be observed in these things.*

It would be misleading to express this by saying that the distinction of "psychical" and "corporeal" no longer existed, but had been replaced by "something neutral." It is not at all a question of a "something," but simply of correlations of a physicalistic character. Only insufficient analysis can lead anyone to say something like: "It cannot yet be ascertained whether the whole sphere of the 'psychical' really admits of physicalistic expression. It is, after all, possible that here and there another type of formulation is required, i.e., concepts not physicalistically definable." This is the last remnant of belief in a "soul" as a separate form of being. When people have observed a running clock and then see it stop, they can easily make use of the capacity of language for creating nouns, and pose the problem, "Where has the 'movement' gone to?" And after it is explained to them that all that can be known about the clock is to be discovered through analysis of the relations between its parts and the surroundings, a sceptic may still object that, although he understands that speculation about the "movement" is pure metaphysics, he is still doubtful whether, for the solution of certain complicated problems relating to the operations of clocks, physicalism entirely suffices.

Without meaning to say that every sociologist must be trained in behaviorism, we can still demand of him that, if he wishes to avoid errors, he must be careful to formulate all his descriptions of human behavior in a wholly straightforward physicalistic fashion. Let him not speak of the "spirit of the age" if it is not completely clear that he means by it certain verbal combinations, forms of worship, modes of architecture, fashions, styles of painting, etc. That he undertakes to predict the behavior of men of other ages on the basis of his knowledge of his own behavior is wholly legitimate, even if sometimes misleading. But "empathy" may not be credited with any peculiar magical power transcending ordinary induction.

With inductions in this or that field, it is always a question of a *decision*. This decision may be characteristic of certain human groups or of whole ages, but is not itself logically deducible. Yet induction always leads, within the physicalistic sphere, to meaningful statements. It must not, for this reason, be confused with the *interpolation of metaphysical constructions*. There are many who concede that they formulate metaphysical constructions, i.e., that they insert meaningless verbal combinations, but nevertheless will not fully appreciate the damage caused by such a procedure. The elimination of such constructions in sociology and psychology, as well as in other fields, must be undertaken not only for the sake of freeing them of superfluities and of avoiding meaningless verbal combinations, which perhaps afford satisfaction to some. The elimination of metaphysics will become *scientifically fruitful* through *obviating the occasion for certain false correlations in the empirical sphere.* It will be seen that one is most likely to overestimate the significance of certain elements in the historical process, which are capable of a physicalistic formulation, when they are believed to be linked with certain metaphysical essences. People often expect from the priest of the transcendent God certain empirically controllable super-achievements which would not be deducible from empirical experience.

There are many who allege in favor of metaphysical constructions that, with their help, better predictions can be made. According to this view, one proceeds from physicalistically formulated observation-statements to the realm of metaphysical word-sequences. By the employment of certain rules which, in the metaphysical sphere, are applied to meaningless word-sequences, this process is supposed to result in predictions consonant with a system of protocol statements. *Even if* results are actually achieved in this way, metaphysics is not essential for prediction in this case, although it may perhaps act as a stimulus, like some narcotic. For if predictions can be made in this roundabout way, "then they can also be *directly* deduced *from the given data.* This is *clear from a purely logical* consideration: if Y follows from X, and Z follows from Y, then Z follows immediately from X."[6] Even if Kepler made use of the world of theological conceptions in arriving at the planetary orbits, this world of conceptions nevertheless does not enter into his scientific statements. Much the same is true of the highly productive fields of psychoanalysis and individual psychology, whose behavioristic transformation will *certainly be no easy task.*

When the metaphysical deviations from the main line of behaviorism have been distinguished in this way, the path will be cleared for a sociology *free of metaphysics.* Just as the behavior of animals can be studied no less than that of machines, stars and stones, so can the behavior of animal groups be investigated. It is possible to take into account both changes in individuals produced by "external" stimuli and those caused by "autonomous" changes "within" living things (e.g., the rhythmical course of a process), just as one can investigate the disintegration of radium, which is not

6. Otto Neurath, *Empirische Soziologie,* p. 57.

influenced by anything external, as well as the decomposition of a chemical compound through the addition of oxygen. Whether analogies to the disintegration of radium play a role within the human body need not be discussed here.

Sociology does not investigate purely statistical variations in animal or, above all, human groups; it is concerned with the *connections among stimuli* occurring between particular individuals. Sometimes, without analyzing these connections in detail, it can determine under certain conditions the total behavior of groups united by common stimuli, and make predictions by means of the laws obtained. How is "social behaviorism," unimpeded by metaphysics, to be pursued? *Just as every other actual science* is pursued. Naturally, in investigating human beings certain correlations result which are not encountered in the study of stars or machines. Social behaviorism attains to laws of a definite type peculiar to itself.

To pursue physicalistic sociology is not to transfer the laws of physics to living things and the groups they form, as some have considered feasible. It is possible to discover comprehensive sociological laws, as well as laws for narrower social areas, without having recourse to micro-structure, and thus being able to base these sociological laws on physical ones. *Whatever sociological laws are discovered without the aid of physical laws in the narrower sense are not necessarily altered by the addition of a subsequently discovered physical substructure.* The sociologist is completely unimpeded in his search for laws. The only stipulation is that he must always speak, in his predictions, of structures which are given in space and time.

V. SOCIOLOGICAL CORRELATIONS

It is as little possible in sociology as in other sciences to state at the outset on the basis of purely theoretical considerations what correlations can be employed with a prospect of success. But it is demonstrable that certain traditional endeavors meet with consistent failure, while other methods, adapted to discovering correlations, are not at present sufficiently cultivated.

Of what type, then, are sociological correlations? How does one arrive, with a certain degree of reliability, at sociological predictions? In order to be able to predict the behavior of a group in a certain respect, it is often necessary to be acquainted with the total life of the group. Variations in the particular modes of behavior distinguishable in the totality of events, the construction of machines, the erection of temples, the forms of marriage, are not "autonomously" calculable. They must be regarded as parts of the whole that is investigated at any given time. In order to know how the construction of temples will change in the future, one must be familiar with the methods of production, the form of social organization, and the modes of religious behavior in the period which is taken as the starting point; one must know the transformation to which *all of these together* are subject.

Not all events prove equally resistant to being employed in such predictions. Given certain conditions, from the mode of production of a historical period one can often roughly infer the next phases in the development of the mode of production and the form of social organization. Then one is in a position to attempt with some success to make further predictions about religious behavior and similar matters with the aid of such previous predictions. Experience shows that the reverse procedure, on the other hand, meets with failure, i.e., it does not seem possible to derive predictions about the mode of production from predictions about religious behavior alone.

But, whether we direct our attention to the methods of production, to religious behavior, to the construction of buildings, or to music, we are always confronted with events which can be physicalistically described.

Many of the social institutions of an age can be properly accounted for only if their distant past is known, while others might, so to speak, be devised at any time given the appropriate stimuli. There is a certain sense in which the presence of cannons acts as a stimulus, producing armed turrets by way of reaction. The dress coats of our day, on the other hand, do not represent a reaction to dancing, and it is only with difficulty that they would be newly devised. But it is comprehensible to us that at some time in the past, a man dressed in a long-skirted coat became the inventor of the dress coat when the skirts of his coat flapped up while he was riding. The coherence between established customs is different in the two cases.

Just as one must be informed about the type of coherence in order to be able to make predictions, so one must know whether the detachment of a certain institution or segment from a social complex is easy or difficult, and whether, in the case of loss, it can be replaced. The state, for example, is a highly stable complex whose operations are, to a considerable extent, independent of the change-over of personnel: even if many judges and soldiers were to die, there would be new ones to take their place. A machine, on the contrary, does not generally replace wheels which have been removed from it.

It is a wholly physicalistic question to what extent the existence of specially conditioned individuals, deviating from the norm, assures the stability of the state structure. The related question of the degree to which such significant individuals are replaceable must be treated separately. The queen bee assumes a special position in the hive, but when a queen bee gets lost, there is the possibility that a new one will emerge. There are always, so to speak, latent queens. How is this in the case of human society?

The extent to which predictions about social complexes can be made without taking into consideration the fate of certain particularly prominent individuals is entirely a concrete sociological question. It is possible to maintain, with good reason, that the creation of bourgeois Europe, once the machine system had imparted to the modern capitalistic transformation its characteristic hue, was predictable at the end of the eighteenth century. On the other hand, one could hardly have predicted Napoleon's Russian campaign and the burning of Moscow. But it would, perhaps, be valid to say that if Napoleon had defeated Russia, the transformation of the social order would have proceeded in the same way as it did in fact proceed. Even a victorious Napoleon would have had to countenance the old feudalism of Central Europe to a certain degree and for a certain time, just as, on another occasion, he re-established the Catholic Church.

The extent to which prediction is possible, or relates to particular individuals, in no way affects the essence of social behaviorism. The movements of a leaf of paper in the wind are equally unpredictable, and yet kinematics, climatology and meteorology are all highly developed sciences. It is no part of the essence of a developed science to be capable of predicting every individual event. That the fate of a single leaf of paper, say, a breeze-blown thousand dollar bill, may especially interest us, is of little concern to scientific investigation. We need not discuss here whether a chronicle of the "accidental" paths of leaves in the wind could eventually lead to a theory of the paths of leaves. Many of the views associated with Rickert and allied thinkers yield no scientific laws even where they can be physicalistically interpreted.

Sociology, like every science, tracks down correlations which can be utilized for predictions. It seeks to lay down its basic conceptions as unambiguously and clearly as possible. One may attempt, for instance, to define groups through *"commercium"* and *"connubium."* One ascertains who trades with whom, or who marries whom. There may emerge clearly distinguishable areas of concentration, together with poorly occupied border areas. And then one could investigate the conditions under which such concentrations vary or even disappear. To discover the correlation of such areas of concentration with the processes of production obtaining at their respective periods is obviously a legitimate sociological task, which might be of importance for the theory of "classes."

One can investigate, for instance, under what conditions matriarchy, ancestor worship, agriculture and similar institutions arise, at what point the founding of cities begins, or what correlations exist between systematic theology and other human activities. One can also ask how the administration of justice is determined by social conditions, although it is questionable whether such limited divisions will exhibit sufficient law-like regularities. It may well be, for instance, that certain events occurring outside the field of law must be added to those involved in the administration of justice, if relations statable as laws are to be found.

What one group recognizes as law, another may regard as outside the legal order. Thus, only correlations among men's statements concerning the "law," or between their behavior and their statements can be established. But it is not possible, without special preliminary work, to contrast "legal events" as such with other events.

It is doubtful whether simple sociological correlations can be determined between the allowed interest rate, on the one hand, and the standard of living of a period, on the other; whether simpler relations do not appear when the "allowed interest rate" and "prohibited usury" are taken together. Thus, the modes of behavior on which unfavorable "legal" and "ethical" judgments are passed could be incorporated into sociology, and the judgments themselves could be included. These disciplines are in every sense branches of sociology, but they are quite different from the "ethics" and "jurisprudence" which are commonly cultivated. The latter yield few or no sociological correlations. They are predominantly metaphysical, or, where free of metaphysics, their methodology and arrangement of statements can only be explained as residues of theology. In part, they yield purely logical deductions, the extraction of certain injunctions from others, or of certain conclusions from given legal assumptions. But all this lies outside the sphere of ordered correlations.

VI. ETHICS AND JURISPRUDENCE AS
REMNANTS OF METAPHYSICS

In its origin, ethics is the discipline which seeks to determine the totality of divine injunctions. It attempts to find out, by means of a logical combination of commandments and prohibitions of a universal kind, whether a given individual act is commanded, permitted or forbidden. The "casuistry" of Catholic moral theologians has extensively elaborated this type of deduction. It is quite obvious that the indeterminateness of divine injunctions and the ambiguity of their meaning preclude any genuine scientific method. The great expenditure on logical deductions was, so to speak, squandered on a worthless object, even though, historically, it prepared the way for the coming logicizing period of science. If the God who issues the commands, as well as events in heaven and hell (which was located by many theologians at the center of the earth) are physicalistically defined, then one is dealing with a non-metaphysical discipline, to be sure, but a highly uncritical one.

But how is a discipline of "ethics" to be defined once God is eliminated? Is it possible to pass meaningfully to a "command-in-itself," to the "categorical imperative"? One might just as well talk of a "neighbor-in-himself without any neighbors," or of a "son-in-himself, who never had a father or mother."

How is one to distinguish certain injunctions or modes of behavior in order to make possible "a new ethics within the context of physicalism"? It seems to be impossible. Men can form joint resolutions and conduct themselves in certain ways, and it is possible to study the consequences of such actions. But what modes of behavior, what directives is one to distinguish as "ethical," so that correlations may then be set up?

The retention of an old name is based on the view that there is something abiding to be discovered, which is common to the old theological or metaphysical and the new empiricist disciplines. When all metaphysical elements, as well as whatever physicalistic theological elements it may contain, have been eliminated from ethics, there remain only statements about certain modes of human behavior or the injunctions directed by some men to others.

One could, however, also conceive of a discipline pursuing its investigations in a wholly behavioristic fashion as part of unified science. Such a discipline would seek to determine the reactions produced by the stimulus of a certain way of living, and whether such ways of living make men more or less happy. It is easy to imagine a thoroughly empirical "felicitology" (*Felicitologie*), on a behavioristic foundation, which could take the place of traditional ethics.

But a non-metaphysical ethics usually seeks to analyze, in one way or another, men's "motivations," as if this provided a suitable groundwork for relations statable as laws. What men assert about the "reasons" for their conduct, however, is essentially more dependent on contingencies than the general run of their behavior. When the general social conditions of a given period are known, the behavior of whole groups can be far more readily predicted than the rationale which individuals will adduce for their conduct. The modes of conduct will be defended in very different fashions, and very few, moreover, will note the correlation between the social situation and average conduct.

These "conflicts of motivations," for the most part metaphysically formulated, are avoided by an empirical sociology, which is intent upon fruitful work. This is the case with Marxism, the most productive sociology of the present day. It endeavors to establish correlations between the social situation and the behavior of entire classes, so that it can then account for the frequently changing verbal sequences which are supposed to "explain the motivation" of the scientifically law-abiding actions which are conditioned in this way. Since Marxism, in its descriptions of relations expressible as laws, makes as little use as possible of what men assert about themselves, the "events in their consciousness," their "ideology," it is related to those schools of "psychology" which accord to the "unconscious" in one form or another a prominent role. Thus it is that *psychoanalysis* and *individual psychology,* by virtue of the fact that they confute and eliminate the motivational psychology of consciousness (today quite obsolete), prepare the way for modern empirical sociology, which seeks, in the spirit of unified science, to discover correlations between actions and the factors that condition them.

And even if psychoanalysis and individual psychology in their present form contain very many metaphysical expressions, nevertheless, through their emphasis on the relation between behavior and its unconscious preconditions, they are precursors of the behavioristic way of thinking and of sociological methodology.

Thus it is permissible to ask whether a certain manner of living yields more or less happiness, since "happiness" can be described wholly behavioristically; it is valid to ask on what depend the demands which masses of men make of one another, what new demands are set, what modes of behavior will emerge in such a situation.

(Claims and modes of behavior in this regard are often fundamentally divergent.) All these are legitimate sociological formulations of problems. Whether it is advisable to characterize them as "ethical" need not be decided here.

The case of "jurisprudence" is a similar one, when it is understood as something other than the sociology of certain social phenomena. But when it takes up the task of establishing whether a system of claims is logically consistent, whether certain conclusions of the statute books can be harmonized with certain observation-statements about legal practice, we are concerned with purely logical investigations. When we determine that the rules of a chemist are logically compatible, we have not yet entered the sphere of the science of chemistry. In order to pursue chemistry, we must establish correlations between certain chemical events and certain temperatures, and other such things. The fact that, despite their essentially metaphysical preliminary formulations, the representatives of certain schools of jurisprudence can produce something logically and scientifically significant does not prevent our rejecting these formulations, as, for example, the following:

The *thinking* of mathematical or logical laws is a psychical act, but the object of mathematics—that which is thought of—is not something *psychical,* neither a mathematical nor a logical "soul," but a specific intellectual reality. For mathematics and logic abstract from the psychological fact of the thinking of such an object. In the same way the state, as the object of a special mode of thought to be distinguished from psychology, is a distinctive reality, but is not the fact of the thinking and willing of such an object. It is an ideal order, a specific system of norms. It resides not in the realm of *nature*—the realm of physical-psychical relations—but in the realm of spirit. The state as obligating authority is a value or—so far as the propositional expression of value is established—a norm, or system of norms. As such, it is essentially different from the specifically real fact of the conceiving or willing of the norm, which is characterized by indifference to value.[7]

Formulations of this type are connected with similar ones on "ethics" and related disciplines, without any attempt having been made to discover how the term "objective goals" is to be fitted into unified science, and without indicating any observation-statements through which "objective goals" as such might be determined. Again:

If the "general theory of the state" asks *what* the state is and *how* it is, i. e., what its possible basic forms and chief components are, politics

---

7. Kelsen, *Allgemeine Staatslehre,* pp. 14 ff.

asks *whether* the state is to be at all, and, if it is, which of its possible forms might be the best. Through this formulation of questions, politics exhibits itself as part of ethics, as the judgment of morality which sets objective goals for human conduct, i. e., which posits as obligatory the content of some actions. But politics, so far as it seeks means appropriate to the realization of these objective goals which are somehow established and assumed by virtue of their establishment; so far, that is, as it fixes those contents of conduct which are shown by experience to cause the effects corresponding substantially to the presupposed goals; to this extent, politics is not ethics, it is not addressed to the normative, prescriptive law. Rather, it is a *technology*, if the term may be used, social technology, and as such directed towards causal-type laws of the connection of means and end.[8]

Even after extensive alteration, most of these views cannot be employed within the body of an empirical sociology, i. e., of a social behaviorism. For what correlation is supposed to be asserted? One may object, however, that it is again a question of showing that combinations of certain rules and legal definitions are logically equivalent to other definitions (although this is something not necessarily noticed at first sight). But then, while such demonstrations are certainly important for practical life, no special metaphysical discussions are required.

It is clear that these tautologies of the legal system will be less prominent when the basic spirit of unified science prevails. People will then be more interested in what effects certain measures produce, and less in whether the ordinances formulated in statute books are logically consistent. No special discipline, certainly, is required to test the logical compatibility of the rules for the administration of a hospital. What one wishes to know is how the joint operation of certain measures affects the standard of health, so that one may act accordingly.

VII. THE EMPIRICAL SOCIOLOGY OF MARXISM

The unified language of physicalism safeguards the scientific method. Statement is linked to statement, law to law. It has been shown how sociology can be incorporated in unified science no less than biology, chemistry, technology or astronomy. The fundamental separation of special "moral sciences" from the "natural sciences" has proved itself theoretically meaningless. But even a purely practical division, sharper than any of the many others that exist has been shown to be inappropriate and wholly uncalled for.

---

8. Kelsen, *op. cit.,* p. 27.

In this connection we have given a sketch of the concept of sociological correlations as applicable within a developed social behaviorism. We have seen that by virtue of this conception, disciplines such as "ethics" and jurisprudence" lose their traditional foundations. Without metaphysics, without distinctions explicable only through reference to metaphysical habits, these disciplines cannot maintain their independence. *Whatever elements of genuine science are contained in them become incorporated into the structure of sociology.*

In this science there gradually converge whatever useful protocol statements and laws economics, ethnology, history and other disciplines have to offer. Sometimes the fact that men alter their modes of reaction plays an important role in sociological thought, and sometimes the starting point is the fact that men do not change in their reaction behavior, but enter into modified relations with one another. Economics, for instance, reckons with a constant human type, and then investigates the consequences of the operation of the given economic order, e. g. the market mechanism. It seeks to determine how crises and unemployment arise, how net profits accrue, etc.

But when it is observed that the given economic order is altered by men, the need arises for sociological laws which describe this change. Investigation of the economic order and its operation is then not sufficient. It is necessary to investigate, in addition, the laws which determine the change in the economic order itself. How certain changes in the mode of production alter stimuli in such a way that men transform their traditional ways of living, often by means of revolutions, is a question investigated by sociologists of the most divergent schools. Marxism is, to a higher degree than any other present-day sociological theory, a system of empirical sociology. The most important Marxist theses employed for prediction are either already formulated in a fairly physicalistic fashion (so far as traditional language made this possible), or they can be so formulated, without the loss of anything essential.

We can see in the case of Marxism how sociological laws are sought for and how relations conformable to law are established. When one attempts to establish the correlation between the modes of production of successive periods and the contemporaneous forms of religious worship, the books, discourses, etc., then one is investigating the *correlation between physicalistic structures.* Marxism lays down, over and above the doctrine of physicalism (materialism) certain special doctrines. When it opposes *one* group of forms as "substructure" to another group as "superstructure" ("historical materialism" as a special physicalistic theory), it proceeds throughout its operations within the confines of social behaviorism. What is involved here is no opposition of the "material" to the "spiritual," i. e., of "essences" with "different types of causality."

The coming decades may be concerned in growing measure with the discovery of such correlations. Max Weber's prodigious attempt to demonstrate the emergence of capitalism from Calvinism clearly shows to how great an extent concrete investigation is obstructed by metaphysical formulations. To a proponent of social behaviorism it seems at once quite natural that certain verbal sequences—the formulation of certain divine commands—should be recognized as dependent on certain modes of production and power situations. But it does not seem very plausible that the way of life of vast numbers of human beings occupied with trade, industry and other matters, should be determined by verbal sequences of individual theologians, or by the deity's injunctions, always very vaguely worded, which the theologians transmit. And yet Max Weber was committed to this point of view. He sought to show that from the "spirit of Calvinism" was born the "spirit of capitalism" and with it the capitalist order.

A Catholic theologian, Kraus, has pointed out that such an overestimation of the influence of theological formulations can only be explained by the fact that he ascribed to spirit a sort of "magical" effect. In the work of Weber and other thinkers, "spirit" is regarded as very closely bound up with words and formulae. Thus we understand Weber's assiduous quest for crucial theological formulations of individual Calvinists, in which the origins of crucial capitalist formulations might be sought. The "rationalism" of one sphere is to spring from that of the other. That theological discourses and writings possess such enormous powers is a supposition which would be formally possible within a physicalistic system. *But experience proves otherwise.* In company with the Marxists, the Catholic theologian mentioned above points out the fact that theological subtleties exercise little influence on human behavior, indeed, that they are scarcely known to the average merchant or professional man. It would be much more plausible to suppose that in England, for example, merchants opposed to the royal monopoly, and usurers desiring to take interest at a higher rate than the Church of England permitted, readily gave their support to a doctrine and a party which turned against the Church and the crown allied with the Church. First the behavior of these men was, to a considerable extent, capitalistically oriented—then they became Calvinists. We should expect to find, in accordance with all our experience of theological doctrines at other times, that these doctrines were subsequently revised and adapted to the system of production and commerce. And, Kraus further shows, in opposition to Weber, that those theological formulations which are "compatible" with capitalism did not appear until later, while Calvinism in its original form was related rather to the dogmas of the anti-capitalist Middle Ages. *Weber's metaphysical starting-point impeded his scientific work, and determined unfavorably his selection of observation-statements.* But without a suitable selection of observation-statements there can be no fruitful scientific work.

Let us analyze a concrete case in somewhat greater detail. With what is the decline of slavery in the ancient world connected?

Many have been inclined to the view that Christian doctrine and the Christian way of life effected the disappearance of slavery, after the Stoic philosophers had impaired the conception of slavery as an eternal institution.

If such an assertion is meant to express a correlation, it is natural to consider, in the first place, whether or not Christianity and slavery are found together. It is then seen that the most oppressive forms of slavery appear at the beginning of the modern era, at a time when Christian states are everywhere expanding their power, when the Christian Churches are vigorous above all in the colonies. Because of the intervention of Catholic theologians motivated by humanitarian considerations, the preservation of the perishing Indian slaves of America was undertaken through the importation of sturdier Negro slaves brought to that continent in shiploads.

It would really be necessary to define in advance with a greater degree of precision what is meant, on the one hand, by "Christian," and, on the other, by "slavery." If the attempt is made to formulate the correlation between them with greater clarity, it must be said that statements of a certain type, religious behavior, etc., never appear in conjunction with the large-scale ownership of slaves. But in this connection, it would be necessary to lay down a definite mode of application. For a man can be a "slave" from the "juristic" standpoint, and, simultaneously, a "master" from the "sociological" point of view. Sociological concepts, however, may be linked only with other sociological concepts.

"Christian dogma" is an extraordinarily indeterminate concept. Many theologians have believed it possible to demonstrate, from the Bible, that God has condemned the Negroes to slavery: when

Ham treated his drunken father Noah irreverently, Noah cursed him and declared that he and his descendants were to be subject to his brothers Shem and Japheth and their descendants. Still other theologians have sought to discover in Christian doctrine arguments against slavery.

It is evident that the sociologist advances much further when he delimits a certain system of men, religious acts, dogmas, etc., and then notes whether it comes into being in conjunction with certain modes of social behavior. This is, of course, a very rough procedure. The attempt must be made to discover not only such simple correlations, but also correlations of greater complexity. Laws must be combined with one another, in order for it to be possible to produce certain predictions.

Some sociological "laws" are valid only for limited periods, just as, in biology, there are laws about ants and about lions in addition to more general laws. That is to say, we are not yet in a position to state precisely on what certain correlations depend: the phrase "historical period" refers to a complicated set of conditions which has not been analyzed. Much confusion is due to the opinion of some analytical sociologists that the laws which they had discovered had to possess the same character as chemical laws, i.e., that they had to hold true under all conceivable earthly conditions. But sociology is concerned for the most part with correlations valid for *limited periods of time*. Marx was justified in asserting that it is senseless to speak of a universal law of population, as Malthus did. But it is possible to state which law of population holds for any given sociological period.

When, for the purpose of clarifying the question, "How does the decline of slavery come about?" one analyzes the conflict between the Northern and Southern States over the freeing of the slaves, one is confronted by a conflict between industrial and plantation states. The emancipation inflicts serious injury on the plantation states. Shouldn't we expect a connection between the freeing of the slaves and the processes of production? How is such a notion to be made plausible?

One attempts to determine the conditions under which slavery offers the slave-owner advantages, and the conditions under which the contrary is the case. If those masters who free their slaves are asked why they do so, only a few will say that they oppose slavery because it does not yield sufficient advantages. Many will inform us, without hypocrisy, that they have been deeply impressed by reading a philosopher who championed the slaves. Others will describe in detail their conflicting motives, will perhaps explain that slavery would really be more advantageous to them, but that the desire to sacrifice, to renounce property, has led them, after a long inner conflict, to the difficult step of freeing their slaves. Anyone accustomed to operate in the spirit of social behaviorism will, above all, keep in mind the very complicated "stimulus" of the way of life based on slave-owning, and then proceed to investigate the "reaction"—retention or freeing of the slaves. He will employ the results of this inquiry to determine how far theological doctrines concerning the emancipation of slaves are to be recognized as "stimulus," how far as "reaction."

If it is shown that relatively simple correlations can be established between the effects of slavery on the masters' tenor of life and the behavior of the master toward the liberation of slaves, and that, as against this, no *simple correlations* can be laid down between the doctrines of the time and the behavior of the slave-owners, then preference will be given to the former mode of investigation.

Thus there will be examined under various conditions the relationship between hunting and slavery, agriculture and slavery, manufacture and slavery. It will be found, for example, that the possession of slaves generally offers no advantage where there are sufficiently numerous free workers who eagerly seek employment in order to avoid starvation. Columella, a Roman agrarian writer of the later period, bluntly says, for example, that the employment of slaves is disadvantageous to anyone who drains fever swamps in the Campagna: the sickness of a slave means loss of interest, while his death results in loss of capital. He goes on to say that it is possible, on the other hand, to obtain free workers on the market at any time, and that the employer is in no way burdened by their sickness or death.

When serious fluctuations in the business situation occur, entrepreneurs find it desirable to be in a position to drop free workers; slaves, like horses, must continue to be fed. When one reads in Strabo, therefore, that in antiquity papyrus shrubs in Egypt were already being cut down in order to maintain the monopoly price, one understands that the universal employment of free labor could not be far away.

The conditions which led to the fluctuating tendencies of early capitalist economic institutions can likewise be investigated. Correlation is added to correlation. It is seen that "free labor" and "the destruction of commodities" seem to be correlated under certain conditions. This is equally true of "plantation slavery" and "a constant market." One can view the Civil War as a conflict between the industrial North, which was not interested in slavery, and the cotton-producing agrarian South, and thereby be able to make extensive predictions.

This does not mean that the religious and ethical opponents of slavery were lying when they said that they directly rejoiced in the emancipation of the slaves, but not in the increase of industrial profits which ensued in the North. That such a desire for the free-ing of the slaves could develop at this time and find so rich a satis-faction is something which the empirical sociologist could deduce, in broad outline, from the total economic situation.

The methods used in the elaboration of a theory of agricultural economics have also been applied by several writers (theologians among them) in the construction of a wholly empirical theory of the "employment of natives," yielding all types of correlations.[9] In combination with other relations expressible as laws one can make all sorts of predictions concerning the fate of slavery in particular countries and territories.

The distribution of grain to freemen but not to slaves, during the later history of Rome, offered slave-owners an additional motive for freeing their slaves. The former master could then re-employ the freedman at a lower cost, and also use his support at elections. It is likewise easy to understand how, during the decline of Rome, the system of the "coloni" and serfdom emerge through the regression of early capitalistic institutions. In order to undertake an enterprise with slave labor, one had to have at one's disposal extensive financial resources, since both workers and implements of production had to be purchased. Under a regime of free labor, the purchase of tools was sufficient. The system of the "coloni" required no invest-ment at all from the owner, who was assured of dues of all kinds. The "free" workers were forced by the whole social order to labor —the death penalty was imposed for idleness—while each slave had to be disciplined by his own master. The master had to protect the health and life of his slave, to care for him just as he had to care for a horse or a bullock, even when it was unruly.

We see how, by means of such analyses, correlations are estab-lished between general social conditions and certain modes of be-havior of limited human groups. The "statements" which these groups make about their own behavior are not essential to these correlations; they can often be added with the help of additional

---

9. Cf. Otto Neurath, "Probleme der Kriegswirtschaftslehre," *Zeitschrift für die gesamten Staatswissenschaften*, 1914, p. 474.

correlations. It is above all in Marxism that empirical sociology is pursued in this way.[10]

A system of empirical sociology in the spirit of social behaviorism, as it has been developed above all in the United States and the U.S.S.R., would have to direct its inquiries primarily to the typical "reactions" of whole groups. But significant historical movements are also often measured or evaluated without such analysis. And it may further be shown that through the development of certain institutions, through the increase in a certain magnitude, a reversal is produced which causes further changes to take a wholly different direction. The primitive "idea of progress," that every magnitude increases indefinitely, is untenable. One must consider the whole system of sociological magnitudes in all its complexity, and then note what changes are predictable. One cannot infer from the growth of large cities up to the present time that the process will continue approximately the same. Rapid growth is especially apt to release stimuli leading to a sudden cessation of growth and perhaps to the reconstitution of many small centers. The expansion of capitalist large-scale industry and the emergence of the proletarian masses dependent on those industries can lead to a situation where the whole capitalist mechanism moves through a series of economic crises towards its ultimate dissolution.

VIII. POSSIBILITIES OF PREDICTION

It is possible to state the extent to which predictions can be successfully made within the sphere of social behaviorism. It is evident that its various *"predictions," i.e., its scientific theories, are sociological events essentially dependent on the social and economic order.* It is only after this is understood that it becomes clear, for example, that under certain conditions certain predictions either do not emerge at all, or cannot be elaborated. Even when an individual believes that he divines the direction of further successful investigation, he can be prevented from finding the collaboration required for sociological research by the indifference, or even the opposition, of other men.

The approach of social changes is difficult to notice. In order to be able to make predictions about events of a new type, one must usually possess a certain amount of new experiences. It is often the changes in the historical process that first give the scientist the

---

10. Cf. for example, Ettore Ciccotti, *Der Untergang der Sklaverei in Altertum* (German translation by Oda Olberg), Berlin, 1910.

necessary data for further investigations. But since sociological investigations also play a certain role as stimuli and instruments in the organization of living, the development of sociology is very closely bound up with social conflicts. Only established schools of sociology, requiring social support, can master, by means of collective labor, the masses of material which must be adapted to a stricter formulation of correlations. This presupposes that the powers which finance such work are favorably inclined towards social behaviorism.

This is in general not the case today. Indeed, there exists in the ruling classes an aversion to social, as well as to individual, behaviorism which is much more than a matter of a scientific doubt, which would be comprehensible in view of the imperfections of this doctrine. The opposition of the ruling circles, which usually find support in the universities of the capitalist countries, is explained sociologically, above all, by the fact that empirical sociology, through its non-metaphysical attitude, reveals the meaninglessness of such expressions as "categorical imperative," "divine injunction," "moral idea," "superpersonal state," etc. In doing this it undermines important doctrines which are useful in the maintenance of the prevailing order. The proponents of "unified science" do not defend *one* world-view among other world-views. Hence the question of tolerance cannot be raised. They declare transcendental theology to be not false, but meaningless. Without disputing the fact that powerful inspiration, and cheering and depressing effects, can be associated with meaningless doctrines, they can in practice "let seven be a holy number," since they do not harass the supporters of these doctrines. But they cannot allow that these claims have any meaning at all, however "hidden," i.e., that they can confirm or confute scientific statements. Even if such reasoning by the pure scientist leaves metaphysics and theology undisturbed, it doubtlessly shakes the reverence for them which is frequently demanded.

All the metaphysical entities whose injunctions men endeavored to obey, and whose "holy" powers they venerated, disappear. In their place there stands as an empirical substitute, confined within the bounds of purely scientific formulations, the actual behavior of groups, whose commands operate as empirical forces on individual men. That groups of men lend strength to individual men pursuing certain modes of action and obstruct others pursuing different modes, is a statement which is wholly meaningful in the context of social behaviorism.

The social behaviorist, too, makes commands, requests and reproaches; *but he does not suppose that these utterances, when connected with propositions, can yield a system.* Words can be employed like whistles, caresses and whiplashes; but when used in this way, they can neither agree with nor contradict propositions. *An injunction can never be deduced* from a system of propositions! This is no "limitation" of the scientific method: it is simply the result of logical analysis. That injunctions and predictions are so frequently linked follows from the fact that both are directed to the future. An injunction is an event which it is assumed will evoke certain changes in the future. A prediction is a statement which it is assumed will agree with a future statement.

The proponents of "unified science" seek, with the help of laws, to formulate predictions in the "unified language of physicalism." This takes place in the sphere of empirical sociology through the development of "social behaviorism." In order to attain to more useful predictions, one can immediately eliminate meaningless verbal sequences by the use of logic. But this is not sufficient. There must follow the elimination of all false formulations. The representatives of modern science, even after they have effected the elimination of metaphysical formulations, must still dispose of false doctrines, for example, astrology, magic, etc. In order to liberate someone from such ideas, the universal acknowledgment accorded to the rules of logic does not, as with the elimination of *meaningless* statements, suffice. One must, if one wishes to see one's own theory prevail, create the groundwork which will lead people to recognize the inadequacy of these theories, which, while *"also physicalistic,"* are uncritical.

The fruitfulness of social behaviorism is demonstrated by the establishment of new correlations and by the successful predictions made on the basis of them. Young people educated in the spirit of physicalism and its unified language will be spared many of the hindrances to scientific work to which we are still at present subjected. A single individual cannot create and employ this successful language, for it is the product of the labor of a generation. Thus, even in the form of social behaviorism, sociology will be able to formulate valid predictions on a large scale only when a generation trained in physicalism sets to work in all departments of science. Despite the fact that we can observe metaphysics on the increase, there is much to show that non-metaphysical doctrines are also spreading and constantly gaining ground as the new "superstructure" erected on the changing economic "substructure" of our age.[11]

11. Cf. Otto Neurath, "Physicalism, the Philosophy of the Vienna Circle," *The Monist*, October 1931.

Analytical Philosophy

15

Philosophy

BY FRANK P. RAMSEY

PHILOSOPHY MUST BE of some use and we must take it seriously; it must clear our thoughts and so our actions. Or else it is a disposition we have to check, and an inquiry to see that this is so; i.e. the chief proposition of philosophy is that philosophy is nonsense. And again we must then take seriously that it is nonsense, and not pretend, as Wittgenstein does, that it is important nonsense!

In philosophy we take the propositions we make in science and everyday life, and try to exhibit them in a logical system with primitive terms and definitions, etc. Essentially a philosophy is a system of definitions or, only too often, a system of descriptions of how definitions might be given.

I do not think it is necessary to say with Moore that the definitions explain what we have hitherto meant by our propositions, but rather that they show how we intend to use them in future. Moore would say they were the same, that philosophy does not change what anyone meant by "This is a table." It seems to me that it might; for meaning is mainly potential, and a change might therefore only be manifested on rare and critical occasions. Also sometimes philosophy should clarify and distinguish notions previously vague and confused, and clearly this is meant to fix our future meaning only.[1] But this is clear, that the definitions are to give at least our future meaning, and not merely to give any pretty way of obtaining a certain structure.

I used to worry myself about the nature of philosophy through excessive scholasticism. I could not see how we could understand

---

This extract is taken from Ramsey's *The Foundations of Mathematics*, copyright 1931 by Routledge and Kegan Paul, London, with whose permission it is here reprinted.

1. But in so far as our past meaning was not utterly confused, philosophy will naturally give that, too. E.g. that paradigm of philosophy, Russell's theory of descriptions.

a word and not be able to recognize whether a proposed definition of it was or was not correct. I did not realize the vagueness of the whole idea of understanding, the reference it involves to a multitude of performances any of which may fail and require to be restored. Logic issues in tautologies, mathematics in identities, philosophy in definitions; all trivial but all part of the vital work of clarifying and organizing our thought.

If we regard philosophy as a system of definitions (and elucidations of the use of words which cannot be nominally defined), the things that seem to me problems about it are these:

(1) What definitions do we feel it up to *philosophy* to provide, and what do we leave to the sciences or feel it unnecessary to give at all?

(2) When and how can we be content without a definition but merely with a description of how a definition might be given? [This point is mentioned above.]

(3) How can philosophical inquiry be conducted without a perpetual *petitio principii?*

(1) Philosophy is not concerned with special problems of definition but only with general ones: it does not propose to define particular terms of art or science, but to settle e.g. problems which arise in the definition of any such term or in the relation of any term in the physical world to the terms of experience.

Terms of art and science, however, must be defined, but not necessarily nominally; e.g. we define mass by explaining how to measure it, but this is not a nominal definition; it merely gives the term "mass" in a theoretical structure a clear relation to certain experimental facts. The terms we do not need to define are those which we know we could define if need arose, like "chair," or those which like "clubs" (the suit of cards) we can translate easily into visual or some other language, but cannot conveniently expand in words.

(2) The solution to what we called in (1) a "general problem of definition" is naturally a description of definitions, from which we learn how to form the actual definition in any particular case. That we so often seem to get no actual *definitions,* is because the solution of the problem is often that nominal definition is inappropriate, and that what is wanted is an explanation of the use of the symbol.

But this does not touch what may be supposed to be the real

difficulty under this head (2); for what we have said applies only to the case in which the word to be defined being merely described (because treated as one of a class), its definition or explanation is also, of course, merely described, but described in such a way that when the actual word is given its actual definition can be derived. But there are other cases in which the word to be defined being given, we are given in return no definition of it but a statement that its meaning involves entities of such-and-such sorts in such-and-such ways, i.e. a statement which *would* give us a definition if we had names for these entities.

As to the use of this, it is plainly to fit the term in connection with variables, to put it as a value of the right complex variable; and it presupposes that we can have variables without names for all their values. Difficult questions arise as to whether we must always be *able* to name all the values, and if so what kind of ability this means, but clearly the phenomenon is in some way possible in connection with sensations for which our language is so fragmentary. For instance, "Jane's voice" is a description of a characteristic of sensations for which we have no name. We could perhaps name it, but can we identify and name the different inflections of which it consists?

An objection often made to these descriptions of definitions of sensory characteristics is that they express what we should find on analysis, but that this kind of analysis changes the sensation analyzed by developing the complexity which it pretends merely to discover. That attention can change our experience is indubitable, but it seems to me possible that sometimes it reveals a pre-existing complexity (i.e. enables us to symbolize this adequately), for this is compatible with any change in incidental facts, anything even except a creation of the complexity.

Another difficulty with regard to descriptions of definitions is that if we content ourselves with them we may get simply nonsense by introducing nonsensical variables, e.g. described variables such as "particular" or theoretical ideas such as "point." We might for instance say that by "patch" we mean an infinite class of points; if so we should be giving up philosophy for theoretical psychology. For in philosophy we analyze *our* thought, in which patch could not be replaced by infinite class of points: we could not determine a particular infinite class extensionally; "This patch is red" is not short for "a is red and b is red etc. . . . ." where a, b, etc., are points. (How would it be if just a were not red?) Infinite classes of points could only come in when we look at the mind from outside and construct a theory of it, in which its sensory field consists of classes of colored points about which it thinks.

Now if we made this theory about our own mind we should have to regard it as accounting for certain *facts,* e.g. that this patch is red; but when we are thinking of other people's minds we have no facts, but are altogether in the realm of theory, and can persuade ourselves that these theoretical constructions exhaust the field. We then turn back on our own minds, and say that what are really happening there are simply these theoretical processes. The clearest instance of this is, of course, materialism. But many other philosophies, e.g. Carnap's, make just the same mistake.

(3) Our third question was how we could avoid *petitio principii,* the danger of which arises somewhat as follows:

In order to clarify my thought the proper method seems to be simply to think out with myself "What do I mean by that?" "What are the separate notions involved in this term?" "Does this really follow from that?" etc., and to test identity of meaning of a proposed definiens and the definiendum by real and hypothetical examples. This we can often do without thinking about the nature of meaning itself; we can tell whether we mean the same or different things by "horse" and "pig" without thinking at all about meaning in general. But in order to settle more complicated questions of the sort we obviously need a logical structure, a system of logic, into which to bring them. These we may hope to obtain by a relatively easy previous application of the same methods; for instance, it should not be difficult to see that for either not-p or not-q to be true is just the same thing as for not both p and q to be true. In this case we construct a logic, and do all our philosophical analysis entirely *unselfconsciously,* thinking all the time of the facts and not about our thinking about them, deciding what we mean without any reference to the nature of meanings. [Of course we could also think about the nature of meaning in an unselfconscious way; i.e. think of a case of meaning before us without reference to our meaning *it.*] This is one method and it may be the right one; but I think it is wrong and leads to an impasse, and I part company from it in the following way.

It seems to me that in the process of clarifying our thought we come to terms and sentences which we cannot elucidate in the obvious manner by defining their meaning. For instance, variable hypotheticals and theoretical terms we cannot define, but we can explain the way in which they are used, and in this explanation we are forced

to look not only at the objects which we are talking about, but at
our own mental states. As Johnson would say, in this part of logic
we cannot neglect the epistemic or subjective side.

Now this means that we cannot get clear about these terms and
sentences without getting clear about meaning, and we seem to get
into the situation that we cannot understand e.g. what we say about
time and the external world without first understanding meaning
and yet we cannot understand meaning without first understanding
certainly time and probably the external world which are involved
in it. So we cannot make our philosophy into an ordered progress to
a goal, but have to take our problems as a whole and jump to a
simultaneous solution; which will have something of the nature of
a hypothesis, for we shall accept it not as the consequence of direct
argument, but as the only one we can think of which satisfies our
several requirements.

Of course, we should not strictly speak of argument, but there
is in philosophy a process analogous to "linear inference" in which
things become successively clear; and since, for the above reason,
we cannot carry this through to the end, we are in the ordinary position of scientists of having to be content with piecemeal improve-
ments: we can make several things clearer, but we cannot make
anything clear.

I find this self-consciousness inevitable in philosophy except in
a very limited field. We are driven to philosophize because we do
not know clearly what we mean; the question is always "What do
I mean by *x*?" And only very occasionally can we settle this without reflecting on meaning. But it is not only an obstacle, this necessity
of dealing with meaning; it is doubtless an essential clue to the truth.
If we neglect it I feel we may get into the absurd position of the
child in the following dialogue: "Say breakfast." "Can't." "What
can't you say?" "Can't say breakfast."

But the necessity of self-consciousness must not be used as a
justification for nonsensical hypotheses; we are doing philosophy not
theoretical psychology, and our analyses of our statements, whether
about meaning or anything else, must be such as we can understand.

The chief danger to our philosophy, apart from laziness and
woolliness, is *scholasticism,* the essence of which is treating what is
vague as if it were precise and trying to fit it into an exact logical
category. A typical piece of scholasticism is Wittgenstein's view that
all our everyday propositions are completely in order and that it is
impossible to think illogically. (This last is like saying that it is impossible to break the rules of bridge because if you break them

you are not playing bridge but, as Mrs. C. says, not-bridge.) Another is the argumentation about acquaintance with before leading to the conclusion that we perceive the past. A simple consideration of the automatic telephone shows that we could react differently to *AB* and *BA* without perceiving the past, so that the argument is substantially unsound. It turns on a play with "acquaintance" which means, first, capacity to symbolize and, secondly, sensory perception. Wittgenstein seems to equivocate in just the same way with his notion of "given."

16

Philosophical Arguments

BY GILBERT RYLE

ROBIN GEORGE COLLINGWOOD held this Waynflete Chair for a lamentably brief time. Yet his literary productivity during this short period was immense. The time is not yet ripe for me to attempt to offer a critical evaluation of these contributions to philosophy, nor, even were I competent, should I on this occasion offer an appreciation of his originality as an historian. He would himself, I think, have desired recognition chiefly for his thoughts on the philosophy of history. About these thoughts, therefore, I submit, with humility and diffidence, a few reflections.

There are many branches of methodical inquiry into the different departments of the world. There are the mathematical sciences, the several natural sciences, and there are the humane or human studies of anthropology, jurisprudence, philosophy, the linguistic and literary studies, and history, which last embraces in one way or another most of the others. There are also many disciplines which teach not truths but arts and skills, such as agriculture, tactics, music, architecture, painting, games, navigation, inference, and scientific method. All theories apply their own several principles and canons of inquiry and all disciplines apply their own several principles and canons of practice. These principles were called by Professor Collingwood their "presuppositions." In other words, all employ their own standards or criteria by which their particular exercises are judged successful or unsuccessful.

Now it is one thing intelligently to apply principles; it is quite another thing to step back to consider them. A scientist who ceases for a moment to try to solve his questions in order to inquire instead why he poses them or whether they are the right questions to pose ceases for the time to be a scientist and becomes a philosopher. This

This is Professor Ryle's Inaugural lecture at Oxford, copyright 1946 by the Clarendon Press, Oxford. It is reprinted here with the kind permission of the author and publisher.

[327]

duality of interests may, as history shows, make him both a good philosopher and a better scientist. The best philosophical theories of mathematics have come from mathematicians who have been forced to try to resolve internal puzzles about the principles of their study, a philosophical exercise which has sometimes led to the origination of new mathematical methods and has often led to the origination of illuminating philosophical views. Every genius is the inventor of new methods and he must therefore be some sort of a critic of principles of method.

Professor Collingwood was an historian who was puzzled about the canons of historical research. He wanted not only to explain certain historical processes and events but also to elucidate what sort of a thing a good historical explanation would be. Nor was this a purely domestic or technological interest. For to see what is an historical explanation, is, among other things, to see how it differs from a chemical, mechanical, biological, anthropological, or psychological theory. The philosopher may, perhaps, begin by wondering about the categories constituting the framework of a single theory or discipline, but he cannot stop there. He must try to co-ordinate the categories of all theories and disciplines. The problem of "Man's place in Nature" is, roughly, the problem of co-ordinating the questions which govern laboratory researches with the questions governing the researches prosecuted in libraries. And this co-ordination is done neither in libraries nor in laboratories but in the philosopher's head.

Professor Collingwood saw more clearly, I think, than did his most eminent predecessors in the philosophy of history that the appearance of a feud or antithesis between Nature and Spirit, that is to say, between the objectives of the natural sciences and those of the human studies, is an illusion. These branches of inquiry are not giving rival answers to the same questions about the same world; nor are they giving separate answers to the same questions about rival worlds; they are giving their own answers to different questions about the same world. Just as physics is neither the foe nor the handmaid of geometry, so history, jurisprudence and literary studies are neither hostile nor ancillary to the laboratory sciences. Their categories, that is, their questions, methods and canons are different. In my predecessor's word, they work with different presuppositions. To establish this point it is necessary to chart these differences. This task Professor Collingwood died too soon to complete but not too soon to begin. He had already made that great philosophic advance of reducing a puzzle to a problem.

Professor Collingwood kept himself aloof from the sparring and the shadow-boxing by which academic philosophers ordinarily strengthen their muscles and discharge their humors. What we lost by this abstention was compensated by the world's gain. For he wrote less for the eyes of his professional associates than for those of the intelligent citizens of the entire republic of letters. In consequence he achieved a style of philosophical writing and, I believe, diction, which at its frequent best is on a level with the higher ranges of English philosophic prose.

THE PROBLEM

Philosophers have in recent years given much consideration to the nature, objectives and methods of their own inquiry. This interest has been due partly to a certain professional hypochondria, since the conspicuous progress made by other studies has induced in philosophers some nervousness about the scale of their own successes. Partly, also, it has been due to the application of modern logical theory to the processes of the mathematical and the inductive sciences, which has automatically led to its application to philosophy. The exposition of the logical credentials of different sorts of scientific conclusions has posed in a bright if painful light the corresponding question about the foundations of philosophical doctrines.

My object is to exhibit the logical structure of a type of arguments which are proper to philosophical thinking. It makes no difference whether these arguments are used polemically in controversies between philosophers or peaceably in private philosophical reflection. For arguments are effective as weapons only if they are logically cogent, and if they are so they reveal connections, the disclosure of which is not the less necessary to the discovery of truth for being also handy in the discomfiture of opponents. The love of truth is not incongruous with a passion for correcting the erring.

Philosophical arguments are not inductions. Both the premises and the conclusions of inductions can be doubted or denied without absurdity. Observed facts and plausible hypotheses have no more illustrative force in philosophy than is possessed by fictions or guesses. Nor have either facts or fancies any evidential force in the resolution of philosophical problems. The evidential force of matters of fact is only to increase or decrease the probability of general or particular hypotheses and it is absurd to describe philosophical propositions as relatively probable or improbable.

On the other hand philosophical arguments are not demonstrations of the Euclidean type, namely deductions of theorems from axioms or postulates. For philosophy has no axioms and it is debarred from taking its start from postulates. Otherwise there could be alternative philosophical doctrines as there are alternative geometries.

A pattern of argument which is proper and even proprietary to philosophy is the *reductio ad absurdum*. This argument moves by extracting contradictions or logical paradoxes from its material. It is the object of this discussion to show how this is possible and why it is necessary.

First it is expedient to distinguish the strong *reductio ad absurdum* from the weak *reductio*. The latter form is used in some of Euclid's demonstrations. He demonstrates the truth of a theorem by deducing from its contradictory consequences which conflict with the axioms of his system or with consequences drawn from them. It should be noticed that this argument proves only either that the required theorem is true if the axioms are true or that both are false, that is, that the contradictory of the required theorem is not compatible with the axioms. The strong reduction consists in deducing from a proposition or a complex of propositions consequences which are inconsistent with each other or with the original proposition. It shows (to express it in a fashion which will have to be amended later) that a proposition is illegitimate because it has logically absurd corollaries. The proposition under investigation is shown to be not merely false but nonsensical.

To prove that arguments of this type belong to philosophy it is enough to mention that it would be proper for a dissentient philosopher to try to demolish this or any other philosophical assertion by exhibiting contradictions latent in it. I am not trying to prove that no other types of argument are proper to philosophy.

On first consideration it will seem that arguments of the type *reductio ad absurdum* can have only a destructive effect. They may be effective in demolishing silly theories and thus possess, besides the pleasing property of defeating opponents, the useful one of clearing the site for subsequent constructive theory. But it will be felt that no demolitions can result in the erection of a new dwelling. I hope to disarm any such objection by showing that (to use another metaphor) *reductio ad absurdum* arguments are neither more nor less nihilist than are threshing operations. Or, to change the picture again, the position will be maintained that philosophical arguments of the type described have something in common with the destruction-tests by which engineers discover the strength of materials. Certainly engineers stretch, twist, compress, and batter bits of metal until they collapse, but it is just by such tests that they determine the strains which the metal will withstand. In somewhat the same way, philosophical arguments bring out the logical powers of the ideas under investigation, by fixing the precise forms of logical mishandling under which they refuse to work.

THE LOGICAL POWERS OF PROPOSITIONS

Every proposition has what will here be called certain "logical powers"; that is to say, it is related to other propositions in various discoverable logical relationships. It follows from some as a consequence and it implies others. It is incompatible with some and merely compatible with others. It is evidence strengthening or weakening the probability of ulterior hypotheses. Further, for any logical powers possessed by a given proposition it is always possible to find or invent an indefinite range of other propositions which can be classed with it as having analogous logical powers or, as it is commonly put, as being of the same logical form.

For the rules of logic are general. Valid arguments exhibit patterns which can be manifested equally well by collocations of any other propositions of the same logical family. Formal logicians learn to extract the logical skeletons of propositions in virtue of which these and any other propositions embodying the same skeletons can function as premises or conclusions of parallel valid arguments.

Now when people are using or considering a given proposition they cannot then and there be attending to all its logical powers. They cannot in one moment be considering it and all the valid arguments into which it might enter and all the fallacious arguments into which it might be improperly coerced. At best their grasp is adequate for them to be able to think out some of these logical powers if they have occasion to do so. Many of the logical powers of a proposition are not noticed at all in the routines of workaday thinking and of these a proportion baffles discovery even when the thinker is concentrating his whole intellectual strength upon the search for them. Thus people can correctly be said to have only a partial grasp of most of the propositions that they consider. They could usually be taken by surprise by certain of the remoter logical connections of their most ordinary propositions.

None the less, though people's understanding of the propositions that they use is in this sense imperfect, there is another sense in which their understanding of some of them may be nearly or quite complete.

For they may have learned from practice or instruction all their logical powers which govern the limited uses to which those propositions are ordinarily put. A boy learns quickly how to use such propositions as *3 × 3 = 9* or *London is due north of Brighton* without ever making the arithmetical or geographical mistakes which would be evidence of an imperfect grasp of such propositions. He does not know the rules governing the logical behavior of these propositions but he knows by wont their logical course down a limited set of familiar tracks.

The fact that people, however intelligent, never achieve a complete appreciation of all the logical powers of the propositions that they use is one which will be seen to have important consequences. It should be noticed that even mastery of the techniques and the theory of formal logic does not in principle modify this situation. The extraction of the logical skeletons of propositions does not reveal the logical powers of those propositions by some trick which absolves the logician from thinking them out. At best it is merely a summary formulation of what his thinking has discovered.

When several different propositions are noticed having something in common (and when this common feature or factor is not itself a constituent proposition) it is convenient and idiomatic, though hazardous, to abstract this common factor and call it (with exceptions) an "idea" or "concept." Thus men learn to fasten on the idea of mortality or the concept of price as that which is common to a range of propositions in which persons are affirmed or denied to be mortal or in which commodities are said to cost so much or to be exchangeable at such and such rates. Later they learn to isolate in the same manner more abstract ideas like those of existence, implication, duty, species, mind, and science.

In the early days of logical speculation these ideas or concepts were construed as being proper parts or substantial bits, an assemblage of two or more of which was supposed to constitute a proposition. They were often technically styled "terms." This erroneous theory has been the source of a multitude of damaging confusions. The truth is that what we label "ideas" or "concepts" are abstractions from the families of propositions of which they are common factors or features. To speak of a given idea is to speak summarily of the family of propositions resembling each other in respect of this common factor. Statements about ideas are general statements about families of propositions.

A natural but disastrous corollary drawn from the erroneous doctrine of terms was the assumption that the rules of logic govern the relations between propositions but have little or no bearing upon their factors. It was, indeed, early discerned that there are logically important differences of type or category between different classes of "terms," "ideas," or "concepts," but the original and traditional classi-fication of a few of these types lent nothing to and borrowed nothing from the study of the rules of inference. (True, certain rules of in-ference were seen to be interlocked with the concepts *all, some,* and *not.* But no niche was found even for these ideas in the table of categories of concepts.)

In fact the distinction between the logical types of ideas is iden-tical with the discrimination between the logical forms of the propo-sitions from which the ideas are abstractions. If one proposition has factors of different types from those of another proposition, those propositions are of different logical forms and have different sorts of logical powers. The rules governing the conjunctions of propositions in valid arguments reflect the logical constitutions of their various abstractible factors and features. There are as many types of terms as there are forms of propositions, just as there are as many uphill as downhill slopes.

It is therefore both proper and necessary to speak not only (at one level of abstraction) of the logical powers of propositions, but also (at a higher level of abstraction) of the logical powers of ideas or concepts. Of course, a description of the logical powers of a given idea is neither more nor less than a description of certain of the logical powers of all propositions similar to one another in having that idea as an abstractible common factor.

As people's understanding of the propositions that they use is always imperfect, in the sense that they never have realized and never could realize all the logical powers of those propositions, so their grasp of ideas or concepts is necessarily incomplete. The risk always exists that confusion or paradox will arise in the course of any hitherto untried operations with those ideas.

THE SOURCES OF LOGICAL PARADOXES

Concepts and propositions carry with them no signal to indicate the logical types to which they belong. Expressions of the same gram-matical patterns are used to express thoughts of multifarious logical sorts. Men naturally, therefore, tend to be blind to the fact that dif-ferent ideas have different logical powers or at least they tend to treat the varieties of logical types as being few in number. Even philosophers have assumed for over two thousand years that Aris-

totle's inventory of ten such types was exhaustive if not over-
elaborate.

What happens when a person assumes an idea to be of one
logical type when it really belongs to another?—when, for example,
he assumes that the ideas *large* or *three* have logical powers similar
to those of *green* or *merry*? The inevitable consequence is that naïve
intellectual operations with those ideas lead directly to logically intolerable results. Concepts of different types cannot be coerced into
similar logical conduct. Some sort of contradiction arises from the
attempt and this, in fortunate cases, compels the thinker to turn
back in his tracks and try to change his treatment of the outraged
concept.

THE DIAGNOSIS AND CURE OF PARADOXES

Here there begins a new sort of inquiry, the deliberate attempt
to discover the real (as distinct from the naïvely anticipated) logical
powers of ideas. The logical absurdities which betray the original
type-confusions give an intellectual shock and set a theoretical problem, the problem of determining with method and with definitive
checks the rules governing the correct manipulation of concepts.

This task can be metaphorically described as the charting of
the logical powers of ideas. The metaphor is helpful in a number
of ways. People often know their way about a locality while quite
unable to describe the distances or directions between different parts
of it or between it and other familiar localities. They may know a
district and still be perplexed when approaching it by an unaccus-
tomed route or in a strange light. Again they may know the district
and still give descriptions of it which entail that two different buildings are in one place or that one building lies in two different directions from a given object.

Our workaday knowledge of the geography of our ideas is in
similar case—even of those ideas with which we can operate effi-
ciently in the daily tasks in which we have been drilled. This workaday knowledge is knowledge but it is knowledge without system and
without checks. It is knowledge by wont and not knowledge by rules.

There is another respect in which the metaphor of maps is useful. Surveyors do not map single objects like the village church.
They put together in one map all the salient features of the area:
the church, the bridge, the railway, the parish boundary, and perhaps the contours. Further, they indicate how this map joins the
maps of the neighboring areas, and how all are co-ordinated with

the points of the compass, the lines of latitude and longitude and standards of measurement. Any error in surveying results in a cartographical contradiction.

The resolution of type-puzzles about the logical powers of ideas demands an analogous procedure. Here too the problem is not to pinpoint separately the locus of this or that single idea but to determine the cross-bearings of all of a galaxy of ideas belonging to the same or contiguous fields. The problem, that is, is not to anatomize the solitary concept, say, of liberty but to extract its logical powers as these bear on those of law, obedience, responsibility, loyalty, government and the rest. Like a geographical survey a philosophical survey is necessarily synoptic. Philosophical problems cannot be posed or solved piecemeal.

This description of the inquiry into the logical powers of ideas as being analogous in some respects to a geographical survey is, of course, of illustrative utility only within narrow limits. In one important respect among many others the analogy breaks down. The correctness of a geographical survey is established by two major sorts of checks; the presence of a cartographical contradiction proves that the survey is erroneous but visual observations are positive evidence of its veracity. In the extraction of the logical powers of ideas there is no process directly corresponding to visual observation. Hence the primacy in philosophical reasoning of the *reductio ad absurdum* argument. The object to which this philosophical destruction-test is applied is the practice of operating with an idea as if it belonged to a certain category, that is as if it had powers corresponding to those of an accepted model. Initially this practice is naïve and unpremeditated. Sometimes it is deliberately recommended and adopted. In this case the destruction-test is being applied to a philosopher's theory.

The earliest philosophical problems are set by contradictions inadvertently encountered in the course of non-philosophical thinking. As every new theory begins certain new concepts come into currency, concepts which are cardinal not merely to its conclusions but even to its questions. Being new their logical powers are still unexplored, and being new they are unthinkingly credited with logical powers similar to those of ideas the discipline of which is familiar. Paradoxical consequences flowing from conventional operations upon them reveal that they have characters of their own. So must horses have startled their first masters by their non-bovine shape and behavior.

When the deliberate attempt is made to find the harness which will fit refractory concepts, the method is adopted of consciously looking for further logical paradoxes and contradictions. The rules governing the logical conduct of an idea are imperfectly grasped so long as there remain unexamined chances that it is still being mishandled. Absurdities are the original goad to philosophical thinking; they continue to be its scalpel.

This process can without injustice to the genealogy of the word be called "dialectical," though there seems no reason to constrict the process within the symmetrical confines of the hallowed double-entry method often associated with its employment. It is also the procedure followed, though not explicitly prescribed, by those who prefer to describe philosophy as being the clarification of ideas, the analysis of concepts, the study of universals and even the search for definitions.

An Objection

At this point it is necessary to face and resolve a difficulty—indeed a contradiction—which threatens to make nonsense of everything that I have said. Its emergence and its resolution may serve as an illustration of my general position.

It has been said that philosophical problems arise from a tendency of propositions (as we inadvertently handle them) to generate absurd consequences. But if the consequences of a proposition are absurd that proposition is absurd and then there can be no such proposition. It is absurd to say that there are absurd propositions. It is logically impossible for there to be a proposition of such a type that there could be no propositions of that type. It seems to follow that the *reductio ad absurdum* can never be applied, though the argument establishing this point itself exemplifies that pattern.

The solution is that expressions and only expressions can be absurd. Only of a given expression such as a sentence, therefore, can it be said that it cannot be construed as expressing a proposition of a certain logical constitution or, perhaps, a proposition of any logical constitution. This is what the *reductio ad absurdum* does. It discloses that a given expression cannot be expressing a proposition of such and such a content with such and such a logical skeleton, since a proposition with certain of these properties would conflict with one with certain of the others. The operation by which this is established is in a certain fashion experimental or hypothetical. *If* the expression is expressing a proposition at all, it cannot be expressing one analogous in these respects to certain familiar propositions and in those respects to others, since the corollaries of part of the hypothesis are at variance with those of another part. It is an hypothetical argument of the pattern known as *ponendo tollens*. In extreme cases it may establish that the expression cannot be expressing a proposition of any pattern; in milder cases it proves only that it cannot be expressing a proposition of certain specified patterns.

For examples, take the two statements "Numbers are eternal" and "Time began a million years ago." Both are linguistically regular statements but the latter sentence expresses no proposition. It tries to say what cannot be significantly said, viz. that there was a moment before which there was no possibility of anything being before anything else, which contains a patent contradiction. The former sentence is nonsensical if construed as expressing a proposition of one type but not if construed in another way. If it is construed as a terse way of saying that numbers are not temporal things or events or, better, that numerical expressions cannot enter into significant expressions as subjects to verbs with tenses, then what it says is true and important. But if it is construed, as childlike people have construed it, as saying that numbers, like tortoises, live a very long time—and in fact however old they get, they cannot die—then it could be shown to be absurd. It is nonsense when construed as an item of biology but true when interpreted as an application of the theory of logical types to arithmetical ideas.

Reductio ad absurdum arguments, therefore, apply to the employment and misemployment of expressions. So it is necessary to recast what was said earlier. Statements about the misreading of the logical powers of propositions and ideas should be reformulated somewhat as follows.

Certain classes of expressions when functioning in certain classes of contexts either have or are unthinkingly supposed to have a certain logical force. And when I speak of an expression as having or being credited with a certain logical force I mean no more than that it expresses or is assumed to express an idea or proposition with certain logical powers, in the sense adumbrated above. It is therefore always possible to inquire what consequential propositions would be true if the expression under investigation expressed or helped to express a proposition the logical powers of which were analogous to those of a known model. It is always initially possible that this logical experiment will reveal that some of the consequences of the assumption conflict with some of its other consequences and thus reveal that the attribution of this logical force to this expression in this use was a false one. The genuine logical force of the expression (if it has a force at all), must therefore be such that the propositions which it helps to express have constitutions which are insured against these and other contradictions.

The Function of the "Reductio ad Absurdum"

The discovery of the logical type to which a puzzle-generating idea belongs is the discovery of the rules governing the valid arguments in which propositions embodying that idea (or any other idea of the same type) can enter as premises or conclusions. It is also the discovery of the general reasons why specific fallacies result from misattributions of it to specific types. In general the former discovery is only approached through the several stages of the latter. The idea is (deliberately or blindly) hypothetically treated as homogeneous with one familiar model after another and its own logical structure emerges from the consecutive elimination of supposed logical properties by the absurdities resulting from the supposals.

This program appears vexatiously circuitous and one is tempted to dream of some direct way of fixing the logical powers of puzzle-generating ideas, which shall share with the method of progressive *reductio* the merit of being rigorous while improving on it by dispensing with trial and error. But, whatever other methods of search may be used, there remains this important fact about its object, that to find or understand a rule it is necessary to appreciate not only what it enforces but also what it permits and what it forbids. People are not fully seized of a logical rule if they have not considered the absurdities against which it prescribes. The boundaries of a right of way are also boundaries of forbidden ground. So no method of discovering the legitimate employments of a concept can dispense with the method of forecasting the logical disasters consequent upon illegitimate operations with it. Before the argument comes to its close, it is necessary to clear up three subsidiary points.

Systematic Ambiguity

It is commonly supposed that a particular concept is precisely indicated by reference to a particular expression, as if for example the idea of equality were unmistakably identified by being described as that for which the word "equality" stands.

There are, of course, in all languages some words which happen to have two or more different meanings. That is how puns are possible. But these ambiguities are of no theoretical interest. They are random in their occurrence, they can be circumvented by simple translation or paraphrases and the different ideas expressed by a pun-word have generally so little connection with one another that the context in which the word is used normally suffices to specify which idea is intended to be conveyed. But there is another sort of elasticity of signification which characterizes the use not of a few but of most or of all expressions and which is such that the paraphrases and translations of an expression with a certain elasticity of significance will normally have a precisely similar elasticity. This sort of ambiguity is systematic in further respects. The various ideas expressed by an expression in its different uses are intimately connected with each other. They are in one way or another different inflections of the same root.

A given word will, in different sorts of context, express ideas of an indefinite range of differing logical types and, therefore, with different logical powers. And what is true of single words is also true of complex expressions and of grammatical constructions.

Consider the adjective "punctual." It can be used to characterize a person's arrival at a place, the person who arrives there, his character, and even the average character of a class of persons. It would be absurd to compare the punctuality of a man on a particular occasion with that of his arrival on that occasion; it would be absurd to compare the punctuality of his character with that of his arrival on a particular occasion; and it would be absurd to compare the punctuality of Naval officers as a class with that of a particular Naval officer. These and similar absurdities show that the word "punctual" undergoes inflections of significance when applied to different types of subjects. There would be the same inflections of significance in French or German and parallel inflections with other words of the same sort, like "tidy" and "industrious." So, where precision is wanted, it is wrong to speak of "the idea" of punctuality, although the word "punctual" does not become a pun-word by having a different logical force for each different type of context in which it is used.

A philosophically more interesting example is afforded by the verb to "exist." It may be true that there exists a cathedral in Oxford, a three-engined bomber, and a square number between 9 and 25. But the naïve passage to the conclusion that there are three existents, a building, a brand of aircraft and a number soon leads to trouble. The senses of "exists" in which the three subjects are said to exist are different and their logical behaviors are different. The discovery of different logical inflections in the forces of expressions is made by the impact upon us of the absurdities resulting from ignoring them; the determination of those differences is done by pressing the search for further such absurdities. Unnoticed systematic ambiguities are a common source of type-confusions and philosophic problems. Philosophers are sometimes found lamenting this readiness of languages to give to one expression the power of expressing an indefinite variety of ideas; some of them even recommend reforms of usage which will pin single meanings to single expressions. But, in fact, the capacity of familiar dictions to acquire new inflections of logical forces is one of the chief factors making original thought possible. A new thought cannot find a new vehicle ready made for it, nor can the discrimination of the logical powers of new ideas precede the birth of the knowledge (by wont) of how to think with them. As some spanners are designed to be adjustable, so as to fit bolts of the same shape but different sizes, so, though undesigned, those linguistic instruments of thought are found to be most handy which are the most readily adjustable. The suggestion that men should coin a different diction to correspond with every difference in the logical powers of ideas assumes, absurdly, that they could be aware of these differences before being taken aback by the paradoxes arising from their naïvely attributed similarities. It is like suggesting that drill should precede the formation of habits or that children should be taught the rules of grammar before learning to talk.

ABSTRACTIONS

I have been speaking so far as if all ideas alike generate philosophical puzzles. But this needs correction. To put it roughly, concrete ideas do not generate such puzzles, abstract ideas do. But this distinction between concrete and abstract as well as that between lower and higher abstractions requires a clarification, of which no more than a sketch can be given here. By a "concrete idea" is meant one the original use of which is to serve as an element in propositions about what exists or occurs in the real world. It could be introduced or explained to an inquirer by confronting him with one or several specimens from the real world, or else by presenting him with physical models, pictures or mental images of specimens. Propositions containing such ideas can be called first-order propositions. Questions about their truth and falsehood can in favorable cases be settled by observation or sets of observations.

Ideas like *spaniel, dog, ache, thunder* in their original use are instances of concrete concepts. In this use they generate no philosophical puzzles, since one learns from the routines of daily experience the scope and the limits of their application. Their "logical geography" is taught by one's daily walks. Such concepts are formed from noticing similarities in the real world.

Quite different from these are what are often called "abstract ideas." It is a negative mark of these that a person cannot be introduced to such concepts by being presented with corresponding realities. Nothing in the world exemplifies *the economic man, the Spaniel* (as this idea occurs e.g. in *the Spaniel is a descendant of the Wolf*), or *2* (as this occurs e.g. in *2 is a prime number*). It is a positive mark of some abstract ideas that they can be expressed by abstract nouns, like "justice," "circularity" and "wickedness"; but this is the exception rather than the rule. The proposition *the economic man buys in the cheapest and sells in the dearest market* is an abstract proposition, though nothing in the vocabulary of the sentence indicates that the proposition is of a different logical type from *the old man buys his tobacco in the neighboring tobacconist's shop.*

Abstract propositions do not directly describe the real world but nor do they directly describe any other world. They apply indirectly to the real world, though there are various types of such indirect application. Arithmetic is not about inventories, but inventories satisfy arithmetical propositions; geometry does not describe Asia, but the geography of Asia is an application of geometry, and so on. To form abstract ideas it is necessary to notice not similarities between things in nature but similarities between propositions about things in nature or, later on, between propositions about propositions about things in nature. . . . But this conclusion has an air of mystery, deriving from the fact that propositions are themselves abstractions. The world does not contain propositions. It contains people believing, supposing and arguing propositions. This amounts (nearly enough) to saying that the world contains linguistic and other expressions, used or usable by no-matter-whom, which expressions, when used, express truths or falsehoods. To talk about a given proposition is therefore to talk about what is expressed by any expression (of no matter what linguistic structure) having the same logical force as some given expression, as such expressions are or might be intelligently used by persons (no matter whom).

This doctrine that to speak of a specified proposition is to speak of persons (no matter who) using expressions (no matter of what sorts) having the same logical force as that of a given expression can be proved. In any particular instance, it is always significant to suggest that there is no such proposition, since the given sentence is absurd, having, perhaps, parts which have correct uses in other contexts but cannot be combined in this way to form a sentence with an integral logical force.

With these safeguards it is correct to say that some propositions are about other propositions and are therefore second- or higher-order propositions. Some higher-order propositions, which form, perhaps, the most numerous class, are only about other propositions in the special sense that they are about partial similarities between otherwise different propositions. For any given proposition there may be found a range of different propositions sharing with it and with each other some one common factor. "Socrates is wise" expresses a proposition having something in common with what is expressed by "Plato sapiens est." This common factor can be expressed by a skeleton sentence of the pattern "so and so is wise" (where "so and so" announces the gap in the skeleton sentence). Similarly the skeleton sentence "if p then q" expresses what is common to a range of hypothetical propositions.

Propositions about such factors of propositions, with certain exceptions, are ordinarily said to be propositions about abstractions or abstract ideas. They are higher-order propositions about isolable features of ranges of lower-order propositions and describe the logical force of skeleton sentences equipollent with a given skeleton sentence. Thus, a proposition about wisdom does not mention Socrates or Plato; facts about Socrates and Plato are irrelevant to its truth. Yet the general fact that there are or might be subjects of whom it could be true that they were wise is not irrelevant to the logical force of the word "wisdom" and it is consequently relevant to the truth of propositions about wisdom. This illustrates the sense in which it has been said that abstract propositions do not describe the world, or any other world, but do indirectly apply to the world. It is always possible to accuse a submitted abstract idea of absurdity or rather to accuse an expression purporting to express an abstract idea of being an absurd expression. Naturally enough language does not provide many nonsensical single words but there frequently occur absurd complex expressions, purporting to express complex concepts, when such a complex is illegitimate. The fact that such accusations are always significant proves that abstract propositions always embody overt or covert inverted commas. (Indeed any abstract proposition if expressed with maximum logical candor would be seen to be describing a tenuous morsel of the real world, namely an expression in inverted commas. But of course it only mentions such an expression as a means of specifying the idea or proposition which is the logical force of that and any equipollent expression.)

There is, of course, an unlimited variety of types and orders of abstract ideas, but all alike can generate philosophical puzzles, just because experience of the real world gives us no drill in their correct use. Mistaken views about abstractions are not rebutted by a bruised shin or a parched throat. Nor does the language used to express abstract ideas vary with their different varieties. The charting of their logical powers consists therefore in the checking of their logical behavior against logical rules, which is the operation described in this lecture, i.e. the elimination by *reductio ad absurdum* of logical powers incorrectly ascribed or ascribable to them.

Another general point can now be established. For any abstract proposition there must be a range of propositions of a lower level, since the abstract proposition describes factors common to them. This implies that corresponding to any abstraction there is at a lower proposition-level an idea being actually used (and not described). There must be at this lower level knowledge by wont of some powers of this idea before there can begin the higher-level research into the rules governing those powers. We must know in practice how to decide whether Socrates is wise or clever before we can debate the abstract question of the relations between wisdom and cleverness. (Hence philosophy is sometimes said to tell us only what we knew before. This is as true as the corresponding statement about Mr. Jourdain's knowledge of prose before his introduction to grammar.)

This indicates what was missing in my prefatory account of the method and effects of philosophical reasoning. This was likened to threshing, which separates the grain from the chaff, discards the chaff and collects the grain. Philosophical reasoning separates the genuine from the erroneously assumed logical powers of abstract ideas by using the *reductio ad absurdum* argument as its flail and winnowing fan, but knowledge by wont of the use of concreter ideas is also necessary as its floor.

CRUCIAL AND CARDINAL IDEAS

Though all abstract ideas alike are liable to generate philosophical puzzles, some demand priority in philosophical examination. Of these one class consists largely of the new theory-shaping ideas which are struck out from time to time in the fields of science, criticism, statesmanship, and philosophy by men of genius. Genius shows itself not so much in the discovery of new answers as in the discovery of new questions. It influences its age not by solving its problems but by opening its eyes to previously unconsidered problems. So the new ideas released by genius are those which give a new direction to inquiry, often amounting to a new method of thinking.

Such crucial ideas, being new, are at the start unco-ordinated with the old. Their potency is quickly recognized but their logical powers have still to be determined, as, correspondingly have those logical powers of the old ideas which have yet to be correlated with the new. The task of assimilating the new crucial ideas into the un-fevered blood-stream of workaday thought is rendered both more urgent and more difficult by the fact that these ideas necessarily begin by being exciting. They shock the settled who execrate them as superstition, and they spell-bind the young who consecrate them into myth. That cloud and this rainbow are not dispelled until philosophers settle the true logical perspectives of the ideas.

Quite distinct from these, though often integral to them, are what may be described as philosophically cardinal ideas, those, namely, the logical unravelling of which leads directly to the unravelling of some complex tangle of interconnected ideas. Once these key-ideas are charted, the geography of a whole region is, at least in outline, fixed. No general clue can be given for predicting which ideas will turn out to have this catalytic power. To discern this is the privilege of philosophic genius.

17

How I See Philosophy

BY FRIEDRICH WAISMANN

I

WHAT PHILOSOPHY IS?[1] I don't know, nor have I a set formula to offer. Immediately I sit down to contemplate the question I am flooded with so many ideas, tumbling over one another, that I cannot do justice to all of them. I can merely make an attempt, a very inadequate one, to sketch with a few strokes what the lie of the land seems to me to be, tracing some lines of thought without entering upon a close-knit argument.

It is, perhaps, easier to say what philosophy is not than what it is. The first thing, then, I should like to say is that philosophy, as it is practised today, is very unlike science; and this in three respects: in philosophy there are no proofs; there are no theorems; and there are no questions which can be decided, Yes or No. In saying that there are no proofs I do not mean to say that there are no arguments. Arguments certainly there are, and first-rate philosophers are recognized by the originality of their arguments; only these do not work in the sort of way they do in mathematics or in the sciences.

There are many things beyond proof: the existence of material objects, of other minds, indeed of the external world, the validity of induction, and so on. Gone are the days when philosophers were trying to prove all sorts of things: that the soul is immortal, that this is the best of all possible worlds and the rest, or to refute, by "irrefutable" argument and with relish, materialism, positivism and what not. Proof, refutation—these are dying words in philosophy (though G. E. Moore still "proved" to a puzzled world that it exists. What

This essay is Dr. Waismann's contribution to *Contemporary British Philosophy*, third series (ed. H. D. Lewis), copyright 1956 by George Allen and Unwin Ltd,, London, with whose kind permission it is here reprinted.

1. This article is in reply to a question put to me by the Editor (of *Contemporary British Philosophy*).

can one say to this—save, perhaps, that he is a great prover before the Lord?).

But can it be *proved* that there are no proofs in philosophy? No; for one thing, such a proof, if it were possible, would by its very existence establish what it was meant to confute. But why suppose the philosopher to have an I.Q. so low as to be unable to learn from the past? Just as the constant failure of attempts at constructing a perpetual motion has in the end led to something positive in physics, so the efforts to construct a philosophical "system," going on for centuries and going out of fashion fairly recently, tell their tale. This, I think, is part of the reason why philosophers today are getting weaned from casting their ideas into deductive moulds, in the grand style of Spinoza.

What I want to show in this article is that it is quite wrong to look at philosophy as though it had for its aim to provide theorems but had lamentably failed to do so. The whole conception changes when one comes to realize that what philosophers are concerned with is something different—neither discovering new propositions nor refuting false ones nor checking and re-checking them as scientists do. For one thing, proofs require premisses. Whenever such premisses have been set up in the past, even tentatively, the discussion at once challenged them and shifted to a deeper level. Where there are no proofs there are no theorems either. (To write down lists of propositions "proved" by Plato or Kant: a pastime strongly to be recommended.) Yet the failure to establish a sort of Euclidean system of philosophy based on some suitable "axioms" is, I submit, neither a mere accident nor a scandal but deeply founded in the nature of philosophy.

Yet there are questions; (and arguments). Indeed, a philosopher is a man who senses as it were hidden crevices in the build of our concepts where others only see the smooth path of commonplaceness before them.

Questions but no answers? Decidedly odd. The oddness may lessen when we take a look at them at closer range. Consider two famous examples: Achilles and the tortoise, and the astonishment of St. Augustine when confronted with the fact of memory. He is amazed, not at some striking feat of memory, but at there being such a thing as memory at all. A sense-impression, say a smell or a taste, floats before us and disappears. One moment it is here and the next it is gone. But in the galleries of the memory pale copies of it are stored up after its death. From there I can drag them out when and as often as I wish, like, and yet strangely unlike, the original—unlike in that they are not perishable like the momentary impression: what was transitory has been arrested and has achieved duration. But who can say how this change comes about?

Here the very fact of memory feels mystifying in a way in which ordinary questions asking for information do not; and *of course* it is not a factual question. What is it?

From Plato to Schopenhauer philosophers are agreed that the source of their philosophizing is wonder. What gives rise to it is nothing recondite and rare but precisely those things which stare us in the face: memory, motion, general ideas. (Plato: What does "horse" mean? A single particular horse? No, for it may refer to *any* horse; *all* the horses, the total class? No, for we may speak of this or that horse. But if it means neither a single horse nor all horses, what *does* it mean?) The idealist is shaken in just the same way when he comes to reflect that he has, in Schopenhauer's words, "no knowledge of the sun but only of an eye that sees a sun, and no knowledge of the earth but only of a hand that feels an earth." Can it be, then, that nothing whatever is known to us except our own consciousness?

In looking at such questions, it seems as if the mind's eye were growing dim and as if everything, even that which ought to be absolutely clear, was becoming oddly puzzling and unlike its usual self. To bring out what seems to be peculiar to these questions one might say that they are not so much questions as tokens of a profound uneasiness of mind. Try for a moment to put yourself into the frame of mind of which Augustine was possessed when he asked: How is it possible to measure time? Time consists of past, present and future. The past can't be measured, it is gone; the future can't be measured, it is not yet here; and the present can't be measured, it has no extension. Augustine knew of course how time is measured and this was not his concern. What puzzled him was how it is *possible* to measure time, seeing that the past hour cannot be lifted out and placed alongside the present hour for comparison. Or look at it this way: what is measured is in the past, the measuring in the present: how can that be?

The philosopher as he ponders over some such problem has the appearance of a man who is deeply disquieted. He seems to be straining to grasp something which is beyond his powers. The words in which such a question presents itself do not quite bring out into the open the real point—which may, perhaps more aptly, be described as the recoil from the incomprehensible. If, on a straight railway journey, you suddenly come in sight of the very station you have just left behind, there will be terror, accompanied perhaps by slight giddiness. That is exactly how the philosopher feels when he says to himself, "Of course time can be measured; but how *can* it?" It is as though, up to now, he had been passing heedlessly over the difficulties, and now, all of a sudden, he notices them and asks himself in alarm, "But how can that be?" That is a sort of question which we only ask when it is the very facts themselves which confound us, when something about them strikes us as preposterous.

Kant, I fancy, must have felt something of the sort when he suddenly found the existence of geometry a puzzle. Here we have propositions as clear and transparent as one would wish, prior, it seems, to all experience; at the same time they apply miraculously to the real world. How is that possible? Can the mind, unaided by experience, in some dark manner actually fathom the properties of real things? Looked upon in this way, geometry takes on a disturbing air.

We all have our moments when something quite ordinary suddenly strikes us as queer—for instance, when time appears to us as a curious thing. Not that we are often in this frame of mind; but on some occasions, when we look at things in a certain way, unexpectedly they seem to change as though by magic: they stare at us with a puzzling expression, and we begin to wonder whether they can possibly be the things we have known all our lives.

"Time flows" we say—a natural and innocent expression, and yet one pregnant with danger. It flows "equably," in Newton's phrase, at an even rate. What can this mean? When something moves, it moves with a definite speed (and speed means: rate of change in time). To ask with what speed time moves, i.e. to ask how quickly time changes in time, is to ask the unaskable. It also flows, again in Newton's phrase, "without relation to anything external." How are we to figure that? Does time flow on irrespective of what happens in the world? Would it flow on even if everything in heaven and on earth came to a sudden standstill as Schopenhauer believed? For if this were not so, he said, time would have to stop with the stopping of the clock and move with the clock's movement. How odd: time flows at the same rate and yet without speed; and perhaps even without anything to occur in it? The expression is puzzling in another way. "I can never catch myself being in the past or in the future," someone might say; "whenever I think or perceive or breathe the word 'now,' I am in the present; therefore I am *always* in the present." In saying this, he may think of the present moment as a bridge as it were from which he is looking down at the "river of time." Time is gliding along underneath the bridge, but the "now" does not take part in the motion. What was future passes into the present (is just below the bridge) and then into the past, while the onlooker, the "self" or the "I," is always in the present. "Time flows *through* the 'now,' " he may feel to be a quite expressive metaphor. Yes, it sounds all right—until he suddenly comes to his senses and, with a start, realizes, "But surely the moment flies?" (Query: How to succeed in wasting time? Answer: In this way, for instance—by trying, with eyes closed or staring vacantly in front of oneself, to catch the present moment as it is flitting by.) He may come now to look at matters in a different way. He sees himself advancing through time towards the future, and with this goes a suggestion of being active, just as at other times he may see himself floating down the stream whether he likes it or not. "What exactly is it that is moving —the events in time or the present moment?" he may wonder. In the first case, it looks to him as if time were moving while he stands still; in the second case as if he were moving through time. "How exactly is it," he may say in a dubious voice, "am I always in the present? Is the present always eluding me?" Both ring true in a way; but they contradict each other. Again, does it make sense to ask, "At what time is the present moment?" Yes, no doubt; but how *can* it, if the "now" is but the fixed point from which the dating of any event ultimately receives its sense?

So he is pulled to and fro: "I am always in the present, yet it slips through my fingers; I am going forward in time—no, I am carried down the stream." He is using different pictures, each in its way quite appropriate to the occasion; yet when he tries to apply them jointly they clash. "What a queer thing time must be," he may say to himself with a puzzled look on his face, "what after all *is* time?" —expecting, half-expecting perhaps, that the answer will reveal to him time's hidden essence. Ranged beyond the intellectual are deeper levels of uneasiness—terror of the inevitability of time's passage, with all the reflections upon life that this forces upon us. Now all these anxious doubts release themselves in the question, "What is time?" (*En passant* this is a hint that *one* answer will never do—will never remove all these doubts that break out afresh on different levels and yet are expressed in the same form of words.)

As we all know what time is and yet cannot say what it is it feels mystifying; and precisely because of its elusiveness it catches our imagination. The more we look at it the more we are puzzled: it seems charged with paradoxes. "What is time? What is this being made up of movement only without anything that is moving?" (Schopenhauer). How funny to have it bottled up! "I've got here

in my hand the most potent, the most enigmatic, the most fleeting
of all essences—Time." (Logan Pearsall Smith of an hour-glass.)
For Shelley it is an "unfathomable sea! whose waves are years," a
"shoreless flood," for Proust—well, why not leave something to the
reader?

But isn't the answer to this that what mystifies us lies in the
noun form "the time"? Having a notion embodied in the form of a
noun almost irresistibly makes us turn round to look for what it is
"the name of." We are trying to catch the shadows cast by the
opacities of speech. A wrong analogy absorbed into the forms of
our language produces mental discomfort; (and the feeling of discomfort, when it refers to language, is a profound one). "All sounds,
all colors . . . evoke indefinite and yet precise emotions, or, as I
prefer to think, call down among us certain disembodied powers
whose footsteps over our hearts we call emotions" (W. B. Yeats).

Yet the answer is a prosaic one: don't ask what time is but how
the *word* "time" is being used. Easier said than done; for if the
philosopher rectifies the use of language, ordinary language has "the
advantage of being in possession of declensions," to speak with
Lichtenberg, and thus renews its spell over him, luring him on into
the shadow chase. It is perhaps only when we turn to languages of
a widely different grammatical structure that the way towards such
possibilities of interpretation is entirely barred. "It is highly probable
that philosophers within the domain of the Ural-Altaic languages
(where the subject-concept is least developed) will look differently
'into the world' and be found on paths of thought different from
those of the Indo-Europeans or Mussulmans" (Nietzsche).

II

It may be well at this point to remind ourselves that the words
"question" and "answer," "problem" and "solution" are not always
used in their most trite sense. It is quite obvious that we often have
to do something very different to find the way out of a difficulty. A
problem of politics is solved by adopting a certain line of action,
the problems of novelists perhaps by the invention of devices for
presenting the inmost thoughts and feelings of their characters; there
is the painter's problem of how to suggest depth or movement on
the canvas, the stylistic problem of expressing things not yet current, not yet turned into cliché; there are a thousand questions of
technology which are answered, not by the discovery of some truth,
but by a practical achievement; and there is of course the "social

question." In philosophy, the real problem is not to find the answer to a given question but to find a sense for it.

To see in what the "solution" of such a "problem" consists let us start with Achilles who, according to Zeno, is to this day chasing the tortoise. Suppose that Achilles runs twice as fast as the tortoise. If the tortoise's start is 1, Achilles will have to cover successively 1, ½, ¼, ⅛, . . . ; this series is endless: so he can never catch the tortoise. "Nonsense!" (a mathematician's voice), "the sum of the infinite series is finite, namely 2, and that settles it." Though perfectly true, his remark is not to the point. It does not remove the sting from the puzzle, the disconcerting idea, namely, that however far we go in the series there is always a next term, that the lead the tortoise has in the race, though naturally getting smaller and smaller, yet never ceases to be: there *can* be no moment when it is strictly zero. It is *this* feature of the case, I suggest, that we do not understand and which throws us into a state of confusion.

But look at it this way. Suppose that we apply the same sort of argument to a minute, then we shall have to argue in some such way as this. Before the minute can be over the first half of it must elapse, then one-quarter of it, then one-eighth of it, and so on *ad infinitum*. This being an endless process, the minute can never come to an end. Immediately we have the argument in this form, the blunder leaps to the eye: we have been confusing two senses of "never," a temporal and a non-temporal one. While it is quite correct to say that the sequence 1, ½, ¼, ⅛, . . . never ends, this sense of the word "never" has nothing whatever to do with time. All it means is that there is no last term in the series, or (what comes to the same) that to any term, no matter how far out in the sequence, a successor can be constructed according to the simple rule "halve it": that is meant here by "never"; whereas in saying, for instance, that man will never find out anything to avert death, "never" is meant in the sense "at no time." It is clear that the mathematical assertion concerning the possibility of going on in the sequence by forming new terms according to the rule does not state anything about actual occurrences in time. The mistake should really be obvious: in saying that, since the start is getting progressively smaller and yet can never cease to be, Achilles can never catch the tortoise, we jump from the mathematical, *non*-temporal to the temporal sense. Had there been two different words in our language to mark these senses the confusion could never have arisen, and the world would be poorer for one of its most attractive paradoxes. But the same word is as a matter of course used with different meanings. Result: something like a conjuring trick. While our attention is diverted, while, "in our mind's eye," we stare fixedly at Achilles as he is speeding along, with each big bound diminishing his distance from the tortoise, the one sense is so innocuously palmed off for the other as to escape notice.

This way of bringing out the fallacy also holds when the other key term is used for presenting the puzzle. As there will "always" be a next term in the sequence, i.e. a next step in the scheme of sub-dividing the race-course (the word "always" looking just as spotless and innocent) we readily fall into the trap of concluding that the tortoise will "always" be ahead of Achilles, eternally to be chased by his pursuer.

Many are the types of bewilderment: there is the obsessional doubt—can I ever know that other people have experiences, that they see, hear and feel as I do? Can I be sure that memory does not always deceive me? Are there really material objects and not only sense-impressions "of" them? There is the doubtlike uneasiness—what sort of being is possessed by numbers? There is the anxiety-doubt—are we really free? This doubt has taken many different forms one of which I shall single out for discussion—the question, namely, whether the law of excluded middle, when it refers to state-ments in the future tense, forces us into a sort of logical Predestina-tion. A typical argument is this. If it is true now that I shall do a certain thing tomorrow, say, jump into the Thames, then no matter how fiercely I resist, strike out with hands and feet like a madman, when the day comes I cannot help jumping into the water; whereas, if this prediction is false now, then whatever efforts I may make, however many times I may nerve and brace myself, look down at the water and say to myself, "One, two, three—," it is impossible for me to spring. Yet that the prediction is either true or false is itself a necessary truth, asserted by the law of excluded middle. From this the startling consequence seems to follow that it is already now decided what I shall do tomorrow, that indeed the entire future is somehow fixed, logically preordained. Whatever I do and whichever way I decide, I am merely moving along lines clearly marked in advance which lead me towards my appointed lot. We are all, in fact, mari-onettes. If we are not prepared to swallow *that,* then—and there is a glimmer of hope in the "then"—there is an alternative open to us. We need only renounce the law of excluded middle for statements of this kind, and with it the validity of ordinary logic, and all will be well. Descriptions of what will happen are, at present, neither true nor false. (This sort of argument was actually propounded by

Lukasiewicz in favor of a three-valued logic with "possible" as a third truth-value alongside "true" and "false.")

The way out is clear enough. The asker of the question has fallen into the error of so many philosophers: of giving an answer before stopping to consider the question. For is he clear what he is asking? He seems to suppose that a statement referring to an event in the future is at present undecided, neither true nor false, but that when the event happens the proposition enters into a sort of new state, that of being true. But how are we to figure the change from "undecided" to "true"? Is it sudden or gradual? At what moment does the statement "it will rain tomorrow" begin to be true? When the first drop falls to the ground? And supposing that it will not rain, when will the statement begin to be false? Just at the end of the day, at 12 p.m. sharp? Supposing that the event *has* happened, that the statement *is* true, will it remain so for ever? If so, in what way? Does it remain uninterruptedly true, at every moment of day and night? Even if there were no one about to give it any thought? Or is it true only at the moments when it is being thought of? In that case, how long does it remain true? For the duration of the thought? We wouldn't know how to answer these questions; this is due not to any particular ignorance or stupidity on our part but to the fact that something has gone wrong with the way the words "true" and "false" are applied here.

If I say, "It is true that I was in America," I am saying that I was in America and no more. That in uttering the words "It is true that—" I take responsibility upon myself is a different matter that does not concern the present argument. The point is that in making a statement prefaced by the words "It is true that" I do not *add* anything to the factual information I give you. *Saying* that something is true is not *making* it true: cp. the criminal lying in court, yet every time he is telling a lie protesting, his hand on his heart, that he is telling the truth.

What is characteristic of the use of the words "true" and "false" and what the pleader of logical determinism has failed to notice is this. "It is true" and "it is false," while they certainly have the force of asserting and denying, are not descriptive. Suppose that someone says, "It is true that the sun will rise tomorrow" all it means is that the sun will rise tomorrow: he is not regaling us with an extra-description of the trueness of what he says. But supposing that he were to say instead, "It is true *now* that the sun will rise tomorrow," this would boil down to something like "The sun will rise tomorrow now"; which is nonsense. To ask, as the puzzle-poser does, "Is it true or false *now* that such-and-such will happen in the future?" is not the sort of question to which an answer can be given: which *is* the answer.

This sheds light on what has, rather solemnly, been termed the "timelessness of truth." It lies in this that the clause "it is true that—" does not allow of inserting a date. To say of a proposition like "Diamond is pure carbon" that it is true on Christmas Eve would be just as poor a joke as to say that it is true in Paris and not in Timbuctoo. (This does not mean that we cannot say in certain circumstances, "Yes, it was true in those days" as this can clearly be paraphrased without using the word "true.")

Now it begins to look a bit less paradoxical to say that when a philosopher wants to dispose of a question the one thing he must not do is: to give an answer. A philosophic question is not solved: it *dis*solves. And in what does the "dissolving" consist? In making the meaning of the words used in putting the question so clear to ourselves that we are released from the spell it casts on us. Confusion was removed by calling to mind the use of language or, so far as the use *can* be distilled into rules, the rules: it therefore *was* a confusion about the use of language, or a confusion about rules. It is here that philosophy and grammar meet.

There is one further point that needs elucidation. When we say of a given assertion, e.g. "It is raining," that it is true we can hardly escape the impression that we say something "about" the assertion, namely, that it has the property of trueness. To make such a statement seems, then, to say *more* than what was asserted originally, namely, that it is raining and that this assertion is true. That, however, leads to queer consequences. For in which sense does it say more? Consider first under which circumstances it would be appropriate to say of two given propositions that the one says "more" than the other. "This is red" says more than "this is colored" for the obvious reason that anyone can conclude from the first statement to the second but no one reversely; similarly "today is Tuesday" says more than "today is a weekday." The criterion, then, suggests itself that, given two propositions p and q, p says more than q, if $\sim p$. q is meaningful and p. $\sim q$ contradictory. The holder of the view that "p is true" says more than p (p standing e.g. for "It is raining"), may now be challenged to explain what he means by that. Is he using the word "more" in the sense just explained? If so, the curious consequence ensues that it must *make sense* to assert the conjunction $\sim p.q$, that is in our case, "It is not true that it is raining and it is raining." Since this obviously is not what he had in mind, what *does* he mean? We are not contradicting him; we merely remind him of how these words have always been used by him, in non-philosophical contexts that is, and then point out that, if he still wants to use them in this sense, to say what he wanted to say lands him in an absurdity. All we do is to make him aware of his own practice. We abstain from any assertion. It is for him to explain what he means. Not that he cannot do it. In ascribing truth to a given statement, he might say, he wants to express perhaps either (i) that it is "in accordance with fact" or something of the sort; or (ii) that he *knows* that it is true. In the first case he is faced with the same dilemma, namely, that it must make sense to say, "It is not in accordance with the facts that it is raining and it is raining"; in the second fresh difficulties are breaking out. For one thing, the words "it is true that—," when uttered by different people, would then mean different things; for another, and this is more fatal to the advocate of fatalism, in construing the words in this sense, he cuts the ground from under his own feet. No one would then be worried by the question whether, supposing that it is false now that he will write a certain letter tomorrow, it follows that it will really be impossible for him to write that letter, that this line of conduct is barred to him, logically barred. For since "it is false now" means in the new sense "he doesn't know yet" nothing follows and the whole question evaporates.

My reason for going into this tangle at some length is that the method applied in unravelling it presents some interesting features. First, we don't *force* our interlocutor. We leave him free to choose, accept or reject any way of using his words. He may depart from ordinary usage—language is not untouchable—if it is only in this way that he can explain himself. He may even use an expression one time in this, another time in that, way. The only thing we insist upon is that he should be aware of what he is doing. If we strictly adhere to this method—going over the argument, asking him at each step whether he is willing to use an expression in a certain way, if not, offering him alternatives, but leaving the decisions to him and only pointing out what their consequences are—no dispute can arise. Disputes arise only if certain steps in this procedure are omitted so that it looks as if we had made an assertion, adding to the world's woes a new apple of discord. This would be the true way of doing philosophy undogmatically. The difficulty of this method lies in

presenting the subject in a manner which can easily be taken in—
in arranging the cases and the ways in which they are connected
through intermediate links so that we can gain a clear synoptic view
of the whole.

Second, we do not use arguments in order to prove or disprove
any "philosophic view." As we have no views we can afford to look
at things as they are.

Next, we only describe; we do not "explain." An explanation,
in the sense of a deductive proof, cannot satisfy us because it pushes
the question "Why just these rules and no other ones?" only one
stage back. In following that method, we do not *want* to give reasons. All we do is to describe a use or tabulate rules. In doing this,
we are not making any discoveries: there is nothing to be discovered
in grammar. Grammar is autonomous and not dictated by reality. Giving reasons, bound as it is to come to an end and leading to something
which cannot further be explained, *ought* not to satisfy us. In grammar we never ask the question "why?"

But isn't the result of this that philosophy itself "dissolves"?
Philosophy eliminates those questions which *can* be eliminated by
such a treatment. Not all of them, though: the metaphysician's crav-
ing that a ray of light may fall on the mystery of the existence of this
world, or on the incomprehensible fact that it is comprehensible,
or on the "meaning of life"—even if such questions *could* be shown
to lack a clear meaning or to be devoid of meaning altogether, they
are *not silenced*. It does nothing to lessen the dismay they rouse in
us. There is something cheap in "debunking" them. The heart's
unrest is not to be stilled by logic. Yet philosophy is not dissolved.
It derives its weight, its grandeur, from the significance of the questions it destroys. It overthrows idols, and it is the importance of these
idols which gives philosophy its importance.

Now it can perhaps be seen why the search for answers fitting
the moulds of the questions fails, is *bound* to fail. They are not real
questions asking for information but "muddles felt as problems"
(Wittgenstein) which wither away when the ground is cleared. If
philosophy advances, it is not by adding new propositions to its list,
but rather by transforming the whole intellectual scene and, as a
consequence of this, by reducing the number of questions which
befog and bedevil us. Philosophy so construed is one of the great
liberating forces. Its task is, in the words of Frege, "to free the
spirit from the tyranny of words by exposing the delusions which
arise, almost inevitably, through the use of a word language."

III

What, only criticism and no meat? The philosopher a fog dispeller? If that were all he was capable of I would be sorry for him and leave him to his devices. Fortunately, this is not so. For one thing, a philosophic question, if pursued far enough, may lead to something positive—for instance, to a more profound understanding of language. Take the sceptical doubts as to material objects, other minds, etc. The first reaction is perhaps to say: these doubts are idle. Ordinarily, when I doubt whether I shall finish this article, after a time my doubt comes to an end. I cannot go on doubting for ever. It's the destiny of doubt to die. But the doubts raised by the sceptic never die. Are they doubts? Are they pseudo-questions? They appear so only when judged by the twin standards of common sense and common speech. The real trouble lies deeper: it arises from the sceptic casting doubt on the very facts which underlie the use of language, those permanent features of experience which make concept formation possible, which in fact are precipitated in the use of our most common words. Suppose that you see an object in front of you quite clearly, say, a pipe, and when you are going to pick it up it melts into thin air, then you may feel, "Lord, I'm going mad" or something of the sort (unless the whole situation is such that you have reason to suspect that it was some clever trick). But what, the sceptic may press now, if such experiences were quite frequent? Would you be prepared to *dis*solve the connection between different sense experiences which form the hard core of our idea of a solid object, to *un*do what language has done—to part with the category of thing-hood? And would you then be living in a phenomenalist's paradise with color patches and the other paraphernalia of the sense-datum theory, in a disobjected, desubstantialized world? To say in such circumstances, "Look, it's just tabling now" would be a joke (for even in the weakened verb forms "tabling," "chairing" an element of the thing-category lingers on). That is why the sceptic struggles to express himself in a language which is not fit for this purpose. He expresses himself misleadingly when he says that he doubts such-and-such *facts:* his doubts cut so deep that they affect the fabric of language itself. For what he doubts is already embodied in the very forms of speech, e.g. in what is condensed in the use of thing-words. The moment he tries to penetrate those deep-sunken layers, he undermines the language in which he ventilates his qualms—with the result that he seems to be talking nonsense. He is not. But in order to make his doubts fully expressible, language would first have to go into the melting-pot. (We can get a glimmering of what is needed from modern science where all the long-established categories—thinghood, causality, position—had to be revolutionized. This required nothing less than the construction of some new language, not the expression of new facts with the old one.)

If we look at the matter in this way the attitude of the sceptic is seen in a new light. He considers possibilities which lie far outside the domain of our current experience. If his doubts are taken seriously, they turn into observations which cast a new and searching light on the subsoil of language, showing what possibilities are open to our thought (though not to ordinary language), and what paths might have been pursued if the texture of our experience were different from what it is. These problems are not spurious: they make us aware of the vast background in which any current experiences are embedded, and to which language has adapted itself; thus they bring out the unmeasured sum of experience stored up in the use of our words and syntactical forms.

For another thing, a question may decide to go in for another career than dissolving: it may pass into science. Frege, for instance, was prompted to his inquiries by philosophical motives, namely, to find a definite answer to the question about the nature of arithmetical truths—whether they are analytic or synthetic, a priori or a posteriori. Starting from this question and pursuing it with all possible rigor, he was led to unearth a whole mine of problems of a scientific nature; and proceeding along these lines, he came to fashion a new instrument, a logic, which in delicacy and range and power far surpassed anything that went by this name before, a subject revealing to this day new and unexpected depths. True, the question from which Frege set out was not too clearly defined owing to the imprecise nature of the Kantian terms in which it was expressed.

A whole chapter might be written on the fate of questions, their curious adventures and transformations—how they change into others and in the process remain, and yet do not remain, the same. The original question may split and multiply almost like a character in a dream play. To mention just a few examples: can logic be characterized completely in a formal way, i.e. without bringing in any extraneous ideas such as the use of language and all that goes with it? Can arithmetic be characterized in any such way, entirely "from within"? Or will any interpretation include some Erdenrest of the empiric? These questions have given rise to extensive research on mathematical interpretation of formal systems. The query how far logical intuition is correct has got ramified into a bunch of questions pertaining to the theory of logical types, the axiom of choice, etc., indeed to a far more fundamental issue, namely, whether ordinary logic itself is "right" as contrasted with the system of inferences evolved by the intuitionists. Or again, are there undecidable questions in mathematics, not in the restricted sense of Gödel, but undecidable in an absolute sense? Are there natural limits to generalization? It is interesting to watch how from a question of this sort, not too precise, somewhat blurred, new and better defined questions detach themselves, the parent question—in Frege's case philosophic *par excellence*—giving rise to a scientist's progeny.

Now something else must be noted—how these questions become, not only precise, but clear (which is not the same thing). To illustrate, can the infinity represented by all natural numbers be compared with the infinity represented by all points in space? That is, can the one be said to be less than, or equal to, the other? When it was first asked, the question had no clear sense—perhaps no sense at all. Yet it guided G. Cantor in his ingenious search. Before set theory was discovered—or should I rather say "invented"?—the question acted as a sort of signpost pointing vaguely to some so far uncharted region of thought. It is perhaps best characterized by saying that it guides our imagination in a given direction, stimulates research along new lines. Such questions do not "dissolve": they are solved, only not in the existing system of thought but rather by constructing a new conceptual system—such as set theory—where the intended and faintly anticipated sense finds its full realization. They are therefore of the nature of incitements to the building of such systems, they point from the not-yet-meaningful to the meaningful.

The question is the first groping step of the mind in its journeyings that lead towards new horizons. The genius of the philosopher shows itself nowhere more strikingly than in the new kind of question he brings into the world. What distinguishes him and gives him his place is the passion of questioning. That his questions are at times not so clear is perhaps of not so much moment as one makes of it. There is nothing like clear thinking to protect one from making discoveries. It is all very well to talk of clarity, but when it becomes an obsession it is liable to nip the living thought in the bud. This, I am afraid, is one of the deplorable results of Logical Positivism, not foreseen by its founders, but only too striking in some of its followers. Look at these people, gripped by a clarity neurosis, haunted by fear, tongue-tied, asking themselves continually, "Oh dear, now does this make perfectly good sense?" Imagine the pioneers of science, Kepler, Newton, the discoverers of non-Euclidean geometry, of field physics, the unconscious, matter waves or heaven knows what, imagine them asking themselves this question at every step—this would have been the surest means of sapping any creative power. No great discoverer has acted in accordance with the motto, "Everything that can be said can be said clearly." And some of the greatest discoveries have even emerged from a sort of primordial fog. (Something to be said for the fog. For my part, I've always suspected that clarity is the last refuge of those who have nothing to say.)

The great mind is the great questioner. An example in point is Kant's problem "How is geometry possible?" The way to its solution was only opened up through the rise of the "axiomatic method." Seeing that the axioms of geometry are capable of an indefinite number of different interpretations and that the particular way they may be interpreted is irrelevant to deductive purposes, Hilbert separated what belongs to the logical form of the axioms from what belongs to their intuitional (or other) content and turned the whole question by saying: a point, a straight line, etc., may be anything that satisfies the axioms. As the business of deduction hinges only on the relations in which the basic terms stand to each other and not on the "content" we associate with them, and as these relations are fully set out in the axioms, the axioms in their totality determine what a "point," a "line," etc., is so far as it is sufficient for deductive needs. Through the rise of this technique it became apparent that the word "geometry," as understood by Kant, covers, in fact, two totally different sciences, mathematical and physical geometry. It was the failure to distinguish between them that produced Kant's perplexity. "So far as the laws of mathematics refer to reality, they are not certain; and so far as they are certain, they do not refer to reality" (Einstein). Kant's credit lies in having *seen* that there is a problem, not in having solved it.

But here a new problem presents itself: How do we know what will satisfy a given question? More generally: How does the answer fit the question? Questions of the current sort ("What is the right time?") show already by their form what sort of answer to expect. They are, so to speak, cheques with a blank to be filled; yet not always so: Augustine's question, "How is it possible to measure time?" or Kant's question, "How is geometry possible?" do not trace out the form of the answer. There is no *obvious* link between question and answer, any more than there is in the case of asking "What is a point?" When Hilbert's idea—that the axioms of geometry jointly provide the "implicit definition" of the basic terms—was first propounded it came totally unexpected; no one had ever thought of that before; on the contrary, many people had an uneasy feeling as if this were a way of evading the issue rather than an answer, amongst them no less a man than Frege. He thought the problem still unsolved.

Now is there anything one can do to make a man like Frege see that the axiomatic method provides the correct answer? Can it, for example, be *proved* to him? The point to which attention must now be drawn, though it should really be obvious, is that such a proof cannot be given, and it cannot because he, the asker, has first to be turned round to see the matter differently. What is required is a change of the entire way of thinking. Indeed, anyone who is puzzled by this problem and yet refuses to accept Hilbert's solution only betrays that he has got stuck in the groove hollowed out by the form in which the question is put. "A point is—" he begins and then stops. What is to be done to help him to get out of the groove or, better still, to make him shift for himself when he feels "cramped" in it, is a *discussion,* not a proof.

Frege behaves not so very unlike a man mystified by the question, "What is time?" We may suggest converting the latter into the question how the word "time" is being used (which would bring him down to earth). But aren't we cheating him? We seem to be holding out the answer to *one* question, but not to that one which he was asking. He may suspect that we are trying to fob him off with the second best we have in store, his original question still remaining an enigma. Similarly Frege: he considered it a scandal that the questions "What is a point?" "What is a number?" were still un-answered.

In either of these cases, the aim of a discussion, in the absence of a proof, can only be to change the asker's attitude. We may, for instance, scrutinize similar, or partially similar, cases, point out that the form of the answer is not always that of the question; by going patiently over such cases, the vast background of analogies against which the question is seen will slowly change. The turning up of a wide field of language loosens the position of certain standards which are so ingrained that we do not see them for what they are; and if we do this in an effective manner, a mind like Frege's will be released from the obsession of seeking strainingly for an answer to fit the mould. Arguments are used in such a discussion, not as proofs though but rather as means to make him see things he had not noticed before: e.g. to dispel wrong analogies, to stress similarities with other cases and in this way to bring about something like a shift of perspective. However, there is no way of proving him wrong or bullying him into mental acceptance of the proposal: when all is said and done the decision is his.

But here more is at stake than loosening a cramped position— it is a question of escaping the domination of linguistic forms. How often are we merely following the channels carved out by numberless repetition of the same modes of expression—as when we say, unsuspectingly, "Time flows" and are, when confronted (say) with Augustine's paradox, suddenly shocked out of complacency. Existing language, by offering us only certain sterotyped moulds of expression, creates habits of thought which it is almost impossible to break. Such a mould is, e.g. the actor-action scheme of the Indo-European languages. How deep their influence is can perhaps be surmised from Descartes' conclusion from thinking to the presence of an agent, an ego, different from the thinking, that does the thinking—a conclusion so natural and convincing to us because it is supported by the whole weight of language. Frege's obsession with the question "What is a number?" is another case. As we can speak of *"the* number five," five, Frege argued, must be the proper name of an entity, a sort of Platonic crystal, indicated by means of the definite article. (A Chinese pupil of mine once informed me that Frege's question is unaskable in Chinese, "five" being used there only as a numeral in contexts like "five friends," five boats," etc.). Again, when we say of a given statement that it is true, we seem to be saying something "about" it—evidence of the power of the subject-predicate cliché. Indeed, so strong is the temptation to construe it in this way, namely, as a statement about a statement, that the idea of a different interpretation scarcely occurs to us. It is important to notice that in doing so we assimilate the expression to analogical forms; but it is no less important to notice that none of these analogies needs to be present to our minds: it is enough if they make themselves felt in a dim, inarticulated way. Such patterns have an effect on us like thousands of explicit analogies: they act upon us, one might say, like a field of force, a language field, that draws our mental gaze in a certain direction. And, I venture to add, it is precisely because of of the fleeting, half-formed, shadow-like nature of these analogies that it is almost impossible to escape their influence. If we are taken in by them, it is our fault. A philosopher, instead of preaching the righteousness of ordinary speech, should learn to be on his guard against the pitfalls ever present in its forms. To use a picture: just as a good swimmer must be able to swim up-stream, so the philosopher should master the unspeakably difficult art of thinking up-speech, against the current of clichés.

Now for another point. When we dissuade a man like Frege from his search, we seem to be hindering him from reaching the aim he set out to reach. Does our discussion clash, then, with his search? And, if so, in which way? First of all, in no clearly definable way; for he is not yet clearly aware what he is aiming at, and the discussion brings him gradually to see things in a different light. How is this change brought about? Well, he first saw the question in analogy with other ones, and these analogies are, one by one, destroyed; or rather, in the course of the discussion they are seen to be misleading. In proportion as the whole conceptual background changes, he comes to see that something is wrong with the way he puts his question, that the attainment of his object is no longer satisfying. It is not that he gives up because he has tried very hard, but in vain, and has now got tired: no, he gives up because he "sees" the question differently. And in what does *this* consist? Well, in the fact that he is now well aware of the analogies which were misleading him, that he sees the question against a different linguistic background (a "figure" sometimes changes when it is seen against a different "ground"), that a certain strain disappears and that he says, with a sigh of relief, "Yes, that's it."

The philosopher contemplates things through the prism of language and, misled (say) by some analogy, suddenly sees things in a new strange light. We can cope with these problems only by digging down to the soil from which they spring. What we do is to light up the mental background from which the question has detached itself; in a clearer perception of some of the crucial concepts the question transforms itself into another one. Not that it has been answered in the current sense. Rather we have removed the factors that prompted the question by a more profound and penetrating analysis. The essence of this process is that it leads the questioner on to some new aspect—and leads him with his spontaneous consent. He agrees to be thus led and therefore ends by abandoning his search. We cannot constrain anyone who is unwilling to follow the new direction of a question; we can only extend the field of vision of the asker, loosen his prejudices, guide his gaze in a new direction: but all this can be achieved only with his consent.

By our critical analysis we try to counteract the influence of the language field, or (what comes to the same) we may help the questioner to gain a deeper insight into the nature of what he is seeking first of all—make him see the build of the concepts and the moulds in which he expresses the question. What matters is more like changing his outlook than proving to him some theorem; or more like increasing his insight. Insight cannot be lodged in a theorem, and this is the deeper reason why the deductive method is doomed to fail: insight cannot be demonstrated by proof.

What it comes to in the end is that the asker of the question, in the course of the discussion, has to make a number of *decisions*. And this makes the philosophical procedure so unlike a logical one. He compares, for instance, the case before him with analogous ones and has to *judge* how far these analogies hold. That is, it is for him to decide how far he is willing to accept these analogies: he has not, like a slave, to follow blindly in their track.

Science is rich in questions of this type. They are not scientific questions properly and yet they exercise scientists, they are philosophic questions and yet they do not exercise philosophers.

What I have wanted to say in this section and have not said, or only half-said:

(1) Philosophy is not only criticism of language: so construed, its aim is too narrow. It is criticizing, dissolving and stepping over *all* prejudices, loosening all rigid and constricting moulds of thought, no matter whether they have their origin in language or somewhere else.

(2) What is essential in philosophy is the breaking through to a *deeper insight*—which is something positive—not merely the dissipation of fog and the exposure of spurious problems.

(3) Insight cannot be lodged in a theorem, and it can therefore not be demonstrated.

(4) Philosophic arguments are, none of them, logically *compelling:* they really screen what actually happens—the quiet and patient undermining of categories over the whole field of thought.

(5) Their purpose is to open our eyes, to bring us to see things in a new way—from a wider standpoint unobstructed by misunderstandings.

(6) The essential difference between philosophy and logic is that logic *constrains* us while philosophy leaves us free: in a philosophic discussion we are led, step by step, to change our angle of vision, e.g. to pass from one way of putting a question to another, and this with our spontaneous agreement—a thing profoundly different from deducing theorems from a given set of premises. Misquoting Cantor one might say: the essence of philosophy lies in its freedom.

IV

There is a notion that philosophy is an exercise of the intellect and that philosophic questions can be settled by argument, and conclusively if one only knew how to set about it. What seems to me queer, however, is that I cannot find any really good hard argument; and more than that, the example just discussed must make it doubtful whether any compelling argument *can* be found. Out of this plight I incline to come to a new and somewhat shocking conclusion: that the thing cannot be done. No philosopher has ever proved anything. The whole claim is spurious. What I have to say is simply this. Philosophic arguments are not deductive; therefore they are not rigorous; and therefore they don't prove anything. Yet they have force.

Before going into the matter, I want to show, quite summarily first, how unplausible the view is that rigorous arguments are applied in philosophy. A first alarming sign can perhaps already be seen in the notorious fact that the ablest minds disagree, that what is indisputable to the one seems to have no force in the eyes of the other. In a clear system of thought such differences are impossible. That they exist in philosophy is weighty evidence that the arguments have none of the logical rigor they have in mathematics and the exact sciences.

Next, arguments, in the way they are thought of, must contain inferences, and inferences must start somewhere. Now where is the philosopher to look for his premises? To science? Then he will "do" science, not philosophy. To statements of everyday life? To particular ones? Then he will never be able to advance a single step beyond them. To general statements? If so, a number of questions raise their ugly heads. By what right does he pass from "some" to "all"? ("To Generalize is to be an Idiot," W. Blake.) Can he be sure that his premises are stated with such clarity and precision that not a ghost of a doubt can creep in? Can he be sure that they contain meat, are not analytic, vacuous, definitions in disguise and the like? Can he be sure that they are true? (How *can* he?) And even supposing, what is not the case, that all these requirements could be met, there is still another task looming before him when it comes to developing the consequences: can he be sure how to operate with the terms? (How *can* he?) I am not letting out a secret when I say that the ordinary rules of logic often break down in natural speech—a fact usually hushed up by logic books. Indeed, the words of common language are so elastic that anyone can stretch their sense to fit his own whims; and with this their "logic" is queered. (Plenty of scope for a "natural logic"; we know that we are *unhappy;* so we *are* unhappy. We *know* that we are unhappy; so we are *great*. Pascal. "If she had perished, she had perished:" does this entail that she has not perished? If so, by what rule? "If I believed that I should be very silly indeed:" does this, or does this not, entail that I don't believe it? Natural language holds logical problems of its own, lots of them.)

This brings me to another point. Ordinary language simply has not got the "hardness," the logical hardness, to cut axioms in it. It needs something like a metallic substance to carve a deductive system out of it such as Euclid's. But common speech? If you begin to draw inferences it soon begins to go "soft" and fluffs up somewhere. You may just as well carve cameos on a cheese *soufflé*. (My point is: language is plastic, yielding to the will to express, even at the price of some obscurity. Indeed, how could it ever express anything that does not conform to the cliché? If logicians had their way, language would become as clear and transparent as glass, but also as brittle as glass: and what would be the good of making an axe of glass that breaks the moment you use it?) But language is not hard. And that is why it is dangerous in philosophy to hunt for premises instead of just going over the ground, standing back and saying: look.

Most philosophic arguments, to ignore constructions *à la* Spinoza, hinge on such points as what "can" and what "cannot" be said or what sort of question it is "proper" and what sort of question it would be "inappropriate" to ask. Much skill and ingenuity has been spent in elucidating such questions as to whether a certain metaphor is "natural," a certain diction "fitting." It would not be right to burke the point that considerations such as these, while apparently pertaining to matters of style, contribute in fact largely to the forcefulness of an argument, indeed play a very real and decisive part in the way they make us look at the subject. In going over, examining and comparing the various modes of expression that center around certain key notions, for instance, "imagination," "memory," "pleasure," we catch the first glimpse of what is sometimes called the "logic" of these notions. Now can any of these things be proved? Can it be proved, for example, that a certain diction is "fitting"? (Remember, no such thing as a definition of a "well-formed formula.") No philosopher has ever made so much as an attempt. Everyone uses words in this way and he leaves it at that; and rightly so. For what sort of reasons *could* he give anyway? Here already, at the very threshold, the idea of a philosophic proof begins to ring hollow.

"Ah, but the ordinary use of language." All right; but even so, it is not that one "cannot" use language differently. To illustrate: "frozen music"—does this "tell" you anything? Perhaps not; yet a saying like "Architecture is frozen music" (Goethe) drives the point home. To say "The arms are full of blunted memories" sounds odd, until you come upon it in Proust's context. The "will to understand" does not even flinch before those bogies of the logician, contradictions: it transforms them, wresting a new sense from the apparent nonsense. ("Dark with excess of light," "the luminous gloom of Plato"—just to remind the reader of two examples of Coleridge.) There are about 303 reasons why we sometimes express ourselves in a contradiction, and understandably so.

Result: it cannot even be proved that a given expression is natural, a metaphor fitting, a question proper (or unaskable), a collocation of words expressive (or devoid of meaning). Nothing of the sort can be demonstrated.

Two other points reinforce what has been said. What we sometimes do in a philosophical discussion is not argue at all but simply raise lots of questions—a method brilliantly employed by Ryle. Indeed, a volley of perplexing questions can certainly not be described as an argument and *a fortiori* not as a logical one, yet it is no less effective in making one turn back in recoil to consider one's views. Lastly, though on the surface the philosopher seems to be engaged in much the same thing as a logician is, for instance, in testing an argument for any loose links in it or in building up an argument, this should not mislead us. For if he were to construct rigorous proofs, where are the theorems established by them? What has he to show as the fruit of his labors?

I have not raised any of these questions wantonly; they force themselves on everyone who tries to arrive at a clear and unbiased view of the matter. Should these difficulties not have their origin in the nature of philosophy itself?

V

I proceed now to consider philosophic arguments, especially those which are regarded as constituting a decisive advance, to see whether they give us any reason for modifying the view advocated here. There are only a few classical cases. One of them is Hume's celebrated argument to show that the relation of cause and effect is intrinsically different from that of ground and consequence. Now in what does this "proof" consist? He *reminds* us of what we have always known: that, while it is self-contradictory to assert the ground and deny the consequence, no such contradiction arises in assuming that a certain event, the "cause," may be followed not by its usual effect but by some other event. If it is asked "Is this a proof?" what is one to say? It certainly is not the sort of proof to be found in a deductive system. Much the same applies to Berkeley's argument when he tells us that, try as he might, he cannot call up in his mind an abstract idea of a triangle, of just a triangle with no particular shape, any more than he can conceive the idea of a man without qualities. Is this a proof? He points out the obvious. (Only it wants a genius to see it.)

To take my own argument against logical fatalism, it is not strict. The decisive step consists in following a certain analogy with other cases. It is analogical, not logical. Similarly the argument used against Zeno is not conclusive. (I have no space to enlarge upon that.)

Now for two more examples, one of the current sort of argument applied today by philosophers, the other taken from Aristotle.

When we say of someone that he "sees" or "hears" an aeroplane, or "descries," "detects" a lark in the sky, or again that he "tastes" or "smells" roast pork, we do not ascribe to him an activity. That "seeing" is not a sort of doing can be illustrated, e.g. by calling attention to the fact that we don't use the continuous present tense. We say "I see the clock," not "I am seeing the clock" (save G. E. Moore, who, oddly enough, regularly says that he "is seeing his right hand"), whereas it is perfectly correct to say "I am looking at the clock, listening to its ticking," and so in the other cases. Again, while it is proper to say "I have forgotten to post the letter," no one would say "I have forgotten to see the letter-box." There is no sense in asking you, when you look at me, whether your seeing is easy or difficult, quick or slowish, careful or heedless, whether you see me deliberately and whether you have now finished seeing me. So, it is argued, perceiving is not a doing (an argument used by myself in lectures).

The point to be labored is that this argument is not conclusive. Odd as it sounds, "I have finished seeing you" *may* be said, though only in very special circumstances. A man with impaired eyesight who, unable to take in the shape as a whole, has perhaps to scan the face bit by bit in search of some characteristic marks might say, and understandably, "Now I have finished seeing you." We too are occasionally in a not much better position, as when, in magnesium light, we look at some scene, and afterwards complain, "Too quick, I couldn't take it in." It would seem then that there is no more than a difference in degree between this case and the normal ones. Odd cases, certainly; but what would you think of a mathematician whose theorems collapse when applied to slightly out-of-the-way curves?

For my next example I choose pleasure. Aristotle, in criticizing Plato, pointed out that if pleasure were a process going on in time I could enjoy something swiftly or slowly—an argument which is almost a bombshell in its destructive power. Certainly, to speak in such terms is very odd and sounds absurd. Yet, if I strain my imagination, I can perhaps bring myself to conceive of a set of circumstances under which it would not be entirely unnatural to say such a thing. In listening to music, for example, when I am following a slow and gentle movement, my enjoying it appears in some respects to be different from what I get when listening to an exciting piece of music. The very quality of my enjoyment seems to change as if something of the slow and gentle or of the wild, intoxicating flow of the music had entered into it. If I say, in the one case, that I was enjoying it leisurely like basking in the sun or sipping wine, in the other that I was suddenly carried away, breathlessly following its onrush and enjoying it like a storm at sea—does this sound like sheer nonsense? So there does seem to be a time factor in pleasure.

Amongst the most powerful weapons in the philosopher's armory are *reductio ad absurdum* and infinite regress arguments. Before proceeding to an appraisal of these forms of reasoning, it will be well to consider how they work in their home land, mathematics.

Let me choose as a typical case the proof that $\sqrt{2}$ is irrational. If it were a rational number, we could find two integers m and n such that

$$m^2 = 2n^2 \tag{1}$$

We may then argue as follows. As m^2 is even, m must be even; hence $m = 2m_1$. Substitution yields

$$2m_1^2 = n^2. \tag{2}$$

As n^2 is even, n must be even; hence $n = 2n_1$. Substitution yields

$$m_1^2 = 2n_1^2. \tag{3}$$

If, then, two integers m and n exist which stand in the relation (1), they must have halves which stand in exactly the same relation (3), and these must have halves which stand in the same relation, and so on *ad infinitum;* which is plainly impossible, m and n being finite. Therefore the tentative assumption (1) cannot hold, and $\sqrt{2}$ cannot be rational. Q.E.D. This is the prototype of a refutation by infinite regress.

Arguments of this type have been applied outside mathematics. However, when I come to look at them a bit more closely I begin to hesitate. An example will illustrate my doubts. An argument propounded against the use of mechanical models is this. If the elastic properties of matter can be explained as being due to electric forces with which the molecules act on each other, it surely is pointless to explain the action of the electric forces as being due to the elastic properties of a mechanical medium, the "ether." To do this is to go round in a circle: elasticity is explained in terms of electric force, and electric force in terms of elasticity; while the attempt to break out of the circle by supposing that the elasticity of the ether is due to "electric forces" acting between the ether particles and these to the elastic properties of a second-order ether is to be pushed into an infinite series of reduction steps. Thus the mechanistic program is faced with a dilemma both horns of which are equally fatal.

A formidable argument—or is it? I can well imagine an undaunted champion of the lost cause retort: "Not a bit of a regress. Yes, the ether is elastic, not, however, in the sense in which a spring is: while elasticity of matter can be reduced to electric force, elasticity of the ether, being an ultimate postulate of the theory, cannot be reduced any further." And with this the argument falls to the ground.

But this is unconvincing, it will be said. I agree; I am not such an imbecile as to plead for retaining mechanical models and the rest. My point is only to see whether this "refutation" is compelling. *It isn't.* The advocate of models is not forcibly dislodged from his position. There is, it would seem, always a way of getting out of the dilemma—of wriggling out if you like—which foils the argument. What is shown in it is merely that to cling to models of this sort becomes, in the circumstances, very unnatural. But to say that something is unnatural is not to say that it is logically impossible: yet this is what the argument should establish. In the mathematical proof cited above no loophole was left for wriggling out. The whole deduction was a "chain of adamant"—precisely the sort of thing the argument under review is not.

Consider now a similar argument. There cannot be any such thing as volitions, it has been said. Volitions were called in by theorists to provide causes not only for what we (intentionally) do but also for mental processes or operations such as controlling an impulse, paying heed to something, and the like. As a consequence of this, acts of will were supposed to be the sort of thing the presence of which makes an action "voluntary," or which—somehow, in some unfathomable way—"gets itself translated" into a bodily or mental act. In fine, volitions were thought of as causes as well as effects of other, mental or physical, occurrences. Now the dilemma: if my pulling of the trigger were the result of a mental act of "willing to pull the trigger," what of this mental act itself? Was it willed or unwilled? If unwilled, it cannot be called voluntary and therefore not a volition; if willed, then we must suppose, according to the theory, that it results from a prior act, namely, "willing to will to pull the trigger," and that from another *ad infinitum,* leaving no possibility for me ever to start.

Brilliant as the argument is, the point to be brought up here is only whether it is logically fatal. Does it really prove that the assumption of acts of willing involves an infinite regress? A believer in such acts need not be cowed into submission. To ask of volitions whether they are themselves voluntary or involuntary acts, he may say, is plain nonsense. Only an *action* can be voluntary or involuntary, not an act of will. It is just the point that an act of will is an act of will and does not issue from any anterior act of will, any more than, in order to recall a thing I must first recall what I want to recall, and before I can even do that I must recall that I want to recall what I want to recall, and so on *ad infinitum*. Just as I can recall a thing without need to call in an act of recalling what I want to recall, so my pulling the trigger may be the direct result of an act of will without the latter issuing from a parent act of will. Thus the whole argument apparently crumbles away.

This is meant not to belittle the argument or detract from its force, but only to get clear as to *what sort* of force it has. If it were conclusive, it would, with its destructive power, do away with a good many more acts and states of mind, not only with volitions—with intending and desiring, for instance. Indeed, precisely similar arguments can be constructed "to deal with them." Intention: though clearly not the sort of thing to be classed as a simple "act," it yet seems somehow to "connect" with what goes on in us before we carry it into action—such as considering, planning, hesitating, choosing. I may, let us say, intend to find a flaw in a given argument, and when I subsequently turn it over in my mind, this will be the result of my intention. Some mental operations, then, *can* arise from an intention, they are "intended." So what of the intention itself? Is it intended or unintended? If the intention is not intended, it is not the intention, and if it is intended it must be due to another intention, and this to yet another *ad infinitum*. Similarly in the case of desire. Suppose that I feel a desire for a certain thing, is this desire itself desired or undesired? Either answer lands us in absurdities.

If the strength of the argument were to lie in its structure it would, with its devastating effect, apply after the exchange of some of its terms for other ones, e.g. "volition" for "intention"—provided, of course, that certain other circumstances essential to the reasoning are the same. Yet, while the first argument sounds, to say the least, very plausible, no one will be duped by its caricatures. So if it *has* any force it cannot owe it to its structure and consequently cannot be of a logical sort. It is meant to refute the existence of a kind of mental thrust; but then we should remember that to prove the non-existence of something is always a precarious business. "No one has ever proved the non-existence of Apollo or Aphrodite" it has been observed; too much weight, then, need perhaps not be laid on this particular case. What is disturbing, however, is the ease with which arguments can be cast into pseudo-deductive moulds. And it is this fact to which I wish to call attention by examining the argument. As has been shown in the preceding discussion, it is not an isolated case. No philosophic argument ends with a Q.E.D. However forceful, it never forces. There is no bullying in philosophy, neither with the stick of logic nor with the stick of language.

VI

In throwing such strong doubts on the power of arguments as used by philosophers I may seem to deny them any value whatever. But such is not my intention. Even if they are lacking in logical rigor this certainly has not prevented an original thinker from using them successfully, or from bringing out something not seen before or not seen so clearly. So in the case I have discussed: something *is* seen in that argument, something *is* made clear, though perhaps not quite in the sense intended by the arguer. If so, something very important has been left out from the picture.

Perhaps our objections have been doing injustice to philosophic arguments. They were, quite mistakenly as I hope to have shown, supposed to be proofs and refutations in a strict sense. But what the philosopher does is something else. *He builds up a case.* First, he makes you see all the weaknesses, disadvantages, shortcomings of a position; he brings to light inconsistencies in it or points out how unnatural some of the ideas underlying the whole theory are by pushing them to their farthest consequences; and this he does with the strongest weapons in his arsenal, reduction to absurdity and infinite regress. On the other hand, he offers you a new way of looking at things not exposed to those objections. In other words, he submits to you, like a barrister, all the facts of his case, and you are in the position of the judge. You look at them carefully, go into the details, weigh the pros and cons and arrive at a verdict. But in arriving at a verdict you are not following a deductive highway, any more than a judge in the High Court does. Coming to a decision, though a rational process, is very unlike drawing conclusions from given premises, just as it is very unlike doing sums. A judge has to judge, we say, implying that he has to use discernment in contrast to applying, machine-like, a set of mechanical rules. There are no computing machines for doing the judge's work nor could there be any—a trivial yet significant fact. When the judge reaches a decision this may be, and in fact often is, a rational result, yet not one obtained by deduction; it does not simply follow from such-and-such: what is required is insight, judgment. Now in arriving at a verdict, you are like a judge in this that you are not carrying out a number of formal logical steps: you have to use discernment, e.g. to descry the pivotal point. Considerations such as these make us see what is already apparent in the use of "rational," that this term has a wider range of application than what can be established deductively. To say that an argument can be rational and yet not deductive is not a sort of contradiction as it would inevitably be in the opposite case, namely, of saying that a deductive argument need not be rational.

This alters the whole picture. The point to be emphasized is that a philosopher may see an important truth and yet be unable to demonstrate it by formal proof. But the fact that his arguments are not logical does nothing to detract from their rationality. To return to our previous example, the argument used against volition, though it is not what it professes to be, logically destructive, nevertheless has a force difficult to resist. Now to what is this due? It does not need much acumen to find the answer. It is the whole arrangement of so many felicitous examples, preceding the argument, and their masterly analysis, which breathes life into its bare bones; aided greatly by the fact that the connection between a mental thrust and a bodily movement is allowed to remain a mystery. The unsatisfactoriness of this position, together with the amassing of hosts of unanswerable questions and very striking examples—this makes the argument so convincing.

What do you find in reading Ryle or Wittgenstein? Lots of examples with little or no logical bone in between. Why so many examples? They speak for themselves; they usually are more transparent than the trouble maker; each one acts as an analogy; together they light up the whole linguistic background with the effect that the case before us is seen in the light they produce. Indeed, examples aptly arranged are often more convincing and, above all, of a more lasting effect than an argument which is anyhow spidery. Not that the "proofs" proffered are valueless: a *reductio ad absurdum* always points to a knot in thought, and so does an infinite regress. But they *point* only. The real strength lies in the examples. All the proofs, in a good book on philosophy, could be dispensed with, without its losing a whit of its convincingness. To seek, in philosophy, for rigorous proofs is to seek for the shadow of one's voice.

In order to forestall misinterpretations which will otherwise certainly arise I have to concede one point: arguments on a small scale, containing a few logical steps only, may be rigorous. The substance of my remarks is that the conception of a whole philosophical view —from Heraclitus to Nietzsche or Bradley—is never a matter of logical steps. A *weltanschauung* like any of these or even a new approach like that of Wittgenstein is never "arrived at," in particular it is not deduced, and once found it can neither be proved nor refuted by strictly logical reasoning; though arguments may play a part in making them acceptable. But some authors have disdained even that.

The one remaining question to be asked is this: if the philosopher's views cannot be derived from any premises how has he ever arrived at them? How can he get to a place to which no road is leading? This leads to a new and deeper problem.

VII

To ask, "What is your aim in philosophy?" and to reply, "To show the fly the way out of the fly-bottle" is . . . well, honor where it is due, I suppress what I was going to say; except perhaps this. There is something deeply exciting about philosophy, a fact not intelligible on such a negative account. It is not a matter of "clarifying thoughts" nor of "the correct use of language" nor of any other of these damned things. What is it? Philosophy is many things and there is no formula to cover them all. But if I were asked to express in one single word what is its most essential feature I would unhesitatingly say: vision. At the heart of any philosophy worth the name is vision and it is from there it springs and takes its visible shape. When I say "vision" I mean it: I do not want to romanticize.

What is characteristic of philosophy is the piercing of that dead crust of tradition and convention, the breaking of those fetters which bind us to inherited preconceptions, so as to attain a new and broader way of looking at things. It has always been felt that philosophy should reveal to us what is hidden. (I am not quite insensitive to the dangers of such a view.) Yet from Plato to Moore and Wittgenstein every great philosopher was led by a sense of vision: without it no one could have given a new direction to human thought or opened windows into the not-yet-seen. Though he may be a good technician, he will not leave his marks on the history of ideas. What is decisive is a new way of seeing and, what goes with it, the will to transform the whole intellectual scene. This is the real thing and everything else is subservient to it.

Suppose that a man revolts against accepted opinion, that he feels "cramped" in its categories; a time may come when he believes, rightly or wrongly, that he has freed himself of these notions; when he has that sense of sudden growth in looking back at the prejudices which held him captive; or a time when he believes, rightly or wrongly, that he has reached a vantage point from which things can be seen to be arranged in clear and orderly patterns while difficulties of long standing dissolve as though by magic. If he is of a philosophic cast of mind he will argue this out with himself and then, perhaps, try to impart what has dawned on him to others. The arguments he will offer, the attacks he will make, the suggestions he will advance are all devised for one end: to win other people over to his own way of looking at things, to change the whole climate of opinion. Though to an outsider he appears to advance all sorts of arguments, this is not the decisive point. What is decisive is that he has seen things from a new angle of vision. Compared to that everything else is secondary. Arguments come only afterwards to lend support to what he has seen. "Big words, not every philosopher, etc.:" but where should one get one's bearings if not from the masters? And besides, once tradition has given way there is always ample scope for specialists to reduce some "pockets of resistance." Unpalatable though it may be, behind the arguments so well-planned, so neat and logical, something else is at work, a will to transform the entire way of thinking. In arguing for his view, the philosopher will, almost against his will, have to undermine current categories and clichés of thinking by exposing the fallacies which underly the established views he is attacking; and not only this, he may go so far as to question the canons of satisfactoriness themselves. In this sense, philosophy is the re-testing of the standards. In every philosopher lives something of the reformer. That is the reason why any advance in science when it touches the standards is felt to be of philosophic significance, from Galileo to Einstein and Heisenberg.

If there is any truth in this, the relation of logic and philosophy appears in a new light. What is at issue is not a conflict between a formal and a less formal or informal logic, nor between the behavior of technical and everyday concepts, but something radically different. It is the difference between drawing a conclusion and seeing, or making one see, a new aspect.

To put the matter in a nutshell, a philosophic argument does more and does less than a logical one: less in that it never establishes anything conclusively; more in that, if successful, it is not content to establish just one isolated point of truth, but effects a change in our whole mental outlook so that, as a result of that, myriads of such little points are brought into view or turned out of sight, as the case may be. Are illustrations necessary? Once Hume had exposed the fallacies of his predecessors when dealing with the notion of causality he had made it impossible for anyone to think along the lines of Spinoza whose world looks to us strange as the moon. Suppose that you look at a picture-puzzle: at first you can see in it only a maze of lines; then, suddenly, you recognize a human face. Can you now, having discovered the face, see the lines as before? Clearly not. As with the maze of lines, so with the muddle cleared up by Hume: to recapture the mood of the past, to travel back into the fog has become impossible—one of the big difficulties of understanding history of philosophy. It is for the same reason that the rise of the linguistic technique in our day has put an end to the great speculative systems of the past.

A philosophy is an attempt to unfreeze habits of thinking, to replace them by less stiff and restricting ones. Of course, these may in time themselves harden, with the result that they clog progress: Kant, the *Alleszermalmer* to his contemporaries, yet proudly upholding his table of categories—which appear to us unduly narrow. The liberator of yesterday may turn into the tyrant of tomorrow.

It can now be seen that the philosopher is not doing what the logician does only less competently but doing something altogether different. A philosophic argument is not an *approximation* of a logical one nor is the latter the ideal the philosopher is striving for. Such an account totally misdescribes what really takes place. Philosophy is not an exercise in formal logic, philosophic arguments are not chains of logical inference, only bungled ones, nor can they by any effort be recast into deductive moulds. What is being confused here is the scientist's aim to find new truths and the philosopher's aim to gain insight. As the two things are so entirely out of scale it is small wonder that the philosopher cannot move in the logician's armor. Not even if the logician himself is fighting the battle. The clash over the law of excluded middle in mathematics is a clash between two parties, each in possession of clear and precisely defined concepts. Yet there seems to be no way of settling the dispute by cogent argument. If it were true that philosophical troubles arise from the loose nature of our everyday concepts, why should such conflicts break out in the exactest of the sciences?

There have never been any absolutely cogent reasons for parting with the law of excluded middle, accepting Darwinism, giving up the Ptolemaic system or renouncing the principle of causality. If any of these things could be demonstrated how does it come that there are always partisans of the "lost causes"? Are they like the unlucky circle-squarers, wasting their time in trying to do what has been shown to be logically impossible? The truth is that conflicts of this type cannot be resolved, not entirely, either by adducing factual evidence or by logical demonstration. Both sides, of course, bring up arguments in the combat but they are not decisive. These are battles never lost and never won irrevocably. It is a typical situation, a recurrent theme in the history of human thought.

Whenever science arrives at a crucial stage where the fundamental notions become uncertain and are held as it were in solution, disputes of an odd kind are breaking out. The mere fact that leading scientists, in spite of differences in temperament, outlook, etc., take part in them, feel bound to do so, should make us reflect. Now what the protagonists avowedly or unavowedly are trying to do is to win their fellow scientists over to their own way of thinking; and to the degree to which their arguments are attempts at changing the whole intellectual attitude they take on a philosophical character. Is this coincidence?

VIII

I have so far spoken of "seeing a new aspect" without making an attempt to explain the term. I hope now to do so, though only perfunctorily, by giving one or two illustrations. There is a sort of paradox connected with the idea of certain discoveries. Descartes, for instance, was the discoverer of analytic geometry. But could he seek for it? To say that he spent years looking for it sounds downright absurd. What we are inclined to say in such a case is: to seek for analytic geometry is not possible—first because it was not seen and then because it was seen. But if he could not seek, how could he find? This leads us straight to the heart of the matter.

Consider first an entirely imaginary case. In the propositional calculus, as it was built up by Frege, two primitive ideas occur, "not" and "or." It was later discovered by Sheffer that the whole calculus can be based on one single idea (his "stroke" function). Of what kind was this discovery? Suppose that Frege, by a curious chance, had written all his logical axioms in the form

$$\sim(.\ .\ .\ .)v\sim(.\ .\ .\ .)$$

i.e. as a sum of two negations, but had none the less mistakenly believed that *two* symbols were required for expressing these laws, namely "$\sim$" and "v." Imagine now that someone else looking at these formulae is struck by what, on our assumption, has escaped Frege, namely that they all have one and the same structure and require therefore only one symbol. In what exactly does his discovery consist? In his *seeing* the formulae in a new way, in his reading a new structure into them. What matters is his apprehension: so long as he does not see the structure of a new system in the old one he has not got it. Anyone may look at the formulae and yet not perceive what Sheffer has perceived, the occurrence of an identical structure. *This* is the discovery, not the introducing of a special symbol for a combination of the old ones. It would have been quite enough, for instance, had Sheffer merely pointed out the constant recurrence of this structure in all the laws without providing his "stroke"; that is inessential.

This example may illustrate what is meant by the "seeing of a new aspect." Seeing such an aspect is often the core of a new discovery. If you look at the formulae, the moment you notice the new structure in them they suddenly seem to change—a phenomenon akin to seeing a figure, say, a drawn cube differently, now as solid and protruding, now as hollow and receding. The one pattern suddenly "jumps" into the other. Similarly in our case, though there are also differences; thus the new aspect, once it has dawned, can steadily be held in mind and has not that perceptual instability. The apprehension of a new pattern in the formulae seems to hold in it actually more of a visual experience, anyhow to be more closely akin to it than it might at first appear. Seeing and interpreting, looking and thinking seem as it were to fuse here.

If it is now asked whether it is possible for anyone to *seek* for the new aspect, what is one to reply? Well, that something *can* be seen in a new way is seen only when it *is* seen in this way. That an aspect is possible is seen only when the aspect has already flashed and not before: that's why the finding cannot be anticipated, not even by the greatest genius. It always comes unbidden and, as it would seem, in a sudden flash.

To take another case, is the calculation

$$(5 + 3)^2 = 5^2 + 2.5.3 + 3^2$$

at the same time a proof that

$$(2 + 3)^2 = 2^2 + 2.2.3 + 3^2 \quad ?$$

Yes and no—depending on how you look at it. (Does it strike you that the 2 in the middle term is a "structural" 2, deriving not from the special numbers but from the general form of the operation?) A man, while reckoning with special numbers only, may yet conceivably do algebra if he sees the special sums in a new way, as the expressions of a general law. (Discovery of algebra as the discovery of an aspect of numerical calculation.)

What goes for these more or less trivial cases goes for Descartes and also for Einstein and Hilbert. They were unable to seek, Einstein for a conceptual gap in the idea of simultaneity, Hilbert for the axiomatic method. Though these discoveries are of a different order altogether, the principle underlying them is the same. None of them has ever "arrived" at his view because he was never travelling. They did not seek, they found (like Picasso). And that is so wrong with the whole way in which such discoveries are so often presented—as if they were the result of a "method" or "procedure," as if the great men arrived at their solutions by drawing logical inferences. This leaves out the most essential thing—the flashing of a new aspect which is *non*-inferential. The moments of seeing cannot be foreseen, any more than they can be planned, forced, controlled, or summoned by will-power.

Is there any truth in what I am saying? I shall not argue. Instead, let me remind you of some observations which will be familiar to you. It is notorious that a philosophy is not made, it grows. You don't choose a puzzle, you are shocked into it. Whoever has pondered some time over some dark problem in philosophy will have noticed that the solution, when it comes, comes with a suddenness. It is not through working very hard towards it that it is found. What happens is rather that he suddenly sees things in a new light—as if a veil had been lifted that screened his view, or as if the scales had fallen from his eyes, leaving him surprised at his own stupidity not to have seen what was there quite plain before him all the time. It is less like finding out something and more like maturing, outgrowing preconceived notions.

To give just one example of vision in philosophy: Wittgenstein saw through a big mistake of his time. It was then held by most philosophers that the nature of such things as hoping and fearing, or intending, meaning and understanding could be discovered through introspection, while others, in particular psychologists, sought to arrive at an answer by experiment, having only obscure notions as to what their results meant. Wittgenstein changed the whole approach by saying: what these words mean shows itself in the way they are used—the nature of understanding reveals itself in grammar, not in experiment. This was at the time quite a revelation and came to him, so far as I remember, suddenly.

The view advocated here is that at the living center of every philosophy is a vision and that it should be judged accordingly. The really important questions to be discussed in the history of philosophy are not whether Leibniz or Kant were consistent in arguing as they did but rather what lies behind the systems they have built. And here I want to end with a few words on metaphysics.

To say that metaphysics is nonsense *is* nonsense. It fails to acknowledge the enormous part played at least in the past by those systems. Why this is so, why they should have such a hold over the human mind I shall not undertake here to discuss. Metaphysicians, like artists, are the antennae of their time: they have a flair for feeling which way the spirit is moving. (There is a Rilke poem about it.) There is something visionary about great metaphysicians as if they had the power to see beyond the horizons of their time. Take, for instance, Descartes' work. That it has given rise to endless metaphysical quibbles is certainly a thing to hold against it. Yet if we attend to the spirit rather than to the words I am greatly inclined to say that there is a certain grandeur in it, a prophetic aspect of the comprehensibility of nature, a bold anticipation of what has been achieved in science at a much later date. The true successors of Descartes were those who translated the spirit of this philosophy into deeds, not Spinoza or Malebranche but Newton and the mathematical description of nature. To go on with some hairsplitting as to what substance is and how it should be defined was to miss the message. It was a colossal mistake. A philosophy is there to be lived out. What goes into the word dies, what goes into the work lives.

Bibliography of Logical Positivism

The range of this bibliography is rather wider than that of the book. It includes works which are either expository or critical not only of logical positivism, in the strict sense, but of every form of modern analytical philosophy. It does not claim to be exhaustive even on the topic of logical positivism: but an effort has been made to list at any rate the most important books and articles that can reasonably be regarded as falling within this field.

The bibliography is divided into three sections: anthologies and compilations; books and monographs; and articles, including contributions to symposia and critical notices of special interest. Contributions by any one writer are listed in chronological order. The references to articles do not give the numbers of the periodicals or proceedings in which they appear, but the dates of the volumes in which these numbers fall. This is in conformity with the practice followed by the other books in this series.

ANTHOLOGIES AND COMPILATIONS

Ayer, A. J. *et al.*, *The Revolution in Philosophy*, London: Macmillan, 1956
Black, M. (ed.), *Philosophical Analysis*, Ithaca: Cornell Univ. Press, 1950
Edwards, P. and Pap, A. (eds.), *A Modern Introduction to Philosophy*, Glencoe: The Free Press; London: Allen and Unwin, 1957
Elton, W. (ed.), *Aesthetics and Language*, Oxford: Basil Blackwell, 1954
Feigl, H. and Brodbeck, M. (eds.), *Readings in the Philosophy of Science*, New York: Appleton-Century-Crofts, 1953
Feigl, H. and Scriven, M. (eds.), *Minnesota Studies in the Philosophy of Science*; Vol. I, *The Foundations of Science and the Concepts of Psychology and Psychoanalysis*, Minneapolis: Univ. of Minnesota Press, 1956

[381]

Feigl, H., Scriven, M. and Maxwell, G. (eds.), *Minnesota Studies in the Phi-
losophy of Science;* Vol. II, *Concepts, Theories, and the Mind-Body
Problem,* Minneapolis: Univ. of Minnesota Press, 1958
Feigl, H. and Sellars, W. (eds.), *Readings in Philosophical Analysis,* New
York: Appleton-Century-Crofts, 1949
Flew, A. G. N. (ed.), *Logic and Language* (first series), Oxford: Blackwell,
1951
    Logic and Language (second series), Oxford: Blackwell, 1953
    Essays in Conceptual Analysis, London: Macmillan, 1956
Flew, A. and Macintyre, A. (eds.), *New Essays in Philosophical Theology,*
London: SCM Press; New York: Macmillan, 1955
Gardiner, P. (ed.), *Theories of History,* Glencoe: The Free Press, 1959
Henle, P., Kallen, H. M. and Langer, S. K. (eds.), *Structure, Method and
Meaning:* Essays in honor of Henry M. Sheffer, New York: Liberal
Arts Press, 1951
Hook, S. (ed.), *American Philosophers at Work,* New York: Criterion Books,
1956
    Determinism and Freedom, New York: New York Univ. Press, 1958
International Encyclopedia of Unified Science, ed. O. Neurath and others:
(combined ed.), vol. I in 2 parts, Chicago: Univ. of Chic. Press, 1955
Laslett, P. (ed.), *The Physical Basis of Mind,* Oxford: Blackwell, 1950
    Politics, Philosophy and Society, Oxford: Blackwell, 1956
Lewis, H. D. (ed.), *Contemporary British Philosophy* (third series), London:
Allen and Unwin, 1956
Linsky, L. (ed.), *Semantics and the Philosophy of Language,* Urbana: Univ.
of Illinois Press, 1952
Macdonald, M. (ed.), *Philosophy and Analysis,* Oxford: Blackwell, 1954
Mace, C. A. (ed.), *British Philosophy in the Mid-Century,* London: Allen
and Unwin; New York: Macmillan, 1957
Mitchell, B. (ed.), *Faith and Logic,* London: Allen and Unwin, 1957
Muirhead, J. H. (ed.), *Contemporary British Philosophy* (first and second
series), London: Allen and Unwin, 1924 and 1925
Munitz, M. K. (ed.), *A Modern Introduction to Ethics,* Glencoe: The Free
Press, 1958
Neurath, O., *et al., Encyclopedia and Unified Science,* Chicago: Univ. of
Chic. Press (Int. Encycl. of Unified Science), 1938
Pears, D. F. (ed.), *The Nature of Metaphysics,* London: Macmillan, 1957
Runes, D. (ed.), *Twentieth Century Philosophy,* New York: Philosophical
Library, 1943
Schilpp, P. A. (ed.), *The Philosophy of G. E. Moore,* Evanston: Northwest-
ern Univ., 1942; 2nd ed. 1952
    The Philosophy of Bertrand Russell, Evanston: Northwestern Univ., 1944
    Albert Einstein: Philosopher-Scientist, New York: Tudor Press, 1949
Sellars, W. and Hospers, J. (eds.), *Readings in Ethical Theory,* New York:
Appleton-Century-Crofts, 1952
Philosophical Studies. Essays in Memory of L. Susan Stebbing, London:
Allen and Unwin, 1948
Wiener, P. P. (ed.), *Readings in Philosophy of Science,* New York: Scribner's,
1953
Philosophical Essays for A. N. Whitehead, London: Longman's, 1936

BOOKS

Ajdukiewicz, K., *Beiträge zur Methodologie der deduktiven Wissenschaften,* Lwow: Verlag der Polnischen Philosophischen Gesellschaft in Lemberg, 1921

Anscombe, G. E. M., *Intention,* Oxford: Basil Blackwell, 1957

Austin, J. L., *Ifs and Cans,* British Academy Annual Philosophical Lecture, London: Oxford Univ. Press, 1956

Ayer, A. J., *Language, Truth and Logic,* London: Gollancz, 1936, 2nd ed. 1946
The Foundations of Empirical Knowledge, London: Macmillan, 1940
Thinking and Meaning, London: H. K. Lewis, 1947
Philosophical Essays, London: Macmillan, 1954
The Problem of Knowledge, London: Macmillan and Penguin Books, 1956

Baier, K., *The Moral Point of View,* Ithaca: Cornell Univ. Press, 1958

Barnes, W. H. F., *The Philosophical Predicament,* London: A. and C. Black, 1950

Bergmann, G., *The Metaphysics of Logical Positivism,* London: Longmans, Green, 1954
Philosophy of Science, Madison: Univ. of Wisconsin Press, 1957

Black, M., *The Nature of Mathematics,* London: Kegan Paul; New York: Harcourt Brace, 1933
Language and Philosophy, Ithaca: Cornell Univ. Press, 1949
Critical Thinking, New York: Prentice Hall, 1952
Problems of Analysis, London: Routledge and Kegan Paul, 1954

Bloomfield, L., *Linguistic Aspects of Science,* Chicago: Univ. of Chic. Press, (Int. Encycl. of Unified Science), 1939

Bochenski, I. M., *Europäische Philosophie der Gegenwart,* Bern: Francke, 1947. Eng. transl. by D. Nicholl and K. Aschenbrenner, *Contemporary European Philosophy,* Berkeley: Univ. of California Press, 1956
Précis de Logique Mathématique, Bussum: F. G. Kroonder, 1949

Braithwaite, R. B., *Scientific Explanation,* Cambridge: Cambridge Univ. Press, 1953

Bridgman, P. W., *The Logic of Modern Physics,* New York: Macmillan, 1927
The Nature of Physical Theory, Princeton: Princeton Univ. Press, 1936
Reflections of a Physicist, New York: Philosophical Library, 1950

Britton, K., *Communication: A Philosophical Study of Language,* London: Routledge and Kegan Paul, 1939

Broad, C. D., *Scientific Thought,* London: Kegan Paul, 1923
The Mind and Its Place in Nature, London: Kegan Paul, 1925

Carnap, R., *Der Raum,* Berlin: Erg. Heft 56 der Kantstudien, 1922
Der logische Aufbau der Welt, Berlin: Weltkreis-Verlag, 1928
Scheinprobleme in der Philosophie, das Fremdpsychische und der Realismusstreit, Berlin, 1928
Abriss der Logistik, Vienna: Springer, 1929
Logische Syntax der Sprache, Vienna: Springer, 1934. Eng. transl., *Logical Syntax of Language,* London: Kegan Paul; New York: Harcourt Brace, 1937

Carnap, R. (*continued*)
   Die Aufgabe der Wissenschaftslogik, Einheitswissenschaft, No. 3, Vienna:
      Gerold, 1934. French transl. (together with that of "Formalwissen-
      schaft und Realwissenschaft," see articles below), *Le problème de
      la logique de la science, science formelle et science du réel*, Paris:
      Actualités Scientifiques 291, Herman, 1935
   Philosophy and Logical Syntax, London: Kegan Paul, 1935
   Foundations of Logic and Mathematics, Chicago: Univ. of Chic. Press
      (Int. Encycl. of Unified Science), 1939
   Introduction to Semantics (Studies in Semantics, vol. I), Cambridge:
      Harvard Univ. Press, 1942
   Formalization of Logic (Studies in Semantics, vol. II), Cambridge: Har-
      vard Univ. Press, 1943
   Meaning and Necessity: A Study in Semantics and Modal Logic, Chi-
      cago: Univ. of Chic. Press, 1947
   Logical Foundations of Probability (Probability and Induction, vol. I),
      Chicago: Univ. of Chic. Press, 1950
   The Nature and Application of Inductive Logic (six sections from *Logical
      Foundations of Probability*), Chicago: Univ. of Chic. Press, 1951
   The Continuum of Inductive Methods, Chicago: Univ. of Chic. Press, 1952
   *Einführung in die symbolische Logik, mit besonderer Berücksichtigung
      ihrer Anwendungen*, Vienna: Springer, 1954. Engl. transl., *Introduc-
      tion to Symbolic Logic*, New York: Dover, 1958
Carnap, R. and Bar-Hillel, Y., *An Outline of the Theory of Semantic Informa-
      tion*, Cambridge: Res. Lab. of Electronics, M.I.T. Report No. 247,
      1952
Carnap, R., Hahn, H. and Neurath, O., *Wissenschaftliche Weltauffassung: Der
      Wiener Kreis*, Vienna: Wolf, 1929
Chisholm, R. M., *Perceiving: A Philosophical Study*, Ithaca: Cornell Univ.
      Press, 1957
Clauberg, K. W. and Dubislav, W., *Systematisches Wörterbuch der Philo-
      sophie*, Leipzig: Meiner, 1923
Copleston, F., *Contemporary Philosophy*, London: Burns and Oates, 1956
Cornforth, M., *Science versus Idealism*, London: Lawrence and Wishart, 1946
   In Defence of Philosophy against Positivism and Pragmatism, London:
      Lawrence and Wishart, 1950
Dray, W., *Laws and Explanation in History*, Oxford: Oxford Univ. Press, 1957
Dubislav, W., *Über die sog. analytischen und synthetischen Urteile*, Berlin,
      1926
   Über die Definition, Berlin, 1927
   Die Philosophie der Mathematik in der Gegenwart, Berlin: Dunker &
      Dunnhaupt, 1932
Dubislav, W. and Clauberg, K. W., *Systematisches Wörterbuch der Philo-
      sophie*, Leipzig: Meiner, 1923
Edwards, P., *The Logic of Moral Discourse*, Glencoe: The Free Press, 1955
Einstein, A., *Geometrie und Erfahrung*, Berlin: Springer, 1921
Ewing, A. C., *The Definition of Good*, New York: Macmillan, 1947
Feigl, H., *Theorie und Erfahrung in der Physik*, Karlsruhe: Braun, 1929
Finlay-Freundlich, E., *Cosmology*, Chicago: Univ. of Chic. Press (Int. Encycl.
      of Unified Science), 1951
Frank, P., *Das Kausalgesetz und seine Grenzen*, Vienna: Springer, 1932
   Das Ende der mechanistischen Physik, Einheitswissenschaft No. 5, Vienna:
      Gerold, 1935

Frank, P. (*continued*)
Interpretations and Misinterpretations of Modern Physics, Paris: Hermann, 1938
Between Physics and Philosophy, Cambridge: Harvard Univ. Press, 1941
Foundations of Physics, Chicago: Univ. of Chic. Press (Int. Encycl. of Unified Science), 1946
Einstein. His Life and Times, New York: Knopf, 1947; London: Jonathan Cape, 1948
Modern Science and Its Philosophy, Cambridge: Harvard Univ. Press, 1949
Relativity: A Richer Truth, Boston: Beacon Press, 1950; London: Cape, 1951
Philosophy of Science, Englewood Cliffs: Prentice-Hall, 1957
Gardiner, P., *The Nature of Historical Explanation,* Oxford: Oxford Univ. Press, 1952
Goodman, N., *The Structure of Appearance,* Cambridge: Harvard Univ. Press, 1951
Fact, Fiction and Forecast, London: Athlone Press, 1954; Cambridge: Harvard Univ. Press, 1955
Hahn, H., *Überflüssige Wesenheiten,* Vienna: Wolf, 1929
Logik, Mathematik und Naturerkennen, Einheitswissenschaft No. 2, Vienna: Gerold, 1933. Eng. transl. in the present volume
Hahn, H., Carnap, R. and Neurath, O., *Wissenschaftliche Weltauffassung: Der Wiener Kreis,* Vienna: Wolf, 1929
Halldén, S. I., *The Logic of Nonsense,* Uppsala: Bokhandeln A-B. Lundequistska, 1949
Emotive Propositions, Stockholm: Almqvist & Wiksell, 1954
Hare, R. M., *The Language of Morals,* Oxford: Clarendon Press, 1952
Hart, H. L. A., *Definition and Theory in Jurisprudence,* Oxford: Clarendon Press, 1953
Helmholtz, H. von, *Schriften zur Erkenntnistheorie,* ed. Schlick, M. and Hertz, P., Berlin: Springer, 1921
Hempel, C. G., *Fundamentals of Concept Formation in Empirical Science,* Chicago: Univ. of Chic. Press (Int. Encycl. of Unified Science), 1952
Hempel, C. G. and Oppenheim, P., *Der Typusbegriff im Lichte der neuen Logik,* Leiden; Sijthoff, 1936
Hill, T. E., *Contemporary Ethical Theories,* New York: Macmillan, 1950
Holloway, J., *Language and Intelligence,* London: Macmillan, 1951
Hospers, J., *Meaning and Truth in the Arts,* Chapel Hill: Univ. of North Carolina Press, 1946
An Introduction to Philosophical Analysis, New York: Prentice-Hall, 1953
Hutten, E. H., *The Language of Modern Physics,* London: Allen and Unwin, 1956
Joad, C. E. M., *A Critique of Logical Positivism,* London: Gollancz; Chicago: Univ. of Chic. Press, 1950
Jordan, Z., *On the Development of Mathematical Logic and of Logical Positivism in Poland,* London: Oxford Univ. Press, 1946
Jorgensen, J., *A Treatise of Formal Logic,* Copenhagen: Levin & Munksgaard; London: Humphrey Milford (Oxford Univ. Press), 1931
Peykologi Paa Biologisk Grundlag (Psychology Based on Biology), Copenhagen, 1941-45
The Development of Logical Empiricism, Chicago: Univ. of Chic. Press (Int. Encycl. of Unified Science), 1951

Kaila, E., *Der Logistische Neupositivismus: Eine kritische Studie*, Turku: Turun Yliopiston julkaisuja, 1930
Über das System der Wirklichkeitsbegriffe, Helsinki: Acta Philosophica Fennica, Fasc. 2, 1936
Über den physikalischen Realitätsbegriff, Helsinki: Acta Philosophica Fennica, Fasc. 4, 1941
Terminal-Kausalität als die Grundlage eines unitarischen Naturbegriffs: eine naturphilosophische Untersuchung, Helsinki: Acta Philosophica Fennica, 1956
Kaufmann, F., *Das Unendliche in der Mathematik und seine Ausschaltung*, Vienna: Deuticke, 1930
Methodology of the Social Sciences, London: Oxford Univ. Press, 1944
Kelsen, H., *Vergeltung und Kausalität*, The Hague: van Stockum, 1941. Eng. transl. *Society and Nature*, Chicago: Univ. of Chic. Press, 1943; London: Kegan Paul, 1946
Kneale, W., *Probability and Induction*, Oxford: Clarendon Press, 1949
Kotarbinski, T., *Elementy teori poznania, logiki formalnej i metodologi nauk* (Elements of the theory of knowledge, formal logic and methodology of science), Lwow, 1929
Kraft, V., *Die Grundlagen einer wissenschaftlichen Wertlehre*, Vienna: Springer, 1937
Mathematik, Logik und Erfahrung, Vienna: Springer, 1947
Einführung in die Philosophie—Philosophie, Weltanschauung, Wissenschaft, Vienna: Springer, 1950
Der Wiener Kreis, Der Ursprung des Neupositivismus, Vienna: Springer, 1950. Eng. transl., *The Vienna Circle*, New York: Philosophical Library, 1953
Lazerowitz, M., *The Structure of Metaphysics*, London: Routledge and Kegan Paul, 1955
Lean, M., *Sense-Perception and Matter*, London: Routledge and Kegan Paul, 1953
Lewis, C. I., *Mind and the World Order*, New York: Scribner, 1929
An Analysis of Knowledge and Valuation, La Salle: Open Court, 1946
Łukasiewicz, J., *Die logischen Grundlagen der Wahrscheinlichkeitsrechnung*, Cracow: Krakauer Akad. d. Wiss., 1913
O nauce (On Science), Lwow, 1934
Mainx, F., *Foundations of Biology*, Chicago: Univ. of Chic. Press (Int. Encycl. of Unified Science), 1955
Malcolm, N., *Ludwig Wittgenstein: A Memoir*, Oxford and New York: Oxford Univ. Press, 1958
Marc-Wogau, K., *Die Theorie der Sinnesdaten*, Uppsala: Universitets Arsskrift, 1945
von Mises, R., *Wahrscheinlichkeit, Statistik und Wahreit*, Vienna: Springer, 1936. Eng. transl., *Probability, Statistics and Truth*, New York: Macmillan; London: William Hodge, 1939
Ernst Mach und die empiristische Wissenschaftsauffassung, Einheitswissenschaft No. 7, 's Gravenhage: W. P. van Stockum, 1938
Kleines Lehrbuch des Positivismus, The Hague: Van Stockum & Son, 1939. Eng. transl., *Positivism: A Study in Human Understanding*, Cambridge: Harvard Univ. Press, 1951
Moore, G. E., *Principia Ethica*, Cambridge: Univ. Press, 1903
Ethics, London: Home University Library, 1912

Moore, G. E. (*continued*)
Philosophical Studies, London: Kegan Paul, 1922
Proof of an External World, British Academy: Annual Philosophical Lecture, 1939
Some Main Problems of Philosophy, London: Allen and Unwin, 1953
Morris, C. W., *Logical Positivism, Pragmatism, and Scientific Empiricism*, Paris: Hermann, 1937
Foundations of the Theory of Signs, Chicago: Univ. of Chic. Press (Int. Encycl. of Unified Science), 1938
Signs, Language, and Behavior, New York: Prentice-Hall, 1946
Naess, A., *Erkenntnis und Wissenschaftliches Verhalten*, Oslo: 1936
"Truth" as Conceived by Those Who Are Not Professional Philosophers, Oslo: 1938
Interpretation and Preciseness, Oslo: 1953
Innforing, Logikk og Metodelaere, Oslo: Universitets Studentkontor, 1949
Naess, A., Christophersen, J. A. and Kvalo, K., *Democracy, Ideology and Objectivity: Studies in the Semantics and Cognitive Analysis of Ideological Controversy*, Oslo: Univ. Press; Oxford, Blackwell, 1956
Nagel, E., *On the Logic of Measurement*, New York: Columbia Univ. Ph.D. Thesis, 1930
Principles of the Theory of Probability, Chicago: Univ. of Chic. Press (Int. Encycl. of Unified Science), 1939
Sovereign Reason, Glencoe: The Free Press, 1954
Logic Without Metaphysics, Glencoe: The Free Press, 1956
Nagel, E. and Newman, J. R., *Gödel's Proof*, New York: New York Univ. Press, 1958
Neurath, O., *Antispengler*, Munich: Callwey, 1921
Empirische Soziologie, Vienna: Springer, 1931
Einheitswissenschaft und Psychologie, Einheitswissenschaft No. 1, Vienna: Springer, 1933
Le développement du Cercle de Vienne et l'avenir de l'empirisme logique, Paris: Hermann, 1935
Was Bedeutet Rationale Wirtschaftsbetrachtung?, Einheitswissenschaft No. 4, Vienna: Gerold, 1935
Foundations of the Social Sciences, Chicago: Univ. of Chic. Press (Int. Encycl. of Unified Science), 1944
Neurath, O., Brunswik, E., Hull, C. L., Mannoury, G. and Woodger, J. H., *Zur Encyklopädie der Einheitswissenschaft, Vorträge, Einheitswissenschaft* No. 6, 's Gravenshage: W. J. von Stockum, 1938
Neurath, O., Carnap, R. and Hahn, H., *Wissenschaftliche Weltauffassung: Der Wiener Kreis*, Vienna: Wolf, 1929
Newman, J. R. and Nagel, E., *Gödel's Proof*, New York: New York Univ. Press, 1958
Nicod, J., *Foundations of Geometry and Induction*, London: Kegan Paul, 1930
Nowell-Smith, P. H., *Ethics*, London: Penguin, 1954; Oxford: Blackwell, 1958
Ogden, C. K. and Richards, I. A., *The Meaning of Meaning*, London: Kegan Paul, 1923
Oppenheim, P., *Die Natürliche Ordnung der Wissenschaften. Grundgesetze der vergleichenden Wissenschaftslehre*, Jena: Gustav Fischer, 1926
Oppenheim, P. and Hempel, C. G., *Der Typusbegriff im Lichte der neuen Logik*, Leiden: Sijthoff, 1936

Pap, A., *The A Priori in Physical Theory*, New York: King's Crown Press, 1946
   Elements of Analytic Philosophy, New York: Macmillan, 1949
   Analytische Erkenntnistheorie, Vienna: Springer-Verlag, 1955
   Semantics and Necessary Truth, New Haven: Yale Univ. Press, 1958
Passmore, J., *A Hundred Years of Philosophy*, London: Duckworth, 1957
Perelman, C. and Olbrechts-Tyteca, L., *Traité de l'Argumentation* (*La nouvelle rhétorique*), Paris: Presses Universitaires de France, 1958
Petzäll, A., *Der Logistische Neupositivismus*, Annales Universitatis Aboensis, Ser. B., Tom. XIII, 1930
   Logistischer Positivismus, Göteborgs Högskolas Arsskrift XXXVII, Göteborg: Wettergren & Kerbers, 1931
Pole, D., *The Later Philosophy of Wittgenstein*, London: Athlone Press, 1958
Popper, K. R., *Logik der Forschung*, Vienna: Springer, 1935. Eng. transl., *The Logic of Scientific Discovery*, London: Hutchinson, 1958
   The Open Society and Its Enemies, London: Kegan Paul, 1945
   The Poverty of Historicism, London: Routledge and Kegan Paul, 1957
Price, H. H., *Perception*, London: Methuen, 1932
   Truth and Corrigibility, Inaugural Lecture, London: Oxford Univ. Press, 1936
   Hume's Theory of the External World, Oxford: Clarendon Press, 1940
   Thinking and Representation, British Academy Lecture, 1946
   Thinking and Experience, London: Hutchinson, 1953
Quine, W. V. O., *From a Logical Point of View*, Cambridge: Harvard Univ. Press, 1953
Ramsey, F. P., *The Foundations of Mathematics and Other Logical Essays*, London: Kegan Paul, 1931
Reichenbach, H., *Relativitätstheorie und Erkenntnis Apriori*, Berlin: Springer, 1920
   Axiomatik der relativistischen Raum-Zeit-Lehre (*Die Wissenschaft* No. 72), Braunschweig: Vieweg, 1924
   Philosophie der Raum-Zeit-Lehre, Berlin and Leipzig: Walter de Gruyter, 1928. Engl. transl., *The Philosophy of Space and Time*, New York: Dover, 1957
   Atom und Kosmos. Das physikalische Weltbild der Gegenwart, Berlin: Deutsche Buch-Gemeinschaft, 1930. Eng. transl., *Atom and Cosmos. The World of Modern Physics*, London: Allen and Unwin, 1932; New York: Macmillan, 1933
   Ziele und Wege der heutigen Naturphilosophie, Leipzig: Meiner, 1931. Eng. transl. in *Selected Essays*, London: Routledge and Kegan Paul, 1959
   Wahrscheinlichkeitslehre. Eine Untersuchung über die logischen und mathematischen Grundlagen der Wahrscheinlichkeitsrechnung, Leiden: Sijthoff, 1935. Eng. transl., *The Theory of Probability. An Inquiry into the Logical and Mathematical Foundations of the Calculus of Probability*, 2nd ed., Berkeley and Los Angeles: Univ. of California Press, 1949
   Experience and Prediction. An Analysis of the Foundations and the Structure of Knowledge, Chicago: Univ. of Chic. Press, 1938
   Philosophic Foundations of Quantum Mechanics, Berkeley and Los Angeles: Univ. of California Press, 1944. Ger. transl., Basel: Birkhauser, 1949

Reichenbach, H. (*continued*)
  Elements of Symbolic Logic, New York: Macmillan, 1947
  The Rise of Scientific Philosophy, Berkeley and Los Angeles: Univ. of
    California Press, 1951. Ger. transl., Berlin-Grunewald: Herbig, 1953
  Nomological Statements and Admissible Operations, Amsterdam: N.-
    Holland Pub. Co., 1954
  The Direction of Time (ed. M. Reichenbach), Berkeley and Los Angeles:
    Univ. of California Press, 1956
Richards, I. A., and Ogden, C. K., *The Meaning of Meaning,* London: Kegan
    Paul, 1923
Robinson, R., *Definition,* Oxford: Clarendon Press, 1950
Rougier, L., *Les paralogismes du rationalisme,* Paris: Alcan, 1920
  La structure des théories déductives, Paris: Alcan, 1921
  Traité de la connaissance, Paris: Gauthier-Villars, 1955
Russell, B., *A Critical Exposition of the Philosophy of Leibniz,* Cambridge:
    Univ. Press, 1900, second ed., London: Allen and Unwin, 1937
  The Principles of Mathematics, Cambridge: Univ. Press, 1903; 2nd ed.,
    London: Allen and Unwin, 1937; New York: Norton, 1938
  Philosophical Essays, London and New York: Longmans, 1910
  The Problems of Philosophy, Home University Library, 1912
  Our Knowledge of the External World, Chicago and London: Open
    Court Publishing Company, 1914. 2nd ed. London: Allen and Un-
    win, 1926.
  Mysticism and Logic, London: Longmans, 1918; now Allen and Unwin
  Introduction to Mathematical Philosophy, London: Allen and Unwin, 1919
  The Analysis of Mind, London: Allen and Unwin; New York: Macmillan,
    1921
  The Analysis of Matter, London: Kegan Paul, 1927
  An Outline of Philosophy, London: Allen and Unwin; New York: Norton,
    1927
  An Inquiry into Meaning and Truth, London: Allen and Unwin; New
    York: Norton, 1940
  A History of Western Philosophy, London: Allen and Unwin; New York:
    Simon and Schuster, 1946
  Human Knowledge: Its Scope and Limits, London: Allen and Unwin;
    New York: Simon and Schuster, 1948
  Logic and Knowledge, Essays 1901-1950 (ed. R. C. Marsh), London:
    Allen and Unwin, 1956
Russell, B. and Whitehead, A. N., *Principia Mathematica,* Cambridge: Univ.
    Press, Vol. I, 1910; Vol. II, 1912; Vol. III, 1913, second ed., 1925-1927
Ryle, G., *Philosophical Arguments.* Inaugural Lecture. London: Oxford Univ.
    Press, 1945. Reprinted in the present volume
  The Concept of Mind, London: Hutchinson, 1949
  Dilemmas, Cambridge: Univ. Press, 1954
Santillana, G. de and Zilsel, E., *The Development of Rationalism and Em-
    piricism,* Chicago: Univ. of Chic. Press (Int. Encycl. of Unified
    Science), 1941
Schächter, J., *Prolegomena zu einer kritischen Grammatik,* Vienna: Springer,
    1935
Schlick, M., *Raum und Zeit in der gegenwärtigen Physik,* Berlin: Springer,
    1917; 2nd ed. 1919. Eng. transl., *Space and Time in Contemporary
    Physics,* Oxford: Clarendon Press, 1920

Schlick, M. (*continued*)
  Allgemeine Erkenntnislehre, Berlin: Springer, 1918
  Vom Sinn des Lebens, Berlin: Weltkreis Verlag, 1927
  Fragen der Ethik, Vienna: Springer, 1930. Eng. transl., *Problems of Ethics,* New York: Prentice-Hall, 1939
  Gesammelte Aufsätze 1926-36, Vienna: Gerold, 1938
  Gesetz, Kausalität und Wahrscheinlichkeit, Vienna: Gerold, 1948
  Grundzüge der Naturphilosophie, posthumous papers ed. W. Holitscher and J. Rauscher, Vienna: Gerold, 1948. Eng. transl., *Philosophy of Nature,* New York: Philosophical Library, 1949
  Natur und Kultur, posthumous papers ed. J. Rauscher, Vienna: Humboldt Verlag, 1952
Schlick, M. and Hertz, P. (eds.), Helmholtz, H., *Schriften zur Erkenntnistheorie,* Berlin: Springer, 1921
Schultzer, B., *Observation and Protocol Statement,* London: Williams and Norgate, 1938
Stebbing, L. S., *Logical Positivism and Analysis,* British Academy Annual Philosophical Lecture, 1933
  Philosophy and the Physicists, London: Methuen, 1937
Stevenson, C. L., *Ethics and Language,* New Haven: Yale Univ. Press, 1945
Strawson, P. F., *Introduction to Logical Theory,* London: Methuen, 1952
Stroll, A., *The Emotive Theory of Ethics,* Berkeley: Univ. of California Press, 1954
Tarski, A., *Einführung in die Mathematische Logik und die Methodologie der Mathematik,* Vienna: Springer, 1937. Eng. transl., *Introduction to Logic and to the Methodology of the Deductive Sciences,* London: Oxford Univ. Press, 1941
  Logic, Semantics, Meta-Mathematics, Oxford: Clarendon Press, 1956
Toulmin, S. E., *The Place of Reason in Ethics,* Cambridge: Univ. Press, 1950
  Philosophy of Science, London: Hutchinson, 1953
  The Uses of Argument, Cambridge: Univ. Press, 1958
Ullman, S., *The Principles of Semantics,* Glasgow: Jackson, 1951; Oxford: Blackwell, 1958
Urmson, J. O., *Philosophical Analysis,* Oxford: Clarendon Press, 1956
Waismann, F., *Einführung in das mathematische Denken,* Vienna: Springer, 1936. Eng. transl., *Introduction to Mathematical Thinking,* London: Hafner, 1951
Warnock, G. J., *English Philosophy Since 1900,* London: Oxford Univ. Press, 1958
Weinberg, J. K., *An Examination of Logical Positivism,* London: Kegan Paul; New York: Harcourt Brace, 1936
Weldon, T. D., *The Vocabulary of Politics,* London: Penguin, 1953
Weyl, H., *Philosophie der Mathematik und Naturwissenschaft,* Munich and Berlin, 1927. Eng. transl. (revised), *Philosophy of Mathematics and Natural Science,* Princeton: Princeton Univ. Press, 1949
White, A. R., *G. E. Moore. A Critical Exposition,* Oxford: Blackwell, 1958
White, M., *Toward Reunion in Philosophy,* Cambridge: Harvard Univ. Press, 1956
Whitehead, A. N., *An Enquiry Concerning the Principles of Natural Knowledge,* Cambridge: Univ. Press, 1919
  The Concept of Nature, Cambridge: Univ. Press, 1920

Whitehead, A. N. and Russell, B., *Principia Mathematica,* Cambridge: Univ. Press, Vol. I, 1910; Vol. II, 1912; Vol. III, 1913, second ed., 1925-1927

Williams, D., *The Ground of Induction,* Cambridge: Harvard Univ. Press, 1947

Wisdom, John, *Interpretation and Analysis.* Psyche Miniature, London: Kegan Paul, 1931

    Problems of Mind and Matter, Cambridge: Univ. Press, 1934

    Other Minds, Oxford: Blackwell, 1952

    Philosophy and Psycho-Analysis, Oxford: Blackwell, 1953

Wisdom, J. O., *Causation and the Foundations of Science,* Paris: Hermann, 1946

    The Metamorphosis of Philosophy, Cairo: Al-Maaref Press, 1947

    Foundations of Inference in Natural Science, London: Methuen, 1952

Wittgenstein, L., *Tractatus Logico-Philosophicus (Logisch-Philosophische Abhandlung),* German version in *Annalen der Naturphilosophie,* 1921; German and English, London: Kegan Paul, 1922

    Philosophical Investigations, Oxford: Blackwell; New York: Macmillan, 1953

    Remarks on the Foundations of Mathematics, Oxford: Blackwell, 1956

    The Blue and Brown Books, Oxford: Blackwell, 1958

Woodger, J. H., *Biological Principles,* London: Kegan Paul, 1929

    The Axiomatic Method in Biology, London: Cambridge Univ. Press, 1937

    The Technique of Theory Construction, Chicago: Univ. of Chic. Press (Int. Encycl. of Unified Science), 1939

    Biology and Language, Cambridge: Cambridge Univ. Press, 1952

von Wright, G. H., *The Logical Problem of Induction,* Helsinki: Acta Philosophica Fennica, Fasc. 3, 1941; 2nd rev. ed., Oxford: Blackwell, 1957

    Den logiska Empirismen, Helsinki, 1943

    A Treatise on Induction and Probability, London: Routledge and Kegan Paul, 1951

Zilsel, E., *Das Anwendungsproblem. Ein philosophischer Versuch über das Gesetz der grossen Zahlen und die Induktion,* Leipzig: Barth, 1916

Zilsel, E. and Santillana, G. de, *The Development of Rationalism and Empiricism,* Chicago: Univ. of Chic. Press (Int. Encycl. of Unified Science), 1941

Zuurdeeg, W. F., *A Research on the Consequences of the Vienna Circle Philosophy for Ethics,* Utrecht: Kemink en Zoon, N. U., 1946

ARTICLES

The following abbreviations are used in this list:

A for *Analysis*
AJ for *Australasian Journal of Psychology and Philosophy*
Arch. F. Sy. Phil. for *Archiv für Systematische Philosophie*
Ar.Soc. for *Proceedings of the Aristotelian Society*
Ar.Soc.Sup. for *Proceedings of the Aristotelian Society, Supplementary Volumes*
BJPS for *The British Journal for the Philosophy of Science*
E for *Erkenntnis*
HJ for *Hibbert Journal*
JP for *Journal of Philosophy*

JSL for *Journal of Symbolic Logic*
JUS for *Journal of Unified Science*
M for *Mind*
P for *Philosophy*
PPR for *Philosophy and Phenomenological Research*
PQ for *Philosophical Quarterly*
PR for *Philosophical Review*
PS for *Philosophy of Science*
PSt for *Philosophical Studies*
Psych. Rev. for *Psychological Review*
Rev.Int.Phil. for *Revue Internationale de Philosophie*
RM for *Review of Metaphysics*
T for *Theoria*

Acton, H. B., "The Expletive Theory of Morals," *A*, 1936-37
  "Is Ethical Relativity Necessary?" *Ar.Soc.Sup.*, 1938
  "Moral Subjectivism," *A*, 1948-49
Adams, E. M., "A Critique of the Emotive Theory of Ethical Terms," *JP*, 1949
  "Word-Magic and Logical Analysis in the Field of Ethics," *JP*, 1950
Aiken, H. D., "Emotive 'Meanings' and Ethical Terms," *JP*, 1944
  "Stevenson's *Ethics and Language*," *JP*, 1945
  "Evaluation and Obligation: Two Functions of Judgments in the Language of Conduct," *JP*, 1950. Reprinted in Sellars, H. and Hospers, J., *Readings in Ethical Theory*
  "The Authority of Moral Judgments," *PPR*, 1951-52
  "Definitions, Factual Premises and Ethical Conclusions," *PR*, 1952
  "The Role of Conventions in Ethics," *JP*, 1952
Ajdukiewicz, K., "Zalozenia logiki tradycyjnej" (Assumptions of Traditional Logic), *Przeglad Filozoficzny*, 1926-27
  "Sprache und Sinn," *E*, 1934
  "Das Weltbild und die Begriffsapparatur," *E*, 1934
  "Der logistische Antiirationalismus in Polen," *E*, 1935-36
  "Die syntaktische Konnexität," *Studia Philosophica*, 1935
  "W sprawie powszechnikow" (On Universals), *Przeglad Filozoficzny*, 1935
  "Die wissenschaftliche Weltperspektive," *E*, 1935. Reprinted in English translation in Feigl, H. and Sellars, W., *Readings in Philosophical Analysis*
  "Logic and Experience," *Synthese*, 1950-51
Aldrich, V. C., "Symbolization and Similarity," *Monist*, 1932
  "A Note on the Empirical Meaning of 'possible'," *A*, 1936-37
  "Some Meanings of 'Vague'," *A*, 1936-37
  "Messrs. Schlick and Ayer on Immortality," *PR*, 1938. Reprinted in Feigl, H. and Sellars, W., *Readings in Philosophical Analysis*
  "The Spirit of the New Positivism," *JP*, 1940

Aldrich, V. C. (*continued*)
  "Pictorial Meaning and Picture Thinking," *Kenyon Review*, 1943. Reprinted in Feigl, H. and Sellars, W., *Readings in Philosophical Analysis*
  "Language, Experience and Pictorial Meaning," *JP*, 1948
  "The Informal Logic of the Employment of Expressions," *PR*, 1954
  "The Last Word on Being Red and Blue All Over," *PSt*, 1954
  "The Origin of the *Apriori*," *JP*, 1954
  "What Appears?," *PR*, 1954
  "Is an After-Image a Sense-Datum?," *PPR*, 1954-55
  "Mr. Quine on Meaning, Naming, and Purporting to Name," *PSt*, 1955
  "Expression by Enactment," *PPR*, 1955-56
Alexander, H. G., "Necessary Truth," *M*, 1957
Alexander, P., "Other People's Experiences," *Ar.Soc.*, 1950-51
  "Complementary Descriptions," *M*, 1956
Alston, W. P., "Are Positivists Metaphysicians?," *PR*, 1954
  "Particulars—Bare and Qualified," *PPR*, 1954-55
  "Pragmatism and the Verifiability Theory of Meaning," *PSt*, 1955
  "Ineffability," *PR*, 1956
  "Is a Sense-Datum Language Necessary?," *PS*, 1957
Ambrose, A., "Finitism in Mathematics, I and II," *M*, 1935
  "Moore's Proof of an External World," in Schilpp, P. A., *The Philosophy of G. E. Moore*, 1942
  "Self-contradictory Suppositions," *M*, 1944
  "The Problem of Justifying Inductive Inference," *JP*, 1947. Reprinted in Hook, S., *American Philosophers at Work*
  "Everett J. Nelson on 'The Relation of Logic to Metaphysics,'" *PR*, 1949
  "The Problem of Linguistic Inadequacy," in Black, M., *Philosophical Analysis*, 1950
  "Linguistic Approaches to Philosophical Problems," *JP*, 1952
  "Wittgenstein on Some Questions in the Foundations of Mathematics," *JP*, 1955
  "On Entailment and Logical Necessity," *Ar.Soc.*, 1955-56
Anderson, J., "The Meaning of Good," *AJ*, 1942
  "Hypotheticals," *AJ*, 1952
Anscombe, G. E. M., "The Reality of the Past," in Black, M., *Philosophical Analysis*, 1950
  "The Principle of Individuation," *Ar.Soc.Sup.*, 1953
  "Aristotle and the Sea Battle," *M*, 1956
  "Intention," *Ar.Soc.*, 1956-57
  "Pretending," *Ar.Soc.Sup.*, 1958
Armstrong, J. H., "Knowledge and Belief," *A*, 1952-53
Ashby, R. W., "Use and Verification," *Ar.Soc.*, 1955-56
von Aster, E., "Kritischer Objektivismus und Neopositivismus," *T*, 1950
  "Physikalistischer und Psychologistischer Positivismus," *T*, 1950
Atkinson, R. F., "'Good' and 'Right' and 'Probable' in *Language, Truth and Logic*," *M*, 1955
Austin, J. L., "Are There A Priori Concepts?," *Ar.Soc.Sup.*, 1939
  "Other Minds," *Ar.Soc.Sup.*, 1946. Reprinted in Flew, A., *Logic and Language* (second series)
  "Truth," *Ar.Soc.Sup.*, 1950
  "How to Talk," *Ar.Soc.*, 1952-53

Austin, J. L. (*continued*)
"A Plea for Excuses," *Ar.Soc.*, 1956-57
"Pretending," *Ar.Soc.Sup.*, 1958
Ayer, A. J., "Atomic Propositions," *A*, 1933-34
"The Genesis of Metaphysics," *A*, 1933-34. Reprinted in Macdonald, M.,
    Philosophy and Analysis
"On Particulars and Universals," *Ar.Soc.*, 1933-34
"Demonstration of the Impossibility of Metaphysics," *M*, 1934. Reprinted
    in Edwards, P. and Pap, A., *A Modern Introduction to Philosophy*
"Internal Relations," *Ar.Soc.Sup.*, 1935
"The Criterion of Truth," *A*, 1935-36. Reprinted in Macdonald, M.,
    Philosophy and Analysis
"The Principle of Verifiability," *M*, 1936
"Concerning the Negation of Empirical Propositions," *E*, 1936-37
"Truth by Convention," *A*, 1936-37
"Verification and Experience," *Ar.Soc.*, 1936-37. Reprinted in the present
    volume
"Does Philosophy Analyse Common Sense?," *Ar.Soc.Sup.*, 1937
"On the Scope of Empirical Knowledge. A Rejoinder to Bertrand Russell,"
    E, 1937-38
"The Terminology of Sense-Data," *M*, 1945. Reprinted in *Philosophical
    Essays*
"Jean-Paul Sartre," *Horizon*, 1945
"Albert Camus," *ibid*.
"Deistic Fallacies," *Polemic*, 1945
"Freedom and Necessity," *Polemic*, 1946. Reprinted in *Philosophical
    Essays*
"The Claims of Philosophy," *Polemic*, 1947. Reprinted in *Reflections on
    Our Age*: Unesco, 1948
"The Principle of Utility," in Keeton, G. W. and Schwarzenberger, G.,
    Jeremy Bentham and the Law, London: Stevens, 1948. Reprinted in
    Philosophical Essays
"Some Aspects of Existentialism," *Rationalist Annual*, 1948
"On the Analysis of Moral Judgements," *Horizon*, 1949. Reprinted in
    Philosophical Essays and in Munitz, M. K., *A Modern Introduction
    to Ethics*
"Basic Propositions," in Black, M., *Philosophical Analysis*, 1950. Re-
    printed in *Philosophical Essays*
"On What There is," *Ar.Soc.Sup.*, 1951. Reprinted in *Philosophical Essays*
"The Philosophy of Science," in Heath, A. E., *Scientific Thought in the
    Twentieth Century*, London: Watts, 1951
"Statements about the Past," *Ar.Soc.*, 1951-52. Reprinted in *Philosophical
    Essays*
"Individuals," *M*, 1952. Reprinted in *Philosophical Essays*
"Negation," *JP*, 1952. Reprinted in *Philosophical Essays*
"Cogito Ergo Sum," *A*, 1952-53
"The Identity of Indiscernibles," in *Proceedings of the XIth International
    Congress of Philosophy*, 1953. Reprinted in *Philosophical Essays*
"L'immutabilité du passé," *Études Philosophiques*, 1953
"One's Knowledge of Other Minds," *T*, 1953. Reprinted in *Philosophical
    Essays*
"Truth," *Rev.Int.Phil.*, 1953

Ayer, A. J. (*continued*)
    "Can There Be a Private Language?," *Ar.Soc.Sup.*, 1954
    "What Is Communication?," in *Studies in Communication*, London: Secker and Warburg, 1955
    "Philosophy at Absolute Zero," *Encounter*, 1955
    'What Is a Law of Nature?," *Rev.Int.Phil.*, 1956
    "Philosophical Scepticism," in Lewis, H. D., *Contemporary British Philosophy* (third series), 1956
    "Perception," in Mace, C. A., *British Philosophy in the Mid-Century*, 1957
    "The Conception of Probability as a Logical Relation," in *Observation and Interpretation: Proceedings of the Ninth Symposium of the Colston Research Society*, 1957
    "Meaning and Intentionality," *Proceedings of the XIIth International Congress of Philosophy*, Venice, 1958
    "Philosophie et langage ordinaire," *Dialectica*, 1958
Ayer, A. J., and Copleston, F. C., "Logical Positivism—a Debate," in Edwards, P. and Pap, A., *A Modern Introduction to Philosophy*
Bachmann, F. and Carnap, R., "Über Extremalaxiome," *E*, 1936-37
Baier, K., "Objectivity in Ethics," *AJ*, 1948
    "Decisions and Descriptions," *M*, 1951
    "The Ordinary Use of Words," *Ar.Soc.*, 1951-52
    "Good Reasons," *PSt*, 1953
    "The Point of View of Morality," *AJ*, 1954
    "Contradiction and Absurdity," *A*, 1954-55
Baier, K. and Toulmin, S. E., "On Describing," *M*, 1952
Bar-Hillel, Y., "Analysis of 'Correct' Language," *M*, 1946
    "Comments on Logical Form," *PSt*, 1951
    "Indexical Expressions," *M*, 1954
    "Logical Syntax and Semantics," *Language*, 1954
Barnes, W. H. F., "A Suggestion about Value," *A*, 1933-34. Reprinted in Sellars, W. and Hospers, J., *Readings in Ethical Theory*
    "Meaning and Verifiability," *P*, 1939
    "The Myth of Sense Data," *Ar.Soc.*, 1944-45
    "Is Philosophy Possible? A Study of Logical Positivism," *P*, 1947
    "Ethics Without Propositions," *Ar.Soc.Sup.*, 1948
    "Talking about Sensations," *Ar.Soc.*, 1953-54
    "On Seeing and Hearing," in Lewis, H. D., *Contemporary British Philosophy* (third series), 1956
Barrett, W., "Logical Empiricism and the History of Philosophy," *JP*, 1939
    "On the Existence of an External World," *JP*, 1939
    "The Present State of the Problem of Induction," *T*, 1940
Barzin, M., "L'empirisme logique," *Rev.Int.Phil.*, 1950
Basson, A. H., "The Existence of Material Objects," *M*, 1946
    "Logic and Fact," *A*, 1947-48
    "The Problem of Substance," *Ar.Soc.*, 1948-49
    "The Immortality of the Soul," *M*, 1950
    "The Logical Status of Supposition," *Ar.Soc.Sup.*, 1951
    "Unsolvable Problems," *Ar.Soc.*, 1956-57
Basson, A. H. and O'Connor, D. J., "Language and Philosophy," *P*, 1947
Baylis, C. A., "Are Some Propositions Neither True Nor False?," *PS*, 1936
    "Critical Comments on the 'Symposium on Meaning and Truth,'" *PPR*, 1944-45

Baylis, C. A. (*continued*)
   "Facts, Propositions, Exemplification and Truth," *M*, 1948
   "Universals, Communicable Knowledge, and Metaphysics," *JP*, 1951
   "The Confirmation of Value Judgments," *PR*, 1952
   "Intrinsic Goodness," *PPR*, 1952-53
   "Logical Subjects and Physical Objects," *PPR*, 1956-57
Beardsley, E., "Imperative Sentences in Relation to Indicatives," *PR*, 1944
Beardsley, M., "Phenomenalism and Determinism," *JP*, 1942
   "Categories," *RM*, 1954
Beck, L. W., "Remarks on the Distinction between Analytic and Synthetic,"
      PPR, 1948-49
   "On the Meta-Semantics of the Problem of the Synthetic *Apriori*," *M*,
      1957
Behman, J., "Sind die mathematischen Urteile analytisch oder synthetisch?,"
      E, 1934
Benjamin, A. C., "Outlines of an Empirical Theory of Meaning," *PS*, 1936
   "The Unholy Alliance of Positivism and Operationalism," *JP*, 1942
   "On Defining Science," *Scientific Monthly*, 1949
   "Operationalism—A Critical Evaluation," *JP*, 1950
   "A Definition of 'Empiricism,' " *PPR*, 1954-55
Bennett, J., "Meaning and Implication," *M*, 1954
Bergmann, G., "On Physicalistic Models of Non-physical Terms," *PS*, 1940
   "On Some Methodological Problems of Psychology," *PS*, 1940. Re-
      printed in Feigl, H. and Brodbeck, M., *Readings in the Philosophy of
      Science*
   "The Subject Matter of Psychology," *PS*, 1940
   "The Logic of Probability," *American Journal of Physics*, 1941
   "An Empiricist Schema of the Psychophysical Problem," *PS*, 1942
   "Remarks Concerning the Epistemology of Scientific Empiricism," *PS*,
      1942
   "Outline of an Empirical Philosophy of Physics," *American Journal of
      Physics*, 1943. Reprinted in Feigl, H. and Brodbeck, M., *Readings
      in the Philosophy of Science*
   "An Empiricist's System of the Sciences," *Scientific Monthly*, 1944
   "Pure Semantics, Sentences and Propositions," *M*, 1944
   "Frequencies, Probabilities and Positivism," *PPR*, 1945-46
   "Remarks on Realism," *PS*, 1946. Reprinted in *The Metaphysics of Logi-
      cal Positivism*
   "Some Comments on Carnap's Logic of Induction," *PS*, 1946
   "Russell on Particulars," *PR*, 1947. Reprinted in *The Metaphysics of
      Logical Positivism*
   "Sense Data, Linguistic Conventions and Existence," *PS*, 1947. Reprinted
      in *The Metaphysics of Logical Positivism*
   "Professor Ayer's Analysis of Knowing," *A*, 1948-49. Reprinted in *The
      Metaphysics of Logical Positivism*
   "Two Criteria for an Ideal Language," *PS*, 1949
   "On Non-perceptual Intuition," *PPR*, 1949-50. Reprinted in *The Meta-
      physics of Logical Positivism*
   "Logical Positivism," in Ferm, V., *A History of Philosophical Systems*,
      1950. Reprinted in *The Metaphysics of Logical Positivism*
   "A Note on Ontology," *PSt*, 1950. Reprinted in *The Metaphysics of
      Logical Positivism*

Bergmann, G. (*continued*)
"Two Cornerstones of Empiricism," *Synthese*, 1950-51. Reprinted in *The Metaphysics of Logical Positivism*
"Logical Atomism, Elementarism and the Analysis of Value," *PS*, 1951. Reprinted in *The Metaphysics of Logical Positivism*
"The Logic of Psychological Concepts," *PS*, 1951
"Two Types of Linguistic Philosophy," *RM*, 1951-52. Reprinted in *The Metaphysics of Logical Positivism*
"The Problem of Relations in Classical Psychology," *PQ*, 1952. Reprinted in *The Metaphysics of Logical Positivism*
"The Identity of Indiscernibles and the Formalist Definition of 'Identity,'" *M*, 1953. Reprinted in *The Metaphysics of Logical Positivism*
"Logical Positivism, Language, and the Reconstruction of Metaphysics," in *Rivista Critica di Storia della Filosofia*, 1953. Reprinted in *The Metaphysics of Logical Positivism*
"The Revolt against Logical Atomism," Parts I and II, *PQ*, 1957 and 1958
Berlin, I., "Induction and Hypothesis," *Ar.Soc.Sup.*, 1937
"Verification," *Ar.Soc.*, 1938-39
"Logical Translation," *Ar.Soc.*, 1949-50
"Empirical Propositions and Hypothetical Statements," *M*, 1950
Black, M., "Philosophical Analysis," *Ar.Soc.*, 1932-33
"A propos of 'Facts,'" *A*, 1933-34
"Is Analysis a Useful Method in Philosophy?," *Ar.Soc.Sup.*, 1934
"The Principle of Verifiability," *A*, 1934-35
"Truth by Convention," *A*, 1936-37
"Vagueness," *PS*, 1937. Reprinted in *Language and Philosophy*
"Some Problems Connected with Language," *Ar.Soc.*, 1938-39. Reprinted as "Wittgenstein's *Tractatus*" in *Language and Philosophy*
"Relations between Logical Positivism and the Cambridge School of Analysis," *JUS*, 1939-40
"Comments on a Recent Version of Phenomenalism," *A*, 1939-40
"Certainty and Empirical Statements," *M*, 1942
"Ogden and Richards' Theory of Interpretation," *JP*, 1942. Reprinted in *Language and Philosophy*
"Schilpp's *The Philosophy of G. E. Moore*," *JP*, 1943
"The Analysis of a Simple Necessary Statement," *JP*, 1943
"The 'Paradox of Analysis,'" *M*, 1944
"Russell's Philosophy of Language," in Schilpp, P. A., *The Philosophy of Bertrand Russell*, 1944. Reprinted in *Language and Philosophy*
"The 'Paradox of Analysis' Again: a Reply," *M*, 1945
"How Can Analysis Be Informative?," *PPR*, 1945-46
"The Limitations of a Behavioristic Semiotic," *PR*, 1947. Reprinted as "The Semiotic of Charles Morris," in *Language and Philosophy*
"The Semantic Definition of Truth," *A*, 1947-48. Reprinted in Macdonald, M., *Philosophy and Analysis*, and in *Language and Philosophy*
"Linguistic Method in Philosophy," *PPR*, 1947-48. Reprinted in *Language and Philosophy*
"Some Questions about Emotive Meaning," *PR*, 1948. Reprinted in *Language and Philosophy*
"Logic and Semantics," in *Philosophical Studies—Essays in Memory of L. Susan Stebbing*, 1948. Reprinted in *Problems of Analysis* as "Carnap on Logic and Semantics"

Bibliography of Logical Positivism

Black, M. (*continued*)
"Carnap's Semantics," *PR*, 1949
"The Definition of Scientific Method," in Stauffer, R. C., *Science and Civilization*, 1949. Reprinted in *Problems of Analysis*
"The Justification of Induction," in *Language and Philosophy*, 1949
"On Speaking with the Vulgar," *PR*, 1949
"Achilles and the Tortoise," *A*, 1950-51. Reprinted in *Problems of Analysis*
"Definition, Presupposition, and Assertion," *PR*, 1952. Reprinted in *Problems of Analysis*
"Phenomenalism," in *Science, Language and Human Rights* (*Proceedings of American Philosophical Association, Eastern Division*), 1952. Reprinted as "The Language of Sense-Data" in *Problems of Analysis*
"The Identity of Indiscernibles," *M*, 1952. Reprinted in *Problems of Analysis*
"Saying and Disbelieving," *A*, 1952-53. Reprinted in *Problems of Analysis*, and in Macdonald, M., *Philosophy and Analysis*
"Metaphor," *Ar.Soc.*, 1954-55
"Why Cannot an Effect Precede its Cause?," *A*, 1955-56
Blanshard, B., "The New Subjectivism in Ethics," *PPR*, 1948-49. Reprinted in Edwards, P. and Pap, A., *A Modern Introduction to Philosophy*
"Subjectivism in Ethics. A Criticism," *PQ*, 1951
Blumberg, A. E., "The Nature of Philosophic Analysis," *PS*, 1935
Blumberg, A. E. and Boas, G., "Some Remarks in Defense of the Operational Theory of Meaning," *JP*, 1931
Blumberg, A. E. and Feigl, H., "Logical Positivism, a New Movement in European Philosophy," *JP*, 1931
Boas, G. and Blumberg, A. E., "Some Remarks in Defense of the Operational Theory of Meaning," *JP*, 1931
Bohnert, H. G., "The Semiotic Status of Commands," *PS*, 1945
"Lewis' Attribution of Value to Objects," *PSt*, 1950
Bouwsma, O. K., "Moore's Theory of Sense-Data," in Schilpp, P. A., *The Philosophy of G. E. Moore*, 1942
"Naturalism," *JP*, 1948
"The Expression Theory of Art," in Black, M., *Philosophical Analysis*, 1950. Reprinted in Elton, W., *Aesthetics and Language*
"The Mystery of Time (or, The Man Who Did Not Know What Time Is)," *JP*, 1954
"Reflections on Moore's Recent Book," *PR*, 1955
Braithwaite, R. B., "Universals and the 'Method of Analysis,'" *Ar.Soc.Sup.*, 1926
"Verbal Ambiguity and Philosophical Analysis," *Ar.Soc.*, 1927-28
"The Nature of Believing," *Ar.Soc.*, 1932-33
"Imaginary Objects," *Ar.Soc.Sup.*, 1933
"Philosophy," in *Cambridge University Studies*, Cambridge Univ. Press, 1933
"Solipsism and 'the Common Sense View of the World,'" *A*, 1933-34
"Propositions about Material Objects," *Ar.Soc.*, 1937-38
"The Relevance of Psychology to Logic," *Ar.Soc.Sup.*, 1938
"Two Ways of Definition by Verification," *E*, 1937-38
"The New Physics and Metaphysical Materialism," *Ar.Soc.*, 1942-43
"Belief and Action," *Ar.Soc.Sup.*, **1946**

Braithwaite, R. B. (*continued*)
"Teleological Explanation," *Ar.Soc.*, 1946-47
"Reducibility," *Ar.Soc.Sup.*, 1952
"Common Action Towards Different Moral Ends," *Ar.Soc.*, 1952-53
"Probability and Induction," in Mace, C. A., *British Philosophy in the Mid-Century*, 1957
Brandt, R., "An Emotional Theory of the Judgment of Moral Words," *Ethics*, 1941-42
"The Emotive Theory of Ethics," *PR*, 1950
"The Status of Empirical Assertion Theories in Ethics," *M*, 1952
"The Languages of Realism and Nominalism," *PPR*, 1956-57
Bridgman, P. W., "Operational Analysis," *PS*, 1938
"Science: Public or Private?," *PS*, 1940
"The Operational Aspect of Meaning," *Synthese*, 1950-51
"The Nature of Some of Our Physical Concepts, I and II," *BJPS*, 1950-52
Britton, K., "Empirical Foundation for Logic," *A*, 1934-35
"Language: Public and Private," *Monist*, 1935
"The Truth of Religious Propositions," *A*, 1935-36
"On Public Objects and Private Objects," *Monist*, 1936
"Reason and the Rules of Language," *Ar.Soc.*, 1938-39
"The Description of Logical Properties," *A*, 1940
"Are Necessary Truths True by Convention?," *Ar.Soc.Sup.*, 1947
"The Nature of Arithmetic—A Reconsideration of Mill's Views," *Ar.Soc.*, 1947-48
"Truth and Knowledge: Some Comments on Russell," *A*, 1947-48
"Seeming," *Ar.Soc.Sup.*, 1952
"What Does a Moral Judgment Commit Me To?," *Ar.Soc.*, 1953-54
"Feelings and their Expression," *P*, 1957
Broad, C. D., "Phenomenalism," *Ar.Soc.*, 1914-15
"Is There Knowledge by Acquaintance?," *Ar.Soc.Sup.*, 1919
"The Character of Cognitive Acts," *Ar.Soc.*, 1920-21
"Critical and Speculative Philosophy," in Muirhead, J. H., *Contemporary British Philosophy* (first series), 1924
"The Principles of Problematic Induction," *Ar.Soc.*, 1927-28
"Is 'Goodness' a Name of a Simple Non-natural Quality?," *Ar.Soc.*, 1933-34
"Mechanical and Teleological Causation," *Ar.Soc.Sup.*, 1935
"Are There Synthetic A Priori Truths?," *Ar.Soc.Sup.*, 1936
"Certain Features in Moore's Ethical Doctrines," in Schilpp, P. A., *The Philosophy of G. E. Moore*, 1942
"Hr. von Wright on the Logic of Induction, I-III," *M*, 1944
"Some of the Main Problems of Ethics," *P*, 1946. Reprinted in Feigl, H. and Sellars, W., *Readings in Philosophical Analysis*
"Some Methods of Speculative Philosophy," *Ar.Soc.Sup.*, 1947
"Some Elementary Reflections on Sense-Perception," *P*, 1952
"The Local Historical Background of Contemporary Cambridge Philosophy," in Mace, C. A., *British Philosophy in the Mid-Century*, 1957
Bronstein, D. J., "Stebbing's Directional Analysis and Basic Facts," *A*, 1934-35
"What Is Logical Syntax?," *A*, 1935-36
"The Meaning of Implication," *M*, 1936
Brotman, H., "Could Space be Four Dimensional?," *M*, 1952. Reprinted in Flew, A., *Essays in Conceptual Analysis*

Brown, D. G., "What the Tortoise Taught Us," *M*, 1954
"Misconceptions of Inference," *A*, 1954-55
"Evaluative Inference," *P*, 1955
"The Nature of Inference," *PR*, 1955
Brown, N., "Sense-data and Material Objects," *M*, 1957
Brown, R. and Watling, J., "Amending the Verification Principle," *A*, 1950-51
"Hypothetical Statements in Phenomenalism," *Synthese*, 1950-51
"Counterfactual Conditionals," *M*, 1952
Buchdahl, G., "Induction and Scientific Method, *M*, 1951
"Inductive Process and Inductive Inference," *AJ*, 1956
"Science and Metaphysics," in Pears, D. F., *The Nature of Metaphysics*, 1957
Buchler, J., "Dr. von Juhos and Physicalism," *A*, 1935-36
"Value-Statements," *A*, 1936-37
"The Class of 'Basic' Sentences," *M*, 1939
"Russell and the Principles of Ethics," in Schilpp, P. A., *The Philosophy of Bertrand Russell*, 1944
Buckley, F. B., "Analysis of 'X Could Have Acted Otherwise,'" *PSt*, 1956
Burks, A. W., "Icon, Index and Symbol," *PPR*, 1948-49
"The Logic of Causal Propositions," *M*, 1951
"Reichenbach's Theory of Probability and Induction," *RM*, 1950-51
"A Theory of Proper Names," *PSt*, 1951
"On the Presuppositions of Induction," *RM*, 1955
Bushkovitch, A. V., "Some Consequences of the Positivistic Interpretation of Physics," *PS*, 1940
Butler, R. J., "The Scaffolding of Russell's Theory of Descriptions," *PR*, 1954
"Aristotle's Sea Fight and Three-Valued Logic," *PR*, 1955
"Language Strata and Alternative Logics," *AJ*, 1955
"A Wittgensteinian on the 'Reality of the Past,'" *PQ*, 1956
Campbell, C. A., "Common-sense Propositions and Philosophical Paradoxes," *Ar.Soc.*, 1944-45
"Ethics without Propositions," *M*, 1950
"Mr. Edwards on 'Ordinary Language and Absolute Certainty,'" *PSt*, 1950
"Is 'Freewill' a Pseudo-Problem?," *M*, 1951. Reprinted in Edwards, P. and Pap, A., *A Modern Introduction to Philosophy*
"Ryle on the Intellect," *PQ*, 1953
Capek, M., "The Development of Reichenbach's Epistemology," *RM*, 1957-58
Capilowish, I. M., "Language Analysis and Metaphysical Inquiry," *PS*, 1949
Capilowish, I. M. and Kaplan, A., "Must There Be Propositions?," *M*, 1939
Carmichael, P., "Prof. Ayer on Individuals," *A*, 1953-54
Carnap, R., "Über die Aufgabe der Physik und die Anwendung des Grundsatzes der Einfachheit," *Kanstudien*, 1923
"Dreidimensionalität des Raumes und Kausalität," *Ann.d.Philos.*, 1924
"Über die Abhängigkeit der Eigenschaften des Raumes von denen der Zeit," *Kanstudien*, 1925
"Eigentliche und uneigentliche Begriffe," *Symposion*, 1927
"Die Mathematik als Zweig der Logik," *Bl.f.Dt.Philos.*, 1930
"Die alte und die neue Logik," *E*, 1930-31. Eng. transl. in the present volume. Fr. transl. in *Actualités Scientifiques*, 1933
"Bericht über Untersuchungen zur allgemeinen Axiomatik," *E*, 1930-31
"Die logizistische Grundlegung der Mathematik," *E*, 1931-32
"Überwindung der Metaphysik durch logische Analyse der Sprache," *E*,

Carnap, R. (*continued*)

1931-32. Eng. transl. in the present volume

"Die physikalische Sprache als Universalsprache der Wissenschaft," *E*, 1931-32. Eng. transl., *The Unity of Science*, London: Kegan Paul, 1934

"Psychologie in physikalischer Sprache," *E*, 1932-33. Eng. transl. in the present volume

"Über Protokollsatze," *E*, 1932-33

"On the Character of Philosophical Problems," *PS*, 1934

"Theoretische Fragen und praktische Entscheidungen," *Natur und Geist*, 1934

"Die Antinomien und die Unvollständigkeit der Mathematik," *Monats. Math.Phys.*, 1934

"Formalwissenschaft und Realwissenschaft," *E*, 1935-36. Reprinted as "Formal and Factual Science" in Feigl, H. and Brodbeck, M., *Readings in the Philosophy of Science*

"Les concepts psychologiques et les concepts physiques sont-ils foncièrement different?," *Revue de Synthese*, 1935

"Die Methode der logischen Analyse," *Actes VIIIème Congrès Intern. de Philos. Scient.*, Paris, 1938

"Wahrheit und Bewährung," *Actes du Congrès Intern. de Philosophie Scientifique, Paris 1935*, 1936

"Über die Einheitssprache der Wissenschaft," *Actes du Congrès Intern. de Philosophie Scientifique, Paris 1935*, 1936

"Exist-t-il des prémisses de la science qui scient incontrolables?," *Scientia*, 1936

"Testability and Meaning, I-IV," *PS*, 1936 and 1937. Reprinted, New Haven: Graduate Philosophy Club, Yale Univ., and (with omissions) in Feigl, H. and Brodbeck, M., *Readings in the Philosophy of Science*

"Logic," in *Factors Determining Human Behavior*, Cambridge: Harvard Univ. Press, 1937

"Einheit der Wissenschaft durch Einheit der Sprache," *Actes IXe Congrès Intern. de Philos.*, Paris, 1937

"Logical Foundations of the Unity of Science," in *Encyclopedia and Unified Science*, Chicago: Univ. of Chic. Press (Int. Encycl. of Unified Science), 1938. Reprinted in Feigl, H. and Sellars, W., *Readings in Philosophical Analysis*

"Science and Analysis of Language," *JUS*, 1940

"The Two Concepts of Probability," *PPR*, 1944-45. Reprinted in Feigl, H. and Sellars, W., *Readings in Philosophical Analysis*, and in Feigl, H. and Brodbeck, M., *Readings in the Philosophy of Science*

"Hall and Bergmann on Semantics," *M*, 1945

"On Inductive Logic," *PS*, 1945

"Remarks on Induction and Truth," *PPR*, 1945-46

"Modalities and Quantification," *JSL*, 1946

"Theory and Prediction in Science," *Science*, 1946

"Probability as a Guide in Life," *JP*, 1947

"On the Application of Inductive Logic," *PPR*, 1947-48

"Remarks on the Paradox of Analysis: A Reply to Leonard Linsky," *PS*, 1949

"Truth and Confirmation," in Feigl, H. and Sellars, W., *Readings in Philosophical Analysis*, 1949

Carnap, R. (*continued*)
"Empiricism, Semantics and Ontology," *Rev.Int.Phil.*, 1950. Reprinted in Linsky, L., *Semantics and the Philosophy of Language*
"The Problem of Relations in Inductive Logic," *PSt*, 1951
"Meaning Postulates," *PSt*, 1952
"On the Comparative Concept of Confirmation," *BJPS*, 1952-53
"Meaning and Synonymy in Natural Languages," *PSt*, 1955. Reprinted in Hook, S., *American Philosophers at Work*
"On Some Concepts of Pragmatics," *PSt*, 1955
"The Methodological Character of Theoretical Concepts," in Feigl, H. and Scriven, M., *Minnesota Studies in the Philosophy of Science*, Vol. I
Carnap, R. and Bachmann, F., "Über Extremalaxiome," *E*, 1936-37
Carritt, E. F., "Moral Positivism and Moral Aestheticism," *P*, 1938. Reprinted in Sellars, W. and Hospers, J., *Readings in Ethical Theory*
Cartwright, R. L., "Ontology and the Theory of Meaning," *PS*, 1954
Chisholm, R. M., "Sextus Empiricus and Modern Empiricism," *PS*, 1941
"The Problem of the Speckled Hen," *M*, 1942
"Russell on the Foundations of Empirical Knowledge," in Schilpp, P. A., *The Philosophy of Bertrand Russell*, 1944
"The Contrary-to-Fact Conditional," *M*, 1946. Reprinted in Feigl, H. and Sellars, W., *Readings in Philosophical Analysis*
"The Problem of Empiricism," *JP*, 1948
"The Theory of Appearing," in Black, M., *Philosophical Analysis*, 1950
"Philosophers and Ordinary Language," *PR*, 1951
"Reichenbach on Observing and Perceiving," *PSt*, 1951
"Verification and Perception," *Rev.Int.Phil.*, 1951
"Comments on the 'Proposal Theory' of Philosophy," *JP*, 1952
"Intentionality and the Theory of Signs," *PSt*, 1952
"Law Statements and Counter-Factual Inference," *A*, 1954-55
"A Note on Carnap's Meaning Analysis," *PSt*, 1955
"Sentences about Believing," *Ar.Soc.*, 1955-56
"Epistemic Statements and the Ethics of Belief," *PPR*, 1955-56
" 'Appear,' 'Take' and 'Evident,' " *JP*, 1956
Church, A., "Logic, Formal," in Runes, D. D., *Dictionary of Philosophy*, 1942
"On Carnap's Analysis of Statements of Assertion and Belief," *A*, 1949-50. Reprinted in Macdonald, M., *Philosophy and Analysis*
"The Need for Abstract Entities in Semantic Analysis," *Proceedings of the Amer. Acad. of Arts and Sciences*, 1951
"Intentional Isomorphism and Identity of Belief," *PSt*, 1954
Chwistek, L., "Zasada sprzeczności w świetle nowszych badań Bertranda Russella" (The Principle of Contradiction in the Light of Recent Investigations of Bertrand Russell), *Rozprawy Akademii Umiejętności*, 1912
"Trzy odczyty odnoszace sie do pojecia istnienia" (Three Lectures Relating to the Concept of Existence), *Przeglad Filozoficzny*, 1917
"Antynomje logiki formalnej" (Antinomies of Formal Logic), *Przeglad Filozoficzny*, 1921
"Über die Antinomien der Prinzipien der Mathematik," *Mathematische Zeitschrift*, 1922
"Zastosowanie metody konstrukcyjnej do teorji poznania" (The Appli-

Chwistek, L. (*continued*)
cation of the Constructive Method to the Theory of Knowledge), *Przeglad Filozoficzny*, 1923
"The Theory of Constructive Types (Principles of Logic and Mathematics)," *Annales de la Société Polonaise de Mathématique*, 1924 and 1925
"Neue Grundlagen der Logik und Mathematik," *Mathematische Zeitschrift*, 1929
"Neue Grundlagen der Logik und Mathematik. Zweite Mitteilung," *Mathematische Zeitschrift*, 1932
"Tragedia werbalnej metafizyki" (The Tragedy of Verbal Metaphysics), *Kwartalnik Filozoficzny*, 1932
"Die nominalistische Grundlegung der Mathematik," *E*, 1932-33
"O granicach nauki" (Concerning the Boundaries of Science), *Sprawozdania Poznanskiego Towarzystwa Przyjaciol Nauk*, 1935
"Rola semantyki racjonalnej w filozofi. Filozoficzne znaczenie logiki semantycznej" (The Role of Semantics in Philosophy. Philosophical Significance of Semantical Logic), *Przeglad Filozoficzny*, 1936
"Rola zasady konsekwencyi w zagadnieniu sprawiedliwosci spolecznej" (The Role of the Principle of Consistency in the Problem of Social Justice), *Przeglad Filozoficzny*, 1936
"Überwindung des Begriffsrealismus," *Studia Philosophica*, 1937
Cobitz, J. L., "The Appeal to Ordinary Language," *A*, 1950-51
Cohen, L. J., "Are Philosophical Theses Relative to Language?," *A*, 1948-49
"Tense Usage and Propositions," *A*, 1950-51. Reprinted in Macdonald, M., *Philosophy and Analysis*
"Three-Valued Ethics," *P*, 1951
"A Relation of Counterfactual Conditionals to Statements of What Makes Sense," *Ar.Soc.*, 1954-55
"On the Use of 'the Use of,' " *P*, 1955
"Theory and Definition in Jurisprudence," *Ar.Soc.Sup.*, 1955
Collingwood, R. G., "On the So-called Idea of Causation," *Ar.Soc.*, 1937-38
Cooley, J. C., "Prof. Goodman's *Fact, Fiction and Forecast*," *JP*, 1957
Copi, I. M., "Modern Logic and the Synthetic A Priori," *JP*, 1949
"Gödel and the Synthetic A Priori: A Rejoinder," *JP*, 1950
"Philosophy and Language," *RM*, 1950-51
"Analytical Philosophy and Analytical Propositions," *PSt*, 1953
"Further Remarks on Definition and Analysis," *PSt*, 1956
Copleston, F. C., "A Note on Verification," *M*, 1950. Reprinted in *Contemporary Philosophy*
"Some Reflections on Logical Positivism," *Dublin Review*, 1950. Reprinted in *Contemporary Philosophy*
"Contemporary British Philosophy," *Gregorianum*, 1953. Reprinted in *Contemporary Philosophy*
"The Function of Metaphysics," *P*, 1953. Reprinted in *Contemporary Philosophy*
"On Seeing and Noticing," *P*, 1954. Reprinted in *Contemporary Philosophy*
"A Further Note on Verification," in *Contemporary Philosophy*, 1956
Copleston, F. C. and Ayer, A. J., "Logical Positivism—A Debate," in Edwards, P. and Pap, A., *A Modern Introduction to Philosophy*, 1957

Cornelius, H., "Zur Kritik der wissenschaftlichen Grundbegriffe," *E*, 1931
Cornforth, M., "Is Analysis a Useful Method in Philosophy?," *Ar.Soc.Sup.*, 1934
Cousin, D. R., "Some Doubts about Knowledge," *Ar.Soc.*, 1935-36
    "Propositions," *Ar.Soc.*, 1948-49
    "Carnap's Theories of Truth," *M*, 1950
    "Truth," *Ar.Soc.Sup.*, 1950
    "How Not to Talk," *A*, 1954-55
Crombie, I. M., "The Possibility of Theological Statements," in Mitchell, B., *Faith and Logic*, 1957
Cross, R. C., "The Emotive Theory of Ethics," *Ar.Soc.Sup.*, 1948
    "Ethical Disagreement," *P*, 1950
Cunningham, G. W., "On the Linguistic Meaning-Situation," *PPR*, 1943-44
Curry, H. B., "Language, Metalanguage, and Formal System," *PR*, 1950
    "Mathematics, Syntactics and Logic," *M*, 1953
Daitz, E., "The Picture Theory of Meaning," *M*, 1953. Reprinted in Flew, A., *Essays in Conceptual Analysis*
Dalkey, N., "The Limits of Meaning," *PPR*, 1943-44
van Dantzig, D., "Carnap's Foundation of Probability Theory," *Synthese*, 1950-51
Demos, R., "Aspects of Positivism," *PPR*, 1952-53
Dewey, J., "Unity of Science as a Social Problem," in Neurath, O. *et al.*, *Encyclopedia and Unified Science*, 1938
Dingler, H., "Über den Aufbau der experimentellen Physik," *E*, 1931-32
Donagan, A., "Recent Criticisms of Russell's Analysis of Existence," *A*, 1951-52
    "The Verification of Historical Theses," *PQ*, 1956
    "Explanation in History," *M*, 1957, reprinted in Gardiner, P., *Theories of History*
Dotterer, R. H., "The Operational Test of Meaninglessness," *Monist*, 1934
Dubislav, W., "Über das Verhältnis der Logik zur Mathematik," *Ann.d.Philos.*, 1925-26
    "Zur kalkülmässigen Charakterisierung der Definitionen," *Ann.d.Philos.*, 1928-29
    "Zur Lehre von den sog. schöpferischen Definitionen," Parts I and II, *Philos.Jahrb.d.Gorresges.*, 1928 and 1929
    "Zur Philosophie der Mathematik und Naturwissenschaft," *Ann.d.Philos.*, 1929
    "Über den sogenannten Gegenstand der Mathematik," *E*, 1930-31
    "Bemerkungen zur Definitionslehre," *E*, 1932-33
Ducasse, C. J., "Verification, Verifiability and Meaningfulness," *JP*, 1936
    "Concerning the Status of So-called 'Pseudo-object' Sentences," *JP*, 1940
    "On the Method of Knowledge in Philosophy," *Cal. Publ. in Phil.*, 1940
    "Propositions, Opinions, Sentences and Facts," *JP*, 1940
    "Truth, Verifiability and Propositions about the Future," *PS*, 1941
    "Moore's Refutation of Idealism," in Schilpp, P. A., *The Philosophy of G. E. Moore*, 1942
    "Propositions, Truth, and the Ultimate Criterion of Truth," *PPR*, 1943-44
    "Facts, Truth, and Knowledge," *PPR*, 1944-45
    "Reality, Science and Metaphysics," *Synthese*, 1950-51
Dummett, M., "Can an Effect Precede its Cause?," *Ar.Soc.Sup.*, 1954

Dummett, M. (*continued*)
"Nominalism," *PR*, 1956
"Constructionalism," *PR*, 1957
Duncan-Jones, A. E., "Ethical Words and Ethical Facts," *M*, 1933
"Universals and Particulars," *Ar.Soc.*, 1933-34
"Definition of Identity of Structure," *A*, 1934-35
"Is Strict Implication the Same as Entailment?," *A*, 1934-35
"Does Philosophy Analyse Common Sense?," *Ar.Soc.Sup.*, 1937
"Further Questions about 'Know' and Think,' " *A*, 1937-38. Reprinted in
    Macdonald, M., *Philosophy and Analysis*
"Lewy's Remarks on Analysis," *A*, 1937-38
"Freedom: An Illustrative Puzzle," *Ar.Soc.*, 1938-39
"More Notes on Assertion," *A*, 1940
"Critical Notice of Stevenson's *Ethics and Language*," *M*, 1945
"Are All Philosophical Questions Questions of Language?," *Ar.Soc.Sup.*,
    1948
"The Concert Ticket," in *Philosophical Studies—Essays in Memory of
    L. Susan Stebbing*, 1948
"Fugitive Propositions," *A*, 1949-50. Reprinted in Macdonald, M., *Phi-
    losophy and Analysis*
"Assertions and Commands," *Ar.Soc.*, 1951-52
"Deadlock in Ethics," *Ar.Soc.Sup.*, 1952
Duncker, K., "Behaviorismus und Gestaltpsychologie (Kritische Bemerkungen
    zu Carnaps 'Psychologie in physikalischer Sprache')," *E*, 1932-33
Dürr, K., "Die Bedeutung der Negation: Grundzüge der empirischen Logik,"
    E, 1935
"Die Einheit der Wissenschaften," *E*, 1937-38
Ebersole, F. B., "Verb Tenses as Expressors and Indicators," *A*, 1951-52
"On Certain Confusions in the Analytic-Synthetic Distinction," *JP*, 1956
Edel, A., "Functional Variability of Ethical Rules," *A*, 1938-39
"The Logical Structure of Moore's Ethical Theory," in Schilpp, P. A.,
    The Philosophy of G. E. Moore, 1942
Edwards, P., "Are Percepts in the Brain," *AJ*, 1942
"Bertrand Russell's Doubts about Induction," *M*, 1949. Reprinted in
    Flew, A., *Logic and Language* (first series), 1951
"Do Necessary Propositions 'Mean Nothing'?," *JP*, 1949
"Necessary Propositions and the Future," *JP*, 1949
"Ordinary Language and Absolute Certainty," *PSt*, 1950
"The Cosmological Argument," *Rationalist Annual*, 1959
Einstein, A., "Physics and Reality," *Journal of the Franklin Institute*, 1936
"Remarks on Bertrand Russell's Theory of Knowledge," in Schilpp, P. A.,
    The Philosophy of Bertrand Russell, 1944
Epstein, J., "Professor Ayer on Sense-Data," *JP*, 1956
"Quine's Gambit Accepted," *JP*, 1958
Evans, E., "Notes on the Symbolic Process," *M*, 1951
Evans, J. L., "On Meaning and Verification," *M*, 1953
Ewing, A. C., "A Defense of Causality," *Ar.Soc.*, 1932-33
"Two Kinds of Analysis," *A*, 1934-35
"Mechanical and Teleological Causation," *Ar.Soc.Sup.*, 1935
"Meaninglessness," *M*, 1937. Reprinted in Edwards, P. and Pap, A., *A
    Modern Introduction to Philosophy*

Ewing, A. C. (*continued*)
   "The Linguistic Theory of A Priori Propositions," *Ar.Soc.*, 1939-40
   "Subjectivism and Naturalism in Ethics," *M*, 1944. Reprinted in Sellars,
      W. and Hospers, J., *Readings in Ethical Theory*
   "The Causal Argument for Physical Objects," *Ar.Soc.Sup.*, 1945
   "Is Metaphysics Impossible?," *A*, 1947-48
   "Philosophical Analysis," in *Philosophical Studies*—Essays in Memory
      of L. Susan Stebbing, 1948
   "Mental Acts," *M*, 1948
   "Moral Subjectivism, a Reply to Professor Acton," *A*, 1948-49
   "Philosophical Analysis In Ethics," *PSt*, 1950
   "Causality and Induction," *PPR*, 1951-52
   "Professor Ryle's Attack on Dualism," *Ar.Soc.*, 1952-53
   "The Relation between Mind and Body as a Problem for the Philosopher,"
      P, 1954
   "The Necessity of Metaphysics," in Lewis, H. D., *Contemporary British
      Philosophy* (third series), 1956
   "Pseudo-Solutions," *Ar.Soc.*, 1956-57
   "Recent Developments in British Ethical Thought," in Mace, C. A.,
      British Philosophy in the Mid-Century
Falk, W. D., "Goading and Guiding," *M*, 1953
Farrell, B. A., "An Appraisal of Therapeutic Positivism, I and II," *M*, 1946
   "Experience," *M*, 1950
   "Intentionality and the Theory of Signs," *PPR*, 1954-55
Feibleman, J. K., "A Reply to Bertrand Russell's Introduction to the Second
      Edition of *The Principles of Mathematics*," in Schilpp, P. A., *The
      Philosophy of Bertrand Russell*, 1944
   "The Metaphysics of Logical Positivism," *RM*, 1951-52
Feigl, H., "Wahrscheinlichkeit und Erfahrung," *E*, 1930-31
   "Logical Analysis of the Psychophysical Problem," *PS*, 1934
   "The Logical Character of the Principle of Induction," *PS*, 1934. Re-
      printed in Feigl, H. and Sellars, W., *Readings in Philosophical
      Analysis*
   "Sense and Nonsense in Scientific Realism," *Actes du Congrès Intern. de
      Philos. Scientifique, Paris 1935*, 1936
   "Moritz Schlick," *E*, 1937-38
   "Logical Empiricism," in Runes, D. D., *Twentieth Century Philosophy*,
      1943. Reprinted in Feigl, H. and Sellars, W., *Readings in Philosophi-
      cal Analysis*
   "Operationism and Scientific Method," *Psych.Rev.*, 1945. Reprinted in
      Feigl, H. and Sellars, W., *Readings in Philosophical Analysis*
   "Some Remarks on the Meaning of Scientific Explanation," *Psych.Rev.*,
      1948. Reprinted in Feigl, H. and Sellars, W., *Readings in Philo-
      sophical Analysis*
   "De Principiis Non Disputandum," in Black, M., *Philosophical Analysis*,
      1950
   "Existential Hypotheses," *PS*, 1950
   "Logical Reconstruction, Realism and Pure Semiotic," *PS*, 1950
   "The Mind-Body Problem in the Development of Logical Empiricism,"
      Rev.Int.Phil., 1950
   "Confirmability and Confirmation," *Rev.Int.Phil.*, 1951
   "Scientific Method without Metaphysical Presuppositions," *PSt*, 1954

Feigl, H. (*continued*)
"Other Minds and the Egocentric Predicament," *JP*, 1958
"The 'Mental' and the 'Physical,' " in Feigl, H., Scriven, M. and Maxwell,
G., *Minnesota Studies in the Philosophy of Science*, Vol. II, 1958
Feigl, H. and Blumberg, A. E., "Logical Positivism, a New Movement in Euro-
pean Philosophy," *JP*, 1931
Feuer, L. S., "Mechanism, Physicalism and the Unity of Science," *PPR*, 1948-49
"The Paradox of Verifiability," *PPR*, 1951-52
"Political Myths and Metaphysics," *PPR*, 1955
Feyerabend, P. K., "Wittgenstein's *Philosophical Investigations*," *PR*, 1955
"A Note on the Paradox of Analysis," *PSt*, 1956
"An Attempt at a Realistic Interpretation of Experience," *Ar.Soc.*, 1957-58
Findlay, J. N., "Some Reactions to Recent Cambridge Philosophy I and II,"
AJ, 1940 and 1941
"Time: A Treatment of Some Puzzles," *AJ*, 1941. Reprinted in Flew, A.,
Logic and Language (first series)
"Gödelian Sentences: A Non-Numerical Approach," *M*, 1942
"Morality by Convention," *M*, 1944
"Can God's Existence Be Disproved?," *M*, 1948. Reprinted in Flew, A.
and MacIntyre, A., *New Essays in Philosophical Theology*
"Recommendations Regarding the Language of Introspection," *PPR*,
1948-49
"Is There Knowledge by Acquaintance?," *Ar.Soc.Sup.*, 1949
"Linguistic Approach to Psycho-Physics," *Ar.Soc.*, 1949-50
"Probability without Nonsense," *PQ*, 1952
"On Having in Mind," *P*, 1953
"Wittgenstein's *Philosophical Investigations*," *Rev.Int.Phil.*, 1953
"The Justification of Attitudes," *M*, 1954
"An Examination of Tenses," in Lewis, H. D., *Contemporary British
Philosophy* (third series)
Firth, R., "Sense-data and the Percept Theory, I and II," *M*, 1949 and 1950
"Radical Empiricism and Perceptual Relativity, I and II," *PR*, 1950
"Phenomenalism," in *Science, Language, and Human Rights*. American
Philosophical Association, Eastern Division, 1952
Fitch, F. B., "The Reality of Propositions," *RM*, 1955-56
Flew, A., "Can an Effect Precede its Cause?," *Ar.Soc.Sup.*, 1954
"Divine Omnipotence and Human Freedom," *HJ*, 1954-55. Reprinted in
a lengthened version in Flew, A. and MacIntyre, A., *New Essays in
Philosophical Theology*
"The Third Maxim," *Rationalist Annual*, 1955
"Philosophy and Language," *PQ*, 1955. Reprinted in *Essays in Concep-
tual Analysis*
"Effects before their Causes? Addenda and Corrigenda," *A*, 1955-56
"Can a Man Witness His Own Funeral?," *HJ*, 1955-56
"Determinism and Validity Again," *Rationalist Annual*, 1958
Flew, A. and MacKinnon, D. M., "Creation," *Church Quarterly Review*, 1955.
Reprinted in Flew, A. and MacIntyre, A., *New Essays in Philosophi-
cal Theology*, 1955
Foot, P. R., "When Is a Principle a Moral Principle?," *Ar.Soc.Sup.*, 1954
Foster, M. B., " 'We' in Modern Philosophy," in Mitchell, B., *Faith and Logic*,
1957

Frank, P., "Kausalgesetz und Erfahrung," *Annalen der Naturphil.*, 1907. Reprinted in Eng. transl. in *Modern Science and Its Philosophy*
"Die Bedeutung der physikalischen Erkenntnistheorie Ernst Machs für das Geistesleben der Gegenwart," *Naturwissenschaften*, 1917. Reprinted in Eng. transl. in *Modern Science and Its Philosophy*
"Wissenschaft und Theologie," *Freier Gedanke*, 1920
"Über die Anschaulichkeit physikalischer Theorien," *Naturwissenschaften*, 1928
"Was bedeuten die gegenwärtigen physikalischen Theorien für die Allgemeine Erkenntnislehre?," *Naturwissenschaften*, 1929, and *E*, 1930-31. Reprinted in Eng. transl. in *Modern Science and Its Philosophy*
"Der Charakter der heutigen physikalischen Theorien," *Scientia*, 1931
"La physique contemporaine manifeste-t-elle une tendence à rintégrer un élément psychique?," *Revue de Synthèse*, 1934. Reprinted in *Modern Science and Its Philosophy*
"Logisierender Empirismus in der Philosophie der U.S.S.R.," *Actes du Congrès Intern. de Philos. Scientifique, Paris 1935*, 1936. Reprinted in *Modern Science and Its Philosophy*
"Positivistische oder metaphysische Auffassung der Physik?," *Scientia*, 1935
"The Mechanical versus the Mathematical Conception of Nature," *PS*, 1937. Reprinted in *Modern Science and Its Philosophy*
"Philosophische Deutungen und Missdeutungen der Quantentheorie," *E*, 1936-37. Reprinted in Eng. transl. in *Modern Science and Its Philosophy*
"Was versteht der Physiker unter der 'Grösse' eines Körpers?," *T*, 1937
"Ernst Mach—The Centenary of His Birth," *E*, 1937-38. Reprinted in *Modern Science and Its Philosophy*
"Physik und Logischer Empirismus," *E*, 1937-38
"The Institute for the Unity of Science, Its Background and Purpose," *Synthese*, 1947
"The Place of Logic and Metaphysics in the Advancement of Modern Science," *PS*, 1948. Reprinted in *Modern Science and Its Philosophy*
"The Problem of Physical Reality," *Synthese*, 1948-49
"Comments on Realistic versus Phenomenalistic Interpretations," *PS*, 1950
"Introduction to the Philosophy of Physical Science, on the Basis of Logical Empiricism," *Synthese*, 1950-51
"Metaphysical Interpretations of Science, I and II," *BJPS*, 1950-51
Fränkel, A., "Die heutigen Gegensätze in der Grundlegung der Mathematik," *E*, 1930-31
Frankel, C., "Empiricism and Moral Imperatives," *JP*, 1953
Frankena, W. K., "The Naturalistic Fallacy," *M*, 1939. Reprinted in Sellars, W. and Hospers, J., *Readings in Ethical Theory*
"Obligation and Value in the Ethics of G. E. Moore," in Schilpp, P. A., *The Philosophy of Moore*, 1942
"Ewing's Case against Naturalistic Theories of Value," *PR*, 1948
"Arguments for Non-Naturalism about Intrinsic Value," *PSt*, 1950
"Obligation and Ability," in Black, M., *Philosophical Analysis*, 1950
"Moral Philosophy at Mid-Century," *PR*, 1951
"Natural and Inalienable Rights," *PR*, 1955
Gallie, W. B., "Solipsistic and Social Theories of Meaning," *Ar.Soc.*, 1937-38
"An Interpretation of Causal Laws," *M*, 1939

Gallie, W. B. (*continued*)
"Dr. Ewing on 'Mental Acts,' " *M*, 1948
"The Function of Philosophical Aesthetics," *M*, 1948. Reprinted in Elton, W., *Aesthetics and Language*
"The Limitations of Analytical Philosophy," *A*, 1948-49
"Pleasure," *Ar.Soc.Sup.*, 1954
"Essentially Contested Concepts," *Ar.Soc.*, 1955-56
"Art as an Essentially Contested Concept," *PQ*, 1956
"What Makes a Subject Scientific?," *BJPS*, 1957-58
Gardiner, P. L., "On Assenting to a Moral Principle," *Ar.Soc.*, 1954-55
"Metaphysics and History," in Pears, D. F., *The Nature of Metaphysics*, 1957
Garnett, A. C., "Must Empiricism Be Materialistic and Behavioristic?," *JP*, 1950
"Mind as Minding," *M*, 1952
Gasking, D. A. T., "Mr. Williams on the A Priori," *A*, 1938-39
"Mathematics and the World," *AJ*, 1940. Reprinted in Flew, A., *Logic and Language* (second series)
"Professor Anderson and the *Tractatus Logico-Philosophicus*," AJ, 1949
"The Philosophy of John Wisdom, I and II," *AJ*, 1954
"Causation and Recipes," *M*, 1955
Geach, P. T., "Designation and Truth," *A*, 1947-48
"Necessary Propositions and Entailment Statements," *M*, 1948
"If's and And's," *A*, 1948-49
"Mr. Ill-Named," *A*, 1948-49
"Russell's Theory of Descriptions," *A*, 1949-50. Reprinted in Macdonald, M., *Philosophy and Analysis*
"Subject and Predicate," *M*, 1950
"On What There Is," *Ar.Soc.Sup.*, 1951
"Form and Existence," *Ar.Soc.*, 1954-55
"Entailment," *Ar.Soc.Sup.*, 1958
"On Frege's Way Out," *M*, 1956
Gellner, E., "Analysis and Ontology," *PQ*, 1950-51
"Knowing How and Validity," *A*, 1951-52
"Contemporary Thought and Politics. Review of Laslett, P., *Philosophy, Politics and Society*," *P*, 1957
"Determinism and Validity," *Rationalist Annual*, 1957
George, F. H., "Meaning and Class," *A*, 1952-53
"Epistemology and the Problem of Perception," *M*, 1957
Ginsburg, E. B., "On the Logical Positivism of the Viennese Circle," *JP*, 1932
Gödel, K., "Über formal unentscheidbare Sätze der Principia Mathematica und verwandter Systeme," *Monats.Math.Phys.*, 1931
"Russell's Mathematical Logic," in Schilpp, P. A., *The Philosophy of Bertrand Russell*, 1944
Gomperz, H., "Interpretation," *E*, 1937-38
"The Meanings of 'Meaning,' " *PS*, 1941
Gonseth, F., "L'idée de la loi naturelle," *E*, 1936-37
Goodman, N., "A Query on Confirmation," *JP*, 1946
"The Problem of Counterfactual Conditionals," *JP*, 1947. Reprinted in *Fact, Fiction and Forecast*, and in Linsky, L., *Semantics and the Philosophy of Language*

Goodman, N. (*continued*)
   "Some Reflections on the Theory of Systems," *PPR*, 1948-49
   "On Likeness of Meaning," *A*, 1949-50. Reprinted in Macdonald, M.,
      Philosophy and Analysis, and in a revised version in Linsky, L.,
      Semantics and the Philosophy of Language
   "Sense and Certainty," *PR*, 1952
   "On Some Differences about Meaning," *A*, 1952-53. Reprinted in Mac-
      donald, M., *Philosophy and Analysis*
   "Reply to an Adverse Ally," *JP*, 1957
Goodman, N. and Quine, W. V., "Steps toward a Constructive Nominalism,"
   JSL, 1947
Goodstein, R. L., "Mathematical Systems," *M*, 1939
   "Wittgenstein's *Remarks on the Foundations of Mathematics*," *M*, 1957
Grant, C. K., "Polar Concepts and Metaphysical Arguments," *Ar.Soc.*, 1955-56
   "On Using Language," *PQ*, 1956
   "Certainty, Necessity and Aristotle's Sea Battle," *M*, 1957
Grelling, K., "Philosophy of the Exact Sciences: Its Present Status in Ger-
      many," *Monist*, 1928
   "Realism and Logic: An Investigation of Russell's Metaphysics," *Monist*,
      1929
   "Bemerkungen zu Dubislavs 'Die Definition,' " *E*, 1932-33
   "Identitas Indiscernibilium," *E*, 1937
Grelling, K. and Oppenheim, P., "Der Gestaltbegriff in Lichte der neuen
      Logik," *E*, 1937-38
Grice, H. P., "Personal Identity," *M*, 1941
   "Meaning," *PR*, 1957
Grice, H. P., Pears, D. F. and Strawson, P. F., "Metaphysics," in Pears, D. F.,
      The Nature of Metaphysics, 1957
Grice, H. P. and Strawson, P. F., "In Defense of a Dogma," *PR*, 1956
Griffiths, A. P., "Formulating Moral Principles," *M*, 1956
Grünbaum, A., "Causality and the Science of Human Behavior," *American
      Scientist*, 1952. Reprinted in Feigl, H. and Brodbeck, M., *Readings
      in the Philosophy of Science*
Haas, W., "On Speaking a Language," *Ar.Soc.*, 1950-51
   "Value-Judgments," *M*, 1953
   "Defeasibility," *M*, 1957
Haggstrom, W. C., "On Careful Reasoning in Ordinary Language," *A*, 1951-52
Hahn, H., "Die Bedeutung der Wissenschaftlichen Weltauffassung, insbesondere
      für Mathematik und Physik," *E*, 1930-31
   "Die Krise der Anschauung," in *Krise und Neuaufbau in den Exakten
      Wissenschaften*, 1933
Hall, E. W., "Of What Use Is Metaphysics?," *JP*, 1936
   "Metaphysics," in Runes, D. D., *Twentieth Century Philosophy*, 1943
   "The Extra-Linguistic Reference of Language, I and II," *M*, 1943 and 1944
   "A Categorical Analysis of Value," *PS*, 1947
   "On the Nature of the Predicate 'Verified,' " *PS*, 1947
   "Stevenson on Disagreement in Attitude," *Ethics*, 1947-48
   "The Metaphysics of Logic," *PR*, 1949
   "On Describing Describing," *M*, 1953
   "Practical Reason(s) and the Deadlock in Ethics," *M*, 1955
   "Ghosts and Categorial Mistakes," *PST*, 1956

Hall, E. W. (*continued*)
 "Logical Subjects and Physical Objects," *PPR*, 1956-57
Hallden, S., "What Is a Word?," *T*, 1951
Hamlyn, D. W., "Behaviour," *P*, 1953
 "A Note on Experience," *A*, 1953-54
 "The Stream of Thought," *Ar.Soc.*, 1955-56
 "Analytic Truths," *M*, 1956
Hampshire, S., "Ideas, Propositions and Signs," *Ar.Soc.*, 1939-40
 "The Progress of Philosophy," *Polemic*, 1946
 "Logical Form," *Ar.Soc.*, 1947-48
 "Are All Philosophical Questions Questions of Language?," *Ar.Soc.Sup.*,
  1948
 "Logical Necessity," *P*, 1948
 "Mr. Strawson on Necessary Propositions and Entailment Statements,"
  M, 1948
 "Subjunctive Conditionals," *A*, 1948-49. Reprinted in Macdonald, M.,
  Philosophy and Analysis
 "Fallacies in Moral Philosophy," *M*, 1949
 "Multiple General Sentences," *A*, 1949-50
 "Ryle's *The Concept of Mind*," *M*, 1950
 "Scepticism and Meaning," *P*, 1950
 "Changing Methods in Philosophy," *P*, 1951
 "The Freedom of the Will," *Ar.Soc.Sup.*, 1951
 "The Analogy of Feeling," *M*, 1952
 "Logic and Appreciation," *World Review*, 1952. Reprinted in Elton, W.,
  Aesthetics and Language
 "Self-Knowledge and the Will," *Rev.Int.Phil.*, 1953
 "Dispositions," *A*, 1953-54
 "Identification and Existence," in Lewis, H. D., *Contemporary British
  Philosophy* (third series), 1956
 "On Referring and Intending," *PR*, 1956
 "The Interpretation of Language: Words and Concepts," in Mace, C. A.,
  British Philosophy in the Mid-Century, 1957
 "Metaphysical Systems," in Pears, D. F., *The Nature of Metaphysics*, 1957
Hanson, N. R., "Mr. Pap on Synonymity," *M*, 1951
 "Professor Ryle's 'Mind,'" *PQ*, 1952
 "A Note on Statement of Fact," *A*, 1952-53
Hardie, C. D., "The Formal Mode of Speech," *A*, 1936-37
 "Logical Positivism and Scientific Theory," *M*, 1938
 "The Necessity of A Priori Propositions," *Ar.Soc.*, 1938-39
Hardie, W. F. R., "The Paradox of Phenomenalism," *Ar.Soc.*, 1945-46
 "Ordinary Language and Perception," *PQ*, 1955
Hare, R. M., "Imperative Sentences," *M*, 1949
 "The Freedom of the Will," *Ar.Soc.Sup.*, 1951
 "Universalisability," *Ar.Soc.*, 1954-55
 "Religion and Morals," in Mitchell, B., *Faith and Logic*, 1957
 "Are Discoveries about the Uses of Words Empirical?," *JP*, 1957
Harré, R., "Dissolving the 'Problem' of Induction," *P*, 1957
 ". . . Is True," *AJ*, 1957
Harrison, J., "Can Ethics Do without Propositions?," *M*, 1950
 "Empiricism in Ethics," *PQ*, 1952

Harrison, J. (*continued*)
  "Mr. Malcolm on 'Knowledge and Belief,' " *A*, 1952-53
  "When Is a Principle a Moral Principle?," *Ar.Soc.Sup.*, 1954
Hart, H. L. A., "The Ascription of Responsibility and Rights," *Ar.Soc.*, 1948-49.
    Reprinted in Flew, A., *Logic and Language* (first series)
  "Is There Knowledge by Acquaintance?," *Ar.Soc.Sup.*, 1949
  "Philosophy of Law and Jurisprudence in Britain (1945-52)," *American
    Journal of Comparative Law*, 1953
  "Are There Any Natural Rights?," *PR*, 1955
  "Theory and Definition in Jurisprudence," *Ar.Soc.Sup.*, 1955
Hartmann, M., "Die methodologischen Grundlagen der Biologie," *E*, 1932-33
Hartnack, J., "The Alleged Privacy of Experience," *JP*, 1952
  "Remarks about Experience," *A*, 1952-53
Hartshorne, R., "Metaphysics for Positivists," *PS*, 1935
  "Anthropomorphic Tendencies in Positivism," *PS*, 1941
Hay, W. H., "C. L. Stevenson and Ethical Analysis," *PR*, 1947
  "Bertrand Russell on the Justification of Induction," *PS*, 1950
  "Professor Carnap and Probability," *PS*, 1952
  "Carnap's *Continuum of Inductive Methods*," *PR*, 1953
Hay, W. H. and Weinberg, J. R., "Concerning Allegedly Necessary Non-
    analytic Propositions," *PSt*, 1951
Heath, A. E., "Communication and Verification," *Ar.Soc.Sup.*, 1934
Heath, P. L., "The Appeal to Ordinary Language," *PQ*, 1952
  "Intentions," *Ar.Soc.Sup.*, 1955
Helmer, O., "Languages with Expressions of Infinite Length," *E*, 1937-38
Helmer, O. and Oppenheim, P., "A Syntactical Definition of Probability and
    Degree of Confirmation," *JSL*, 1945
Hempel, C. G., "On the Logical Positivists' Theory of Truth," *A*, 1934-35
  "Some Remarks on 'Facts' and Propositions," *A*, 1934-35
  "The Logical Analysis of Psychology," *Revue de Synthèse*, 1935. Re-
    printed in Feigl, H. and Sellars, W., *Readings in Philosophical Anal-
    ysis*
  "Über den Gehalt von Wahrscheinlichkeitsaussagen," *E*, 1935-36
  "Some Remarks on Empiricism," *A*, 1935-36
  "Eine rein topologische Form nichtaristotelischer Logik," *E*, 1936-37
  "Le Problème de la Verité," *T*, 1937
  "On the Logical Form of Probability-Statements," *E*, 1937-38
  "Vagueness and Logic," *PS*, 1939
  "The Function of General Laws in History," *JP*, 1942. Reprinted in
    Feigl, H. and Sellars, W., *Readings in Philosophical Analysis*, and
    in Gardiner, P., *Theories of History*
  "A Purely Syntactical Definition of Confirmation," *JSL*, 1943
  "Geometry and Empirical Science," *American Math. Monthly*, 1945. Re-
    printed in Feigl, H. and Sellars, W., *Readings in Philosophical Anal-
    ysis*
  "On the Nature of Mathematical Truth," *American Math. Monthly*, 1945.
    Reprinted in Feigl, H. and Sellars, W., *Readings in Philosophical
    Analysis*, and in Feigl, H. and Brodbeck, M., *Readings in the Philos-
    ophy of Science*
  "Studies in the Logic of Confirmation, I and II," *M*, 1945
  "A Note on Semantic Realism," *PS*, 1950

Hempel, C. G. (*continued*)
"Problems and Changes in the Empiricist Criterion of Meaning," *Rev. Int. Phil.*, 1950. Reprinted in Linsky, L., *Semantics and the Philosophy of Language*, and in the present volume
"General System Theory and the Unity of Science," *Human Biology*, 1951
"The Concept of Cognitive Significance," *Proceedings of American Academy of Arts and Sciences*, 1951
"Reflections on Nelson Goodman's *The Structure of Appearance*," *PR*, 1953
Hempel, C. G. and Oppenheim, P., "L'importance logique de la notion de type," *Actes du Congrès Intern. de Philosophie Scientifique, Paris 1935*, 1936
"A Definition of 'Degree of Confirmation,' " *PS*, 1945
"Studies in the Logic of Explanation," *PS*, 1948. Reprinted as "The Logic of Explanation" in Feigl, H. and Brodbeck, M., *Readings in the Philosophy of Science*.
Henderson, G. P., "Metaphysical Thinking," *PQ*, 1953
"Causal Implication," *M*, 1954
"Discussion: Nelson Goodman's *Fact, Fiction and Forecast*," *PQ*, 1956
Henle, P., "Method in Ethics," *Ethics*, 1943
"On the Certainty of Empirical Statements," *JP*, 1947
"Mysticism and Semantics," *PPR*, 1948-49
"The Problem of Meaning," *Proceedings and Addresses of the American Phil. Assn.*, 1956
"The Nature of Analysis," *JP*, 1957
"Do We Discover Our Uses of Words?," *JP*, 1957
Herbst, P., "The Nature of Facts," *AJ*, 1952. Reprinted in Flew, A., *Essays in Conceptual Analysis*
Hertz, P., "Über den Kausalbegriff im Makroskopischen besonders in der Classischen Physik," *E*, 1930-31
"Kritische Bemerkungen zu Reichenbachs Behandlung des Humeschen Problems," *E*, 1936-37
"Regelmässigkeit, Kausalität und Zeitrichtung," *E*, 1936-37
"Sprache und Logik," *E*, 1937-38
Heyting, A., "Die intuitionistische Grundlegung der Mathematik," *E*, 1931-32
"Mathematische Grundlagenforschung Intuitionismus-Beweistheorie," *Ergebnisse der Mathematik*, 1934
Hicks, G. Dawes, "Is There Knowledge by Acquaintance?," *Ar.Soc.Sup.*, 1919
"The Nature of Sensible Appearances," *Ar.Soc.Sup.*, 1926
Hirst, R. J., "Perception, Science, and Common Sense," *M*, 1951
"Mathematics and Truth," *PQ*, 1953
"Sensing and Observing," *Ar.Soc.Sup.*, 1954
Hobart, R. E., "Free Will as Involving Determination and Inconceivable Without It," *M*, 1936
Hofstadter, A., "On Semantic Problems," *JP*, 1938
"Causality and Necessity," *JP*, 1949
"The Causal Universal," *JP*, 1949
"Explanation and Necessity," *PPR*, 1950-51
"Professor Ryle's Category-Mistake," *JP*, 1951
"The Myth of the Whole; A Consideration of Quine's View of Knowledge," *JP*, 1954

Hofstadter, A. (*continued*)
  "Does Intuitive Knowledge Exist?," *PSt*, 1955
Hofstadter, A. and McKinsey, J. C. C., "On the Logic of Imperatives," *PS*, 1939
Hohenemser, K., "Beitrag zu den Grundlagenproblemen in der Wahrschein-lichkeitsrechnung," *E*, 1931-32
Holland, R. F., "The Empiricist Theory of Memory," *M*, 1954
  "Religious Discourse and Theological Discourse," *AJ*, 1956
Holloway, J., "Ethical Qualities," *Ar.Soc.*, 1947-48
Holzapfel, W., "Bemerkungen zur Wissenschaftslehre des Wiener Kreises," *E*, 1937-38
Hosiasson, J., "Definicja rozumowania indukcyjnego" (A Definition of Inductive Reasoning), *Przeglad Filozoficzny*, 1928
  "Why Do We Prefer Probabilities Relative to Many Data?," *M*, 1931
  "La théorie des probabilités est-elle une logique généralisée? Analyse critique," *Actes du Congrès International de Philosophie Scientifique, Paris 1935*, 1936
  "Induction et Analogie," *M*, 1941
Hospers, J., "On Explanation," *JP*, 1946. Reprinted as "What Is Explanation?" in Flew, A., *Essays in Conceptual Analysis*
  "Meaning and Free Will," *PPR*, 1949-50. Reprinted in part in Sellars, W. and Hospers, J., *Readings in Ethical Theory*
  "The Concept of Artistic Expression," *Ar.Soc.*, 1954-55
Hudson, H., "Achievement Expressions," *A*, 1955-56
Hughes, G. E., "Is There Knowledge by Acquaintance?," *Ar.Soc.Sup.*, 1949
Hung, T., "Moritz Schlick and Modern Empiricism," *PPR*, 1948-49
Hutten, E. H., "On Semantics and Physics," *Ar.Soc.*, 1948-49
  "Induction as a Semantic Problem," *A*, 1949-50
  "Probability-Sentences," *M*, 1952
  "Natural and Scientific Language," *P*, 1954
Isenberg, A., "Critical Communication," *PR*, 1949. Reprinted in Elton, W., *Aesthetics and Language*
  "The Esthetic Function of Language," *JP*, 1949
Jensen, J. C., "Ethical Propositions and Their Foundation," *T*, 1941
Johansen, H., "Die Russelsche Theorie der definiten Deskriptionen vom Standpunkt der Sprachwissenschaft aus betrachtet," *T*, 1952
Jones, J. R., "Our Knowledge of Other Persons," *P*, 1950
  "Simple Particulars," *PSt*, 1950
  "Dr. Moore's Revised Directions for Picking Out Visual Sense Data," *PQ*, 1950-51
  "What Do We Mean by an 'Instance'?," *A*, 1950-51
  "Sense Data: A Suggested Source of the Fallacy," *M*, 1954
Jorgensen, J., "Über die Ziele und Probleme der Logistik," *E*, 1932-33
  "Die logischen Grundlagen der Wissenschaft," *Actes du VIIIe Congrès Intern. de Philosophie, Prague 1936*, 1936
  "Imperatives and Logic," *E*, 1937-38
  "Reflexions on Logic and Language," *JUS*, 1939-40
  "Remarks concerning the Concept of Mind and the Problem of Other People's Minds," *T*, 1949
von Juhos, B., "Kritische Bemerkungen zur Wissenschaftstheorie des Physi-kalismus," *E*, 1934
  "Empiricism and Physicalism," *A*, 1934-35

von Juhos, B. (*continued*)
"Some Modes of Speech of Empirical Science," *A*, 1935-36
"Negationsformen empirischer Sätze," *E*, 1936
"The Truth of Empirical Statements," *A*, 1936-37
"Principles of Logical Empiricism," *M*, 1937
"The Empirical and the Grammatical Doubt," *A*, 1937-38
"Empirische Sätze und Logische Konstanten," *JUS*, 1939-40
Kaila, E., "Der Satz vom Ausgleich des Zufalls und das Kausalprinzip," *Annales Universitatis Fennicoe Aboensis*, 1924
"Die Prinzipien der Wahrscheinlichkeitslogik," *Annales Universitatis Fennicae Aboensis*, 1926
"Beiträge zu einer synthetischen Philosophie;" *Annales Universitatis Fennicae Aboensis*, 1928
"Probleme der Deduktion," *Annales Universitatis Fennicae Aboensis*, 1928
"Rudolf Carnap's *Logische Syntax der Sprache*," *T*, 1936
"Logistik und Metaphysik," *T*, 1942
"Physikalismus und Phänomenalismus," *T*, 1942
"Logik und Psychophysik. Ein Beitrag zur theoretischen Psychologie," *T*, 1944
"Wenn . . . so . . . ," *T*, 1945
Kalish, D., "Meaning and Truth," *Univ. of Calif. Publications in Philosophy*, 1950
"Logical Form," *M*, 1952
Kaminsky, J., "Analytic and Synthetic Moral Judgments," *JP*, 1949
"Metaphysics and the Problem of Synonymity," *PPR*, 1953-54
Kanger, S., "The Morning Star Paradox," *T*, 1957
Kaplan, A., "Are Moral Judgments Assertions?," *PR*, 1942
"Definition and Specification of Meaning," *JP*, 1946
"What Good Is 'Truth'?", *PPR*, 1954-55
Kaplan, A. and Capilowish, L. M., "Must There Be Propositions?," *M*, 1939
Kaufman, A. S., "The Analytic and the Synthetic," *PR*, 1953
Kaufmann, F., "Bemergungen zum Grundlagenstreit in Logik und Mathematik," *E*, 1931-32
"Verification, Meaning and Truth," *PPR*, 1943-44
"Scientific Procedure and Probability," *PPR*, 1945-46
"Three Meanings of 'Truth'," *JP*, 1948
"Rudolf Carnap's Analysis of 'Truth,' " *PPR*, 1948-49
Kazemier, B. H., "Remarks on Logical Positivism," *Synthese*, 1946
Keene, G. B., "Mathematical Statements—A Reply to Mr. Hirst," *PQ*, 1955
"Analytical Statements and Mathematical Truth," *A*, 1955-56
Kemeny, J. G., "Carnap on Probability," *RM*, 1951-52
"A Contribution to Inductive Logic," *PPR*, 1952-53
"The Use of Simplicity in Induction," *PR*, 1953
Kemeny, J. G. and Oppenheim, P., "On Reduction," *PSt*, 1956
King, H. R., "Professor Ryle and *The Concept of Mind*," *JP*, 1951
Kneale, M., "Logical and Metaphysical Necessity," *Ar.Soc.*, 1937-38
"What Is the Mind-Body Problem?," *Ar.Soc.*, 1949-50
Kneale, W. C., "The Objects of Acquaintance," *Ar.Soc.*, 1933-34
"Is Existence a Predicate?", *Ar.Soc.Sup.*, 1936. Reprinted in Feigl, H. and Sellers, W., *Readings in Philosophical Analysis*

[416]   *Bibliography of Logical Positivism*

Kneale, W. C. (*continued*)
"Verifiability," *Ar.Soc.Sup.*, 1945
"Truths of Logic," *Ar.Soc.*, 1945-46
"Are Necessary Truths True by Convention?," *Ar.Soc.Supp.*, 1947
"What Can Logic Do for Philosophy?," *Ar.Soc.Sup.*, 1948
"Experience and Introspection," *Ar.Soc.*, 1949-50
"Natural Laws and Contrary to Fact Conditionals," *A*, 1949-50. Reprinted in Macdonald, M., *Philosophy and Analysis*
"Objectivity in Morals," *P*, 1950. Reprinted in Sellars, W. and Hospers, J., *Readings in Ethical Theory*
"Sensation and the Physical World," *PQ*, 1950-51
"Gottlob Frege and Mathematical Logic," in Ayer, A. J. *et al.*, *The Revolution in Philosophy*, 1956
"The Province of Logic," in Lewis, H. D., *Contemporary British Philosophy* (third series), 1956
Knight, H., "The Use of 'Good' in Aesthetic Judgments," *Ar.Soc.*, 1935-36. Reprinted in Elton, W., *Aesthetics and Language*
Kokoszynska, M., "Über den Absoluten Wahrheitsbegriff und einige andere semantische Begriffe," *E*, 1936-37
"Bemerkungen über die Einheitswissenschaft," *E*, 1937-38
Körner, S., "Are All Philosophical Questions, Questions of Language?", *Ar.Soc. Sup.*, 1948
"Entailment and the Meaning of Words," *A*, 1949-50
"On Theoretical and Practical Appropriateness," *Ar.Soc.*, 1951-52
"On Laws of Nature," *M*, 1953
"Truth as a Predicate," *A*, 1954-55
"Some Remarks on Philosophical Analysis," *JP*, 1957
"Reference, Vagueness and Necessity," *PR*, 1957
"Some Types of Philosophical Thinking," in Mace, C. A., *British Philosophy in the Mid-Century*
Kotarbinski, T., "O istocie doswiadczenia wewnetrznego" (On the Essence of Introspective Experience), *Przeglad Filosoficzny*, 1922
"Le réalisme radical," *Proceedings of the 7th Intern. Cong. of Philosophy, Oxford, 1930*, 1931
"Grundlinien und Tendenzen der Philosophie in Polen," *Slavische Rundschau*, 1933
"The Fundamental Ideas of Pansomatism," *M*, 1955
Kraft, J., "Das Problem der Geisteswissenschaft," *E*, 1936-37
Kraft, V., "Grundformen der wissenschaftlichen Methoden," *S-B d. Wiener Akad. der Wissenschaften*, 1925
"Die Grösse eines Körpers gemäss der Relativitätstheorie," *T*, 1940
"Über Moralbegründung," *T*, 1940
"Die Grösse eines Körpers gemäss der Relativitätstheorie-Diskussion," *T*, 1941
"Logik und Erfahrung," *T*, 1946
Ladd, J., "Value Judgments, Emotive Meaning, and Attitudes," *JP*, 1949
"Ethics and Explanation," *JP*, 1952
Laird, J., "Positivism, Empiricism and Metaphysics," *Ar.Soc.*, 1938-39
Lake, B., "Necessary and Contingent Statements," *A*, 1951-52
"A Study of the Irrefutability of Two Aesthetic Theories," in Elton, W., *Aesthetics and Language*, 1954

Lambert, K. J., "On Naming and Claiming," *PSt,* 1956

Langford, C. H., "Moore's Notion of Analysis," in Schilpp, P. A., *The Philosophy of G. E. Moore,* 1942

"A Proof that Synthetic A Priori Propositions Exist," *JP,* 1949

"The Institutional Use of 'The,'" *PPR,* 1949-50

Langford, C. H. and Langford, M., "Logic, I and II," *PPR,* 1951-52 and 1952-53

"Introduction to Logic," *PPR,* 1953-54

"Strict, Causal and Material Propositions," *JP,* 1954

Lazerowitz, M., "The Principle of Verifiability," *M,* 1937

"Tautologies and the Matrix Method," *M,* 1937

"Meaninglessness and Conventional Use," *A,* 1937-38

"The Null Class of Premises," *M,* 1938

"Strong and Weak Verification I," *M,* 1939. Reprinted in *The Structure of Metaphysics*

"Self-Contradictory Propositions," *PS,* 1940

"Moore's Paradox," in Schilpp, P. A., *The Philosophy of G. E. Moore,* 1942. Reprinted in *The Structure of Metaphysics*

"The Existence of Universals," *M,* 1946. Reprinted in *The Structure of Metaphysics*

"The Positivistic Use of 'Nonsense,'" *M,* 1946. Reprinted in *The Structure of Metaphysics*

"Are Self-Contradictory Expressions Meaningless?", *PR,* 1949. Reprinted in *The Structure of Metaphysics*

"Strong and Weak Verification II," *M,* 1950. Reprinted in *The Structure of Metaphysics*

"Substratum," in Black, M., *Philosophical Analysis,* 1950. Reprinted in *The Structure of Metaphysics*

"Negative Terms," *A,* 1951-52. Reprinted in Macdonald, M., *Philosophy and Analysis* and in *The Structure of Metaphysics*

"The Paradox of Motion," *Ar.Soc.,* 1951-52. Reprinted in *The Structure of Metaphysics*

"Logical Necessity," in *The Structure of Metaphysics,* 1955

"The Nature of Metaphysics," in *The Structure of Metaphysics,* 1955

Lejewski, C., "Logic and Existence," *BJPS,* 1954-55

"Proper Names," *Ar.Soc.Sup.,* 1957

Lenz, J. W., "Carnap on Defining 'Degree of Confirmation,'" *PS,* 1956

Lenzen, V. F., "Physical Causality," *Univ. of Calif. Publ. in Philosophy,* 1932

"A Positivistic Theory of Possibility," *Univ. of Calif. Publ. in Philosophy,* 1934

"The Interaction between Subject and Object in Observation," *E,* 1936-37

"Experience and Convention in Physical Theory," *E,* 1937-38

"The Concept of Reality in Physical Theory," *PR,* 1945

Leonard, H. S., "Ethical Predicates," *JP,* 1949

"The Logic of Existence," *PSt,* 1956

Lewis, C. I., "A Pragmatic Conception of the A Priori," *JP,* 1923. Reprinted in Feigl, H. and Sellars, W., *Readings in Philosophical Analysis*

"Alternative Systems of Logic," *Monist,* 1932

"Experience and Meaning," *PR,* 1934. Reprinted in Feigl, H. and Sellars, W., *Readings in Philosophical Analysis*

Lewis, C. I. (*continued*)
"Some Logical Considerations concerning the Mental," *JP*, 1941. Reprinted in Feigl, H. and Sellars, W., *Readings in Philosophical Analysis*
"The Modes of Meaning," *PPR*, 1943-44. Reprinted in Linsky, L., *Semantics and the Philosophy of Language*
"Professor Chisholm and Empiricism," *JP*, 1948
"The Given Element in Empirical Knowledge," *PR*, 1952
"Realism or Phenomenalism?", *PR*, 1955
"Some Suggestions Concerning Metaphysics of Logic," in Hook, S., *American Philosophers at Work*
Lewy, C., "A Note on Empirical Propositions," *A*, 1937-38
"Some Remarks on Analysis," *A*, 1937-38
"On the 'Justification' of Induction," *A*, 1938-39
"Some Notes on Assertion," *A*, 1939-40. Reprinted in Macdonald, M., *Philosophy and Analysis*
"Is the Notion of Disembodied Existence Self-Contradictory?," *Ar.Soc.*, 1942-43
"On the Relation of Some Empirical Propositions to Their Evidence," *M*, 1944
"Entailment and Empirical Propositions," *M*, 1946
"Equivalence and Identity," *M*, 1946
"The Terminology of Sense-Data," *M*, 1946
"Why Are the Calculuses of Logic and Arithmetic Applicable to Reality?," *Ar.Soc.Sup.*, 1946
"Truth and Significance," *A*, 1947-48. Reprinted in Macdonald, M., *Philosophy and Analysis*
"Carnap's *Meaning and Necessity*," *M*, 1949
"Entailment and Necessary Propositions," in Black, M., *Philosophical Analysis*, 1950
"Entailment," *Ar.Soc.Sup.*, 1958
Lieb, I. C., "Wittgenstein's *Investigations*," *RM*, 1954-55
Lindenbaum-Hosiasson, J., "Bemerkungen über die Zurückführung der physischen auf psychische Begriffe," *E*, 1937-38
Linsky, L., "Some Notes on Carnap's Concept of Intensional Isomorphism and the Paradox of Analysis," *PS*, 1949
"A Note on Carnap's 'Truth and Confirmation,' " *PSt*, 1950
"On Using Inverted Commas," *Methodos*, 1950
"On Understanding Philosophical Writings," *PPR*, 1954-55
"Wittgenstein on Language and Some Problems of Philosophy, *JP*, 1957
Lloyd, A. C., "Empiricism, Sense Data and Scientific Languages," *M*, 1950
"Thinking and Language," *Ar.Soc.Sup.*, 1951
Long, P., "Natural Laws and So-called Accidental General Statements," *A*, 1952-53
Lucas, J. R., "The Soul," in Mitchell, B., *Faith and Logic*, 1957
Łukasiewicz, J., "O logice trójwartościowej" (On Three-valued Logic), *Ruch Filozoficzny*, 1920
"Philosophische Bemerkungen zu mehrwertigen Systemen des Aussagenkalküls," *Comptes rendus des séances de la Société des Sciences et des Lettres de Varsovie*, 1930
"Zur Geschichte der Aussagenlogik," *E*, 1935
"Bedeutung der logischen Analyse für die Erkenntnis," *Actes du VIIIe Congrès Intern. de Philosophie, Prague 1936*, 1936

Łukasiewicz, J. (*continued*)
"Die Logik und das Grundlagenproblem," *Les entretiens de Zurich sur les fondéments et la méthode des sciences mathématiques,* 1938
"The Principle of Individuation," *Ar.Soc.Sup.,* 1953
Łukasiewicz, J. and Tarski, A., "Untersuchungen über den Aussagenkalkül," *Comptes rendus des séances de la Société des Sciences et des Lettres de Varsovie,* 1930. Eng. transl. in Tarski, A., *Logic, Semantics, Metamathematics*
Lundberg, G. A., "The Concept of Law in the Social Sciences," *PS,* 1938
"Contemporary Positivism in Sociology," *Amer. Sociol. Rev.,* 1939
"Operational Definitions in the Social Sciences," *Amer. Journal of Sociol.,* 1941-42
Mabbott, J. D., "Negation," *Ar.Soc.Sup.,* 1929
"True and False in Morals," *Ar.Soc.,* 1948-49
"The Specious Present," *M,* 1955
Macdonald, M., "Verification and Understanding," *Ar.Soc.,* 1933-34
"Language and Reference," *A,* 1936-37
"Induction and Hypothesis," *Ar.Soc.Sup.,* 1937
"The Philosopher's Use of Analogy," *Ar.Soc.,* 1937-38. Reprinted in Flew, A., *Logic and Language* (first series)
"Things and Processes," *A,* 1938-39. Reprinted in *Philosophy and Analysis*
"Necessary Propositions," *A,* 1940
"The Language of Political Theory," *Ar.Soc.,* 1940-41. Reprinted in Flew, A., *Logic and Language* (first series)
"Natural Rights," *Ar.Soc.,* 1946-47. Reprinted in Laslett, P., *Philosophy, Politics and Society*
"Some Distinctive Features of Arguments Used in Criticism of the Arts," *Ar.Soc.Sup.,* 1949. Reprinted in Elton, W., *Aesthetics and Language*
"Ethics and the Ceremonial Use of Language," in Black, M., *Philosophical Analysis,* 1950
"Professor Ryle on the Concept of Mind," *PR,* 1951
"Art and Imagination," *Ar.Soc.,* 1952-53
"Linguistic Philosophy and Perception," *P,* 1953
"Sleeping and Waking," *M,* 1953
"Language in Fiction," *Ar.Soc.Sup.,* 1954
Mace, C. A., "Representation and Expression," *A,* 1933-34. Reprinted in Macdonald, M., *Philosophy and Analysis*
"Metaphysics and Emotive Language," *A,* 1934-35
"Mechanical and Teleological Causation," *Ar.Soc.Sup.,* 1935. Reprinted in Feigl, H. and Sellars, W., *Readings in Philosophical Analysis*
"Physicalism," *Ar.Soc.,* 1936-37
"Self Identity," *Ar.Soc.Sup.,* 1939
"On How We Know that Material Things Exist," in Schilpp, P. A., *The Philosophy of G. E. Moore,* 1942
"The Logic of Elucidation," in *Philosophical Studies—Essays in Memory of L. Susan Stebbing,* 1948
"Some Implications of Analytical Behaviorism," *Ar.Soc.,* 1948-49
"Introspection and Analysis," in Black, M., *Philosophical Analysis,* 1950
"Some Trends in the Philosophy of Mind," in *British Philosophy in the Mid-Century,* 1957
MacIntyre, A., "A Note on Immortality," *M,* 1955

MacIntyre, A. (*continued*)
   "Visions," in Flew, A., and MacIntyre, A., *New Essays in Philosophical Theology*, 1955
   "The Logical Status of Religious Belief," in Toulmin, *et al.*, *Metaphysical Beliefs*, 1957
MacIver, A. M., "Demonstratives and Proper Names," *A*, 1935-36. Reprinted in Macdonald, M., *Philosophy and Analysis*
   "Token, Type and Meaning," *A*, 1936-37
   "Some Questions about 'Know' and 'Think,' " *A*, 1937-38. Reprinted in Macdonald, M., *Philosophy and Analysis*
   "More about Some Old Logical Puzzles," *A*, 1938-39
   "Metaphor," *A*, 1940
Mackie, J., "A Refutation of Morals," *AJ*, 1946
   "The Nature of Facts," *AJ*, 1952
   "Responsibility and Language," *AJ*, 1955
MacKinnon, D. M., "Are There A Priori Concepts?," *Ar.Soc.Sup.*, 1939
   "What Is a Metaphysical Statement?," *Ar.Soc.*, 1940-41
   "Verifiability," *Ar.Soc.Sup.*, 1945
MacKinnon, D. M. and Flew, A., "Creation," *Church Quarterly Review*, 1955. Reprinted in Flew, A. and MacIntyre, A., *New Essays in Philosophical Theology*
Macnabb, D. G. C., "Phenomenalism," *Ar.Soc.*, 1940-41
   "The Causal Argument for Physical Objects," *Ar.Soc.Sup.*, 1945
Malcolm, N., "Are Necessary Propositions Really Verbal?," *M*, 1940
   "The Nature of Entailment," *M*, 1940
   "Certainty and Empirical Statements," *M*, 1942
   "Moore and Ordinary Language," in Schilpp, P. A., *The Philosophy of G. E. Moore*, 1942
   "Defending Common Sense," *PR*, 1949
   "Russell's *Human Knowledge*," *PR*, 1950
   "The Verification Argument," in Black, M., *Philosophical Analysis*, 1950
   "Philosophy for Philosophers," *PR*, 1951
   "Knowledge and Belief," *M*, 1952
   "Direct Perception," *PQ*, 1953
   "Moore's Use of 'Know,' " *M*, 1953
   "On Knowledge and Belief," *A*, 1953-54
   "Wittgenstein's *Philosophical Investigations*," *PR*, 1954
   "Dreaming and Skepticism," *PR*, 1956
   "Knowledge of Other Minds," *JP*, 1958
Malfitano, G., "L'unité de l'expérience scientifique selon la positivité véritable conventionellement définée," *E*, 1937-38
Mannoury, G., "Signifische Analyse der Willensprache als Grundlage einer physikalistischen Sprachsynthese," *E*, 1937-38
Marc-Wogau, K., "Bemerkungen zum Begriff 'Sinnesdatum' in der Diskussion der letzten Jahre," *T*, 1950
   "Der Zweifel Descartes und das *Cogito ergo sum*," *T*, 1956
Margenau, H., "Metaphysical Elements in Physics," *Rev. of Modern Physics*, 1941
   "On the Frequency Theory of Probability," *PPR*, 1945-46
Marhenke, P., "Moore's Analysis of Sense-Perception," in Schilpp, P. A., *The Philosophy of G. E. Moore*, 1942

Marhenke, P. (*continued*)
"The Criterion of Significance," *Proceedings and Addresses of the Amer. Phil. Assn.*, 1950. Reprinted in Linsky, L., *Semantics and the Philosophy of Language*
"Phenomenalism," in Black, M., *Philosophical Analysis*, 1950
"Propositions and Sentences," *Univ. of Calif. Publ. in Philosophy*, 1950
Martin, C. B., "Mr. Geach on Mention and Use," *M*, 1949
"Mr. Hanson on Statements of Fact," *A*, 1952-53
"A Religious Way of Knowing," *M*, 1952. Reprinted in Flew, A. and MacIntyre, A., *New Essays in Philosophical Theology*
Martin, R. M., "Some Comments on Truth and Designation," *A*, 1949-50
"On Inscriptions," *PPR*, 1950-51
"On Tarski's 'Semantic Conception of Truth,' " *PPR*, 1950-51
"On 'Analytic,' " *PSt*, 1952
"On the Berkeley-Russell Theory of Proper Names," *PPR*, 1952-53
"On Woodger's Analysis of Biological Language," *RM*, 1954-55
Masterman, M., "Words," *Ar.Soc.*, 1953-54
"Metaphysical and Ideographic Language," in Mace, C. A., *British Philosophy in the Mid-Century*, 1957
Mates, B., "Synonymity," *Univ. of Calif. Publ. in Philosophy*, 1950. Reprinted in Linsky, L., *Semantics and the Philosophy of Language*
"Analytic Sentences," *PR*, 1951
Mayo, B., "Events and Language," *A*, 1949-50. Reprinted in Macdonald, M., *Philosophy and Analysis*
"Is There a Case for the General Will?," *P*, 1950. Reprinted in Laslett, P., *Philosophy, Politics and Society*
"Facts, Feelings and Attitudes," *Ar.Soc.*, 1950-51
"The Logical Status of Supposition," *Ar.Soc.Sup.*, 1951
" 'Rules' of Language," *PSt*, 1951
"Ethics and Moral Controversy," *PQ*, 1954
"Rule-Making and Rule-Breaking," *A*, 1954-55
"Commitments and Reasons," *M*, 1955
"Conditional Statements," *PR*, 1957
McKinney, J. P., "The Status of Theoretical Entities," *AJ*, 1956
"Philosophical Implications of Logical Analysis," *HJ*, 1957
McKinsey, J. C. C. and Hofstadter, A., "On the Logic of Imperatives," *PS*, 1939
McPherson, T., "Ramsey on Rules," *A*, 1951-52
"Positivism and Religion," *PPR*, 1953-54. Reprinted as "Religion as the Inexpressible," in Flew, A. and MacIntyre, A., *New Essays in Philosophical Theology*, 1955
Meckler, L., "The Value-Theory of C. I. Lewis," *JP*, 1950
"Normative and Descriptive Expressions," *JP*, 1953
"On Goodman's Refutation of Synonymy," *A*, 1953-54
"Are 'Indubitable' Statements Necessary?," *M*, 1955
"An Analysis of Belief-Sentences," *PPR*, 1955-56
Mehlberg, H., "Essais sur la théorie causale du temps, I and II," *Studia Philosophica*, 1935 and 1937
"Positivisme et Science, I," *Studia Philosophica*, 1939-40
Melden, A. I., "On the Method of Ethics," *JP*, 1948
"Action," *PR*, 1956
"On Promising," *M*, 1956

Mellor, W. W., "Believing the Meaningless," *A*, 1954-55
   "Three Problems about Other Minds," *M*, 1956
Menger, K., "Intuitionismus," *Zeitschrift f. deutsche Philosophie*, 1930
   "Die neue Logik," in *Krise und Neuaufbau in den exakten Wissenschaften*, 1933
   "The New Logic," *PS*, 1937
Miller, D. L., "Two Kinds of Certainty," *PS*, 1940
Miller, D. S., " 'Descartes' Myth' and Professor Ryle's Fallacy," *JP*, 1951
von Mises, R., "Wahrscheinlichkeitsrechnung," *Naturwissenschaften*, 1919
   "Über die Wahrscheinlichkeit seltener Ereignisse," *Zeitschrift für Angewandte Mathematik und Mechanik*, 1921
   "Über das Gesetz der grossen Zahlen und die Häufigkeitstheorie der Wahrscheinlichkeit," *Naturwissenschaften*, 1927
   "Über kausale und statistische Gesetzmässigkeit in der Physik," *E*, 1930-31
von Mises, R. and Pollaczek-Geiringer, H., "Probability," *Encycl. of Social Sciences*, 1932
Moore, A., "Verifiability and Phenomenalism," *JP*, 1950
   "The Emotive Theory and Rational Methods in Moral Controversy," *M*, 1951
   "The Principles of Induction," *JP*, 1952
Moore, G. E., "The Nature of Judgment," *M*, 1899
   "The Refutation of Idealism," *M*, 1903. Reprinted in *Philosophical Studies* and in Ewing, A. C. (ed.), *The Idealist Tradition*
   "The Nature and Reality of Objects of Perception," *Ar.Soc.*, 1905-6. Reprinted in *Philosophical Studies*
   "Professor James's 'Pragmatism,' " *Ar.Soc.*, 1907-8. Reprinted in *Philosophical Studies*
   "Hume's Philosophy," *The New Quarterly*, 1909. Reprinted in *Philosophical Studies*, and in Feigl, H. and Sellars, W., *Readings in Philosophical Analysis*
   "The Status of Sense-Data," *Ar.Soc.*, 1913-14. Reprinted in *Philosophical Studies*
   "Are the Materials of Sense Affections of the Mind?," *Ar.Soc.*, 1916-17
   "The Conception of Reality," *Ar.Soc.*, 1917-18. Reprinted in *Philosophical Studies*
   "Some Judgments of Perception," *Ar.Soc.*, 1918-19. Reprinted in *Philosophical Studies*
   "Is There Knowledge by Acquaintance?," *Ar.Soc.Sup.*, 1919
   "External and Internal Relations," *Ar.Soc.*, 1919-20. Reprinted in *Philosophical Studies*
   "The Character of Cognitive Acts," *Ar.Soc.*, 1920-21
   "Are the Characteristics of Particular Things Universal or Particular?," *Ar.Soc.Sup.*, 1923
   "A Defence of Common Sense," in Muirhead, J. H., *Contemporary British Philosophy* (second series), 1925
   "The Nature of Sensible Appearances," *Ar.Soc.Sup.*, 1926
   "Facts and Propositions," *Ar.Soc.Sup.*, 1927
   "Indirect Knowledge," *Ar.Soc.Sup.*, 1929
   "Is Goodness a Quality?," *Ar.Soc.Sup.*, 1932
   "Imaginary Objects," *Ar.Soc.Sup.*, 1933
   "Is Existence a Predicate?," *Ar.Soc.Sup.*, 1936. Reprinted in Flew, A., *Logic and Language* (second series)

Moore, G. E. (*continued*)
"A Reply to My Critics," in Schilpp, P. A., *The Philosophy of G. E. Moore*, 1942
"Russell's 'Theory of Descriptions,'" in Schilpp, P. A., *The Philosophy of Bertrand Russell*, 1944
"Addendum to My 'Reply,'" in Schilpp, P. A., *The Philosophy of G. E. Moore* (second edition), 1952
"Wittgenstein's Lectures in 1930-1933, I-III," *M*, 1954 and 1955
"Visual Sense-Data," in *British Philosophy in Mid-Century*, 1957
Morgenbesser, S., "On the Justification of Beliefs and Attitudes," *JP*, 1954
Morris, C. W., "Truth, Action and Verification," *Monist*, 1932
"Philosophy of Science and Science of Philosophy," *PS*, 1935
"The Relation of the Formal and Empirical Sciences within Scientific Empiricism," *E*, 1935
"Some Aspects of Recent American Scientific Philosophy," *E*, 1935
"The Concept of Meaning in Pragmatism and Logical Positivism," *Proceedings of the 8th Intern. Congress of Philosophy*, 1934 (Prague, 1936)
"Science and Discourse," *Synthese*, 1946
Mothersill, M., "The Use of Normative Language," *JP*, 1955
Mundle, C. W. K., "How Specious Is the Specious Present?," *M*, 1954
Murdoch, I., "Thinking and Language," *Ar.Soc.Sup.*, 1951
"Metaphysics and Ethics," in Pears, D. F., *The Nature of Metaphysics*, 1957
Murphy, A. E., "Two Versions of Critical Philosophy," *Ar.Soc.*, 1937-38
"Moore's 'Defense of Common Sense,'" in Schilpp, P. A., *The Philosophy of G. E. Moore*, 1942
Myhill, J., "Two Ways of Ontology in Modern Logic," *RM*, 1951-52
"Some Philosophical Implications of Mathematical Logic. Three Classes of Ideas," *RM*, 1952-53
Naess, A., "Common-Sense and Truth," *T*, 1938
"Über die Funktion der Verallgemeinerung," *E*, 1937-38
"Toward a Theory of Interpretation and Preciseness," *T*, 1949. Reprinted in Linsky, L., *Semantics and the Philosophy of Language*
"Synonymity as Revealed by Intuition," *PR*, 1957
Nagel, E., "Intuition, Consistency, and the Excluded Middle," *JP*, 1929
"Nature and Convention," *JP*, 1929
"Review of A. S. Eddington's *The Nature of the Physical World*," *The Symposium*, 1930. Reprinted as Part I of "Eddington's Philosophy of Physical Science" in *Sovereign Reason*
"Measurement," *E*, 1931-32
"A Frequency Theory of Probability," *JP*, 1933
"Verifiability, Truth and Verification," *JP*, 1934. Reprinted in *Logic without Metaphysics*
"Carnap's *Logische Syntax der Sprache*," *JP*, 1935
"The Logic of Reduction in the Sciences," *E*, 1935
"Impressions and Appraisals of Analytic Philosophy in Europe, I and II," *JP*, 1936. Reprinted in *Logic without Metaphysics*
"The Meaning of Probability," *Journal of Amer. Statistical Assn.*, 1936
"Reichenbach's *Wahrscheinlichkeitslehre*," *M*, 1936
"Some Theses in the Philosophy of Logic," *PS*, 1938
"Probability and the Theory of Knowledge," *PS*, 1939. Reprinted in *Sovereign Reason*

Nagel, E. (*continued*)

"Charles S. Peirce, Pioneer of Modern Empiricism," *PS,* 1940. Reprinted in *Sovereign Reason*

"Mr. Russell on Meaning and Truth," *JP,* 1941. Reprinted in *Sovereign Reason*

"Recent Philosophies of Science," *Kenyon Review,* 1941. Reprinted in *Sovereign Reason*

"Operational Analysis as an Instrument for the Critique of Linguistic Signs," *JP,* 1942

"Malicious Philosophies of Science," *Partisan Review,* 1943. Reprinted in *Sovereign Reason*

"Logic without Ontology," in Krikorian, Y., *Naturalism and the Human Spirit,* 1944. Reprinted in Feigl, H., and Sellars, W., *Readings in Philosophical Analysis* and in *Logic without Metaphysics*

"Russell's Philosophy of Science," in Schilpp, P. A., *The Philosophy of Bertrand Russell,* 1944. Reprinted in *Sovereign Reason*

"Critical Notice of Schilpp's *The Philosophy of G. E. Moore,*" *M,* 1944

"Truth and Knowledge of the Truth," *PPR,* 1944-45. Reprinted in *Logic without Metaphysics*

"Probability and Non-demonstrative Inference," *PPR,* 1944-45

"Some Reflections on the Use of Language in the Natural Sciences," *JP,* 1945

"Sovereign Reason," in Hook, S. and Konvitz, M. R., *Freedom and Experience,* 1947. Reprinted in *Sovereign Reason* and in Ewing, A. C., *The Idealist Tradition*

"William's *The Ground of Induction,*" *JP,* 1947

"Carnap's *Meaning and Necessity,*" *JP,* 1948

"The Basis of Human Knowledge," *The Nation,* 1949. Reprinted in *Sovereign Reason*

"In Defense of Logic without Metaphysics," *PR,* 1949. Reprinted in *Logic without Metaphysics*

"The Meaning of Reduction in the Natural Sciences," in Stauffer, R. C., *Science and Civilization,* 1949

"Einstein's Philosophy of Science," *Kenyon Review,* 1950. Reprinted in *Logic without Metaphysics*

"Reichenbach's *The Theory of Probability,*" *JP,* 1950

"Science and Semantic Realism," *PS,* 1950

"Mechanistic Explanation and Organismic Biology," *PPR,* 1950-51. Reprinted in Hook, S., *American Philosophers at Work*

"The Logic of Historical Analysis," *Scientific Monthly,* 1952. Reprinted in Feigl, H. and Brodbeck, M., *Readings in the Philosophy of Science* and in Gardiner, P., *Theories of History*

"Wholes, Sums and Organic Unities," *PSt,* 1952

"On the Method of 'Verstehen' as the Sole Method of Philosophy," *JP* 1953

"A Budget of Problems in the Philosophy of Science," *PR,* 1957

Nakhnikian, G. and Salmon, W. C., " 'Exists' as a Predicate," *PR,* 1957

Nelson, E. J., "Deductive Systems and the Absoluteness of Logic, *M,* 1933

"Professor Reichenbach on Induction," *JP,* 1935

"Contradiction and the Presupposition of Existence," *M,* 1946

"The Relation of Logic to Metaphysics," *PPR,* 1948-49, and *PR,* 1949

"The Verification Theory of Meaning," *PR,* 1954

Neurath, O., "Eindeutigkeit und Kommutativität des logischen Produktes 'ab,'" *Arch. f. syst. Phil.*, 1909
"Definitionsgleichheit und symbolische Gleichheit," *Arch. f. Syst. Phil.*, 1910
"Das Problem des Lustmaximums," *Jahrb. d. Philos. Ges. a.d. Univ. Wien*, 1912
"Die Verirrten des Cartesius und das Auxiliarmotiv," *Jahrb. d. Philos. Ges. a.d. Univ. Wien*, 1913
"Wege der Wissenschaftlichen Weltauffassung," *E*, 1930-31
"Physicalism: The Philosophy of the Viennese Circle," *Monist*, 1931
"Physikalismus," *Scientia*, 1931
"Soziologie im Physikalismus," *E*, 1931-32. Reprinted in Engl. transl. in the present volume
"Protokollsätze," *E*, 1932-33. Reprinted in Engl. transl. in the present volume
"Radikaler Physikalismus und 'Wirkliche Welt,'" *E*, 1934
"Einheit der Wissenschaft als Aufgabe," *E*, 1935
"Pseudorationalismus der Falsifikation," *E*, 1935
"Den Logiska empirismen och Wienerkretsen," *T*, 1936
"Soziologische Prognosen," *E*, 1937
"Unified Science and its Encyclopedia," *PS*, 1937
"The Departmentalization of Unified Science," *E*, 1937-38
"Unified Science as Encyclopedic Integration," in Neurath *et al.*, *Encyclopedia and Unified Science*, 1938
"Universal Jargon and Terminology," *Ar.Soc.*, 1940-41
Neurath, O. and Hahn-Neurath, O., "Zum Dualismus in der Logik," *Arch. f. syst. Phil.*, 1909
Nielsen, K., "The Functions of Moral Discourse," *PQ*, 1957
Northrop, F. S. C., "The Significance of Epistemic Correlations in Scientific Method," *JUS*, 1939
"The Importance of Deductively Formulated Theory in Ethics and Social and Legal Science," in Henle, P., Kallen, H. M. and Langer, S. K., *Structure, Method and Meaning*, 1951
Nowell-Smith, P. H., "Subjectivism and the Empiricists," *A*, 1938-39
"Philosophical Theories," *Ar.Soc.*, 1947-48
"Freewill and Moral Responsibility," *M*, 1948. Reprinted in Munitz, M. K., *A Modern Introduction to Ethics*
"Science and Politics," *Ar.Soc.Sup.*, 1949
"Fugitive Propositions," *A*, 1949-50. Reprinted in Macdonald, M., *Philosophy and Analysis*
"Miracles," *HJ*, 1949-50. Reprinted in Flew, A. and MacIntyre, A., *New Essays in Philosophical Theology*
"Determinists and Libertarians," *M*, 1954
"Psycho-analysis and Moral Language," *Rationalist Annual*, 1954
"Are Historical Events Unique?," *Ar.Soc.*, 1956-57
O'Connor, D. J., "Pragmatic Paradoxes," *M*, 1948
"Is There a Problem about Free-Will?," *Ar.Soc.*, 1948-49
"Some Consequences of Professor A. J. Ayer's Verification Principle, *A*, 1949-50
"The Analysis of Conditional Sentences," *M*, 1951
"Philosophy and Ordinary Language," *JP*, 1951
"Names and Universals," *Ar.Soc.*, 1952-53
"The Identity of Indiscernibles," *A*, 1953-54

O'Connor, D. J. (*continued*)
  "Incompatible Properties," *A*, 1954-55
  "Awareness and Communication," *JP*, 1955
  "Causal Statements," *PQ*, 1956
  "Validity and Standards," *Ar.Soc.*, 1956-57
  "Determinism and Predictability," *BJPS*, 1956-57
O'Connor, D. J. and Basson, A. H., "Language and Philosophy," *P*, 1947
Olds, M. E., "Synonymity: Extensional Isomorphism," *M*, 1956
Oliver, D., "Logic and Necessity," *JP*, 1950
  "A Reexamination of the Problem of Induction," *JP*, 1952
Oppenheim, F. E., "Outline of a Logical Analysis of Law," *PS*, 1944
Oppenheim, P. and Grelling, K., "Der Gestaltbegriff im Lichte der neuen
    Logik," *E*, 1937-38
Oppenheim, P. and Helmer, O., "A Syntactical Definition of Probability and
    Degree of Confirmation," *JSL*, 1945
Oppenheim, P., and Hempel, C. G., "L'importance logique de la notion de
    type," *Actes du Congrès Intern. de Philosophie Scientifique, Paris
    1935*, 1936
  "Studies in the Logic of Explanation," *PS*, 1948. Reprinted as "The Logic
    of Explanation" in Feigl, H. and Brodbeck, M., *Readings in the
    Philosophy of Science*
Oppenheim, P. and Kemeny, J. G., "On Reduction," *PSt*, 1956
Orr, S. S., "Some Reflections on the Cambridge Approach to Philosophy, I
    and II," *AJ*, 1946
O'Shaughnessy, B., "The Origin of Pain," *A*, 1954-55
  "The Limits of the Will," *PR*, 1956
  "The Location of Sound," *M*, 1957
Ossowska, M., "W sprawie podstaw semantyki" (On the Question of the
    Foundation of Semantics), *Przeglad Filozoficzny*, 1925
Ossowski, S., "Analiza pojecia znaku" (Analysis of the Notion of Sign),
    Przeglad Filozoficzny, 1926
Oxienstierna, G., "Was versteht der Physiker unter der 'Grösse' eines Körpers?
    Bemerkungen zu Philipp Frank's vorherstehendem Artikel," *T*, 1937
Palmieri, L. E., "Verification and Descriptive Predicates," *PPR*, 1954-55
  "Entailment and Contradiction," *PPR*, 1956-57
Pap, A., "The Meaning of Necessity," *JP*, 1943
  "The Different Kinds of A Priori," *PR*, 1944
  "Indubitable Existential Statements," *M*, 1946
  "A Note on Logic and Existence," *M*, 1947
  "A Semantic Examination of Realism," *JP*, 1947
  "Logical Nonsense," *PPR*, 1948-49
  "Synonymity and Logical Equivalence," *A*, 1948-49
  "Are All Necessary Propositions Analytic?," *PR*, 1949
  "Are Individual Concepts Necessary?," *PSt*, 1950
  "Logic and the Concept of Entailment," *JP*, 1950
  "Ostensive Definition and Empirical Certainty," *M*, 1950
  "Other Minds and the Principle of Verifiability," *Rev.Int.Phil.*, 1951
  "Note on the 'Semantic' and the 'Absolute' Concept of Truth," *PSt*, 1952
  "Philosophical Analysis, Translation Schemas and the Regularity Theory
    of Causation," *JP*, 1952
  "Semantic Analysis and Psycho-Physical Dualism," *M*, 1952

Pap, A. (*continued*)
"Logic, Existence and the Theory of Descriptions," *A*, 1952-53
"The Linguistic Hierarchy and the Vicious-Circle Principle," *PSt*, 1954
"Propositions, Sentences and the Semantic Definition of Truth," *T*, 1954
"Belief, Synonymity and Analysis," *PSt*, 1955
"Beliefs and Propositions," *PS*, 1957
"Fact, Fiction and Forecast," *RM*, 1955
"Once More: Colors and the Synthetic A Priori," *PR*, 1957
Pasch, A., "Empiricism: One 'Dogma' or Two?," *JP*, 1956
Passmore, J. A., Logical Positivism, I-III," *AJ*, 1943, 1944, 1948
"Philosophy and Scientific Method," *Ar.Soc.*, 1948-49
"Reflections on *Logic and Language*," *AJ*, 1952
"Professor Ryle's Use of 'Use' and 'Usage,' " *PR*, 1954
"Intentions," *Ar.Soc.Sup.*, 1955
"Christianity and Positivism," *AJ*, 1957
Paton, H. J., "The Alleged Independence of Goodness," in Schilpp, P. A.,
The Philosophy of G. E. Moore, 1942
"The Emotive Theory of Ethics," *Ar.Soc.Sup.*, 1948
"Fifty Years of Philosophy," in Lewis, H. D., *Contemporary British
Philosophy* (third series), 1956
Paul, G. A., "The Analysis of Sense-Data," *A*, 1935-36
"Is There a Problem about Sense Data?," *Ar.Soc.Sup.*, 1936. Reprinted
in Flew, A., *Logic and Language* (first series)
"Lenin's Theory of Perception," *A*, 1937-38. Reprinted in Macdonald, M.,
Philosophy and Analysis
"G. E. Moore: Analysis, Common Usage, and Common Sense," in Ayer,
A. J. et al., *The Revolution in Philosophy*, 1956
"Wittgenstein," *ibid.*
Peach, B., "A Nondescriptive Theory of the Analytic," *PR*, 1952
"Logical and Practical Contradictions," *A*, 1953-54
Pears, D. F., "Hypotheticals," *A*, 1949-50. Reprinted in Macdonald, M.,
Philosophy and Analysis
"Synthetic Necessary Truth," *M*, 1950
"Time, Truth and Inference," *Ar.Soc.*, 1950-51. Reprinted in Flew, A.,
Essays in Conceptual Analysis
"The Logical Status of Supposition," *Ar.Soc.Sup.*, 1951
"Universals," *PQ*, 1950-51. Reprinted in Flew, A., *Logic and Language*
(second series)
"Incompatibilities of Colors," in Flew, A., *Logic and Language* (second
series), 1953
"The Identity of Indiscernibles," *M*, 1955
"Logical Atomism: Russell and Wittgenstein," in Ayer, A. J. et al., *The
Revolution in Philosophy*, 1956
Pears, D. F., Grice, H. P. and Strawson, P. F., "Metaphysics," in *The Nature
of Metaphysics*, 1957
Penelmum, T., "The Logic of Pleasure," *PPR*, 1957
Penttilä, A. and Saarnio, U., "Einige grundlegende Tatsachen der Worttheorie
neben Bemerkungen über die sogenannten unvollständigen Symbole,"
E, 1934
Peters, R. S., "Observationalism in Psychology," *M*, 1951
"Motives and Causes," *Ar.Soc.Sup.*, 1952

Pinsky, L. O., "Positivism and Realism," *M*, 1954
Place, U. T. and Smart, J. J. C., "Contradictories and Entailment," *PPR*, 1954-55
Popper, K. R., "What is Dialectic?," *M*, 1940
"Are Contradictions Embracing?," *M*, 1943
"The Poverty of Historicism," *Economica*, 1944
"Why Are the Calculuses of Logic and Arithmetic Applicable to Reality?," *Ar.Soc.Sup.*, 1946
"Logic without Assumptions," *Ar.Soc.*, 1946-47
"New Foundations for Logic," *M*, 1947, with Corrections and Additions, *M*, 1948
"What Can Logic Do for Philosophy?," *Ar.Soc.Sup.*, 1948
"A Note on Natural Laws and So-Called 'Contrary-to-Fact Conditionals,' " *M*, 1949
"Indeterminism in Quantum Physics and in Classical Physics, I and II," *BJPS*, 1950-51
"The Nature of Philosophical Problems and their Roots in Science," *BJPS*, 1952-53
"The Principle of Individuation," *Ar.Soc.Sup.*, 1953
"Self-Reference and Meaning in Ordinary Language," *M*, 1954
"Degree of Confirmation," *BJPS*, 1954-55
"A Note on the Body-Mind Problem," *A*, 1954-55
"A Note on Tarski's Definition of Truth," *M*, 1955
"Three Views concerning Human Knowledge," in Lewis, H. D., *Contemporary British Philosophy* (third series), 1956
"Philosophy of Science: A Personal Report," in Mace, C. A., *British Philosophy in the Mid-Century*, 1957
Popper-Lynkeus, J., "Über die Grundbegriffe der Philosophie und die Gewissheit unserer Erkenntnisse (aus dem literarischen Nachlass herausgegeben von Margit Ornstein)," *E*, 1932-33
Porteous, A. J. D., "Are There Synthetic A Priori Truths?," *Ar.Soc.Sup.*, 1936
Pratt, J. B., "Logical Positivism and Professor Lewis," *JP*, 1934
Price, H. H., "The Nature of Sensible Appearances," *Ar.Soc.Sup.*, 1926
"Mill's View of the External World," *Ar.Soc.*, 1926-27
"Negation," *Ar.Soc.Sup.*, 1929
"Our Knowledge of Other Minds," *Ar.Soc.*, 1931-32
"Some Considerations about Belief," *Ar.Soc.*, 1934-35
"Logical Positivism and Theology," *P*, 1935
"Memory-Knowledge," *Ar.Soc.Sup.*, 1936
"Our Evidence for the Existence of Other Minds," *P*, 1938
"Critical Notice of A. J. Ayer's *The Foundations of Empirical Knowledge*," *M*, 1941
"The Causal Argument for Physical Objects," *Ar.Soc.Sup.*, 1945
"Clarity Is Not Enough," *Ar.Soc.Sup.*, 1945
"Ayer's *Thinking and Meaning*," *P*, 1948
"British Philosophy between the Wars," *Horizon*, 1949
"Image Thinking," *Ar.Soc.*, 1951-52
"Seeming," *Ar.Soc.Sup.*, 1952
"Belief and Will," *Ar.Soc.Sup.*, 1954
"Discussion: Professor Ayer's Essays," *PQ*, 1955
"The Argument from Illusion," in Lewis, H. D., *Contemporary British Philosophy* (third series), 1956

Price-Williams, D. R., "Proprioception and Personal Identity," *PPR*, 1956-57
Prichard, H. A., "The Sense-Datum Fallacy," *Ar.Soc.Sup.*, 1938
Prior, A. N., "Can Religion Be Discussed?," *AJ*, 1942. Reprinted in Flew A. and MacIntyre, A., *New Essays in Philosophical Theology*
"Facts Propositions and Entailment," *M*, 1948
"Is Necessary Existence Possible?," *PPR*, 1954-55
Putnam, H., "Synonymity and the Analysis of Belief Sentences," *A*, 1953-54
"Mathematics and the Existence of Abstract Entities," *PSt*, 1956
"Reds, Greens and Logical Analysis," *PR*, 1956
"Psychological Concepts, Explication, and Ordinary Language," *JP*, 1957
Quine, W. V., "Ontological Remarks on the Propositional Calculus," *M*, 1934
"Truth by Convention," in *Philosophical Essays for A. N. Whitehead*, 1936. Reprinted in Feigl, H. and Sellars, W., *Readings in Philosophical Analysis*
"Designation and Existence," *JP*, 1939. Reprinted in Feigl, H. and Sellars, W., *Readings in Philosophical Analysis*
"Notes on Existence and Necessity," *JP*, 1943. Reprinted in Linsky, L., *Semantics and the Philosophy of Language*
"The Problem of Interpreting Modal Logic," *JSL*, 1947
"On Universals," *JSL*, 1947
"On What There Is," *RM*, 1948-49. Reprinted in *From a Logical Point of View*, and in Linsky, L., *Semantics and the Philosophy of Language*
"Identity, Ostension and Hypostasis," *JP*, 1950. Reprinted in *From a Logical Point of View*
"Goodman's *The Structure of Appearance*," *JP*, 1951
"On Carnap's Views on Ontology," *PSt*, 1951
"Ontology and Ideology," *PSt*, 1951
"On What There is," *Ar.Soc.Sup.*, 1951
"Semantics and Abstract Objects," *Proceedings of the American Academy of Arts and Sciences*, 1951
"Two Dogmas of Empiricism," *PR*, 1951. Reprinted in *From a Logical Point of View*
"Mr. Strawson on Logical Theory," *M*, 1953
"On a So-Called Paradox," *M*, 1953
"The Problem of Meaning in Linguistics," in *From a Logical Point of View*, 1953
"On Frege's Way Out," *M*, 1955
"Quantifiers and Propositional Attitudes," *JP*, 1956
"The Scope and Language of Science," *BJPS*, 1957-58
Quine, W. F. and Goodman, N., "Steps toward a Constructive Nominalism," *JSL*, 1947
Quinton, A., "Seeming," *Ar.Soc.Sup.*, 1952
"On Punishment," *A*, 1953-54. Reprinted in Laslett, P., *Philosophy, Politics and Society*
"The Problem of Perception," *M*, 1955
"Properties and Classes," *Ar.Soc.*, 1957-58
Ramsey, F., "Critical Notice of Wittgenstein's *Tractatus Logico-Philosophicus*," *M*, 1923. Reprinted in *The Foundations of Mathematics*
"Universals," *M*, 1925. Reprinted in *The Foundations of Mathematics*
"The Foundations of Mathematics," *Proceedings of the London Mathematical Society*, 1926. Reprinted in *The Foundations of Mathematics*

Ramsey, F. (*continued*)
"Universals and the 'Method of Analysis,' " *Ar.Soc.Sup.*, 1926
"Facts and Propositions," *Ar.Soc.Sup.*, 1927. Reprinted in *The Foundations of Mathematics*
Rand, R., "Kotarbinski's Philosophie," *E*, 1937-38
"Die Logik der Forderungssätze," *Int. Zeitschrift f. Theorie d. Rechts*, 1939
Rankin, K. W., "Linguistic Analysis and the Justification of Induction," *PQ*, 1955
"Causal Modalities and Alternative Action," *PQ*, 1957
Ranulf, S., "Positivism and Sociology," *T*, 1942
Raphael, D. D., "Universals, Resemblance and Identity," *Ar.Soc.*, 1954-55
"Linguistic Performances and Descriptive Meaning," *M*, 1956
Rees, D. A., "The Meaning of 'Survival,' " *A*, 1951-52
Reichenbach, H., "Der Begriff der Wahrscheinlichkeit fur die mathematische Darstellung der Wirklichkeit," *Zeitschrift für Philosophie und philosophische Kritik*, 1916
"Über die physikalischen Voraussetzungen der Wahrscheinlichkeitsrechnung," *Zeitschrift fur Physik*, 1920 and 1921
"Die physikalischen Voraussetzungen der Wahrscheinlichkeitsrechnung," *Die Naturwissenschaften*, 1920
"Philosophische Kritik der Wahrscheinlichkeitsrechnung," *Die Naturwissenschaften*, 1920
"Die Einsteinsche Raumlehre," *Die Umschau*, 1920
"Bericht über eine Axiomatik der Einsteinchen Raum-Zeit-Lehre," *Physikalische Zeitschrift*, 1921
"Die Einsteinsche Bewegungslehre," *Die Umschau*, 1921
"La signification philosophique de la théorie de la relativité," *Revue Philosophique de la France et de l'Etranger*, 1922
"Der gegenwärtige Stand der Relativitätsdiskussion," *Logos*, 1921-22. Eng. transl., "The Present State of the Discussion on Relativity," in *Selected Essays*
"Die Bewegungslehre bei Newton, Leibniz und Huyghens," *Kantstudien*, 1924
"Die relativistische Zeitlehre," *Scientia*, 1924
"Die Kausalstruktur der Welt und der Unterschied von Vergangenheit und Zukunft," *Bayerische Akademie der Wissenschaften, Sitzungsberichte*, 1925
"Wahrscheinlichkeitsgesetze und Kausalgesetze," *Die Umschau*, 1925
"Lichtgeschwindigkeit und Gleichzeitigkeit," *Annalen der Philosophie*, 1927
"Metaphysik und Naturwissenschaft," *Symposion*, 1927
"Wandlungen im physikalischen Weltbild," *Zeitschrift für angewandte Chemie*, 1928
"Das Kausalproblem in der gegenwärtigen Physik," *Zeitschrift für angewandte Chemie*, 1929
"Neuere Forschungsergebnisse in der Naturphilosophie," *Forschungen und Fortschritte*, 1929
"Ziele und Wege der physikalischen Erkenntnis," *Handbuch der Physik*, 1929
"Probleme und Denkweisen der gegenwärtigen Physik," *Deutsche Rundschau*, 1930

Reichenbach, H. (*continued*)
"Die philosophische Bedeutung der modernen Physik," *E,* 1930-31
"Kausalität und Wahrscheinlichkeit," *E,* 1930-31. Eng. transl., "Causality and Probability," in *Selected Essays*
"Das Kausalproblem in der Physik," *Naturwissenschaften,* 1931
"Axiomatik der Wahrscheinlichkeitsrechnung," *Mathematische Zeitschrift,* 1931-32
"Bemerkungen zum Wahrscheinlichkeitsproblem," *E,* 1931-32
"Der physikalische Wahrheitsbegriff," *E,* 1931-32
"Zum Anschaulichkeitsproblem der Geometrie," *E,* 1931-32
"Wahrscheinlichkeitslogik," *Sitzungsberichte der Preussischen Akademie der Wissenschaften, Phys.-Math. Klasse,* 1932
"Die Kausalbehauptung und die Möglichkeit ihrer empirischen Nachprüfung," *E,* 1932-33. Eng. transl., "The Principle of Causality and the Possibility of Its Empirical Confirmation," in *Selected Essays*
"Die logischen Grundlagen des Wahrscheinlichkeitsbegriffs," *E,* 1932-33. Eng. transl., "The Logical Foundations of the Concept of Probability," in Feigl, H. and Sellars, W., *Readings in Philosophical Analysis,* and in Feigl, H. and Brodbeck, M., *Readings in the Philosophy of Science*
"Kausalität und Wahrscheinlichkeit in der gegenwärtigen Physik," *Unterrichtsblätter für Mathematik und Naturwissenschaften,* 1933
"Bemerkungen zu Carl Hempels Versuch einer finitistischen Deutung des Wahrscheinlichkeitsbegriffs," *E,* 1935
"Bemerkungen zu Karl Marbes statistischen Untersuchungen zur Wahrscheinlichkeitsrechnung," *E,* 1935
"Über Induktion und Wahrscheinlichkeit. Bemerkungen zu Karl Poppers *Logik der Forschung*," *E,* 1935
"Wahrscheinlichkeitslogik," *E,* 1935
"Die Bedeutung des Wahrscheinlichkeitsbegriffs für die Erkenntnis," *Actes du VIIIème Congrès Intern. de Philosophie, Prague 1934,* 1936
"Die Induktion als Methode der wissenschaftlichen Erkenntnis," *Actes du Congrès Intern. de Philosophie Scientifique, Paris 1935,* 1936
"L'empirisme logistique et la désagréation de l'a priori," *Actes du Congrès Intern. de Philosophie Scientifique, Paris 1935,* 1936
"Logistic Empiricism in Germany and the Present State of its Problems," *JP,* 1936
"Wahrscheinlichkeitslogik als Form wissenschaftlichen Denkens," *Actes du Congrès Intern. de Philosophie Scientifique, Paris 1935,* 1936
"Warum ist die Anwendung der Induktionsregel für uns notwendige Bedingung von Voraussagen?," *E,* 1936-37
"Causalité et induction," *Bulletin de la Société Française de Philosophie,* 1937
"La philosophie scientifique: une esquisse de ses traits principaux," *Travaux de IXème Congrès Intern. de Philosophie, Paris,* 1937
"Les fondements logiques du calcul des probabilités," *Annales de l'Institut Henri Poincaré,* 1937
"On Probability and Induction," *PS,* 1938
"Dewey's Theory of Science," in Schilpp, P. A., *The Philosophy of John Dewey,* 1939

Reichenbach, H. (*continued*)
  "Bemerkungen zur Hypothesenwahrscheinlichkeit," *JUS*, 1939-40
  "Über die semantische und die Objekt-auffassung von Wahrscheinlich-keitsausdrücken," *JUS*, 1939-40
  "On the Justification of Induction," *JP*, 1940. Reprinted in Feigl, H. and Sellars, W., *Readings in Philosophical Analysis*
  "On Meaning," *JUS*, 1940
  "Bertrand Russell's Logic," in Schilpp, P. A., *The Philosophy of Bertrand Russell*, 1944
  "Reply to Donald C. William's Criticism of the Frequency Theory of Probability," *PPR*, 1944-45
  "The Principle of Anomaly in Quantum Mechanics," *Dialectica*, 1948. Reprinted in Feigl, H. and Brodbeck, M., *Readings in the Philosophy of Science*
  "Rationalism and Empiricism: an Inquiry into the Roots of Philosophical Error," *PR*, 1948
  "The Philosophical Analysis of Quantum Mechanics," *Library of the 10th Intern. Congress of Philosophy, Amsterdam, 1948*, 1949
  "Philosophical Foundations of Probability," *Proceedings of the Berkeley Symposium on Mathematical Statistics and Probability*, 1949
  "On Observing and Perceiving," *PSt*, 1951
  "The Philosophical Significance of the Theory of Relativity," in Schilpp, P. A., *Albert Einstein: Philosopher-Scientist*, 1951. Reprinted in Feigl, H. and Brodbeck, M., *Readings in the Philosophy of Science*, and in Wiener, P. P., *Readings in Philosophy of Science*
  "Über die erkenntnistheoretische Problemlage und den Gebrauch einer dreiwertigen Logik in der Quantenmechanik," *Zeitschrift für Naturforschung*, 1951
  "The Verifiability Theory of Meaning," *Proceedings of the Amer. Acad. of Arts and Sciences*, 1951. Reprinted in Feigl, H. and Brodbeck, M., *Readings in the Philosophy of Science*
  "Are Phenomenal Reports Absolutely Certain?," *PR*, 1952
  "The Syllogism Revised," *PS*, 1952
  "Les fondements logiques de la mécanique des quanta," *Annales de l'Institut Henri Poincaré*, 1952-53
Rescher, N., "The Identity of Indiscernibles: A Reinterpretation," *JP*, 1955
  "Translation as a Tool of Philosophical Analysis," *JP*, 1956
Rhees, R., "Science and Politics," *Ar.Soc.Sup.*, 1949
  "Can There Be a Private Language?," *Ar.Soc.Sup.*, 1954
Richards, I. A., "Multiple Definition," *Ar.Soc.*, 1933-34
  "Emotive Meaning Again," *PR*, 1948
Ritchie, A. D., "The Errors of Logical Positivism," *P*, 1937
Robinson, R., "Mr. Ryle on Propositions," *M*, 1931
  "The Emotive Theory of Ethics," *Ar.Soc.Sup.*, 1948
Rollins, C. D., "Professor Ayer's Query on 'Other Minds'," *A*, 1947-48
  "Are There Indubitable Existential Statements?," *M*, 1949
  "The Philosophical Denial of Sameness of Meaning," *A*, 1950-51
  "Ordinary Language and Procustean Beds," *M*, 1951
  "Logic and Description," *JP*, 1956
Ross, A., "Imperatives and Logic," *T*, 1941
  "On the Logical Nature of Propositions of Value," *T*, 1945

Rothenberg, B., "Zur Krise der Wissenschaft und übder den logistischen Neo-Positivismus," *Synthese,* 1939

Rougier, L., "La Scolastique et la logique," *E,* 1935
"Le Langage de la Physique est-il Universel et Autonome?," *E,* 1937-38
"The Relativity of Logic," *PPR,* 1941-42

Rubin, E., "Bemerkungen über unser Wissen von anderen Menschen," *E,* 1936-37

Rudner, R., "Formal and Non-Formal," *PS,* 1949
"The Ontological Status of the Esthetic Object," *PPR,* 1949-50
"Counter-Intuitivity and the Method of Analysis," *PSt,* 1950
"On Semiotic Aesthetics," *Journal of Aesthetics and Art Criticism,* 1951

Ruja, H., "The Logic of Logical Positivism," *JP,* 1936

Russell, B., "Sur la logique des relations avec des applications à la théorie des séries," *Rivista di matematica,* 1900-01. Reprinted in Eng. transl. as "The Logic of Relations" in *Logic and Knowledge*
"G. E. Moore's *Principia Ethica,*" *Independent Review,* 1904
"Meinong's Theory of Complexes and Assumptions, I-III," *M,* 1904
"On Denoting," *M,* 1905. Reprinted in *Logic and Knowledge,* and in Feigl, H. and Sellars, W., *Readings in Philosophical Analysis*
"The Nature of Truth," *M,* 1906.
"On the Nature of Truth," *Ar.Soc.,* 1906-07. Reprinted as "The Monistic Theory of Truth" in *Philosophical Essays*
"The Study of Mathematics," *New Quarterly,* 1907. Reprinted in *Philosophical Essays,* and in *Mysticism and Logic*
"Pragmatism," *Edinburgh Review,* 1909. Reprinted in *Philosophical Essays*
"Knowledge by Acquaintance and Knowledge by Description," *Ar.Soc.,* 1910-11. Reprinted in *Mysticism and Logic*
"On the Relation of Universals and Particulars," *Ar.Soc.,* 1911-12. Reprinted in *Logic and Knowledge*
"On the Notion of Cause," *Ar.Soc.,* 1912-13. Reprinted in *Mysticism and Logic*
"Mysticism and Logic," *HJ,* 1913-14. Reprinted in *Mysticism and Logic*
"On the Nature of Acquaintance," *Monist,* 1914. Reprinted in *Logic and Knowledge*
"The Relation of Sense-Data to Physics," *Scientia,* 1914. Reprinted in *Mysticism and Logic*
"The Ultimate Constituents of Matter," *Monist,* 1915. Reprinted in *Mysticism and Logic*
"The Philosophy of Logical Atomism, I-VII," *Monist,* 1918 and 1919. Reprinted in Marsh, R. C., *Logic and Knowledge*
"On Propositions: What They Are and How They Mean," *Ar.Soc.Sup.,* 1919. Reprinted in *Logic and Knowledge*
"Introduction to Ludwig Wittgenstein's *Tractatus Logico-Philosophicus,* 1922
"Logical Atomism," in Muirhead, J. H., *Contemporary British Philosophy* (first series), 1924. Reprinted in this volume, and in *Logic and Knowledge*
"C. D. Broad's *The Mind and its Place in Nature,*" *M,* 1926
"F. P. Ramsey's *The Foundations of Mathematics,*" *M,* 1931
"The Limits of Empiricism," *Ar.Soc.,* 1935-36
"On Verification," *Ar.Soc.,* 1937-38

Russell, B. (continued)
"On the Importance of Logical Form," in Encyclopedia and Unified Science, 1938
"The Relevance of Psychology to Logic," Ar.Soc.Sup., 1938
"Dewey's New Logic," in Schilpp, P. A., The Philosophy of John Dewey, 1939
"The Philosophy of Santayana," in Schilpp, P. A., The Philosophy of George Santayana, 1940
"Reply to Criticisms," in Schilpp, P. A., The Philosophy of Bertrand Russell, 1944
"Logical Positivism," Polemic, 1946
"The Problem of Universals," Polemic, 1946
"Logical Positivism," Rev.Int.Phil., 1950. Reprinted in Logic and Knowledge
"Ludwig Wittgenstein," M, 1951
"The Cult of 'Common Usage,'" BJPS, 1952-53. Reprinted in Portraits from Memory
"Philosophical Analysis," HJ, 1955-56
"Logic and Ontology," JP, 1957
"Mr. Strawson on Referring," M, 1957
"What is 'Mind?,'" JP, 1958
Russell, L. J., "Communication and Verification," Ar.Soc.Sup., 1934
"Epistemology and the Ego-centric Predicament," in Philosophical Studies —Essays in Memory of L. Susan Stebbing, 1948
"Von Mises' Kleines Lehrbuch des Positivismus," M, 1940
"Probability," Ar.Soc.Sup., 1950
Ryle, G., "Negation," Ar.Soc.Sup., 1929
"Are There Propositions?," Ar.Soc., 1929-30
"Systematically Misleading Expressions," Ar.Soc., 1931-32. Reprinted in Flew, A., Logic and Language (first series)
"Phenomenology," Ar.Soc.Sup., 1932
"Imaginary Objects," Ar.Soc.Sup., 1933
"About," A, 1933-34
"Mr. Collingwood and the Ontological Argument," M, 1935
"Internal Relations," Ar.Soc.Sup., 1935
"Unverifiability-by-me," A, 1936-37
"Back to the Ontological Argument," M, 1937
"Induction and Hypothesis," Ar.Soc.Sup., 1937
"Taking Sides in Philosophy," P, 1937
"Categories," Ar.Soc., 1937-38. Reprinted in Flew, A., Logic and Language (second series)
"Conscience and Moral Convictions," A, 1940. Reprinted in Macdonald, M., Philosophy and Analysis
"Knowing How and Knowing That," Ar.Soc., 1945-46
"Why Are the Calculuses of Logic and Arithmetic Applicable to Reality?," Ar.Soc.Sup., 1946
"Carnap's Meaning and Necessity," P, 1949
"'If,' 'So' and 'Because,'" in Black, M., Philosophical Analysis, 1950
"Logic and Professor Anderson," AJ, 1950
"Feelings," PQ, 1950-51. Reprinted in Elton, W., Aesthetics and Language
"Heterologicality," A, 1950-51. Reprinted in Macdonald, M., Philosophy and Analysis

Ryle, G. (*continued*)
"Thinking and Language," *Ar.Soc.Sup.*, 1951
"Ludwig Wittgenstein," *A*, 1951-52
"Ordinary Language," *PR*, 1953
"Pleasure," *Ar.Soc.Sup.*, 1954
"Proofs in Philosophy," *Rev.Int.Phil.*, 1954
"Sensation," in Lewis, H. D., *Contemporary British Philosophy* (third series), 1956
"The Theory of Meaning," in Mace, C. A., *British Philosophy in the Mid-Century*, 1957
Rynin, D., "The Nature of Communication," *JP*, 1932
"A Critical Essay on Johnson's Philosophy of Language," in Johnson, A. B., *A Treatise on Language*, 1947
"Probability and Meaning," *JP*, 1947
"Definitions of 'Value' and the Logic of Value Judgments," *JP*, 1948
"Remarks on M. Schlick's Essay 'Positivism and Realism,'" *Synthese*, 1948-49
"Meaning and Formation Rules," *JP*, 1949
"The Dogma of Logical Pragmatism," *M*, 1956
"A Vindication of Logical Positivism," *Proceedings and Addresses of Amer. Philosophical Assn.*, *1956*, 1957
"The Autonomy of Morals," *M*, 1957
Saarnio, U., "Zur heterologischen Paradoxie," *T*, 1937
Saarnio, U. and Penttilä, A., "Einige grundlegende Tatsachen der Worttheorie nebst Bemerkungen über die sogenannten unvollständigen Symbole," *E*, 1934
Salmon, W. C., "The Uniformity of Nature," *PPR*, 1953-54
"Regular Rules of Induction," *PR*, 1956
Salmon, W. C. and Nakhnikian, G., " 'Exists' as a Predicate," *PR*, 1957
Scheffler, I., "The New Dualism," *JP*, 1950
"Anti-Naturalist Restrictions in Ethics," *JP*, 1953
"An Inscriptional Approach to Indirect Quotation," *A*, 1953-54
"On Justification and Commitment," *JP*, 1954
"Prospects of a Modest Empiricism, I and II," *RM*, 1956-57
Schlick, M., "Gas Grundproblem der Ästhetik in entwicklungsgeschichtlicher Beleuchtung," *Archiv f. d. gesamte Psychologie*, 1910
"Die Grenze der naturwissenschaftlichen und philosophischen Begriffsbildung," *Viertelj. f. Wiss. Phil. u. Soz.*, 1910
"Das Wesen der Wahrheit nach der modernen Logik," *ibid.*
"Gibt es intuitive Erkenntnis?," *Viertelj. f. Wiss. Phil. u. Soz.*, 1913
"Die philosophische Bedeutung des Relativitätsprinzips," *Zeitschrift für Philosophie und philosophische Kritik*, 1915
"Idealität des Raumes, Introjektion und psychophysisches Problem," *Viertelj. f. Wiss. Phil. u. Soz.*, 1916
"Erscheinung und Wesen," *Kantstudien*, 1918-19
"Naturphilosophische Betrachtungen über das Kausalprinzip," *Naturwissenschaften*, 1920
"Kritizistische oder empiristische Deutung der neuen Physik?," *Kantstudien*, 1921
"Helmholtz als Erkenntnistheoretiker," in *Helmholtz als Physiker, Physiologe und Philosoph*, Karlsruhe, 1922

Schlick, M. (*continued*)

"Die Relativitätstheorie in der Philosophie," *Verhandlungen der Gesellschaft deutscher Naturforscher und Ärzte*, 1922

"Erleben, Erkennen, Metaphysik," *Kantstudien*, 1926

"Erkenntnistheorie und moderne Physik," *Scientia*, 1929

"Gibt es ein materiales Apriori?," *Wissenschaftlicher Jahresbericht der philosophischen Gesellschaft an der Universität zu Wien für das Vereinsjahr*, 1930-31. Eng. transl. in Feigl, H. and Sellars, W., *Readings in Philosophical Analysis*

"La relativité de l'espace," *Nouvelles littéraires*, 1930

"Die Wende der Philosophie," *E*, 1930-31. Reprinted in *Gesammelte Aufsätze*, Eng. transl. in the present volume

"Die Kausalität in der gegenwärtigen Physik," *Naturwissenschaften*, 1931. Reprinted in *Gesammelte Aufsätze* and in *Gesetz, Kausalität und Wahrscheinlichkeit*

"The Future of Philosophy," *Publ. in Philos. of the College of the Pacific*, 1932. Reprinted in *Gesammelte Aufsätze*, and in Bronstein, D., Krikorian, Y. and Wiener, P., *Basic Problems in Philosophy*

"A New Philosophy of Experience," *Publ. in Philos. of the College of the Pacific*, 1932. Reprinted in *Gesammelte Aufsätze*

"Causality in Everyday Life and in Recent Science," *Publ. in Philos. of the University of Calif.*, 1932. Reprinted in *Gesammelte Aufsätze*, and in Feigl, H. and Sellars, W., *Readings in Philosophical Analysis*

"Positivismus und Realismus," *E*, 1932-33. Reprinted in *Gesammelte Aufsätze*. Eng. transl. in *Synthese*, 1948-49, and the present volume

"Über den Begriff der Ganzheit," *Wissenschaftlicher Jahresbericht der philosophischen Gesellschaft an der Universität zu Wien für das Vereinsjahr*, 1933-34 and 1934-35, and *E*, 1935. Reprinted in *Gesammelte Aufsätze*, and in *Gesetz, Kausalität und Wahrscheinlichkeit*

"Les énoncés scientifiques et la réalité du monde extérieur," *Actualités scientifiques*, 1934

"Über das Fundament der Erkenntnis," *E*, 1934. Reprinted in *Gesammelte Aufsätze*. Eng. transl. in the present volume; Fr. transl., Paris: Hermann, 1935

"Philosophie und Naturwissenschaft," *E*, 1934

"Facts and Propositions," *A*, 1934-35. Reprinted in Macdonald, M., *Philosophy and Analysis*

"De la relation entre les notions psychologiques et les notions physiques," *Revue de Synthèse*, 1935. Eng. transl. in Feigl, H. and Sellars, W., *Readings in Philosophical Analysis*

"Unanswerable Questions?," *The Philosopher*, 1935. Reprinted in *Gesammelte Aufsätze*

"Sind die Naturgesetze Konventionen?," *Actes du Congrès Intern. de Philos. Scientifique, Paris 1935*, 1936. Reprinted in *Gesammelte Aufsätze* and in *Gesetz, Kausalität, und Wahrscheinlichkeit*. Eng. transl. in Feigl, H. and Brodbeck, M., *Readings in the Philosophy of Science*

"Gesetz und Wahrscheinlichkeit," *Actes du Congrès Intern. de Philos. Scientifique, Paris 1935*, 1936. Reprinted in *Gesammelte Aufsätze* and *Gesetz, Kausalität und Wahrscheinlichkeit*

"Meaning and Verification," *PR*, 1936. Reprinted in *Gesammelte Auf-*

Bibliography of Logical Positivism [437]

Schlick, M. (*continued*)

  sätze, and in Feigl, H. and Sellars, W., *Readings in Philosophical Analysis*

  "Quantentheorie und Erkennbarheit der Natur," *E*, 1936-37. Reprinted in *Gesammelte Aufsätze* and *Gesetz, Kausalität und Wahrscheinlichkeit*

  "L'école de Vienne et la philosophie traditionelle," *Travaux du IXème Congrès Intern. de Philosophie, Paris,* 1937

  "Form and Content, an Introduction to Philosophical Thinking. Three Lectures, delivered in the University of London in Nov. 1932," in *Gesammelte Aufsätze,* 1938

Schultzer, B., "Empiricism as a Logical Problem," *T*, 1949

Scriven, M., "Paradoxical Announcements," *M*, 1951

  "Definitions in Analytical Philosophy," *PSt*, 1954

  "Language in Fiction," *Ar.Soc.Sup.*, 1954

Segerstedt, T. T., "Imperative Propositions and Judgments of Value," *T*, 1945

Sellars, R. W., "The Meaning of True and False," *PPR*, 1944-45

Sellars, W., "Epistemology and the New Way of Words," *JP*, 1947

  "Pure Pragmatics and Epistemology," *PS*, 1947

  "Realism and the New Way of Words," *PPR*, 1947-48. Reprinted in Feigl, H. and Sellars, W., *Readings in Philosophical Analysis*

  "Concepts as Involving Laws and Inconceivable without Them," *PS*, 1948

  "On the Logic of Complex Particulars," *M*, 1949

  "Language, Rules and Behavior," in Hook, S., *John Dewey: Philosopher of Science and Freedom,* 1950

  "Quotation Marks, Sentences and Propositions," *PPR*, 1949-50

  "Gestalt Qualities and the Paradox of Analysis," *PSt*, 1950

  "The Identity of Linguistic Expressions and the Paradox of Analysis," *PSt,* 1950

  "Mind, Meaning and Behavior," *PSt*, 1952

  "Particulars," *PPR*, 1952-53

  "Inference and Meaning," *M*, 1953

  "Is There a Synthetic A Priori?," *PS*, 1953

  "A Semantical Solution of the Mind-Body Problem," *Methodos*, 1953

  "Presupposing," *PR*, 1954

  "Some Reflections on Language Games," *PS*, 1954

  "Logical Subjects and Physical Objects," *PPR*, 1956-57

Sesonke, A., "On the Skepticism of *Ethics and Language*," *JP*, 1953

  " 'Cognitive' and 'Normative,' " *PPR*, 1956

  "Truth in Art," *JP*, 1956

Shearn, M., "Other People's Sense-Data," *Ar.Soc.*, 1949-50

  "Russell's Analysis of Existence," *A*, 1950-51

Shwayder, D. S., "Some Remarks on "Synonymity' and the Language of the Semanticists," *PSt*, 1954

  "Achilles Unbound," *JP*, 1955

  "Self-Defeating Pronouncements," *A*, 1955-56

  "≡," *M*, 1956

Smart, H. R., "Language Games," *PQ*, 1957

Smart, J. J. C., "The River of Time," *M*, 1949. Reprinted in Flew, A., *Essays in Conceptual Analysis*

  "Whitehead and Russell's Theory of Types," *A*, 1949-50

Smart, J. J. C. (*continued*)
"Excogitation and Induction," *AJ*, 1950
"Reason and Conduct," *P*, 1950
"Theory Construction," *PPR*, 1950-51. Reprinted in Flew, A., *Logic and Language* (second series)
"The Moving 'Now,'" *AJ*, 1953
"The Temporal Asymmetry of the World," *A*, 1953-54
"The Existence of God," *Church Quarterly Review*, 1955. Reprinted in Flew, A. and MacIntyre, A., *New Essays in Philosophical Theology* and in Edwards, P. and Pap, A., *A Modern Introduction to Philosophy*
"Metaphysics, Logic and Theology," in Flew, A. and MacIntyre, A., *New Essays in Philosophical Theology*, 1955
"Spatializing Time," *M*, 1955
"The Reality of Theoretical Entities," *AJ*, 1956
"Plausible Reasoning in Philosophy," *M*, 1957
Smart, J. J. C. and Place, U. T., "Contradictories and Entailment," *PPR*, 1954-55
Smullyan, A., "Aspects," *PR*, 1955
"The Concept of Empirical Knowledge," *PR*, 1956
"The Concept of Empirical Language," *ibid.*
Somerville, J., "Logical Empiricism and the Problem of Causality in Social Science," *E*, 1936-37
Spillsbury, R. J., "Dispositions and Phenomenalism," *M*, 1953
Stace, W. T., "The Refutation of Realism," *M*, 1936. Reprinted in Feigl, H. and Sellars, W., *Readings in Philosophical Analysis* and in Edwards, P. and Pap, A., *A Modern Introduction to Philosophy*
"Metaphysics and Meaning," *M*, 1935. Reprinted in Edwards, P. and Pap, A., *A Modern Introduction to Philosophy*
"Positivism," *M*, 1944
"Are All Empirical Statements Hypotheses?," *JP*, 1947
Stanley, R. L., "A Theory of Subjunctive Conditionals," *PPR*, 1956-57
Stebbing, L. S., "The Nature of Sensible Appearances," *Ar.Soc.Sup.*, 1926
"Substances, Events, and Facts," *JP*, 1932
"The Method of Analysis in Metaphysics," *Ar.Soc.*, 1932-33
"The A Priori," *Ar.Soc.Sup.*, 1933
"Constructions," *Ar.Soc.*, 1933-34
"Communication and Verification," *Ar.Soc.Sup.*, 1934
"Directional Analysis and Basic Facts," *A*, 1934-35
"Carnap's *Logische Syntax der Sprache, Die Aufgabe der Wissenchafts-logik, Philosophy and Logical Syntax, The Unity of Science*, *M*, 1935
"Sounds, Shapes, and Words," *Ar.Soc.Sup.*, 1935
"Ayer's *Language, Truth and Logic*, *M*," 1936
"Carnap's *Logical Syntax of Language*," *P*, 1938
"Some Puzzles about Analysis," *Ar.Soc.*, 1938-39
"Moore's Influence," in Schilpp, P. A., *The Philosophy of G. E. Moore*, 1942
Stenius, F., "Linguistic Structure and the Structure of Experience," *T*, 1954
Stevenson, C. L., "The Emotive Meaning of Ethical Terms," *M*, 1937. Reprinted in Sellars, W. and Hospers, J., *Readings in Ethical Theory*, and in the present volume

Stevenson, C. L. (*continued*)
"Ethical Judgments and Avoidability," *M*, 1938. Reprinted in Sellars, W. and Hospers, J., *Readings in Ethical Theory*
"Persuasive Definitions," *M*, 1938. Reprinted in Hook, S., *American Philosophers at Work*
"Moore's Arguments against Certain Forms of Ethical Naturalism," in Schilpp, P. A., *The Philosophy of G. E. Moore*, 1942
"Some Relations between Philosophy and the Study of Language," *A*, 1947-48
"Meaning: Descriptive and Emotive," *PR*, 1948
"The Nature of Ethical Disagreement," in Feigl, H. and Sellars, W., *Readings in Philosophical Analysis*, 1949 Reprinted in Edwards, P. and Pap, A., *A Modern Introduction to Philosophy*, and in Munitz, M. K., *A Modern Introduction to Ethics*
"The Emotive Concept of Ethics and its Cognitive Implications," *PR*, 1950
"Interpretation and Evaluation in Aesthetics," in Black, M., *Philosophical Analysis*, 1950
"Critical Notice of Nowell-Smith's *Ethics*," *M*, 1955
"On 'What Is a Poem'?," *PR*, 1957
Storer, T., "The Logic of Value Imperatives," *PS*, 1946
"The Philosophical Relevance of a 'Behavioristic Semiotic,' " *PS*, 1948
"On Communication," *PSt*, 1950
"On Defining 'Soluble,' " *A*, 1950-51
Stout, G. F., "The Status of Sense Data," *Ar.Soc.*, 1913-14
"Are the Characteristics of Particular Things Universal or Particular?," *Ar.Soc.Sup.*, 1923
"Mechanical and Teleological Causation," *Ar.Soc.Sup.*, 1935
"Phenomenalism," *Ar.Soc.*, 1938-39
Strauss, M., "Ungenauigkeit, Wahrscheinlichkeit und Unbestimmtheit," *E*, 1936-37
"Komplementarität und Kausalität im Lichte der Logischen Syntax," *E*, 1936-37
"Mathematics as Logical Syntax—A Method to Formalize the Language of a Physical Theory," *E*, 1937-38
Strawson, P. F., "Necessary Propositions and Entailment Statements," *M*, 1948
"Truth," *A*, 1948-49. Reprinted in Macdonald, M., *Philosophy and Analysis*
"Ethical Intuitionism," *P*, 1949. Reprinted in Sellars, W. and Hospers, J., *Readings in Ethical Theory*
"On Referring," *M*, 1950. Reprinted in Flew, A., *Essays in Conceptual Analysis*
"Truth," *Ar.Soc.Sup.*, 1950
"Particular and General," *Ar.Soc.*, 1953-54
"Presupposing: a Reply to Mr. Sellars," *PR*, 1954
"Wittgenstein's *Philosophical Investigations*, M, 1954
"A Logician's Landscape," *P*, 1955
"Construction and Analysis," in Ayer, A. J. *et al.*, *The Revolution in Philosophy*, 1956
"Singular Terms, Ontology and Identity," *M*, 1956
"Logical Subjects and Physical Objects," *PPR*, 1956-57
"*Logic and Knowledge* by Bertrand Russell," *PQ*, 1957

Strawson, P. F. (*continued*)
  "Professor Ayer's *The Problem of Knowledge*," *P*, 1957
  "Proper Names," *Ar.Soc.Sup.*, 1957
  "Propositions, Concepts and Logical Truths," *PQ*, 1957
Strawson, P. F. and Grice, H. P., "In Defense of a Dogma," *PR*, 1956
Strawson, P. F., Grice, H. P. and Pears, D. F., "Metaphysics," in Pears, D. F.,
  The Nature of Metaphysics, 1957
Stroll, A., "A Problem concerning the Analysis of Belief Sentences," *A*, 1953-54
  "Is Everyday Language Inconsistent?," *M*, 1954
  "On 'The,'" *PPR*, 1955-56
Strzelewicz, W., "Über Moralbegründung. Bemerkungen zu Victor Krafts Auf-
  satz," *T*, 1941
Tarski, A., "O wyrazie pierwotnym logistyki," *Przeglad Filozoficzny*, 1923.
  Reprinted in a modified version in two parts: "Sur le terme primitif
  de la logistique," *Fundamenta Mathematicae*, 1923, and "Sur les
  truth-functions au sens de MM. Russell et Whitehead," *Fundamenta
  Mathematicae*, 1924, and in Eng. transl., "On the Primitive Term of
  Logistic," in *Logic, Semantics, Metamathematics*
  "Remarques sur les notions fondamentales de la méthodologie des mathé-
  matiques," *Annales de la Société Polonaise de Mathématique, 1929*.
  Reprinted in an expanded version as "Über einige fundamentalen
  Begriffe der Mathematik," *Comptes rendus des séances de la So-
  ciété des Sciences et des Lettres de Varsovie*, 1930, and in Eng.
  transl., "On Some Fundamental Concepts of Metamathematics," in
  Logic, Semantics, Metamathematics
  "Fundamentale Begriffe der Methodologie der deduktiven Wissenschaften,
  I," *Monatsh. Math. Phys.*, 1930. Eng. transl. in *Logic, Semantics,
  Metamathematics*
  "Pojecie prawdy w jtzykach nauk dedukcyjnych," *Travaux de la Société
  des Sciences et des Lettres de Varsovie, Classe III, Sciences mathé-
  matiques et physiques*, 1933. Reprinted as "Der Wahrheitsbegriff in
  den formalisierten Sprachen" in *Studia Philosophica*, 1935, and as
  "The Concept of Truth in Formalized Languages" in *Logic, Seman-
  tics, Metamathematics*
  "Einige methodologische Untersuchungen über die Definierbarkeit der
  Begriffe," *E*, 1935. Eng. transl. in *Logic, Semantics, Metamathematics*
  "Grundlegung der wissenschaftlichen Semantik," *Actes du Congrès Intern.
  de Philosophie Scientifique, Paris 1935*, 1936. Eng. transl. in *Logic,
  Semantics, Metamathematics*, and Polish transl. in *Przeglad Filozo-
  ficzny*, 1936
  "Über den Begriff der logischen Folgerung," *Actes du Congrès Intern. de
  Philosophie Scientifique, Paris 1935*, 1936. Eng. transl. in *Logic,
  Semantics, Metamathematics*, and Polish transl. in *Przeglad Filozo-
  ficzny*, 1936
  "On Undecidable Statements in Enlarged Systems of Logic and the Con-
  cept of Truth," *JSL*, 1939
  "The Semantic Conception of Truth and the Foundations of Semantics,"
  PPR, 1943-44. Reprinted in Feigl, H. and Sellars, W., *Readings in
  Philosophical Analysis*, and in Linsky, L., *Semantics and the Philos-
  ophy of Language*
Tarski, A. and Łukasiewicz, J., "Untersuchungen über den Aussagenkalkül,"

Tarski, A. and Łukasiewicz, J. (*continued*)
   Comptes rendus des séances de la Société des Sciences et des Lettres de Varsovie, 1930. Eng. transl. in *Logic, Semantics, Metamathematics*
Taylor, D., "Fallacies in Moral Philosophy. S. Hampshire," *M*, 1951
Taylor, R., "Mr. Black on Temporal Paradoxes," *A*, 1951-52
   "Negative Things," *JP*, 1952
   "Mr. Wisdom on Temporal Paradoxes," *A*, 1952-53
   "Ayer's Analysis of Negation," *PSt*, 1953
   "Disputes about Synonymy," *PR*, 1954
   "Spatial and Temporal Analogies and the Concept of Identity," *JP*, 1955
   "The Problem of Future Contingencies," *PR*, 1957
Terrell, D. B., "On a Supposed Synthetic Entailment," *PSt*, 1951
   "What You Will, or The Limits of Analysis," *PSt*, 1952
   "A Remark on Good Reasons," *PSt*, 1953
Thompson, M., "What Are Law-Statements About?," *JP*, 1955
   "On Category Differences," *PR*, 1957
Thomson, J. F., "A Note on Truth," *A*, 1948-49
   "The Argument from Analogy and Our Knowledge of Other Minds," *M*, 1951
   "Some Remarks on Synonymy," *A*, 1951-52
   "Reducibility," *Ar.Soc.Sup.*, 1952
   "Tasks and Super-Tasks," *A*, 1954-55
Tolman, E. C., "An Operational Analysis of 'Demand,' " *E*, 1936-37
Tomas, V., "Ethical Disagreements and the Emotive Theory of Values, *M*, 1951
Toms, E., "Facts and Entailment," *M*, 1948
   "Non-Existence and Universals," *PQ*, 1956
Toulmin, S., "A Defence of 'Synthetic Necessary Truth,' " *M*, 1949
   "Probability," *Ar.Soc.Sup.*, 1950. Reprinted in Flew, A., *Essays in Conceptual Analysis*
   "Is There a Fundamental Problem in Ethics?," *AJ*, 1955
   "Contemporary Scientific Mythology," in Toulmin, *et al.*, *Metaphysical Beliefs*, 1957
Toulmin, S. and Baier, K., "On Describing," *M*, 1952
University of California Associates, "The Freedom of the Will," in *Knowledge and Society*, 1938. Reprinted in Feigl, H. and Sellars, W., *Readings in Philosophical Analysis* and in Munitz, M. K., *A Modern Introduction to Ethics*
Urban, W. M., "Value Propositions and Verifiability," *JP*, 1937
   "The Dialectic of Meaning and Truth: Truth as Immanent in Discourse," *PPR*, 1943-44
Urmson, J. O., "Are Necessary Truths True by Convention?," *Ar.Soc.Sup.*, 1947
   "Two of the Senses of 'Probable,' " *A*, 1947-48. Reprinted in Macdonald, M., *Philosophy and Analysis*
   "On Grading," *M*, 1950. Reprinted in Flew, A., *Logic and Language* (second series)
   "Motives and Causes," *Ar.Soc.Sup.*, 1952
   "Parenthetical Verbs," *M*, 1952. Reprinted in Flew, A., *Essays in Conceptual Analysis*
   "Some Questions Concerning Validity," *Rev.Int.Phil.*, 1953. Reprinted in Flew, A., *Essays in Conceptual Analysis*
   "Recognition," *Ar.Soc.*, 1955-56

[442]   *Bibliography of Logical Positivism*

Ushenko, A., "The Problem of General Propositions," *Monist,* 1933
  "The Problem of Semantics," *JP,* 1942
  "Russell's Critique of Empiricism," in Schilpp, P. A., *The Philosophy of Bertrand Russell,* 1944
  "Undecidable Statements and Meta-Language," *M,* 1944
  "A Note on the Semantic Conception of Truth," *PPR,* 1944-45
Veatch, H., "Formalism and/or Intentionality in Logic," *PPR,* 1950-51
Vesey, G. N. A., "Unthinking Assumptions and their Justification," *M,* 1954
  "Seeing and Seeing As," *Ar.Soc.,* 1955-56
Vogel, T., "Bemerkungen zur Aussagentheorie des radikalen Physikalismus," *E,* 1934
Waismann, F., "Die Natur des Reduzibilitätsaxioms," *Monats. Math. Phys.,* 1928
  "Logische Analyse des Wahrscheinlichkeitsbegriffs," *E,* 1930-31
  "Über den Begriff der Identität," *E,* 1936-37
  "Ist die Logik eine deduktive Theorie?," *E,* 1937-38
  "The Relevance of Psychology to Logic," *Ar.Soc.Sup.,* 1938. Reprinted in Feigl, H. and Sellars, W., *Readings in Philosophical Analysis*
  "Verifiability," *Ar.Soc.Sup.,* 1945. Reprinted in Flew, A., *Logic and Language* (first series)
  "Are There Alternative Logics?," *Ar.Soc.,* 1945-46
  "The Many-Level Structure of Language," *Synthese,* 1946
  "Analytic-Synthetic, I-VI," *A,* 1949-53
  "Language Strata," in Flew, A., *Logic and Language* (second series), 1953
  "How I See Philosophy," in Lewis, H. D., *Contemporary British Philosophy* (third series), 1956. Reprinted in the present volume
Walker, E. R., "Verification and Probability," *JP,* 1947
Walsh, W. H., "Analytic-Synthetic," *Ar.Soc.,* 1953-54
Walter, W., "Einheitswissenschaft als Basis der Wissenschaftsgeschichte," *E,* 1937-38
Wang, H., "The Existence of Material Objects," *M,* 1948
  "What Is an Individual?," *PR,* 1953
  "A Question of Knowledge," *A,* 1953-54
  "Notes on the Analytic-Synthetic Distinction," *T,* 1955
  "On Formalization," *M,* 1955
Warnock, G. J., "Concepts and Schematism," *A,* 1948-49
  "Metaphysics in Logic," *Ar.Soc.,* 1950-51. Reprinted in Flew, A., *Essays in Conceptual Analysis*
  "Empirical Propositions and Hypothetical Statements," *M,* 1951
  "Verification and the Use of Language," *Rev.Int.Phil.,* 1951
  "Reducibility," *Ar.Soc.Sup.,* 1952
  "Every Event Has a Cause," in Flew, A., *Logic and Language* (second series), 1953
  "Seeing," *Ar.Soc.,* 1954-55
  "Analysis and Imagination," in Ayer, A. J. et al., *The Revolution in Philosophy,* 1956
  "Criticisms of Metaphysics," in Pears, D. F., *The Nature of Metaphysics,* 1957
Waters, B., "Positivistic and Activistic Theories of Causation, *JP,* 1938
  "Basic Sentences and Incorrigibility," *PS,* 1942
Watkins, J. W. N., "Between Analytical and Empirical," *P,* 1957

Watkins, J. W. N. (*continued*)
  "Confirmable and Influential Metaphysics," *M*, 1958
  "After the Revolution in Philosophy," *The Rationalist Annual*, 1958
Watling, J., "The Causal Theory of Perception," *M*, 1950
  "The Sum of an Infinite Series," *A*, 1952-53
  "Propositions Asserting Causal Connections," *A*, 1953-54
  "Ayer on Other Minds," *T*, 1954
  "Inference from the Known to the Unknown," *Ar.Soc.*, 1954-55
  "The Problem of Contrary-to-Fact Conditionals," *A*, 1956-57
  "Entailment," *Ar.Soc.Sup.*, 1958
Watling, J. and Brown, R., "Amending the Verification Principle," *A.*, 1950-51
  "Hypothetical Statements in Phenomenalism," *Synthese*, 1950-51
  "Counterfactual Conditions," *M*, 1952
Weinberg, C. B., "Protocols, Communicability, and Pointer Readings," *JP*, 1938
Weinberg, J. R., "Our Knowledge of Other Minds," *PR*, 1946
  "The Idea of Causal Efficacy," *JP*, 1950
  "Contrary-to-Fact Conditionals," *JP*, 1951
  "Concerning Undefined Descriptive Predicates of Higher Levels," *M*, 1954
Weinberg, J. R. and Hay, W. H., "Concerning Allegedly Necessary Non-
    analytic Propositions," *PSt*, 1951
Weiss, P., "The Logic of Semantics," *JP*, 1942
Weissmann, A., "The Meaning of Identity," *PPR*, 1955-56
Weitz, M., "Does Art Tell the Truth?," *PPR*, 1942-43
  "Analysis and the Unity of Russell's Philosophy," in Schilpp, P. A., *The
    Philosophy of Bertrand Russell*, 1944
  "Philosophy and the Abuse of Language," *JP*, 1947
  "Analysis and Real Definition," *PSt*, 1950
  "Professor Ryle's 'Logical Behaviorism,' " *JP*, 1951
  "Oxford Philosophy," *PR*, 1953
  "Analytic Statements," *M*, 1954
Weldon, T. D., "Science and Politics," *Ar.Soc.Sup.*, 1949
  "Appraisals," *P*, 1950
  "Political Principles," in Laslett, P., *Philosophy, Politics and Society*, 1956
Wells, D. A., "Basic Propositions in Ayer and Russell," *JP*, 1954
Welsh, P., "On the Nature of Inference," *PR*, 1957
Werkmeister, W. H., "Seven Theses of Logical Positivism Critically Exam-
    ined, I and II," *PR*, 1937
  "The Meaning of 'Meaning' Re-examined," *PR*, 1938
  "On 'Describing a World,' " *PPR*, 1950-51
  "Problems of Value Theory," *PPR*, 1951-52
Wheatley, J. M. O., "Deliberative Questions," *A*, 1954-55
White, A. R., "Mr. Hampshire and Prof. Ryle on Dispositions," *A*, 1953-54
  "A Note on Meaning and Verification," *M*, 1954
  "On Claiming to Know," *PR*, 1957
  "Truth as Appraisal," *M*, 1957
White, M. G., "Probability and Confirmation," *JP*, 1939
  "Historical Explanation," *M*, 1943. Reprinted with postscript in Gardiner,
    P., *Theories of History*
  "The Attack on the Historical Method," *JP*, 1945
  "A Note on the 'Paradox of Analysis,' " *M*, 1945
  "Analysis and Identity: A Rejoinder," *M*, 1945

White, M. G. (*continued*)
"The Analytic and the Synthetic: An Untenable Dualism," in Hook, S., *John Dewey: Philosopher of Science and Freedom*, 1950. Reprinted in Linsky, L., *Semantics and the Philosophy of Language*
"A Finitistic Approach to Philosophical Theses," *PR*, 1951
"Ontological Clarity and Semantic Obscurity," *JP*, 1951
Whiteley, C. H., "Truth by Convention," *A*, 1936-37
"On Meaning and Verifiability," *A*, 1938-39
"On the Justification of Induction," *A*, 1940
"Hempel's Paradoxes of Confirmation," *M*, 1945
"Can Philosophical Theories Transcend Experience?," *Ar.Soc.Sup.*, 1946
"More about Probability," *A*, 1947-48. Reprinted in Macdonald, M., *Philosophy and Analysis*
"On Understanding," *M*, 1949
"Rationality in Morals," *Ar.Soc.*, 1949-50
"Note on the Concept of Mind," *A*, 1955-56
Whitrow, G. J., "On the Synthetic Aspect of Mathematics," *P*, 1950
Wick, W. A., "Moral Problems, Moral Philosophy and Metaethics," *PR*, 1953
Wiener, P. P., "Some Metaphysical Assumptions and Problems of Neo-Positivism," *JP*, 1935
"Philosophical, Scientific and Ordinary Language," *JP*, 1948
Wienpahl, P. D., "Philosophy of Ethics, Ethics, and Moral Theory," *JP*, 1948
"Are All Signs Signs?," *PR*, 1949
"Frege's *Sinn und Bedeutung*," *M*, 1950
"Concerning Moral Responsibility," *A*, 1952-53
Will, F. L., "Verifiability and the External World," *PS*, 1940
"Is There a Problem of Induction?," *JP*, 1942
"The Contrary-to-Fact Conditional," *M*, 1947
"Will the Future Be Like the Past?," *M*, 1947. Reprinted in Flew, A., *Logic and Language* (second series), and in Edwards, P. and Pap, A., *A Modern Introduction to Philosophy*
"Donald Williams' Theory of Induction," *PR*, 1948
"Generalization and Evidence," in Black, M., *Philosophical Analysis*, 1950
"Kneale's Theories of Probability and Induction," *PR*, 1954
"The Justification of Theories," *PR*, 1955
Williams, B. A. O., "Tertullian's Paradox," in Flew, A. and MacIntyre, A., *New Essays in Philosophical Theology*, 1955
"Personal Identity and Individuation," *Ar.Soc.*, 1956-57
"Metaphysical Arguments," in Pears, D. F., *The Nature of Metaphysics*, 1957
Williams, D. C., "Ethics as Pure Postulate," *PR*, 1933. Reprinted in Sellars, W. and Hospers, J., *Readings in Ethical Theory*
"Analysis, Analytic Propositions, and Real Definitions," *A*, 1935-36
"The Nature and Variety of the A Priori," *A*, 1937-38
"The Realistic Interpretation of Scientific Sentences," *E*, 1937-38
"On the Derivation of Probabilities from Frequencies," *PPR*, 1944-45
"The Challenging Situation in the Philosophy of Probability," *PPR*, 1945-46
"Induction and the Future," *M*, 1948
"The Myth of Passage," *JP*, 1951. Reprinted in Hook, S., *American Philosophers at Work*

Williams, D. C. (*continued*)
  "The Sea Fight Tomorrow," in Henle, P., Kallen, H. M. and Langer, S. K., *Structure, Method and Meaning*, 1951
  "Professor Carnap's Philosophy of Probability," *PPR*, 1952-53
  "On the Direct Probability of Inductions," *M*, 1953
  "On the Elements of Being, I and II," *RM*, 1953-54
Williams, G., "International Law and the Controversy Concerning the Word 'Law'," *British Yearbook of International Law*, 1945. Reprinted in Laslett, P., *Philosophy, Politics and Society*
  "Language and the Law," *Law Quarterly Review I-V*, 1945 and 1946
Willis, R., "The Phenomenalist Theory of the World," *M*, 1957
Wilson, N. L., "Description and Designation," *JP*, 1953
  "In Defense of Proper Names against Descriptions," *PSt*, 1953
  "Property Designation and Description," *PR*, 1953
  "Space, Time, and Individuals," *JP*, 1955
  "Existence Assumptions and Contingent Meaningfulness," *M*, 1956
Winch, P. G., "Necessary and Contingent Truths," *A*, 1952-53
Wisdom, John, "Time, Fact and Substance," *Ar.Soc.*, 1928-29
  "Logical Constructions, I-V," *M*, 1931-33
  "Ostentation," *Psyche*, 1933. Reprinted in *Philosophy and Psycho-Analysis*
  "Is Analysis a Useful Method in Philosophy?," *Ar.Soc.Sup.*, 1934. Reprinted in *Philosophy and Psycho-Analysis*
  "God and Evil," *M*, 1935
  "Philosophical Perplexity," *Ar.Soc.*, 1936-37. Reprinted in *Philosophy and Psycho-Analysis*
  "Metaphysics and Verification," *M*, 1938. Reprinted in *Philosophy and Psycho-Analysis*
  "Other Minds, I-VIII," *M*, 1940-43. Reprinted in *Other Minds*
  "Moore's Technique," in Schilpp, P. A., *The Philosophy of G. E. Moore*, 1942. Reprinted in *Philosophy and Psycho-Analysis*
  "Waddington's *Science and Ethics*," *M*, 1943. Reprinted in *Philosophy and Psycho-Analysis*
  "Philosophy, Anxiety and Novelty," *M*, 1944. Reprinted in *Philosophy and Psycho-Analysis*
  "Gods," *Ar.Soc.*, 1944-45. Reprinted in Flew, A., *Logic and Language* (first series), and in *Philosophy and Psycho-Analysis*
  "Other Minds," *Ar.Soc.Sup.*, 1946
  "Philosophy and Psycho-Analysis," *Polemic*, 1946. Reprinted in *Philosophy and Psycho-Analysis*
  "Bertrand Russell and Modern Philosophy," *Politics and Letters*, 1947. Reprinted in *Philosophy and Psycho-Analysis*
  "Note on the New Edition of Professor Ayer's *Language, Truth and Logic*," *M*, 1948. Reprinted in *Philosophy and Psycho-Analysis*
  "Things and Persons," *Ar.Soc.Sup.*, 1948. Reprinted in *Philosophy and Psycho-Analysis*
  "The Concept of Mind," *Ar.Soc.*, 1949-50. Reprinted in *Other Minds*
  "A Note on Probability," in Black, M., *Philosophical Analysis*, 1950. Reprinted in *Philosophy and Psycho-Analysis*
  "Metaphysics," *Ar.Soc.*, 1950-51. Reprinted in *Other Minds*
  "Ludwig Wittgenstein," *M*, 1952

Wisdom, John (*continued*)
"Philosophy, Metaphysics and Psychoanalysis," in *Philosophy and Psycho-Analysis*, 1953
Foreword to Moore, G. E., *Some Main Problems of Philosophy*, 1953
Foreword to Lazerowitz, M., *The Structure of Metaphysics*, 1955
Wisdom, J. O., "Solipsism," *A*, 1933-34
"The Analysis of Sense-Data," *A*, 1934-35
"Why Achilles Does Not Fail to Catch the Tortoise," *M*, 1941
"Positivism," *M*, 1945
"Perception-Statements," *Ar.Soc.*, 1948-49
"A New Model for the Mind-Body Relationship," *BJPS*, 1951-52
Wittgenstein, L., "Some Remarks on Logical Form," *Ar.Soc.Sup.*, 1929
Wollheim, R., "Privacy," *Ar.Soc.*, 1950-51
"Sensing and Observing," *Ar.Soc.Sup.*, 1954
"F. H. Bradley," in Ayer, A. J. et al., *The Revolution in Philosophy*, 1956
Wood, O., "The Force of Linguistic Rules," *Ar.Soc.*, 1950-51
Woodger, J. R., "The Formalization of Psychological Theory," *E*, 1937-38
"Science Without Properties," *BJPS*, 1951-52
Woozley, A. D., "Dispositions," *M*, 1948
"Knowing and Not Knowing," *Ar.Soc.*, 1952-53
"Ordinary Language and Common Sense," *M*, 1953
Wright, G. H. von, "Der Wahrscheinlichkeitsbegriff in der modernen Erkennt-nisphilosophie," *T*, 1938
"Carnap's Theory of Probability," *PR*, 1951
"Deontic Logic," *M*, 1951
"Ludwig Wittgenstein, a Biographical Sketch," *PR*, 1955. Reprinted in Malcolm, N., *Ludwig Wittgenstein—A Memoir*
Xenakis, J., "Ordinary Language and Ordinary Belief," *PSt*, 1954
Yolton, J. W., "A Defense of Sense Data," *M*, 1948
"Linguistic and Epistemological Dualism," *M*, 1953
Zawirski, Z., "O wiecznym powrocie swiatow" (The Everlasting Return of the Worlds), *Kwartalnik Filozoficzny*, 1927
"Über das Verhältnis der mehrwertigen Logik zur Wahrscheinlichkeits-rechnung," *Studia Philosophica*, 1935
"Über die Anwendung der mehrwertigen Logik in der empirischen Wissenschaft," *E*, 1936-37
Ziedins, R., "Conditions of Observation and States of Observers," *PR*, 1956
Ziff, P., "Art and the 'Object of Art'," *M*, 1951. Reprinted in Elton, W., *Aesthetics and Language*
Zilsel, E., "Die Asymmetrie der Kausalität und die Einsinnigkeit der Zeit," *Naturwissenschaften*, 1927
"Bemerkungen zur Wissenschaftslogik," *E*, 1932-33
"Physics and the Problem of Historico-Sociological Laws," *PS*, 1941. Reprinted in Feigl, H. and Brodbeck, M., *Readings in the Philosophy of Science*
"The Genesis of the Concept of Physical Law," *PR*, 1942
Zinkernagel, P., "On the Problem of Objective Reality as Conceived in the Empiricist Tradition," *M*, 1955

Index

Ackerman, W., 135
Adjuciewicz, K., 6, 7, 241
Analogy, 229, 373; arguments from, 176, 177
Analysis, 5, 324; critical, 363; logical, 7, 76, 124 n., 133, 145, 169, 177, 293, 317; logical, and philosophical problems, 8; logical, and philosophy, 77; logical, as business of philosophy, 47; philosophical, 23, 28; *see also* Definition
Antinomies, logical, 139
Aquinas, 134
Aristotle, 333, 334, 368, 369
Arithmetic, 200, 341; *see also* Logic
St. Augustine, 218, 346, 347, 360, 362
Austin, J. L., 9, 28
Avenarius, R., 4, 85, 86, 291
Axiom(s), 346; and philosophy, 330; of geometry, 360; doubtful, 31; *see also* Geometry, Logic, Mathematics
Axiomatization, 136
Ayer, A. J., 6, 8, 110 n., 112 n., 114, 115, 116, 123 n., 124 n.

Bar-Hillel, Y., 8
Behavior, 21, 189, 294, 296, 304, 305, 306, 307, 312; meaningful, 181, 182; moral, 263; of groups 301, 316; physical, 181; understandable, 182; *see also* Psychology
Behaviorism, 181, 286, 296, 297, 299, 300, 316; social, 296, 301, 303, 308-310, 313, 315-317
Behmann, H., 135
Benjamin, A. C., 108 n.
Bentham, 4
Bergson, 80
Berkeley, 16, 17, 97, 368
Bernays, P., 135

Black, M., 8, 165 n., 199n.
Blake, William, 365
Blondlot, R., 91
Blumberg, A. E., 106 n.
Bolzmann, L., 4
Boole, G., 134
Bradley, F. H., 32, 41, 42, 43, 46, 374
Braithwaite, R. B., 6
Brentano, F., 4
Bridgman, P. W., 120 n.

Calvinism, 310, 311
Cantor, G., 32, 359, 364
Capitalism, 310, 311
Carnap, R., 3, 4, 7, 8, 13, 18, 20, 21, 22, 24, 25, 26, 27, 28, 107 n., 110 n., 117, 119, 120, 122 n., 124 n., 125 n., 128 n., 133 n., 147 n., 165 n., 199 n., 201, 202 n., 203, 204, 205, 206, 207, 208, 209, 210, 213 n., 231, 233 n., 235, 236, 237, 238, 282, 290, 298, 324
Causation, 242
Chisholm, R. M., 120 n,
Church, A., 8, 116
Chwistek, L., 6, 135
Ciccotti, E., 215 n.
Cognition, 219, 222, 223, 227; of the good, 250
Coleridge, S. T., 367
Collingwood, R. G., 327, 328, 329
Common-sense, 8, 101, 110 n., 356
Comte, A., 4, 83
Concepts, 13, 17, 24, 133, 145, 146, 232, 233, 248, 288, 334-336, 338, 341, 342, 376; and the given, 144; clarification of, 283; dispositional, 186, 187, 197; kinematic, 186; limiting, 286; logical, powers of, 333; of the good, 250, 251, 253, 255, 256, 261; of mathematics,

[447]

Kant (*continued*)
253, 256, 259, 346, 348, 360, 376, 380
Kaplan, A., 122 n.
Kelsen, H., 307 n., 308 n.
Kepler, 360
Knowledge, 10, 56, 144, 148, 151, 171, 210, 212, 220, 221, 227, 334, 340, 343; a priori, 152; and ethics, 247, 248; and positivism, 90; and reality, 226; as intuition, 102; as sensation, 102; basis of, 20, 213, 216, 222, 223, 226; certainty of human, 209; empirical, 278, 279; intersubjective, 211; limitation of human, 72, 73; metaphysical, 72; non-analytic, 108; of facts, 152; of other minds, 177; of physiology, 175; origin of, 221; scientific, 17, 125, 284; scientific, of the good, 261; systems of, 219, 222; theory of, 133, 136, 209, 292, 293; thinking and, 149; see also Empiricism, Rationalism
Kotarbinsky, T., 6, 7
Kraft, V., 3, 7
Kraus, O., 310, 311
Kronecker, L., 25

Laas, E., 85
Langford, C. H., 120 n.
Language, 19, 21, 23, 24, 26, 27, 55, 110 n., 116, 117, 152, 157, 167, 177, 179, 205, 214, 219, 237, 238, 241, 271, 285, 289, 295, 323, 340, 342, 343, 350, 354, 358, 362-364, 366, 372, 374; and contemporary British philosophy, 5; and type confusion, 75; constituents, 61; current uses of, 7; empiricist, 116-118, 120-123, 128 n.; games, 27; ideal, 199; influence on philosophy, 38; intersubjective, 205, 206; logical, construction of, 45; logical syntax of, 6; of everyday life, 287; of physics, 287; of science, 28, 199, 200, 202, 203; ordinary use of, 9; phenomenalistic, 201; protocol, 165, 182, 188, 201, 202, 205-207; structure of,

24; subject-predicate, 39; system, 24, 166, 235; see also Meaning
Lazerowitz, M., 8
Leibniz, 4, 32, 44, 54, 134, 135, 137, 139, 380
Lesnievsky, S., 6, 135
Leverrier, U. J. J., 151, 160
Lewin, K., 284
Lewis, C. I., 120 n.
Lichtenberg, G. C., 350
Locke, 19
Logic, 8, 22, 74, 96, 114, 117, 134, 150, 152, 236, 282, 284-286, 317, 322, 324, 358, 372, 376; and mathematics, 134, 307; and metaphysics, 60, 143; and numbers, 135; and symbolic method, 136; applied, 134; as method of philosophizing, 133 ff., laws of, 151, 153; mathematics as branch of, 140, 143; natural, 366; of relations, 137; of science, 24; philosophy and, 24, 134, 364, 376; propositions of, 158; tautological character of, 141, 142, 143; three-valued, 353; traditional, 133, 134; see also Empiricism, Rationalism
Łukasiewicz, J., 6, 135, 353

Mach, E., 4, 9, 85, 86, 139, 174, 208, 282
Malcolm, N., 8
Malebranche, 380
Malthus, 312
Mannoury, G., 6
Marc-Wogau, K., 7
Marx, 4, 167, 312
Marxism, 7, 9, 306, 308, 309, 315
Material mode of speech, 25, 165 ff., 237 ff.
Materialism, 324, 345
Mathematics, 135, 150, 158, 159, 282, 284, 285, 286, 322, 370, 377; and logic, 134, 307; and reality, 360; as branch of logic, 140, 143; foundations of, 32, 135; laws of, 151; propositions of, 158; sentences of, as analytic, 143; sentences of, as tautologics, 142; undecidable questions in, 359; see